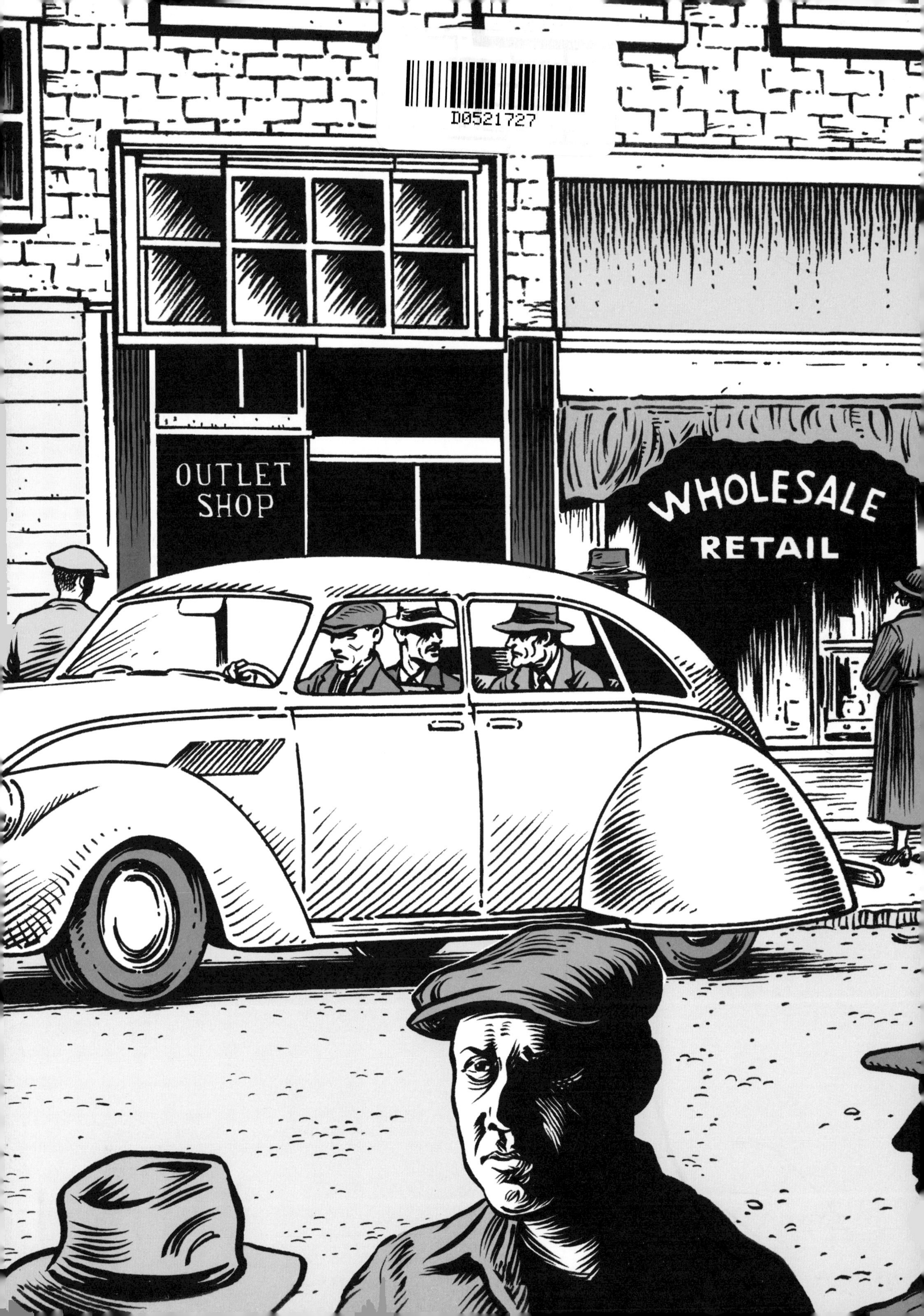
OUTLET
SHOP
WHOLESALE
RETAIL

ON THE ROPES

Also by James Vance and Dan E. Burr

Kings in Disguise

ON THE ROPES

JAMES VANCE *and* DAN E. BURR

Lettering and Halftones by Debbie Freiberg

W. W. Norton & Company

NEW YORK • LONDON

For information about permission to reproduce selections from this book,
write to Permissions, W. W. Norton & Company, Inc.,
500 Fifth Avenue, New York, NY 10110

For information about special discounts for bulk purchases, please contact
W. W. Norton Special Sales at specialsales@wwnorton.com or 800-233-4830

Manufacturing through Asia Pacific Offset
Book design by Joe Lops
Production manager: Anna Oler

Library of Congress Cataloging-in-Publication Data

Vance, James, 1953–
On the ropes / James Vance and Dan E. Burr. — 1st ed.
p. cm.
ISBN 978-0-393-06220-5 (hardcover)
1. Circus—Comic books, strips, etc. 2. Graphic novels.
I. Burr, Dan, 1951– II. Title.
PN6727.V36O5 2013
741.5'973—dc23
2012037353

W. W. Norton & Company, Inc.
500 Fifth Avenue, New York, N.Y. 10110
www.wwnorton.com

W. W. Norton & Company Ltd.
Castle House, 75/76 Wells Street, London W1T 3QT

1 2 3 4 5 6 7 8 9 0

This book exists thanks to two irreplaceable people: Carlton Winters, who produced the original version for the stage many years ago and whose full-blooded talent brought Gordon Corey to remarkable life; and Kate Worley, whose belief in its predecessor lifted me out of the darkest times of my life and inspired me to do no less than my best. Thanks also to Dan Burr, without whose participation I wouldn't have considered climbing back into Fred Bloch's world; to Jodi Berg, who showed me it was possible to be sane again, after a fashion; and to the brilliant children named Brigid, Jacob, Kaitlyn, and Sarah, who never stop reminding me of the many flavors of being alive. *On the Ropes* is for all of you.

—J. V.

I want to express my thanks to my wife, art assistant, and valued critic, Debbie Freiberg, who provided the excellent coloring for the cover illustration and who continues to inspire and encourage me; to Dave Schreiner and Denis Kitchen for their support, patience, and belief in me; and to James Vance for his special vision and hard work, and for providing me with a wonderful script to interpret.

—D. B.

ON THE ROPES

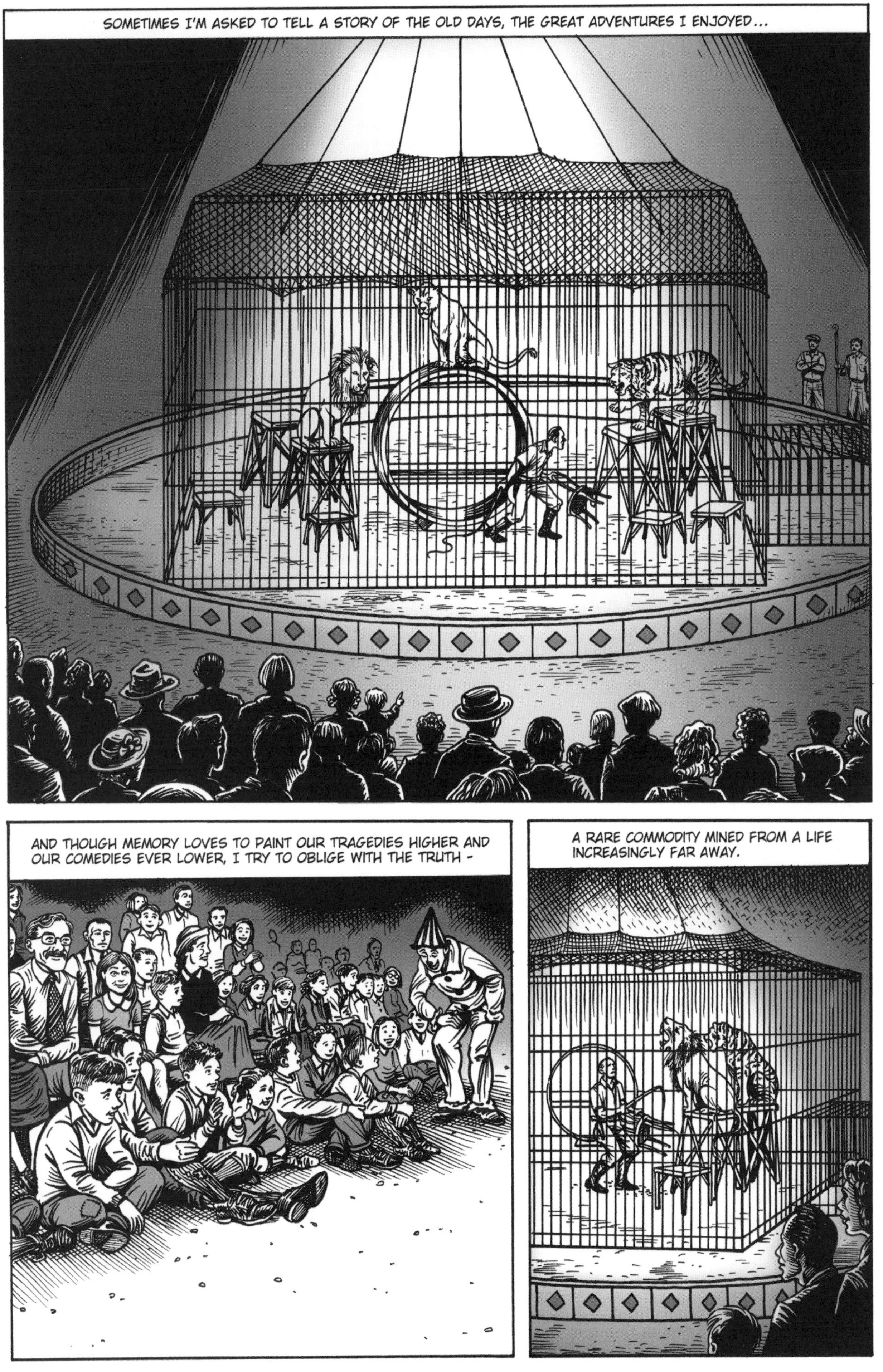
SOMETIMES I'M ASKED TO TELL A STORY OF THE OLD DAYS, THE GREAT ADVENTURES I ENJOYED...
AND THOUGH MEMORY LOVES TO PAINT OUR TRAGEDIES HIGHER AND OUR COMEDIES EVER LOWER, I TRY TO OBLIGE WITH THE TRUTH -
A RARE COMMODITY MINED FROM A LIFE INCREASINGLY FAR AWAY.

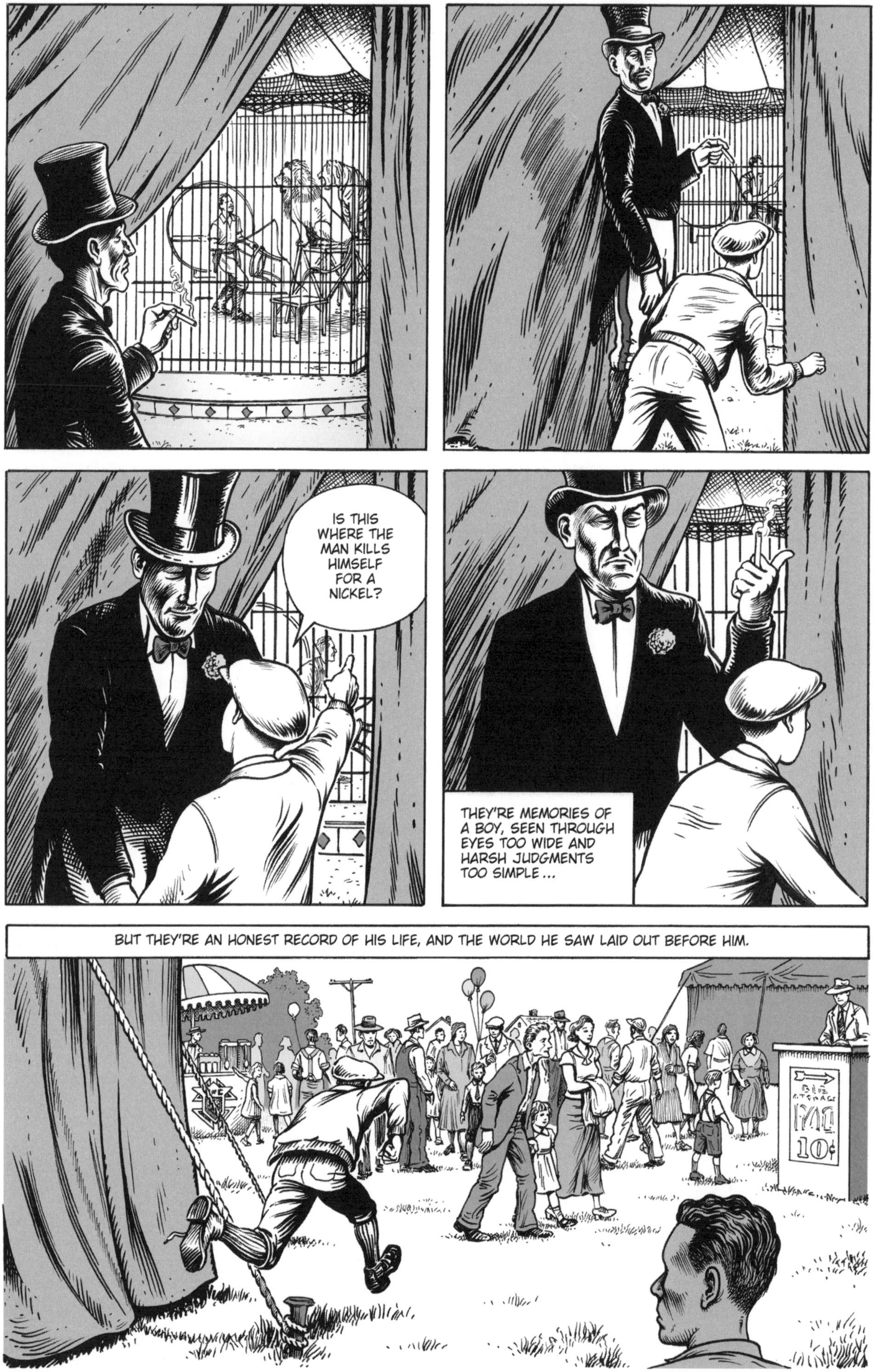
IS THIS WHERE THE MAN KILLS HIMSELF FOR A NICKEL?
THEY'RE MEMORIES OF A BOY, SEEN THROUGH EYES TOO WIDE AND HARSH JUDGMENTS TOO SIMPLE ...
BUT THEY'RE AN HONEST RECORD OF HIS LIFE, AND THE WORLD HE SAW LAID OUT BEFORE HIM.
10¢

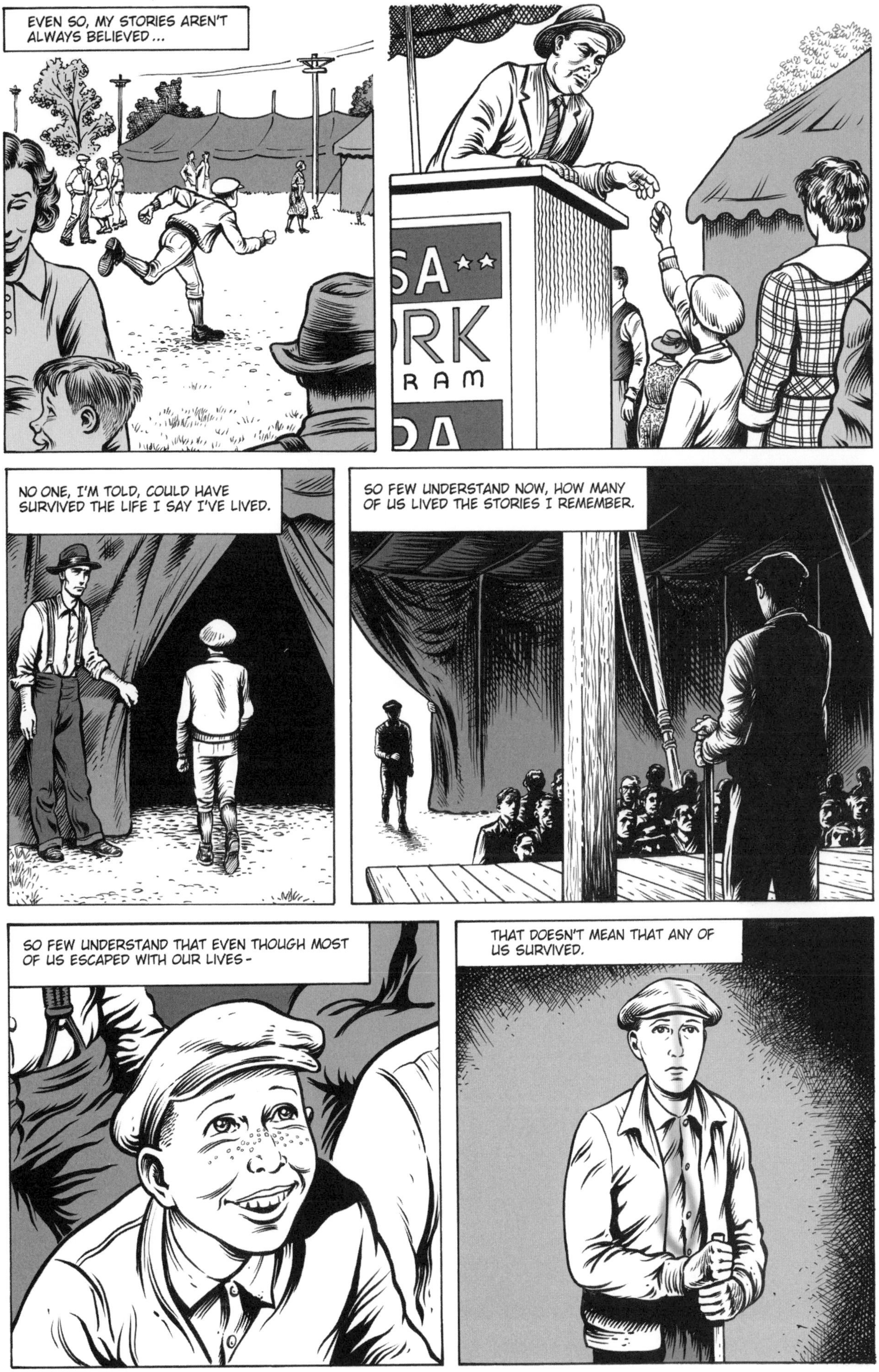
EVEN SO, MY STORIES AREN'T ALWAYS BELIEVED...
NO ONE, I'M TOLD, COULD HAVE SURVIVED THE LIFE I SAY I'VE LIVED.
SO FEW UNDERSTAND NOW, HOW MANY OF US LIVED THE STORIES I REMEMBER.
SO FEW UNDERSTAND THAT EVEN THOUGH MOST OF US ESCAPED WITH OUR LIVES -
THAT DOESN'T MEAN THAT ANY OF US SURVIVED.

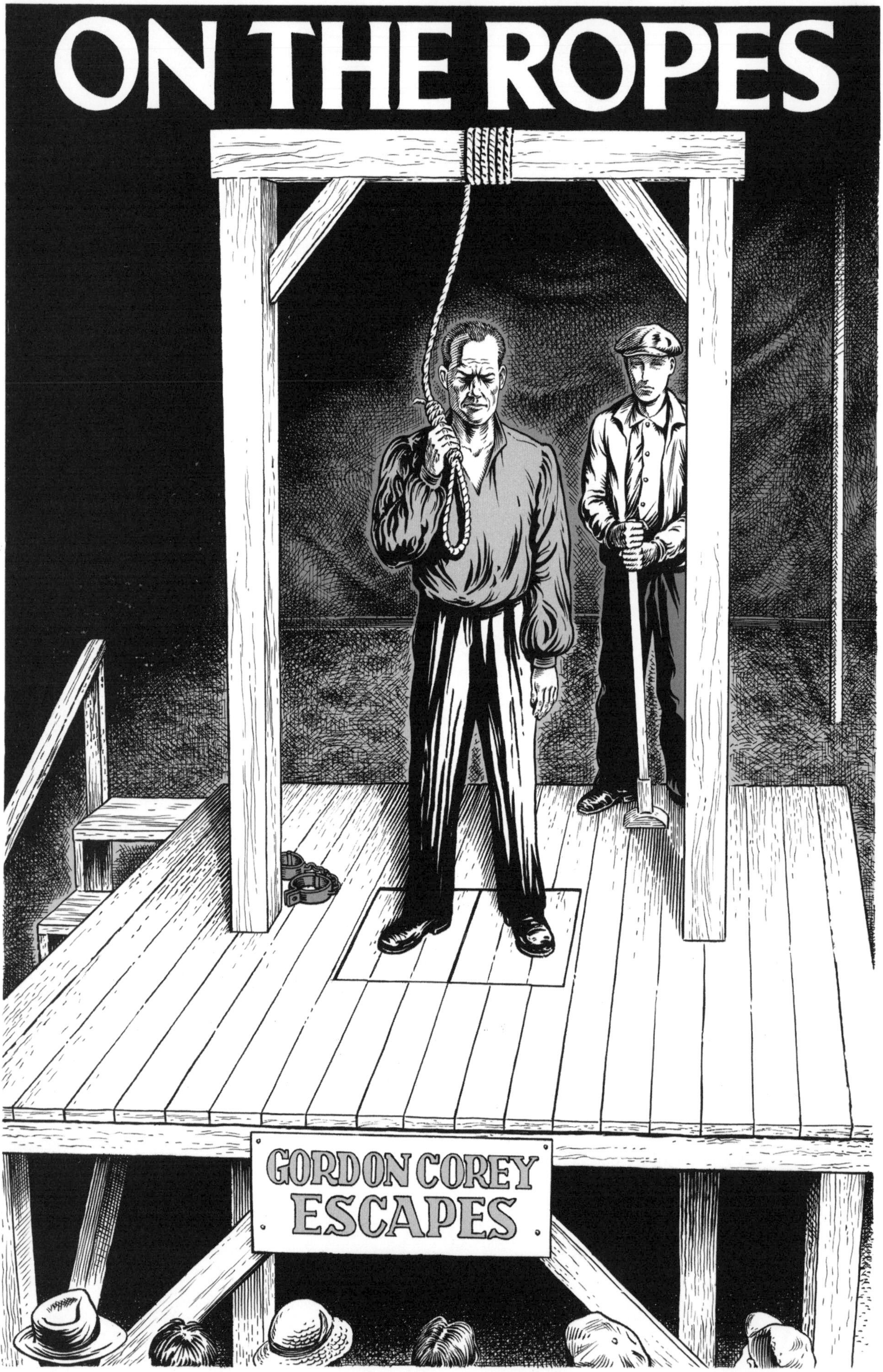
ON THE ROPES
GORDON COREY
ESCAPES

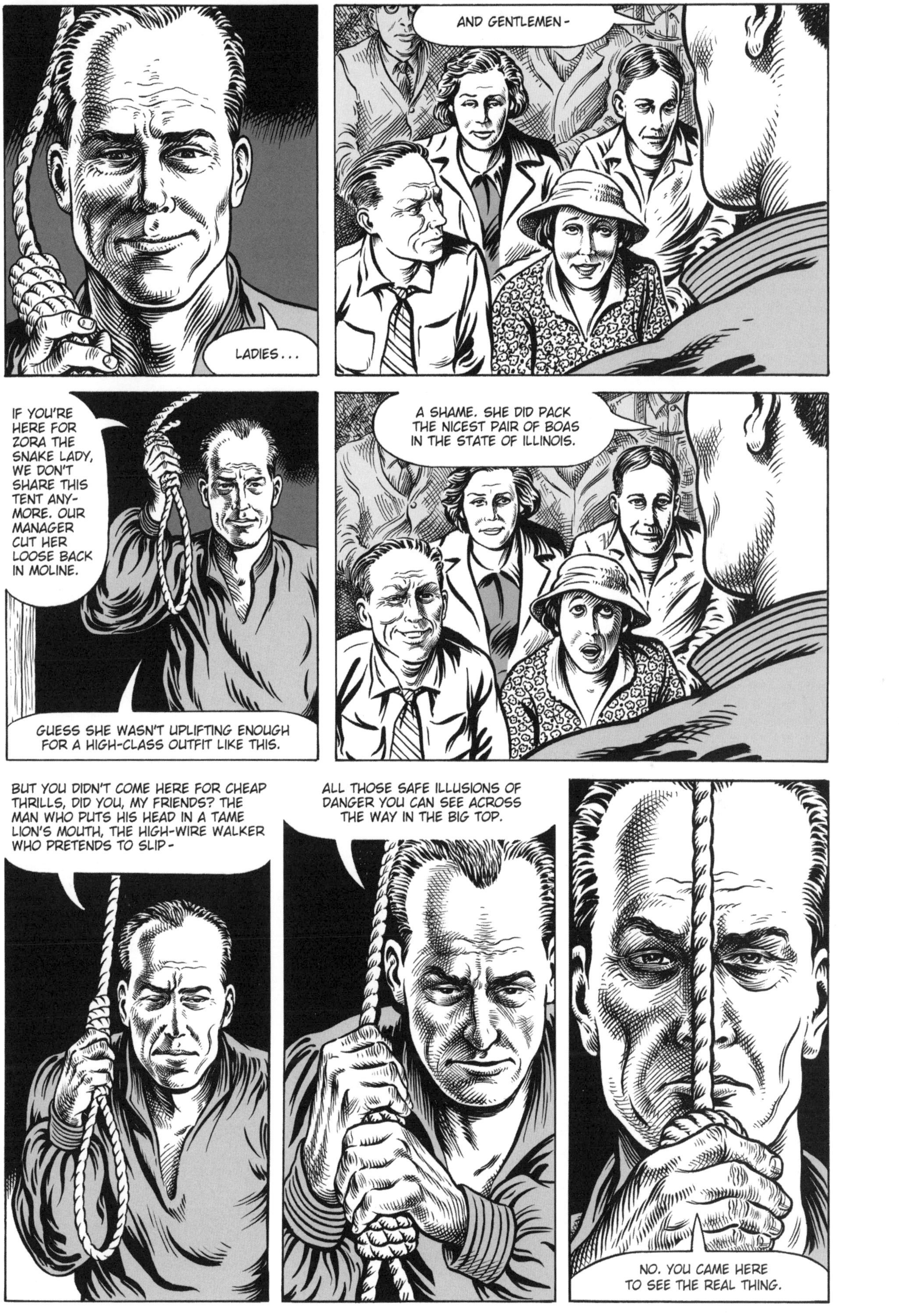
LADIES . . .
AND GENTLEMEN-
IF YOU'RE HERE FOR ZORA THE SNAKE LADY, WE DON'T SHARE THIS TENT ANY-MORE. OUR MANAGER CUT HER LOOSE BACK IN MOLINE.
GUESS SHE WASN'T UPLIFTING ENOUGH FOR A HIGH-CLASS OUTFIT LIKE THIS.
A SHAME. SHE DID PACK THE NICEST PAIR OF BOAS IN THE STATE OF ILLINOIS.
BUT YOU DIDN'T COME HERE FOR CHEAP THRILLS, DID YOU, MY FRIENDS? THE MAN WHO PUTS HIS HEAD IN A TAME LION'S MOUTH, THE HIGH-WIRE WALKER WHO PRETENDS TO SLIP-
ALL THOSE SAFE ILLUSIONS OF DANGER YOU CAN SEE ACROSS THE WAY IN THE BIG TOP.
NO. YOU CAME HERE TO SEE THE REAL THING.

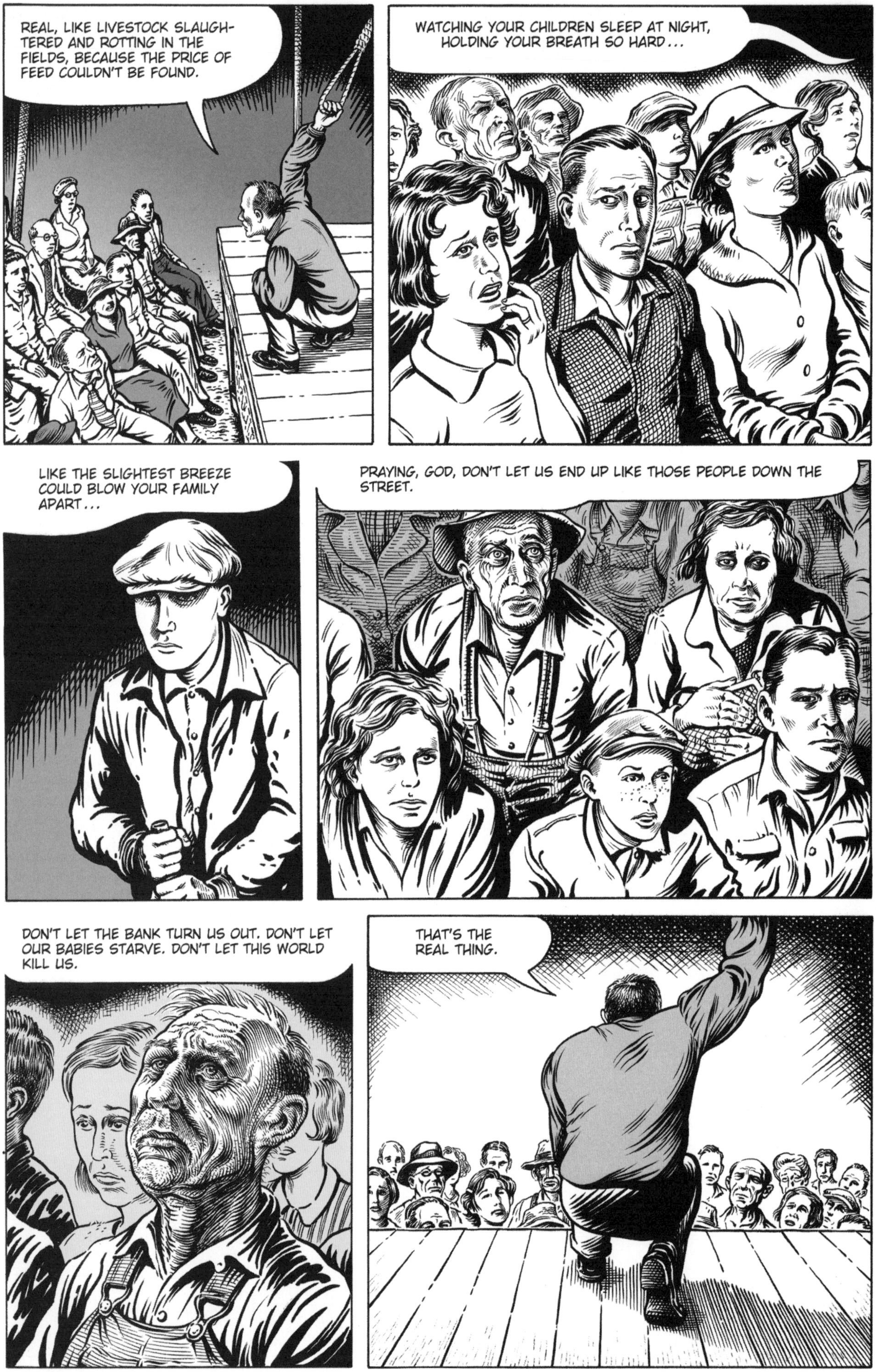
REAL, LIKE LIVESTOCK SLAUGHTERED AND ROTTING IN THE FIELDS, BECAUSE THE PRICE OF FEED COULDN'T BE FOUND.
WATCHING YOUR CHILDREN SLEEP AT NIGHT, HOLDING YOUR BREATH SO HARD...
LIKE THE SLIGHTEST BREEZE COULD BLOW YOUR FAMILY APART...
PRAYING, GOD, DON'T LET US END UP LIKE THOSE PEOPLE DOWN THE STREET.
DON'T LET THE BANK TURN US OUT. DON'T LET OUR BABIES STARVE. DON'T LET THIS WORLD KILL US.
THAT'S THE REAL THING.

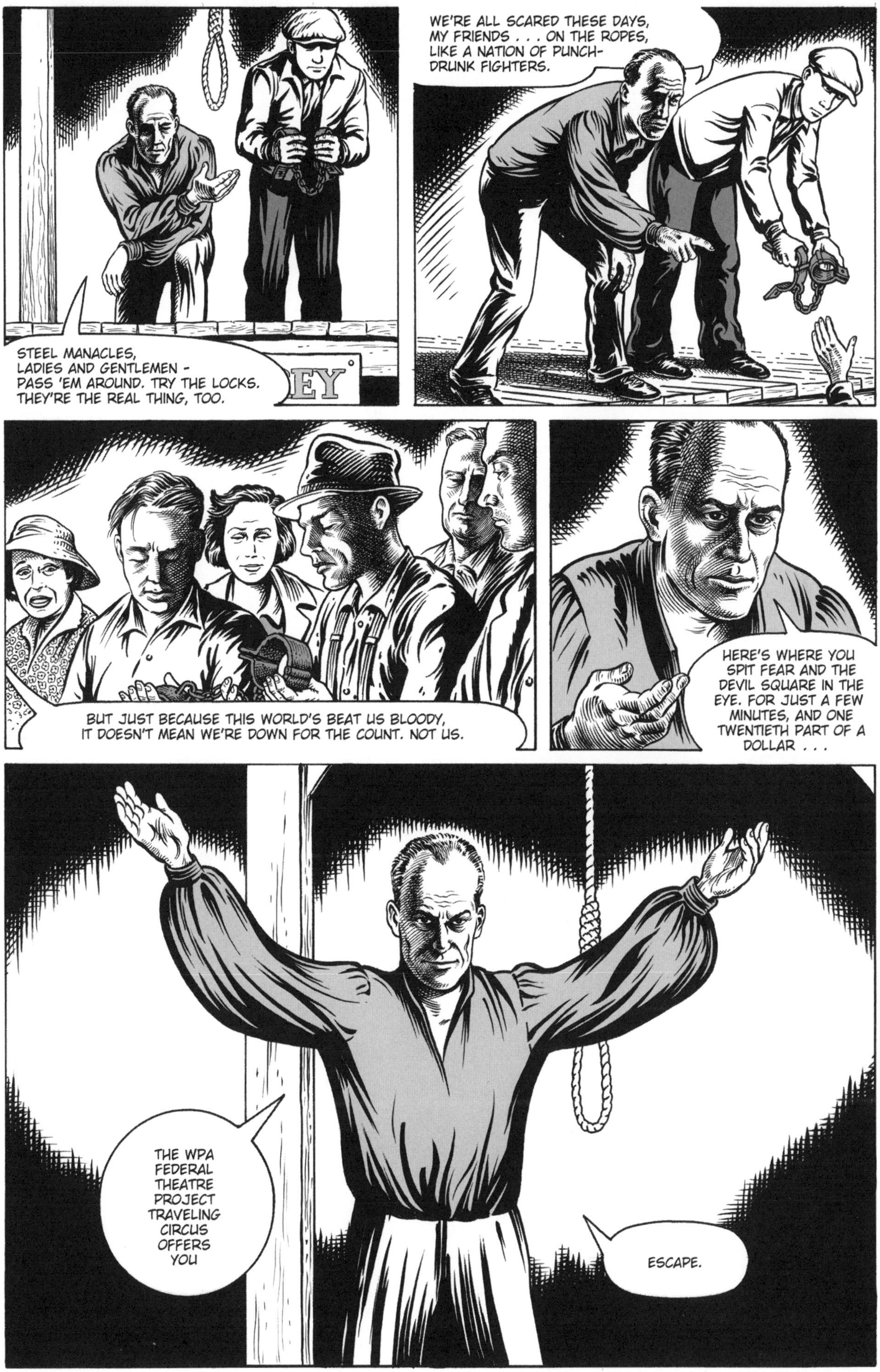
STEEL MANACLES, LADIES AND GENTLEMEN - PASS 'EM AROUND. TRY THE LOCKS. THEY'RE THE REAL THING, TOO.
EY
WE'RE ALL SCARED THESE DAYS, MY FRIENDS . . . ON THE ROPES, LIKE A NATION OF PUNCH-DRUNK FIGHTERS.
BUT JUST BECAUSE THIS WORLD'S BEAT US BLOODY, IT DOESN'T MEAN WE'RE DOWN FOR THE COUNT. NOT US.
HERE'S WHERE YOU SPIT FEAR AND THE DEVIL SQUARE IN THE EYE. FOR JUST A FEW MINUTES, AND ONE TWENTIETH PART OF A DOLLAR . . .
THE WPA FEDERAL THEATRE PROJECT TRAVELING CIRCUS OFFERS YOU
ESCAPE.

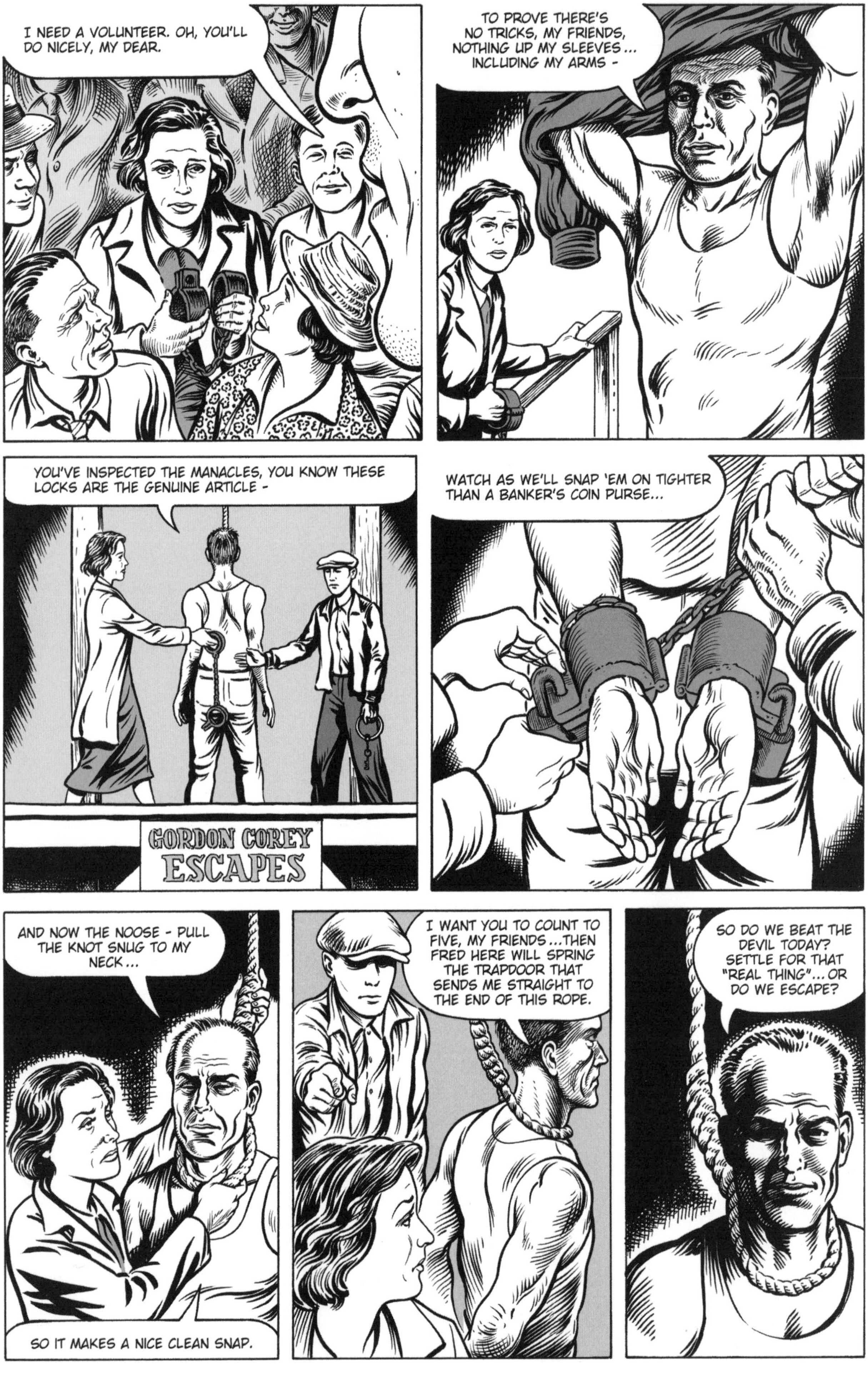
I NEED A VOLUNTEER. OH, YOU'LL DO NICELY, MY DEAR.
TO PROVE THERE'S NO TRICKS, MY FRIENDS, NOTHING UP MY SLEEVES ... INCLUDING MY ARMS -
YOU'VE INSPECTED THE MANACLES, YOU KNOW THESE LOCKS ARE THE GENUINE ARTICLE -
GORDON COREY ESCAPES
WATCH AS WE'LL SNAP 'EM ON TIGHTER THAN A BANKER'S COIN PURSE...
AND NOW THE NOOSE - PULL THE KNOT SNUG TO MY NECK ...
SO IT MAKES A NICE CLEAN SNAP.
I WANT YOU TO COUNT TO FIVE, MY FRIENDS ... THEN FRED HERE WILL SPRING THE TRAPDOOR THAT SENDS ME STRAIGHT TO THE END OF THIS ROPE.
SO DO WE BEAT THE DEVIL TODAY? SETTLE FOR THAT "REAL THING" ... OR DO WE ESCAPE?

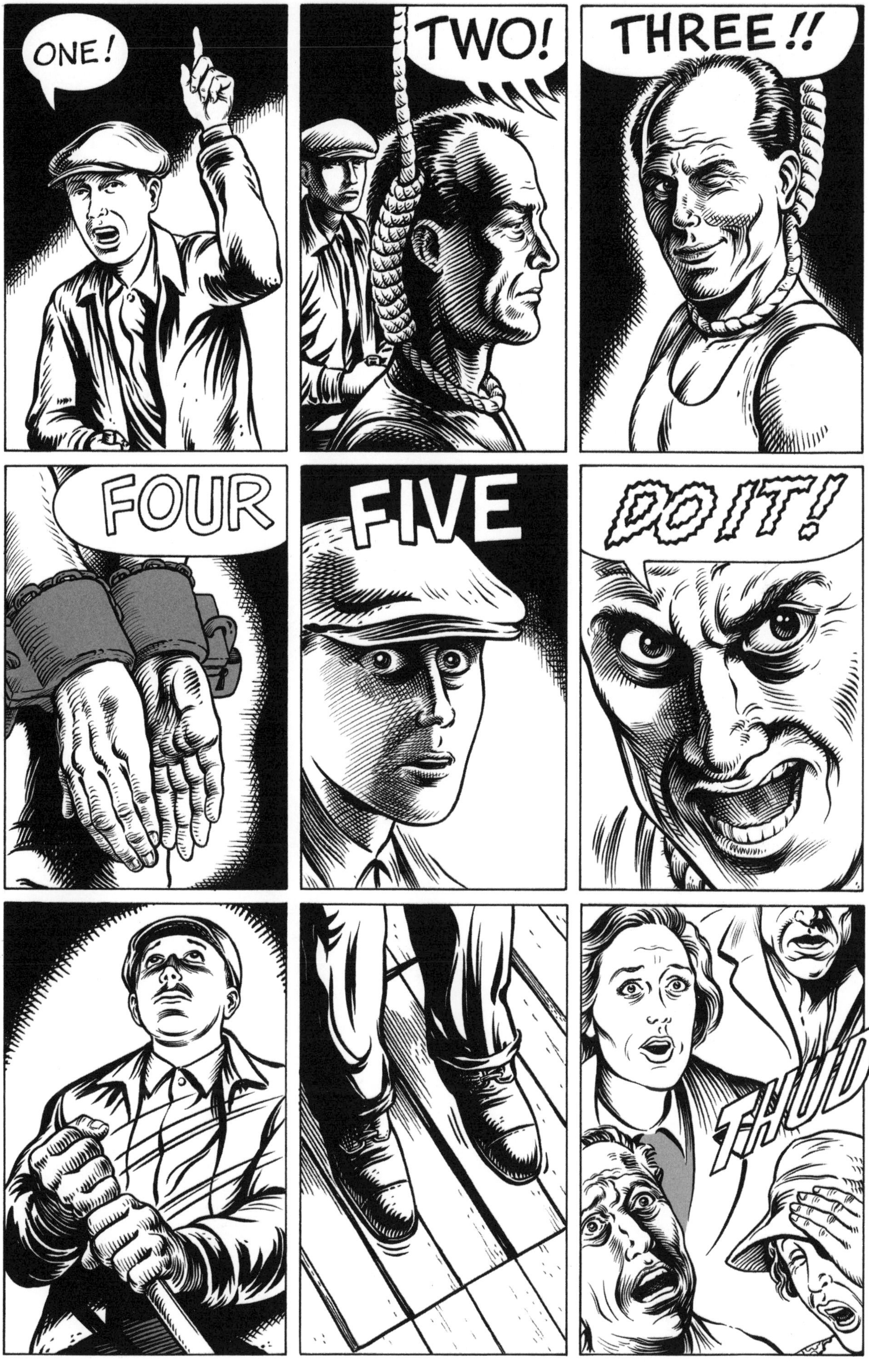
ONE!
TWO!
THREE!!
FOUR
FIVE
DO IT!
THUD

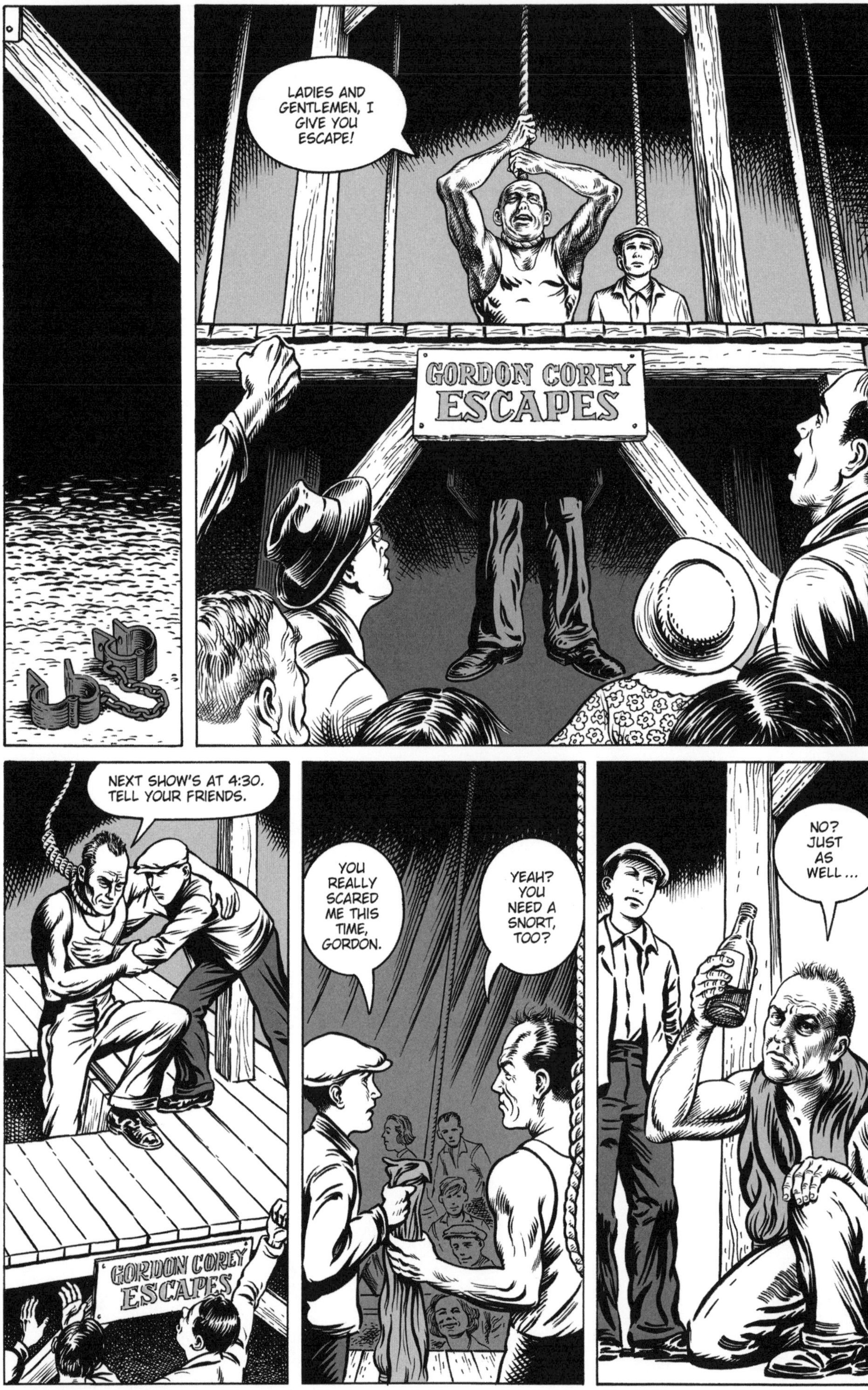
LADIES AND GENTLEMEN, I GIVE YOU ESCAPE!
GORDON COREY ESCAPES
NEXT SHOW'S AT 4:30. TELL YOUR FRIENDS.
GORDON COREY ESCAPES
YOU REALLY SCARED ME THIS TIME, GORDON.
YEAH? YOU NEED A SNORT, TOO?
NO? JUST AS WELL ...

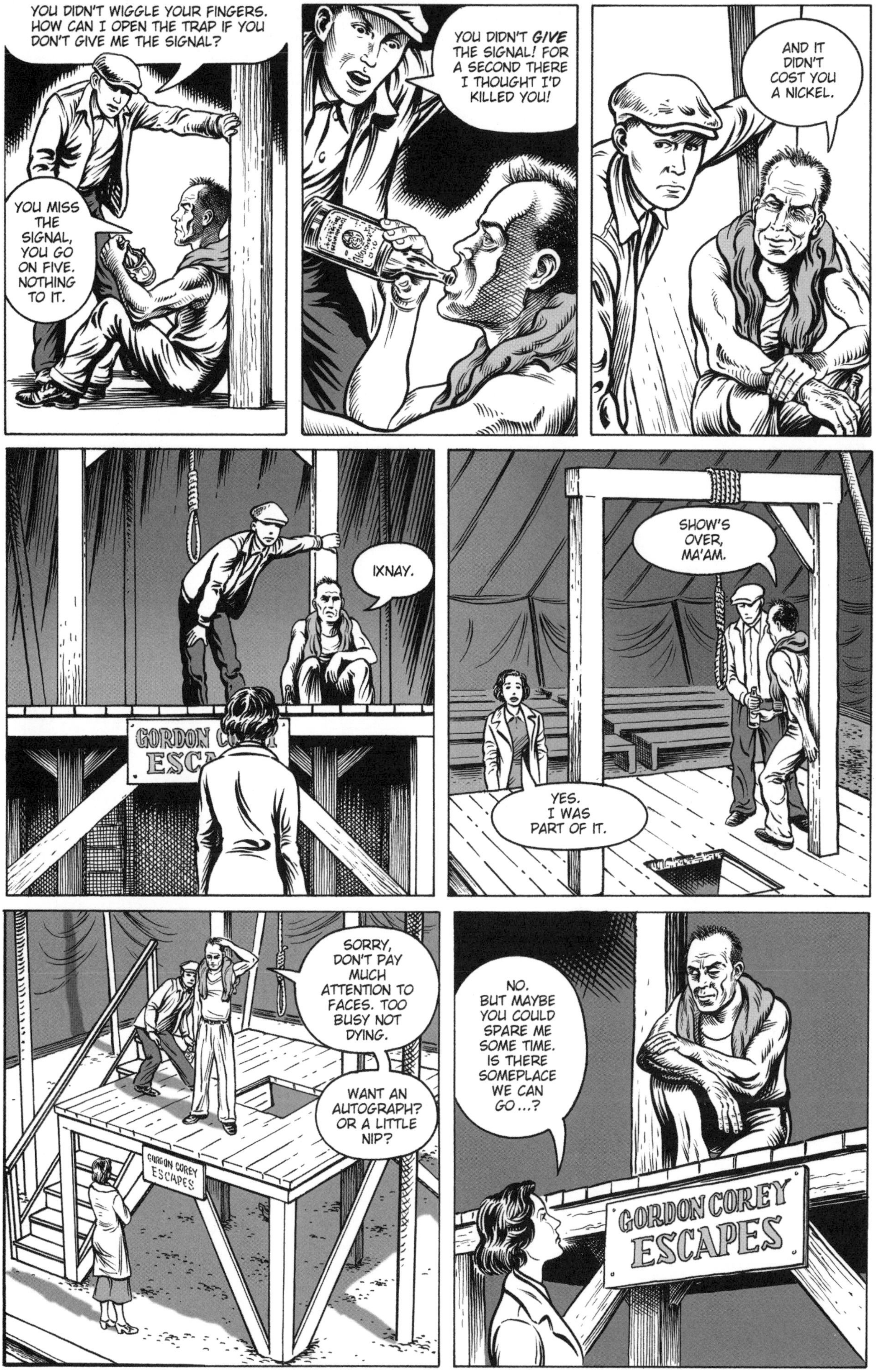

YOU DIDN'T WIGGLE YOUR FINGERS. HOW CAN I OPEN THE TRAP IF YOU DON'T GIVE ME THE SIGNAL?
YOU MISS THE SIGNAL, YOU GO ON FIVE. NOTHING TO IT.
YOU DIDN'T GIVE THE SIGNAL! FOR A SECOND THERE I THOUGHT I'D KILLED YOU!
AND IT DIDN'T COST YOU A NICKEL.
IXNAY.
GORDON COREY ESCAPES
SHOW'S OVER, MA'AM.
YES. I WAS PART OF IT.
SORRY, DON'T PAY MUCH ATTENTION TO FACES. TOO BUSY NOT DYING.
WANT AN AUTOGRAPH? OR A LITTLE NIP?
GORDON COREY ESCAPES
NO. BUT MAYBE YOU COULD SPARE ME SOME TIME. IS THERE SOMEPLACE WE CAN GO...?
GORDON COREY ESCAPES

WELL, THERE'S NOT MUCH TIME BETWEEN SHOWS, BUT WE COULD GET GOOD AND ACQUAINTED AFTER SUPPER...

SORRY, I HAVE TO BE ON A TRAIN TONIGHT.

GOLDEN COREY ESCAPES

STORY OF MY LIFE –

BUT MAYBE WE COULD TALK BETWEEN SHOWS. I THINK I COULD SELL A MAGAZINE PIECE ON YOU.

ON THE LEVEL?

"A SYMBOL OF HOPE FOR THE DESPERATE," OR SOMETHING. I HAVE A FRIEND AT THE *AMERICAN MERCURY*... OR *LIBERTY* MIGHT BE INTERESTED.

YOU HEAR THAT, FRED? YOU WANT TO BE ON THE COVER OF *LIBERTY*?

OR WHAT'S THAT ONE YOU LIKE? *SPICY ADVENTURES*?

JUST WHEN THERE'S NOTHING ELSE TO READ...

INTERVIEW MY MAN FRED, WHY DON'T YOU? HE'LL GAS ABOUT "THE DESPERATE" 'TIL THAT NOOSE STARTS LOOKING GOOD TO YOU.

MR. COREY, I'M OFFERING YOU SOME PUBLICITY–

NOT INTERESTED. NOT IN THE *MERCURY*, NOT IN *LIBERTY*...

BUT IF YOU DECIDE TO TRY A SPICY ADVENTURE, YOU COME LOOK ME UP, OKAY?

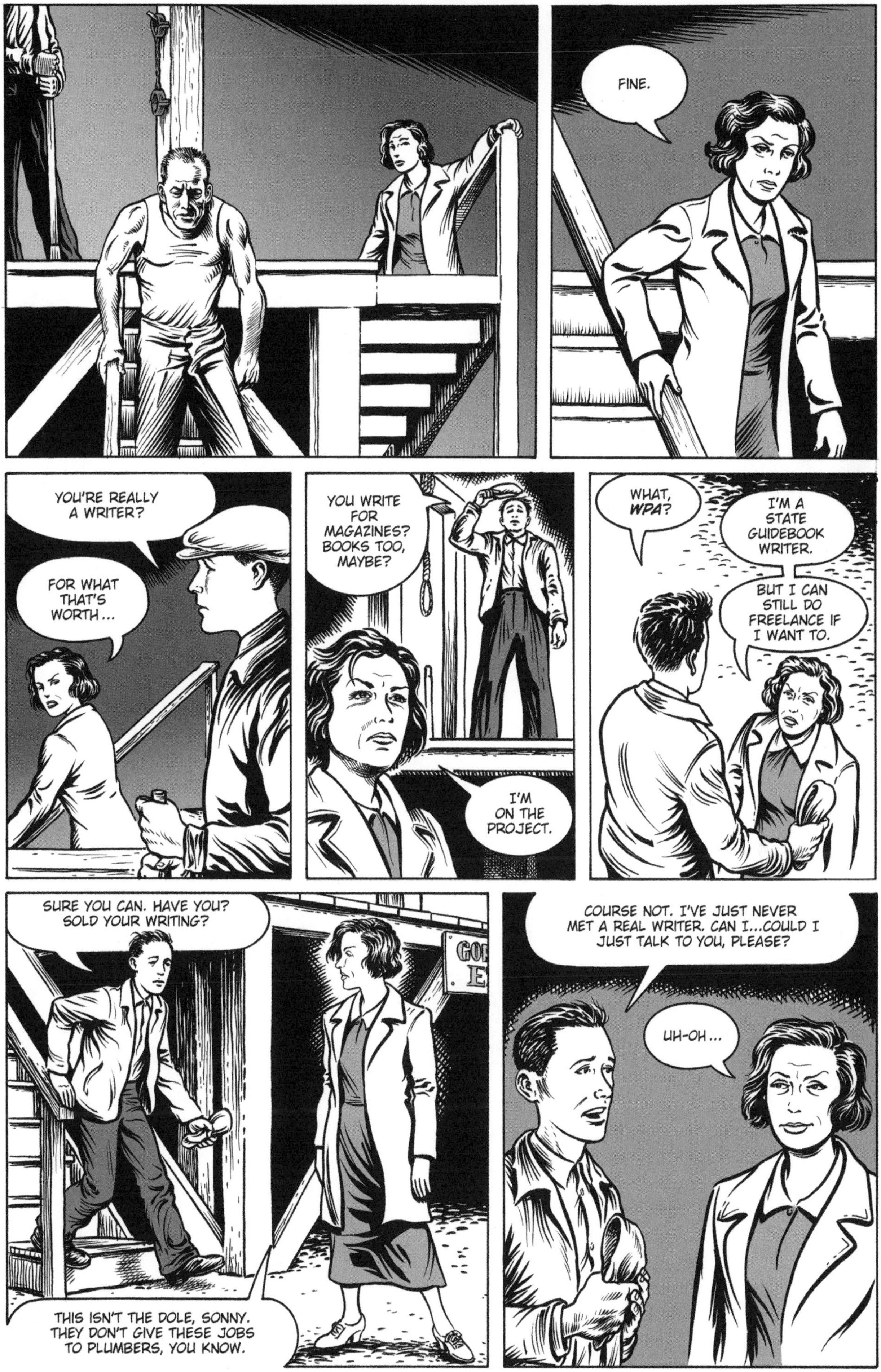
FINE.
YOU'RE REALLY A WRITER?
FOR WHAT THAT'S WORTH...
YOU WRITE FOR MAGAZINES? BOOKS TOO, MAYBE?
I'M ON THE PROJECT.
WHAT, WPA?
I'M A STATE GUIDEBOOK WRITER.
BUT I CAN STILL DO FREELANCE IF I WANT TO.
SURE YOU CAN. HAVE YOU? SOLD YOUR WRITING?
THIS ISN'T THE DOLE, SONNY. THEY DON'T GIVE THESE JOBS TO PLUMBERS, YOU KNOW.
COURSE NOT. I'VE JUST NEVER MET A REAL WRITER. CAN I...COULD I JUST TALK TO YOU, PLEASE?
UH-OH...

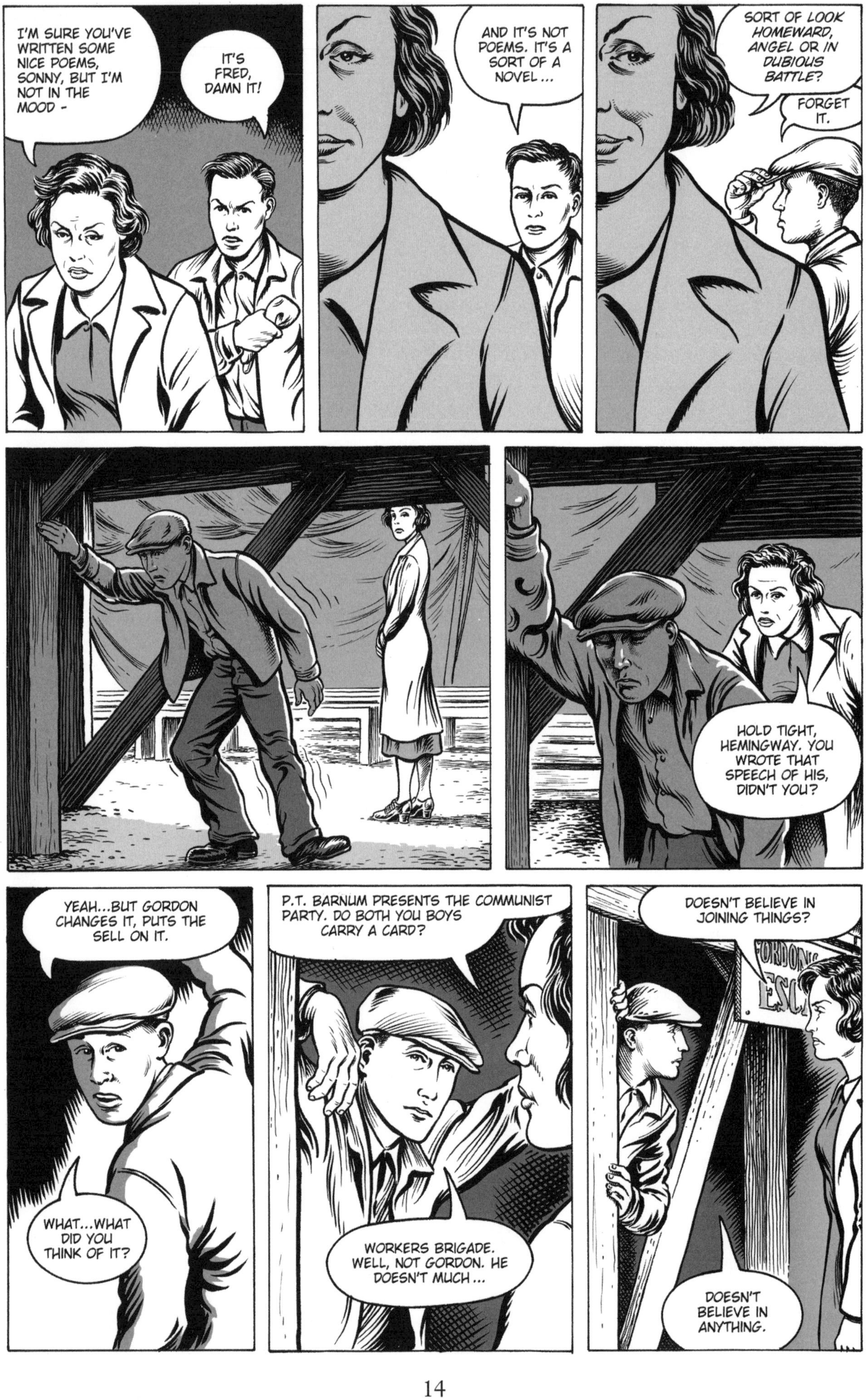
I'M SURE YOU'VE WRITTEN SOME NICE POEMS, SONNY, BUT I'M NOT IN THE MOOD -
IT'S FRED, DAMN IT!
AND IT'S NOT POEMS. IT'S A SORT OF A NOVEL ...
SORT OF *LOOK HOMEWARD, ANGEL* OR *IN DUBIOUS BATTLE*?
FORGET IT.
HOLD TIGHT, HEMINGWAY. YOU WROTE THAT SPEECH OF HIS, DIDN'T YOU?
YEAH...BUT GORDON CHANGES IT, PUTS THE SELL ON IT.
WHAT...WHAT DID YOU THINK OF IT?
P.T. BARNUM PRESENTS THE COMMUNIST PARTY. DO BOTH YOU BOYS CARRY A CARD?
WORKERS BRIGADE. WELL, NOT GORDON. HE DOESN'T MUCH ...
DOESN'T BELIEVE IN JOINING THINGS?
DOESN'T BELIEVE IN ANYTHING.

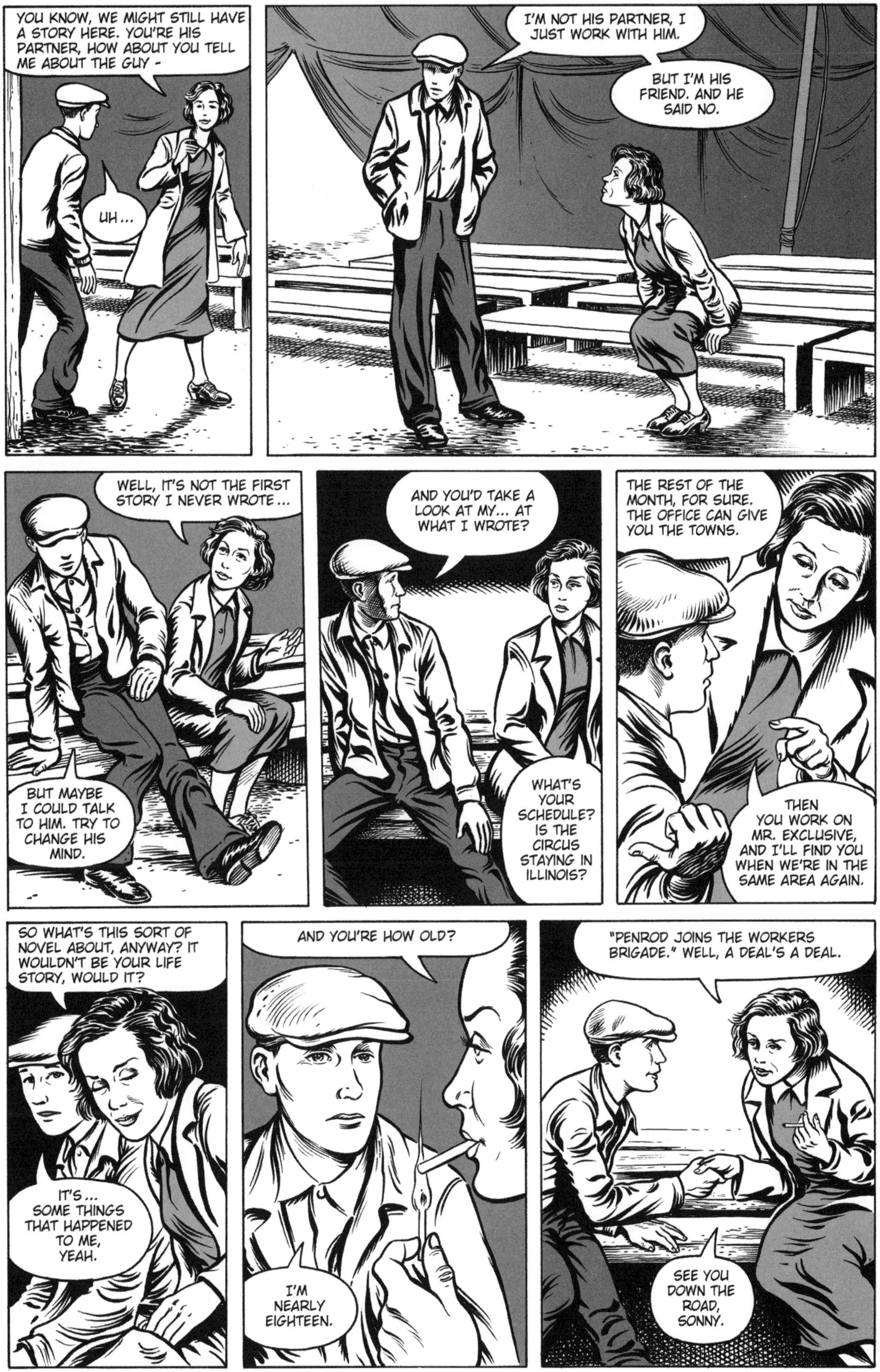
YOU KNOW, WE MIGHT STILL HAVE A STORY HERE. YOU'RE HIS PARTNER, HOW ABOUT YOU TELL ME ABOUT THE GUY -
UH...
I'M NOT HIS PARTNER, I JUST WORK WITH HIM.
BUT I'M HIS FRIEND. AND HE SAID NO.
WELL, IT'S NOT THE FIRST STORY I NEVER WROTE...
BUT MAYBE I COULD TALK TO HIM. TRY TO CHANGE HIS MIND.
AND YOU'D TAKE A LOOK AT MY... AT WHAT I WROTE?
WHAT'S YOUR SCHEDULE? IS THE CIRCUS STAYING IN ILLINOIS?
THE REST OF THE MONTH, FOR SURE. THE OFFICE CAN GIVE YOU THE TOWNS.
THEN YOU WORK ON MR. EXCLUSIVE, AND I'LL FIND YOU WHEN WE'RE IN THE SAME AREA AGAIN.
SO WHAT'S THIS SORT OF NOVEL ABOUT, ANYWAY? IT WOULDN'T BE YOUR LIFE STORY, WOULD IT?
IT'S... SOME THINGS THAT HAPPENED TO ME, YEAH.
AND YOU'RE HOW OLD?
I'M NEARLY EIGHTEEN.
"PENROD JOINS THE WORKERS BRIGADE." WELL, A DEAL'S A DEAL.
SEE YOU DOWN THE ROAD, SONNY.

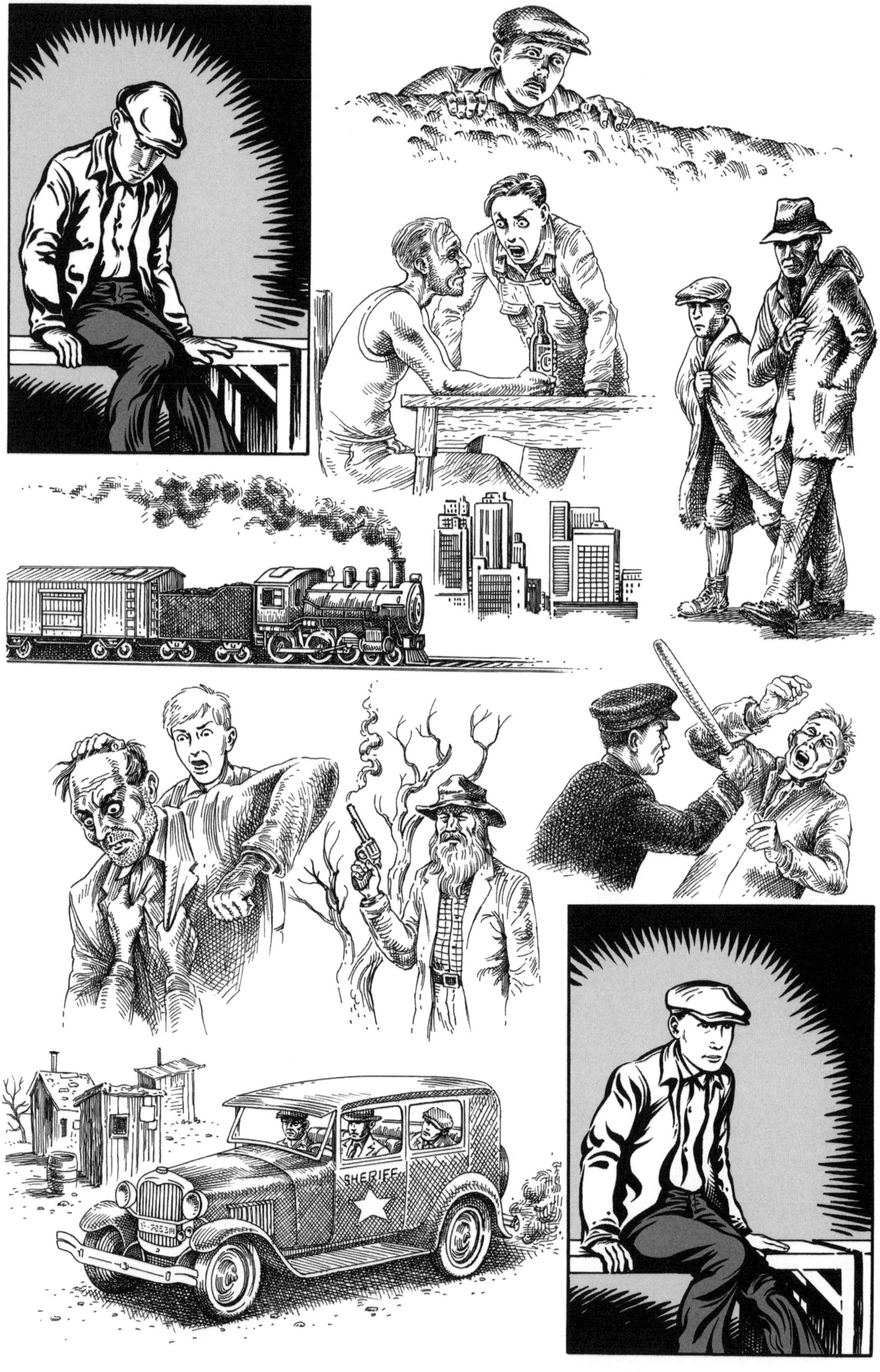
SHERIFF

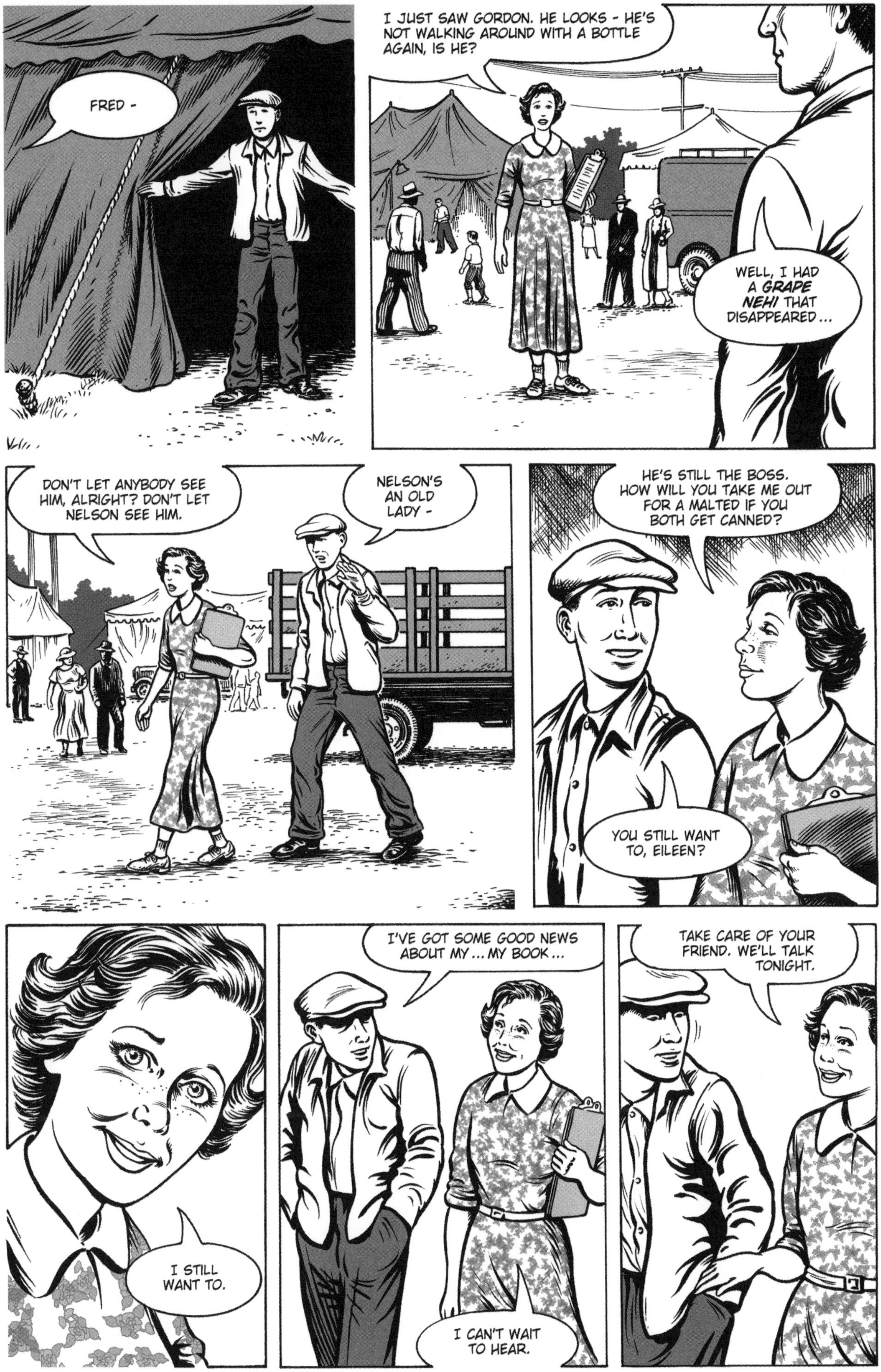
FRED -
I JUST SAW GORDON. HE LOOKS - HE'S NOT WALKING AROUND WITH A BOTTLE AGAIN, IS HE?
WELL, I HAD A GRAPE NEHI THAT DISAPPEARED...
DON'T LET ANYBODY SEE HIM, ALRIGHT? DON'T LET NELSON SEE HIM.
NELSON'S AN OLD LADY -
HE'S STILL THE BOSS. HOW WILL YOU TAKE ME OUT FOR A MALTED IF YOU BOTH GET CANNED?
YOU STILL WANT TO, EILEEN?
I STILL WANT TO.
I'VE GOT SOME GOOD NEWS ABOUT MY ... MY BOOK ...
I CAN'T WAIT TO HEAR.
TAKE CARE OF YOUR FRIEND. WE'LL TALK TONIGHT.

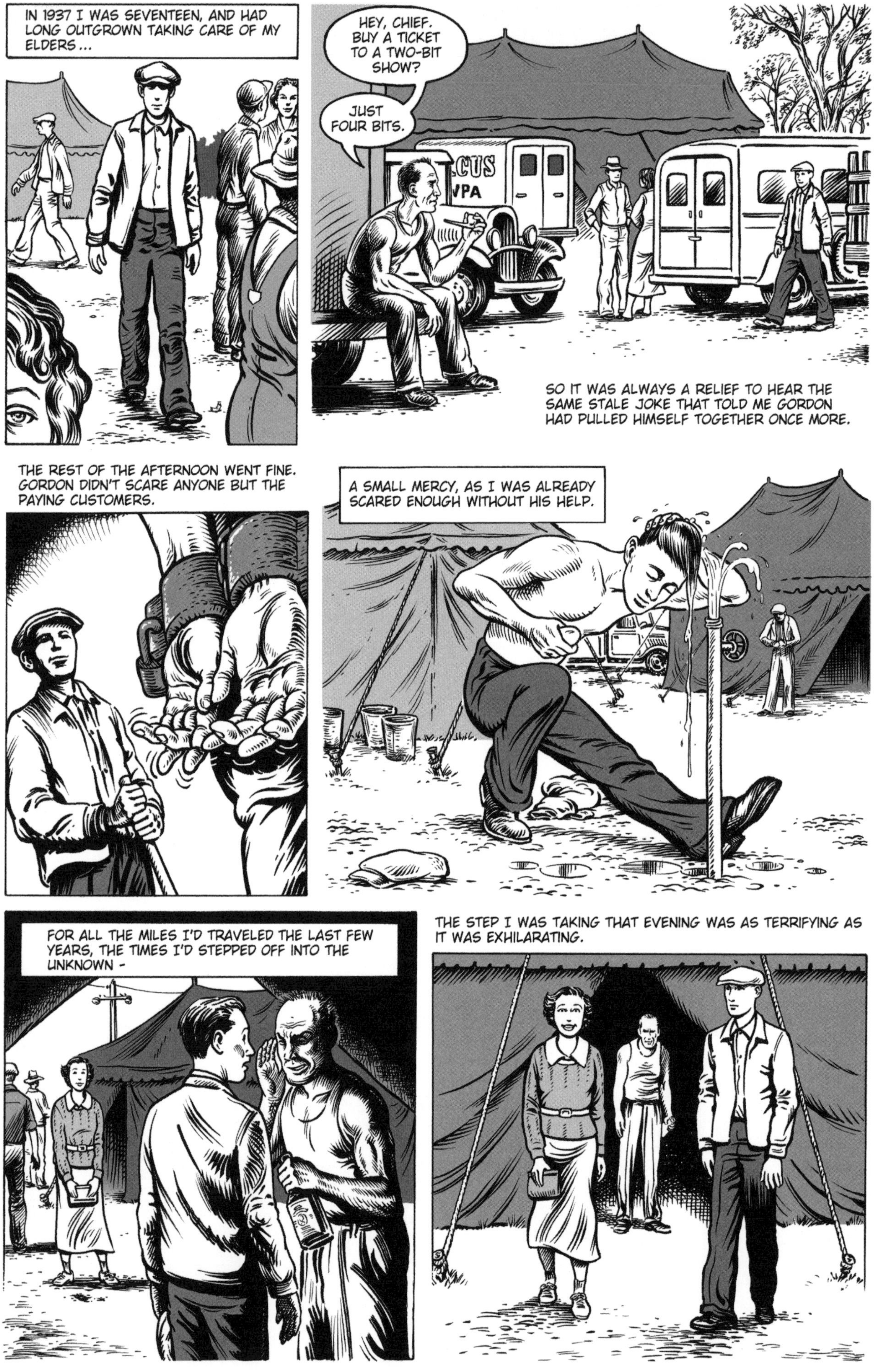
IN 1937 I WAS SEVENTEEN, AND HAD LONG OUTGROWN TAKING CARE OF MY ELDERS...
HEY, CHIEF. BUY A TICKET TO A TWO-BIT SHOW?
JUST FOUR BITS.
SO IT WAS ALWAYS A RELIEF TO HEAR THE SAME STALE JOKE THAT TOLD ME GORDON HAD PULLED HIMSELF TOGETHER ONCE MORE.
THE REST OF THE AFTERNOON WENT FINE. GORDON DIDN'T SCARE ANYONE BUT THE PAYING CUSTOMERS.
A SMALL MERCY, AS I WAS ALREADY SCARED ENOUGH WITHOUT HIS HELP.
FOR ALL THE MILES I'D TRAVELED THE LAST FEW YEARS, THE TIMES I'D STEPPED OFF INTO THE UNKNOWN -
THE STEP I WAS TAKING THAT EVENING WAS AS TERRIFYING AS IT WAS EXHILARATING.

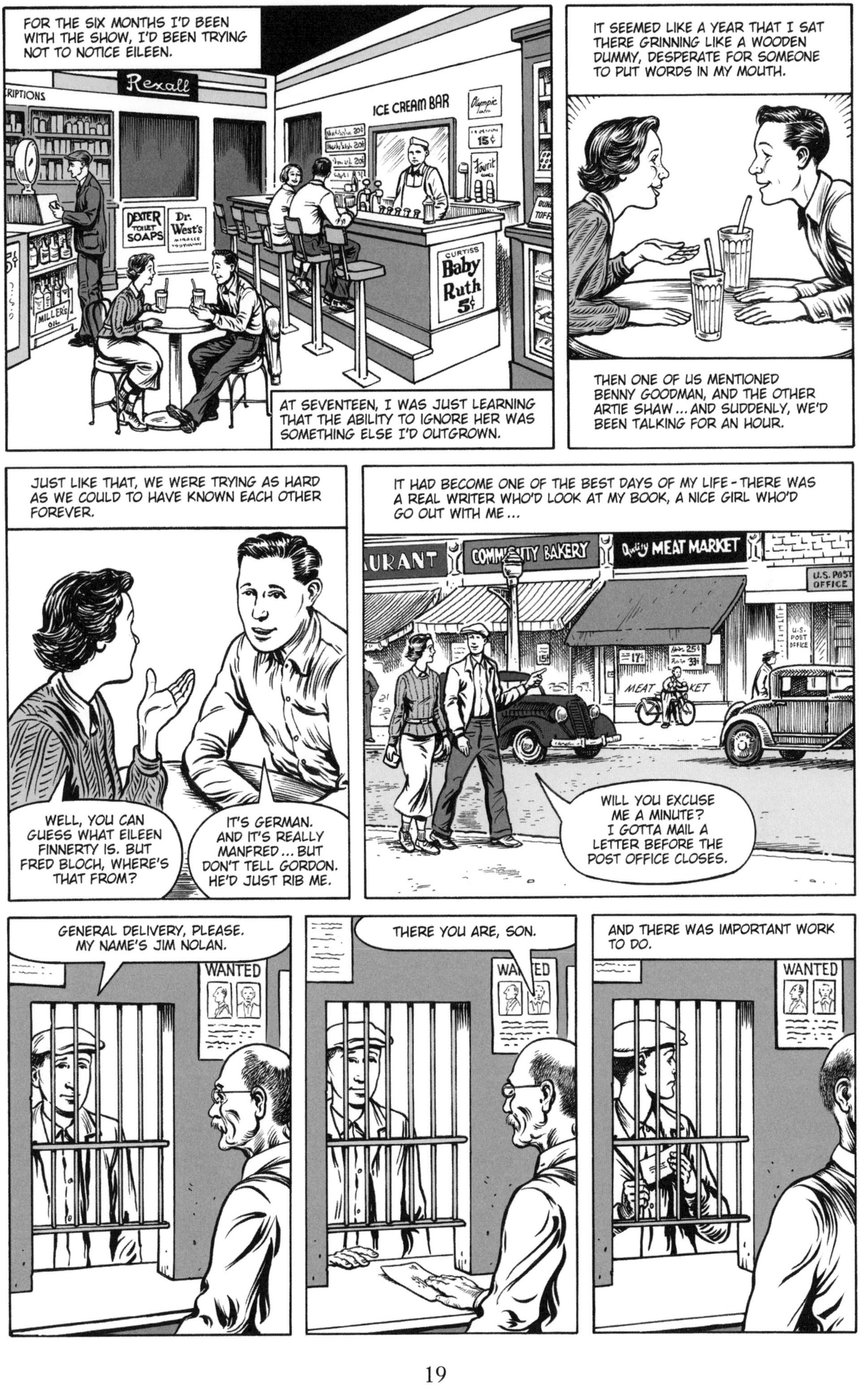
FOR THE SIX MONTHS I'D BEEN WITH THE SHOW, I'D BEEN TRYING NOT TO NOTICE EILEEN.
Rexall
ICE CREAM BAR
DEXTER TOILET SOAPS
Dr. West's
CURTISS Baby Ruth 5¢
MILLER'S OIL
AT SEVENTEEN, I WAS JUST LEARNING THAT THE ABILITY TO IGNORE HER WAS SOMETHING ELSE I'D OUTGROWN.
IT SEEMED LIKE A YEAR THAT I SAT THERE GRINNING LIKE A WOODEN DUMMY, DESPERATE FOR SOMEONE TO PUT WORDS IN MY MOUTH.
THEN ONE OF US MENTIONED BENNY GOODMAN, AND THE OTHER ARTIE SHAW ... AND SUDDENLY, WE'D BEEN TALKING FOR AN HOUR.
JUST LIKE THAT, WE WERE TRYING AS HARD AS WE COULD TO HAVE KNOWN EACH OTHER FOREVER.
WELL, YOU CAN GUESS WHAT EILEEN FINNERTY IS. BUT FRED BLOCH, WHERE'S THAT FROM?
IT'S GERMAN. AND IT'S REALLY MANFRED ... BUT DON'T TELL GORDON. HE'D JUST RIB ME.
IT HAD BECOME ONE OF THE BEST DAYS OF MY LIFE - THERE WAS A REAL WRITER WHO'D LOOK AT MY BOOK, A NICE GIRL WHO'D GO OUT WITH ME ...
COMMUNITY BAKERY
MEAT MARKET
U.S. POST OFFICE
WILL YOU EXCUSE ME A MINUTE? I GOTTA MAIL A LETTER BEFORE THE POST OFFICE CLOSES.
GENERAL DELIVERY, PLEASE. MY NAME'S JIM NOLAN.
WANTED
THERE YOU ARE, SON.
AND THERE WAS IMPORTANT WORK TO DO.
WANTED

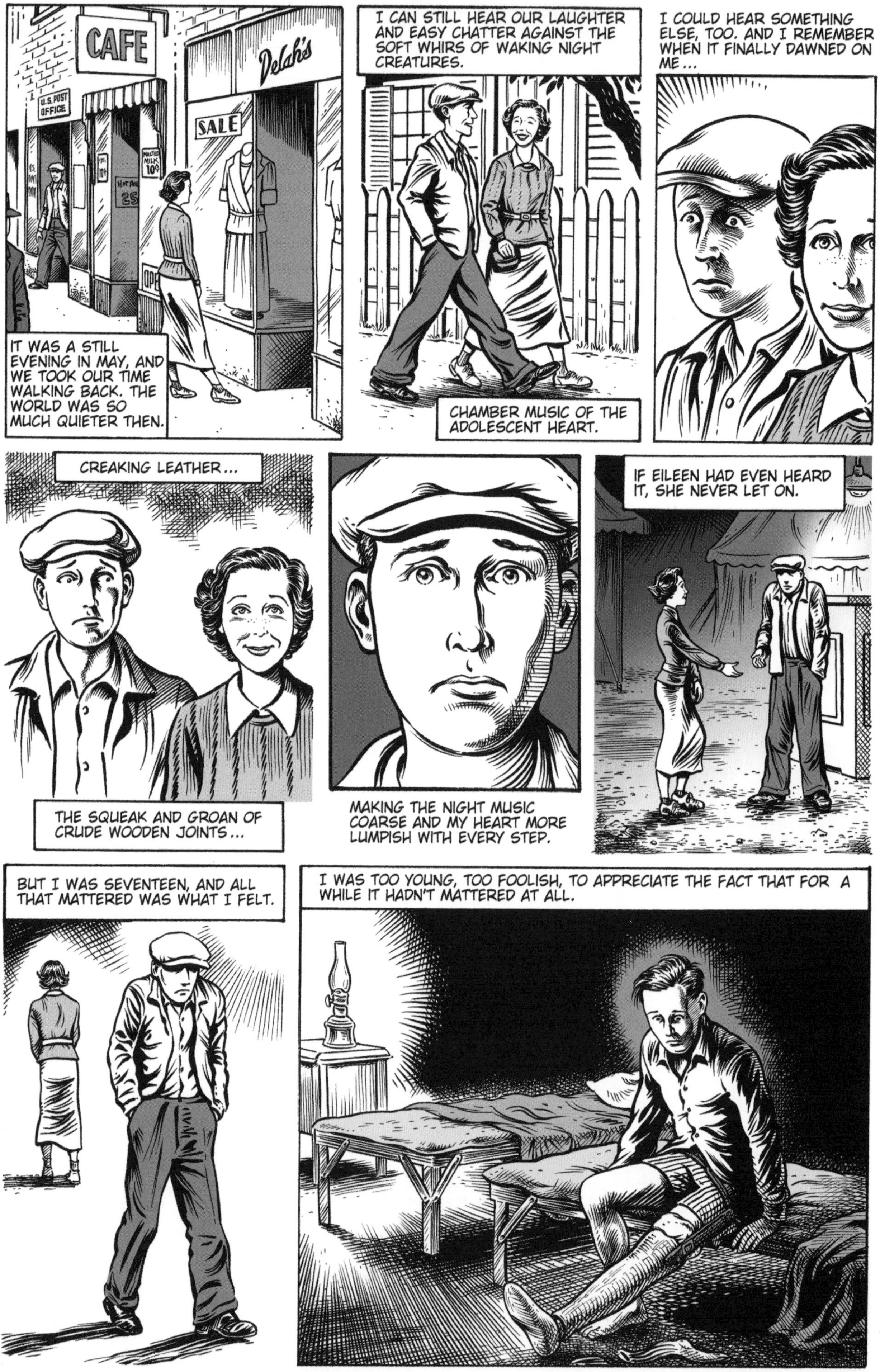
CAFE
U.S. POST OFFICE
Delah's
SALE
IT WAS A STILL EVENING IN MAY, AND WE TOOK OUR TIME WALKING BACK. THE WORLD WAS SO MUCH QUIETER THEN.
I CAN STILL HEAR OUR LAUGHTER AND EASY CHATTER AGAINST THE SOFT WHIRS OF WAKING NIGHT CREATURES.
CHAMBER MUSIC OF THE ADOLESCENT HEART.
I COULD HEAR SOMETHING ELSE, TOO. AND I REMEMBER WHEN IT FINALLY DAWNED ON ME...
CREAKING LEATHER...
THE SQUEAK AND GROAN OF CRUDE WOODEN JOINTS...
MAKING THE NIGHT MUSIC COARSE AND MY HEART MORE LUMPISH WITH EVERY STEP.
IF EILEEN HAD EVEN HEARD IT, SHE NEVER LET ON.
BUT I WAS SEVENTEEN, AND ALL THAT MATTERED WAS WHAT I FELT.
I WAS TOO YOUNG, TOO FOOLISH, TO APPRECIATE THE FACT THAT FOR A WHILE IT HADN'T MATTERED AT ALL.

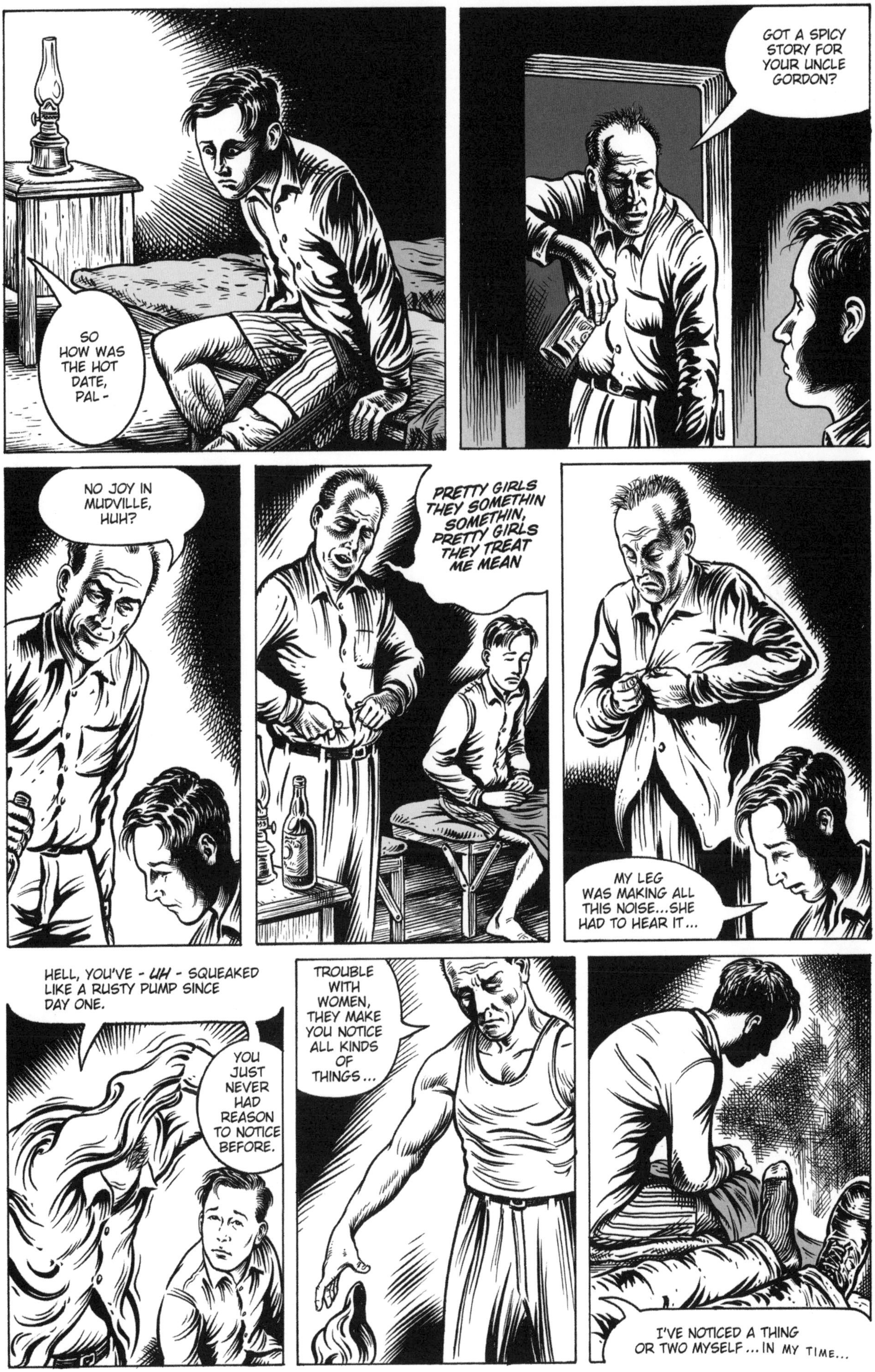
SO HOW WAS THE HOT DATE, PAL-
GOT A SPICY STORY FOR YOUR UNCLE GORDON?
NO JOY IN MUDVILLE, HUH?
PRETTY GIRLS THEY SOMETHIN SOMETHIN, PRETTY GIRLS THEY TREAT ME MEAN
MY LEG WAS MAKING ALL THIS NOISE...SHE HAD TO HEAR IT...
HELL, YOU'VE - UH - SQUEAKED LIKE A RUSTY PUMP SINCE DAY ONE.
YOU JUST NEVER HAD REASON TO NOTICE BEFORE.
TROUBLE WITH WOMEN, THEY MAKE YOU NOTICE ALL KINDS OF THINGS...
I'VE NOTICED A THING OR TWO MYSELF...IN MY TIME...

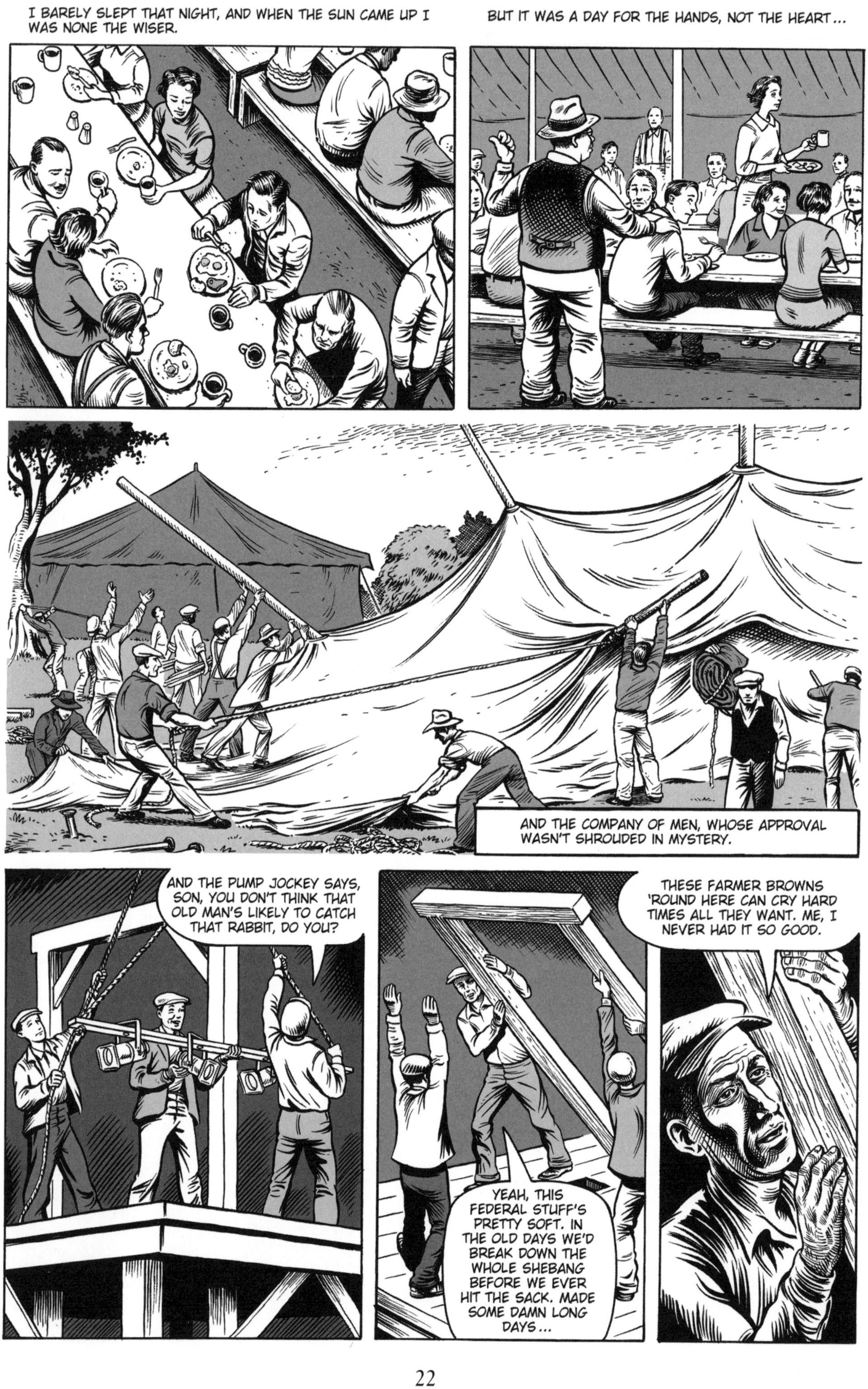
I BARELY SLEPT THAT NIGHT, AND WHEN THE SUN CAME UP I WAS NONE THE WISER.
BUT IT WAS A DAY FOR THE HANDS, NOT THE HEART...
AND THE COMPANY OF MEN, WHOSE APPROVAL WASN'T SHROUDED IN MYSTERY.
AND THE PUMP JOCKEY SAYS, SON, YOU DON'T THINK THAT OLD MAN'S LIKELY TO CATCH THAT RABBIT, DO YOU?
YEAH, THIS FEDERAL STUFF'S PRETTY SOFT. IN THE OLD DAYS WE'D BREAK DOWN THE WHOLE SHEBANG BEFORE WE EVER HIT THE SACK. MADE SOME DAMN LONG DAYS...
THESE FARMER BROWNS 'ROUND HERE CAN CRY HARD TIMES ALL THEY WANT. ME, I NEVER HAD IT SO GOOD.

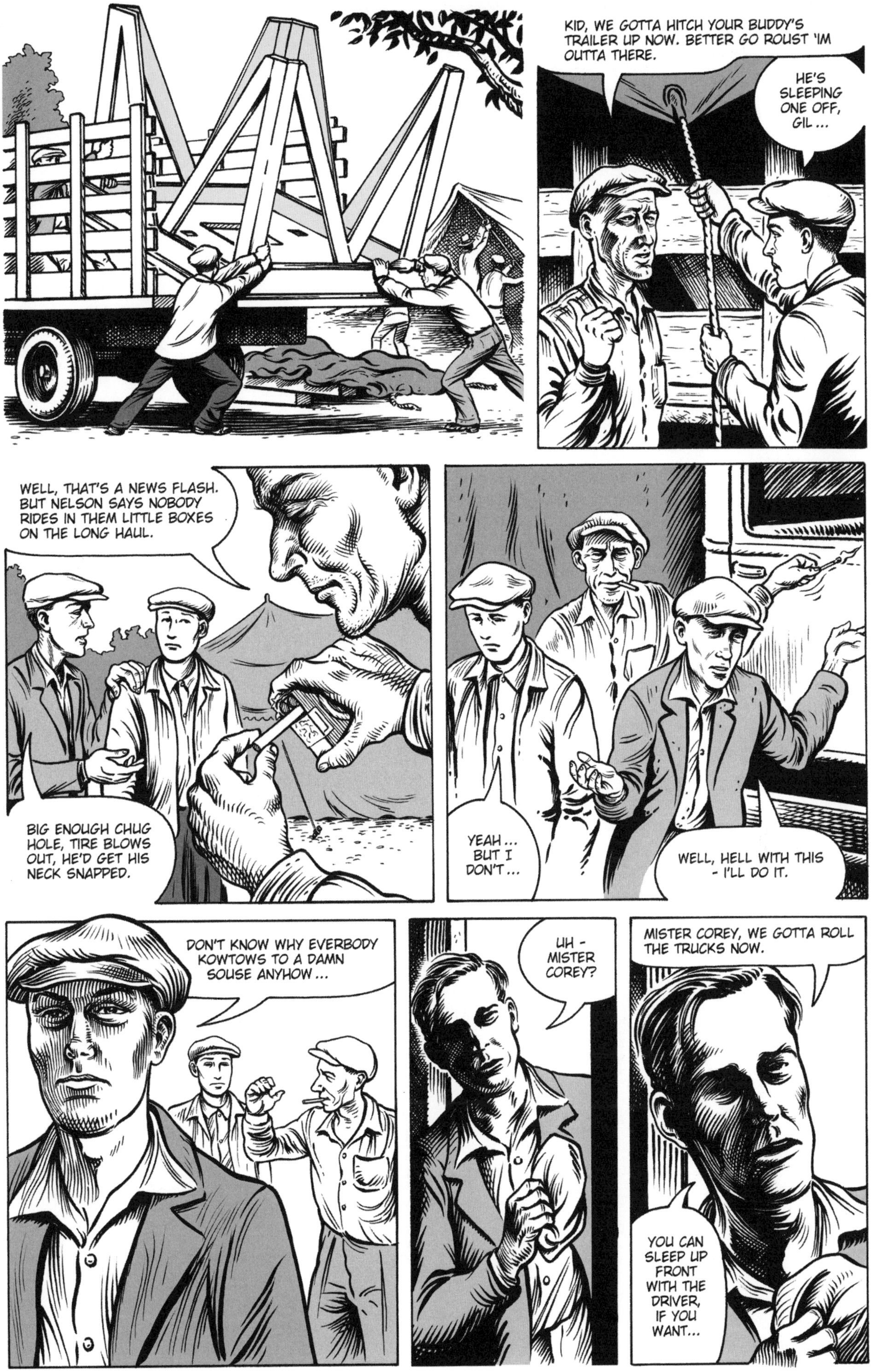
KID, WE GOTTA HITCH YOUR BUDDY'S TRAILER UP NOW. BETTER GO ROUST 'IM OUTTA THERE.
HE'S SLEEPING ONE OFF, GIL ...
WELL, THAT'S A NEWS FLASH. BUT NELSON SAYS NOBODY RIDES IN THEM LITTLE BOXES ON THE LONG HAUL.
BIG ENOUGH CHUG HOLE, TIRE BLOWS OUT, HE'D GET HIS NECK SNAPPED.
YEAH ... BUT I DON'T ...
WELL, HELL WITH THIS - I'LL DO IT.
DON'T KNOW WHY EVERBODY KOWTOWS TO A DAMN SOUSE ANYHOW ...
UH - MISTER COREY?
MISTER COREY, WE GOTTA ROLL THE TRUCKS NOW.
YOU CAN SLEEP UP FRONT WITH THE DRIVER, IF YOU WANT...

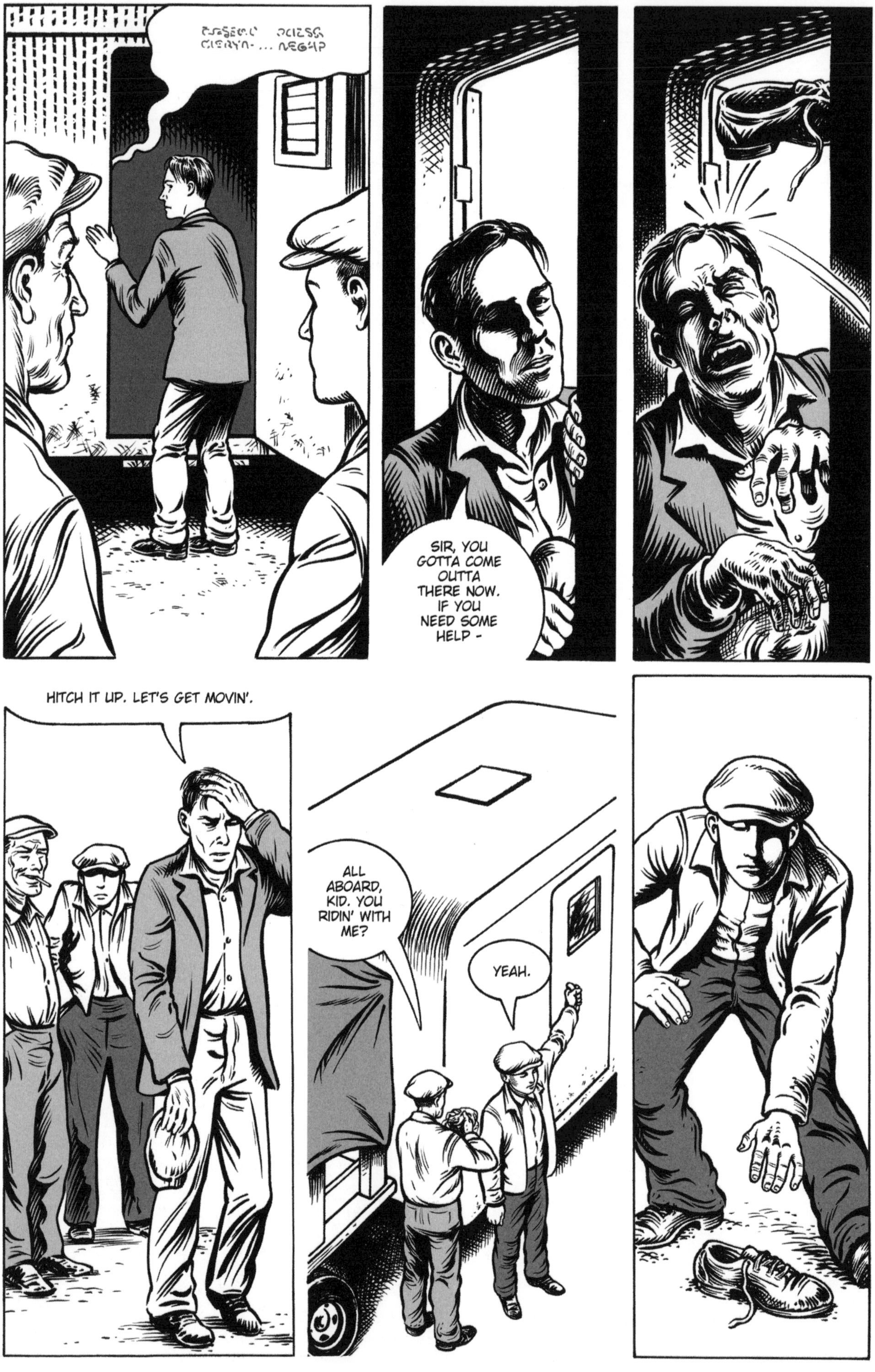
SIR, YOU GOTTA COME OUTTA THERE NOW. IF YOU NEED SOME HELP -
HITCH IT UP. LET'S GET MOVIN'.
ALL ABOARD, KID. YOU RIDIN' WITH ME?
YEAH.

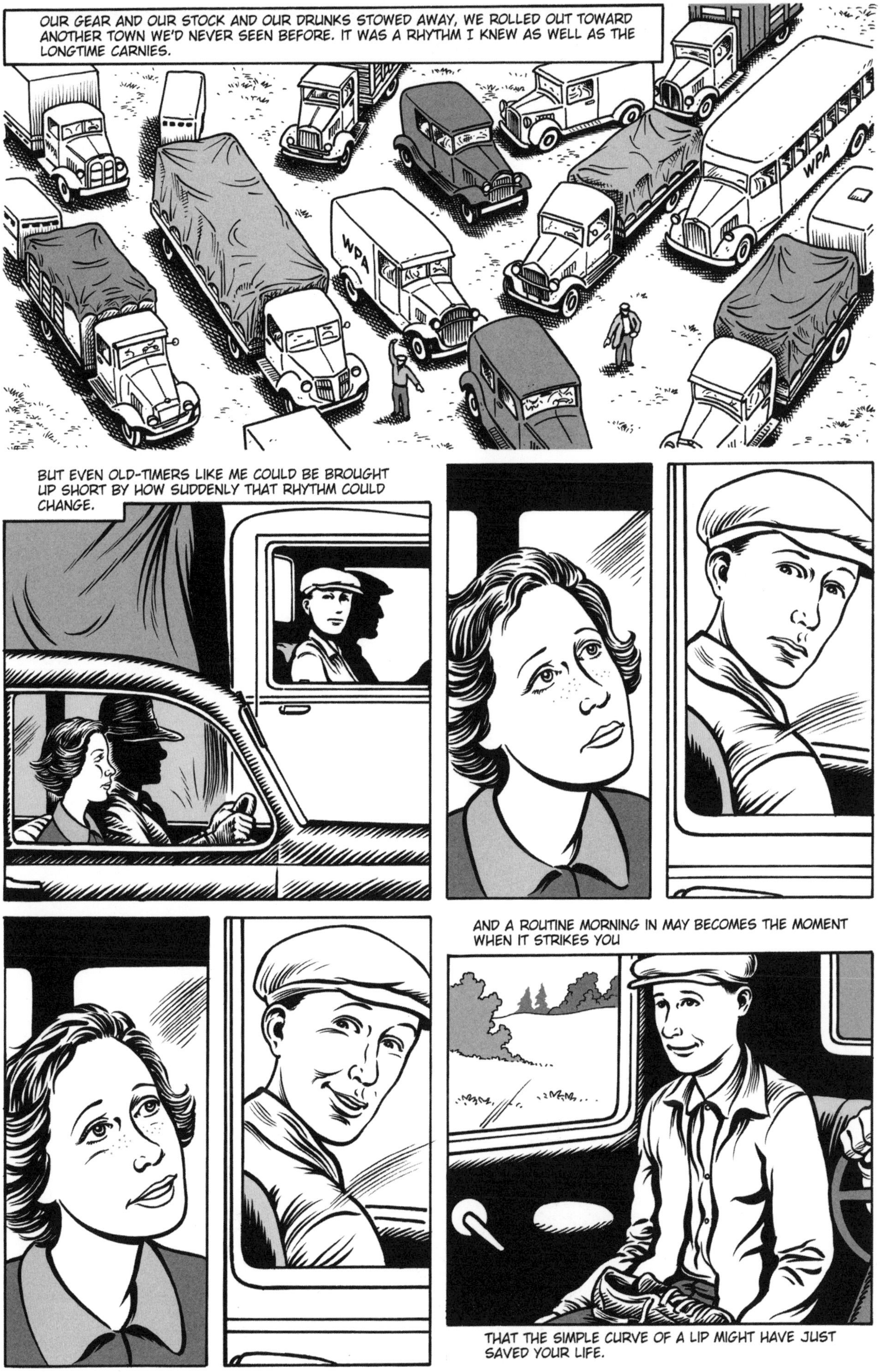
OUR GEAR AND OUR STOCK AND OUR DRUNKS STOWED AWAY, WE ROLLED OUT TOWARD ANOTHER TOWN WE'D NEVER SEEN BEFORE. IT WAS A RHYTHM I KNEW AS WELL AS THE LONGTIME CARNIES.
WPA
WPA
BUT EVEN OLD-TIMERS LIKE ME COULD BE BROUGHT UP SHORT BY HOW SUDDENLY THAT RHYTHM COULD CHANGE.
AND A ROUTINE MORNING IN MAY BECOMES THE MOMENT WHEN IT STRIKES YOU
THAT THE SIMPLE CURVE OF A LIP MIGHT HAVE JUST SAVED YOUR LIFE.

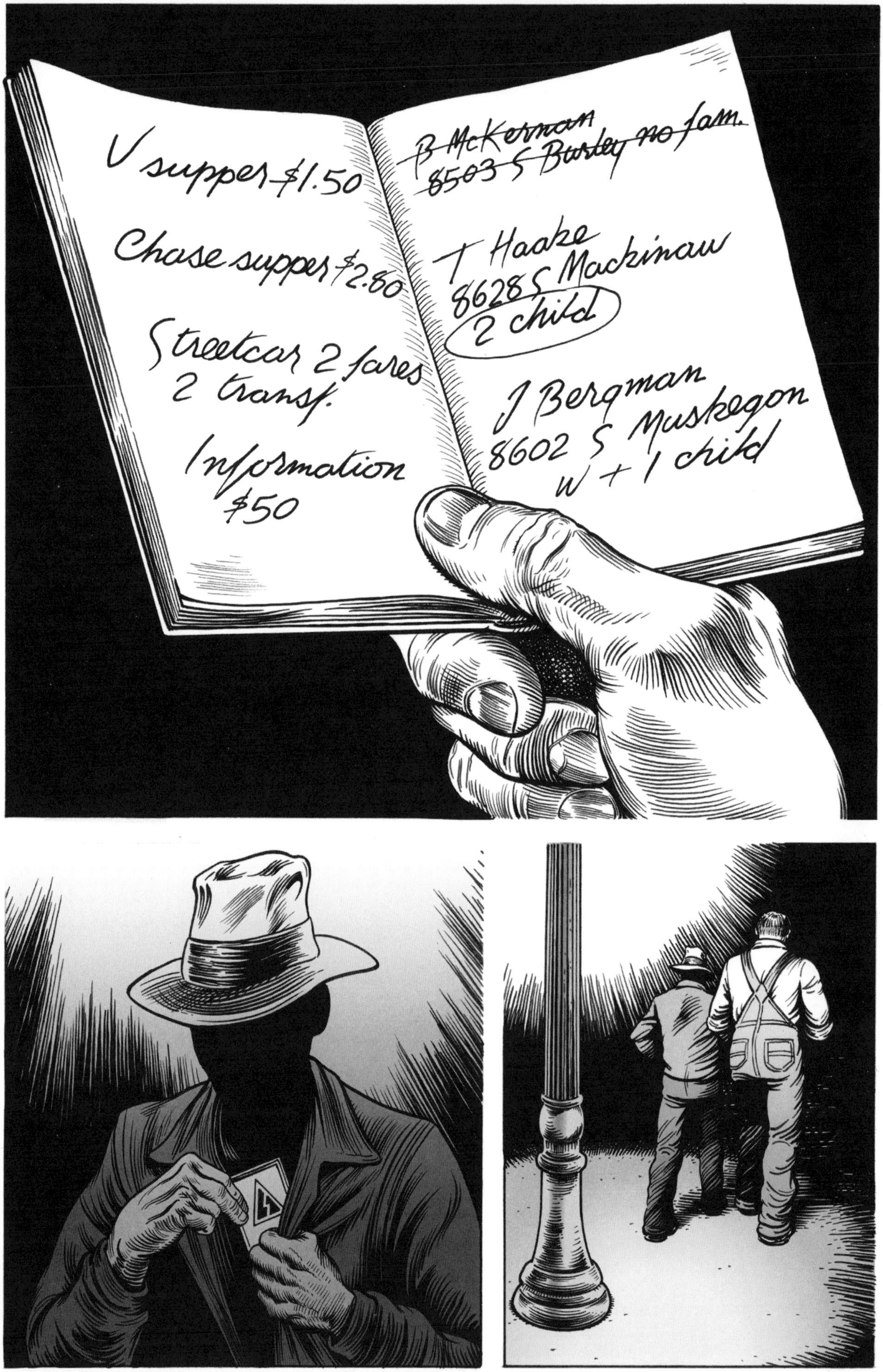
V supper $1.50
Chase supper $2.80
Streetcar 2 fares
2 transf.
Information
$50
B McKernan
8503 S Burley no fam.
T Haake
8628 S Mackinaw
2 child
J Bergman
8602 S Muskegon
w + 1 child

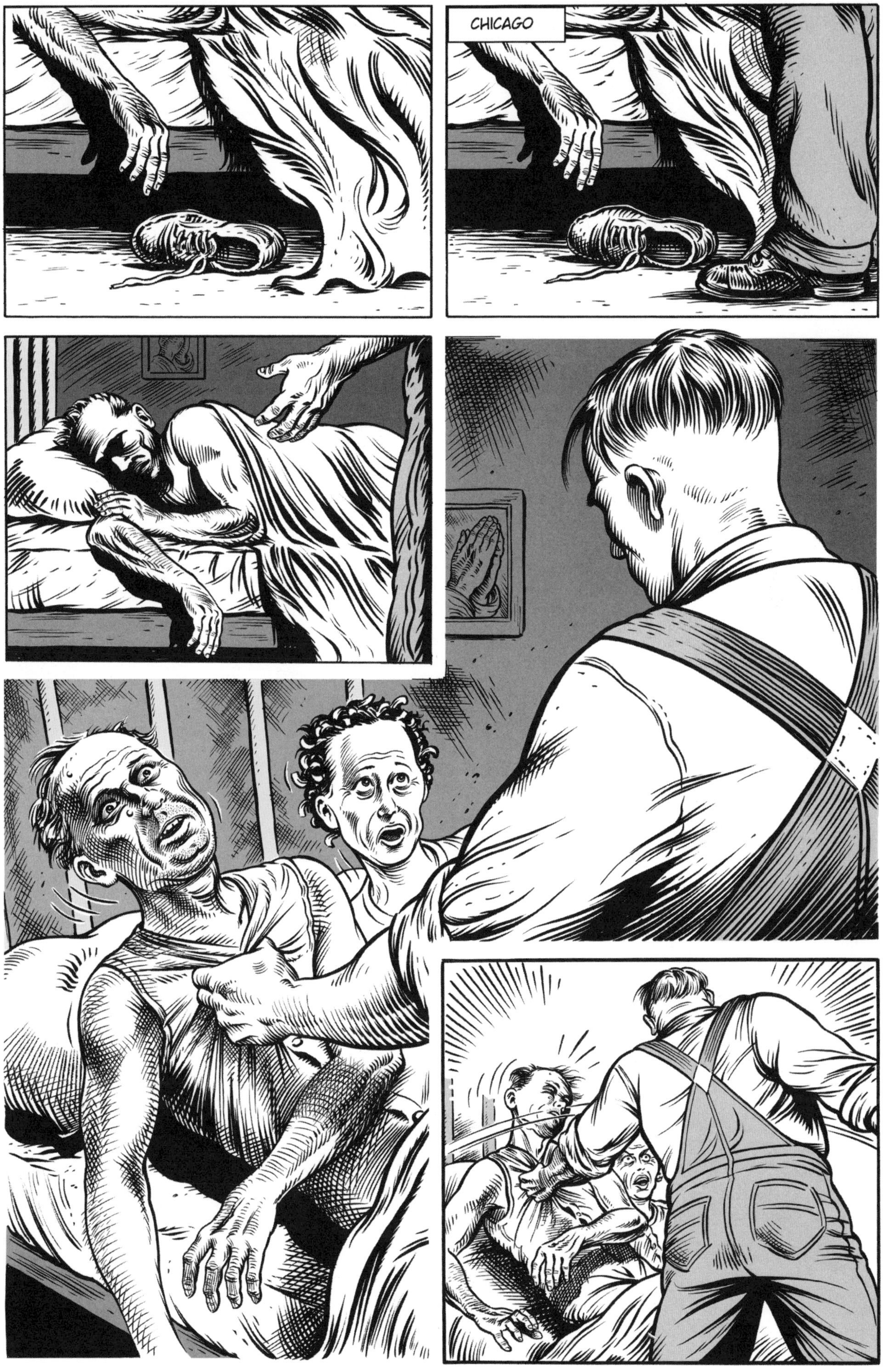
CHICAGO

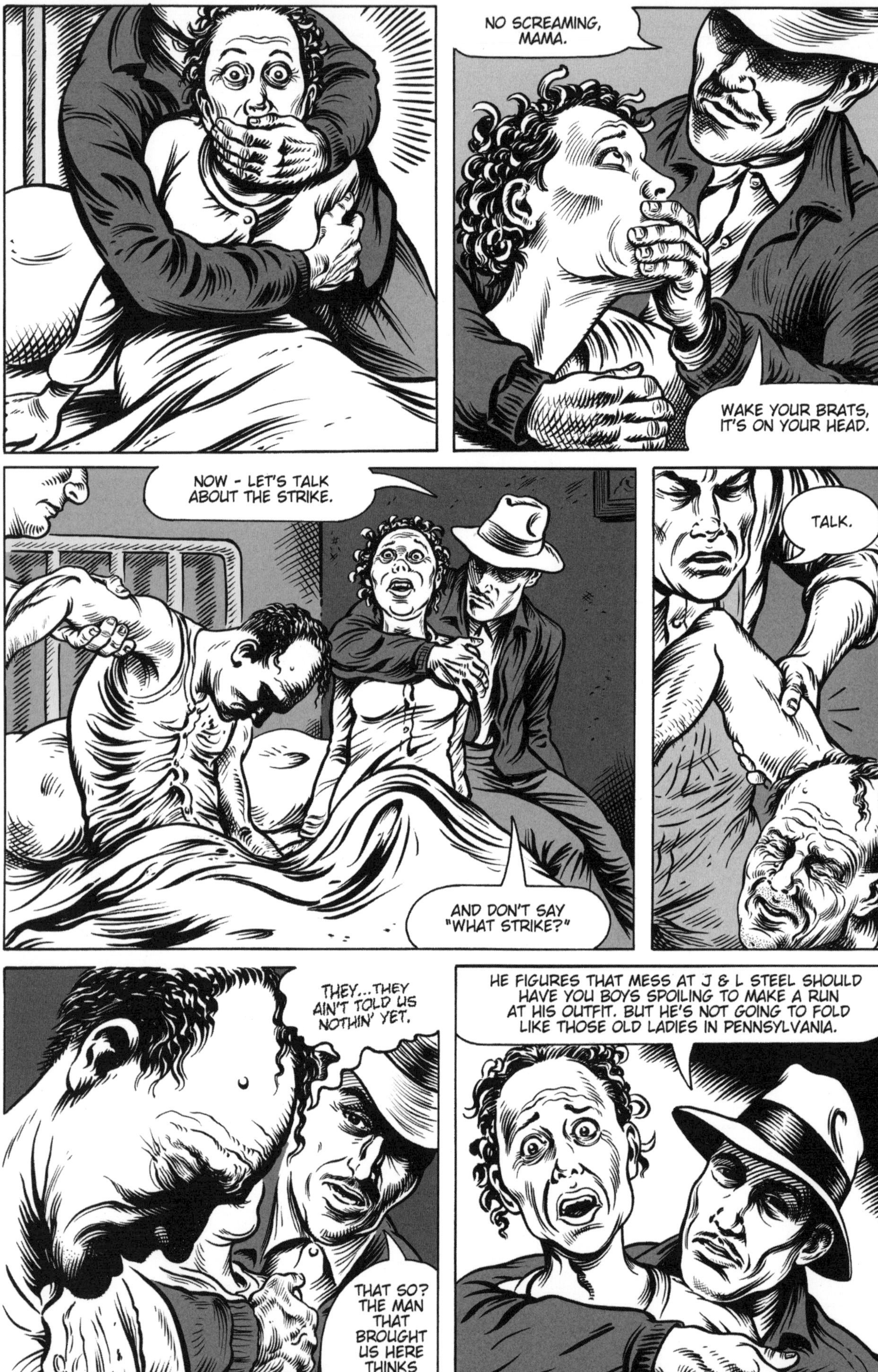
NO SCREAMING, MAMA.
WAKE YOUR BRATS, IT'S ON YOUR HEAD.
NOW - LET'S TALK ABOUT THE STRIKE.
AND DON'T SAY "WHAT STRIKE?"
TALK.
THEY... THEY AIN'T TOLD US NOTHIN' YET.
THAT SO? THE MAN THAT BROUGHT US HERE THINKS DIFFERENT.
HE FIGURES THAT MESS AT J & L STEEL SHOULD HAVE YOU BOYS SPOILING TO MAKE A RUN AT HIS OUTFIT. BUT HE'S NOT GOING TO FOLD LIKE THOSE OLD LADIES IN PENNSYLVANIA.

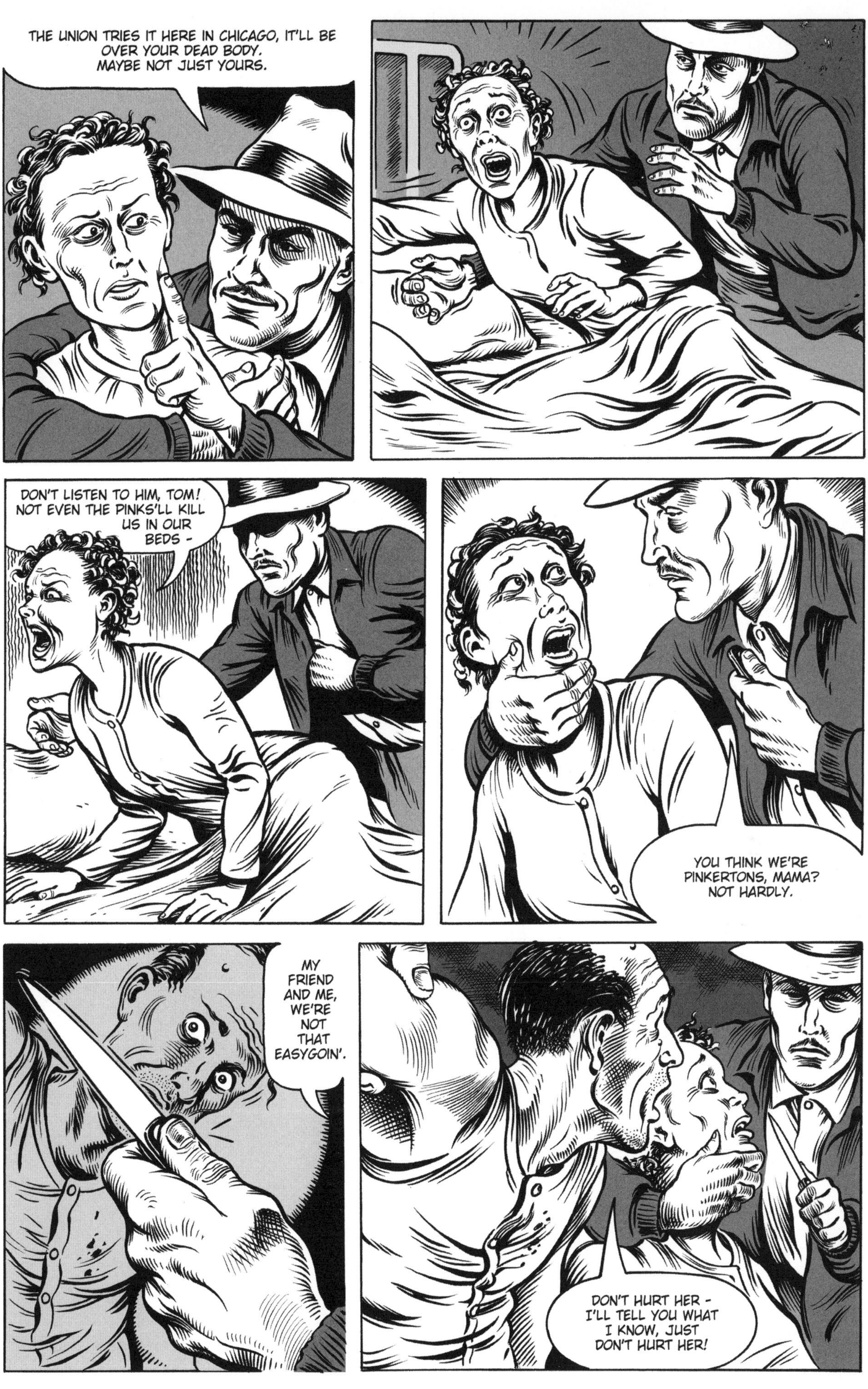
THE UNION TRIES IT HERE IN CHICAGO, IT'LL BE OVER YOUR DEAD BODY. MAYBE NOT JUST YOURS.
DON'T LISTEN TO HIM, TOM! NOT EVEN THE PINKS'LL KILL US IN OUR BEDS -
YOU THINK WE'RE PINKERTONS, MAMA? NOT HARDLY.
MY FRIEND AND ME, WE'RE NOT THAT EASYGOIN'.
DON'T HURT HER - I'LL TELL YOU WHAT I KNOW, JUST DON'T HURT HER!

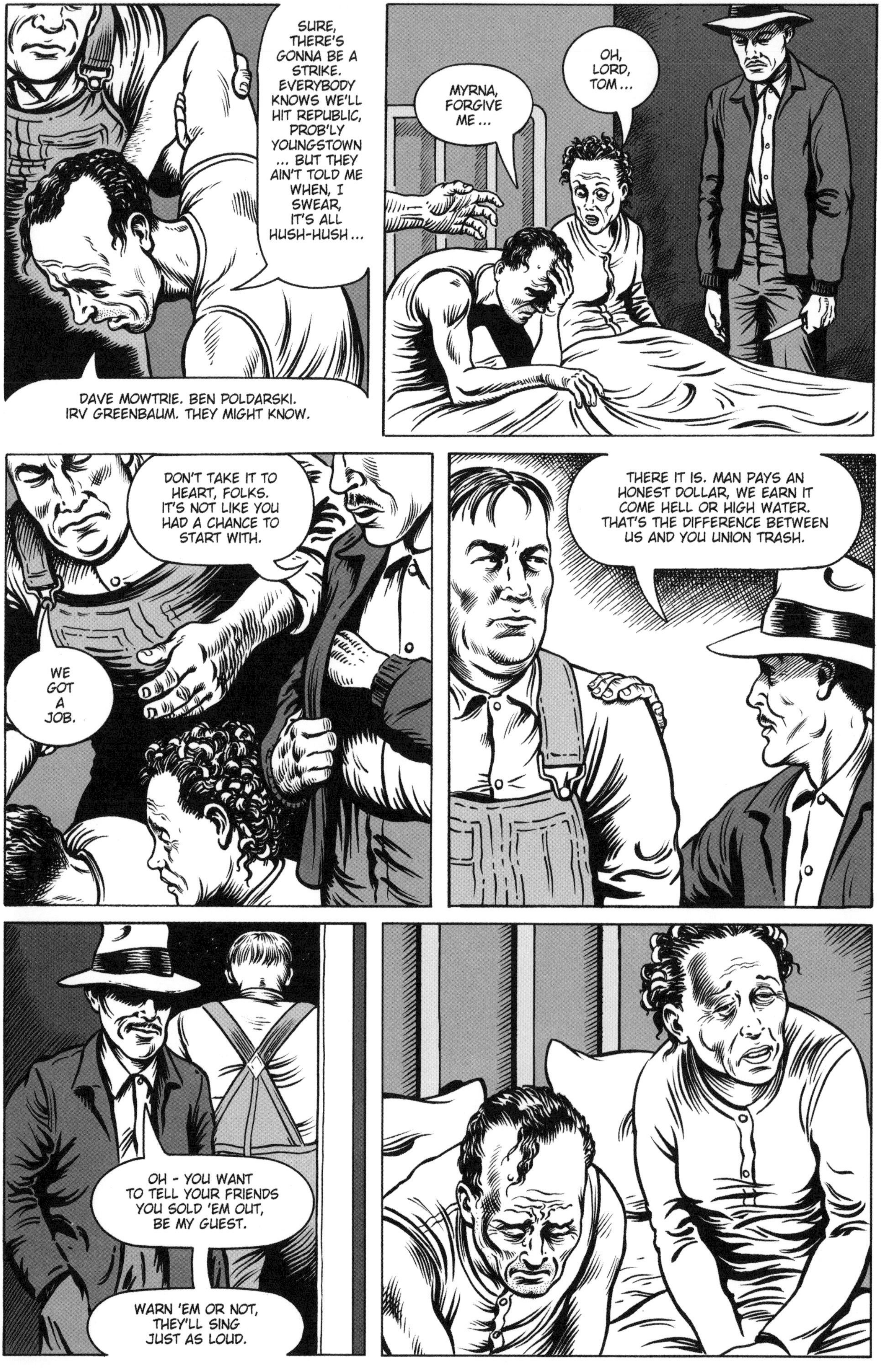
SURE, THERE'S GONNA BE A STRIKE. EVERYBODY KNOWS WE'LL HIT REPUBLIC, PROB'LY YOUNGSTOWN ... BUT THEY AIN'T TOLD ME WHEN, I SWEAR, IT'S ALL HUSH-HUSH ...
DAVE MOWTRIE. BEN POLDARSKI. IRV GREENBAUM. THEY MIGHT KNOW.
MYRNA, FORGIVE ME ...
OH, LORD, TOM ...
DON'T TAKE IT TO HEART, FOLKS. IT'S NOT LIKE YOU HAD A CHANCE TO START WITH.
WE GOT A JOB.
THERE IT IS. MAN PAYS AN HONEST DOLLAR, WE EARN IT COME HELL OR HIGH WATER. THAT'S THE DIFFERENCE BETWEEN US AND YOU UNION TRASH.
OH - YOU WANT TO TELL YOUR FRIENDS YOU SOLD 'EM OUT, BE MY GUEST.
WARN 'EM OR NOT, THEY'LL SING JUST AS LOUD.

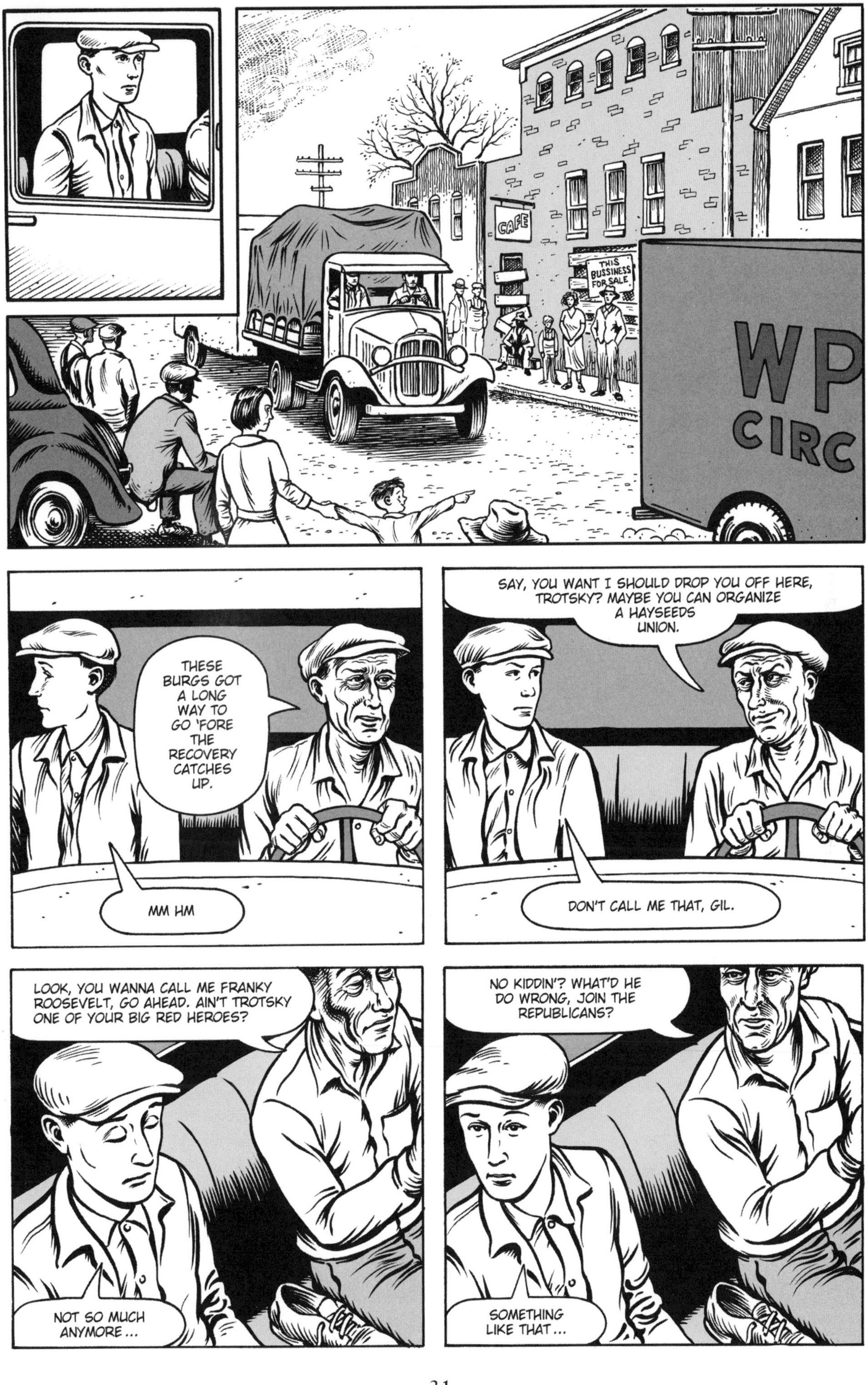
CAFE
THIS BUSSINESS FOR SALE
WP
CIRC
THESE BURGS GOT A LONG WAY TO GO 'FORE THE RECOVERY CATCHES UP.
MM HM
SAY, YOU WANT I SHOULD DROP YOU OFF HERE, TROTSKY? MAYBE YOU CAN ORGANIZE A HAYSEEDS UNION.
DON'T CALL ME THAT, GIL.
LOOK, YOU WANNA CALL ME FRANKY ROOSEVELT, GO AHEAD. AIN'T TROTSKY ONE OF YOUR BIG RED HEROES?
NOT SO MUCH ANYMORE...
NO KIDDIN'? WHAT'D HE DO WRONG, JOIN THE REPUBLICANS?
SOMETHING LIKE THAT...

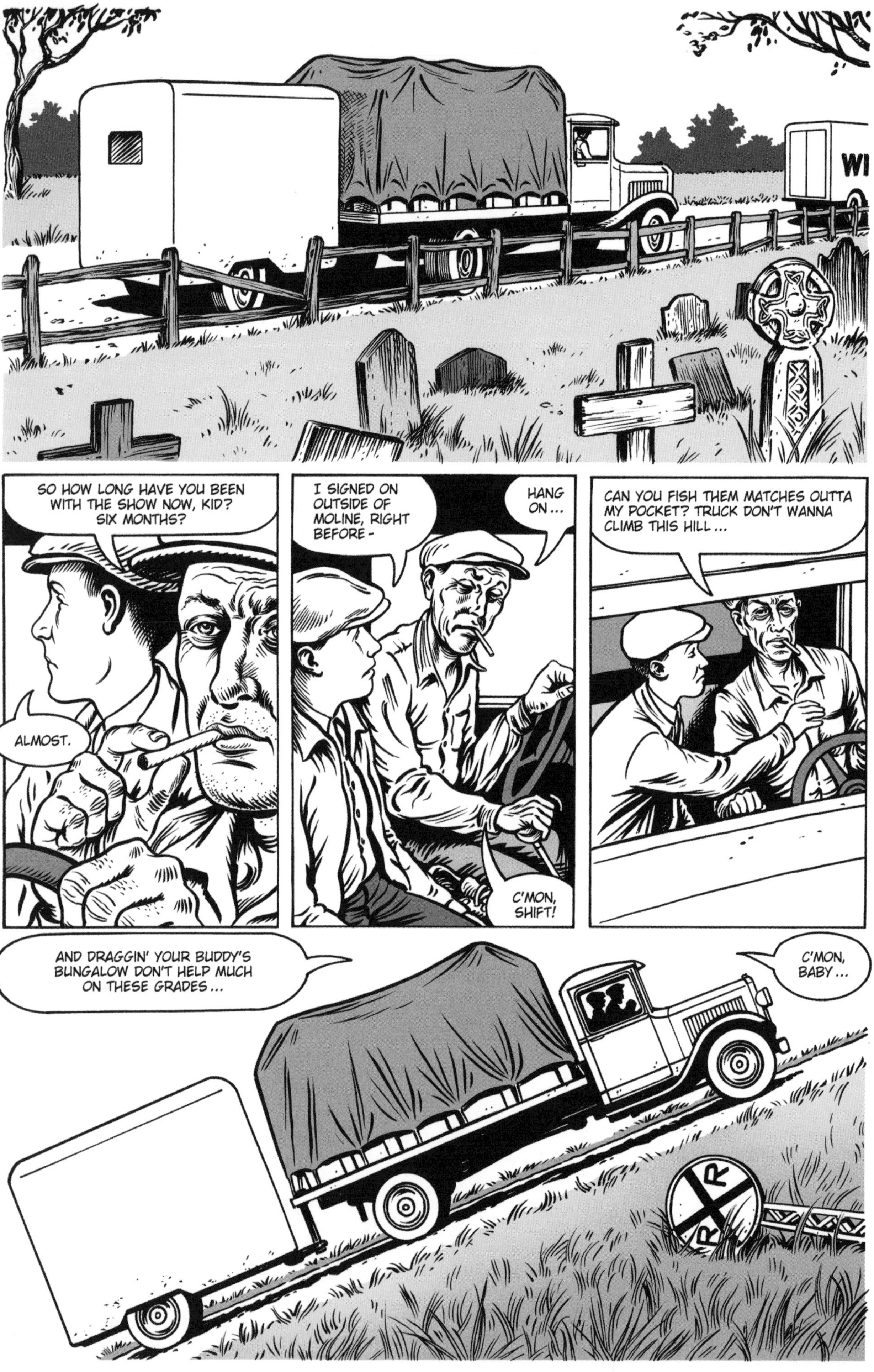

SO HOW LONG HAVE YOU BEEN WITH THE SHOW NOW, KID? SIX MONTHS?
ALMOST.
I SIGNED ON OUTSIDE OF MOLINE, RIGHT BEFORE -
HANG ON...
C'MON, SHIFT!
CAN YOU FISH THEM MATCHES OUTTA MY POCKET? TRUCK DON'T WANNA CLIMB THIS HILL...
AND DRAGGIN' YOUR BUDDY'S BUNGALOW DON'T HELP MUCH ON THESE GRADES...
C'MON, BABY...

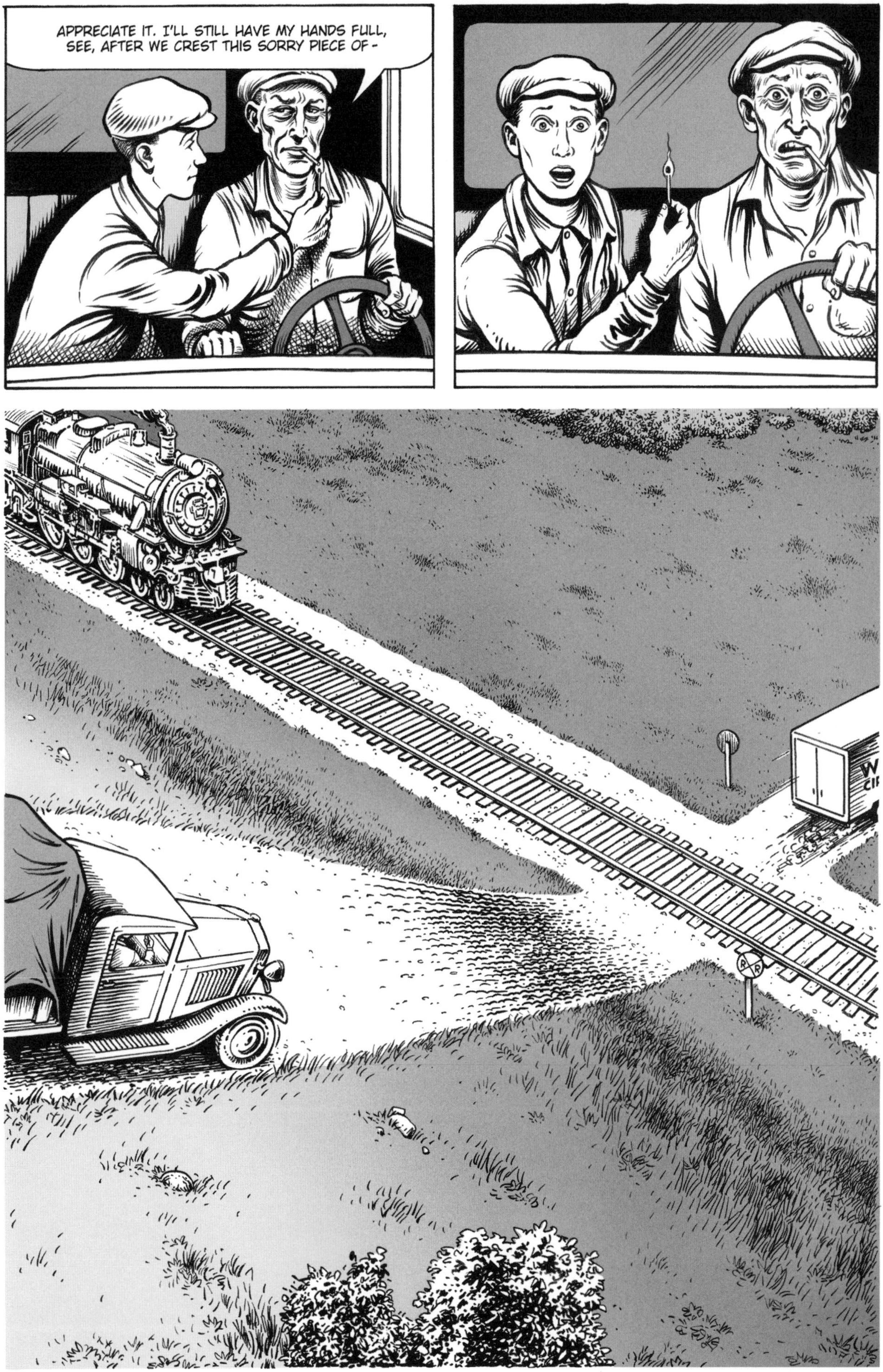
APPRECIATE IT. I'LL STILL HAVE MY HANDS FULL, SEE, AFTER WE CREST THIS SORRY PIECE OF -

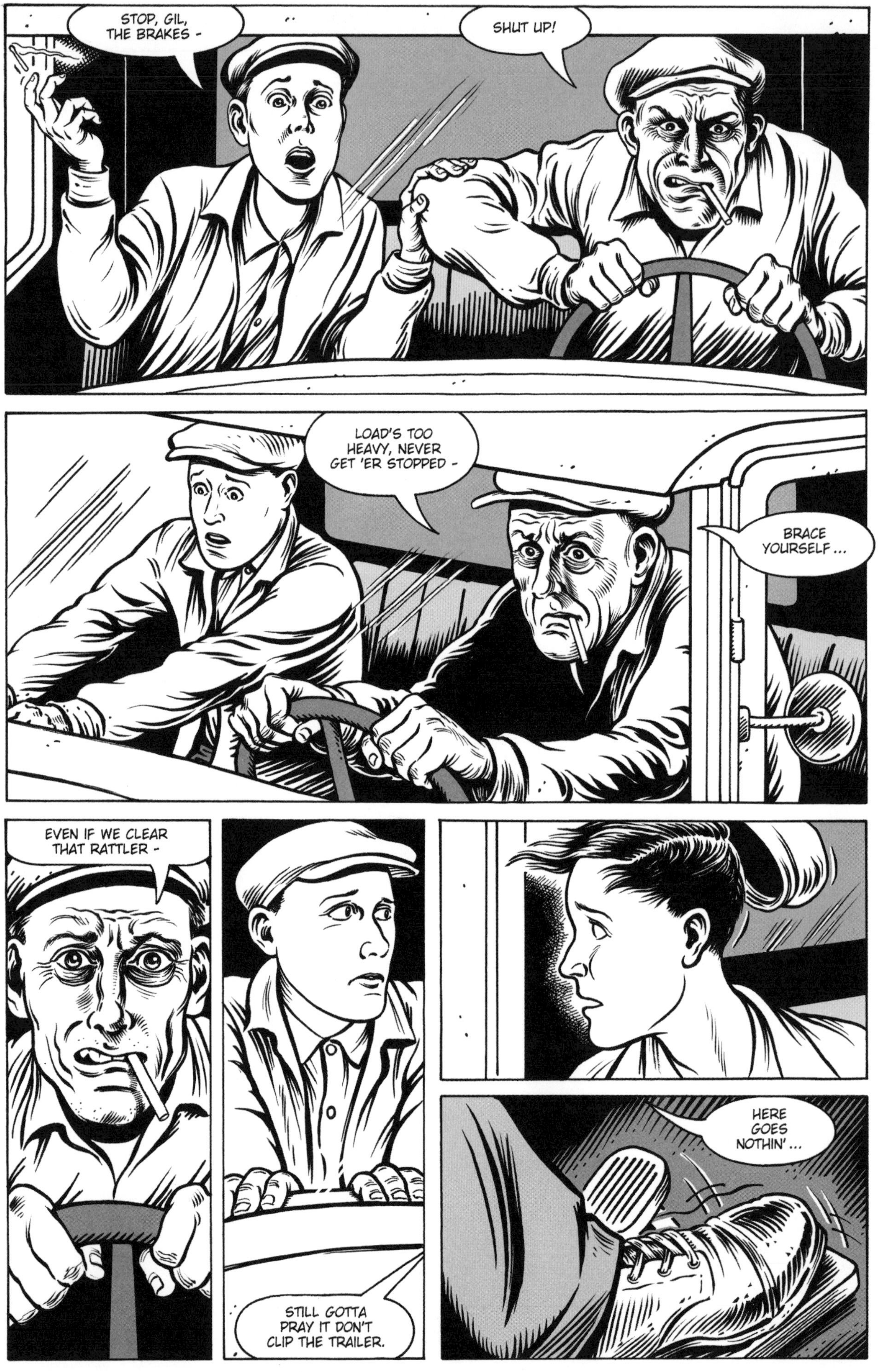
STOP, GIL, THE BRAKES -
SHUT UP!
LOAD'S TOO HEAVY, NEVER GET 'ER STOPPED -
BRACE YOURSELF ...
EVEN IF WE CLEAR THAT RATTLER -
STILL GOTTA PRAY IT DON'T CLIP THE TRAILER.
HERE GOES NOTHIN' ...

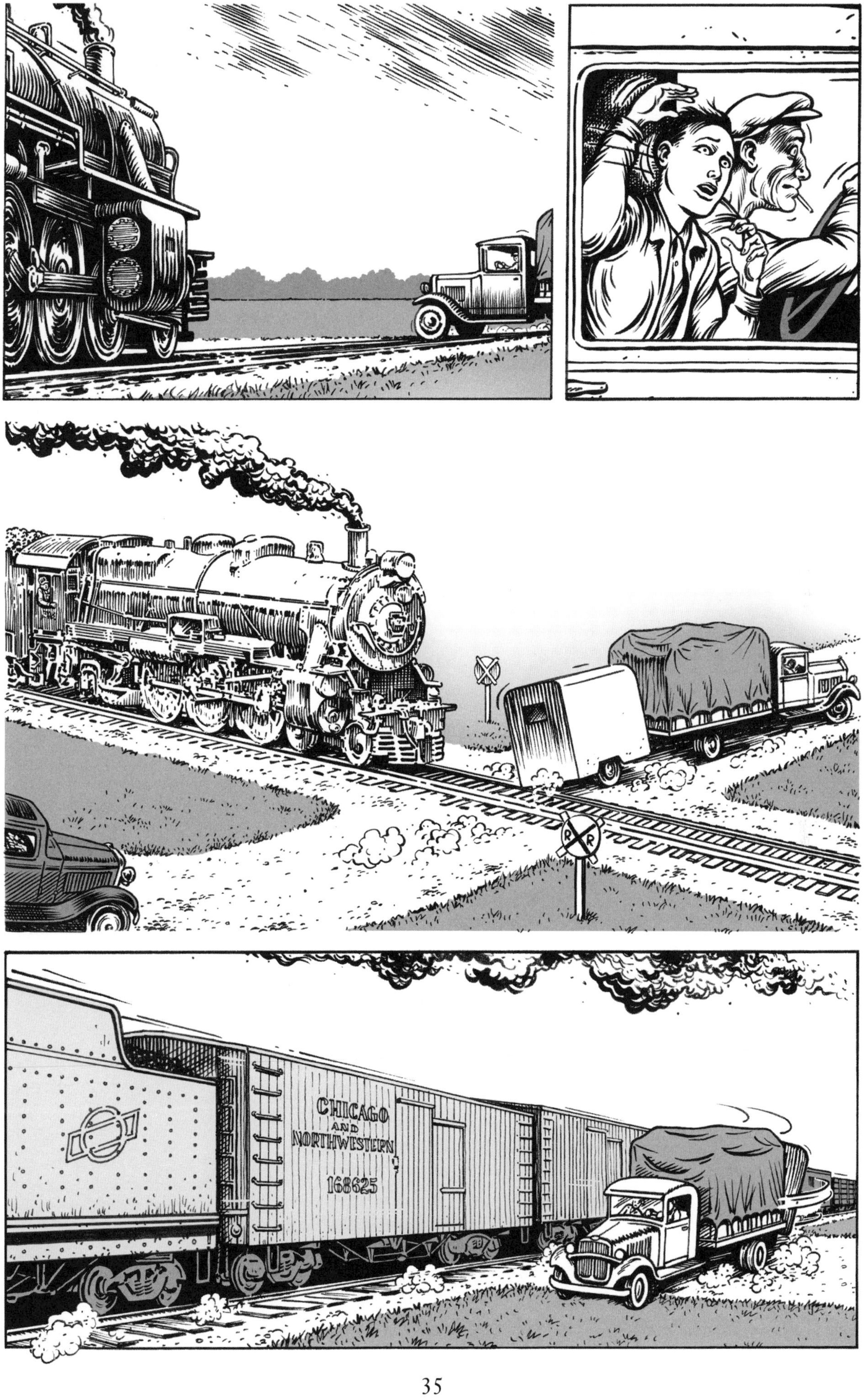
R R
CHICAGO
AND
NORTHWESTERN
168625

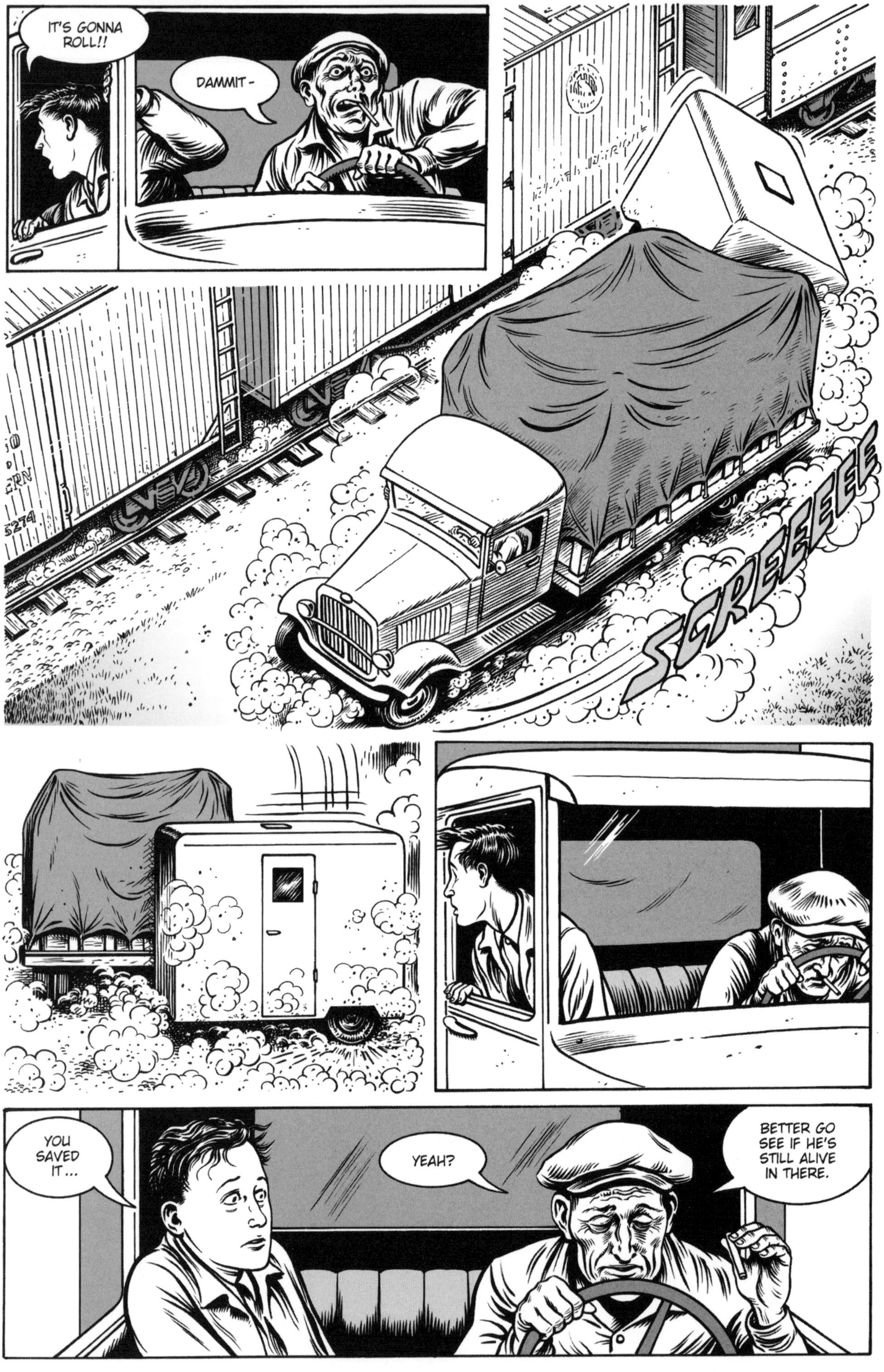
IT'S GONNA ROLL!!
DAMMIT-
SCREEEEE
YOU SAVED IT...
YEAH?
BETTER GO SEE IF HE'S STILL ALIVE IN THERE.

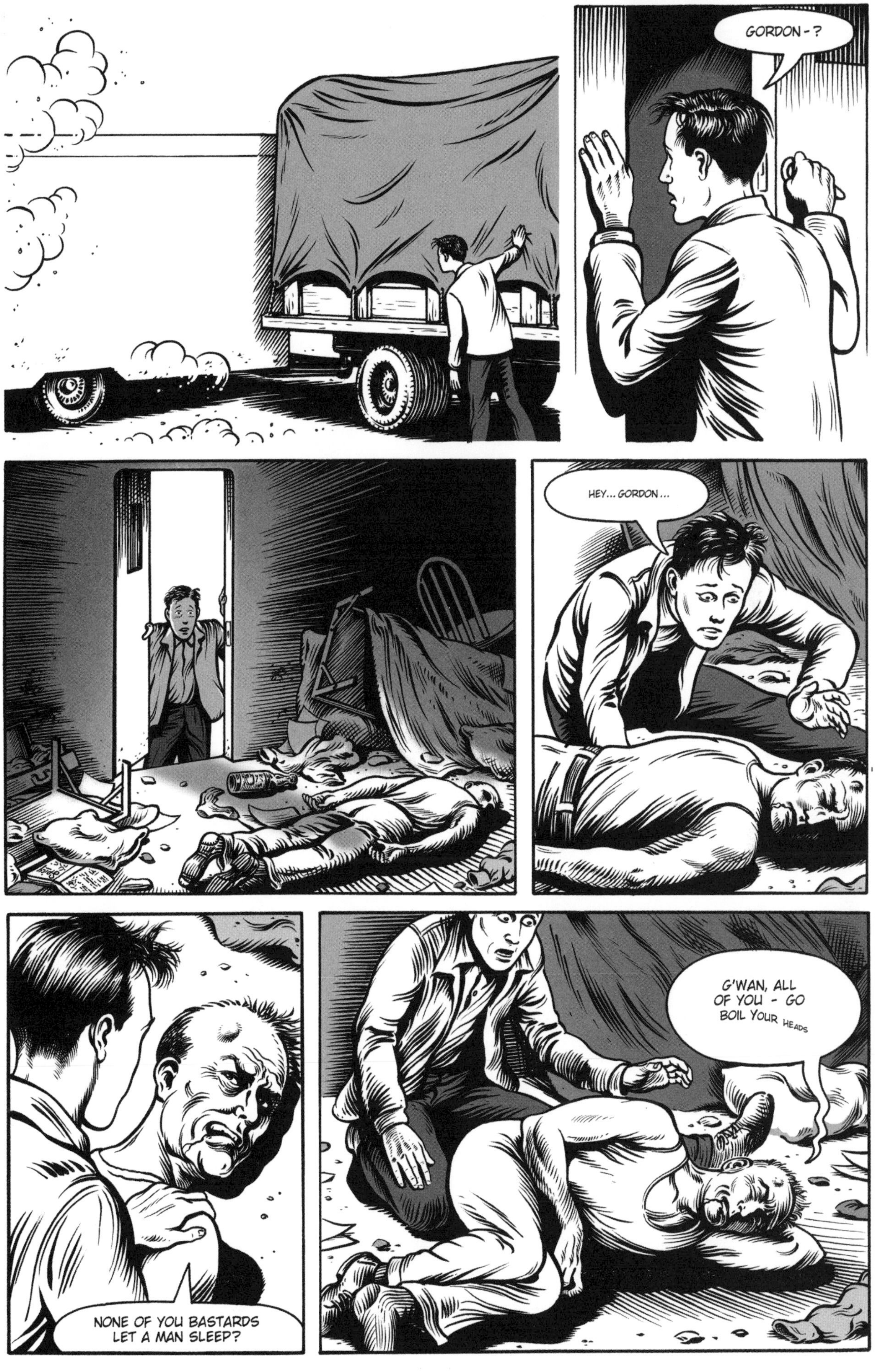
GORDON - ?
HEY... GORDON...
NONE OF YOU BASTARDS LET A MAN SLEEP?
G'WAN, ALL OF YOU - GO BOIL YOUR HEADS

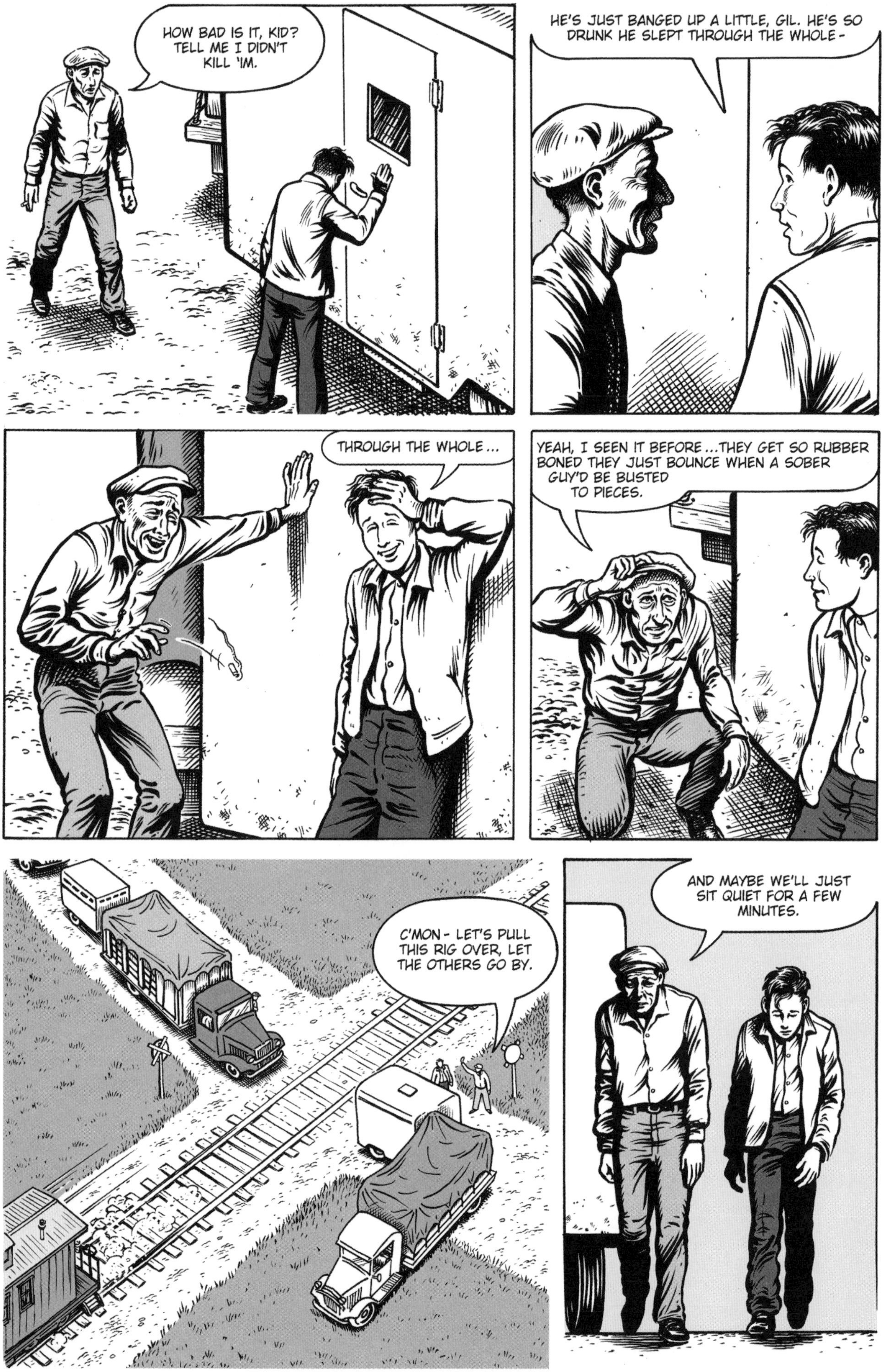
HOW BAD IS IT, KID? TELL ME I DIDN'T KILL 'IM.
HE'S JUST BANGED UP A LITTLE, GIL. HE'S SO DRUNK HE SLEPT THROUGH THE WHOLE -
THROUGH THE WHOLE...
YEAH, I SEEN IT BEFORE...THEY GET SO RUBBER BONED THEY JUST BOUNCE WHEN A SOBER GUY'D BE BUSTED TO PIECES.
C'MON - LET'S PULL THIS RIG OVER, LET THE OTHERS GO BY.
AND MAYBE WE'LL JUST SIT QUIET FOR A FEW MINUTES.

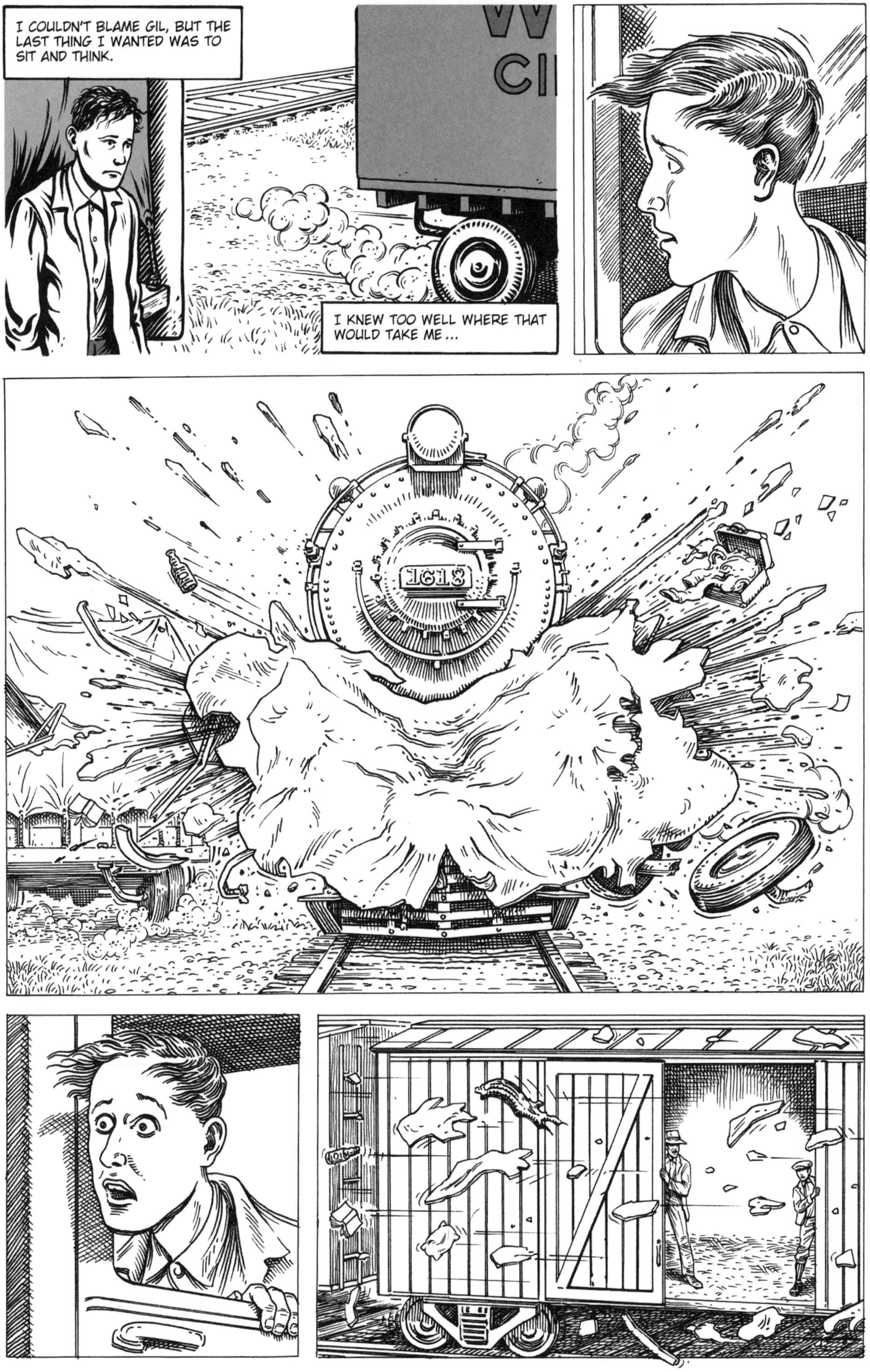
I COULDN'T BLAME GIL, BUT THE LAST THING I WANTED WAS TO SIT AND THINK.
I KNEW TOO WELL WHERE THAT WOULD TAKE ME...
1618

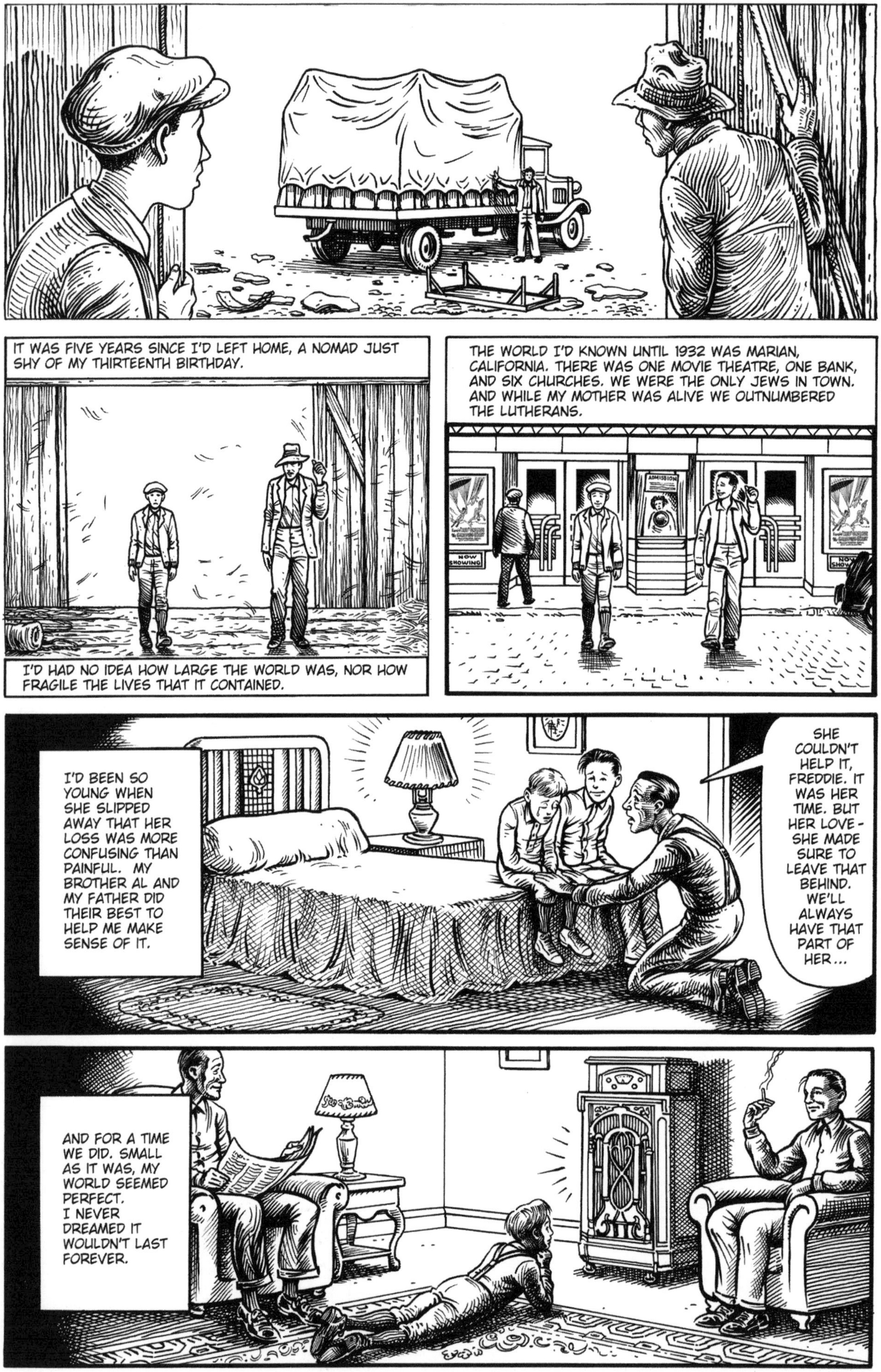
IT WAS FIVE YEARS SINCE I'D LEFT HOME, A NOMAD JUST SHY OF MY THIRTEENTH BIRTHDAY.
I'D HAD NO IDEA HOW LARGE THE WORLD WAS, NOR HOW FRAGILE THE LIVES THAT IT CONTAINED.
THE WORLD I'D KNOWN UNTIL 1932 WAS MARIAN, CALIFORNIA. THERE WAS ONE MOVIE THEATRE, ONE BANK, AND SIX CHURCHES. WE WERE THE ONLY JEWS IN TOWN. AND WHILE MY MOTHER WAS ALIVE WE OUTNUMBERED THE LUTHERANS.
NOW SHOWING
I'D BEEN SO YOUNG WHEN SHE SLIPPED AWAY THAT HER LOSS WAS MORE CONFUSING THAN PAINFUL. MY BROTHER AL AND MY FATHER DID THEIR BEST TO HELP ME MAKE SENSE OF IT.
SHE COULDN'T HELP IT, FREDDIE. IT WAS HER TIME. BUT HER LOVE-SHE MADE SURE TO LEAVE THAT BEHIND. WE'LL ALWAYS HAVE THAT PART OF HER...
AND FOR A TIME WE DID. SMALL AS IT WAS, MY WORLD SEEMED PERFECT. I NEVER DREAMED IT WOULDN'T LAST FOREVER.

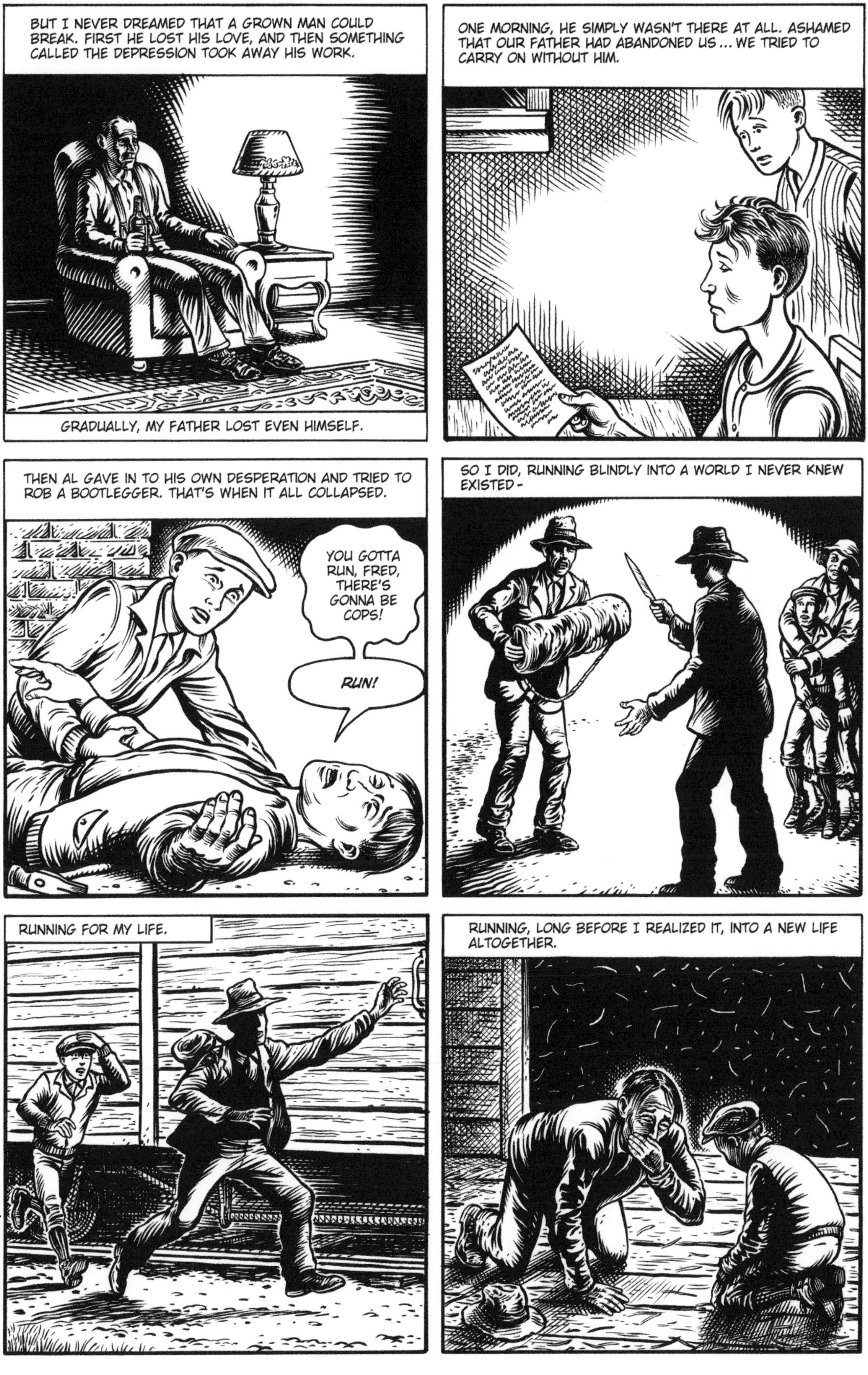
BUT I NEVER DREAMED THAT A GROWN MAN COULD BREAK. FIRST HE LOST HIS LOVE, AND THEN SOMETHING CALLED THE DEPRESSION TOOK AWAY HIS WORK.
GRADUALLY, MY FATHER LOST EVEN HIMSELF.
ONE MORNING, HE SIMPLY WASN'T THERE AT ALL. ASHAMED THAT OUR FATHER HAD ABANDONED US ... WE TRIED TO CARRY ON WITHOUT HIM.
THEN AL GAVE IN TO HIS OWN DESPERATION AND TRIED TO ROB A BOOTLEGGER. THAT'S WHEN IT ALL COLLAPSED.
YOU GOTTA RUN, FRED, THERE'S GONNA BE COPS!
RUN!
SO I DID, RUNNING BLINDLY INTO A WORLD I NEVER KNEW EXISTED–
RUNNING FOR MY LIFE.
RUNNING, LONG BEFORE I REALIZED IT, INTO A NEW LIFE ALTOGETHER.

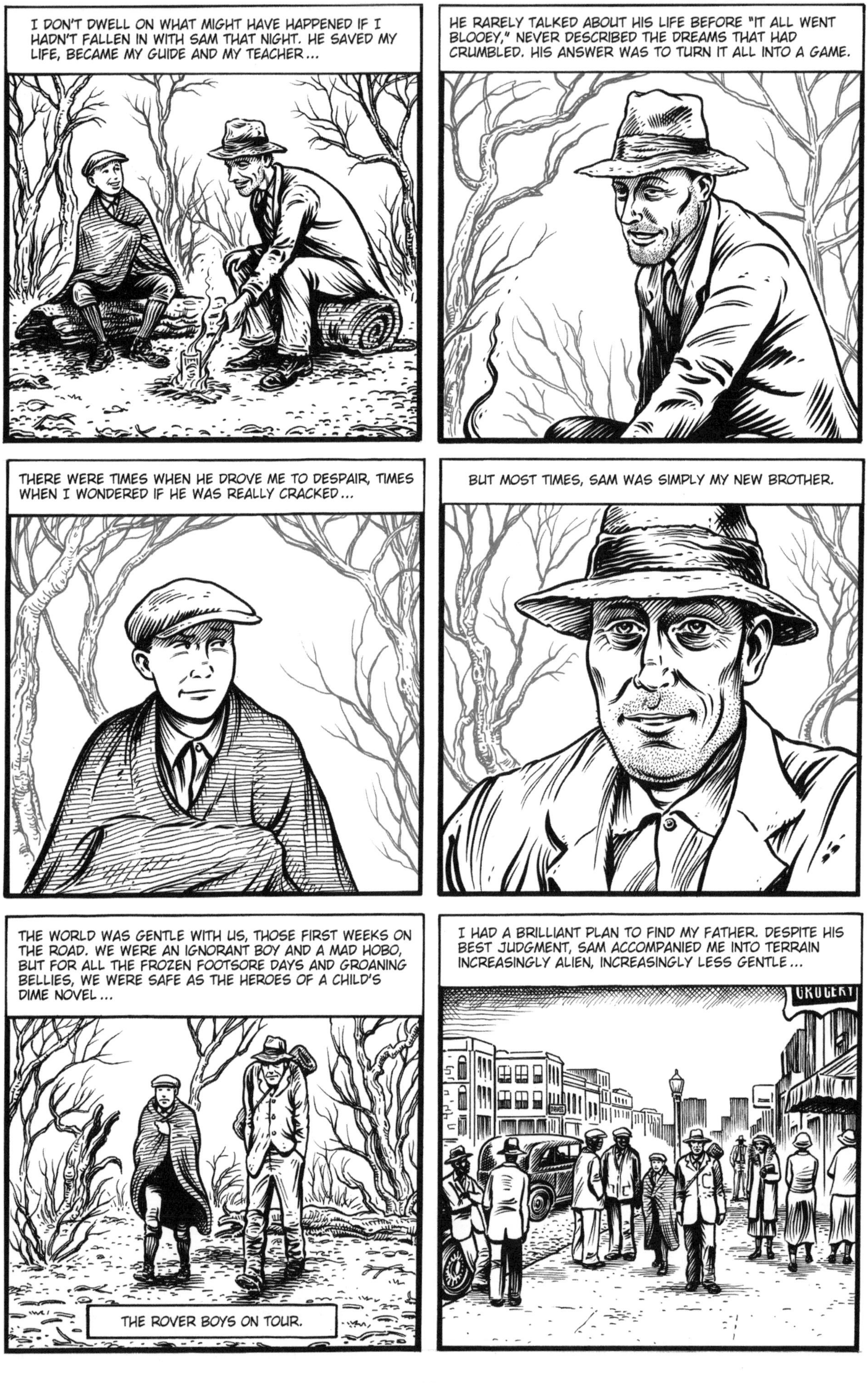
I DON'T DWELL ON WHAT MIGHT HAVE HAPPENED IF I HADN'T FALLEN IN WITH SAM THAT NIGHT. HE SAVED MY LIFE, BECAME MY GUIDE AND MY TEACHER...
HE RARELY TALKED ABOUT HIS LIFE BEFORE "IT ALL WENT BLOOEY," NEVER DESCRIBED THE DREAMS THAT HAD CRUMBLED. HIS ANSWER WAS TO TURN IT ALL INTO A GAME.
THERE WERE TIMES WHEN HE DROVE ME TO DESPAIR, TIMES WHEN I WONDERED IF HE WAS REALLY CRACKED...
BUT MOST TIMES, SAM WAS SIMPLY MY NEW BROTHER.
THE WORLD WAS GENTLE WITH US, THOSE FIRST WEEKS ON THE ROAD. WE WERE AN IGNORANT BOY AND A MAD HOBO, BUT FOR ALL THE FROZEN FOOTSORE DAYS AND GROANING BELLIES, WE WERE SAFE AS THE HEROES OF A CHILD'S DIME NOVEL...
THE ROVER BOYS ON TOUR.
I HAD A BRILLIANT PLAN TO FIND MY FATHER. DESPITE HIS BEST JUDGMENT, SAM ACCOMPANIED ME INTO TERRAIN INCREASINGLY ALIEN, INCREASINGLY LESS GENTLE...
GROCERY

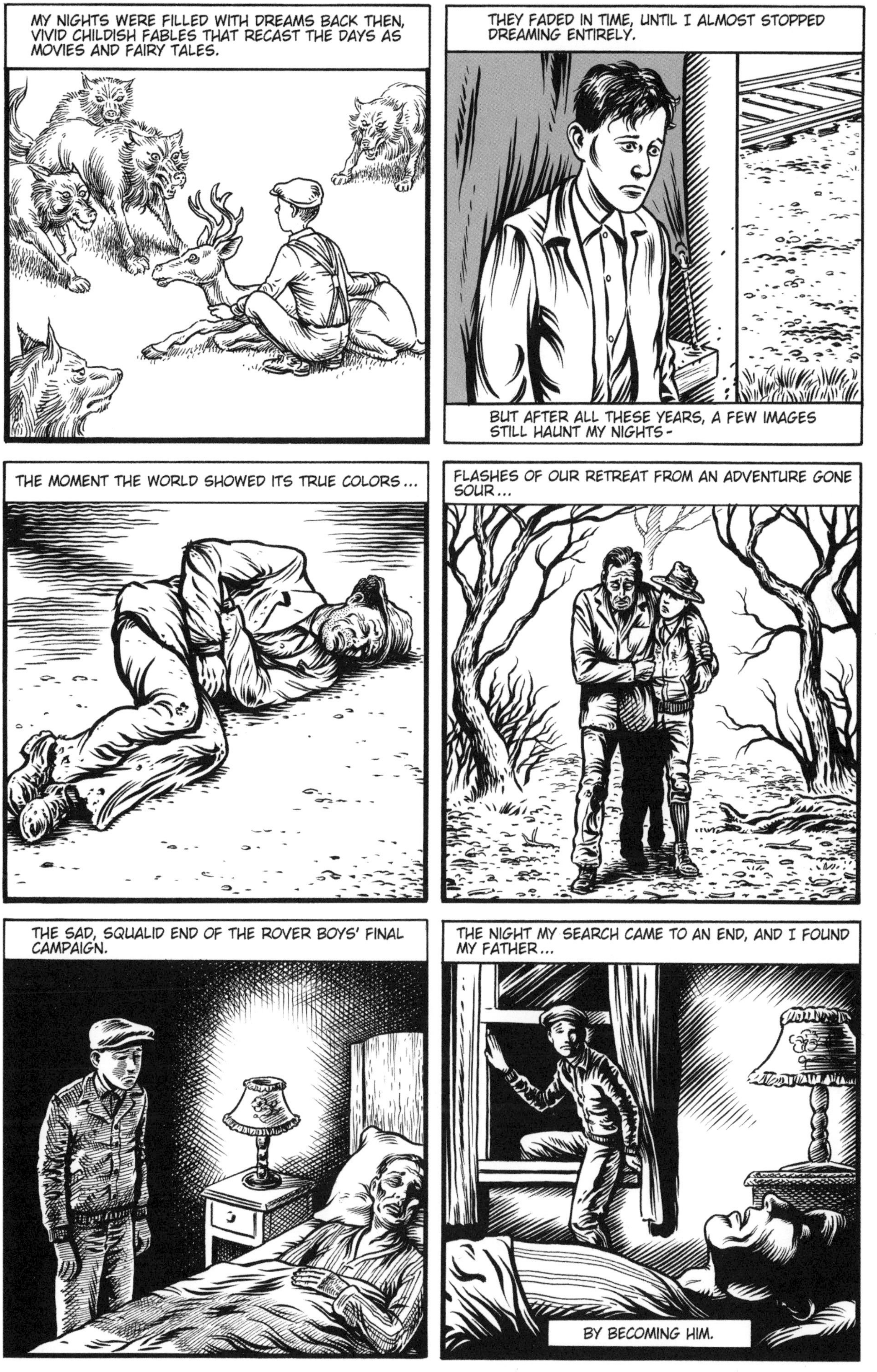
MY NIGHTS WERE FILLED WITH DREAMS BACK THEN, VIVID CHILDISH FABLES THAT RECAST THE DAYS AS MOVIES AND FAIRY TALES.
THEY FADED IN TIME, UNTIL I ALMOST STOPPED DREAMING ENTIRELY.
BUT AFTER ALL THESE YEARS, A FEW IMAGES STILL HAUNT MY NIGHTS -
THE MOMENT THE WORLD SHOWED ITS TRUE COLORS...
FLASHES OF OUR RETREAT FROM AN ADVENTURE GONE SOUR...
THE SAD, SQUALID END OF THE ROVER BOYS' FINAL CAMPAIGN.
THE NIGHT MY SEARCH CAME TO AN END, AND I FOUND MY FATHER...
BY BECOMING HIM.

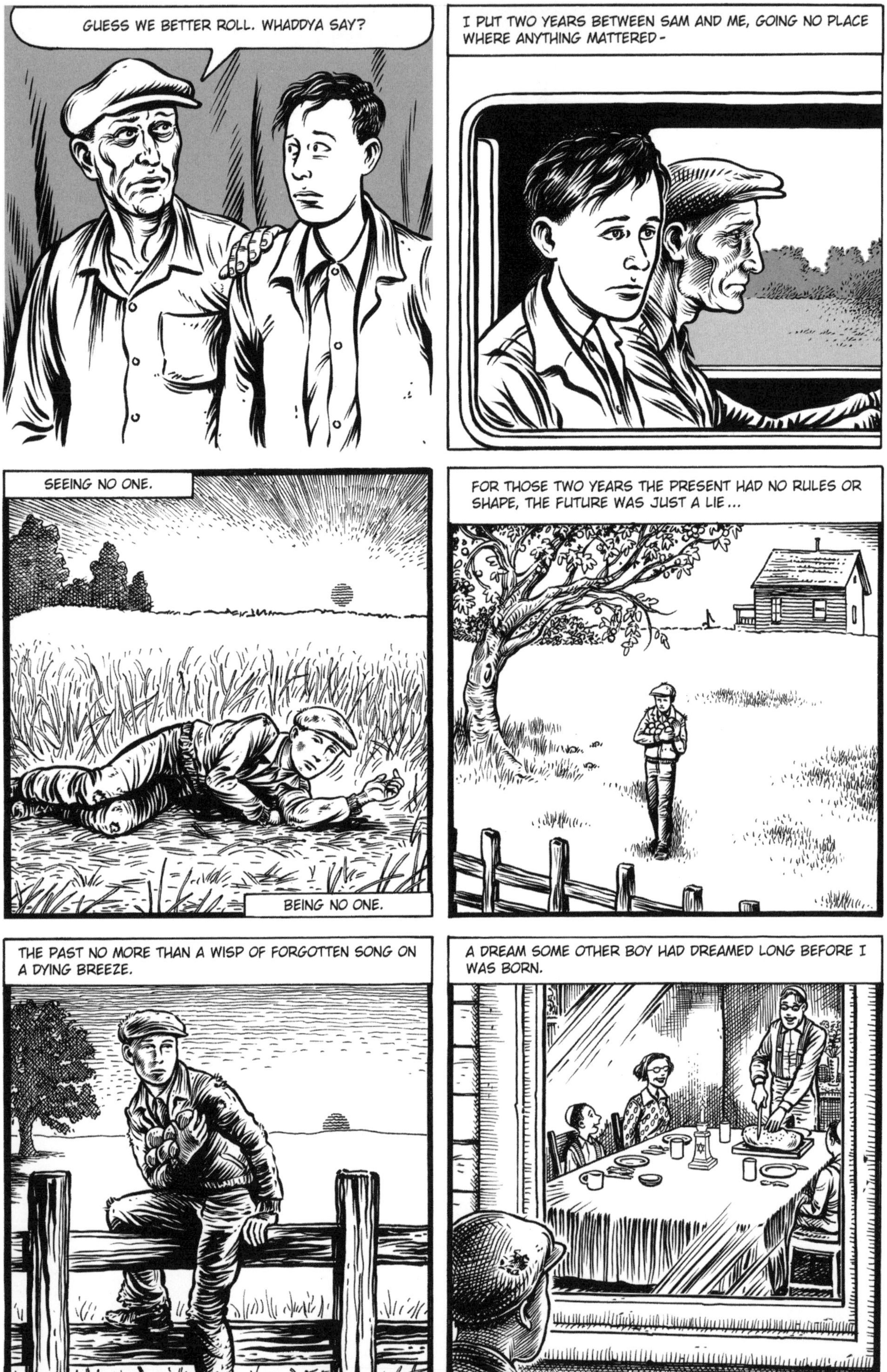

GUESS WE BETTER ROLL. WHADDYA SAY?
I PUT TWO YEARS BETWEEN SAM AND ME, GOING NO PLACE WHERE ANYTHING MATTERED -
SEEING NO ONE.
BEING NO ONE.
FOR THOSE TWO YEARS THE PRESENT HAD NO RULES OR SHAPE, THE FUTURE WAS JUST A LIE...
THE PAST NO MORE THAN A WISP OF FORGOTTEN SONG ON A DYING BREEZE.
A DREAM SOME OTHER BOY HAD DREAMED LONG BEFORE I WAS BORN.

I'D GIVEN MYSELF UP TO THE ROAD, WHERE NOTHING AHEAD COULD CUT YOU AS BADLY AS WHAT YOU'D LEFT BEHIND.

JUST KEEP MOVING, I TOLD MYSELF, AND MAYBE SOMEDAY I'D ESCAPE FROM SAM —

AND THE KNOWLEDGE THAT WHAT HAD BROUGHT HIM DOWN HAD HAPPENED BECAUSE OF ME.

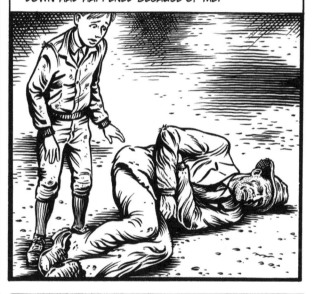

I COULDN'T DO THAT TO ANYONE, EVER AGAIN.

I WOULDN'T LIVE THROUGH THAT, EVER AGAIN.

I JUST HAD TO KEEP REMEMBERING: DON'T LET ANYONE GET THAT CLOSE.

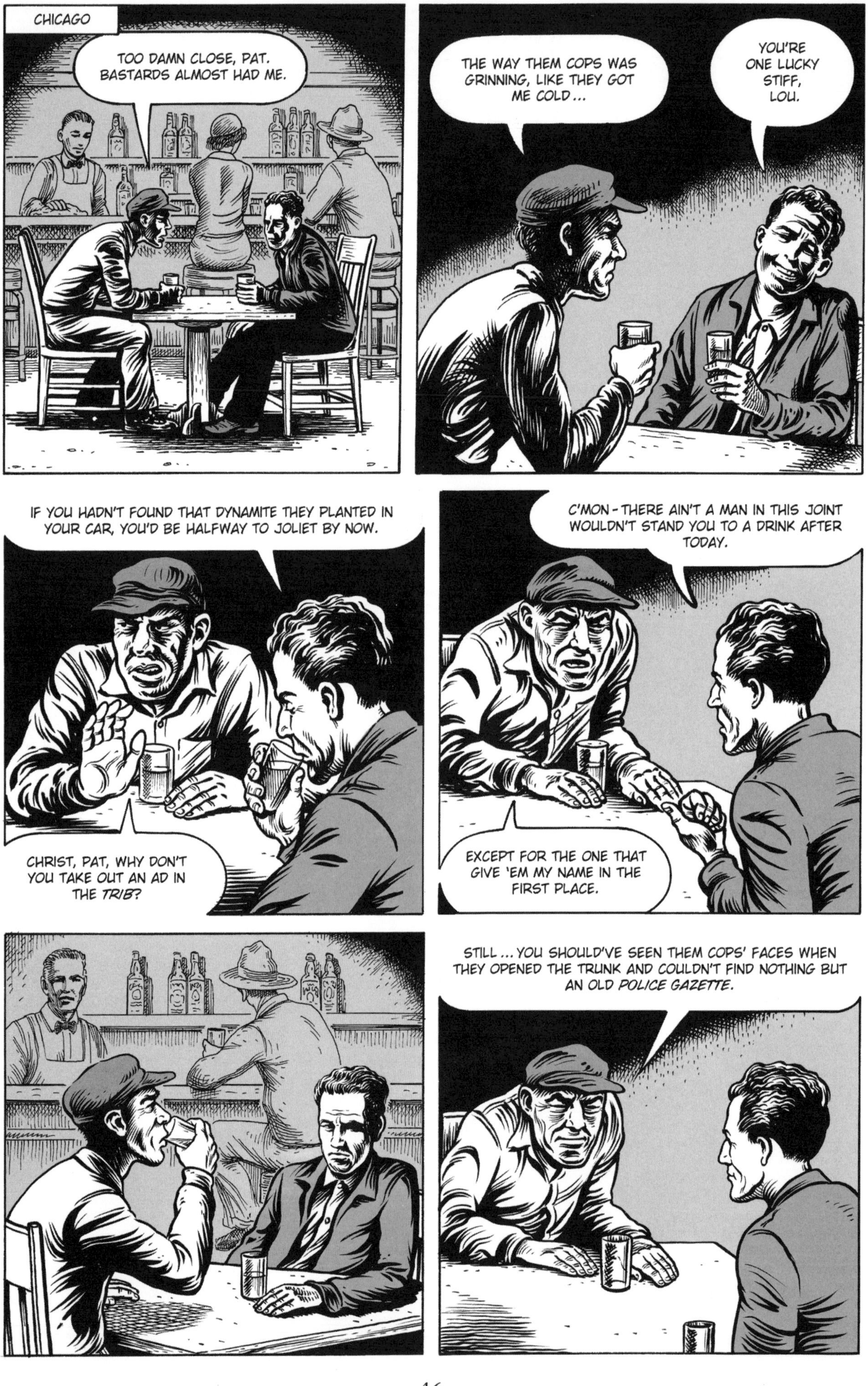
CHICAGO
TOO DAMN CLOSE, PAT. BASTARDS ALMOST HAD ME.
THE WAY THEM COPS WAS GRINNING, LIKE THEY GOT ME COLD...
YOU'RE ONE LUCKY STIFF, LOU.
IF YOU HADN'T FOUND THAT DYNAMITE THEY PLANTED IN YOUR CAR, YOU'D BE HALFWAY TO JOLIET BY NOW.
CHRIST, PAT, WHY DON'T YOU TAKE OUT AN AD IN THE *TRIB*?
C'MON - THERE AIN'T A MAN IN THIS JOINT WOULDN'T STAND YOU TO A DRINK AFTER TODAY.
EXCEPT FOR THE ONE THAT GIVE 'EM MY NAME IN THE FIRST PLACE.
STILL ... YOU SHOULD'VE SEEN THEM COPS' FACES WHEN THEY OPENED THE TRUNK AND COULDN'T FIND NOTHING BUT AN OLD *POLICE GAZETTE*.

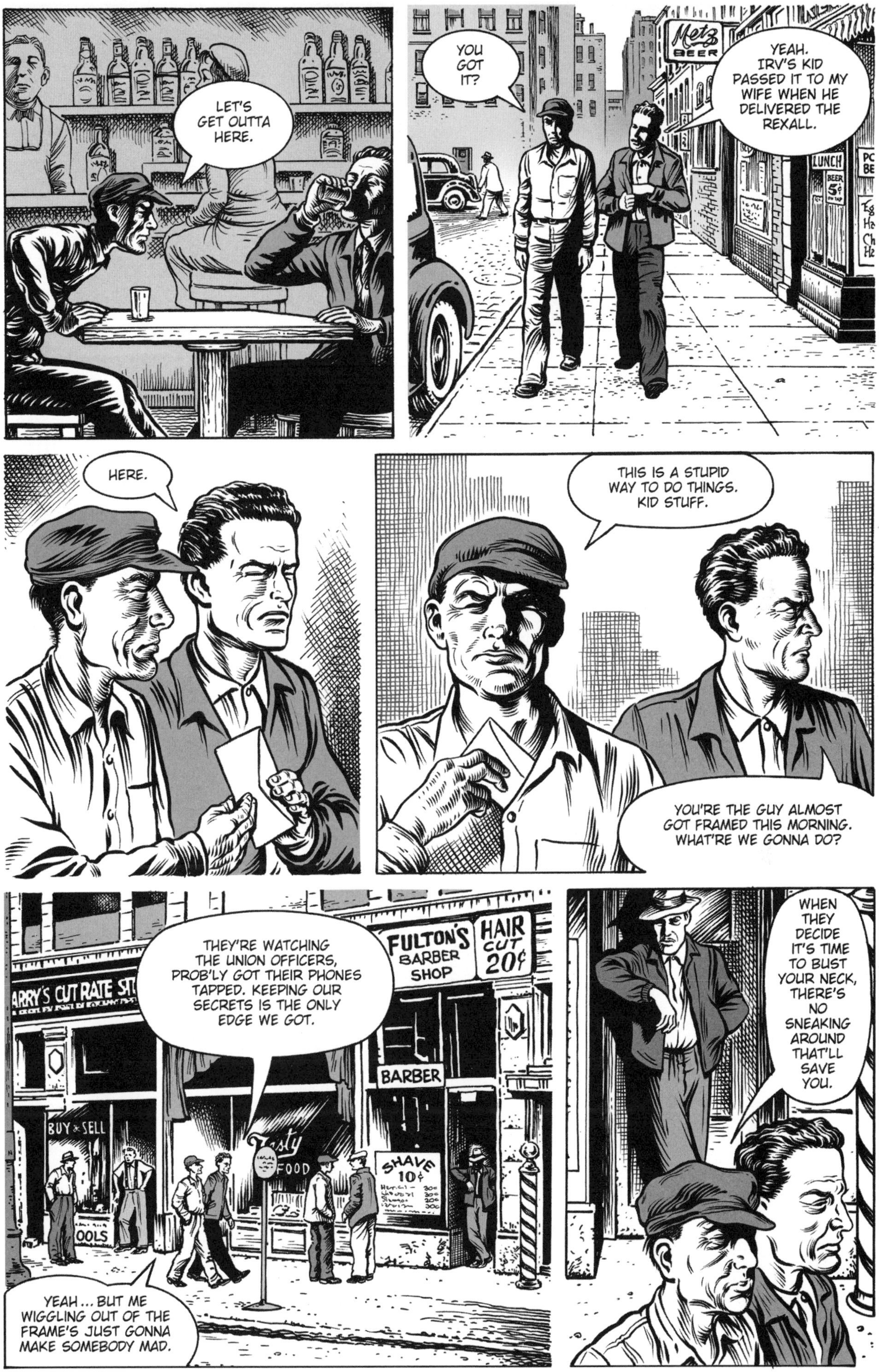
LET'S GET OUTTA HERE.
YOU GOT IT?
Metz BEER
YEAH. IRV'S KID PASSED IT TO MY WIFE WHEN HE DELIVERED THE REXALL.
LUNCH
BEER 5¢
HERE.
THIS IS A STUPID WAY TO DO THINGS. KID STUFF.
YOU'RE THE GUY ALMOST GOT FRAMED THIS MORNING. WHAT'RE WE GONNA DO?
ARRY'S CUT RATE ST
FULTON'S BARBER SHOP
HAIR CUT 20¢
THEY'RE WATCHING THE UNION OFFICERS, PROB'LY GOT THEIR PHONES TAPPED. KEEPING OUR SECRETS IS THE ONLY EDGE WE GOT.
BARBER
BUY & SELL
FOOD
SHAVE 10¢
OOLS
YEAH... BUT ME WIGGLING OUT OF THE FRAME'S JUST GONNA MAKE SOMEBODY MAD.
WHEN THEY DECIDE IT'S TIME TO BUST YOUR NECK, THERE'S NO SNEAKING AROUND THAT'LL SAVE YOU.

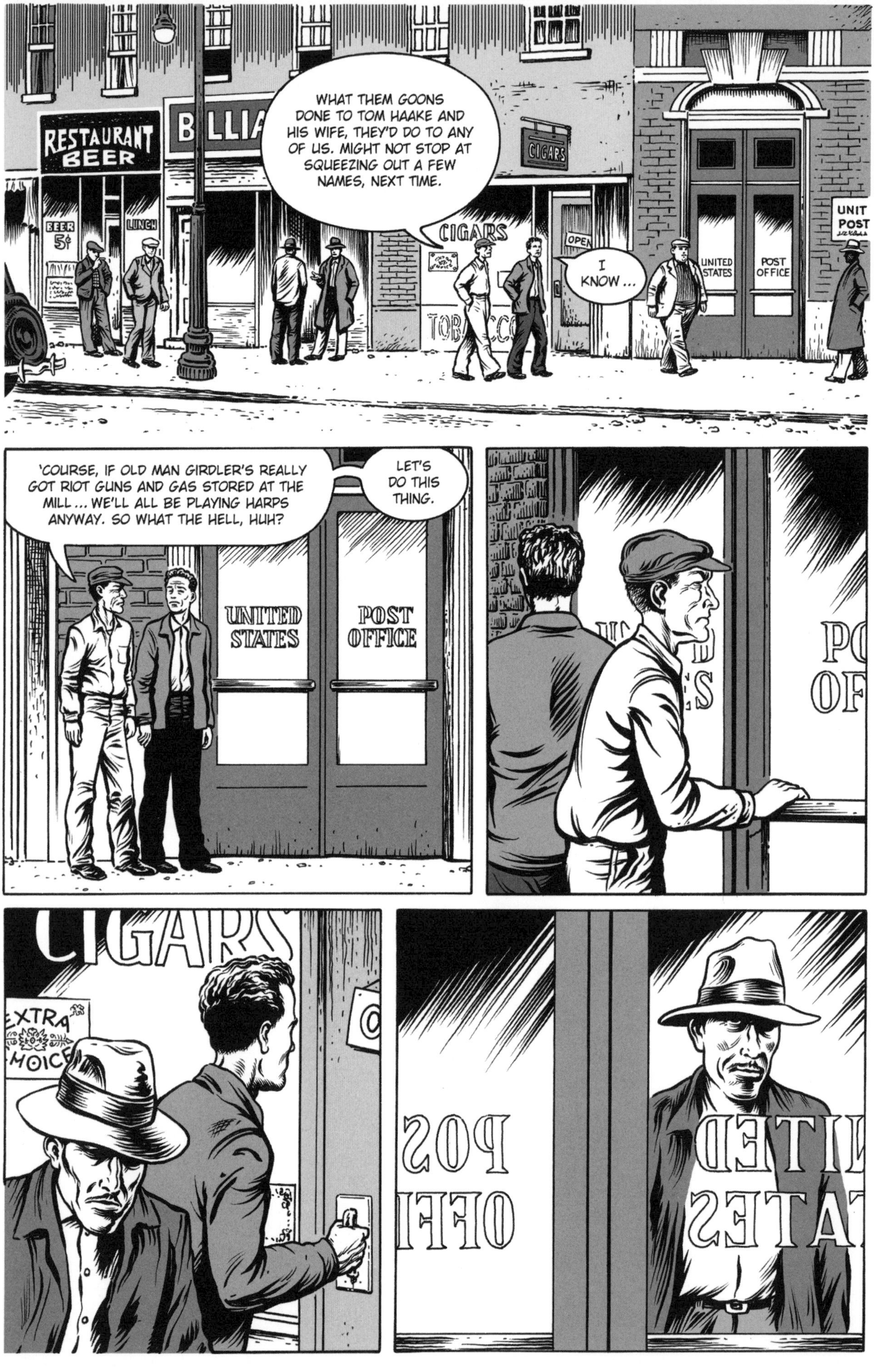
RESTAURANT BEER
CIGARS
WHAT THEM GOONS DONE TO TOM HAAKE AND HIS WIFE, THEY'D DO TO ANY OF US. MIGHT NOT STOP AT SQUEEZING OUT A FEW NAMES, NEXT TIME.
BEER 5¢
LUNCH
CIGARS
OPEN
I KNOW...
UNITED STATES
POST OFFICE
'COURSE, IF OLD MAN GIRDLER'S REALLY GOT RIOT GUNS AND GAS STORED AT THE MILL... WE'LL ALL BE PLAYING HARPS ANYWAY. SO WHAT THE HELL, HUH?
LET'S DO THIS THING.
UNITED STATES
POST OFFICE
CIGARS
EXTRA

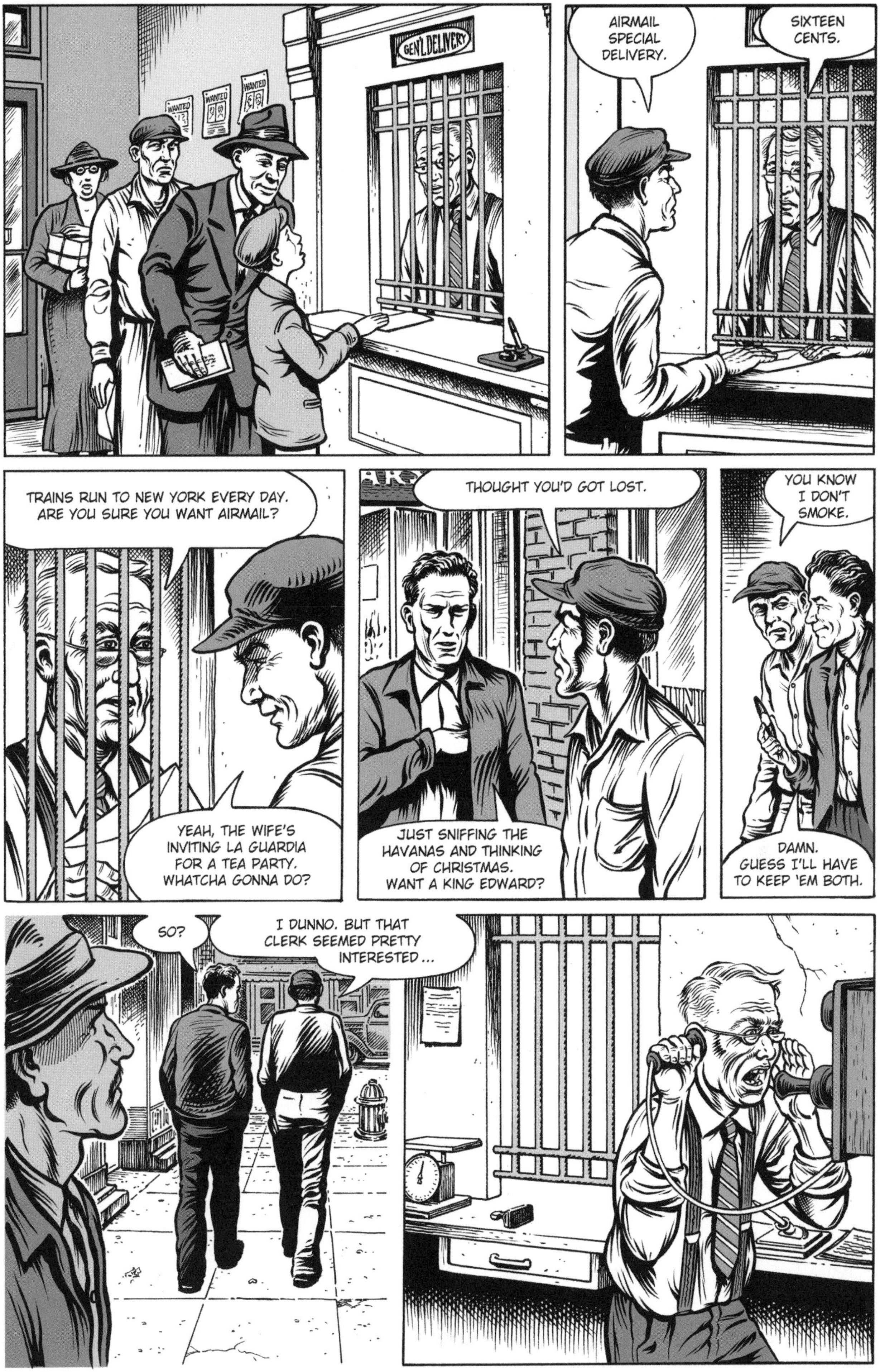
GEN'L DELIVERY
AIRMAIL SPECIAL DELIVERY.
SIXTEEN CENTS.
TRAINS RUN TO NEW YORK EVERY DAY. ARE YOU SURE YOU WANT AIRMAIL?
YEAH, THE WIFE'S INVITING LA GUARDIA FOR A TEA PARTY. WHATCHA GONNA DO?
THOUGHT YOU'D GOT LOST.
JUST SNIFFING THE HAVANAS AND THINKING OF CHRISTMAS. WANT A KING EDWARD?
YOU KNOW I DON'T SMOKE.
DAMN. GUESS I'LL HAVE TO KEEP 'EM BOTH.
SO?
I DUNNO. BUT THAT CLERK SEEMED PRETTY INTERESTED ...

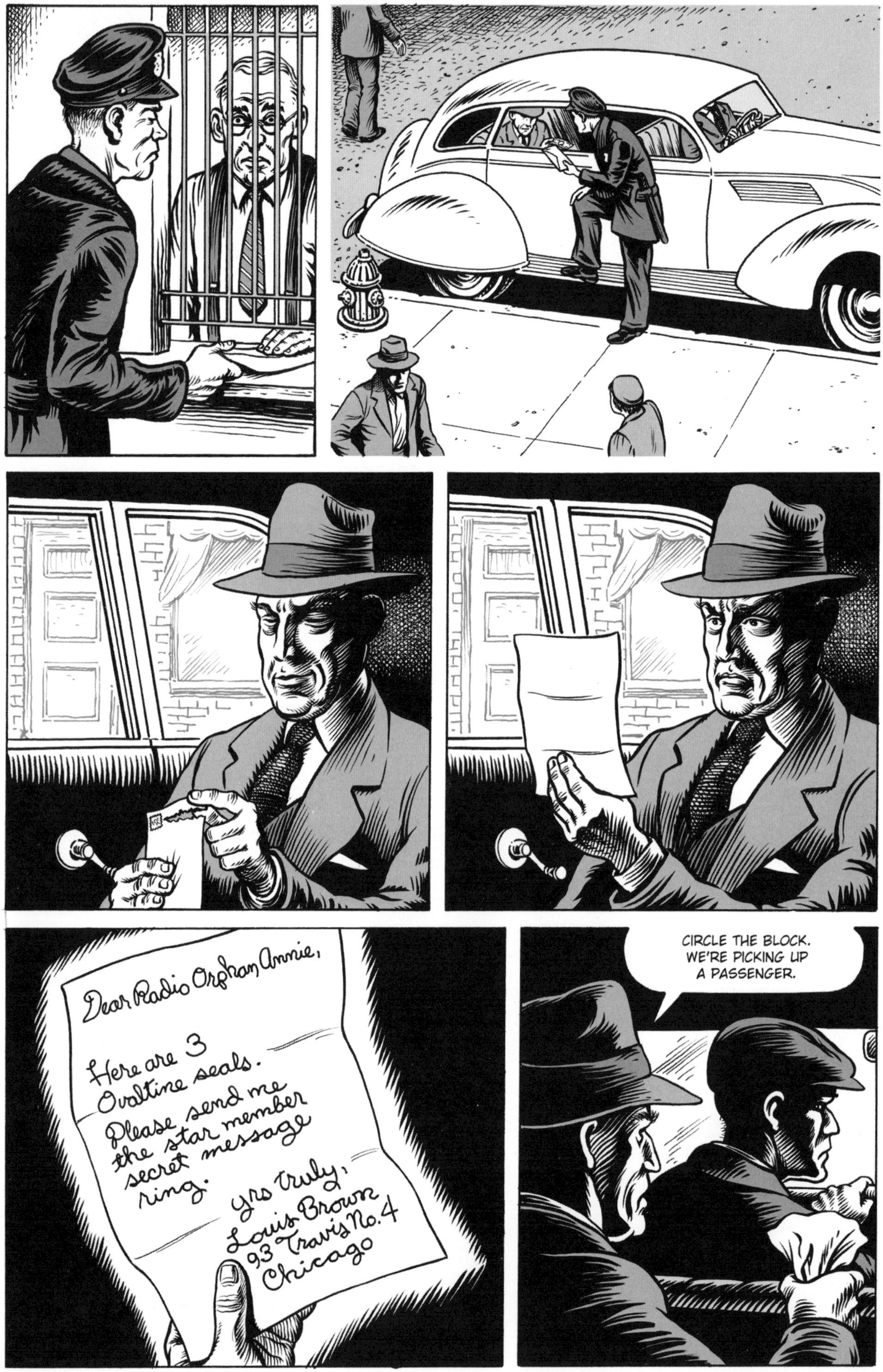
Dear Radio Orphan Annie,
Here are 3 Ovaltine seals. Please send me the star member secret message ring.
yrs truly, Louis Brown 93 Travis No. 4 Chicago
CIRCLE THE BLOCK. WE'RE PICKING UP A PASSENGER.

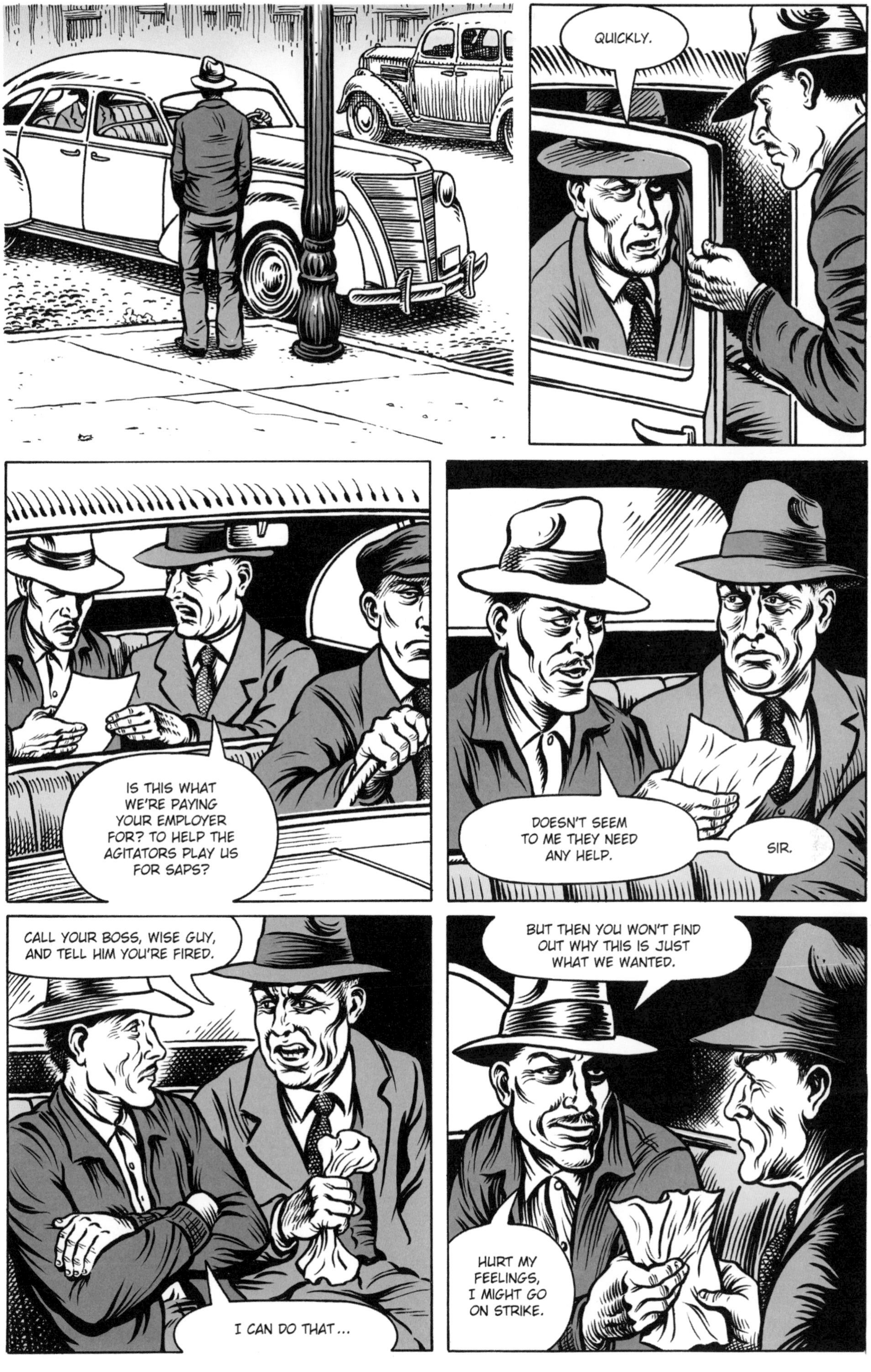
QUICKLY.
IS THIS WHAT WE'RE PAYING YOUR EMPLOYER FOR? TO HELP THE AGITATORS PLAY US FOR SAPS?
DOESN'T SEEM TO ME THEY NEED ANY HELP.
SIR.
CALL YOUR BOSS, WISE GUY, AND TELL HIM YOU'RE FIRED.
I CAN DO THAT...
BUT THEN YOU WON'T FIND OUT WHY THIS IS JUST WHAT WE WANTED.
HURT MY FEELINGS, I MIGHT GO ON STRIKE.

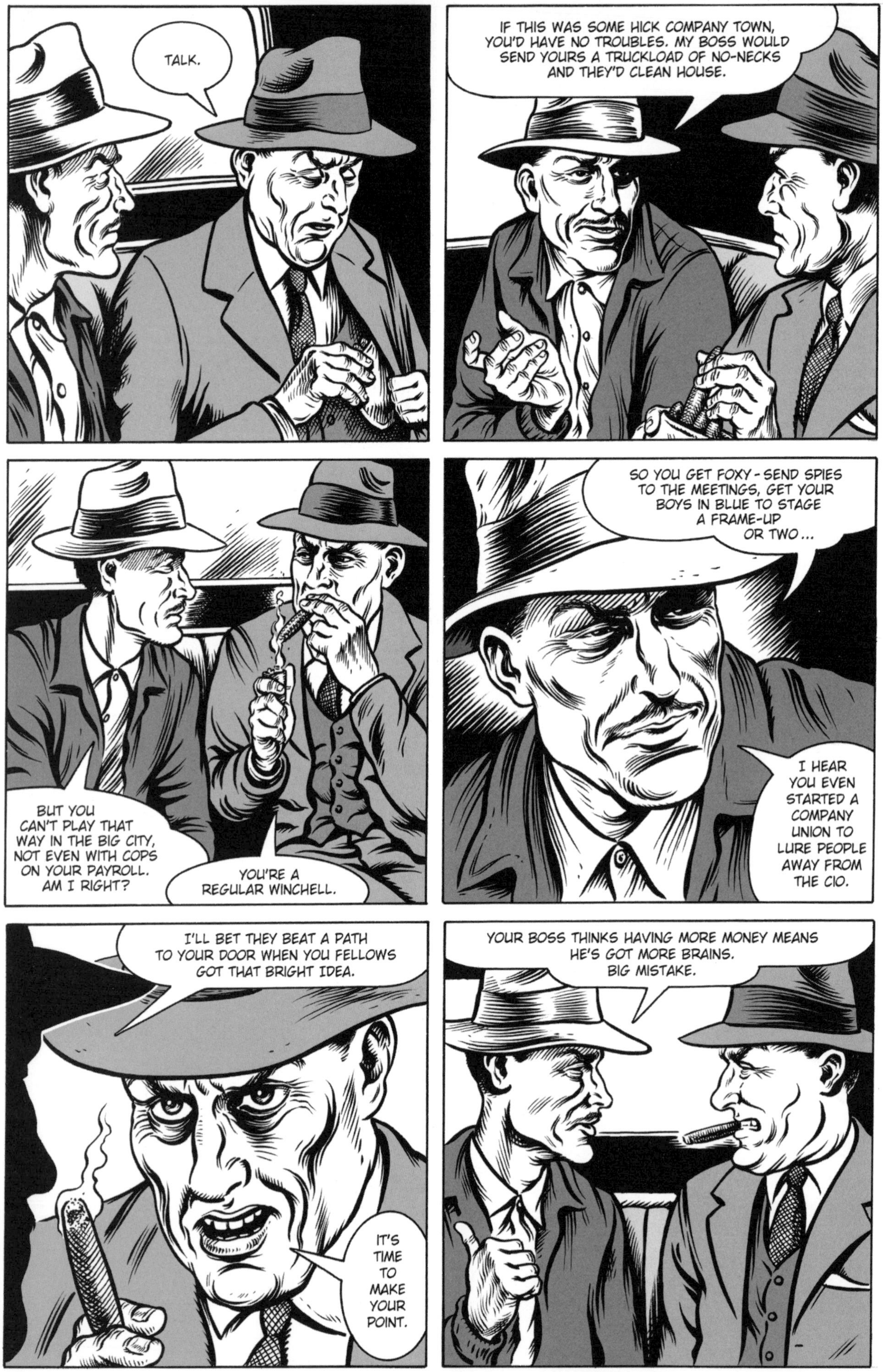
TALK.
IF THIS WAS SOME HICK COMPANY TOWN, YOU'D HAVE NO TROUBLES. MY BOSS WOULD SEND YOURS A TRUCKLOAD OF NO-NECKS AND THEY'D CLEAN HOUSE.
BUT YOU CAN'T PLAY THAT WAY IN THE BIG CITY, NOT EVEN WITH COPS ON YOUR PAYROLL. AM I RIGHT?
YOU'RE A REGULAR WINCHELL.
SO YOU GET FOXY - SEND SPIES TO THE MEETINGS, GET YOUR BOYS IN BLUE TO STAGE A FRAME-UP OR TWO...
I HEAR YOU EVEN STARTED A COMPANY UNION TO LURE PEOPLE AWAY FROM THE CIO.
I'LL BET THEY BEAT A PATH TO YOUR DOOR WHEN YOU FELLOWS GOT THAT BRIGHT IDEA.
IT'S TIME TO MAKE YOUR POINT.
YOUR BOSS THINKS HAVING MORE MONEY MEANS HE'S GOT MORE BRAINS. BIG MISTAKE.

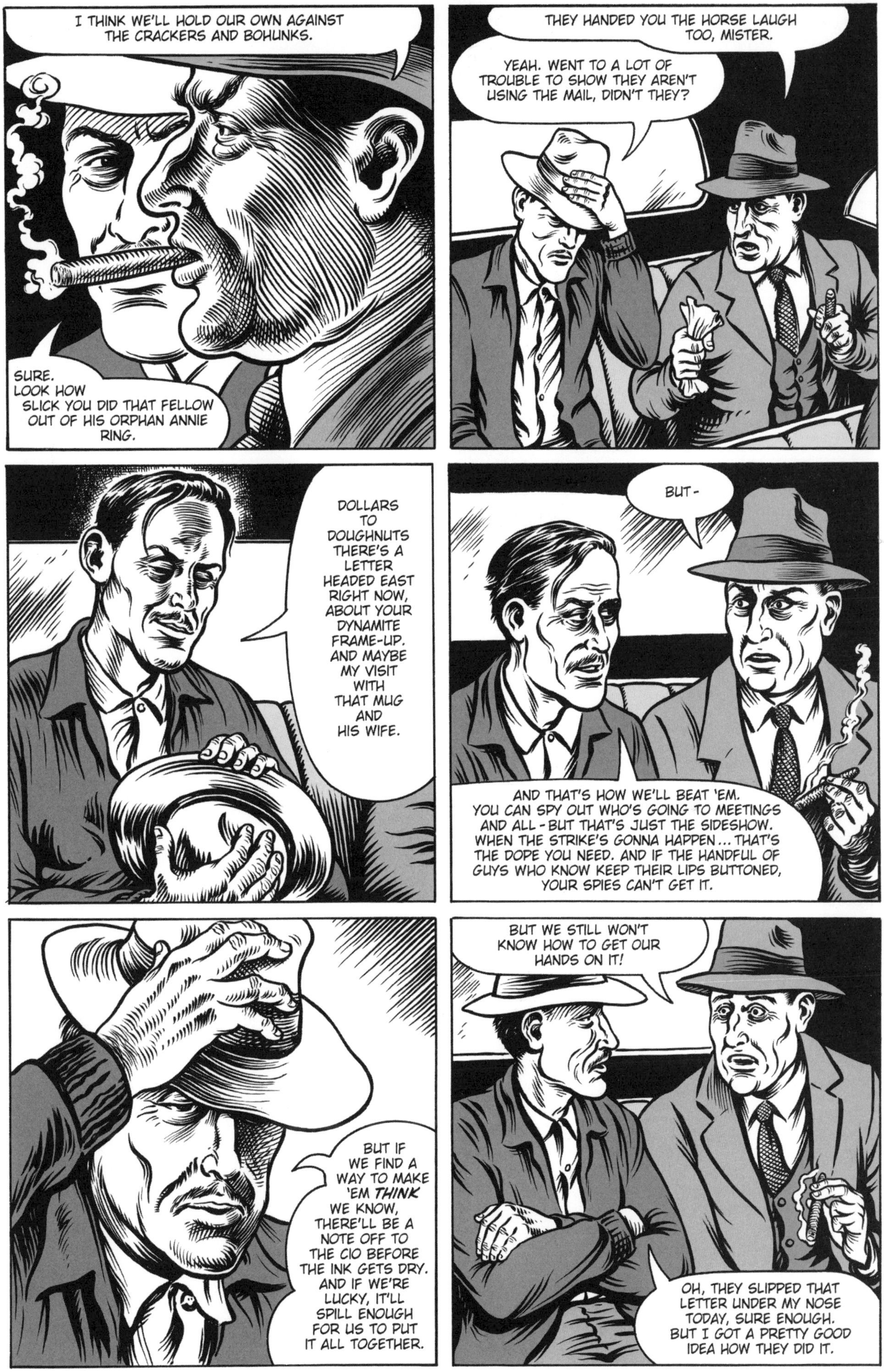
I THINK WE'LL HOLD OUR OWN AGAINST THE CRACKERS AND BOHUNKS.
SURE. LOOK HOW SLICK YOU DID THAT FELLOW OUT OF HIS ORPHAN ANNIE RING.
THEY HANDED YOU THE HORSE LAUGH TOO, MISTER.
YEAH. WENT TO A LOT OF TROUBLE TO SHOW THEY AREN'T USING THE MAIL, DIDN'T THEY?
DOLLARS TO DOUGHNUTS THERE'S A LETTER HEADED EAST RIGHT NOW, ABOUT YOUR DYNAMITE FRAME-UP. AND MAYBE MY VISIT WITH THAT MUG AND HIS WIFE.
BUT-
AND THAT'S HOW WE'LL BEAT 'EM. YOU CAN SPY OUT WHO'S GOING TO MEETINGS AND ALL - BUT THAT'S JUST THE SIDESHOW. WHEN THE STRIKE'S GONNA HAPPEN... THAT'S THE DOPE YOU NEED. AND IF THE HANDFUL OF GUYS WHO KNOW KEEP THEIR LIPS BUTTONED, YOUR SPIES CAN'T GET IT.
BUT IF WE FIND A WAY TO MAKE 'EM *THINK* WE KNOW, THERE'LL BE A NOTE OFF TO THE CIO BEFORE THE INK GETS DRY. AND IF WE'RE LUCKY, IT'LL SPILL ENOUGH FOR US TO PUT IT ALL TOGETHER.
BUT WE STILL WON'T KNOW HOW TO GET OUR HANDS ON IT!
OH, THEY SLIPPED THAT LETTER UNDER MY NOSE TODAY, SURE ENOUGH. BUT I GOT A PRETTY GOOD IDEA HOW THEY DID IT.

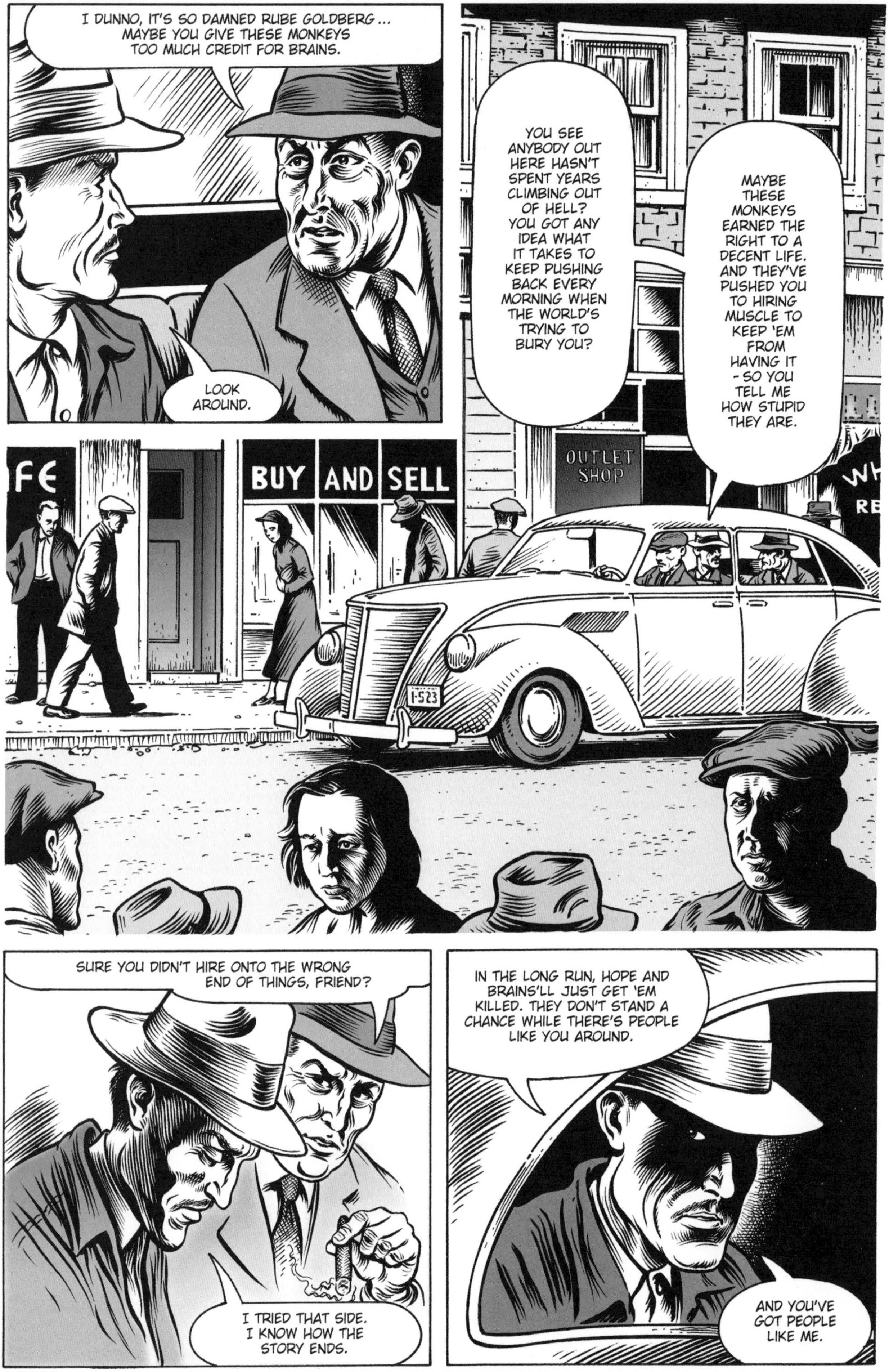

I DUNNO, IT'S SO DAMNED RUBE GOLDBERG ... MAYBE YOU GIVE THESE MONKEYS TOO MUCH CREDIT FOR BRAINS.
LOOK AROUND.
YOU SEE ANYBODY OUT HERE HASN'T SPENT YEARS CLIMBING OUT OF HELL? YOU GOT ANY IDEA WHAT IT TAKES TO KEEP PUSHING BACK EVERY MORNING WHEN THE WORLD'S TRYING TO BURY YOU?
MAYBE THESE MONKEYS EARNED THE RIGHT TO A DECENT LIFE. AND THEY'VE PUSHED YOU TO HIRING MUSCLE TO KEEP 'EM FROM HAVING IT - SO YOU TELL ME HOW STUPID THEY ARE.
BUY AND SELL
OUTLET SHOP
I-523
SURE YOU DIDN'T HIRE ONTO THE WRONG END OF THINGS, FRIEND?
I TRIED THAT SIDE. I KNOW HOW THE STORY ENDS.
IN THE LONG RUN, HOPE AND BRAINS'LL JUST GET 'EM KILLED. THEY DON'T STAND A CHANCE WHILE THERE'S PEOPLE LIKE YOU AROUND.
AND YOU'VE GOT PEOPLE LIKE ME.

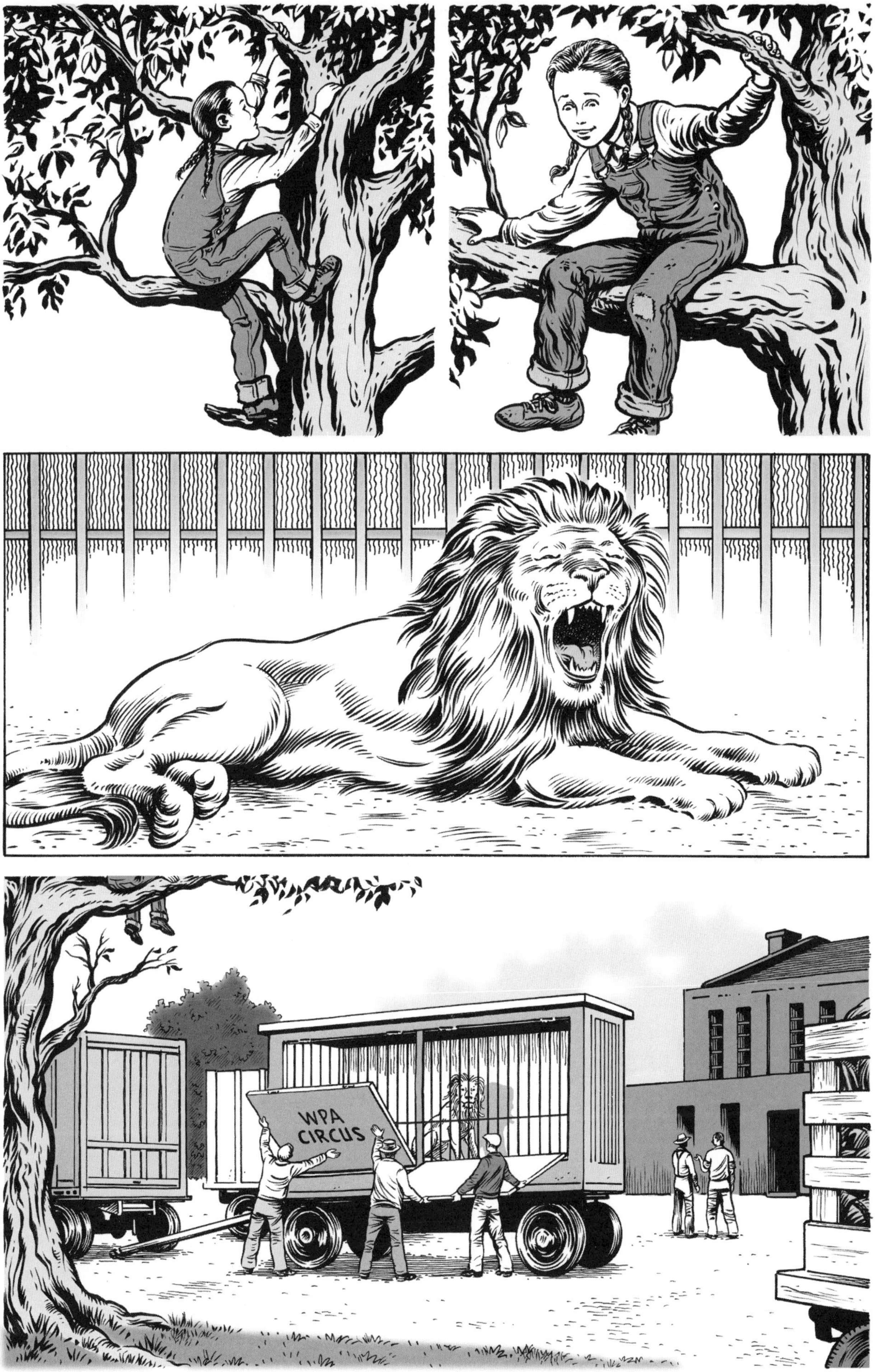
WPA
CIRCUS

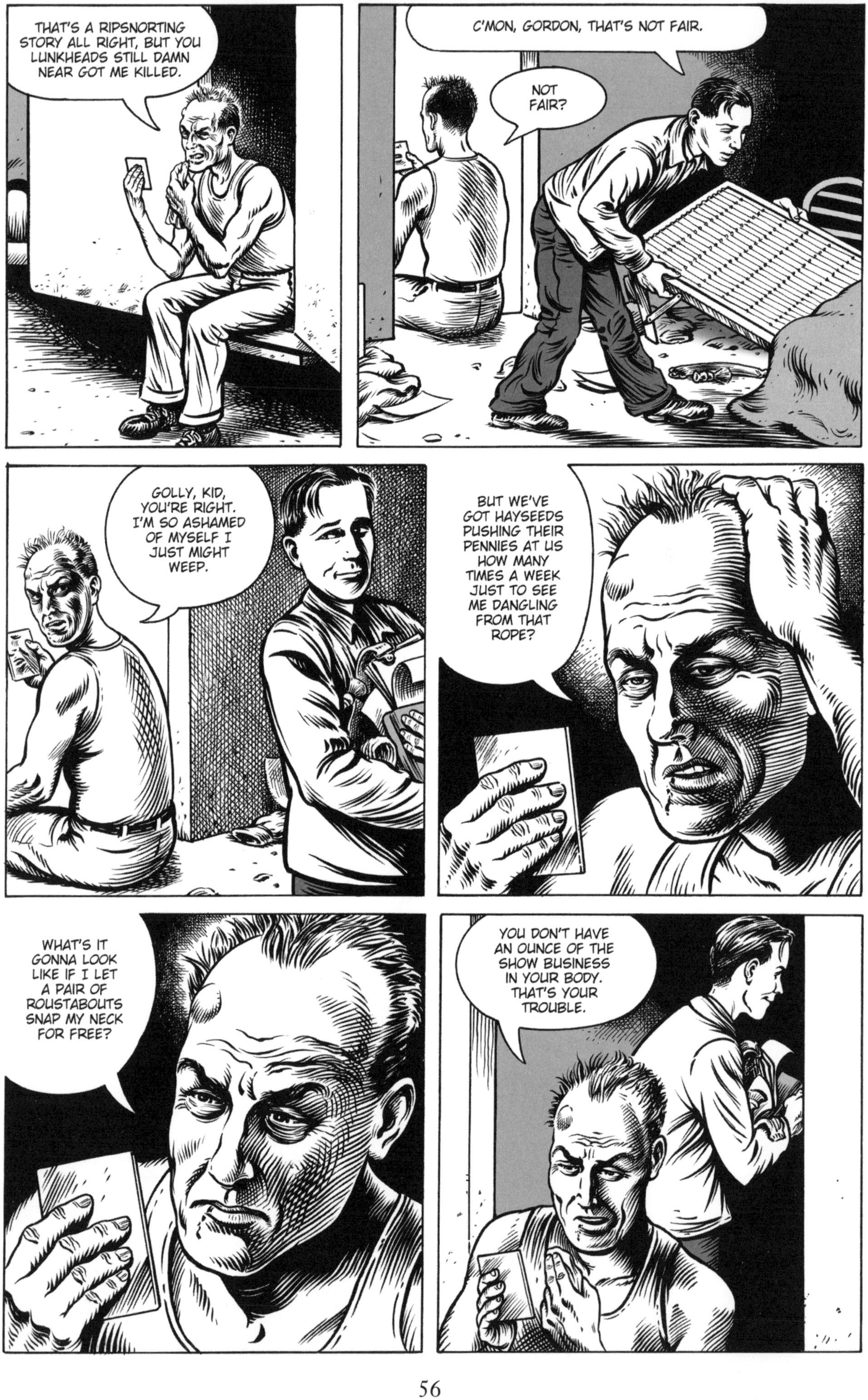
THAT'S A RIPSNORTING STORY ALL RIGHT, BUT YOU LUNKHEADS STILL DAMN NEAR GOT ME KILLED.
C'MON, GORDON, THAT'S NOT FAIR.
NOT FAIR?
GOLLY, KID, YOU'RE RIGHT. I'M SO ASHAMED OF MYSELF I JUST MIGHT WEEP.
BUT WE'VE GOT HAYSEEDS PUSHING THEIR PENNIES AT US HOW MANY TIMES A WEEK JUST TO SEE ME DANGLING FROM THAT ROPE?
WHAT'S IT GONNA LOOK LIKE IF I LET A PAIR OF ROUSTABOUTS SNAP MY NECK FOR FREE?
YOU DON'T HAVE AN OUNCE OF THE SHOW BUSINESS IN YOUR BODY. THAT'S YOUR TROUBLE.

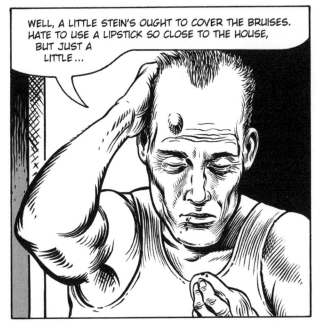

WELL, A LITTLE STEIN'S OUGHT TO COVER THE BRUISES. HATE TO USE A LIPSTICK SO CLOSE TO THE HOUSE, BUT JUST A LITTLE...

FRED, I'VE GOT AN OLD MAKEUP KIT IN MY DUFFEL—SEE IF IT'S STILL IN ONE PIECE, WILL YOU?

AA -!

BROKEN GLASS IN HERE, GORDON. IT'S ALL OVER YOUR STUFF.

OH, HELL, DON'T TELL ME I LEFT A BOTTLE IN THERE.

THERE'S STUFF IN THERE THAT CAN'T AFFORD TO GET SOAKED.

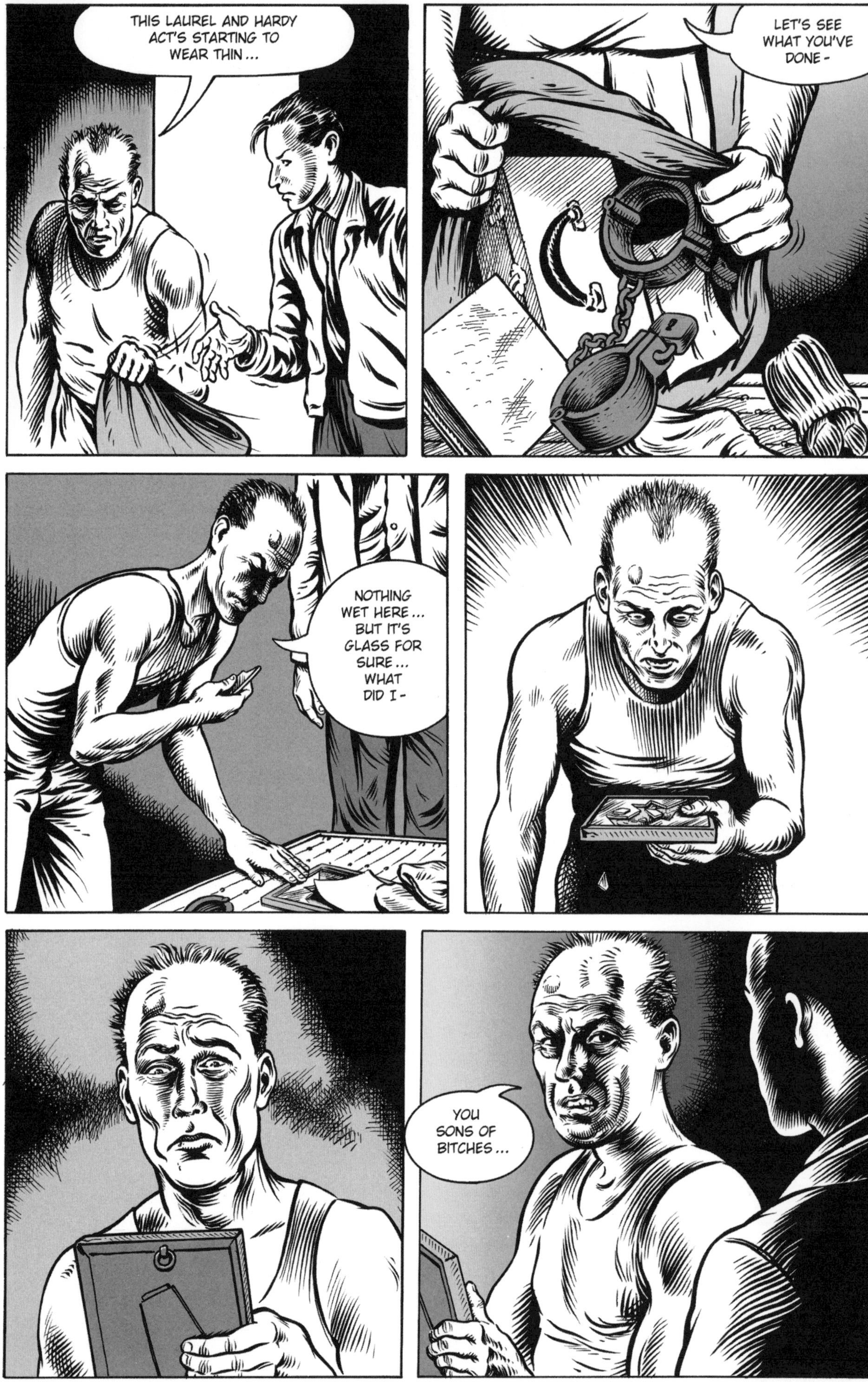
THIS LAUREL AND HARDY ACT'S STARTING TO WEAR THIN...
LET'S SEE WHAT YOU'VE DONE -
NOTHING WET HERE... BUT IT'S GLASS FOR SURE... WHAT DID I-
YOU SONS OF BITCHES...

WHERE THE HELL'S THE TRASH BARREL?

I SAID, WHERE'S THE GOD—

THERE'S ONE BY THE MESS TENT.

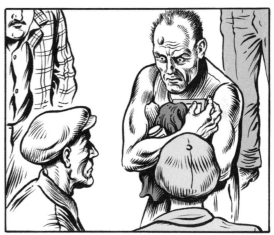

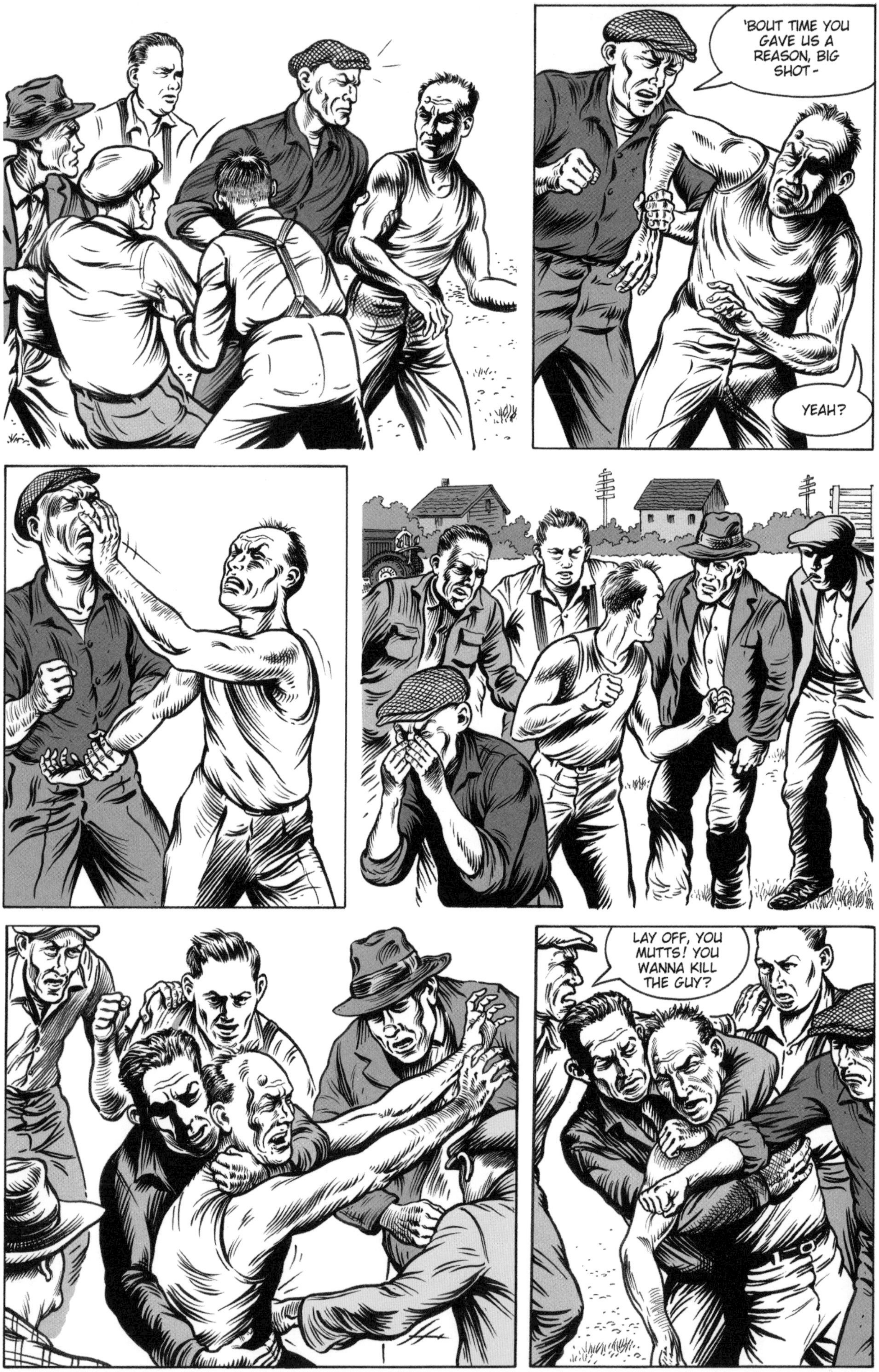
'BOUT TIME YOU GAVE US A REASON, BIG SHOT -
YEAH?
LAY OFF, YOU MUTTS! YOU WANNA KILL THE GUY?

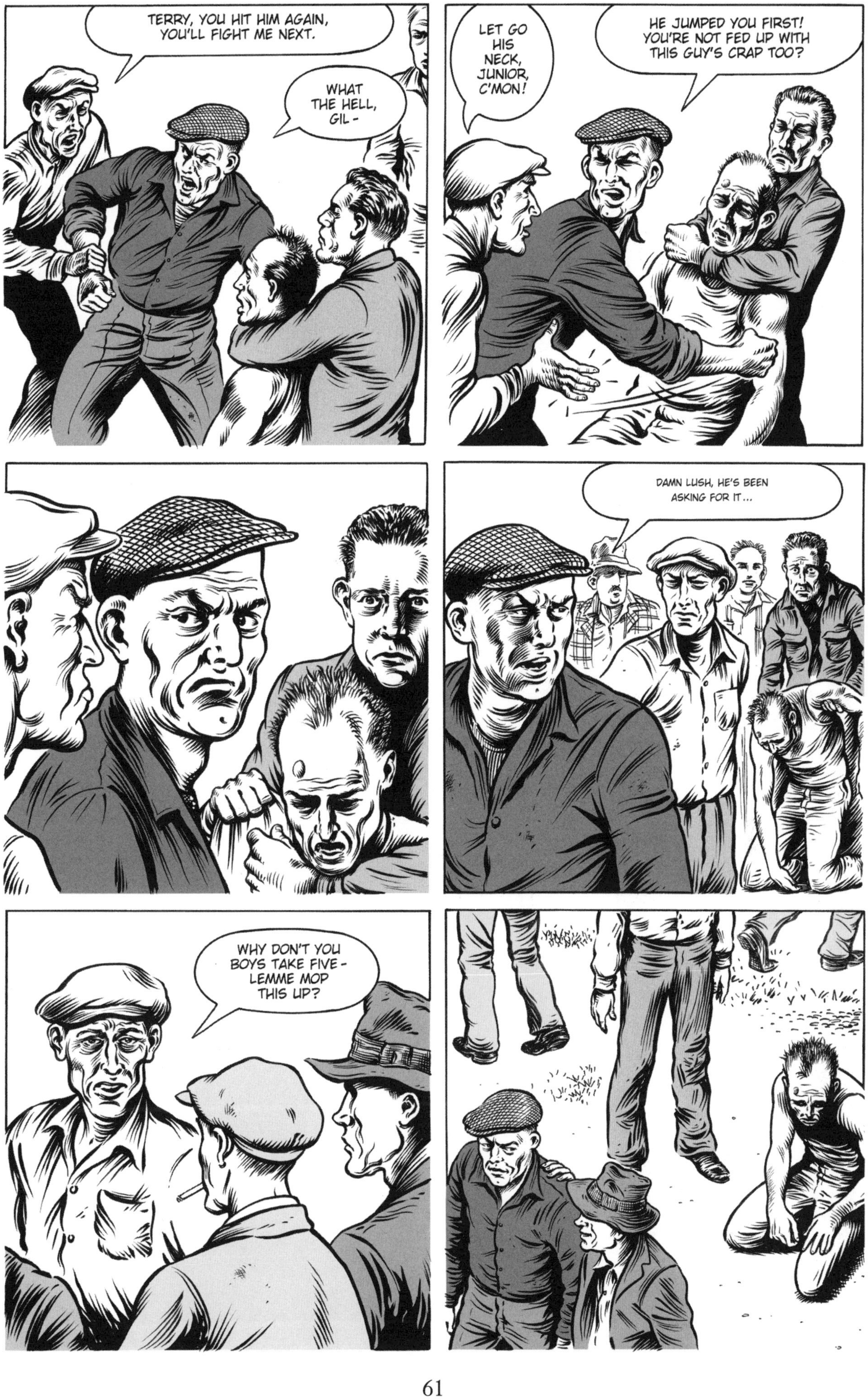
TERRY, YOU HIT HIM AGAIN, YOU'LL FIGHT ME NEXT.
WHAT THE HELL, GIL -
LET GO HIS NECK, JUNIOR, C'MON!
HE JUMPED YOU FIRST! YOU'RE NOT FED UP WITH THIS GUY'S CRAP TOO?
DAMN LUSH, HE'S BEEN ASKING FOR IT...
WHY DON'T YOU BOYS TAKE FIVE - LEMME MOP THIS UP?

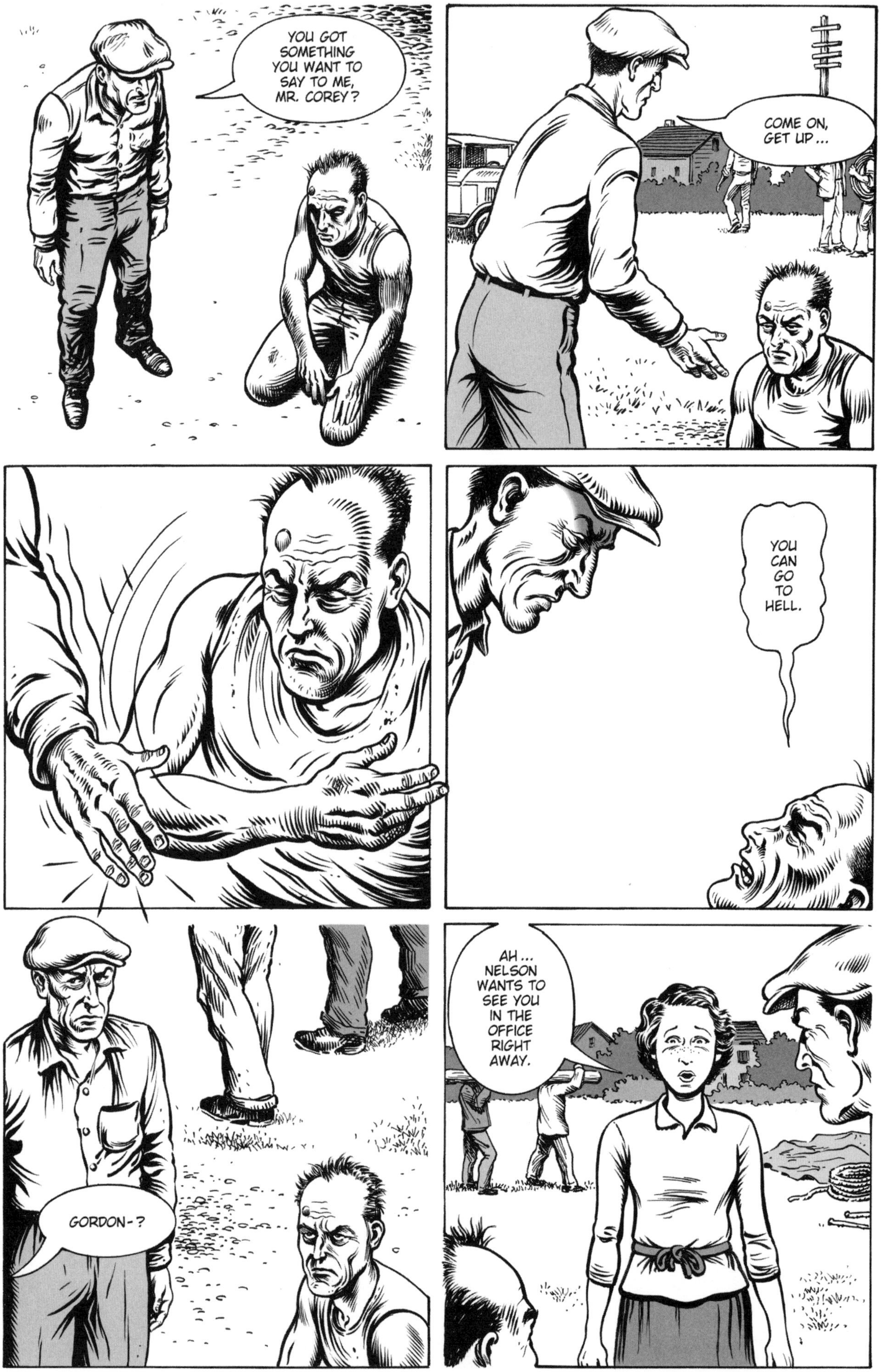
YOU GOT SOMETHING YOU WANT TO SAY TO ME, MR. COREY?
COME ON, GET UP...
YOU CAN GO TO HELL.
GORDON-?
AH... NELSON WANTS TO SEE YOU IN THE OFFICE RIGHT AWAY.

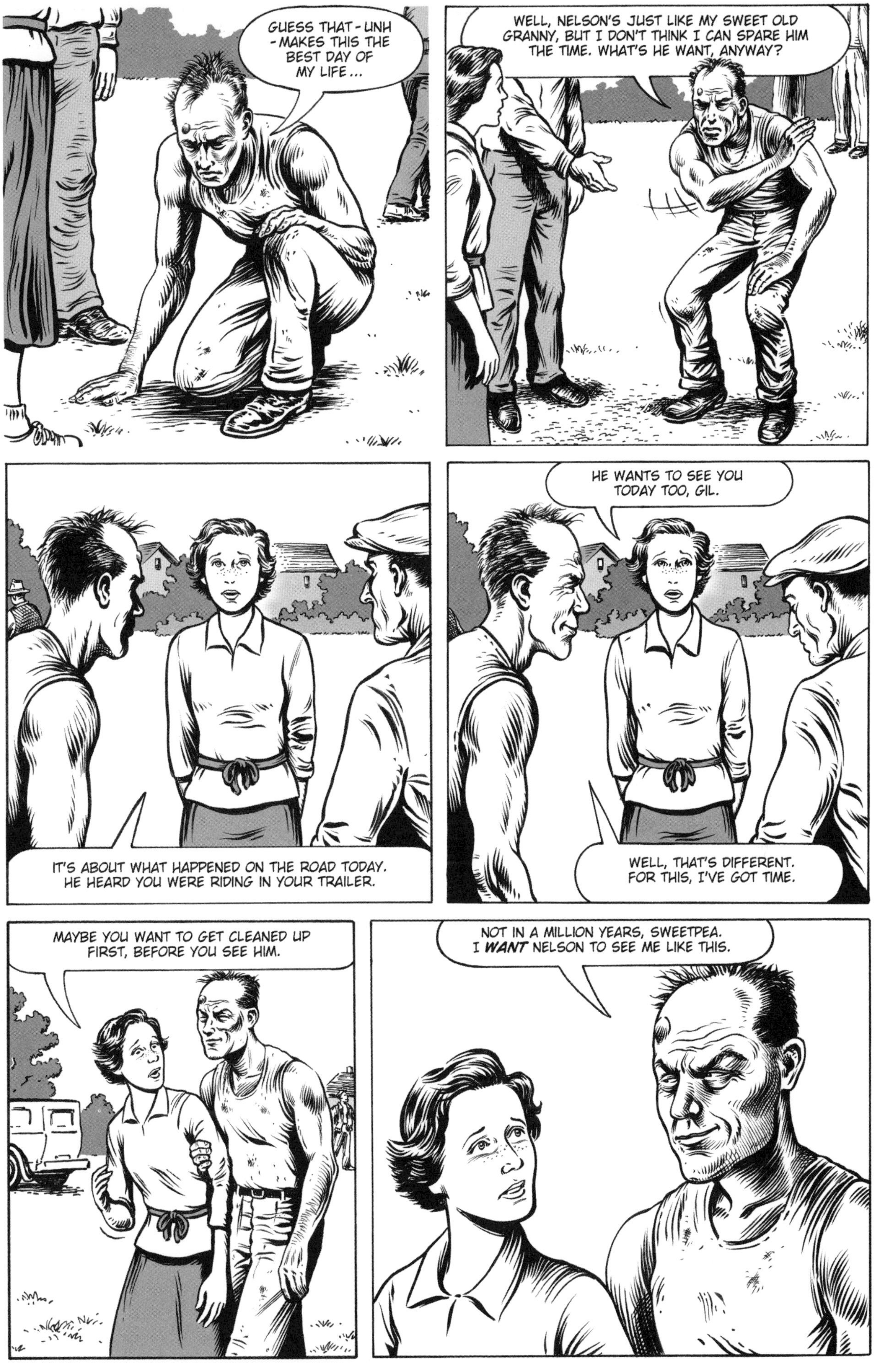
GUESS THAT - UNH - MAKES THIS THE BEST DAY OF MY LIFE...
WELL, NELSON'S JUST LIKE MY SWEET OLD GRANNY, BUT I DON'T THINK I CAN SPARE HIM THE TIME. WHAT'S HE WANT, ANYWAY?
IT'S ABOUT WHAT HAPPENED ON THE ROAD TODAY. HE HEARD YOU WERE RIDING IN YOUR TRAILER.
HE WANTS TO SEE YOU TODAY TOO, GIL.
WELL, THAT'S DIFFERENT. FOR THIS, I'VE GOT TIME.
MAYBE YOU WANT TO GET CLEANED UP FIRST, BEFORE YOU SEE HIM.
NOT IN A MILLION YEARS, SWEETPEA. I *WANT* NELSON TO SEE ME LIKE THIS.

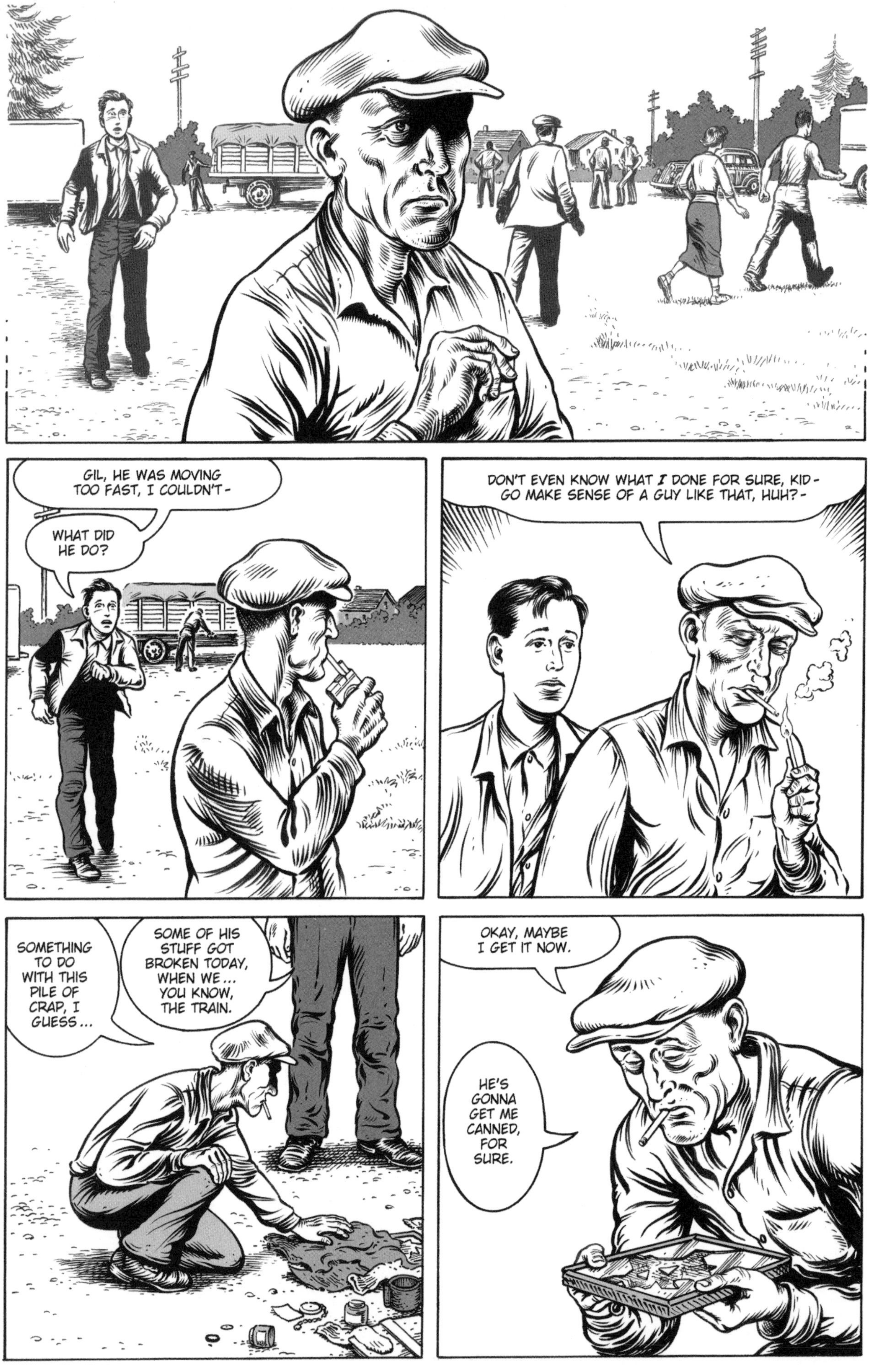
GIL, HE WAS MOVING TOO FAST, I COULDN'T-
WHAT DID HE DO?
DON'T EVEN KNOW WHAT I DONE FOR SURE, KID-
GO MAKE SENSE OF A GUY LIKE THAT, HUH?-
SOMETHING TO DO WITH THIS PILE OF CRAP, I GUESS...
SOME OF HIS STUFF GOT BROKEN TODAY, WHEN WE... YOU KNOW, THE TRAIN.
OKAY, MAYBE I GET IT NOW.
HE'S GONNA GET ME CANNED, FOR SURE.

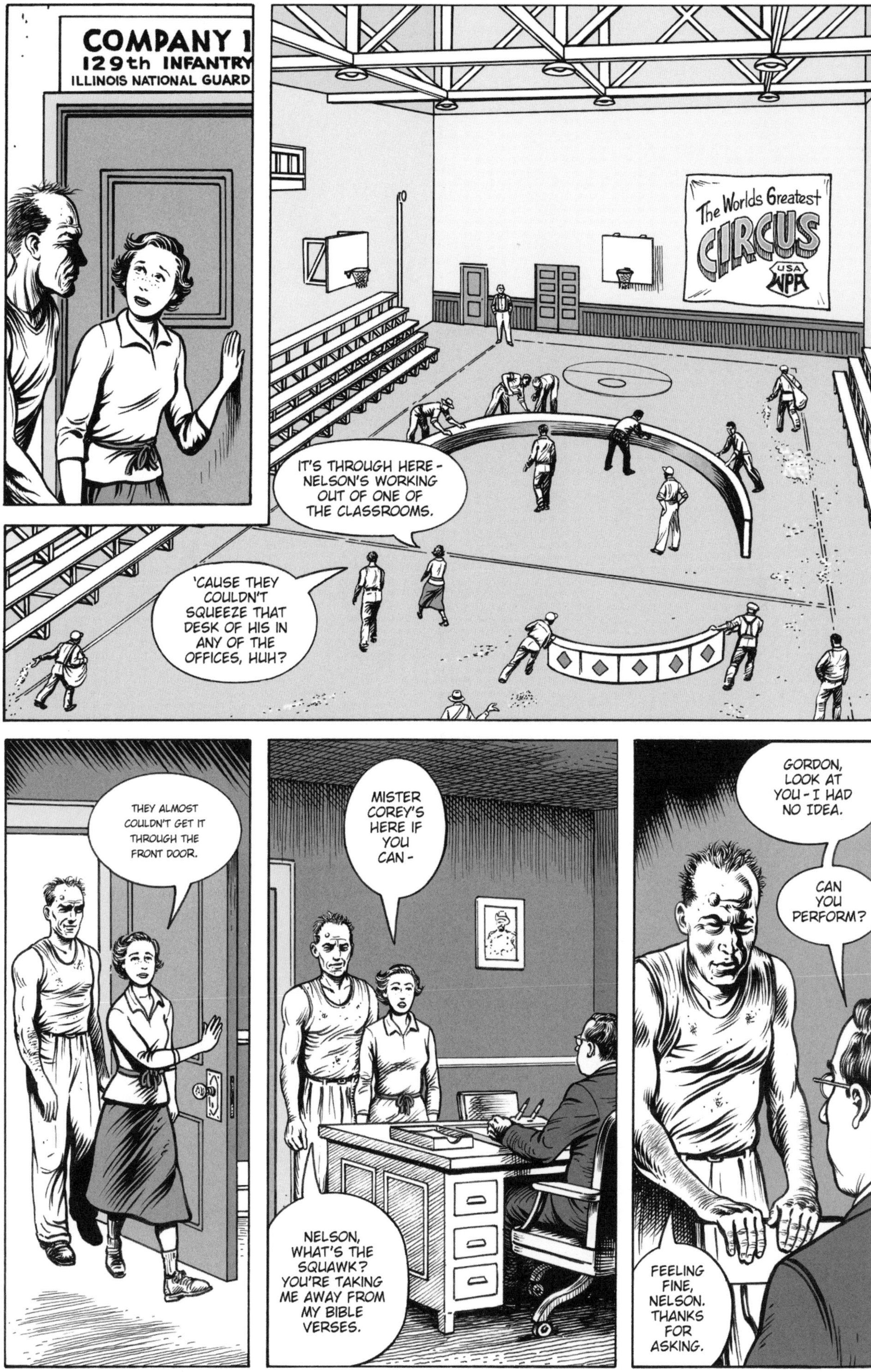

COMPANY I
129th INFANTRY
ILLINOIS NATIONAL GUARD
The Worlds Greatest CIRCUS
USA WPA
IT'S THROUGH HERE - NELSON'S WORKING OUT OF ONE OF THE CLASSROOMS.
'CAUSE THEY COULDN'T SQUEEZE THAT DESK OF HIS IN ANY OF THE OFFICES, HUH?
THEY ALMOST COULDN'T GET IT THROUGH THE FRONT DOOR.
MISTER COREY'S HERE IF YOU CAN -
NELSON, WHAT'S THE SQUAWK? YOU'RE TAKING ME AWAY FROM MY BIBLE VERSES.
GORDON, LOOK AT YOU - I HAD NO IDEA.
CAN YOU PERFORM?
FEELING FINE, NELSON. THANKS FOR ASKING.

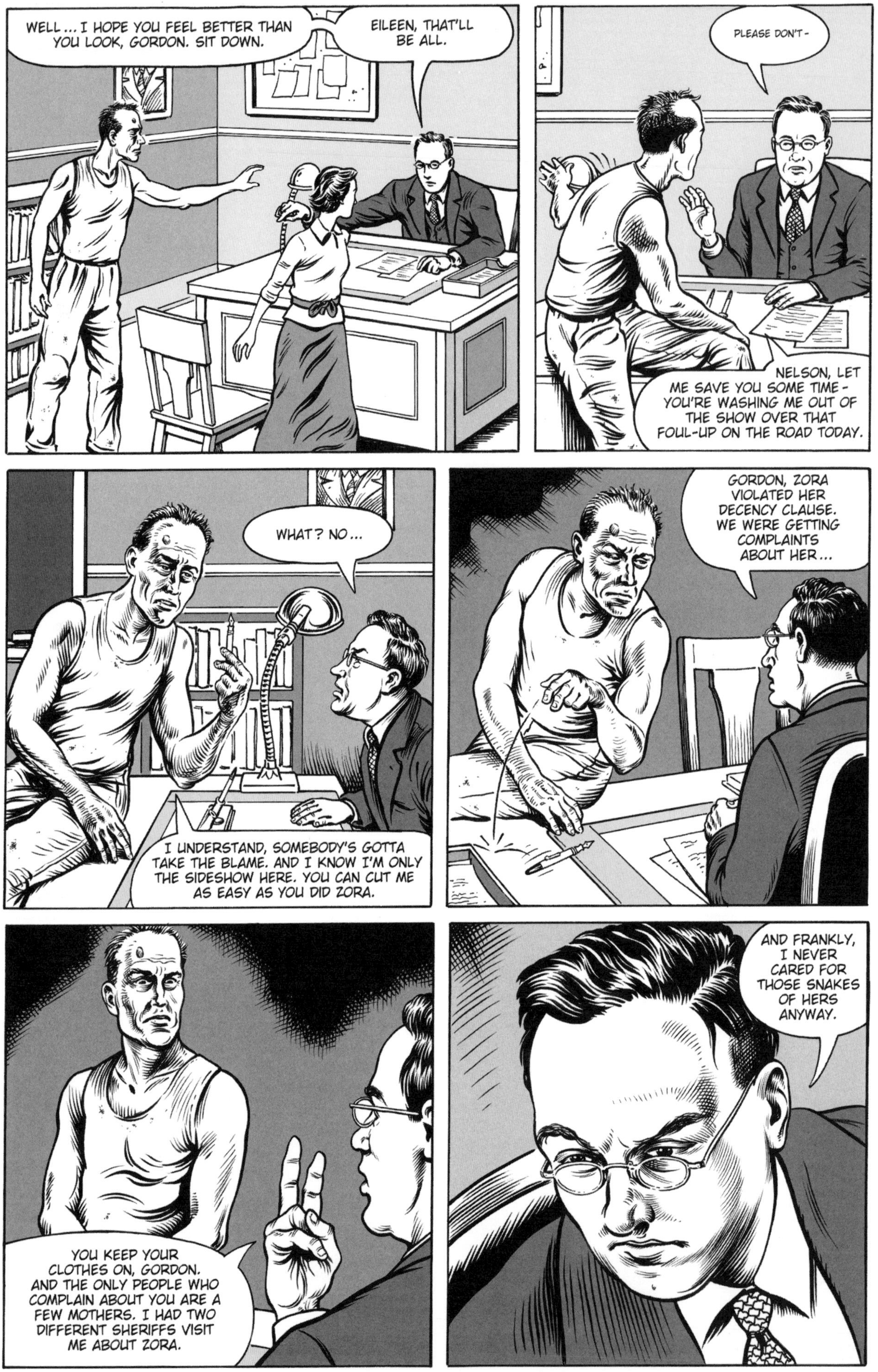

WELL ... I HOPE YOU FEEL BETTER THAN YOU LOOK, GORDON. SIT DOWN.
EILEEN, THAT'LL BE ALL.
PLEASE DON'T -
NELSON, LET ME SAVE YOU SOME TIME - YOU'RE WASHING ME OUT OF THE SHOW OVER THAT FOUL-UP ON THE ROAD TODAY.
WHAT? NO ...
I UNDERSTAND, SOMEBODY'S GOTTA TAKE THE BLAME. AND I KNOW I'M ONLY THE SIDESHOW HERE. YOU CAN CUT ME AS EASY AS YOU DID ZORA.
GORDON, ZORA VIOLATED HER DECENCY CLAUSE. WE WERE GETTING COMPLAINTS ABOUT HER ...
YOU KEEP YOUR CLOTHES ON, GORDON. AND THE ONLY PEOPLE WHO COMPLAIN ABOUT YOU ARE A FEW MOTHERS. I HAD TWO DIFFERENT SHERIFFS VISIT ME ABOUT ZORA.
AND FRANKLY, I NEVER CARED FOR THOSE SNAKES OF HERS ANYWAY.

BUT THE PUBLIC DOES EXPECT A SIDESHOW OF SOME KIND.

IN FACT, I'M INTERVIEWING A... UH... BEARDED LADY NEXT WEEK. AND A GENTLEMAN WHO CLAIMS TO BE MADE OF RUBBER.

YOU CAN LAUGH, GORDON, BUT YOU AREN'T CARRYING THE RESPONSIBILITY OF A FEDERAL PROGRAM ON YOUR SHOULDERS.

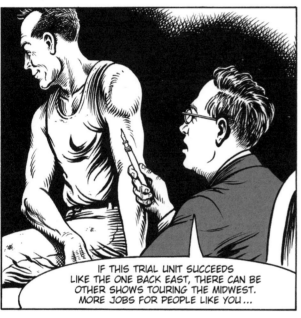

IF THIS TRIAL UNIT SUCCEEDS LIKE THE ONE BACK EAST, THERE CAN BE OTHER SHOWS TOURING THE MIDWEST. MORE JOBS FOR PEOPLE LIKE YOU...

ANYWAY...

I KNOW WE HAVE OUR DIFFERENCES, GORDON, BUT YOU'RE AN ASSET TO THIS UNIT. YOU WON'T BE BLAMED FOR WHAT HAPPENED TODAY.

BUT VALUABLE EQUIPMENT WAS ALMOST DAMAGED. AND YOU COULD HAVE BEEN KILLED. SOMEONE HAS TO BE HELD ACCOUNTABLE.

SO I THOUGHT YOU SHOULD HEAR FROM ME THAT YOU'LL BE NEEDING A NEW ASSISTANT.

WAIT A MINUTE, FRED WASN'T DRIVING THAT TRUCK—

OH, I'M LETTING MR. GILBERT GO, TOO. THEY WERE EQUALLY NEGLIGENT.

I REALIZE YOU'RE FOND OF THE BOY, BUT WE BOTH KNOW HE DOESN'T REALLY BELONG HERE. NOT REALLY SHOW FOLK, IS HE?

C'MON, NELSON, THIS ISN'T A REGULAR SHOW, THIS IS WPA. CAN'T YOU LEAVE THE KID ALONE? GET GIL TRANSFERRED TO A ROAD CREW OR SOMETHING, IF THAT'S EASIER...

OUT OF THE QUESTION.

I'M NOT GOING TO HAVE A GRIEVANCE FILED OVER UNEQUAL TREATMENT.

WE GAVE THESE PEOPLE WORK WHEN THEY WERE DESPERATE—

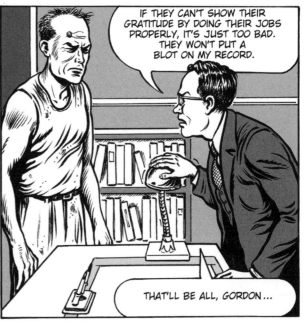

IF THEY CAN'T SHOW THEIR GRATITUDE BY DOING THEIR JOBS PROPERLY, IT'S JUST TOO BAD. THEY WON'T PUT A BLOT ON MY RECORD.

THAT'LL BE ALL, GORDON...

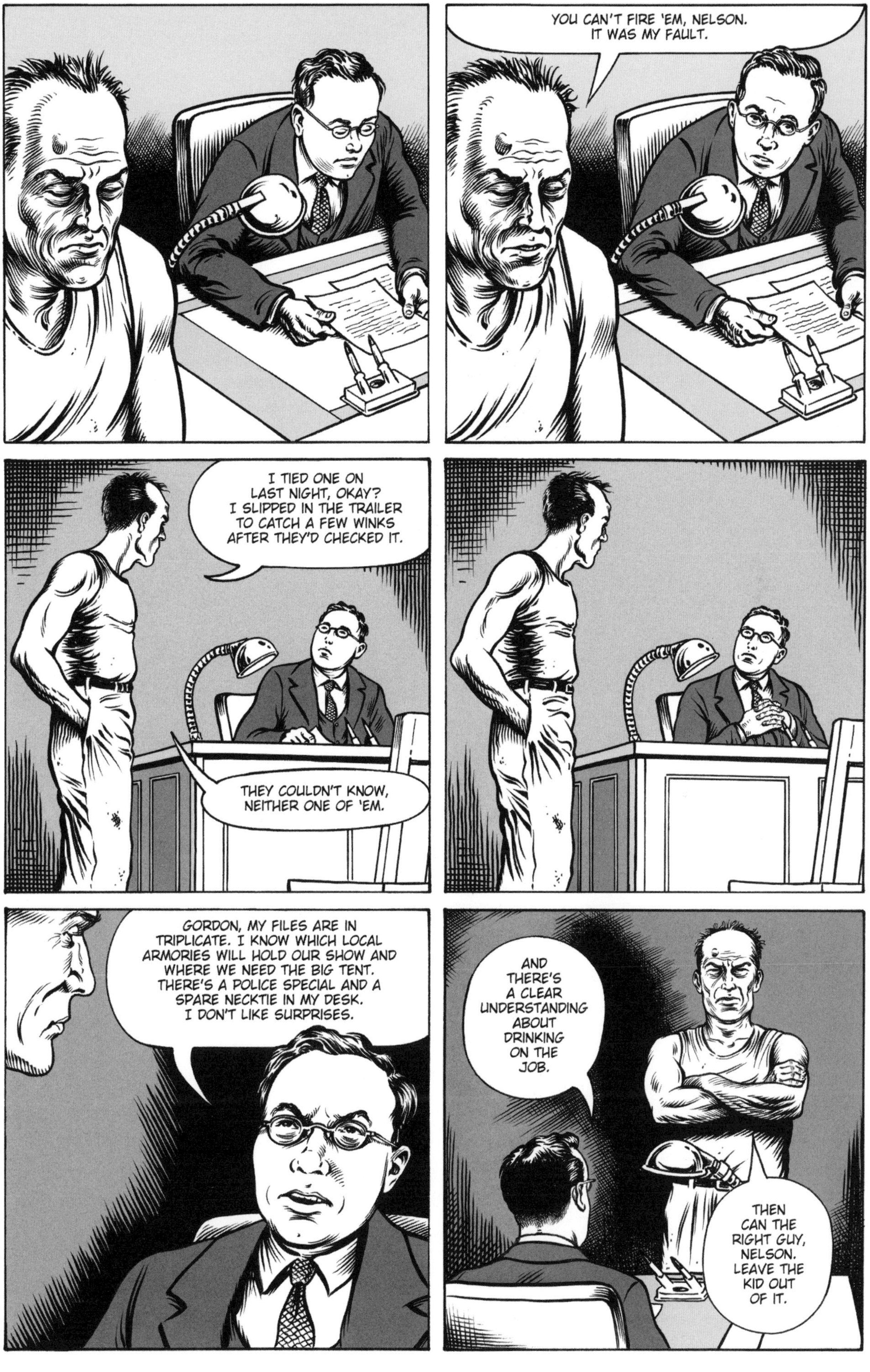
YOU CAN'T FIRE 'EM, NELSON. IT WAS MY FAULT.
I TIED ONE ON LAST NIGHT, OKAY? I SLIPPED IN THE TRAILER TO CATCH A FEW WINKS AFTER THEY'D CHECKED IT.
THEY COULDN'T KNOW, NEITHER ONE OF 'EM.
GORDON, MY FILES ARE IN TRIPLICATE. I KNOW WHICH LOCAL ARMORIES WILL HOLD OUR SHOW AND WHERE WE NEED THE BIG TENT. THERE'S A POLICE SPECIAL AND A SPARE NECKTIE IN MY DESK. I DON'T LIKE SURPRISES.
AND THERE'S A CLEAR UNDERSTANDING ABOUT DRINKING ON THE JOB.
THEN CAN THE RIGHT GUY, NELSON. LEAVE THE KID OUT OF IT.

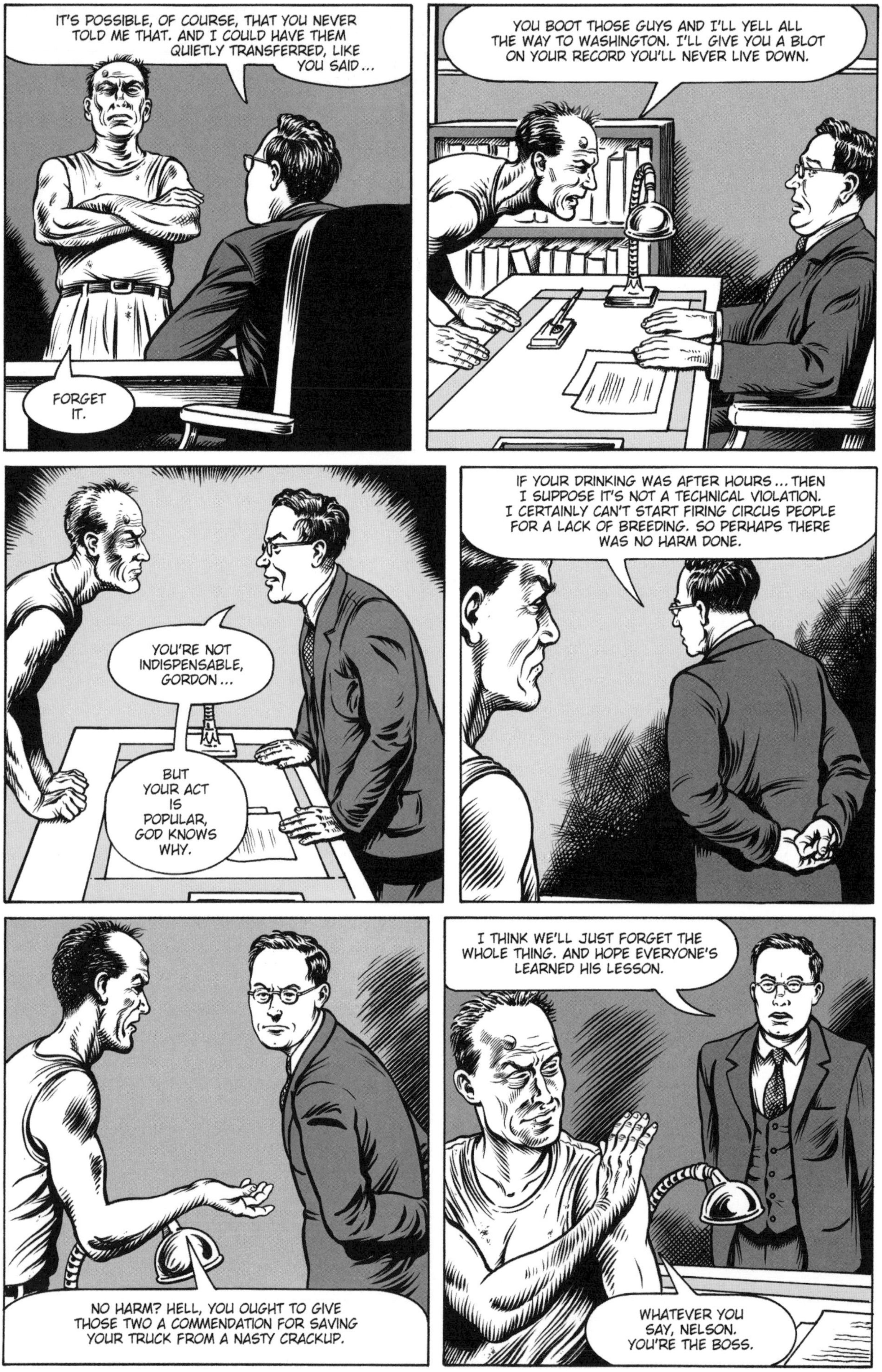
IT'S POSSIBLE, OF COURSE, THAT YOU NEVER TOLD ME THAT. AND I COULD HAVE THEM QUIETLY TRANSFERRED, LIKE YOU SAID...
FORGET IT.
YOU BOOT THOSE GUYS AND I'LL YELL ALL THE WAY TO WASHINGTON. I'LL GIVE YOU A BLOT ON YOUR RECORD YOU'LL NEVER LIVE DOWN.
YOU'RE NOT INDISPENSABLE, GORDON...
BUT YOUR ACT IS POPULAR, GOD KNOWS WHY.
IF YOUR DRINKING WAS AFTER HOURS... THEN I SUPPOSE IT'S NOT A TECHNICAL VIOLATION. I CERTAINLY CAN'T START FIRING CIRCUS PEOPLE FOR A LACK OF BREEDING. SO PERHAPS THERE WAS NO HARM DONE.
NO HARM? HELL, YOU OUGHT TO GIVE THOSE TWO A COMMENDATION FOR SAVING YOUR TRUCK FROM A NASTY CRACKUP.
I THINK WE'LL JUST FORGET THE WHOLE THING. AND HOPE EVERYONE'S LEARNED HIS LESSON.
WHATEVER YOU SAY, NELSON. YOU'RE THE BOSS.

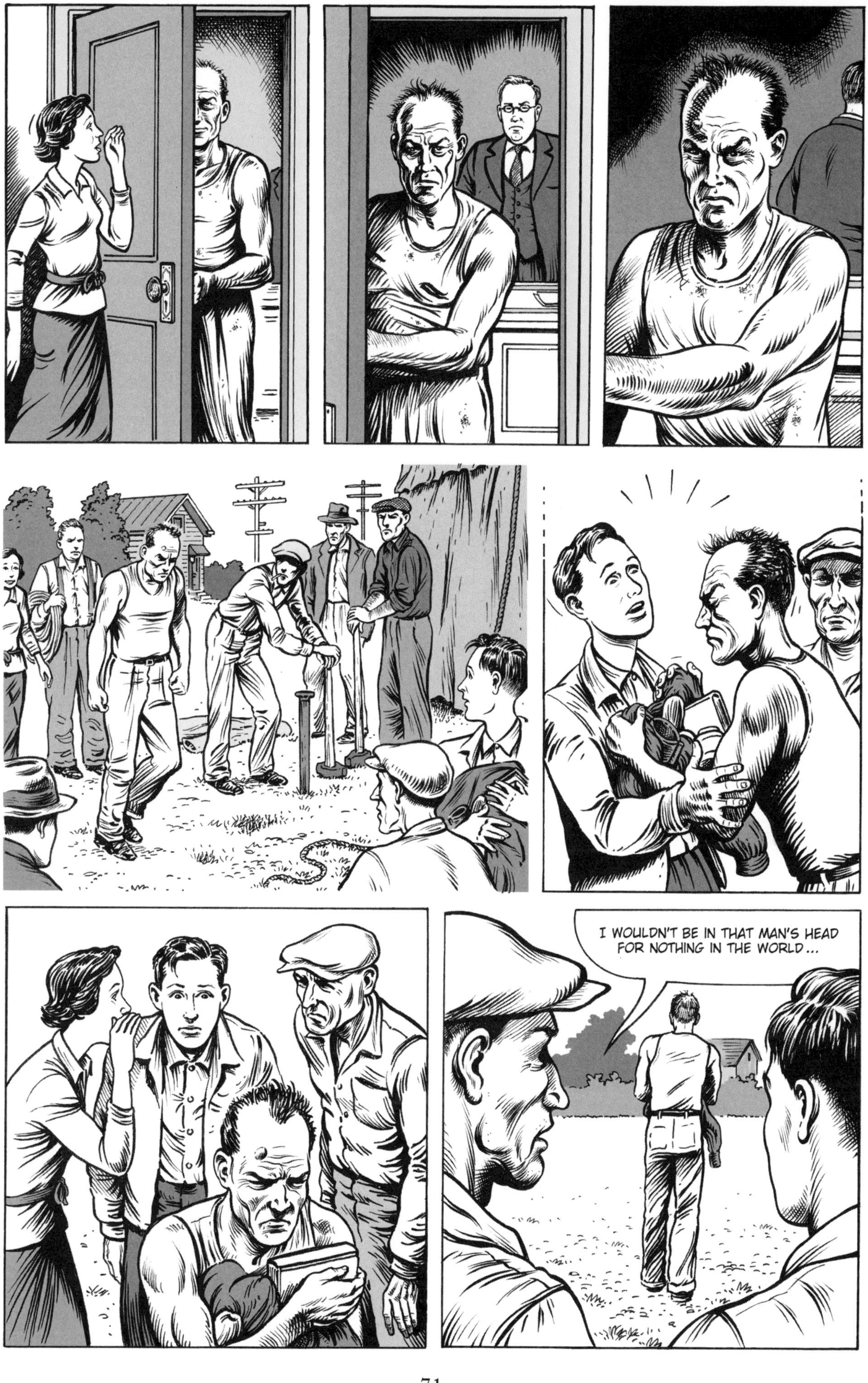
I WOULDN'T BE IN THAT MAN'S HEAD FOR NOTHING IN THE WORLD...

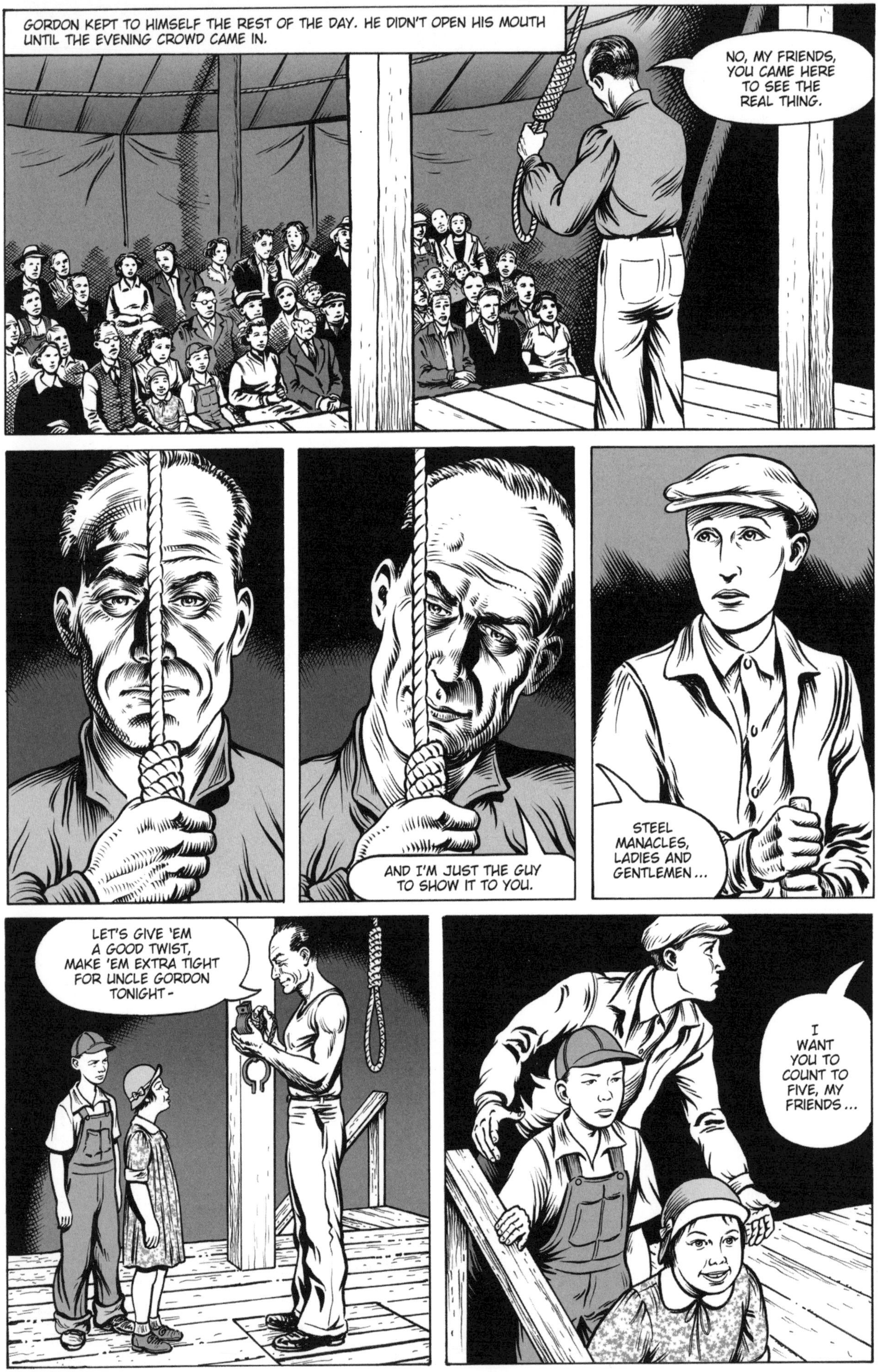
GORDON KEPT TO HIMSELF THE REST OF THE DAY. HE DIDN'T OPEN HIS MOUTH UNTIL THE EVENING CROWD CAME IN.
NO, MY FRIENDS, YOU CAME HERE TO SEE THE REAL THING.
AND I'M JUST THE GUY TO SHOW IT TO YOU.
STEEL MANACLES, LADIES AND GENTLEMEN...
LET'S GIVE 'EM A GOOD TWIST, MAKE 'EM EXTRA TIGHT FOR UNCLE GORDON TONIGHT -
I WANT YOU TO COUNT TO FIVE, MY FRIENDS...

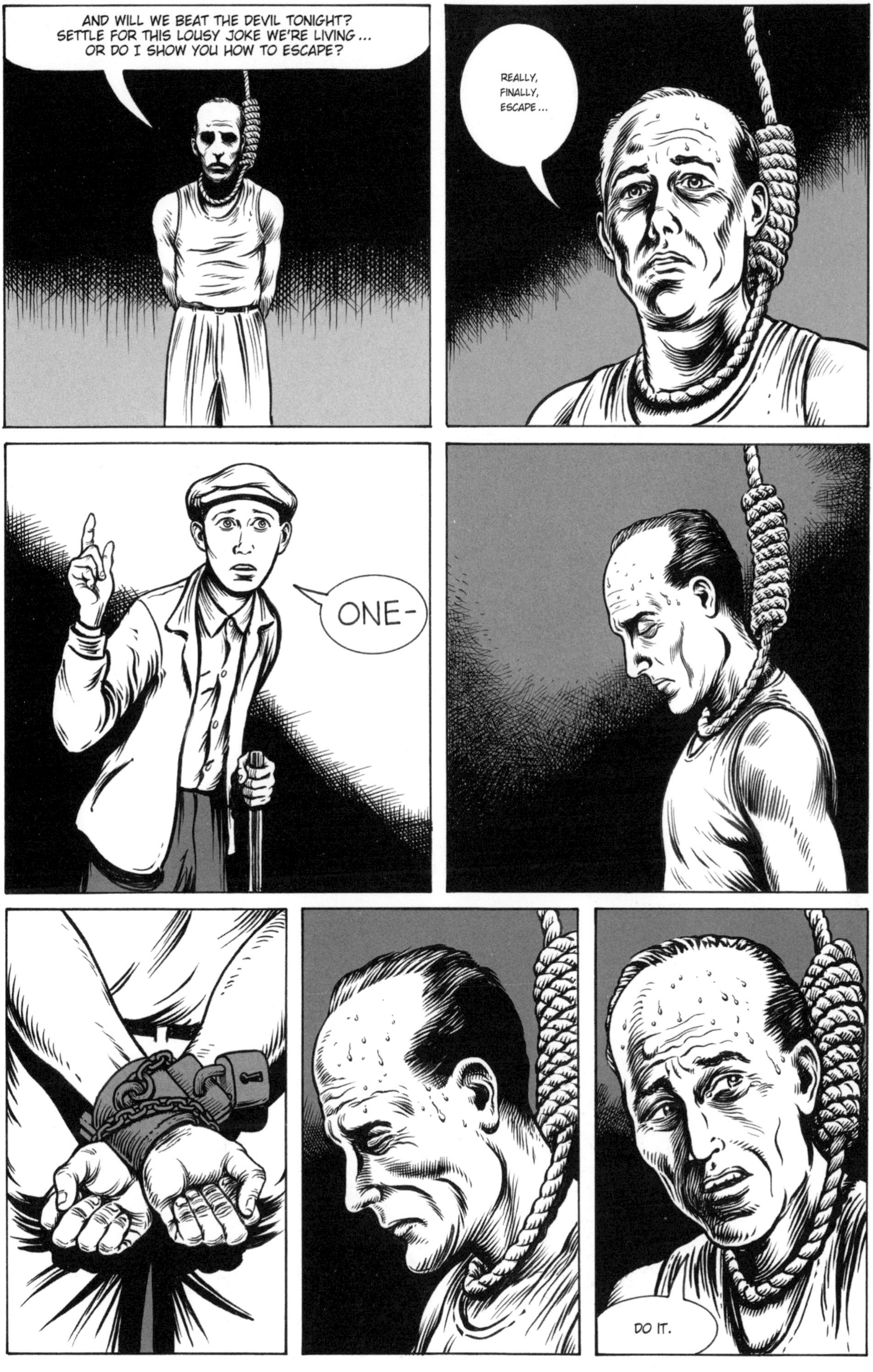
AND WILL WE BEAT THE DEVIL TONIGHT? SETTLE FOR THIS LOUSY JOKE WE'RE LIVING... OR DO I SHOW YOU HOW TO ESCAPE?
REALLY, FINALLY, ESCAPE...
ONE-
DO IT.

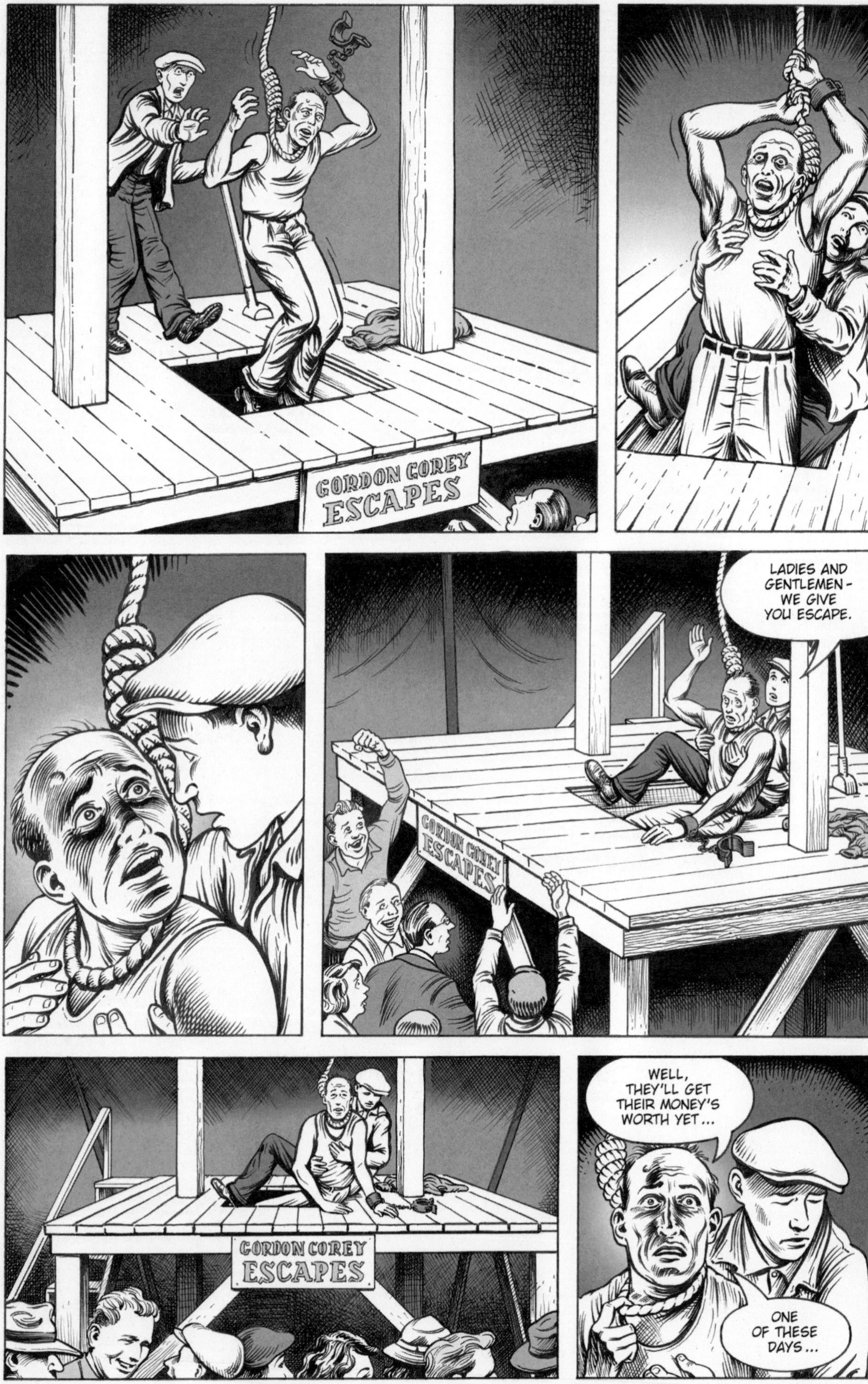
GORDON COREY
ESCAPES
GORDON COREY
ESCAPES
LADIES AND GENTLEMEN - WE GIVE YOU ESCAPE.
GORDON COREY
ESCAPES
WELL, THEY'LL GET THEIR MONEY'S WORTH YET...
ONE OF THESE DAYS...

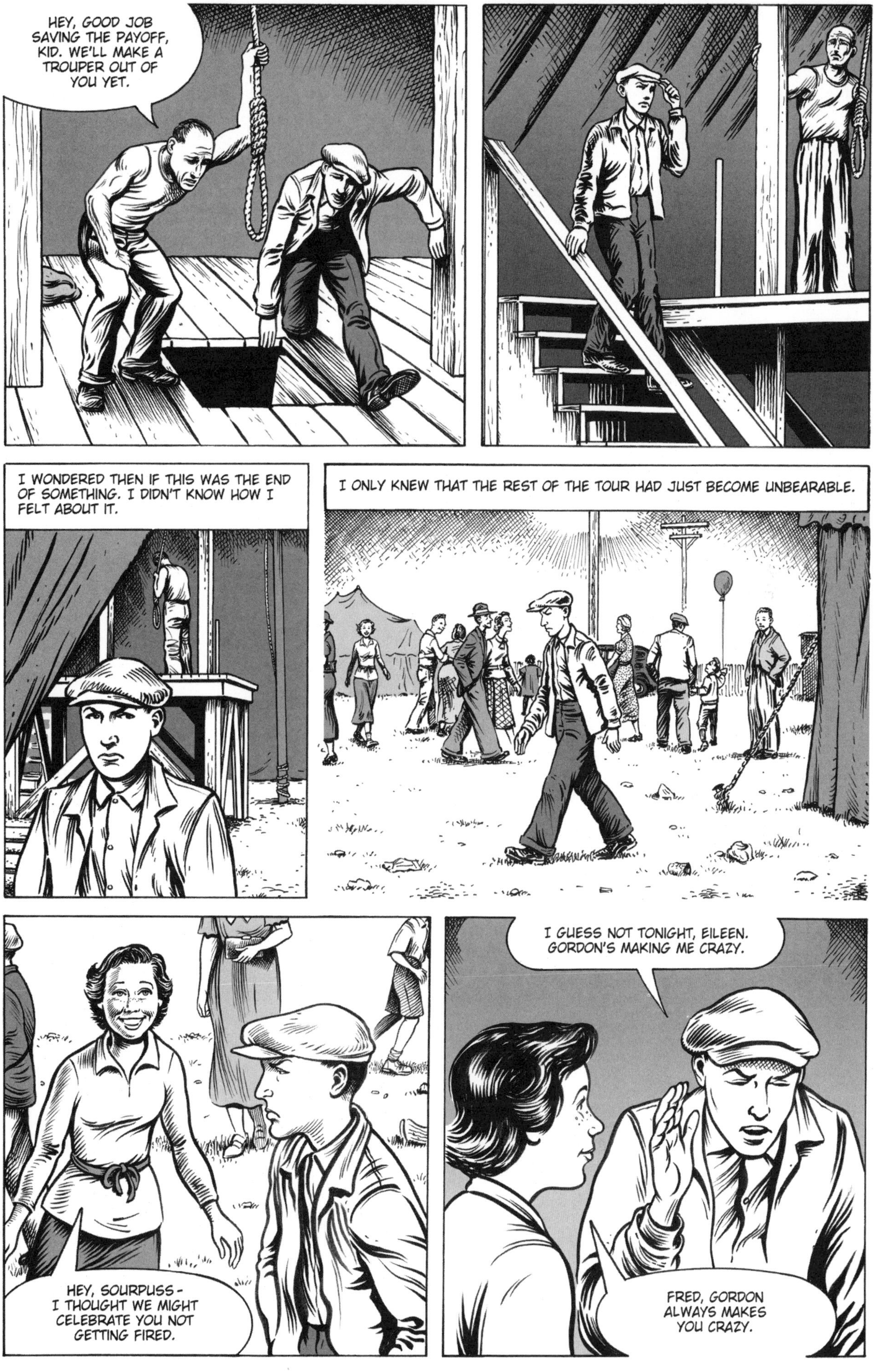
HEY, GOOD JOB SAVING THE PAYOFF, KID. WE'LL MAKE A TROUPER OUT OF YOU YET.
I WONDERED THEN IF THIS WAS THE END OF SOMETHING. I DIDN'T KNOW HOW I FELT ABOUT IT.
I ONLY KNEW THAT THE REST OF THE TOUR HAD JUST BECOME UNBEARABLE.
HEY, SOURPUSS - I THOUGHT WE MIGHT CELEBRATE YOU NOT GETTING FIRED.
I GUESS NOT TONIGHT, EILEEN. GORDON'S MAKING ME CRAZY.
FRED, GORDON ALWAYS MAKES YOU CRAZY.

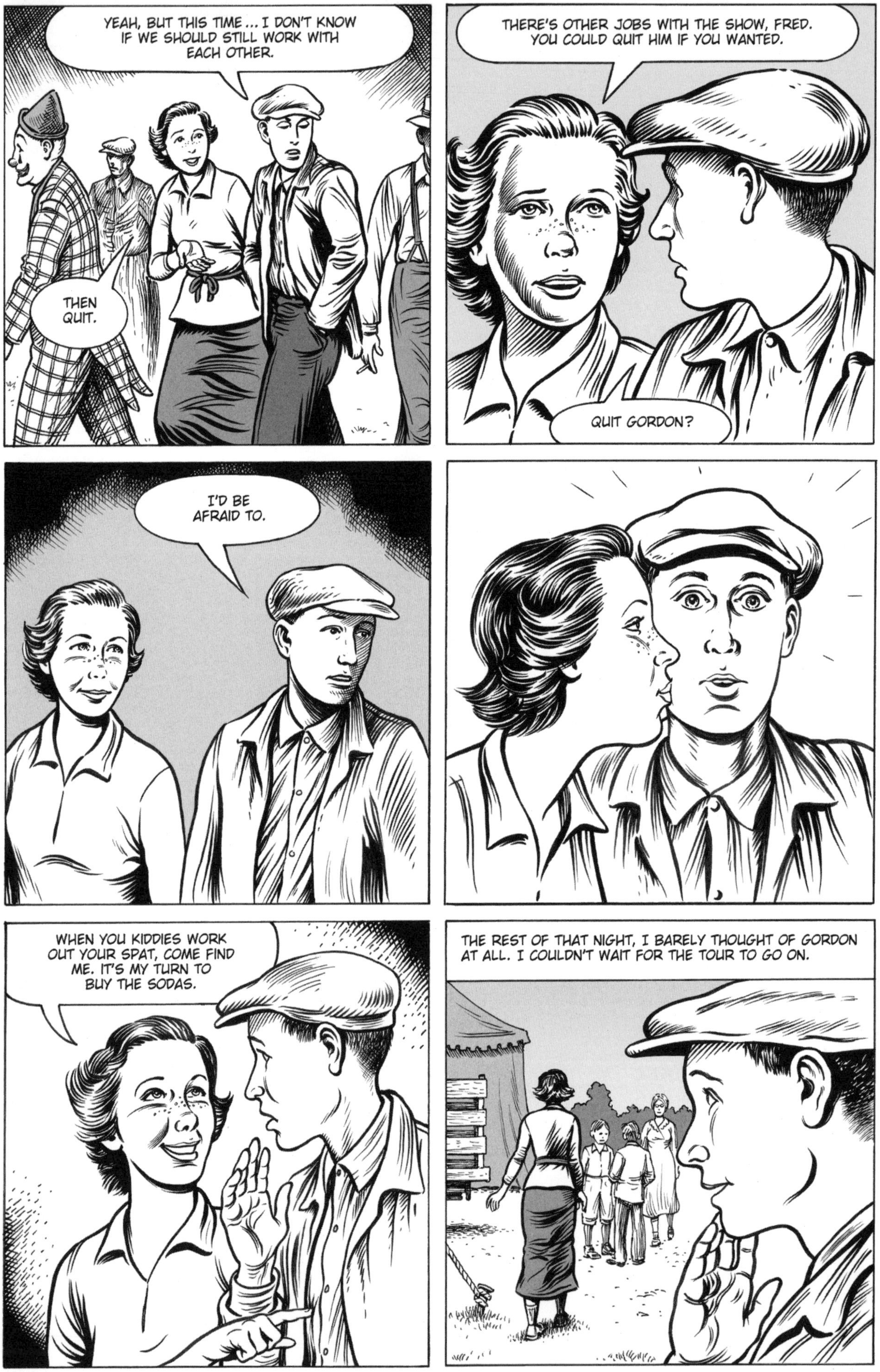
YEAH, BUT THIS TIME... I DON'T KNOW IF WE SHOULD STILL WORK WITH EACH OTHER.
THEN QUIT.
THERE'S OTHER JOBS WITH THE SHOW, FRED. YOU COULD QUIT HIM IF YOU WANTED.
QUIT GORDON?
I'D BE AFRAID TO.
WHEN YOU KIDDIES WORK OUT YOUR SPAT, COME FIND ME. IT'S MY TURN TO BUY THE SODAS.
THE REST OF THAT NIGHT, I BARELY THOUGHT OF GORDON AT ALL. I COULDN'T WAIT FOR THE TOUR TO GO ON.

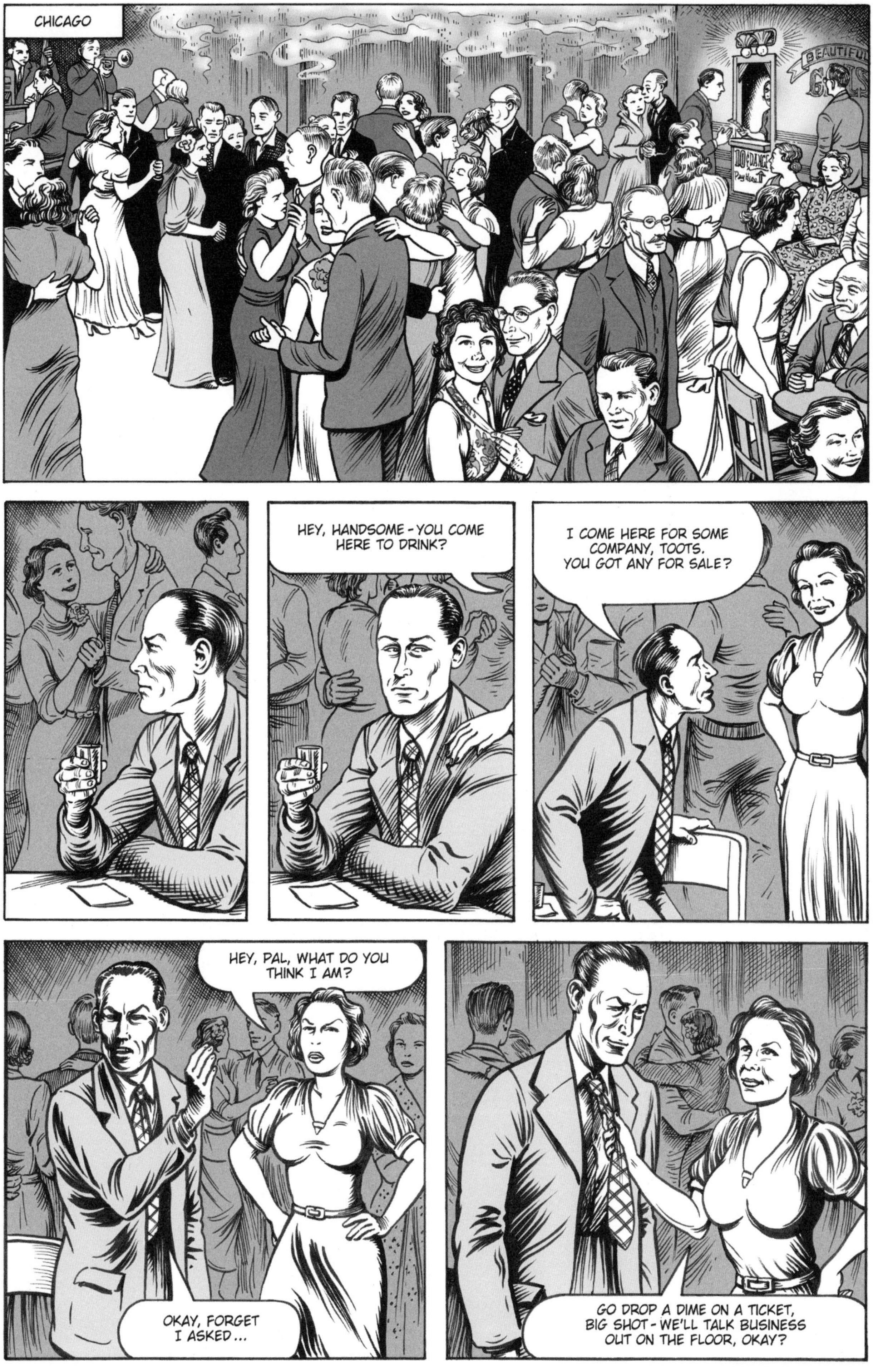
CHICAGO
10¢ DANCE
Pay Here
BEAUTIFUL
HEY, HANDSOME - YOU COME HERE TO DRINK?
I COME HERE FOR SOME COMPANY, TOOTS. YOU GOT ANY FOR SALE?
HEY, PAL, WHAT DO YOU THINK I AM?
OKAY, FORGET I ASKED...
GO DROP A DIME ON A TICKET, BIG SHOT - WE'LL TALK BUSINESS OUT ON THE FLOOR, OKAY?

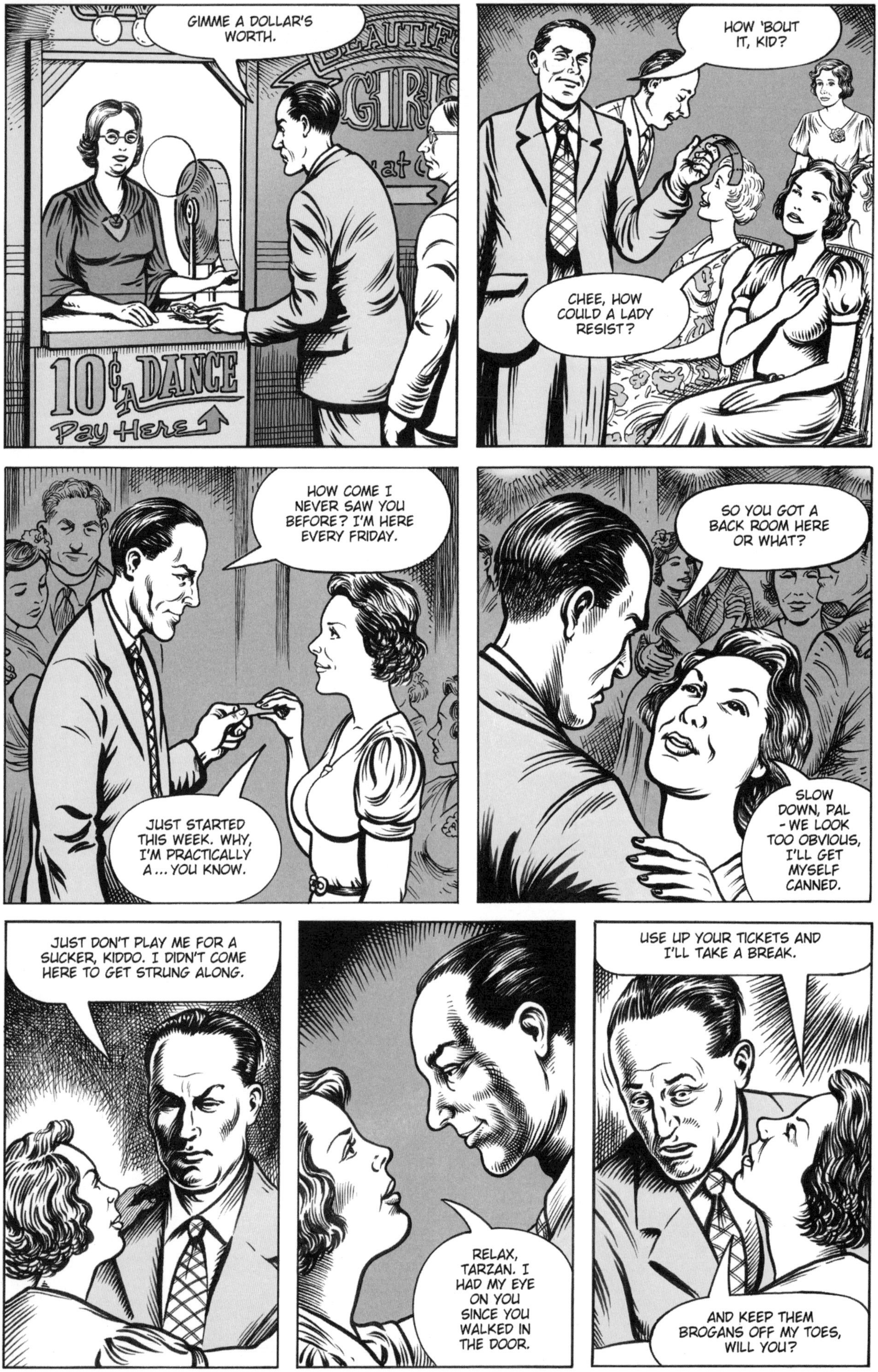
GIMME A DOLLAR'S WORTH.
BEAUTIFUL GIRLS
10¢ A DANCE
Pay Here
HOW 'BOUT IT, KID?
CHEE, HOW COULD A LADY RESIST?
HOW COME I NEVER SAW YOU BEFORE? I'M HERE EVERY FRIDAY.
JUST STARTED THIS WEEK. WHY, I'M PRACTICALLY A... YOU KNOW.
SO YOU GOT A BACK ROOM HERE OR WHAT?
SLOW DOWN, PAL - WE LOOK TOO OBVIOUS, I'LL GET MYSELF CANNED.
JUST DON'T PLAY ME FOR A SUCKER, KIDDO. I DIDN'T COME HERE TO GET STRUNG ALONG.
RELAX, TARZAN. I HAD MY EYE ON YOU SINCE YOU WALKED IN THE DOOR.
USE UP YOUR TICKETS AND I'LL TAKE A BREAK.
AND KEEP THEM BROGANS OFF MY TOES, WILL YOU?

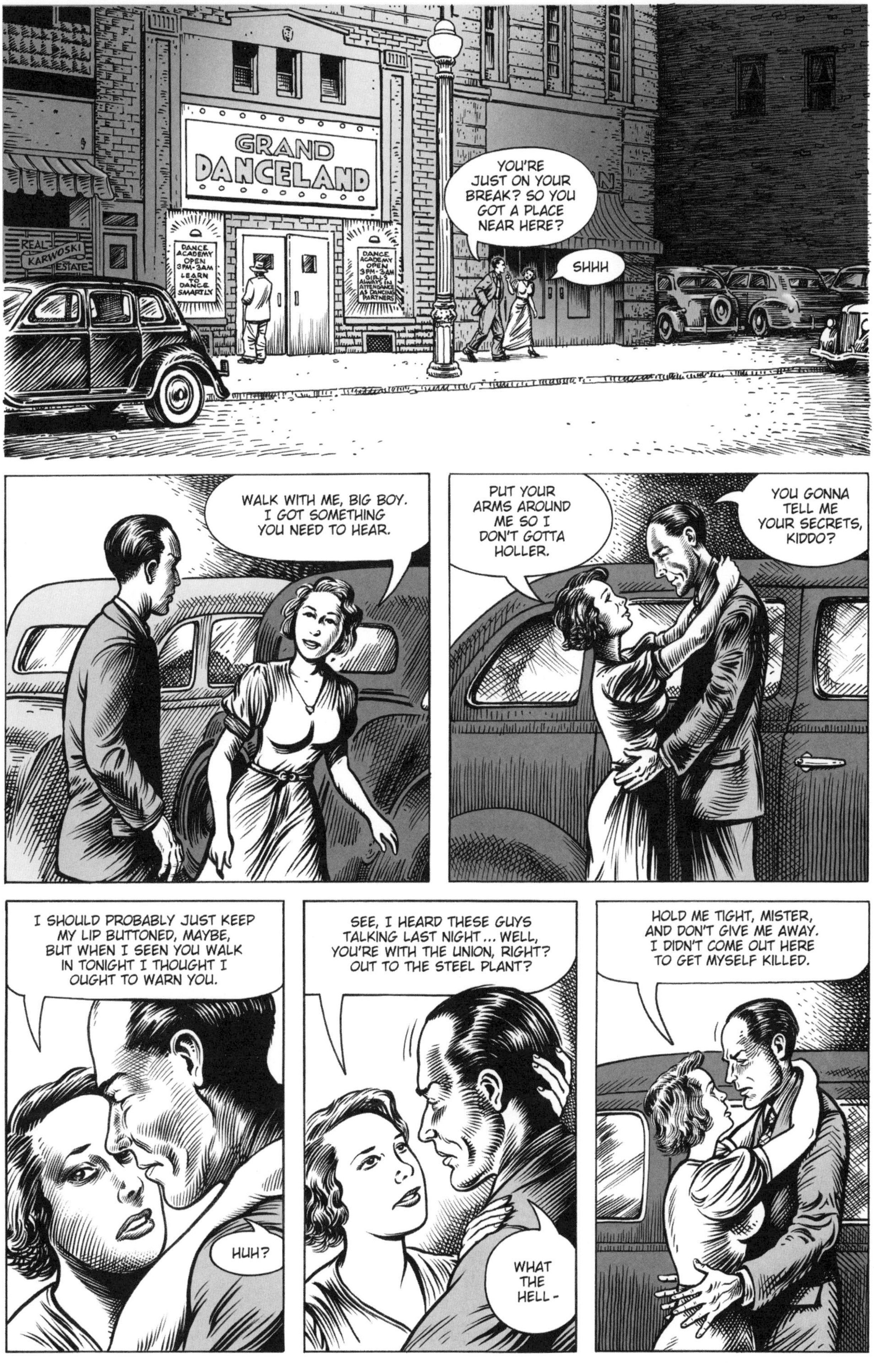
GRAND DANCELAND
YOU'RE JUST ON YOUR BREAK? SO YOU GOT A PLACE NEAR HERE?
SHHH
WALK WITH ME, BIG BOY. I GOT SOMETHING YOU NEED TO HEAR.
PUT YOUR ARMS AROUND ME SO I DON'T GOTTA HOLLER.
YOU GONNA TELL ME YOUR SECRETS, KIDDO?
I SHOULD PROBABLY JUST KEEP MY LIP BUTTONED, MAYBE, BUT WHEN I SEEN YOU WALK IN TONIGHT I THOUGHT I OUGHT TO WARN YOU.
HUH?
SEE, I HEARD THESE GUYS TALKING LAST NIGHT ... WELL, YOU'RE WITH THE UNION, RIGHT? OUT TO THE STEEL PLANT?
WHAT THE HELL -
HOLD ME TIGHT, MISTER, AND DON'T GIVE ME AWAY. I DIDN'T COME OUT HERE TO GET MYSELF KILLED.

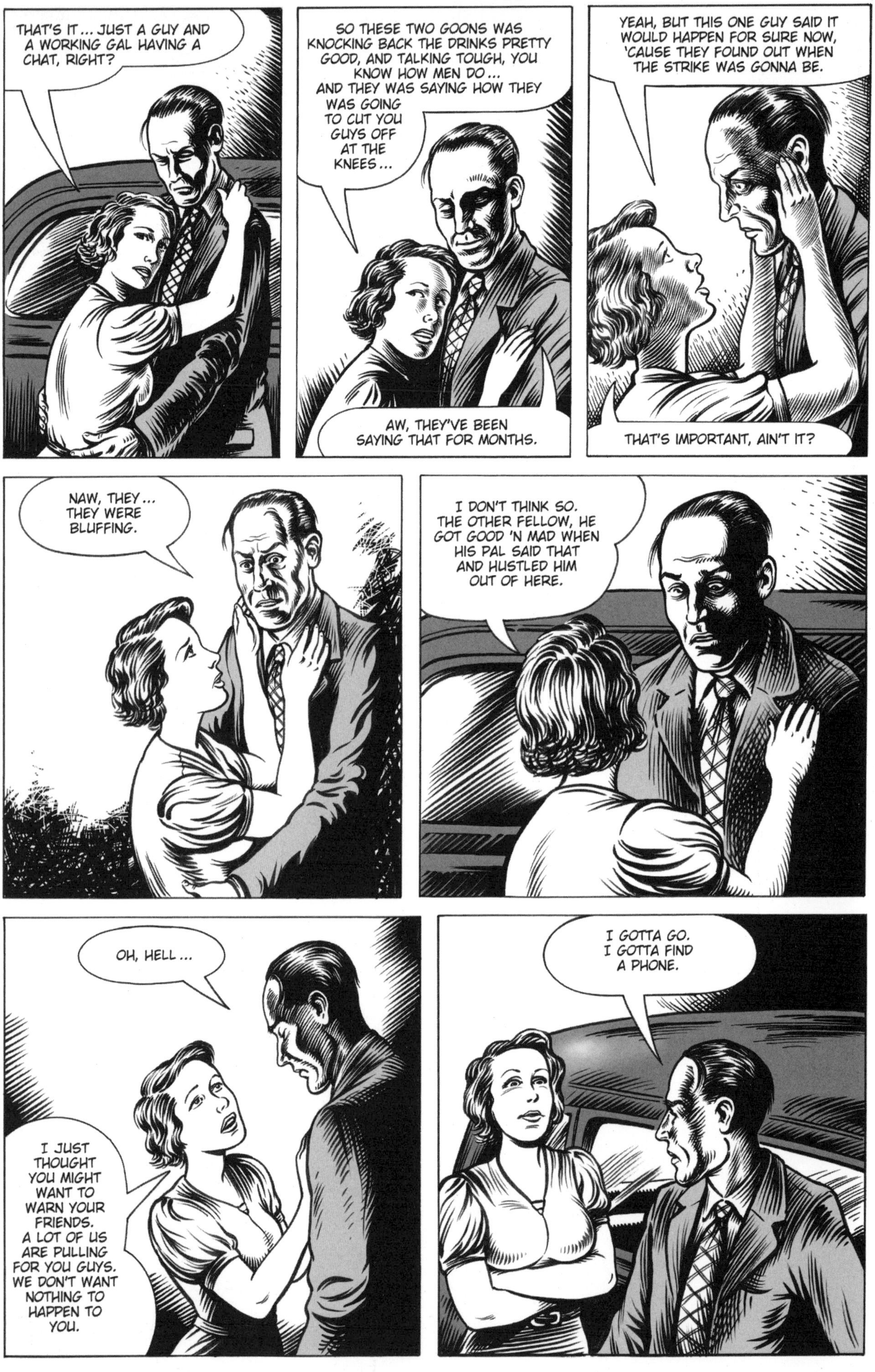
THAT'S IT... JUST A GUY AND A WORKING GAL HAVING A CHAT, RIGHT?
SO THESE TWO GOONS WAS KNOCKING BACK THE DRINKS PRETTY GOOD, AND TALKING TOUGH, YOU KNOW HOW MEN DO... AND THEY WAS SAYING HOW THEY WAS GOING TO CUT YOU GUYS OFF AT THE KNEES...
AW, THEY'VE BEEN SAYING THAT FOR MONTHS.
YEAH, BUT THIS ONE GUY SAID IT WOULD HAPPEN FOR SURE NOW, 'CAUSE THEY FOUND OUT WHEN THE STRIKE WAS GONNA BE.
THAT'S IMPORTANT, AIN'T IT?
NAW, THEY... THEY WERE BLUFFING.
I DON'T THINK SO. THE OTHER FELLOW, HE GOT GOOD 'N MAD WHEN HIS PAL SAID THAT AND HUSTLED HIM OUT OF HERE.
OH, HELL...
I JUST THOUGHT YOU MIGHT WANT TO WARN YOUR FRIENDS. A LOT OF US ARE PULLING FOR YOU GUYS. WE DON'T WANT NOTHING TO HAPPEN TO YOU.
I GOTTA GO. I GOTTA FIND A PHONE.

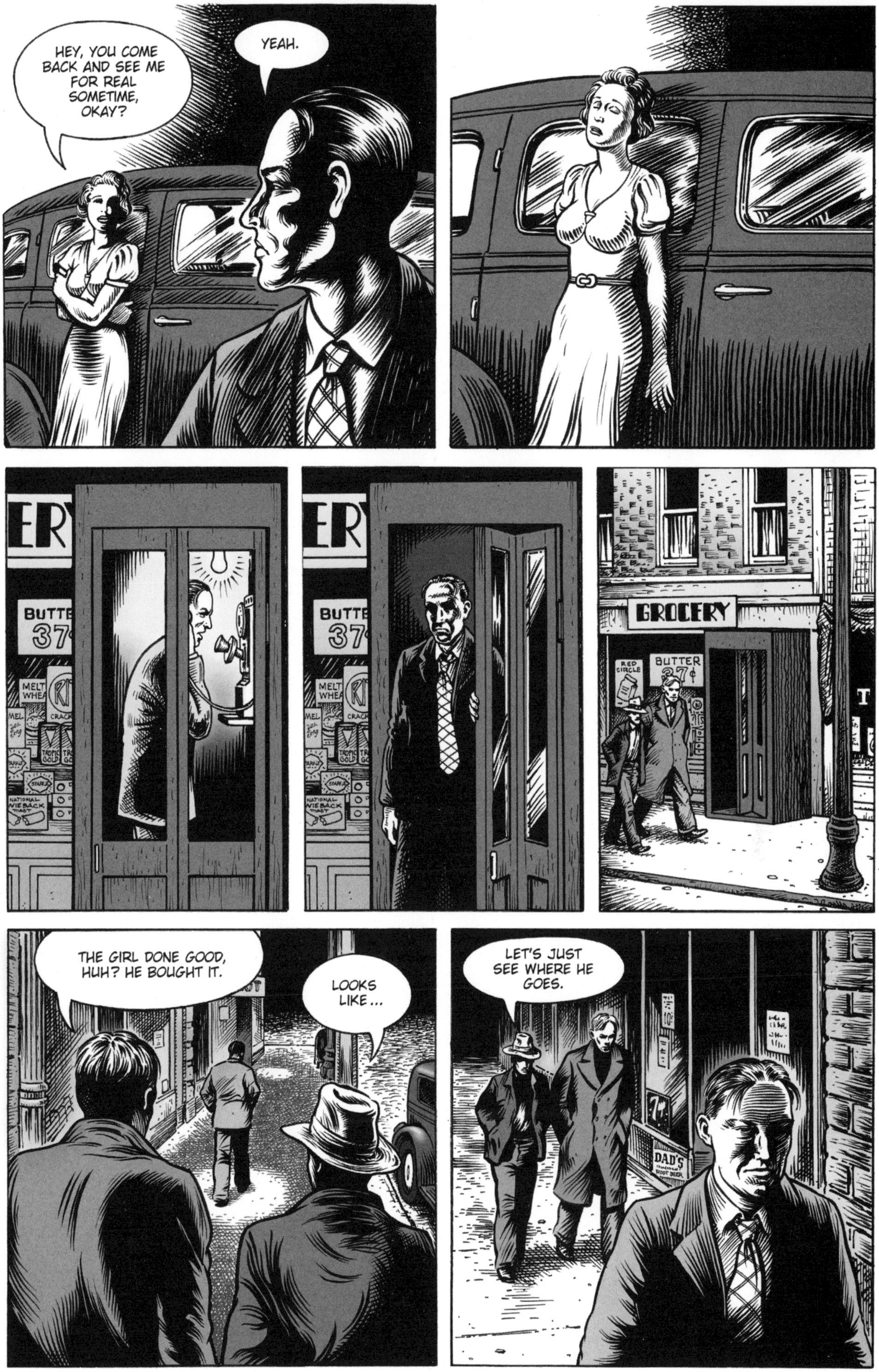

HEY, YOU COME BACK AND SEE ME FOR REAL SOMETIME, OKAY?
YEAH.
GROCERY
BUTTER 37¢
RED CIRCLE
THE GIRL DONE GOOD, HUH? HE BOUGHT IT.
LOOKS LIKE...
LET'S JUST SEE WHERE HE GOES.
DAD'S

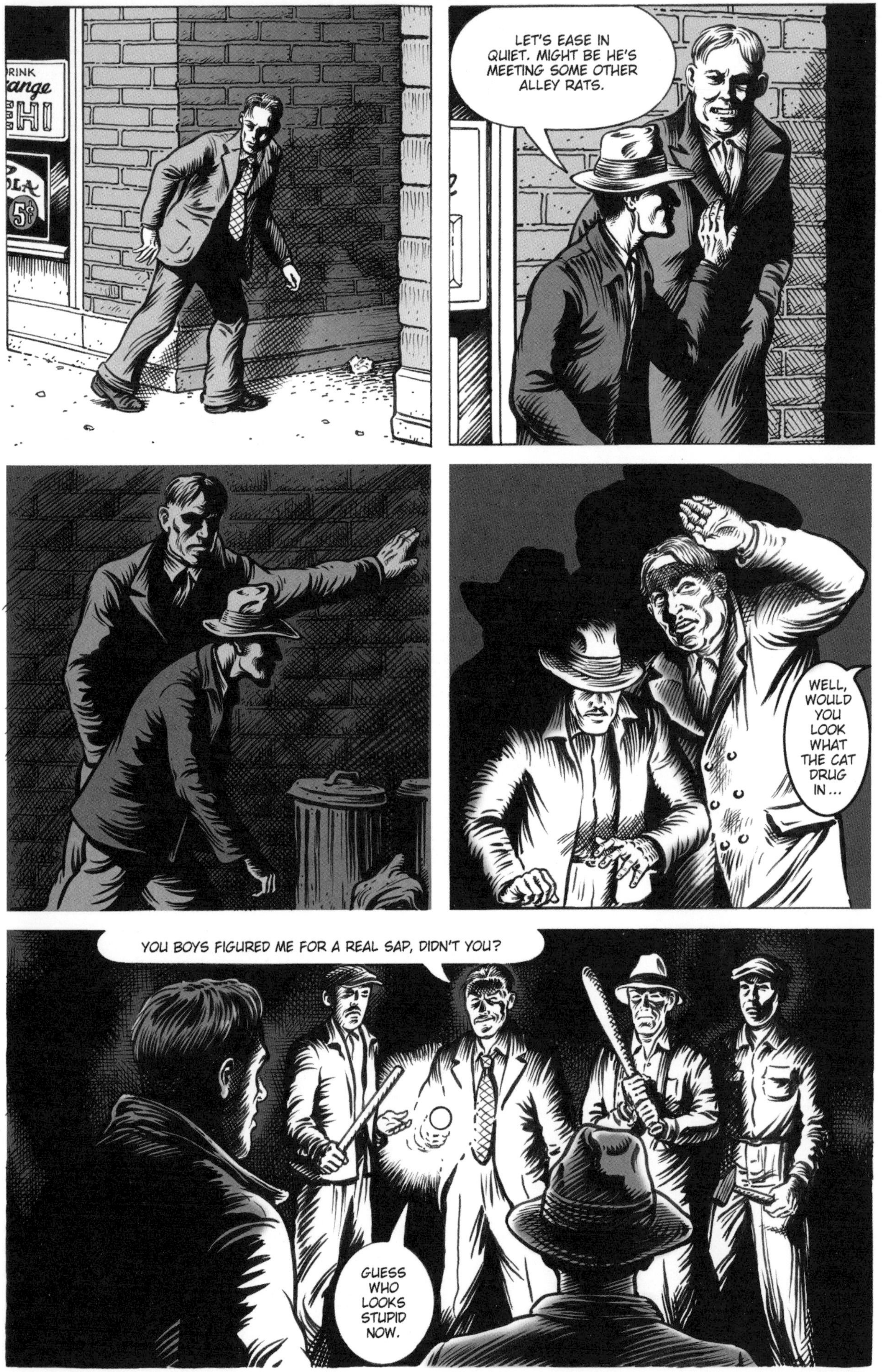
DRINK
5¢
LET'S EASE IN QUIET. MIGHT BE HE'S MEETING SOME OTHER ALLEY RATS.
WELL, WOULD YOU LOOK WHAT THE CAT DRUG IN...
YOU BOYS FIGURED ME FOR A REAL SAP, DIDN'T YOU?
GUESS WHO LOOKS STUPID NOW.

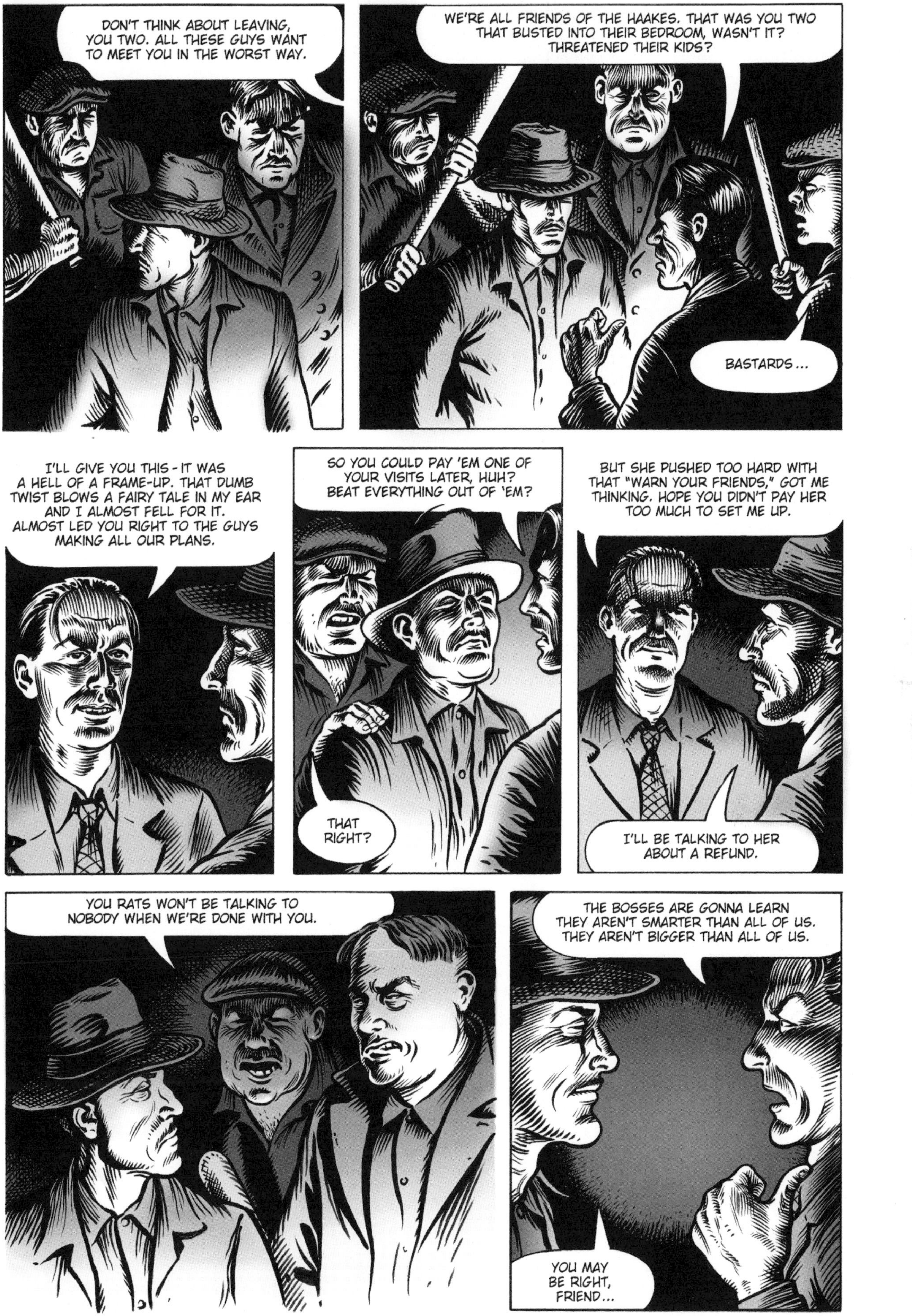
DON'T THINK ABOUT LEAVING, YOU TWO. ALL THESE GUYS WANT TO MEET YOU IN THE WORST WAY.
WE'RE ALL FRIENDS OF THE HAAKES. THAT WAS YOU TWO THAT BUSTED INTO THEIR BEDROOM, WASN'T IT? THREATENED THEIR KIDS?
BASTARDS...
I'LL GIVE YOU THIS - IT WAS A HELL OF A FRAME-UP. THAT DUMB TWIST BLOWS A FAIRY TALE IN MY EAR AND I ALMOST FELL FOR IT. ALMOST LED YOU RIGHT TO THE GUYS MAKING ALL OUR PLANS.
SO YOU COULD PAY 'EM ONE OF YOUR VISITS LATER, HUH? BEAT EVERYTHING OUT OF 'EM?
THAT RIGHT?
BUT SHE PUSHED TOO HARD WITH THAT "WARN YOUR FRIENDS," GOT ME THINKING. HOPE YOU DIDN'T PAY HER TOO MUCH TO SET ME UP.
I'LL BE TALKING TO HER ABOUT A REFUND.
YOU RATS WON'T BE TALKING TO NOBODY WHEN WE'RE DONE WITH YOU.
THE BOSSES ARE GONNA LEARN THEY AREN'T SMARTER THAN ALL OF US. THEY AREN'T BIGGER THAN ALL OF US.
YOU MAY BE RIGHT, FRIEND...

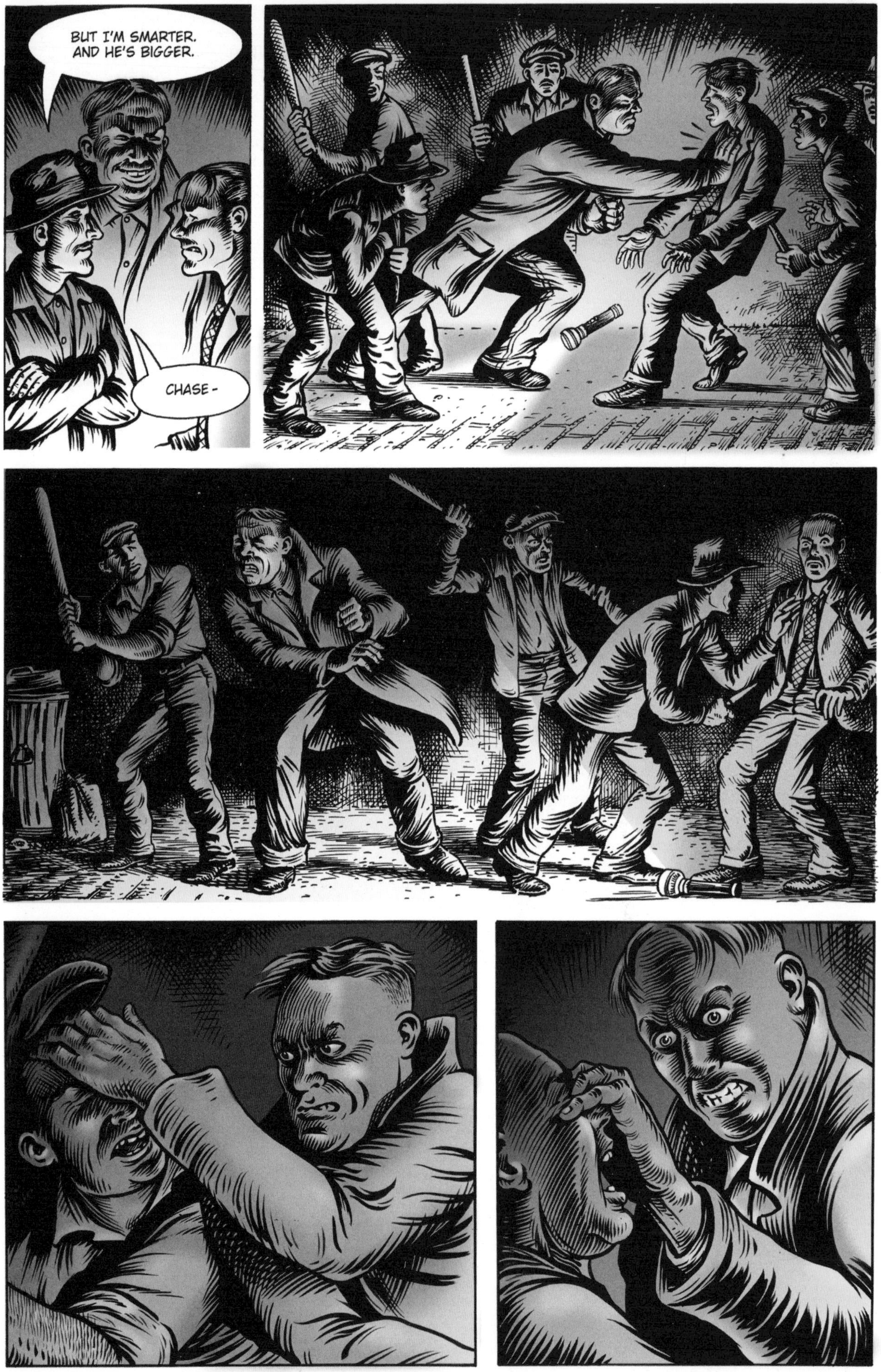
BUT I'M SMARTER.
AND HE'S BIGGER.
CHASE-

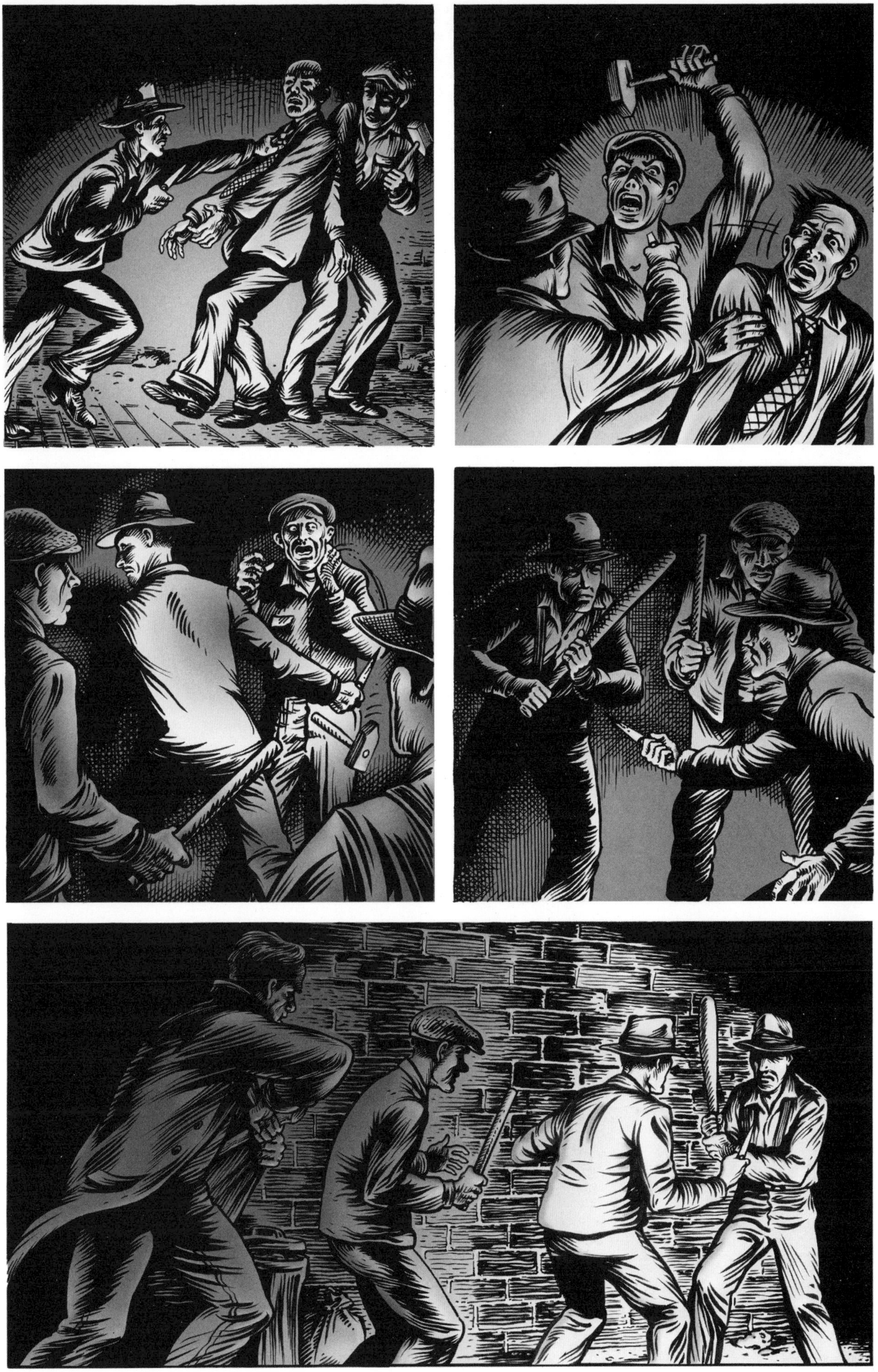

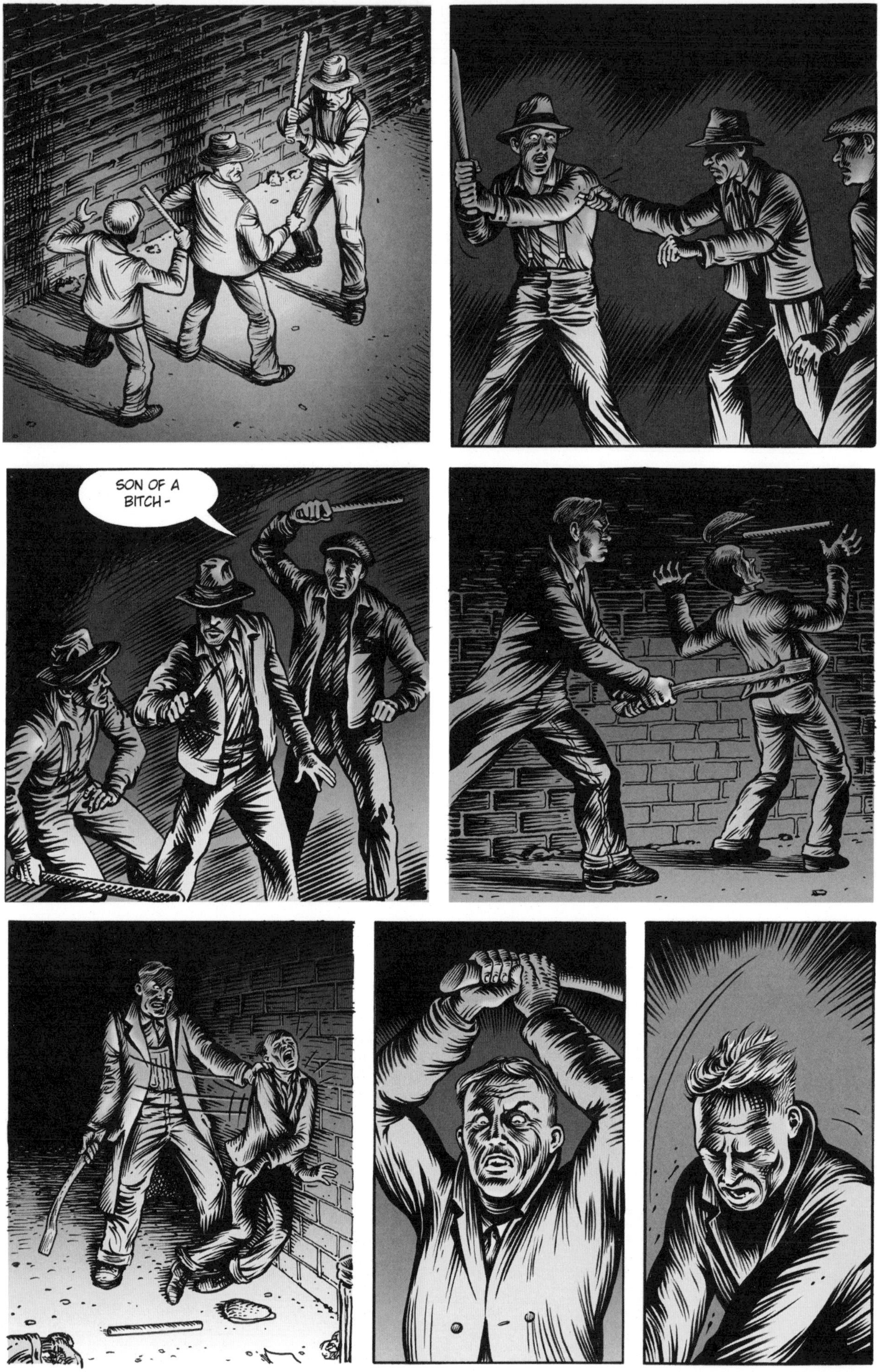
SON OF A BITCH -

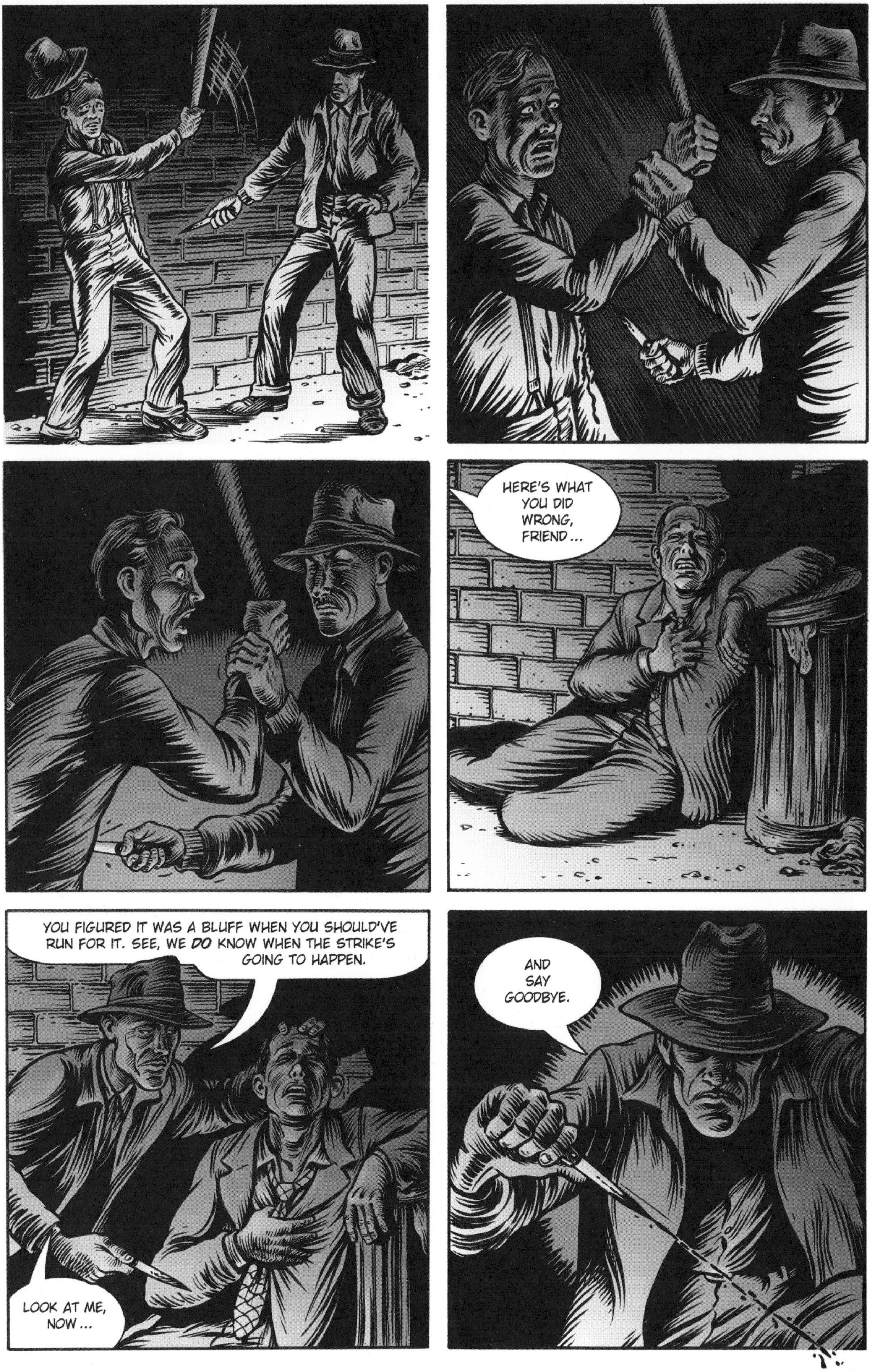
HERE'S WHAT YOU DID WRONG, FRIEND...
YOU FIGURED IT WAS A BLUFF WHEN YOU SHOULD'VE RUN FOR IT. SEE, WE *DO* KNOW WHEN THE STRIKE'S GOING TO HAPPEN.
LOOK AT ME, NOW...
AND SAY GOODBYE.

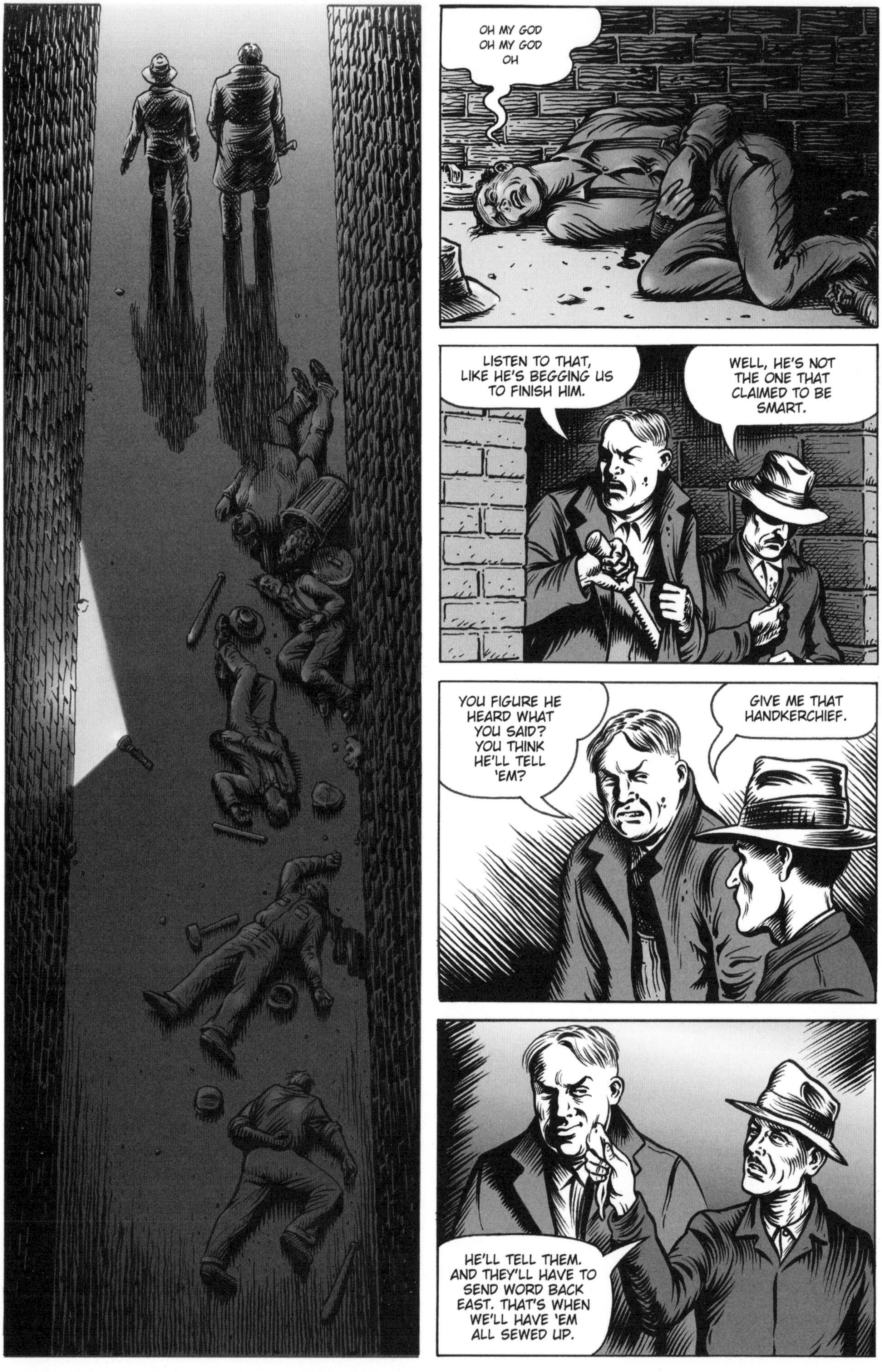
OH MY GOD
OH MY GOD
OH
LISTEN TO THAT, LIKE HE'S BEGGING US TO FINISH HIM.
WELL, HE'S NOT THE ONE THAT CLAIMED TO BE SMART.
YOU FIGURE HE HEARD WHAT YOU SAID? YOU THINK HE'LL TELL 'EM?
GIVE ME THAT HANDKERCHIEF.
HE'LL TELL THEM. AND THEY'LL HAVE TO SEND WORD BACK EAST. THAT'S WHEN WE'LL HAVE 'EM ALL SEWED UP.

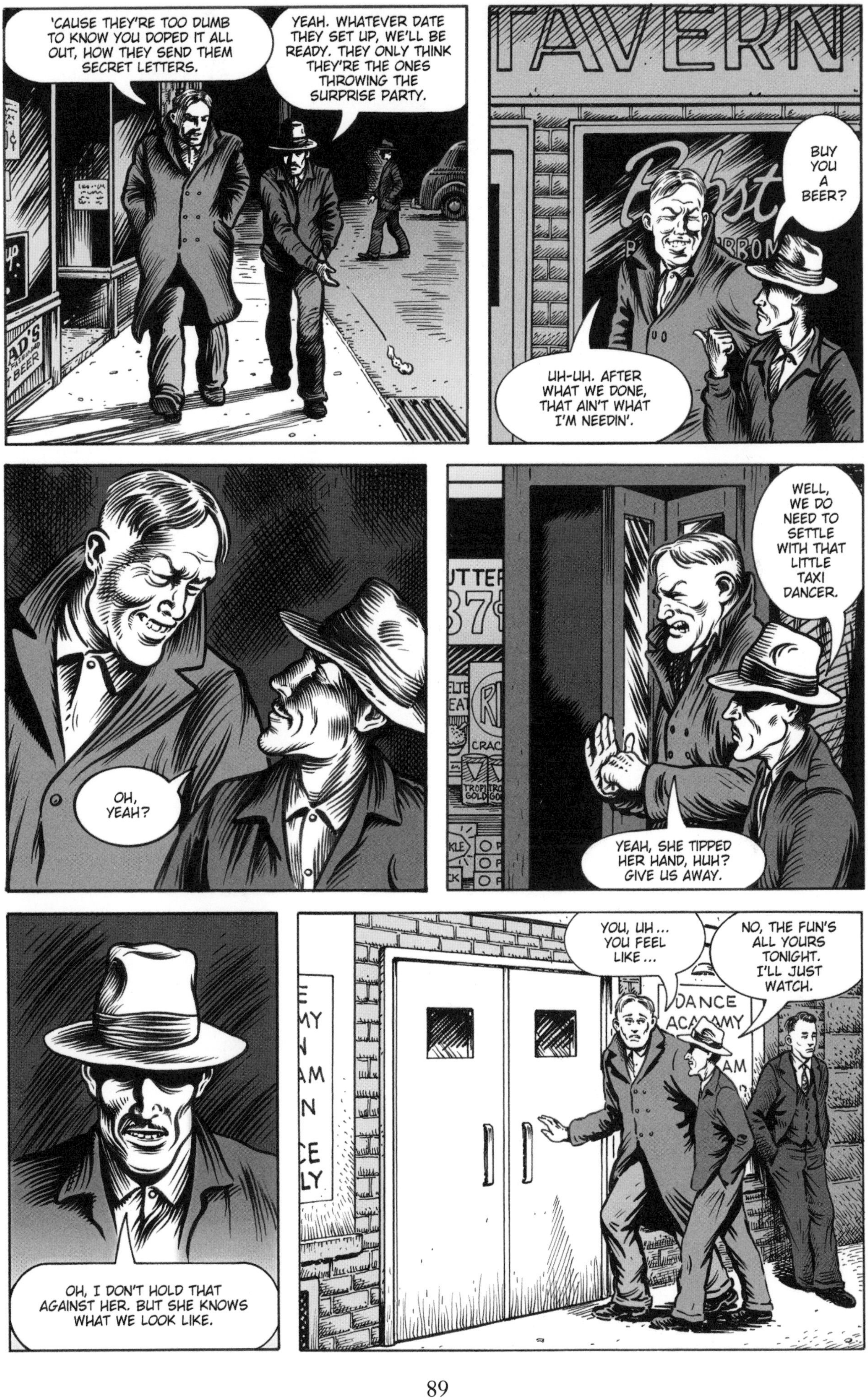
'CAUSE THEY'RE TOO DUMB TO KNOW YOU DOPED IT ALL OUT, HOW THEY SEND THEM SECRET LETTERS.
YEAH. WHATEVER DATE THEY SET UP, WE'LL BE READY. THEY ONLY THINK THEY'RE THE ONES THROWING THE SURPRISE PARTY.
TAVERN
BUY YOU A BEER?
UH-UH. AFTER WHAT WE DONE, THAT AIN'T WHAT I'M NEEDIN'.
OH, YEAH?
WELL, WE DO NEED TO SETTLE WITH THAT LITTLE TAXI DANCER.
YEAH, SHE TIPPED HER HAND, HUH? GIVE US AWAY.
OH, I DON'T HOLD THAT AGAINST HER. BUT SHE KNOWS WHAT WE LOOK LIKE.
YOU, UH... YOU FEEL LIKE...
NO, THE FUN'S ALL YOURS TONIGHT. I'LL JUST WATCH.
DANCE ACADAMY

IT HAD BEEN A GOOD NIGHT FOR THE BUTCHERS.

THE LOCALS HAD CLEANED THEM OUT OF CANDY APPLES, AND THE MEMORY OF POPCORN AND PRETZELS STILL RODE THE BREEZE LONG AFTER THE CROWD HAD LEFT.

I ALWAYS RELISHED THAT HOUR AFTER THE ALL-OUT-AND-OVER... THE BALLY AND CLAMOR REDUCED TO MURMURS AND THE DISTANT SHUFFLING OF CARDS, THE SNORTS OF THE STOCK AS THEY SETTLED IN THEIR CAGES.

IT WAS A GOOD TIME TO THINK.

FOR A WHILE, ON MY OWN, I COULD DREAM OF SHAPING MY PAST INTO SOME KIND OF A FUTURE...

IGNORE HOW THE QUIET WOULD TURN TO SULLEN SILENCE, HOW THE STENCH OF CHEAP HOOCH HAD COME TO HAUNT THE TRAILER.

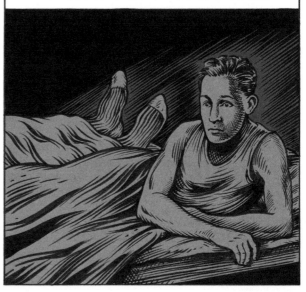

SOMETIMES I COULD IGNORE IT FOR HALF THE NIGHT.

BUT SOONER OR LATER I'D FIND MYSELF WONDERING AGAIN, WHAT IT WAS LIKE...

TO LIVE EVERY DAY WITH THORNS BENEATH YOUR SKIN.

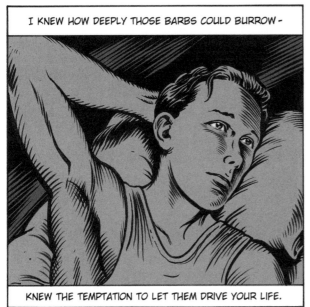

I KNEW HOW DEEPLY THOSE BARBS COULD BURROW—

KNEW THE TEMPTATION TO LET THEM DRIVE YOUR LIFE.

IT HAD NEARLY HAPPENED TO ME...

NOT SO LONG BEFORE...

ON THE DAY THAT EVERYTHING CHANGED.

91

SAM HAD TOLD ME, "THERE'S AS MANY WAYS HOPPING A FREIGHT CAN GO SOUR AS THERE'S FOOLS LIKE US WILLING TO TRY IT."

"YOU GOT YOUR RUNG THAT'S GREASY, OR RUSTED THROUGH..."

"YOUR BRAKEMAN ON THE PROD WITH A BILLY IN HIS MITT..."

"EVEN YOUR HANDS AND EYES CAN PLAY YOU WRONG IF YOU'VE RUN TOO LONG WITH AN EMPTY BELLY."

I'LL NEVER KNOW WHICH ONE IT WAS THAT DAY –

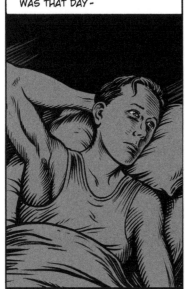

ALL I REMEMBER IS THAT SENSE OF THE WORLD WHIPPING AWAY –

THE DIN OF THE WHEELS AS THEY GNASHED ALONG THE TRACK –

AND NOTHING MORE.

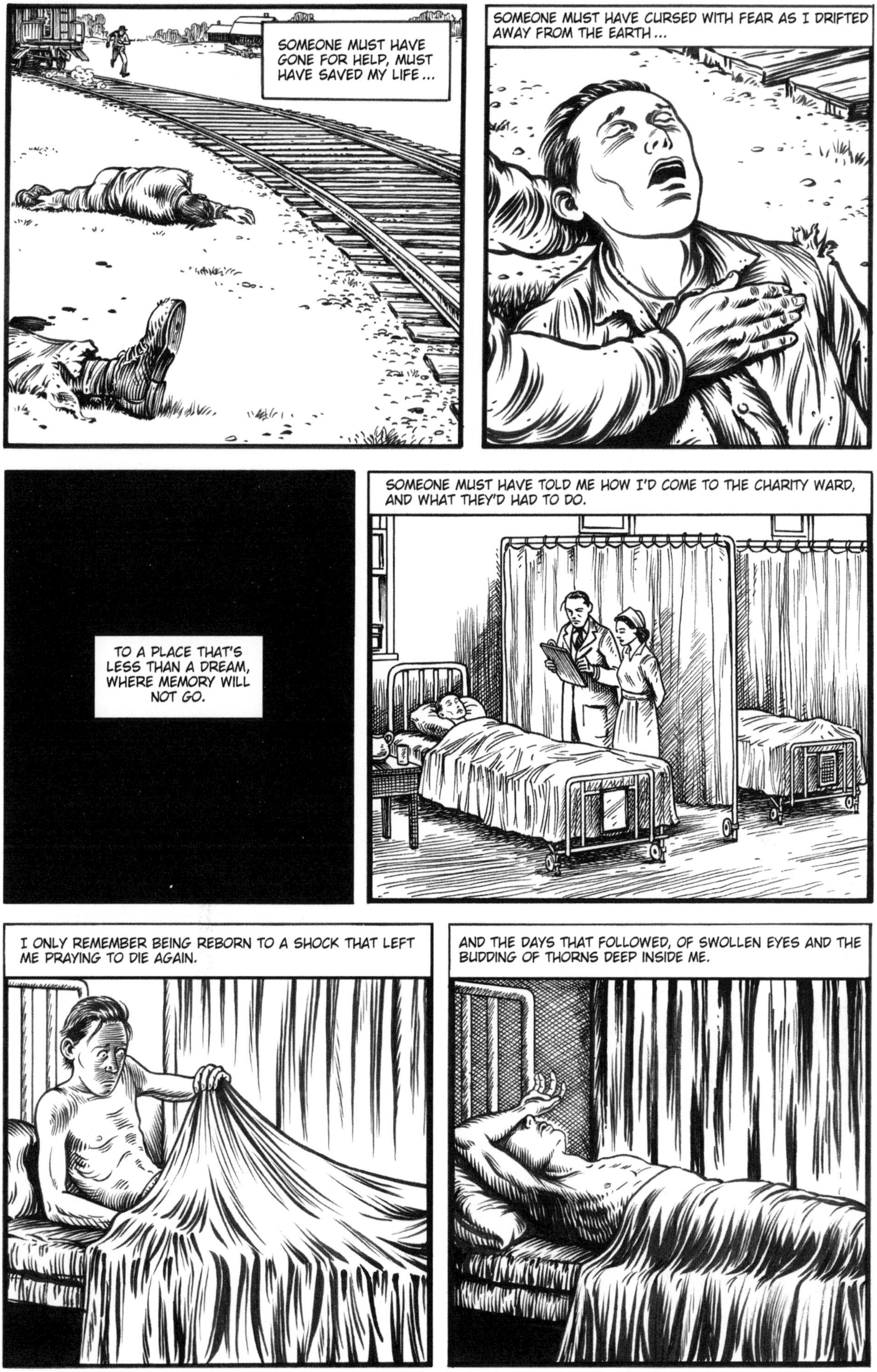
SOMEONE MUST HAVE GONE FOR HELP, MUST HAVE SAVED MY LIFE...
SOMEONE MUST HAVE CURSED WITH FEAR AS I DRIFTED AWAY FROM THE EARTH...
TO A PLACE THAT'S LESS THAN A DREAM, WHERE MEMORY WILL NOT GO.
SOMEONE MUST HAVE TOLD ME HOW I'D COME TO THE CHARITY WARD, AND WHAT THEY'D HAD TO DO.
I ONLY REMEMBER BEING REBORN TO A SHOCK THAT LEFT ME PRAYING TO DIE AGAIN.
AND THE DAYS THAT FOLLOWED, OF SWOLLEN EYES AND THE BUDDING OF THORNS DEEP INSIDE ME.

EVEN THE WARD'S CHARITY ONLY STRETCHED SO FAR, BUT I WAS GLAD TO BE RID OF IT.

THEIR CONCERN WAS UNBEARABLE, THEIR EYES WERE ALWAYS ON ME, THEIR PATIENCE WITH MY BITTERNESS HAD BECOME A PRISON.

HOSPITAL QUIET

SO I WAS FREE AGAIN.

POT ROAST 25¢
CHICKENS 3¢
PORK

REFUGE MISSION
COME UNTO ME
MATTHEW 11:28
FOR RENT

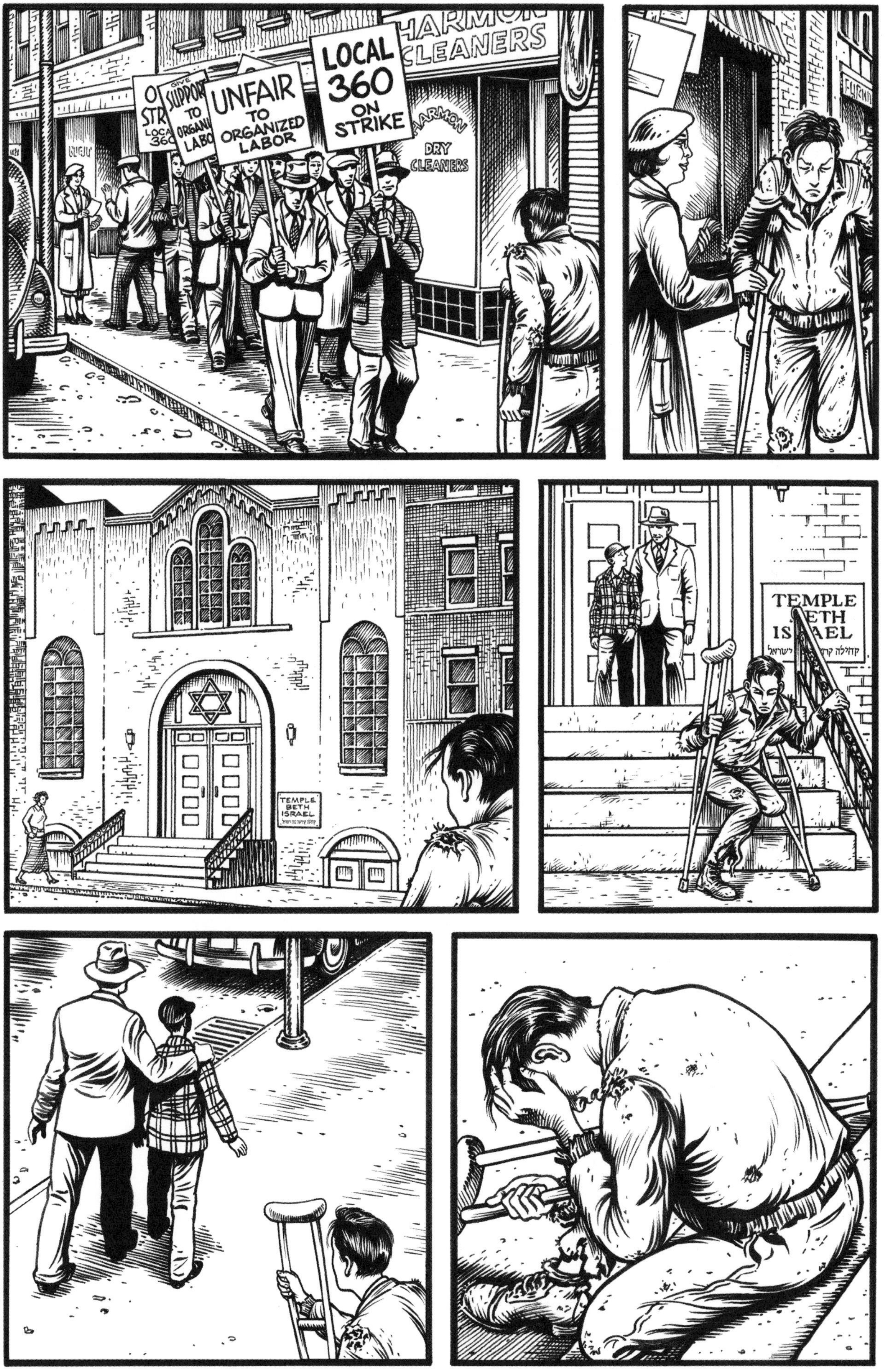
UNFAIR TO ORGANIZED LABOR
LOCAL 360 ON STRIKE
CLEANERS
DRY CLEANERS
TEMPLE BETH ISRAEL

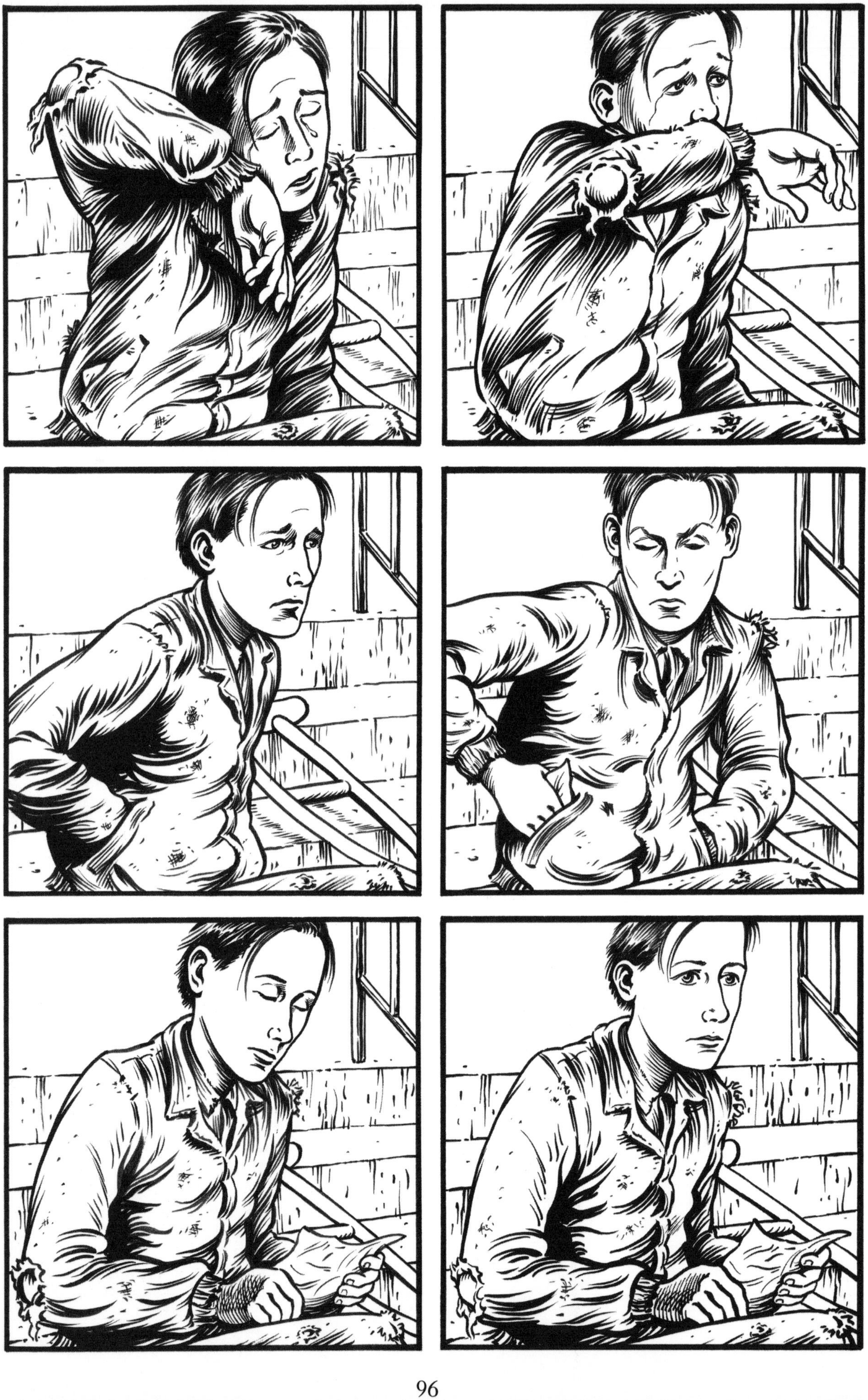

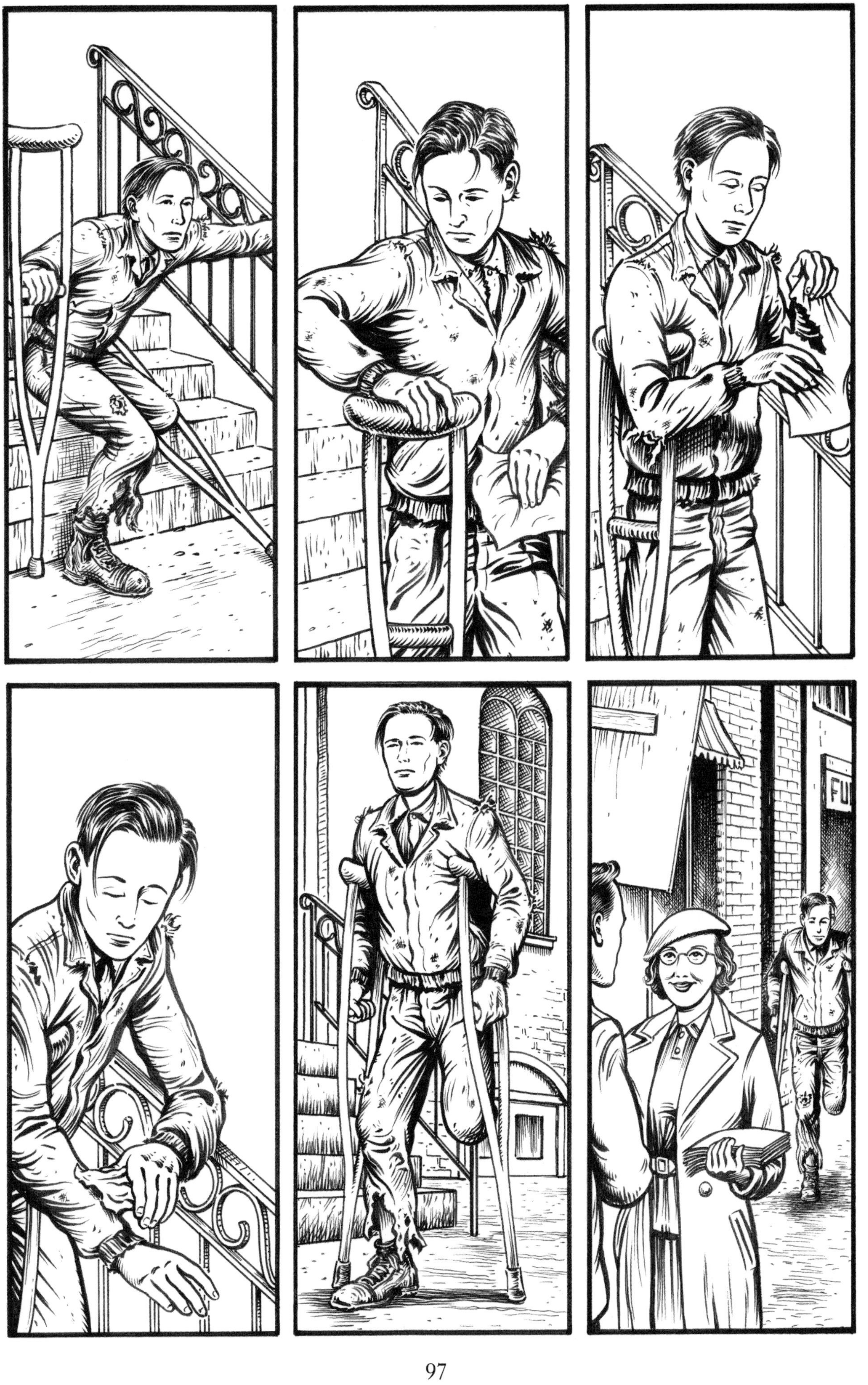

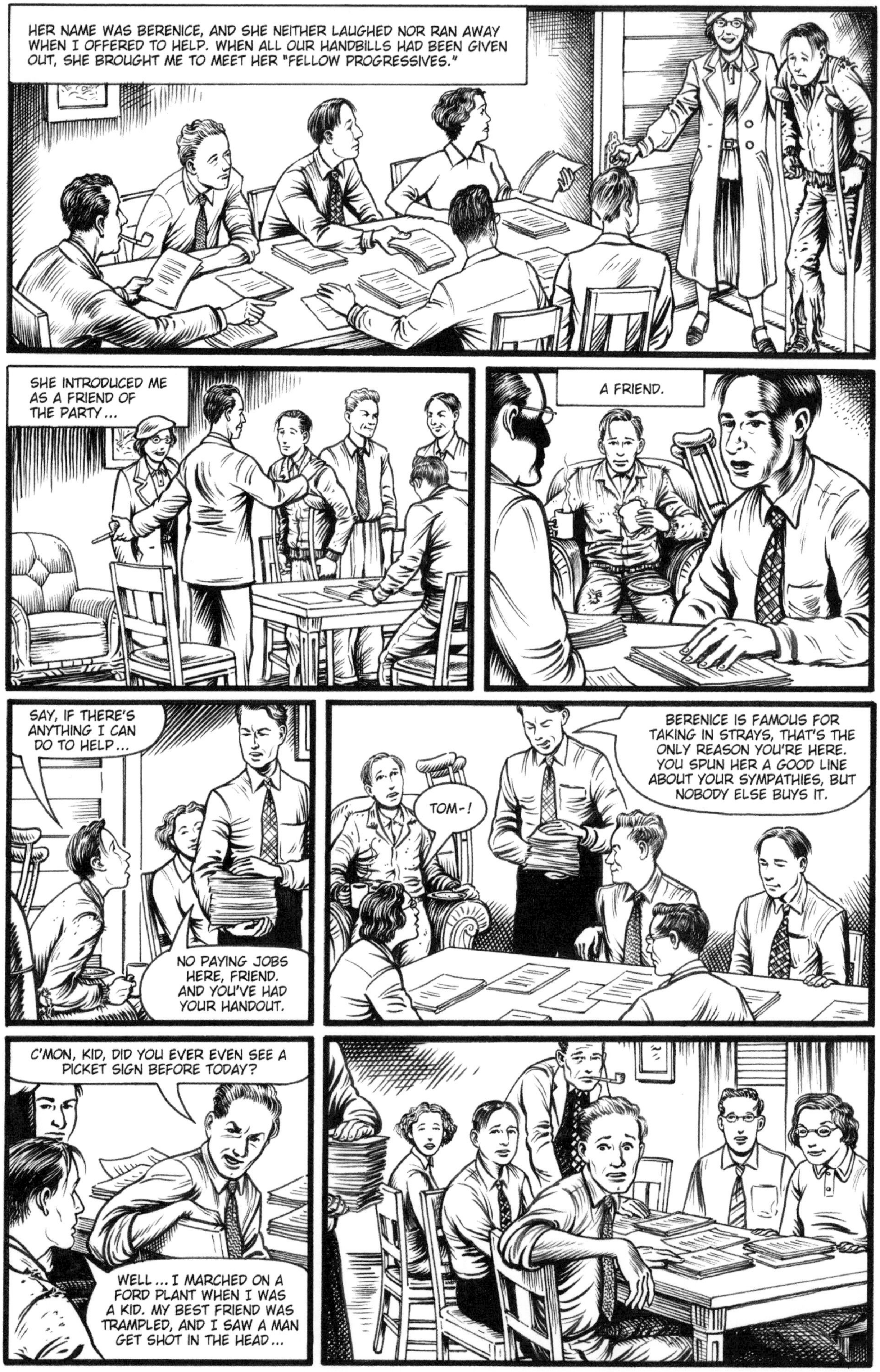
HER NAME WAS BERENICE, AND SHE NEITHER LAUGHED NOR RAN AWAY WHEN I OFFERED TO HELP. WHEN ALL OUR HANDBILLS HAD BEEN GIVEN OUT, SHE BROUGHT ME TO MEET HER "FELLOW PROGRESSIVES."
SHE INTRODUCED ME AS A FRIEND OF THE PARTY...
A FRIEND.
SAY, IF THERE'S ANYTHING I CAN DO TO HELP...
NO PAYING JOBS HERE, FRIEND. AND YOU'VE HAD YOUR HANDOUT.
BERENICE IS FAMOUS FOR TAKING IN STRAYS, THAT'S THE ONLY REASON YOU'RE HERE. YOU SPUN HER A GOOD LINE ABOUT YOUR SYMPATHIES, BUT NOBODY ELSE BUYS IT.
TOM-!
C'MON, KID, DID YOU EVER EVEN SEE A PICKET SIGN BEFORE TODAY?
WELL... I MARCHED ON A FORD PLANT WHEN I WAS A KID. MY BEST FRIEND WAS TRAMPLED, AND I SAW A MAN GET SHOT IN THE HEAD...

IF THEY HADN'T BAITED ME I NEVER WOULD HAVE MENTIONED IT. WHO COULD DREAM THAT HIS NIGHTMARE WOULD BE A LEGEND TO SOMEONE ELSE?

THE FIRST TIME I REALIZED THAT I HAD A STORY TO TELL.

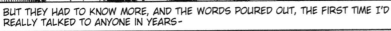

BUT THEY HAD TO KNOW MORE, AND THE WORDS POURED OUT, THE FIRST TIME I'D REALLY TALKED TO ANYONE IN YEARS—

WELL...I THINK WE'D BETTER FIND YOU SOMETHING TO DO HERE.

I'LL SHOW YOU HOW TO COLLATE THESE SHEETS.

SAY, SPORT, MAKE SURE YOU KEEP MY STUFF IN ORDER, OKAY? I WORKED HARD FILLING UP THESE PAGES.

YOU WROTE ALL THIS?

MEL WAS *BMOC* UNTIL YOU CAME IN, FRED.

WELL...SURE YOU ARE. I'D GIVE ANYTHING TO BE ABLE TO DO WHAT YOU CAN DO.

NICE TO SEE *SOMEONE* APPRECIATES HARD WORK.

99

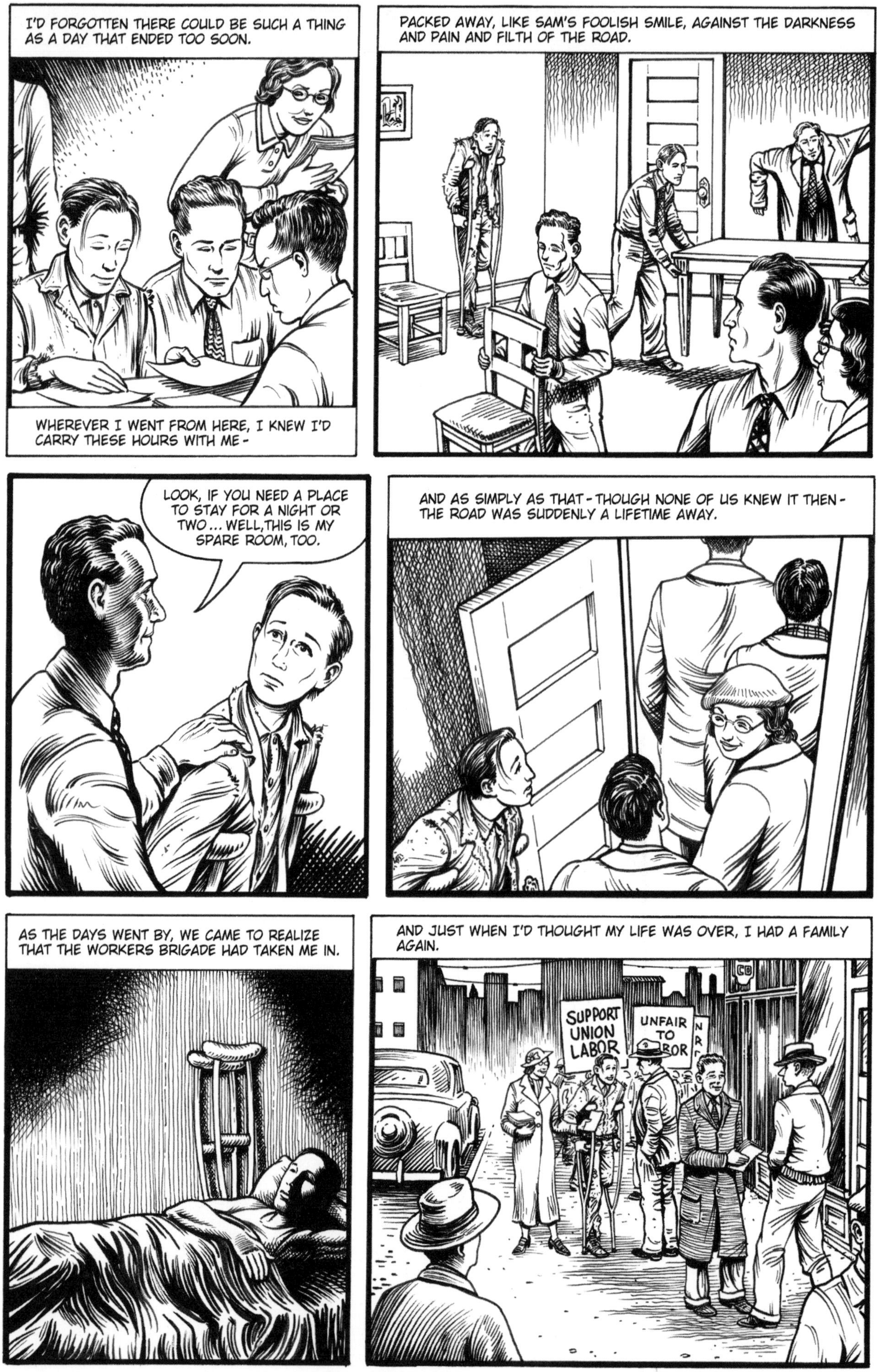
I'D FORGOTTEN THERE COULD BE SUCH A THING AS A DAY THAT ENDED TOO SOON.
WHEREVER I WENT FROM HERE, I KNEW I'D CARRY THESE HOURS WITH ME -
PACKED AWAY, LIKE SAM'S FOOLISH SMILE, AGAINST THE DARKNESS AND PAIN AND FILTH OF THE ROAD.
LOOK, IF YOU NEED A PLACE TO STAY FOR A NIGHT OR TWO... WELL, THIS IS MY SPARE ROOM, TOO.
AND AS SIMPLY AS THAT - THOUGH NONE OF US KNEW IT THEN - THE ROAD WAS SUDDENLY A LIFETIME AWAY.
AS THE DAYS WENT BY, WE CAME TO REALIZE THAT THE WORKERS BRIGADE HAD TAKEN ME IN.
AND JUST WHEN I'D THOUGHT MY LIFE WAS OVER, I HAD A FAMILY AGAIN.
SUPPORT UNION LABOR
UNFAIR TO

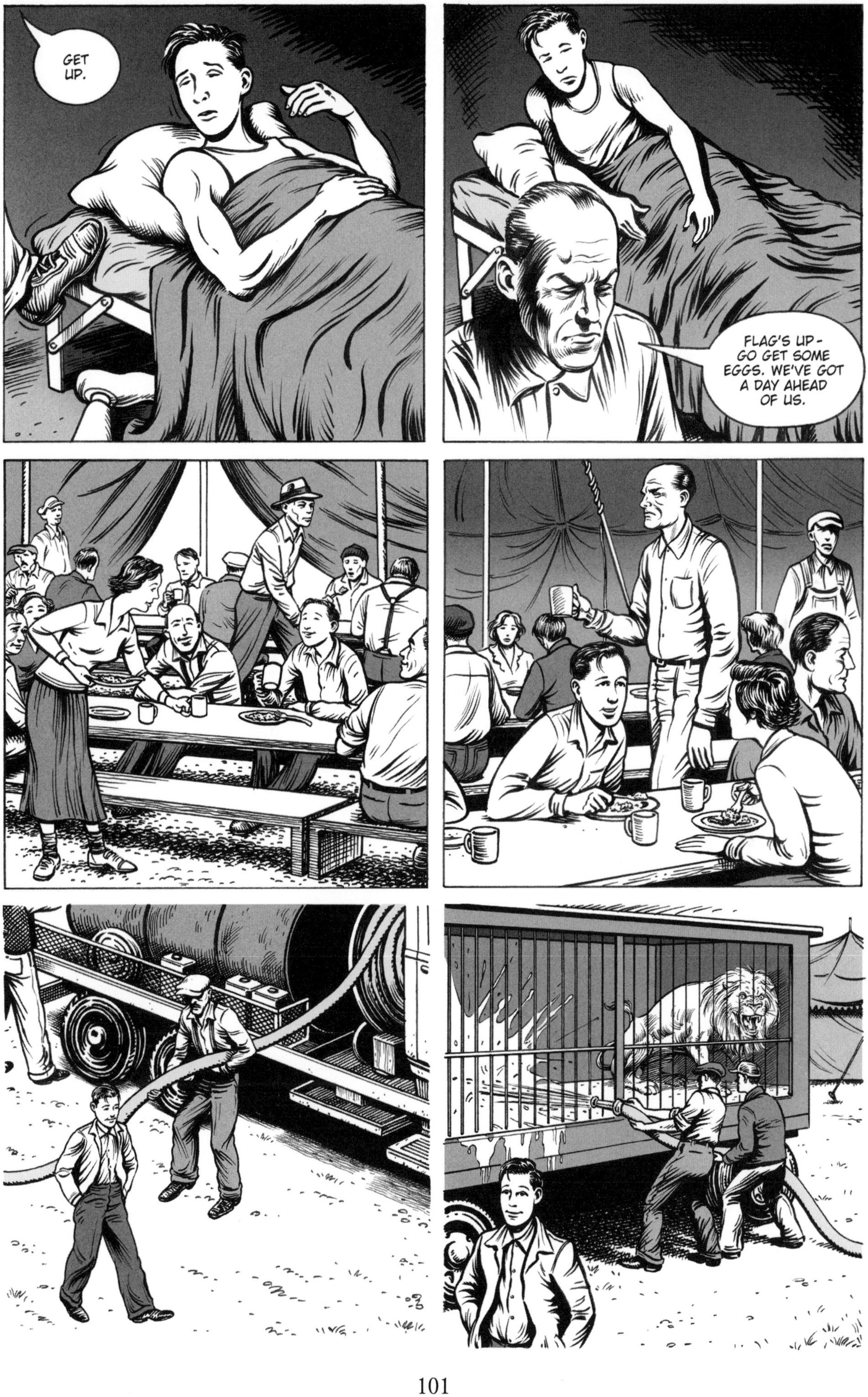
GET UP.
FLAG'S UP - GO GET SOME EGGS. WE'VE GOT A DAY AHEAD OF US.

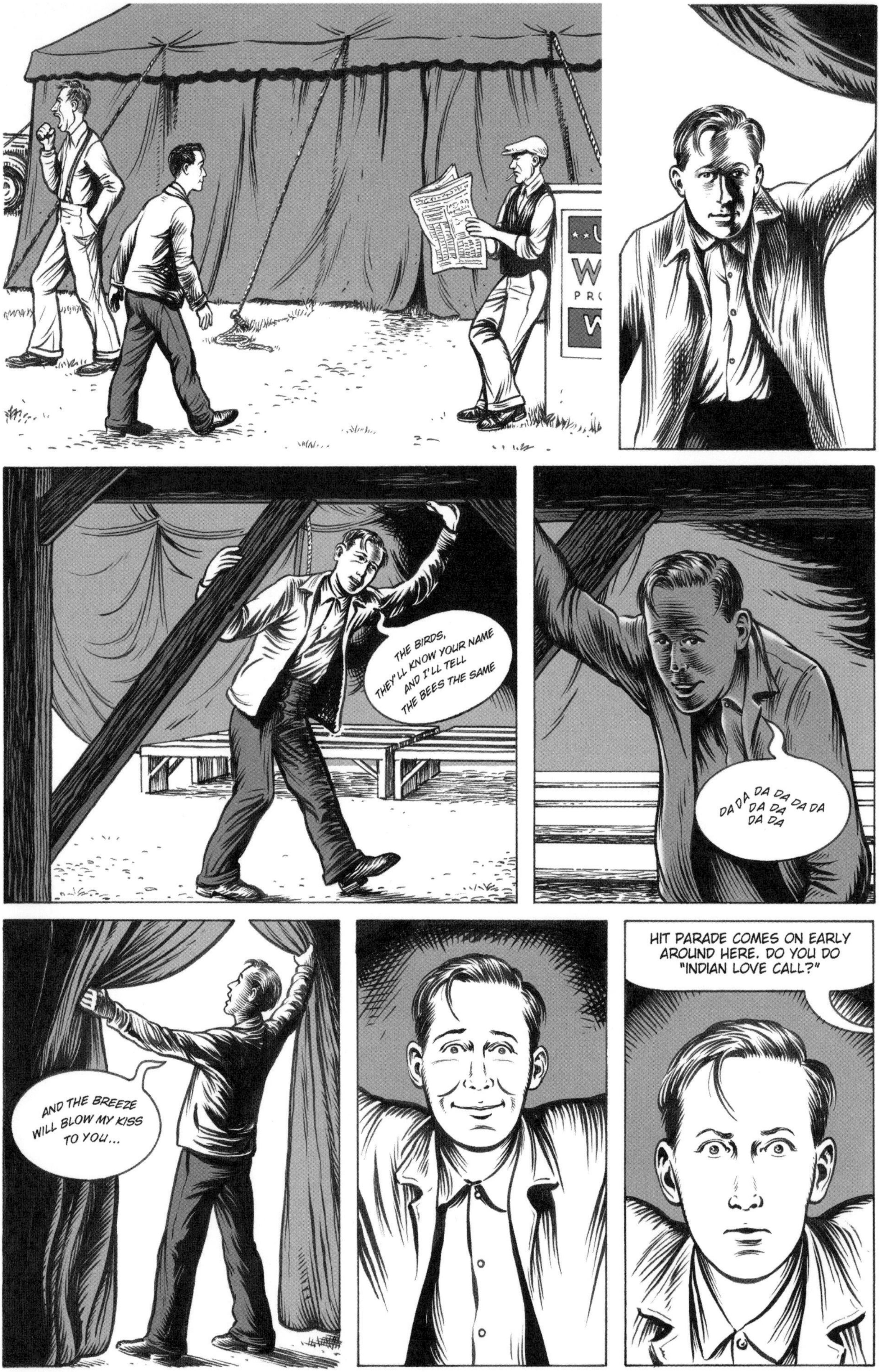
THE BIRDS, THEY'LL KNOW YOUR NAME AND I'LL TELL THE BEES THE SAME
DA DA DA DA DA DA DA DA DA DA
AND THE BREEZE WILL BLOW MY KISS TO YOU...
HIT PARADE COMES ON EARLY AROUND HERE. DO YOU DO "INDIAN LOVE CALL?"

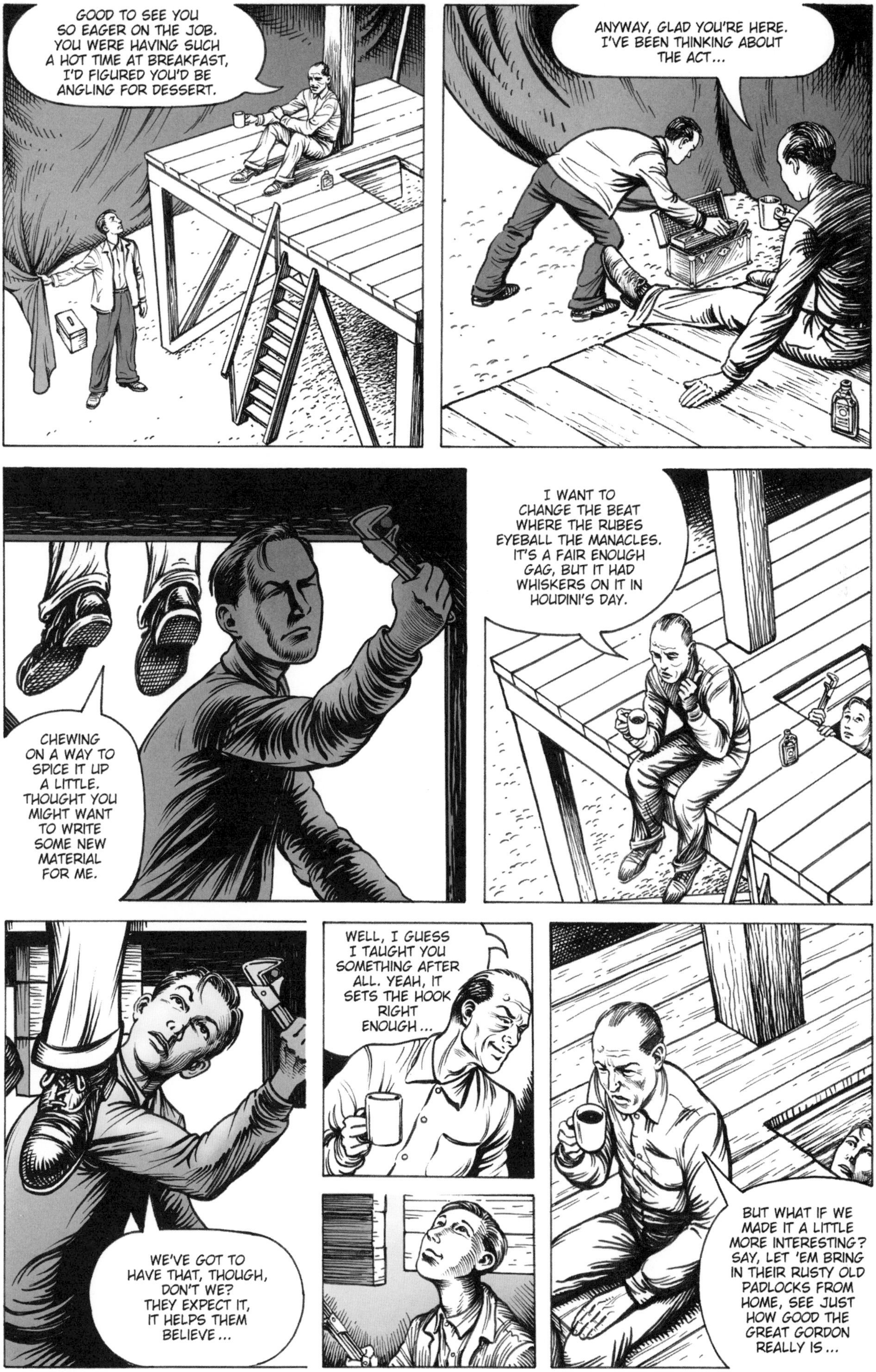
GOOD TO SEE YOU SO EAGER ON THE JOB. YOU WERE HAVING SUCH A HOT TIME AT BREAKFAST, I'D FIGURED YOU'D BE ANGLING FOR DESSERT.
ANYWAY, GLAD YOU'RE HERE. I'VE BEEN THINKING ABOUT THE ACT...
CHEWING ON A WAY TO SPICE IT UP A LITTLE. THOUGHT YOU MIGHT WANT TO WRITE SOME NEW MATERIAL FOR ME.
I WANT TO CHANGE THE BEAT WHERE THE RUBES EYEBALL THE MANACLES. IT'S A FAIR ENOUGH GAG, BUT IT HAD WHISKERS ON IT IN HOUDINI'S DAY.
WE'VE GOT TO HAVE THAT, THOUGH, DON'T WE? THEY EXPECT IT, IT HELPS THEM BELIEVE...
WELL, I GUESS I TAUGHT YOU SOMETHING AFTER ALL. YEAH, IT SETS THE HOOK RIGHT ENOUGH...
BUT WHAT IF WE MADE IT A LITTLE MORE INTERESTING? SAY, LET 'EM BRING IN THEIR RUSTY OLD PADLOCKS FROM HOME, SEE JUST HOW GOOD THE GREAT GORDON REALLY IS...

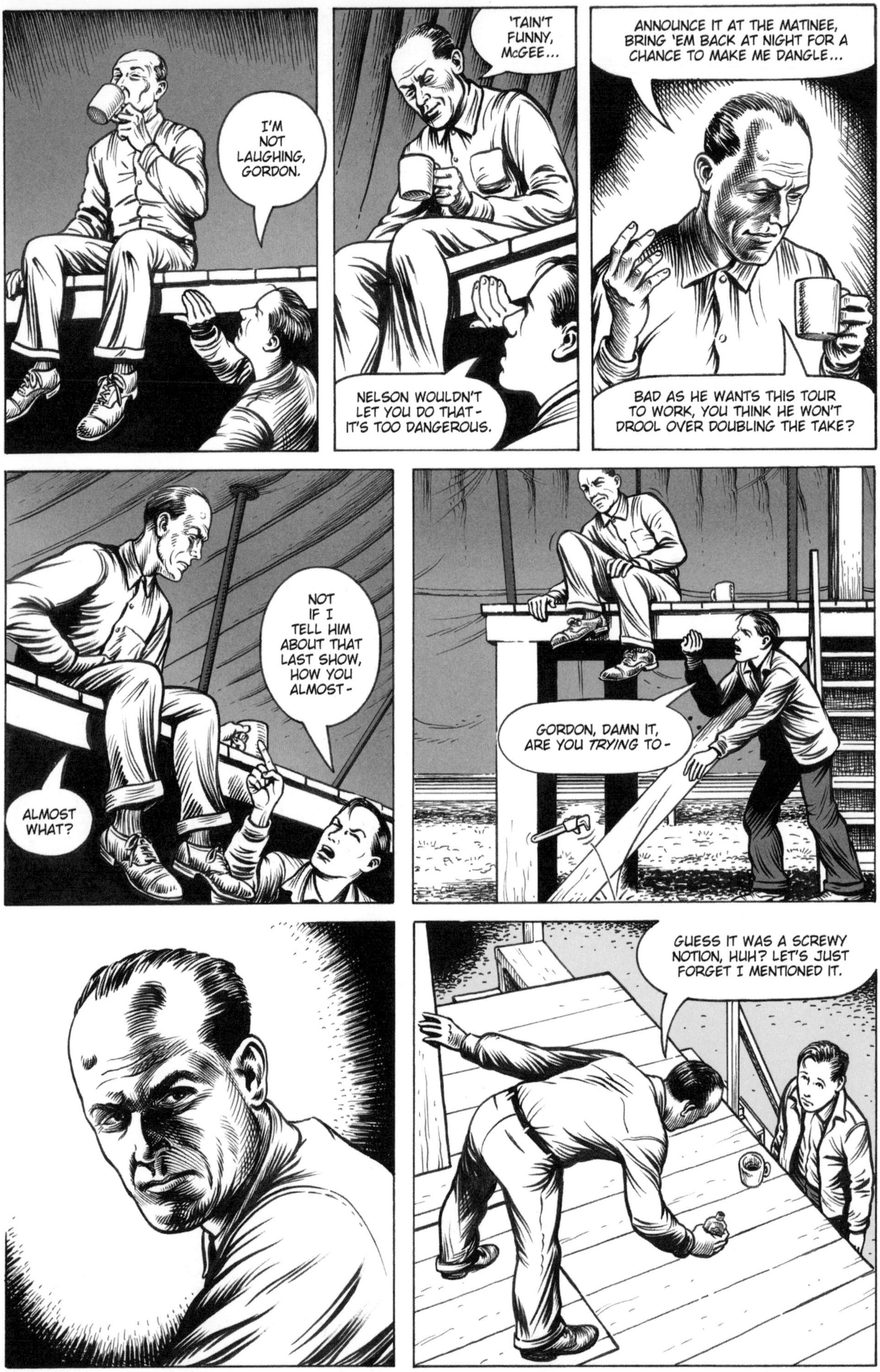
I'M NOT LAUGHING, GORDON.
'TAIN'T FUNNY, McGEE...
NELSON WOULDN'T LET YOU DO THAT- IT'S TOO DANGEROUS.
ANNOUNCE IT AT THE MATINEE, BRING 'EM BACK AT NIGHT FOR A CHANCE TO MAKE ME DANGLE...
BAD AS HE WANTS THIS TOUR TO WORK, YOU THINK HE WON'T DROOL OVER DOUBLING THE TAKE?
NOT IF I TELL HIM ABOUT THAT LAST SHOW, HOW YOU ALMOST-
ALMOST WHAT?
GORDON, DAMN IT, ARE YOU *TRYING* TO-
GUESS IT WAS A SCREWY NOTION, HUH? LET'S JUST FORGET I MENTIONED IT.

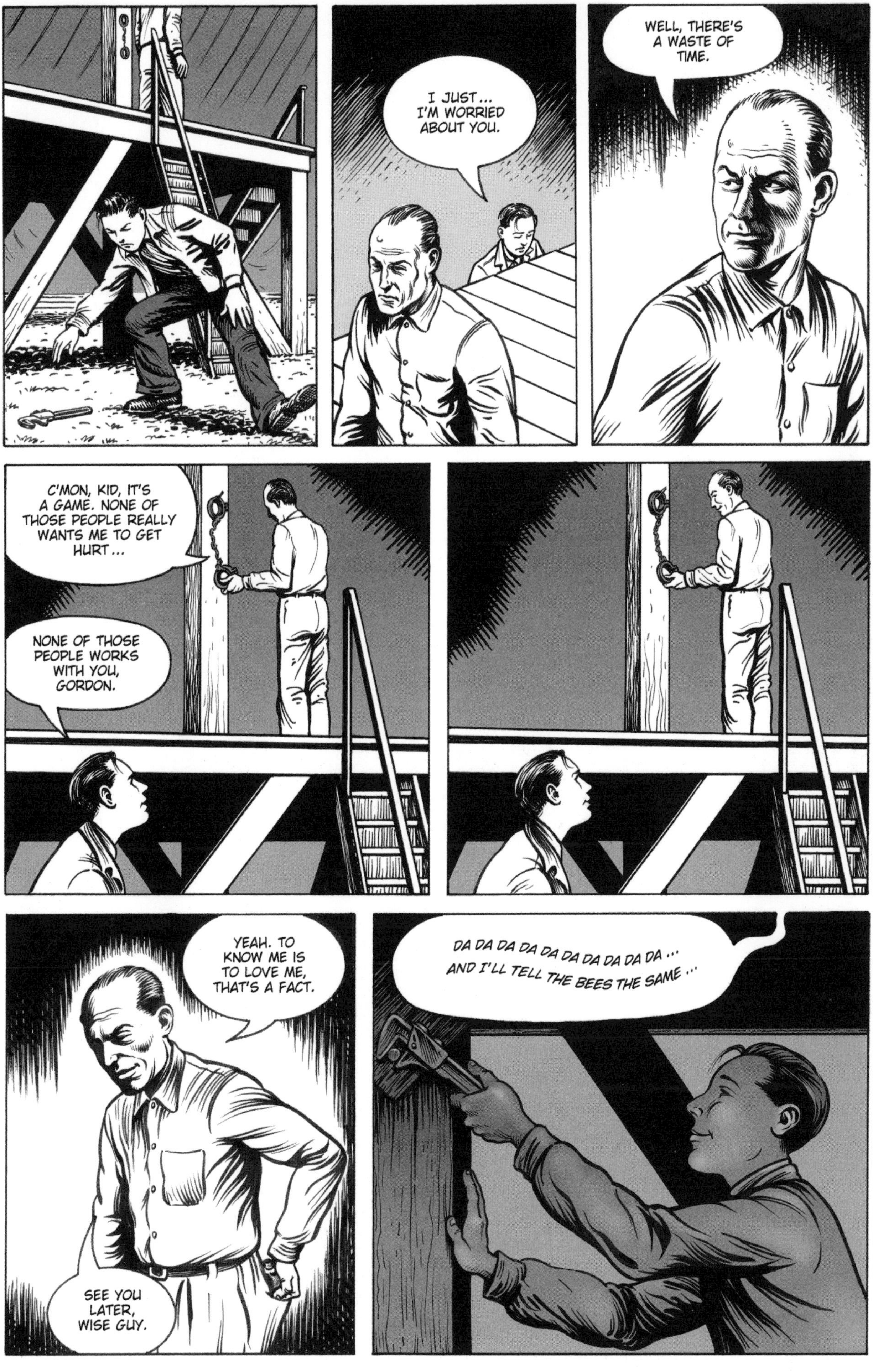
I JUST... I'M WORRIED ABOUT YOU.
WELL, THERE'S A WASTE OF TIME.
C'MON, KID, IT'S A GAME. NONE OF THOSE PEOPLE REALLY WANTS ME TO GET HURT...
NONE OF THOSE PEOPLE WORKS WITH YOU, GORDON.
YEAH. TO KNOW ME IS TO LOVE ME, THAT'S A FACT.
SEE YOU LATER, WISE GUY.
DA DA DA DA DA DA DA DA DA DA DA...
AND I'LL TELL THE BEES THE SAME...

YOU SEE HOW IT WORKS...

IT'S ALWAYS TWO GUYS, JUST CHEWING THE RAG, NATURAL AS CAN BE...

AND TWICE AS HARD TO MUSCLE IN BROAD DAYLIGHT.

THEN ONE PEELS OFF AT THE POST OFFICE, SO THEY DON'T DRAW SUSPICION. THAT'S HOW THEY FOOL THE STEEL BOYS.

BUT HOW DO THEY SWITCH THEM LETTERS?

THEY DON'T.

I USED TO WORK WITH A TRICKY LITTLE GUY WHO'D HAVE IT FIGURED OUT BY NOW. SEE IF YOU CAN, CHASE.

TRICKY GUYS GIVE ME A PAIN.

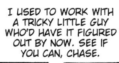

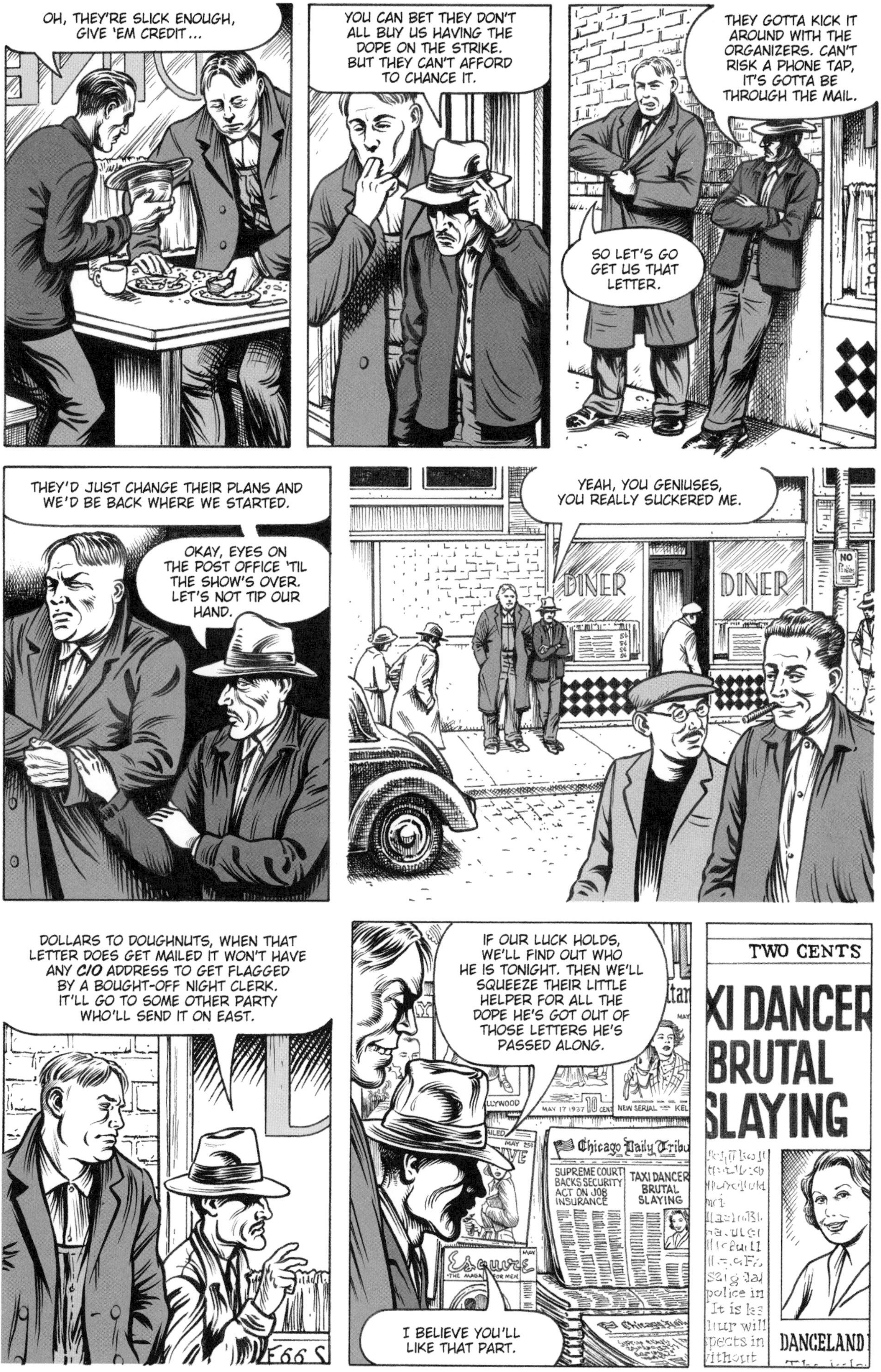
OH, THEY'RE SLICK ENOUGH, GIVE 'EM CREDIT...
YOU CAN BET THEY DON'T ALL BUY US HAVING THE DOPE ON THE STRIKE. BUT THEY CAN'T AFFORD TO CHANCE IT.
THEY GOTTA KICK IT AROUND WITH THE ORGANIZERS. CAN'T RISK A PHONE TAP, IT'S GOTTA BE THROUGH THE MAIL.
SO LET'S GO GET US THAT LETTER.
THEY'D JUST CHANGE THEIR PLANS AND WE'D BE BACK WHERE WE STARTED.
OKAY, EYES ON THE POST OFFICE 'TIL THE SHOW'S OVER. LET'S NOT TIP OUR HAND.
YEAH, YOU GENIUSES, YOU REALLY SUCKERED ME.
DINER
DINER
DOLLARS TO DOUGHNUTS, WHEN THAT LETTER DOES GET MAILED IT WON'T HAVE ANY C/O ADDRESS TO GET FLAGGED BY A BOUGHT-OFF NIGHT CLERK. IT'LL GO TO SOME OTHER PARTY WHO'LL SEND IT ON EAST.
IF OUR LUCK HOLDS, WE'LL FIND OUT WHO HE IS TONIGHT. THEN WE'LL SQUEEZE THEIR LITTLE HELPER FOR ALL THE DOPE HE'S GOT OUT OF THOSE LETTERS HE'S PASSED ALONG.
MAY 17 1937
NEW SERIAL
Chicago Daily Tribu
SUPREME COURT BACKS SECURITY ACT ON JOB INSURANCE
TAXI DANCER BRUTAL SLAYING
I BELIEVE YOU'LL LIKE THAT PART.
TWO CENTS
XI DANCER BRUTAL SLAYING
DANCELAND

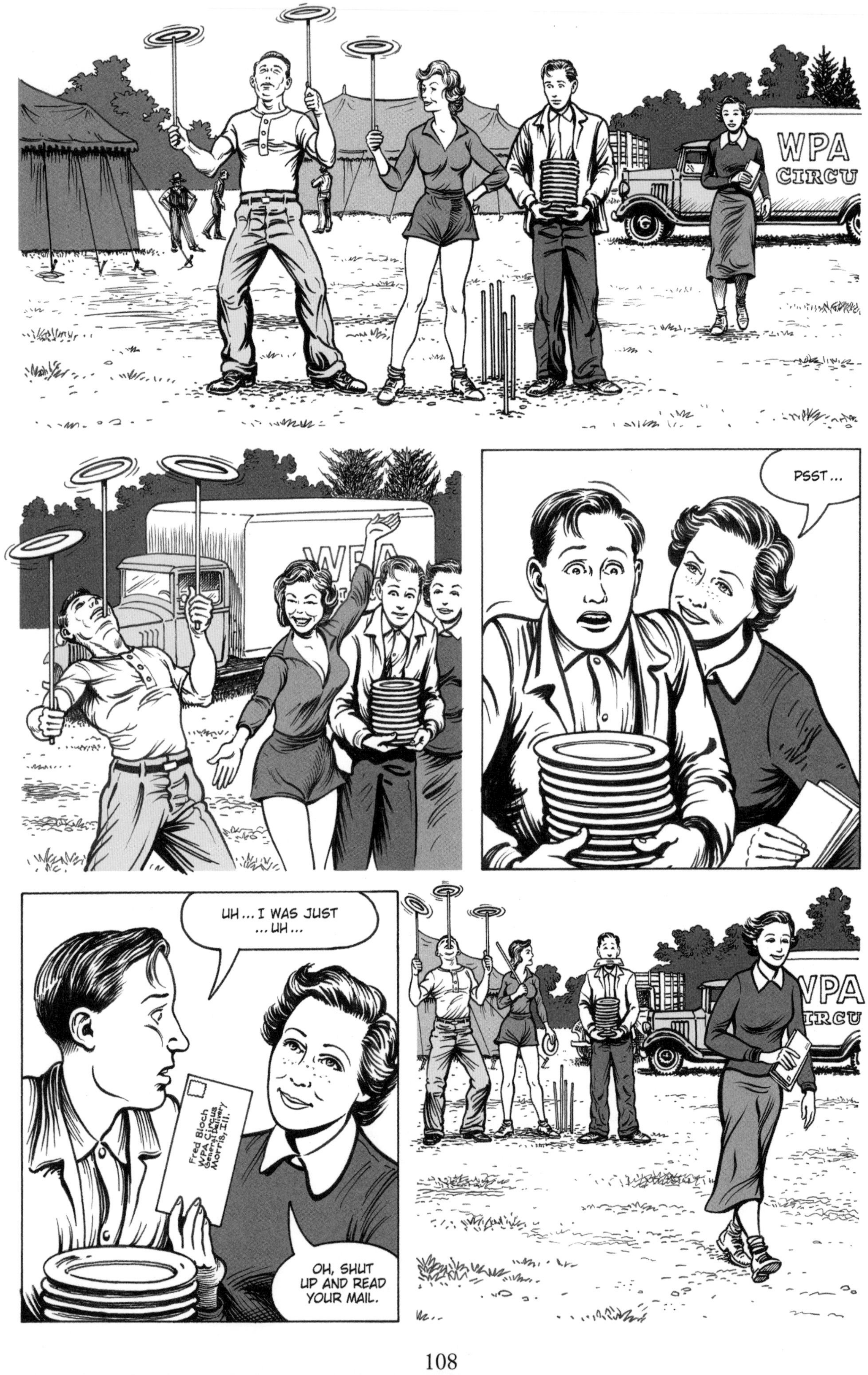
WPA
CIRCU
PSST...
UH... I WAS JUST ...UH...
Fred Bloch
WPA Circus
General Delivery
Morris, Ill.
OH, SHUT UP AND READ YOUR MAIL.

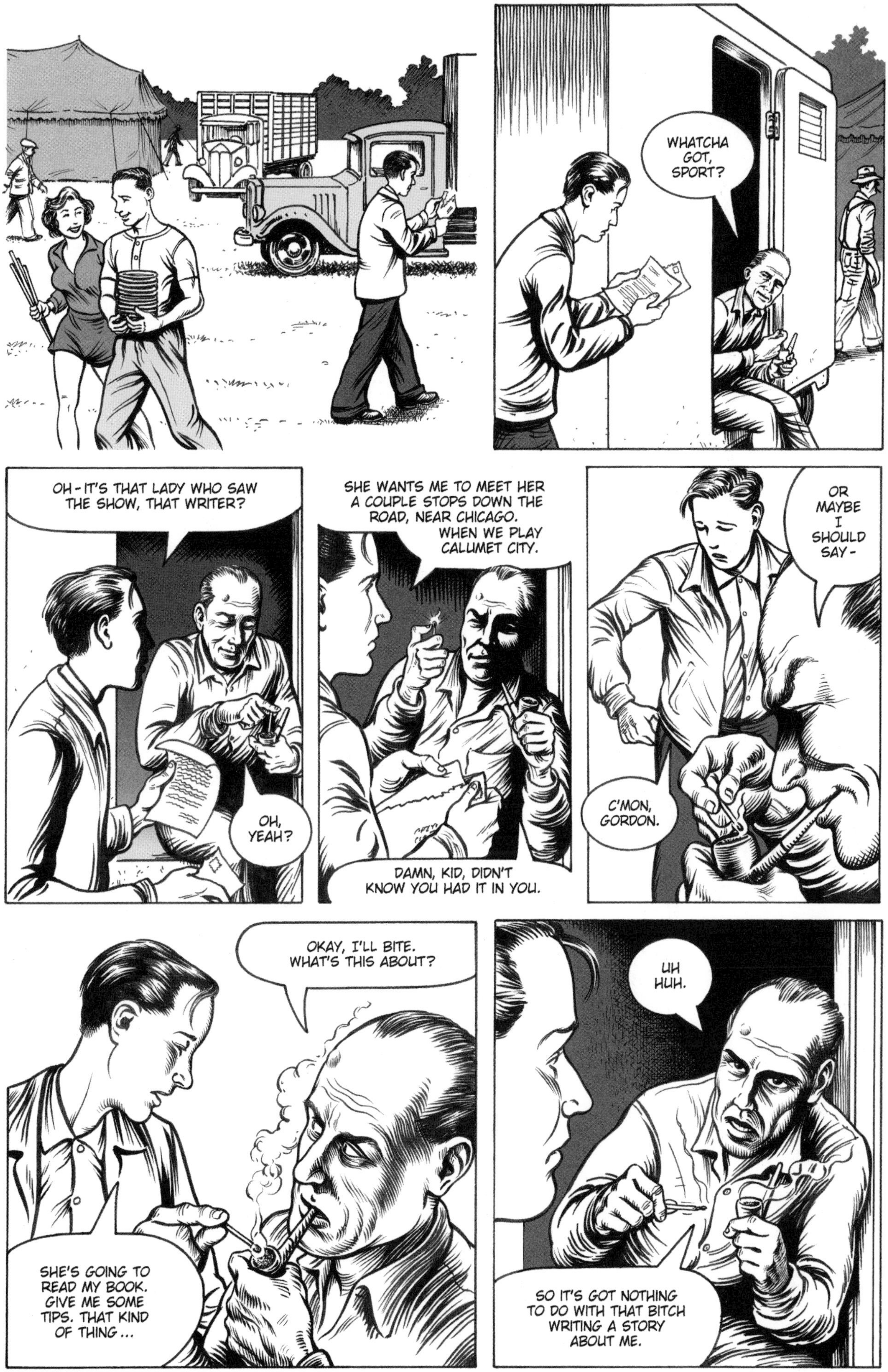
WHATCHA GOT, SPORT?
OH - IT'S THAT LADY WHO SAW THE SHOW, THAT WRITER?
OH, YEAH?
SHE WANTS ME TO MEET HER A COUPLE STOPS DOWN THE ROAD, NEAR CHICAGO.
WHEN WE PLAY CALUMET CITY.
DAMN, KID, DIDN'T KNOW YOU HAD IT IN YOU.
OR MAYBE I SHOULD SAY -
C'MON, GORDON.
OKAY, I'LL BITE. WHAT'S THIS ABOUT?
SHE'S GOING TO READ MY BOOK. GIVE ME SOME TIPS. THAT KIND OF THING...
UH HUH.
SO IT'S GOT NOTHING TO DO WITH THAT BITCH WRITING A STORY ABOUT ME.

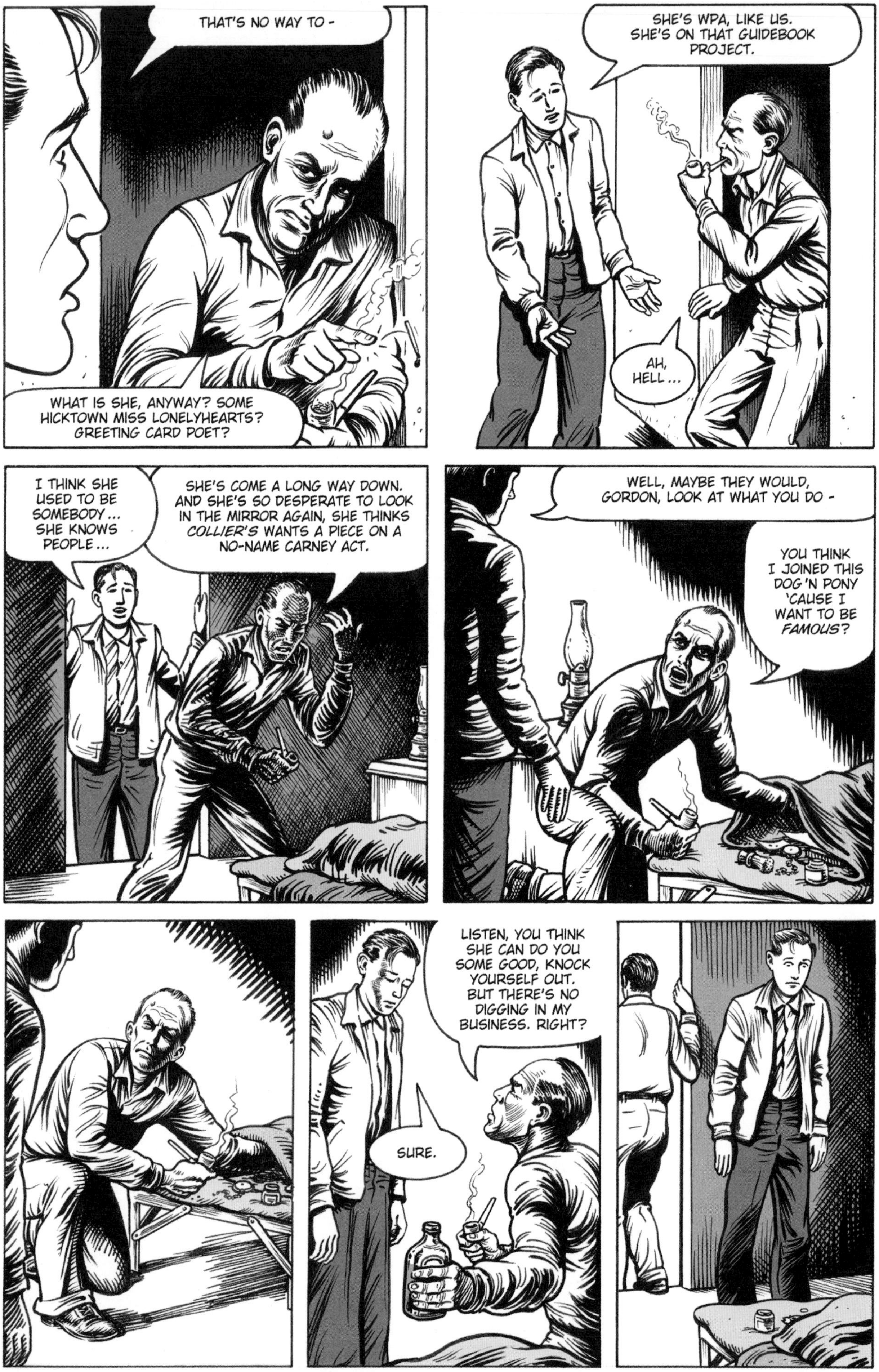
THAT'S NO WAY TO -
WHAT IS SHE, ANYWAY? SOME HICKTOWN MISS LONELYHEARTS? GREETING CARD POET?
SHE'S WPA, LIKE US. SHE'S ON THAT GUIDEBOOK PROJECT.
AH, HELL...
I THINK SHE USED TO BE SOMEBODY... SHE KNOWS PEOPLE...
SHE'S COME A LONG WAY DOWN. AND SHE'S SO DESPERATE TO LOOK IN THE MIRROR AGAIN, SHE THINKS *COLLIER'S* WANTS A PIECE ON A NO-NAME CARNEY ACT.
WELL, MAYBE THEY WOULD, GORDON, LOOK AT WHAT YOU DO -
YOU THINK I JOINED THIS DOG 'N PONY 'CAUSE I WANT TO BE *FAMOUS*?
LISTEN, YOU THINK SHE CAN DO YOU SOME GOOD, KNOCK YOURSELF OUT. BUT THERE'S NO DIGGING IN MY BUSINESS. RIGHT?
SURE.

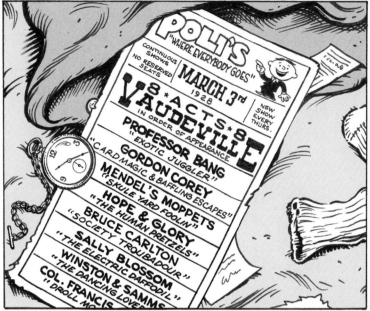

POLI'S
"WHERE EVERYBODY GOES"

CONTINUOUS
SHOWS
NO RESERVED
SEATS

MARCH 3rd
1926

NEW
SHOW
EVERY
THURS.

8 *ACTS* 8
VAUDEVILLE
IN ORDER OF APPEARANCE

PROFESSOR BANG
"EXOTIC JUGGLER"

GORDON COREY
CARD MAGIC & BAFFLING ESCAPES

MENDEL'S MOPPETS
"SKULE YARD FOOLIN'"

HOPE & GLORY
"THE HUMAN PRETZELS"

BRUCE CARLTON
"SOCIETY TROUBADOUR"

SALLY BLOSSOM
"THE ELECTRIC DAFFODIL"

WINSTON & SAMMS
"THE DANCING LOVE..."

COL. FRANCIS M...
"DROLL M..."

VARIETY Thursday, April 17, 1930

ESCAPER IN CUFFS AFTER SOCKO FINISH

Escape artist Gordon Corey was arrested for assault Tuesday after a brawl with comic Elmer Starr on the stage of Milwaukee's Modjeska Theatre. Starr is expected to return to the bill next week.

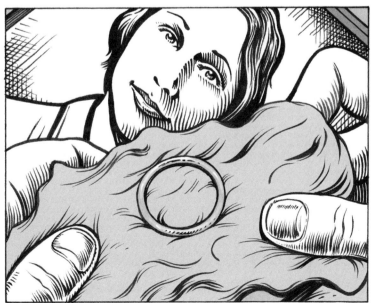

111

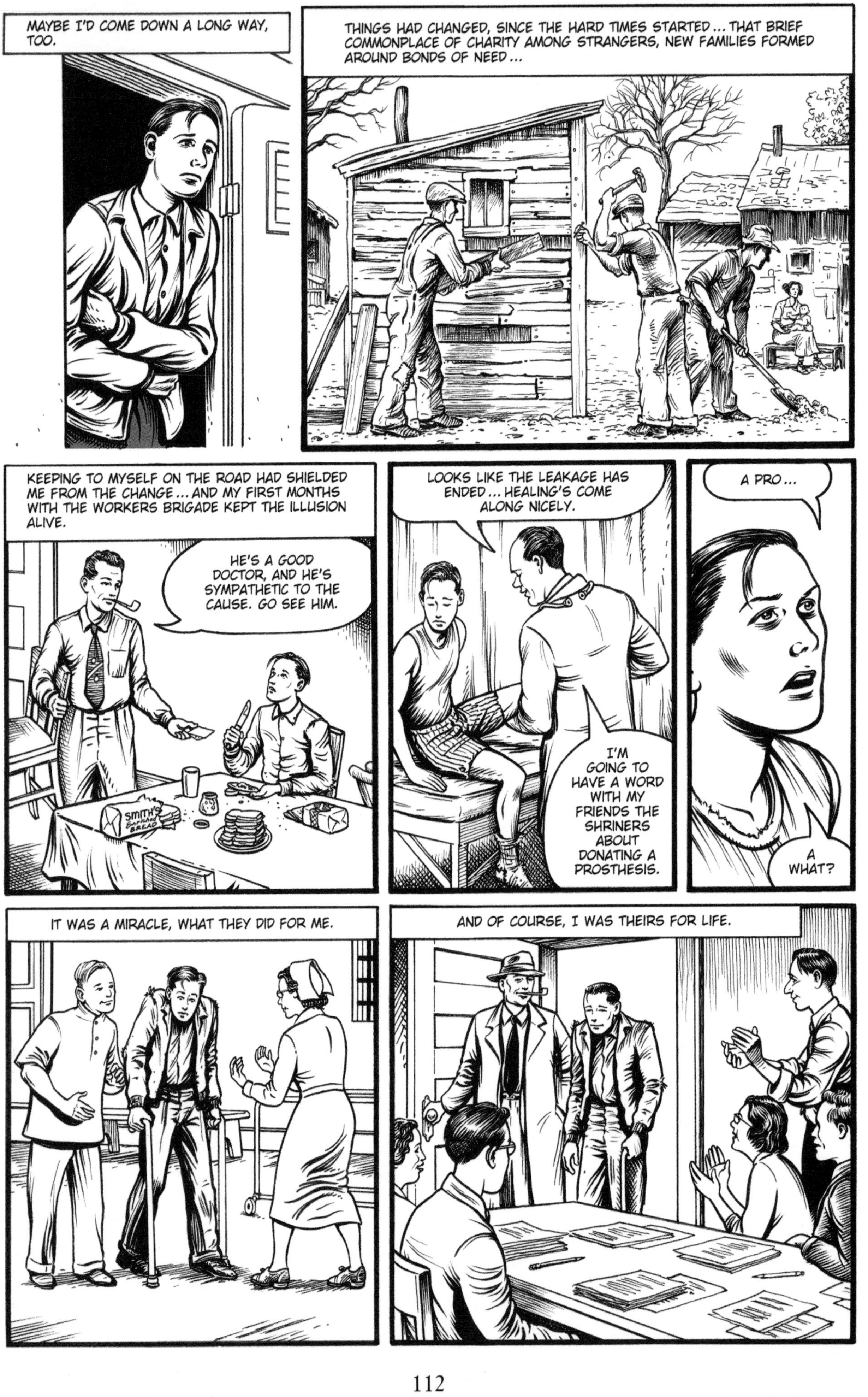
MAYBE I'D COME DOWN A LONG WAY, TOO.
THINGS HAD CHANGED, SINCE THE HARD TIMES STARTED... THAT BRIEF COMMONPLACE OF CHARITY AMONG STRANGERS, NEW FAMILIES FORMED AROUND BONDS OF NEED...
KEEPING TO MYSELF ON THE ROAD HAD SHIELDED ME FROM THE CHANGE... AND MY FIRST MONTHS WITH THE WORKERS BRIGADE KEPT THE ILLUSION ALIVE.
HE'S A GOOD DOCTOR, AND HE'S SYMPATHETIC TO THE CAUSE. GO SEE HIM.
SMITH'S Enriched BREAD
LOOKS LIKE THE LEAKAGE HAS ENDED... HEALING'S COME ALONG NICELY.
I'M GOING TO HAVE A WORD WITH MY FRIENDS THE SHRINERS ABOUT DONATING A PROSTHESIS.
A PRO...
A WHAT?
IT WAS A MIRACLE, WHAT THEY DID FOR ME.
AND OF COURSE, I WAS THEIRS FOR LIFE.

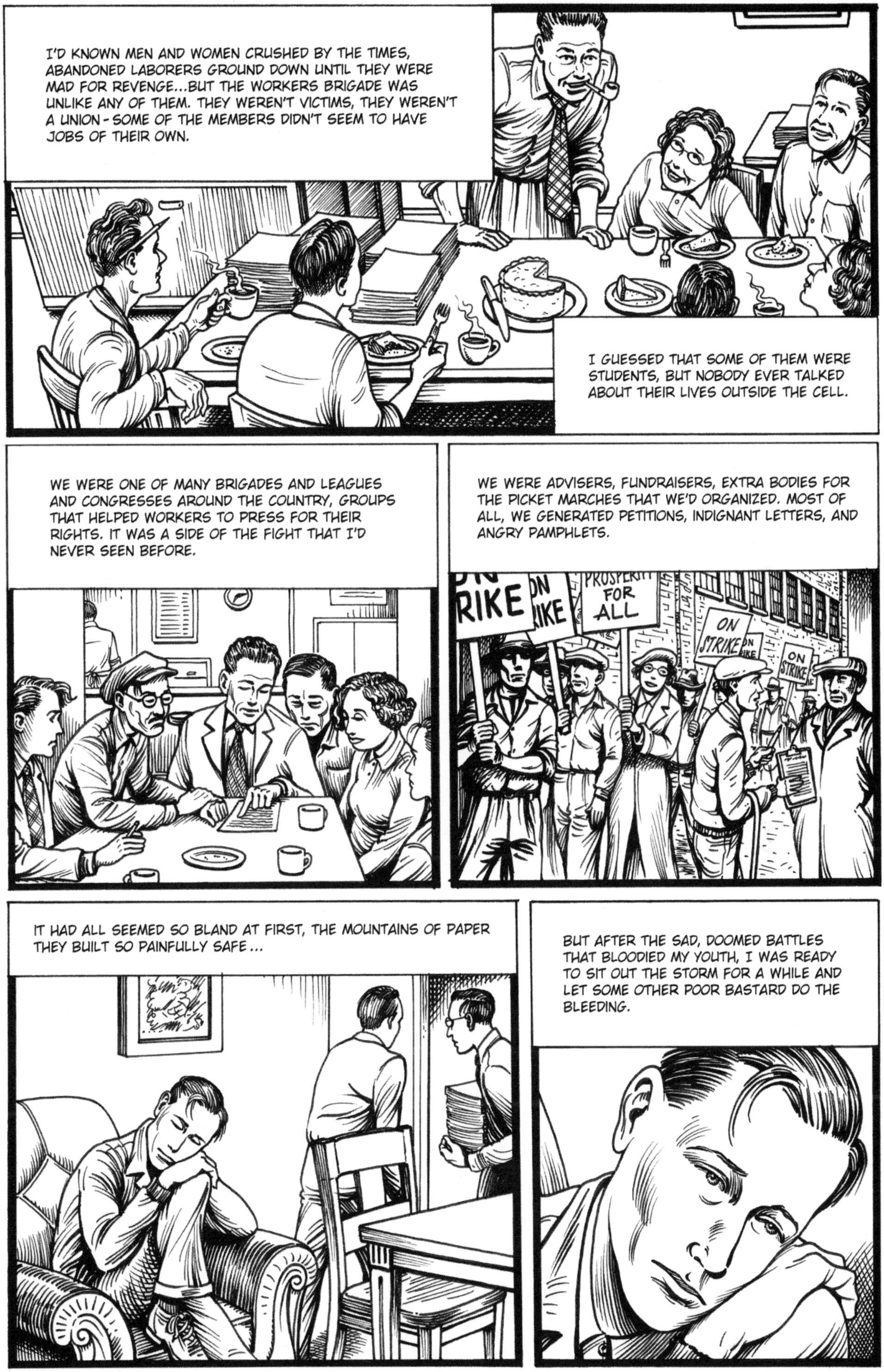
I'D KNOWN MEN AND WOMEN CRUSHED BY THE TIMES, ABANDONED LABORERS GROUND DOWN UNTIL THEY WERE MAD FOR REVENGE...BUT THE WORKERS BRIGADE WAS UNLIKE ANY OF THEM. THEY WEREN'T VICTIMS, THEY WEREN'T A UNION - SOME OF THE MEMBERS DIDN'T SEEM TO HAVE JOBS OF THEIR OWN.
I GUESSED THAT SOME OF THEM WERE STUDENTS, BUT NOBODY EVER TALKED ABOUT THEIR LIVES OUTSIDE THE CELL.
WE WERE ONE OF MANY BRIGADES AND LEAGUES AND CONGRESSES AROUND THE COUNTRY, GROUPS THAT HELPED WORKERS TO PRESS FOR THEIR RIGHTS. IT WAS A SIDE OF THE FIGHT THAT I'D NEVER SEEN BEFORE.
WE WERE ADVISERS, FUNDRAISERS, EXTRA BODIES FOR THE PICKET MARCHES THAT WE'D ORGANIZED. MOST OF ALL, WE GENERATED PETITIONS, INDIGNANT LETTERS, AND ANGRY PAMPHLETS.
FOR ALL
ON STRIKE
ON STRIKE
IT HAD ALL SEEMED SO BLAND AT FIRST, THE MOUNTAINS OF PAPER THEY BUILT SO PAINFULLY SAFE...
BUT AFTER THE SAD, DOOMED BATTLES THAT BLOODIED MY YOUTH, I WAS READY TO SIT OUT THE STORM FOR A WHILE AND LET SOME OTHER POOR BASTARD DO THE BLEEDING.

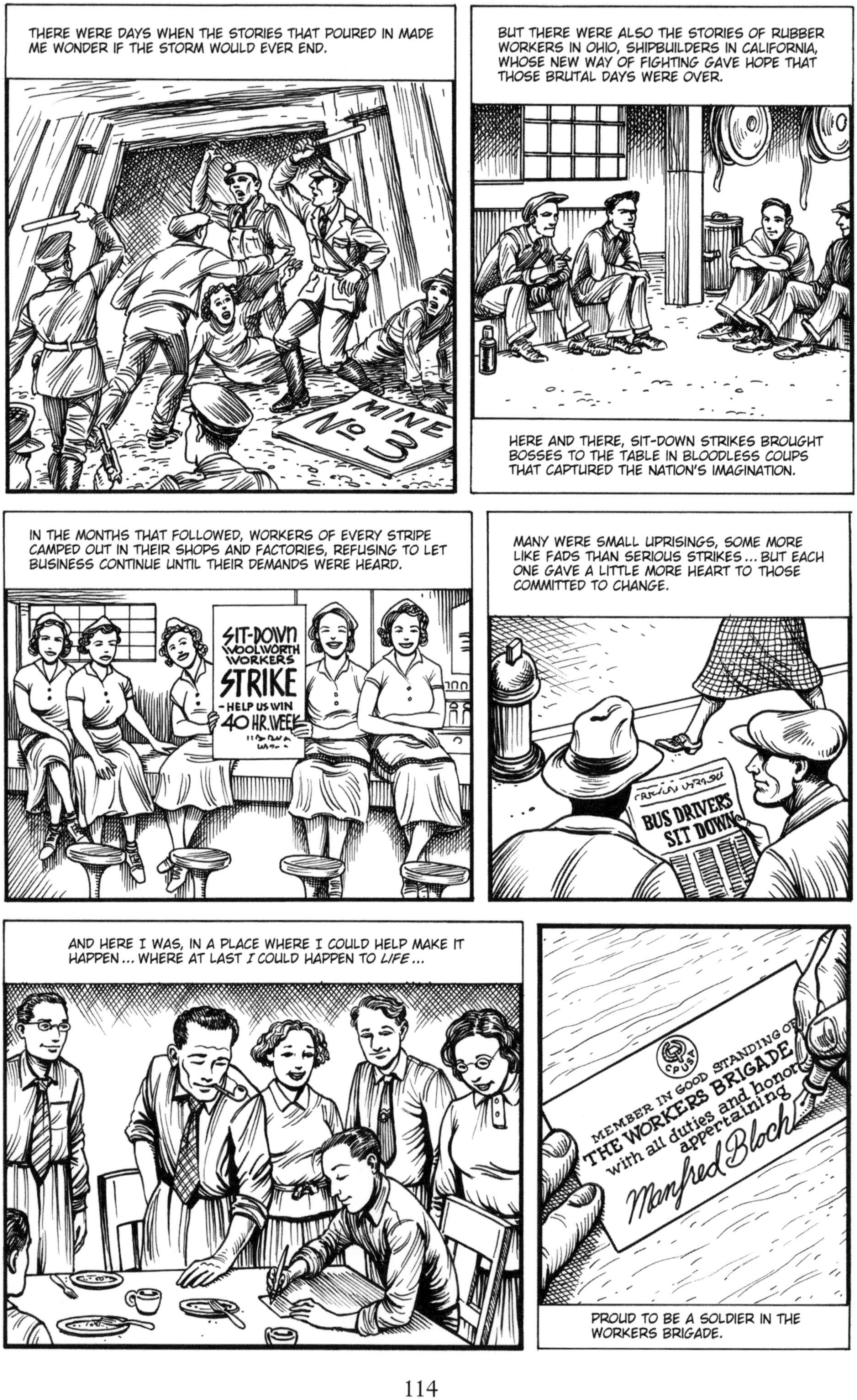
THERE WERE DAYS WHEN THE STORIES THAT POURED IN MADE ME WONDER IF THE STORM WOULD EVER END.
MINE No 3
BUT THERE WERE ALSO THE STORIES OF RUBBER WORKERS IN OHIO, SHIPBUILDERS IN CALIFORNIA, WHOSE NEW WAY OF FIGHTING GAVE HOPE THAT THOSE BRUTAL DAYS WERE OVER.
HERE AND THERE, SIT-DOWN STRIKES BROUGHT BOSSES TO THE TABLE IN BLOODLESS COUPS THAT CAPTURED THE NATION'S IMAGINATION.
IN THE MONTHS THAT FOLLOWED, WORKERS OF EVERY STRIPE CAMPED OUT IN THEIR SHOPS AND FACTORIES, REFUSING TO LET BUSINESS CONTINUE UNTIL THEIR DEMANDS WERE HEARD.
SIT-DOWN
WOOLWORTH WORKERS
STRIKE
-HELP US WIN
40 HR. WEEK
MANY WERE SMALL UPRISINGS, SOME MORE LIKE FADS THAN SERIOUS STRIKES... BUT EACH ONE GAVE A LITTLE MORE HEART TO THOSE COMMITTED TO CHANGE.
BUS DRIVERS SIT DOWN
AND HERE I WAS, IN A PLACE WHERE I COULD HELP MAKE IT HAPPEN... WHERE AT LAST *I* COULD HAPPEN TO *LIFE*...
CPUSA
MEMBER IN GOOD STANDING OF
THE WORKERS BRIGADE
with all duties and honor
appertaining
Manfred Bloch
PROUD TO BE A SOLDIER IN THE WORKERS BRIGADE.

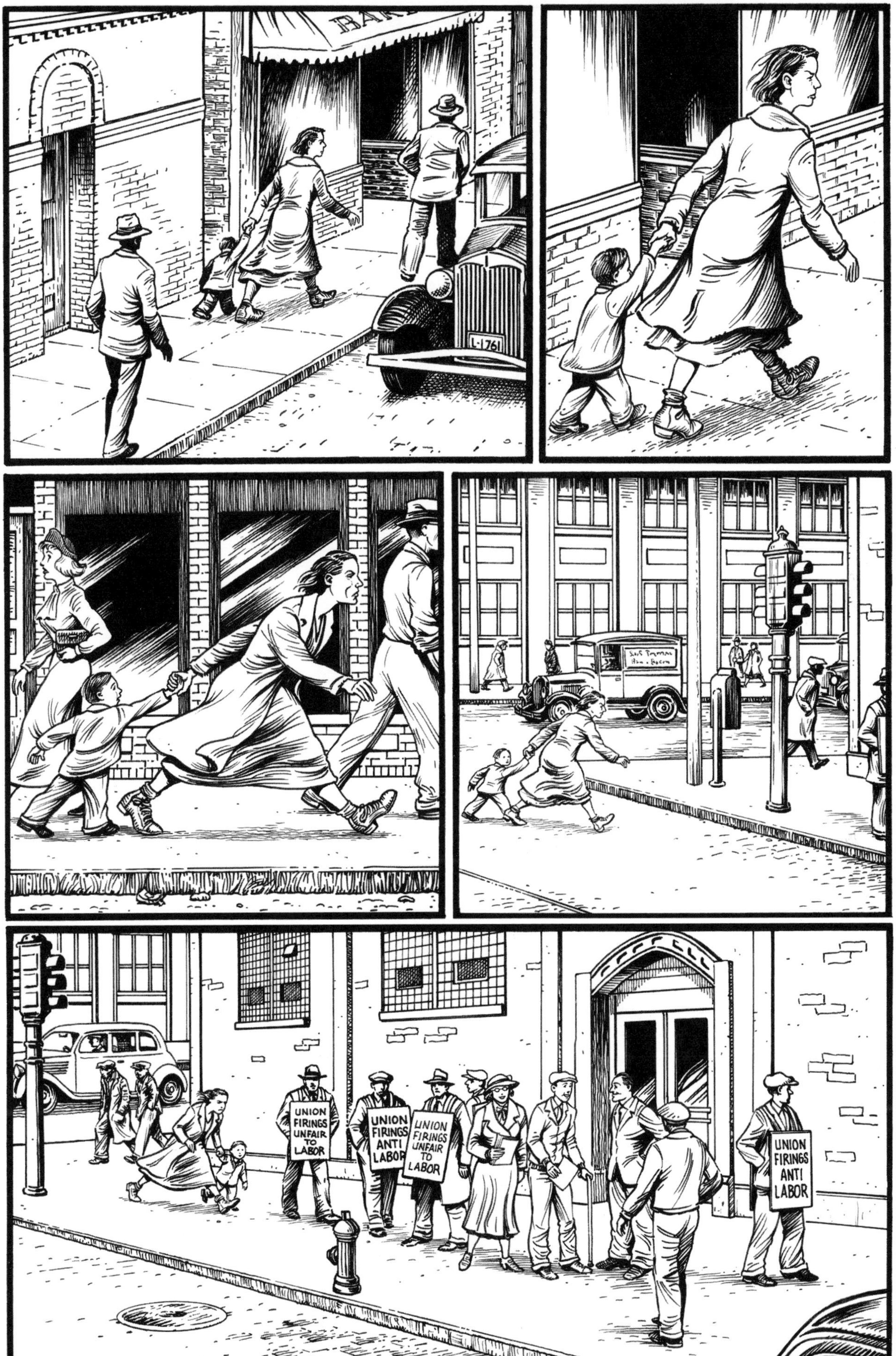
L-1761
UNION FIRINGS UNFAIR TO LABOR
UNION FIRINGS ANTI LABOR
UNION FIRINGS UNFAIR TO LABOR
UNION FIRINGS ANTI LABOR

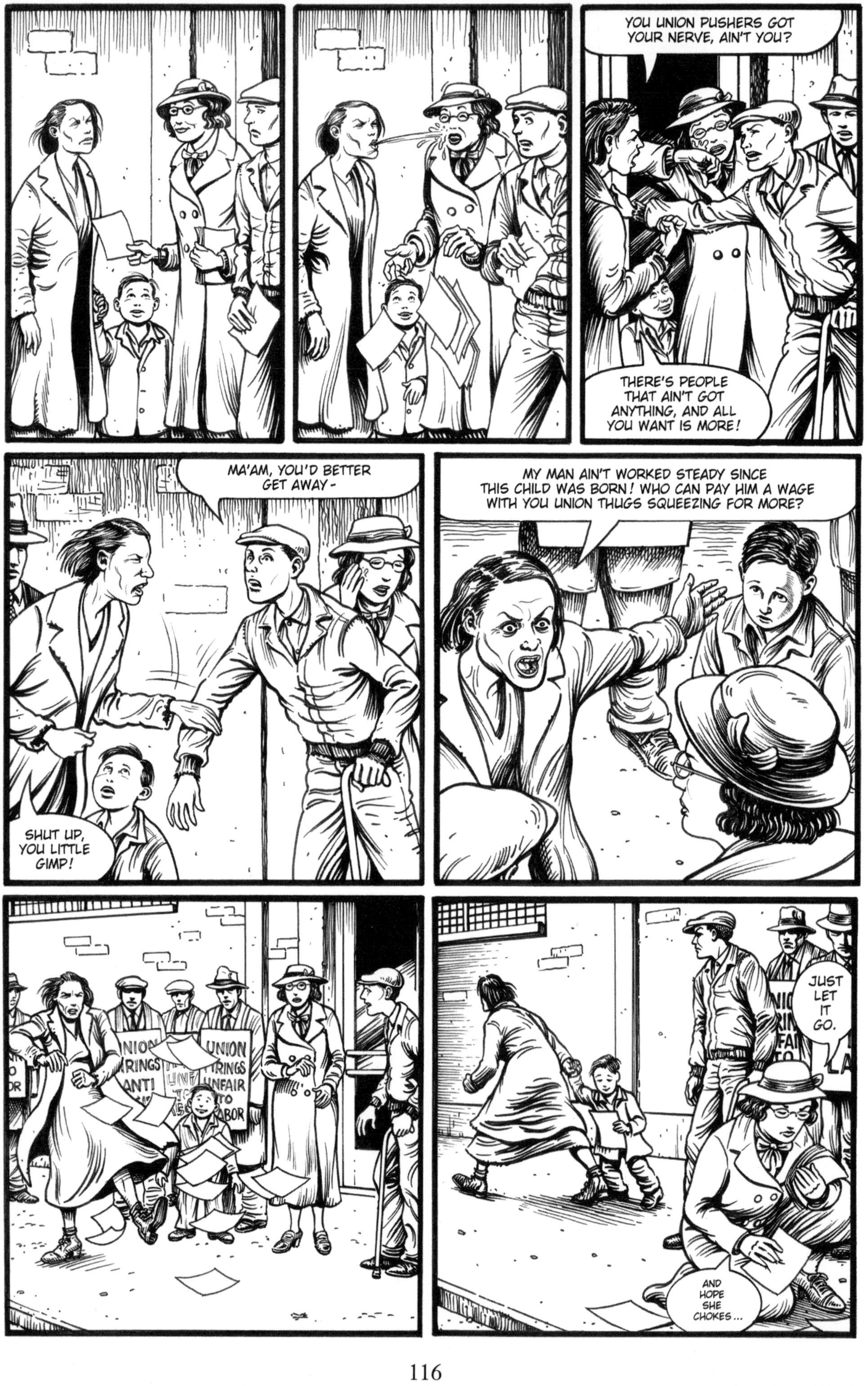
YOU UNION PUSHERS GOT YOUR NERVE, AIN'T YOU?
THERE'S PEOPLE THAT AIN'T GOT ANYTHING, AND ALL YOU WANT IS MORE!
MA'AM, YOU'D BETTER GET AWAY-
SHUT UP, YOU LITTLE GIMP!
MY MAN AIN'T WORKED STEADY SINCE THIS CHILD WAS BORN! WHO CAN PAY HIM A WAGE WITH YOU UNION THUGS SQUEEZING FOR MORE?
JUST LET IT GO.
AND HOPE SHE CHOKES...

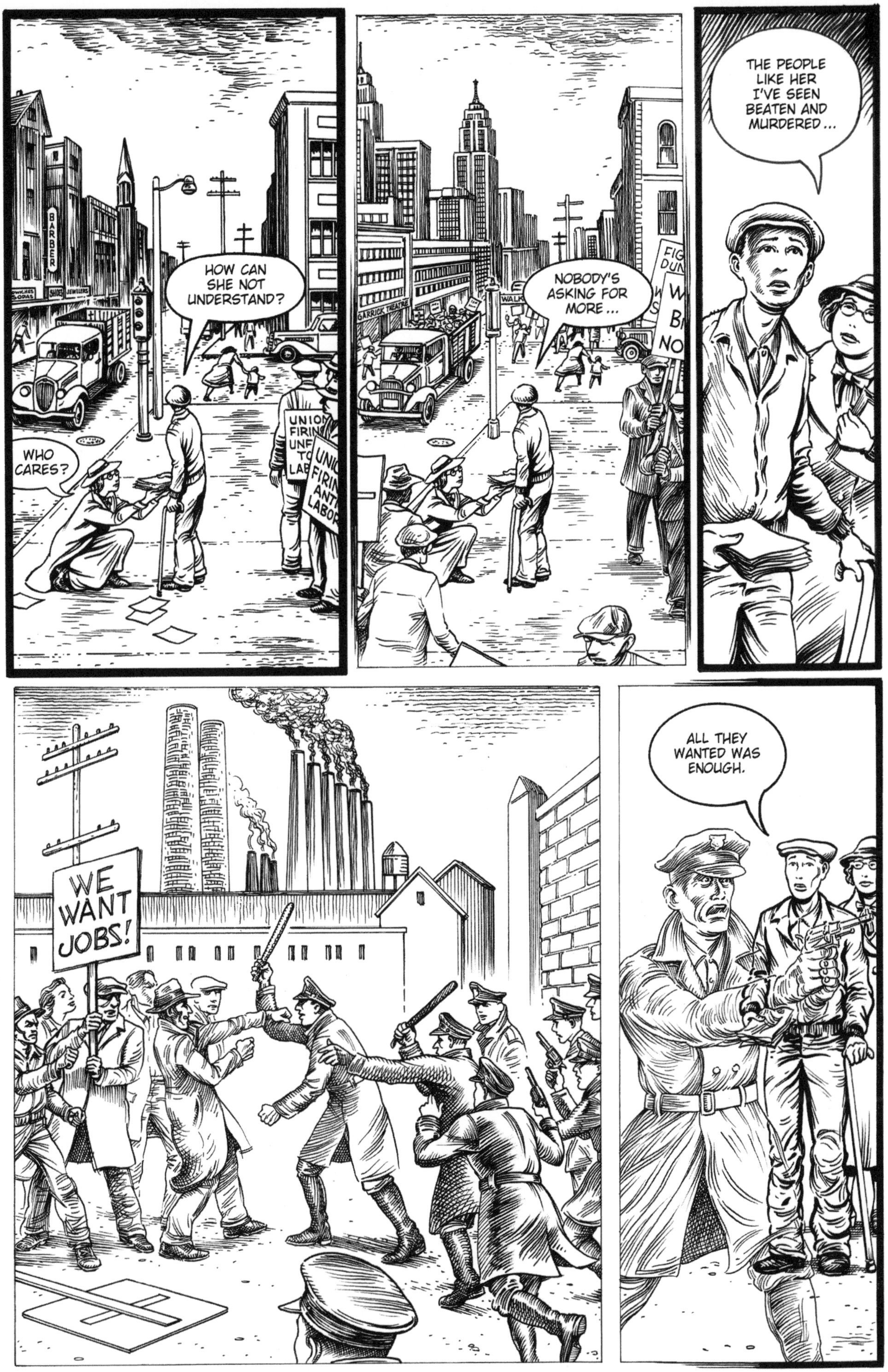
BARBER
HOW CAN SHE NOT UNDERSTAND?
WHO CARES?
GARRICK THEATRE
NOBODY'S ASKING FOR MORE...
THE PEOPLE LIKE HER I'VE SEEN BEATEN AND MURDERED...
WE WANT JOBS!
ALL THEY WANTED WAS ENOUGH.

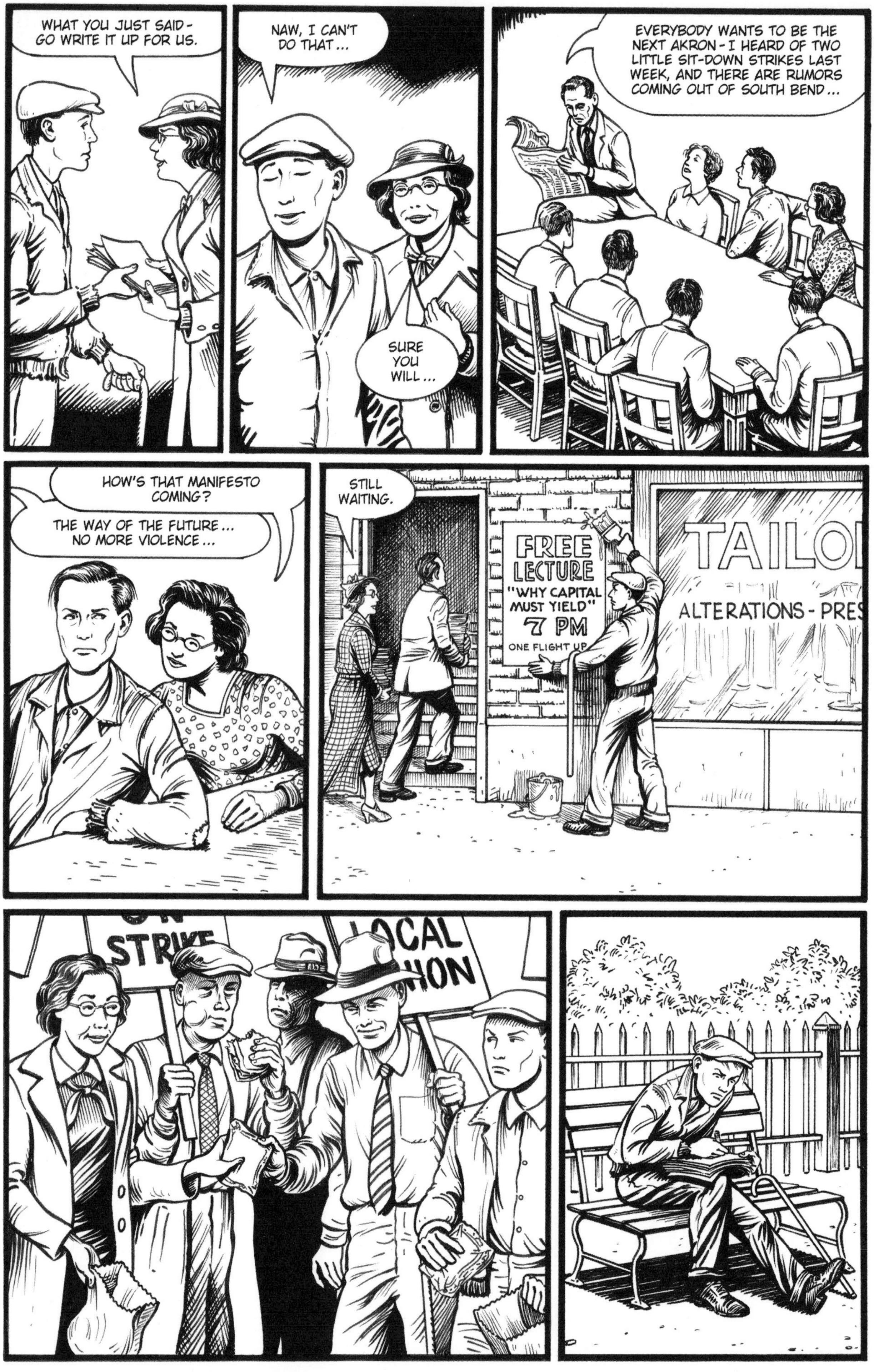
WHAT YOU JUST SAID - GO WRITE IT UP FOR US.
NAW, I CAN'T DO THAT...
SURE YOU WILL...
EVERYBODY WANTS TO BE THE NEXT AKRON - I HEARD OF TWO LITTLE SIT-DOWN STRIKES LAST WEEK, AND THERE ARE RUMORS COMING OUT OF SOUTH BEND...
HOW'S THAT MANIFESTO COMING?
THE WAY OF THE FUTURE... NO MORE VIOLENCE...
STILL WAITING.
FREE LECTURE "WHY CAPITAL MUST YIELD" 7 PM ONE FLIGHT UP
ALTERATIONS - PRES
STRIKE
LOCAL

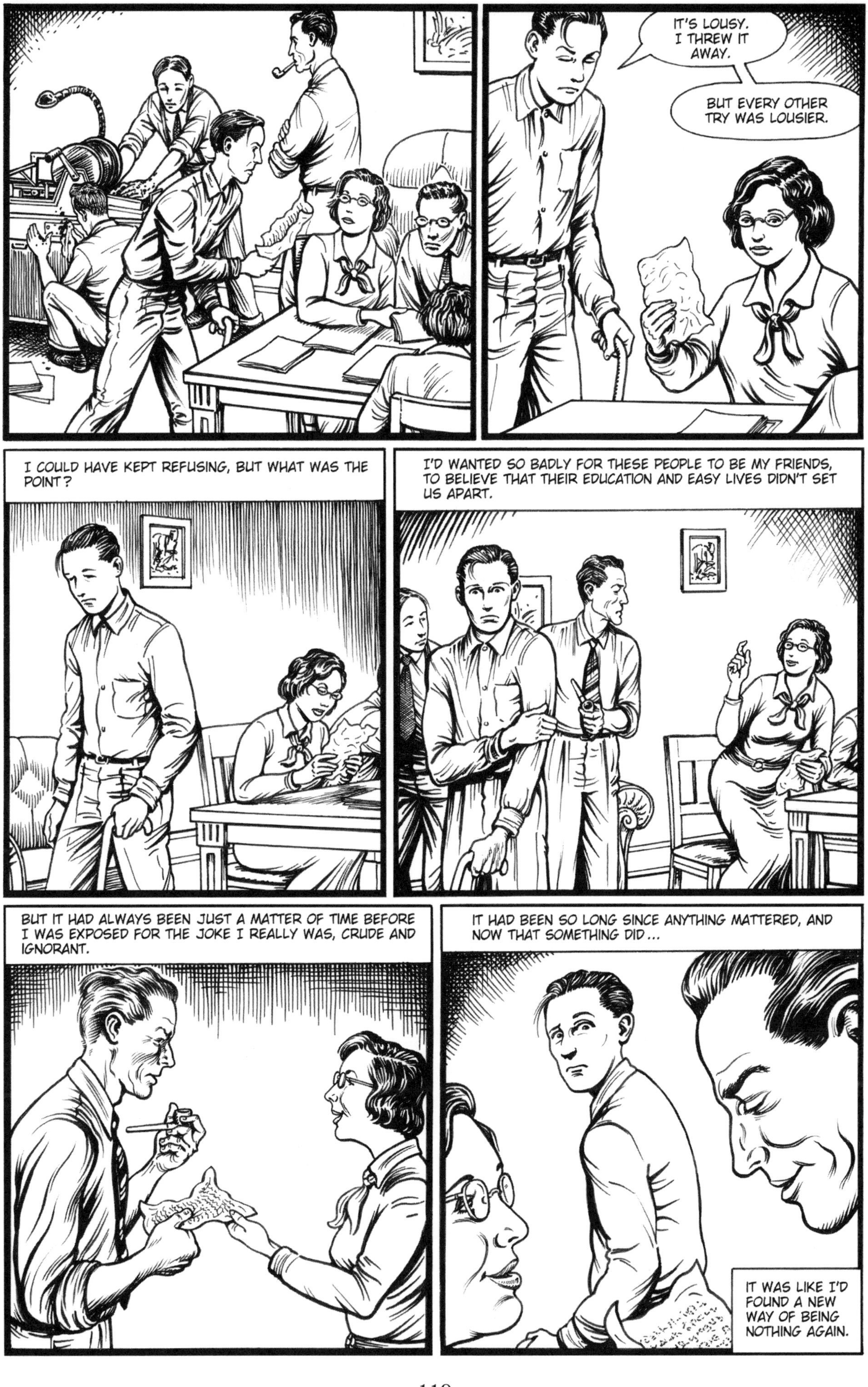
IT'S LOUSY. I THREW IT AWAY.
BUT EVERY OTHER TRY WAS LOUSIER.
I COULD HAVE KEPT REFUSING, BUT WHAT WAS THE POINT?
I'D WANTED SO BADLY FOR THESE PEOPLE TO BE MY FRIENDS, TO BELIEVE THAT THEIR EDUCATION AND EASY LIVES DIDN'T SET US APART.
BUT IT HAD ALWAYS BEEN JUST A MATTER OF TIME BEFORE I WAS EXPOSED FOR THE JOKE I REALLY WAS, CRUDE AND IGNORANT.
IT HAD BEEN SO LONG SINCE ANYTHING MATTERED, AND NOW THAT SOMETHING DID...
IT WAS LIKE I'D FOUND A NEW WAY OF BEING NOTHING AGAIN.

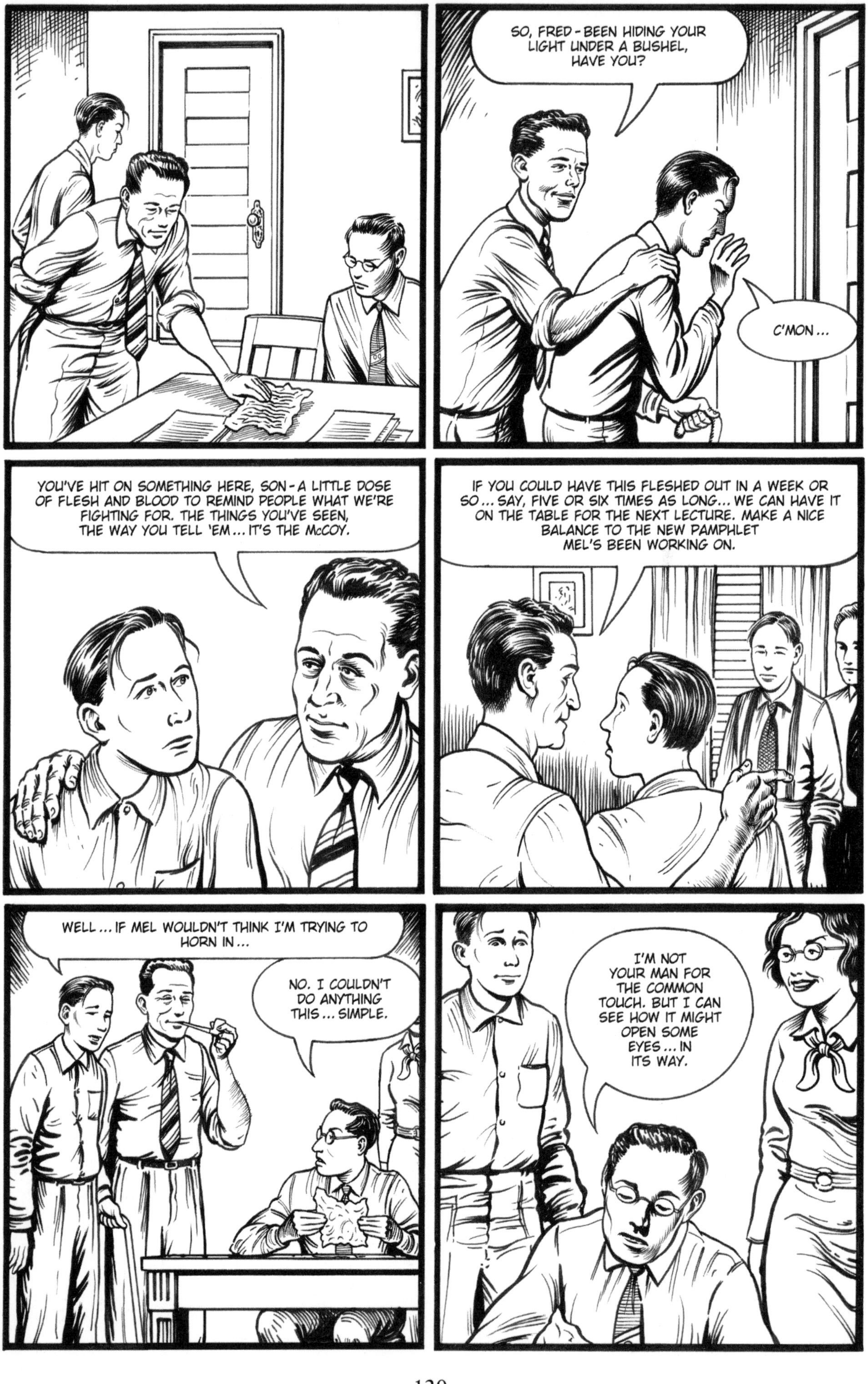
SO, FRED - BEEN HIDING YOUR LIGHT UNDER A BUSHEL, HAVE YOU?
C'MON...
YOU'VE HIT ON SOMETHING HERE, SON - A LITTLE DOSE OF FLESH AND BLOOD TO REMIND PEOPLE WHAT WE'RE FIGHTING FOR. THE THINGS YOU'VE SEEN, THE WAY YOU TELL 'EM... IT'S THE McCOY.
IF YOU COULD HAVE THIS FLESHED OUT IN A WEEK OR SO... SAY, FIVE OR SIX TIMES AS LONG... WE CAN HAVE IT ON THE TABLE FOR THE NEXT LECTURE. MAKE A NICE BALANCE TO THE NEW PAMPHLET MEL'S BEEN WORKING ON.
WELL... IF MEL WOULDN'T THINK I'M TRYING TO HORN IN...
NO. I COULDN'T DO ANYTHING THIS... SIMPLE.
I'M NOT YOUR MAN FOR THE COMMON TOUCH. BUT I CAN SEE HOW IT MIGHT OPEN SOME EYES... IN ITS WAY.

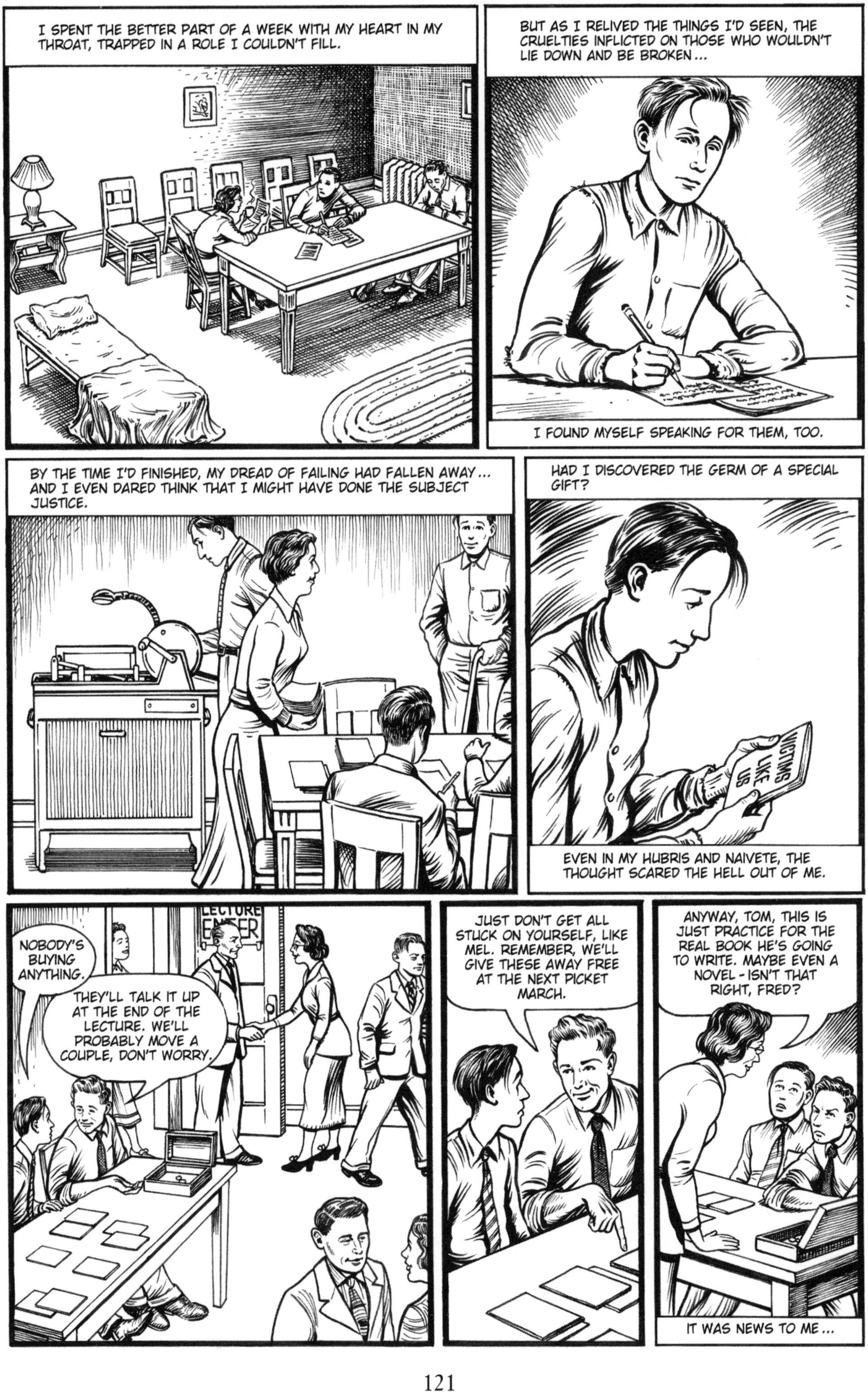
I SPENT THE BETTER PART OF A WEEK WITH MY HEART IN MY THROAT, TRAPPED IN A ROLE I COULDN'T FILL.
BUT AS I RELIVED THE THINGS I'D SEEN, THE CRUELTIES INFLICTED ON THOSE WHO WOULDN'T LIE DOWN AND BE BROKEN...
I FOUND MYSELF SPEAKING FOR THEM, TOO.
BY THE TIME I'D FINISHED, MY DREAD OF FAILING HAD FALLEN AWAY... AND I EVEN DARED THINK THAT I MIGHT HAVE DONE THE SUBJECT JUSTICE.
HAD I DISCOVERED THE GERM OF A SPECIAL GIFT?
VICTIMS LIKE US
EVEN IN MY HUBRIS AND NAIVETE, THE THOUGHT SCARED THE HELL OUT OF ME.
LECTURE
ENTER
NOBODY'S BUYING ANYTHING.
THEY'LL TALK IT UP AT THE END OF THE LECTURE. WE'LL PROBABLY MOVE A COUPLE, DON'T WORRY.
JUST DON'T GET ALL STUCK ON YOURSELF, LIKE MEL. REMEMBER, WE'LL GIVE THESE AWAY FREE AT THE NEXT PICKET MARCH.
ANYWAY, TOM, THIS IS JUST PRACTICE FOR THE REAL BOOK HE'S GOING TO WRITE. MAYBE EVEN A NOVEL - ISN'T THAT RIGHT, FRED?
IT WAS NEWS TO ME...

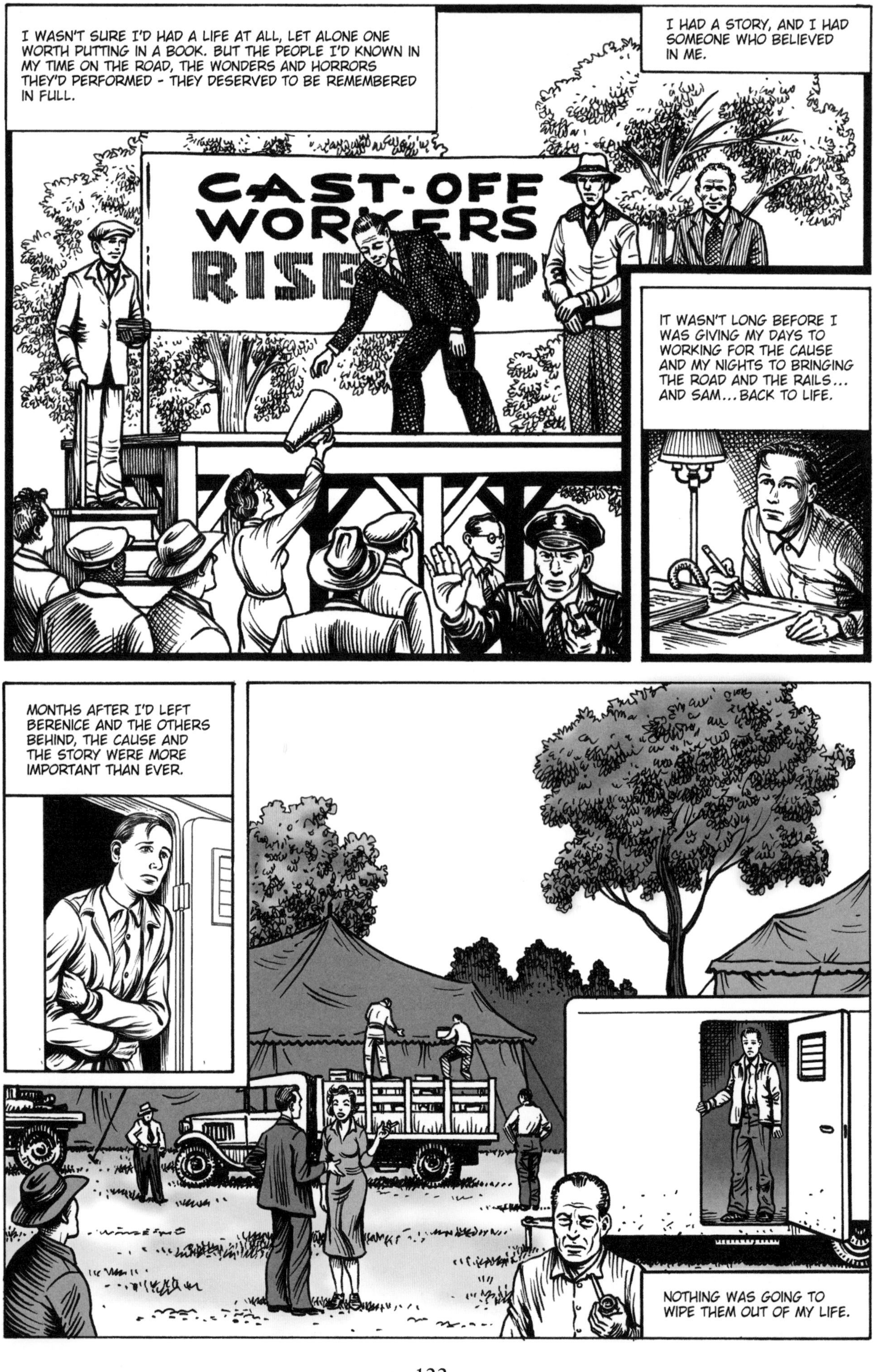
I WASN'T SURE I'D HAD A LIFE AT ALL, LET ALONE ONE WORTH PUTTING IN A BOOK. BUT THE PEOPLE I'D KNOWN IN MY TIME ON THE ROAD, THE WONDERS AND HORRORS THEY'D PERFORMED - THEY DESERVED TO BE REMEMBERED IN FULL.
I HAD A STORY, AND I HAD SOMEONE WHO BELIEVED IN ME.
CAST-OFF WORKERS RISE UP!
IT WASN'T LONG BEFORE I WAS GIVING MY DAYS TO WORKING FOR THE CAUSE AND MY NIGHTS TO BRINGING THE ROAD AND THE RAILS... AND SAM... BACK TO LIFE.
MONTHS AFTER I'D LEFT BERENICE AND THE OTHERS BEHIND, THE CAUSE AND THE STORY WERE MORE IMPORTANT THAN EVER.
NOTHING WAS GOING TO WIPE THEM OUT OF MY LIFE.

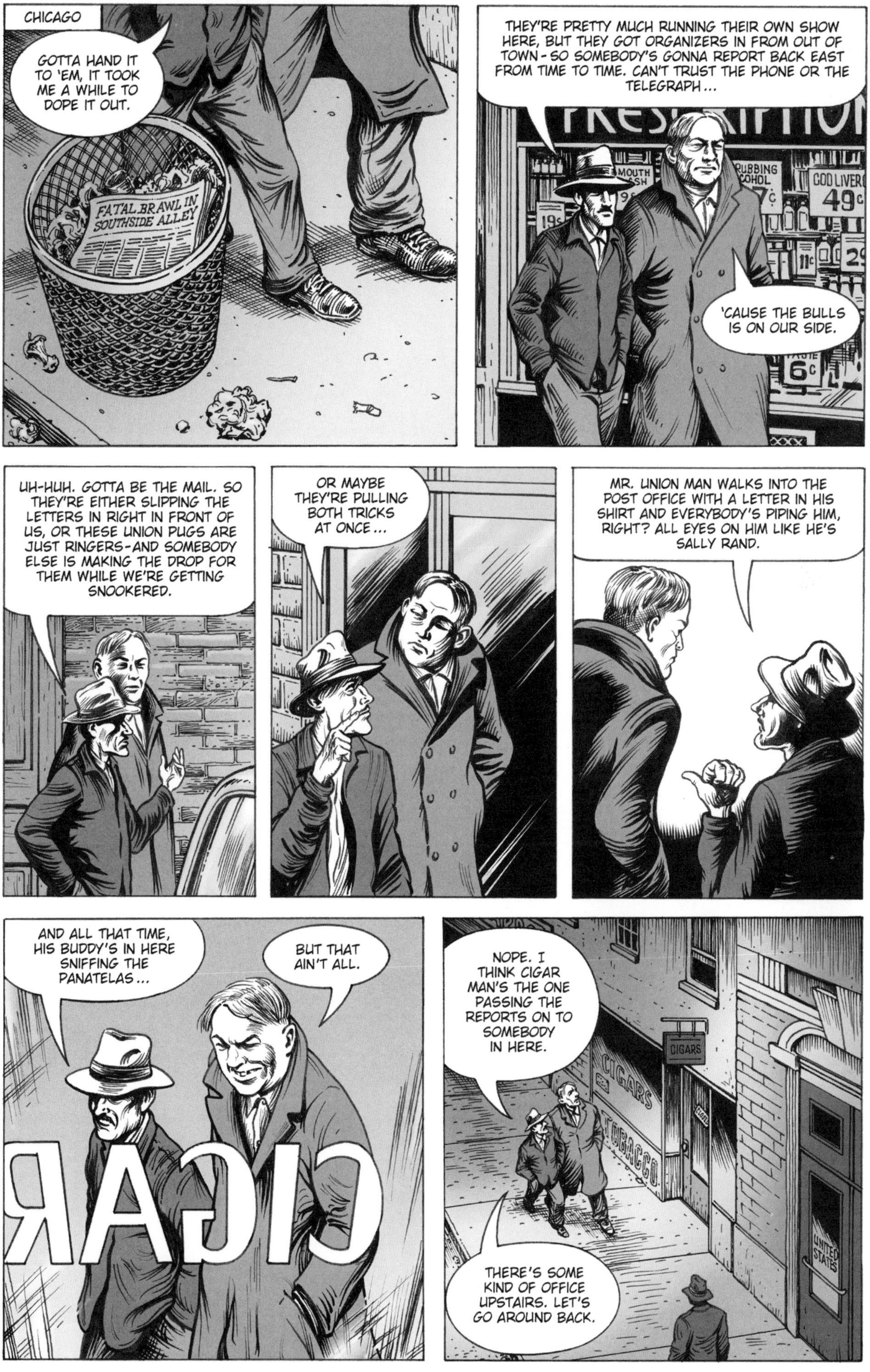
CHICAGO
GOTTA HAND IT TO 'EM, IT TOOK ME A WHILE TO DOPE IT OUT.
FATAL BRAWL IN SOUTHSIDE ALLEY
THEY'RE PRETTY MUCH RUNNING THEIR OWN SHOW HERE, BUT THEY GOT ORGANIZERS IN FROM OUT OF TOWN - SO SOMEBODY'S GONNA REPORT BACK EAST FROM TIME TO TIME. CAN'T TRUST THE PHONE OR THE TELEGRAPH...
'CAUSE THE BULLS IS ON OUR SIDE.
UH-HUH. GOTTA BE THE MAIL. SO THEY'RE EITHER SLIPPING THE LETTERS IN RIGHT IN FRONT OF US, OR THESE UNION PUGS ARE JUST RINGERS - AND SOMEBODY ELSE IS MAKING THE DROP FOR THEM WHILE WE'RE GETTING SNOOKERED.
OR MAYBE THEY'RE PULLING BOTH TRICKS AT ONCE...
MR. UNION MAN WALKS INTO THE POST OFFICE WITH A LETTER IN HIS SHIRT AND EVERYBODY'S PIPING HIM, RIGHT? ALL EYES ON HIM LIKE HE'S SALLY RAND.
AND ALL THAT TIME, HIS BUDDY'S IN HERE SNIFFING THE PANATELAS...
BUT THAT AIN'T ALL.
NOPE. I THINK CIGAR MAN'S THE ONE PASSING THE REPORTS ON TO SOMEBODY IN HERE.
CIGARS
THERE'S SOME KIND OF OFFICE UPSTAIRS. LET'S GO AROUND BACK.

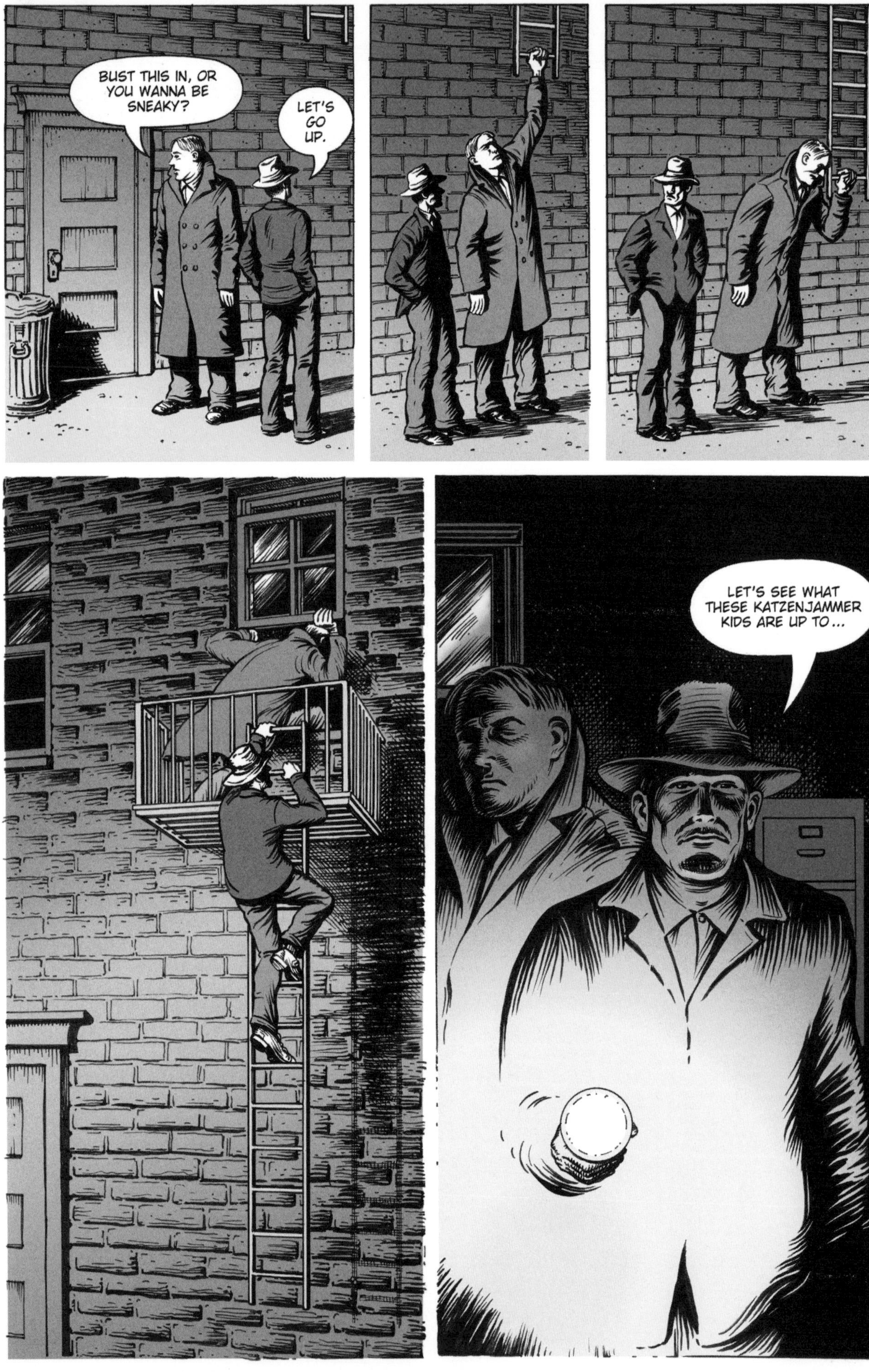
BUST THIS IN, OR YOU WANNA BE SNEAKY?
LET'S GO UP.
LET'S SEE WHAT THESE KATZENJAMMER KIDS ARE UP TO...

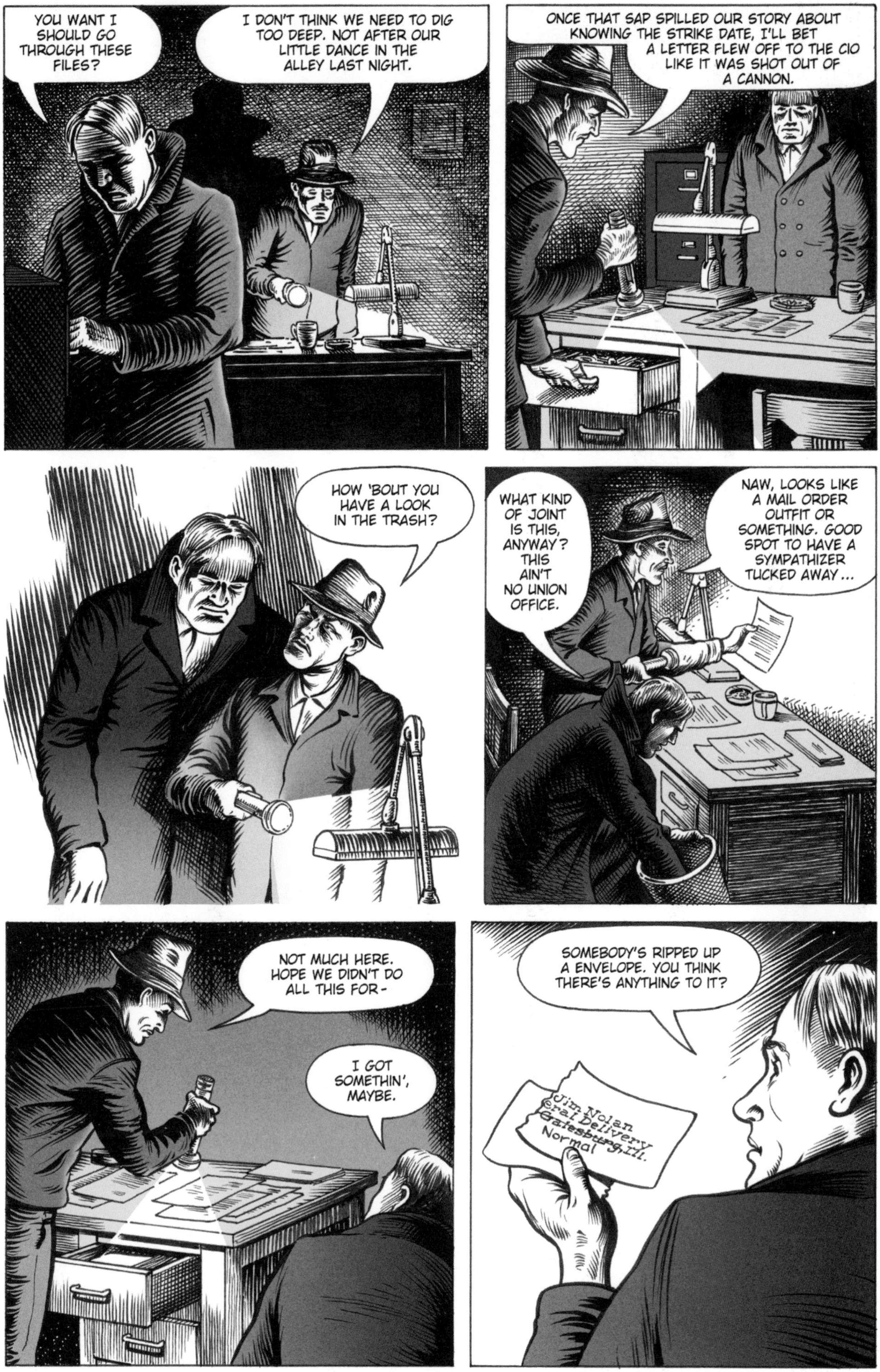
YOU WANT I SHOULD GO THROUGH THESE FILES?
I DON'T THINK WE NEED TO DIG TOO DEEP. NOT AFTER OUR LITTLE DANCE IN THE ALLEY LAST NIGHT.
ONCE THAT SAP SPILLED OUR STORY ABOUT KNOWING THE STRIKE DATE, I'LL BET A LETTER FLEW OFF TO THE CIO LIKE IT WAS SHOT OUT OF A CANNON.
HOW 'BOUT YOU HAVE A LOOK IN THE TRASH?
WHAT KIND OF JOINT IS THIS, ANYWAY? THIS AIN'T NO UNION OFFICE.
NAW, LOOKS LIKE A MAIL ORDER OUTFIT OR SOMETHING. GOOD SPOT TO HAVE A SYMPATHIZER TUCKED AWAY...
NOT MUCH HERE. HOPE WE DIDN'T DO ALL THIS FOR-
I GOT SOMETHIN', MAYBE.
SOMEBODY'S RIPPED UP A ENVELOPE. YOU THINK THERE'S ANYTHING TO IT?
Jim Nolan
eral Delivery
Galesburg, Ill.
Normal

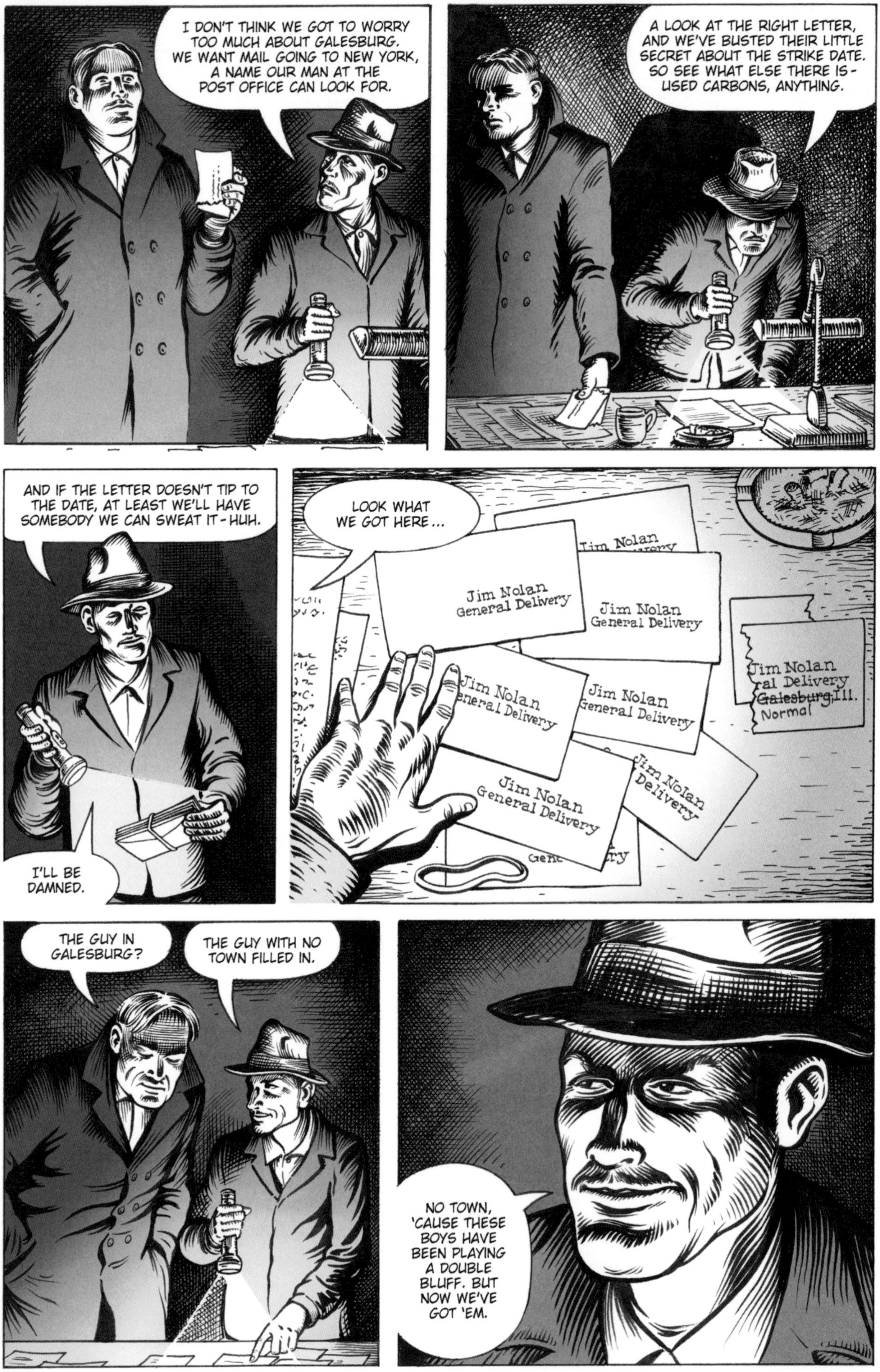
I DON'T THINK WE GOT TO WORRY TOO MUCH ABOUT GALESBURG. WE WANT MAIL GOING TO NEW YORK, A NAME OUR MAN AT THE POST OFFICE CAN LOOK FOR.
A LOOK AT THE RIGHT LETTER, AND WE'VE BUSTED THEIR LITTLE SECRET ABOUT THE STRIKE DATE. SO SEE WHAT ELSE THERE IS - USED CARBONS, ANYTHING.
AND IF THE LETTER DOESN'T TIP TO THE DATE, AT LEAST WE'LL HAVE SOMEBODY WE CAN SWEAT IT - HUH.
I'LL BE DAMNED.
LOOK WHAT WE GOT HERE...
Jim Nolan General Delivery
Jim Nolan General Delivery
Jim Nolan General Delivery
Jim Nolan General Delivery
Jim Nolan General Delivery
Jim Nolan Delivery
Jim Nolan
al Delivery
Galesburg, Ill.
Normal
THE GUY IN GALESBURG?
THE GUY WITH NO TOWN FILLED IN.
NO TOWN, 'CAUSE THESE BOYS HAVE BEEN PLAYING A DOUBLE BLUFF. BUT NOW WE'VE GOT 'EM.

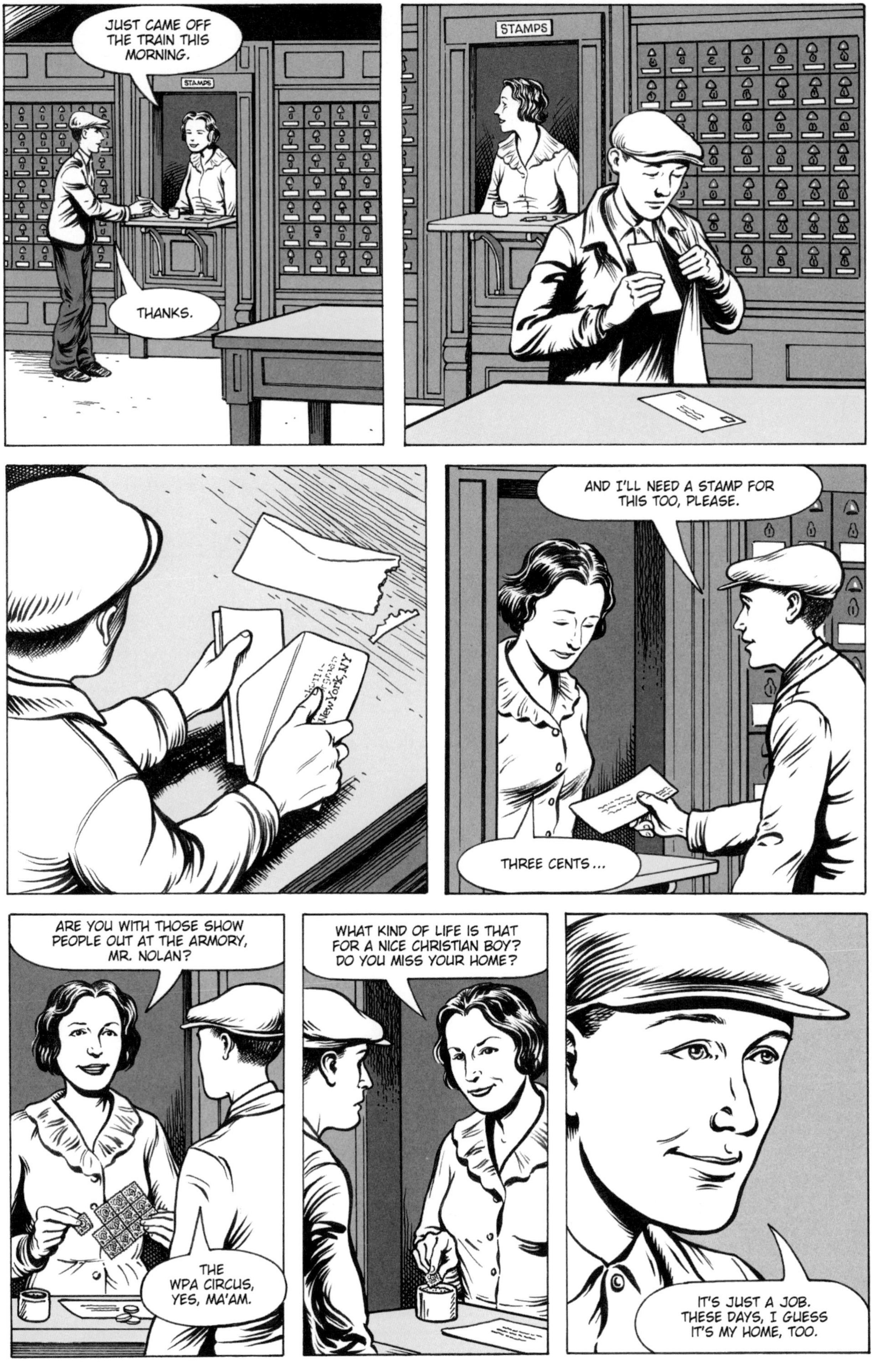
JUST CAME OFF THE TRAIN THIS MORNING.
STAMPS
THANKS.
STAMPS
New York, NY
AND I'LL NEED A STAMP FOR THIS TOO, PLEASE.
THREE CENTS...
ARE YOU WITH THOSE SHOW PEOPLE OUT AT THE ARMORY, MR. NOLAN?
THE WPA CIRCUS, YES, MA'AM.
WHAT KIND OF LIFE IS THAT FOR A NICE CHRISTIAN BOY? DO YOU MISS YOUR HOME?
IT'S JUST A JOB. THESE DAYS, I GUESS IT'S MY HOME, TOO.

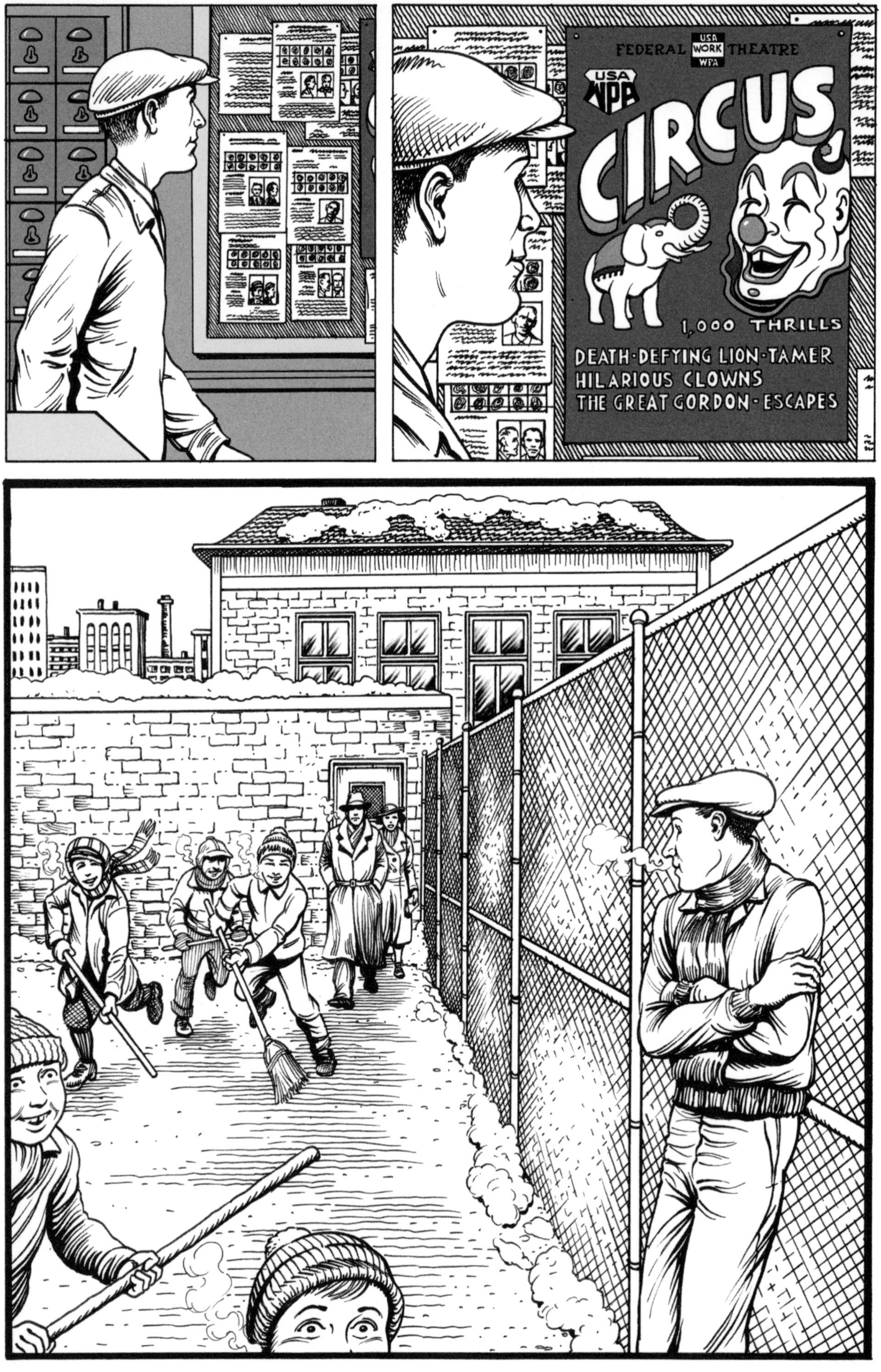
FEDERAL USA WORK WPA THEATRE
USA WPA
CIRCUS
1,000 THRILLS
DEATH-DEFYING LION-TAMER
HILARIOUS CLOWNS
THE GREAT GORDON-ESCAPES

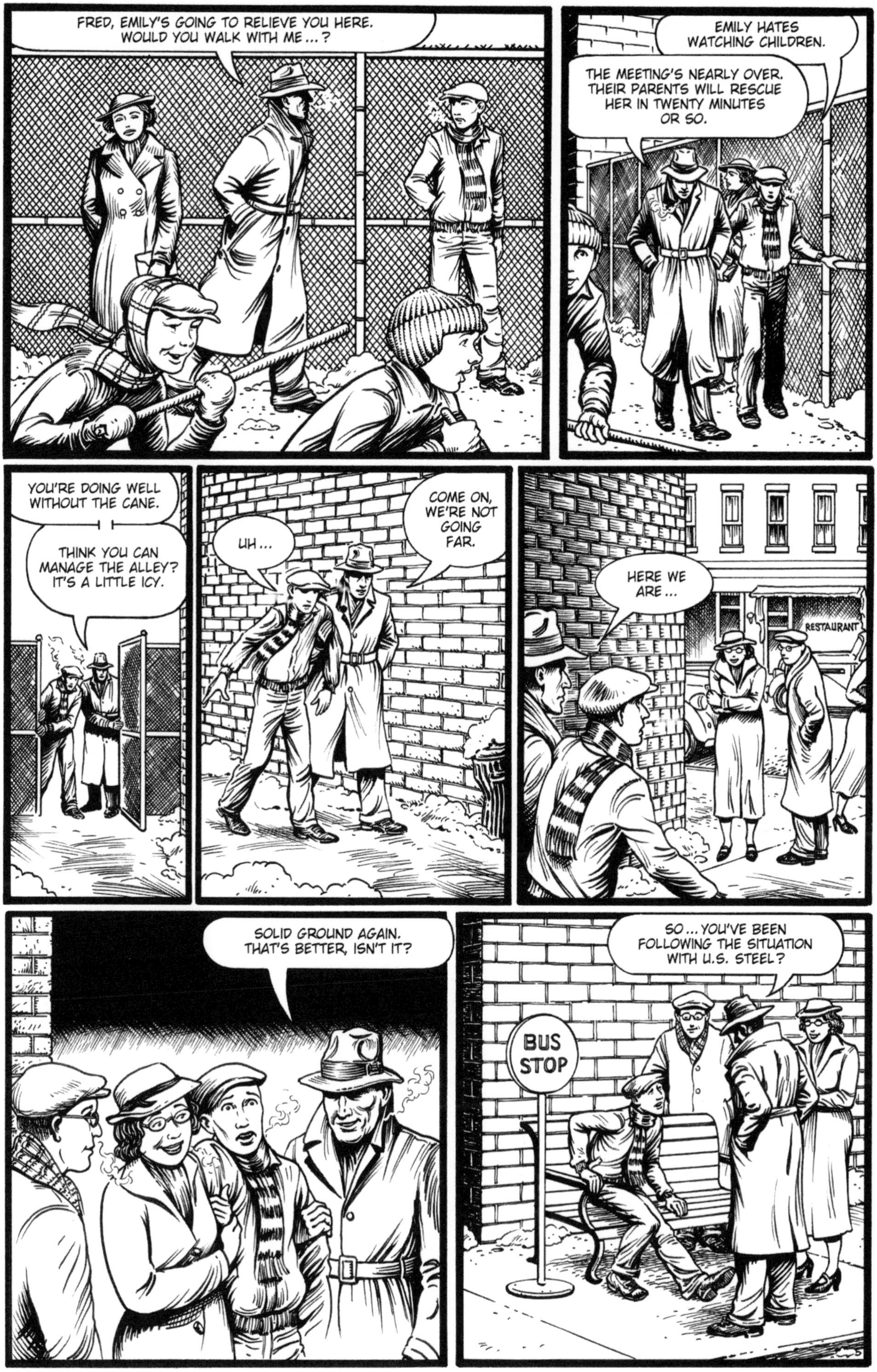
FRED, EMILY'S GOING TO RELIEVE YOU HERE. WOULD YOU WALK WITH ME ...?
EMILY HATES WATCHING CHILDREN.
THE MEETING'S NEARLY OVER. THEIR PARENTS WILL RESCUE HER IN TWENTY MINUTES OR SO.
YOU'RE DOING WELL WITHOUT THE CANE.
THINK YOU CAN MANAGE THE ALLEY? IT'S A LITTLE ICY.
UH ...
COME ON, WE'RE NOT GOING FAR.
HERE WE ARE ...
RESTAURANT
SOLID GROUND AGAIN. THAT'S BETTER, ISN'T IT?
SO ... YOU'VE BEEN FOLLOWING THE SITUATION WITH U.S. STEEL?
BUS STOP

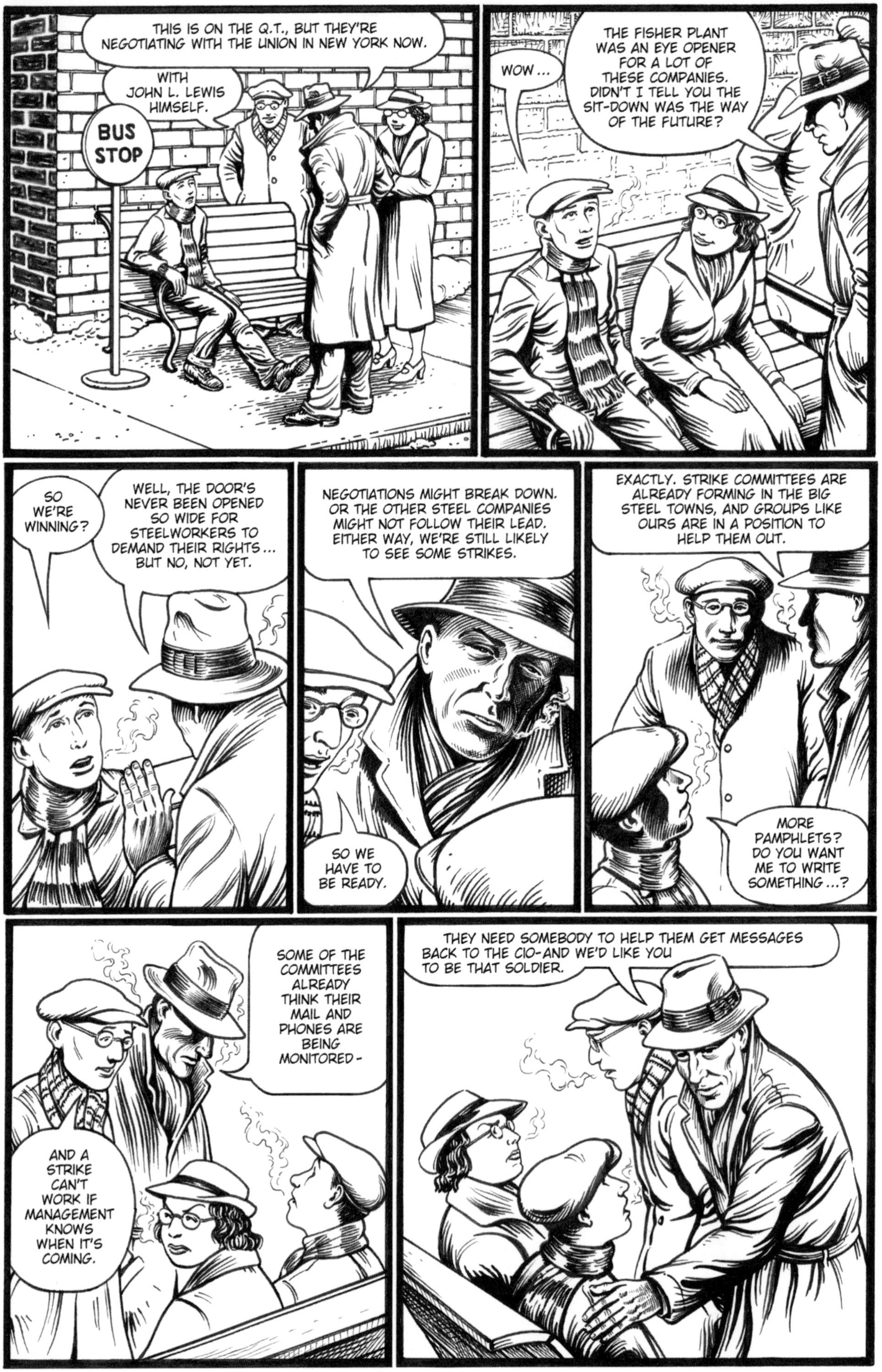
THIS IS ON THE Q.T., BUT THEY'RE NEGOTIATING WITH THE UNION IN NEW YORK NOW.
WITH JOHN L. LEWIS HIMSELF.
BUS STOP
WOW ...
THE FISHER PLANT WAS AN EYE OPENER FOR A LOT OF THESE COMPANIES. DIDN'T I TELL YOU THE SIT-DOWN WAS THE WAY OF THE FUTURE?
SO WE'RE WINNING?
WELL, THE DOOR'S NEVER BEEN OPENED SO WIDE FOR STEELWORKERS TO DEMAND THEIR RIGHTS ... BUT NO, NOT YET.
NEGOTIATIONS MIGHT BREAK DOWN. OR THE OTHER STEEL COMPANIES MIGHT NOT FOLLOW THEIR LEAD. EITHER WAY, WE'RE STILL LIKELY TO SEE SOME STRIKES.
SO WE HAVE TO BE READY.
EXACTLY. STRIKE COMMITTEES ARE ALREADY FORMING IN THE BIG STEEL TOWNS, AND GROUPS LIKE OURS ARE IN A POSITION TO HELP THEM OUT.
MORE PAMPHLETS? DO YOU WANT ME TO WRITE SOMETHING ...?
SOME OF THE COMMITTEES ALREADY THINK THEIR MAIL AND PHONES ARE BEING MONITORED -
AND A STRIKE CAN'T WORK IF MANAGEMENT KNOWS WHEN IT'S COMING.
THEY NEED SOMEBODY TO HELP THEM GET MESSAGES BACK TO THE CIO - AND WE'D LIKE YOU TO BE THAT SOLDIER.

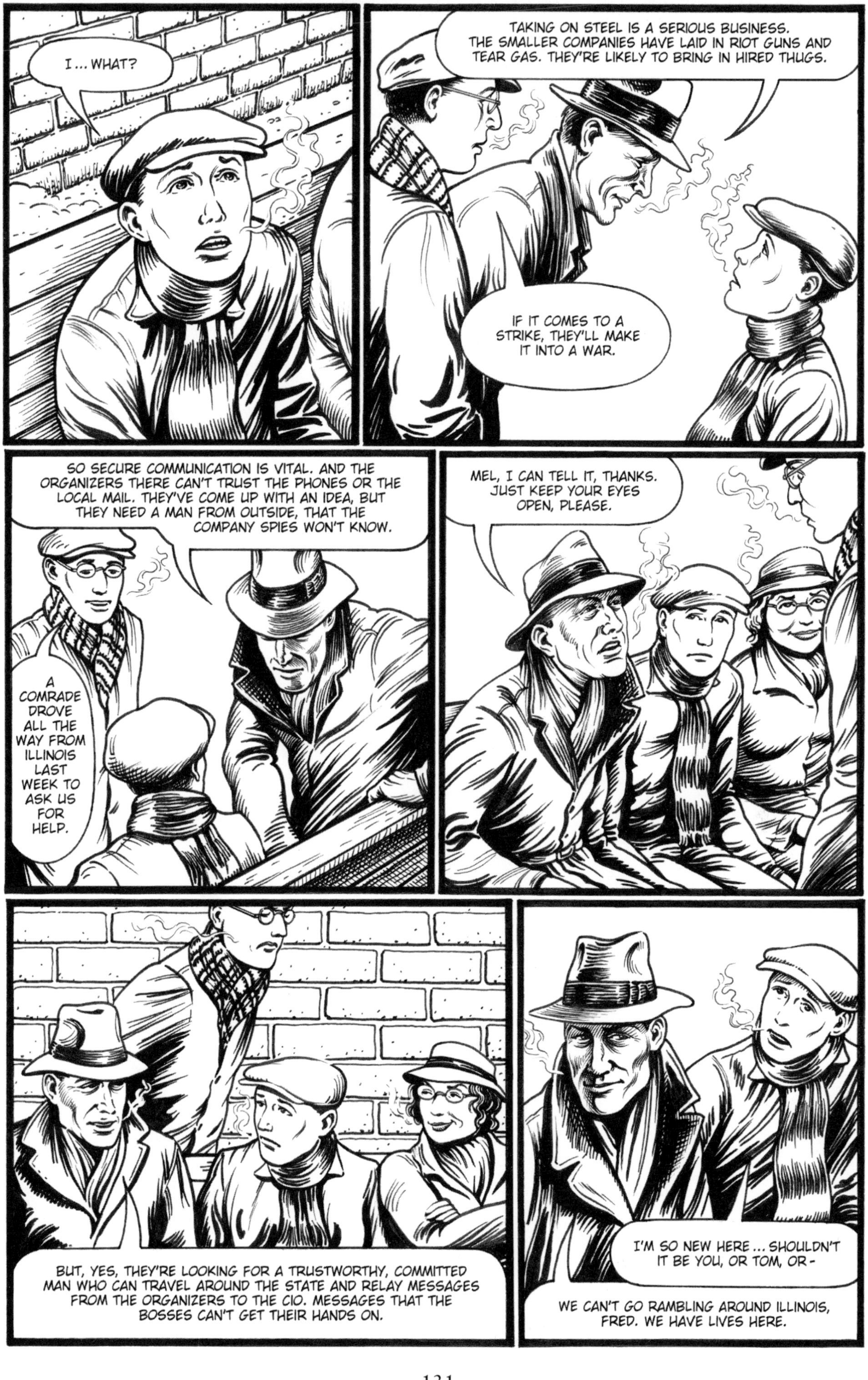
I ... WHAT?
TAKING ON STEEL IS A SERIOUS BUSINESS. THE SMALLER COMPANIES HAVE LAID IN RIOT GUNS AND TEAR GAS. THEY'RE LIKELY TO BRING IN HIRED THUGS.
IF IT COMES TO A STRIKE, THEY'LL MAKE IT INTO A WAR.
SO SECURE COMMUNICATION IS VITAL. AND THE ORGANIZERS THERE CAN'T TRUST THE PHONES OR THE LOCAL MAIL. THEY'VE COME UP WITH AN IDEA, BUT THEY NEED A MAN FROM OUTSIDE, THAT THE COMPANY SPIES WON'T KNOW.
A COMRADE DROVE ALL THE WAY FROM ILLINOIS LAST WEEK TO ASK US FOR HELP.
MEL, I CAN TELL IT, THANKS. JUST KEEP YOUR EYES OPEN, PLEASE.
BUT, YES, THEY'RE LOOKING FOR A TRUSTWORTHY, COMMITTED MAN WHO CAN TRAVEL AROUND THE STATE AND RELAY MESSAGES FROM THE ORGANIZERS TO THE CIO. MESSAGES THAT THE BOSSES CAN'T GET THEIR HANDS ON.
I'M SO NEW HERE ... SHOULDN'T IT BE YOU, OR TOM, OR-
WE CAN'T GO RAMBLING AROUND ILLINOIS, FRED. WE HAVE LIVES HERE.

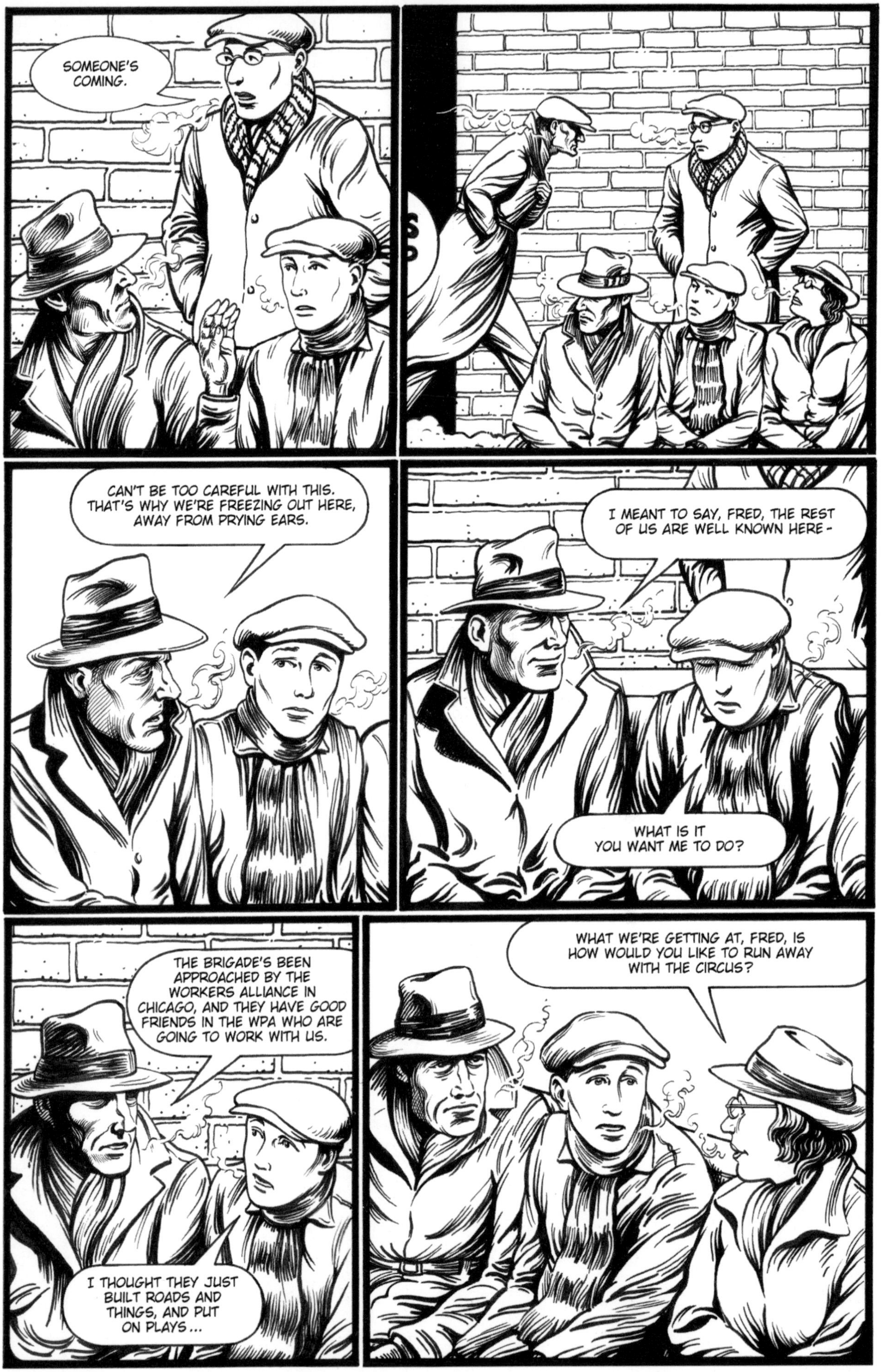
SOMEONE'S COMING.
CAN'T BE TOO CAREFUL WITH THIS. THAT'S WHY WE'RE FREEZING OUT HERE, AWAY FROM PRYING EARS.
I MEANT TO SAY, FRED, THE REST OF US ARE WELL KNOWN HERE -
WHAT IS IT YOU WANT ME TO DO?
THE BRIGADE'S BEEN APPROACHED BY THE WORKERS ALLIANCE IN CHICAGO, AND THEY HAVE GOOD FRIENDS IN THE WPA WHO ARE GOING TO WORK WITH US.
I THOUGHT THEY JUST BUILT ROADS AND THINGS, AND PUT ON PLAYS...
WHAT WE'RE GETTING AT, FRED, IS HOW WOULD YOU LIKE TO RUN AWAY WITH THE CIRCUS?

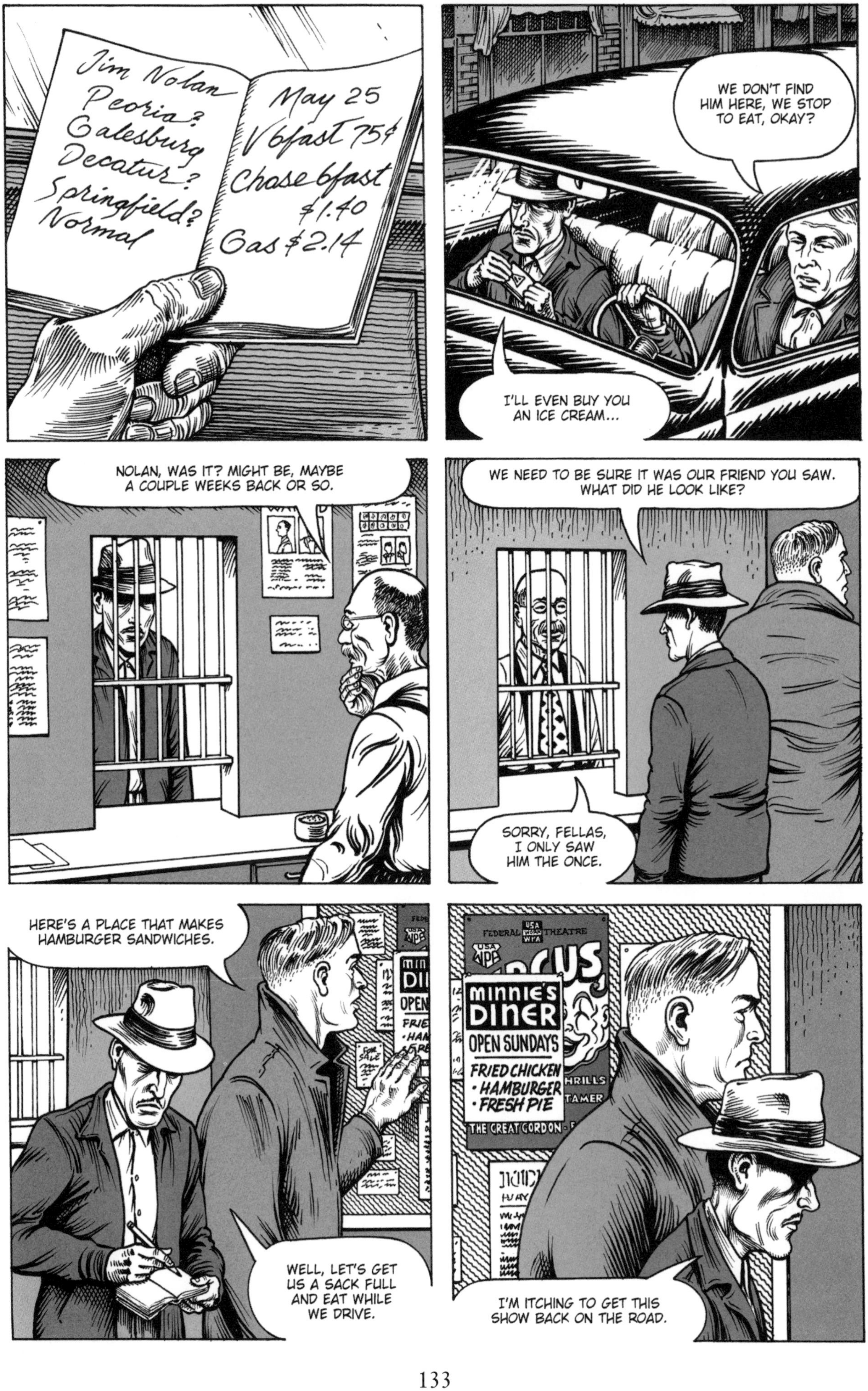
Jim Nolan
Peoria?
Galesburg
Decatur?
Springfield?
Normal
May 25
V bfast 75¢
Chase bfast
$1.40
Gas $2.14
WE DON'T FIND HIM HERE, WE STOP TO EAT, OKAY?
I'LL EVEN BUY YOU AN ICE CREAM...
NOLAN, WAS IT? MIGHT BE, MAYBE A COUPLE WEEKS BACK OR SO.
WE NEED TO BE SURE IT WAS OUR FRIEND YOU SAW. WHAT DID HE LOOK LIKE?
SORRY, FELLAS, I ONLY SAW HIM THE ONCE.
HERE'S A PLACE THAT MAKES HAMBURGER SANDWICHES.
WELL, LET'S GET US A SACK FULL AND EAT WHILE WE DRIVE.
FEDERAL THEATRE
USA WORK WPA
minnie's DINER
OPEN SUNDAYS
FRIED CHICKEN
• HAMBURGER
• FRESH PIE
THE GREAT GORDON
I'M ITCHING TO GET THIS SHOW BACK ON THE ROAD.

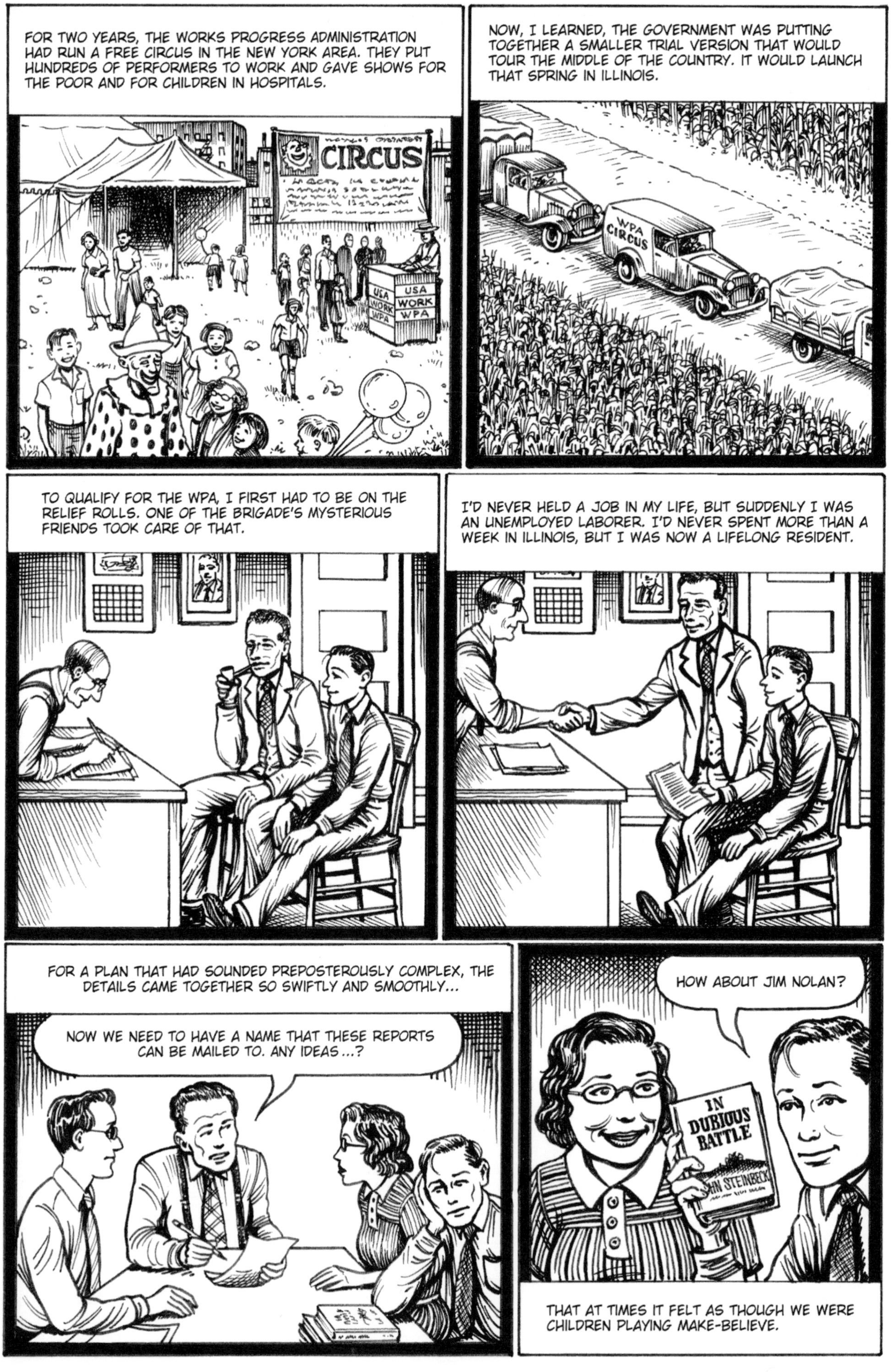
FOR TWO YEARS, THE WORKS PROGRESS ADMINISTRATION HAD RUN A FREE CIRCUS IN THE NEW YORK AREA. THEY PUT HUNDREDS OF PERFORMERS TO WORK AND GAVE SHOWS FOR THE POOR AND FOR CHILDREN IN HOSPITALS.
CIRCUS
USA WORK WPA
USA WORK WPA
NOW, I LEARNED, THE GOVERNMENT WAS PUTTING TOGETHER A SMALLER TRIAL VERSION THAT WOULD TOUR THE MIDDLE OF THE COUNTRY. IT WOULD LAUNCH THAT SPRING IN ILLINOIS.
WPA CIRCUS
TO QUALIFY FOR THE WPA, I FIRST HAD TO BE ON THE RELIEF ROLLS. ONE OF THE BRIGADE'S MYSTERIOUS FRIENDS TOOK CARE OF THAT.
I'D NEVER HELD A JOB IN MY LIFE, BUT SUDDENLY I WAS AN UNEMPLOYED LABORER. I'D NEVER SPENT MORE THAN A WEEK IN ILLINOIS, BUT I WAS NOW A LIFELONG RESIDENT.
FOR A PLAN THAT HAD SOUNDED PREPOSTEROUSLY COMPLEX, THE DETAILS CAME TOGETHER SO SWIFTLY AND SMOOTHLY...
NOW WE NEED TO HAVE A NAME THAT THESE REPORTS CAN BE MAILED TO. ANY IDEAS ...?
HOW ABOUT JIM NOLAN?
IN DUBIOUS BATTLE
THAT AT TIMES IT FELT AS THOUGH WE WERE CHILDREN PLAYING MAKE-BELIEVE.

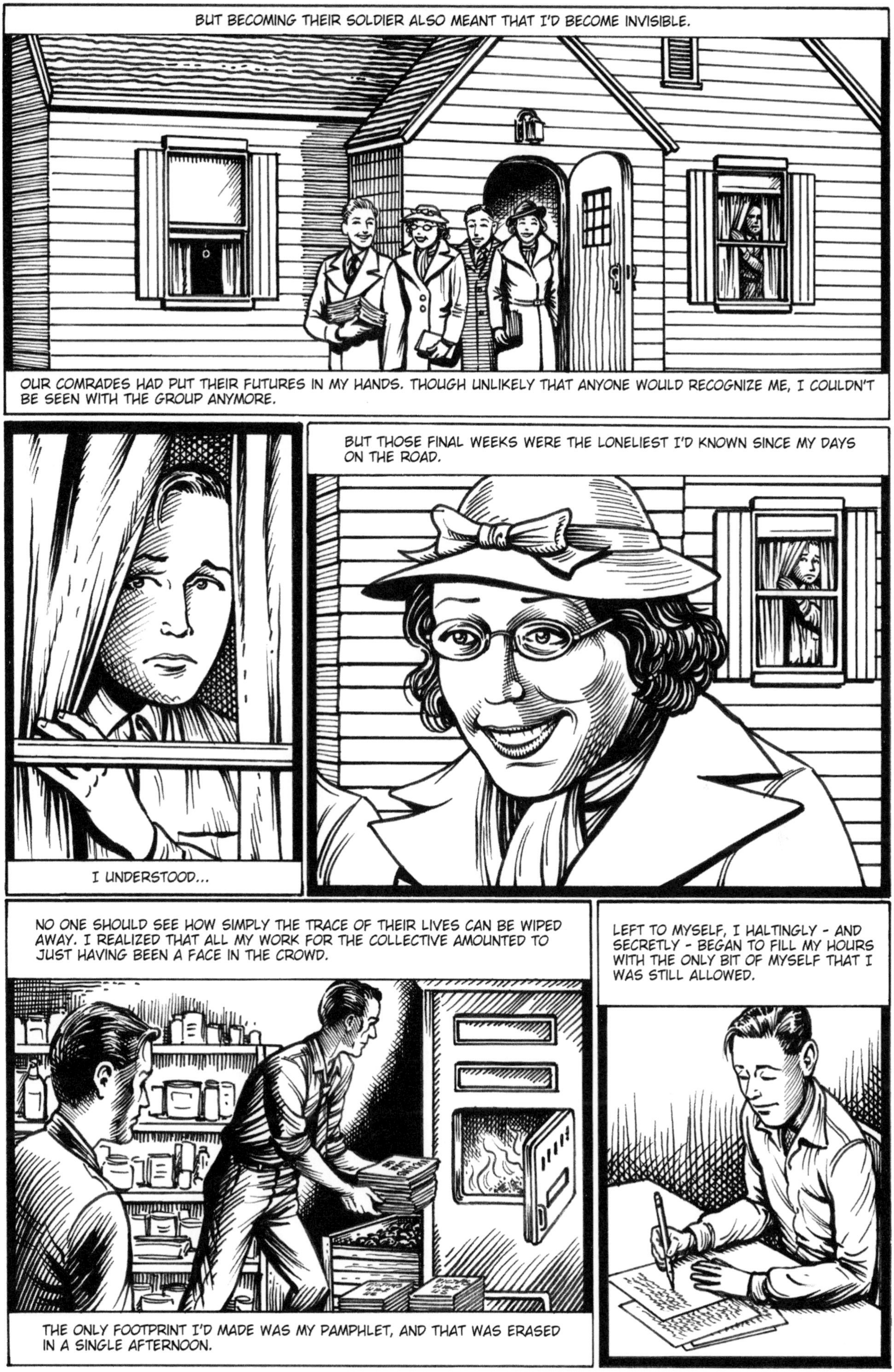
BUT BECOMING THEIR SOLDIER ALSO MEANT THAT I'D BECOME INVISIBLE.
OUR COMRADES HAD PUT THEIR FUTURES IN MY HANDS. THOUGH UNLIKELY THAT ANYONE WOULD RECOGNIZE ME, I COULDN'T BE SEEN WITH THE GROUP ANYMORE.
I UNDERSTOOD...
BUT THOSE FINAL WEEKS WERE THE LONELIEST I'D KNOWN SINCE MY DAYS ON THE ROAD.
NO ONE SHOULD SEE HOW SIMPLY THE TRACE OF THEIR LIVES CAN BE WIPED AWAY. I REALIZED THAT ALL MY WORK FOR THE COLLECTIVE AMOUNTED TO JUST HAVING BEEN A FACE IN THE CROWD.
THE ONLY FOOTPRINT I'D MADE WAS MY PAMPHLET, AND THAT WAS ERASED IN A SINGLE AFTERNOON.
LEFT TO MYSELF, I HALTINGLY - AND SECRETLY - BEGAN TO FILL MY HOURS WITH THE ONLY BIT OF MYSELF THAT I WAS STILL ALLOWED.

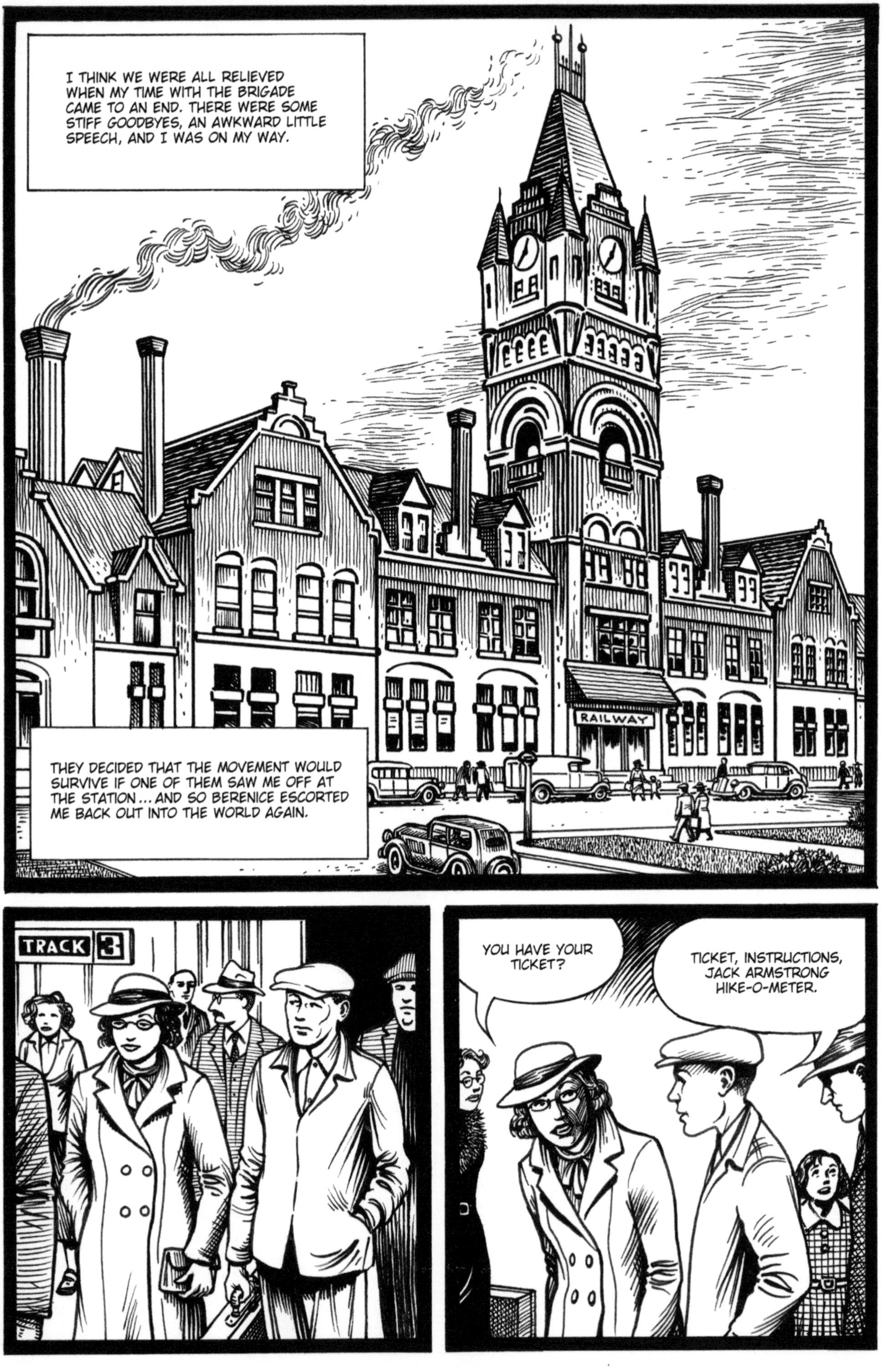
I THINK WE WERE ALL RELIEVED WHEN MY TIME WITH THE BRIGADE CAME TO AN END. THERE WERE SOME STIFF GOODBYES, AN AWKWARD LITTLE SPEECH, AND I WAS ON MY WAY.
RAILWAY
THEY DECIDED THAT THE MOVEMENT WOULD SURVIVE IF ONE OF THEM SAW ME OFF AT THE STATION... AND SO BERENICE ESCORTED ME BACK OUT INTO THE WORLD AGAIN.
TRACK 3
YOU HAVE YOUR TICKET?
TICKET, INSTRUCTIONS, JACK ARMSTRONG HIKE-O-METER.

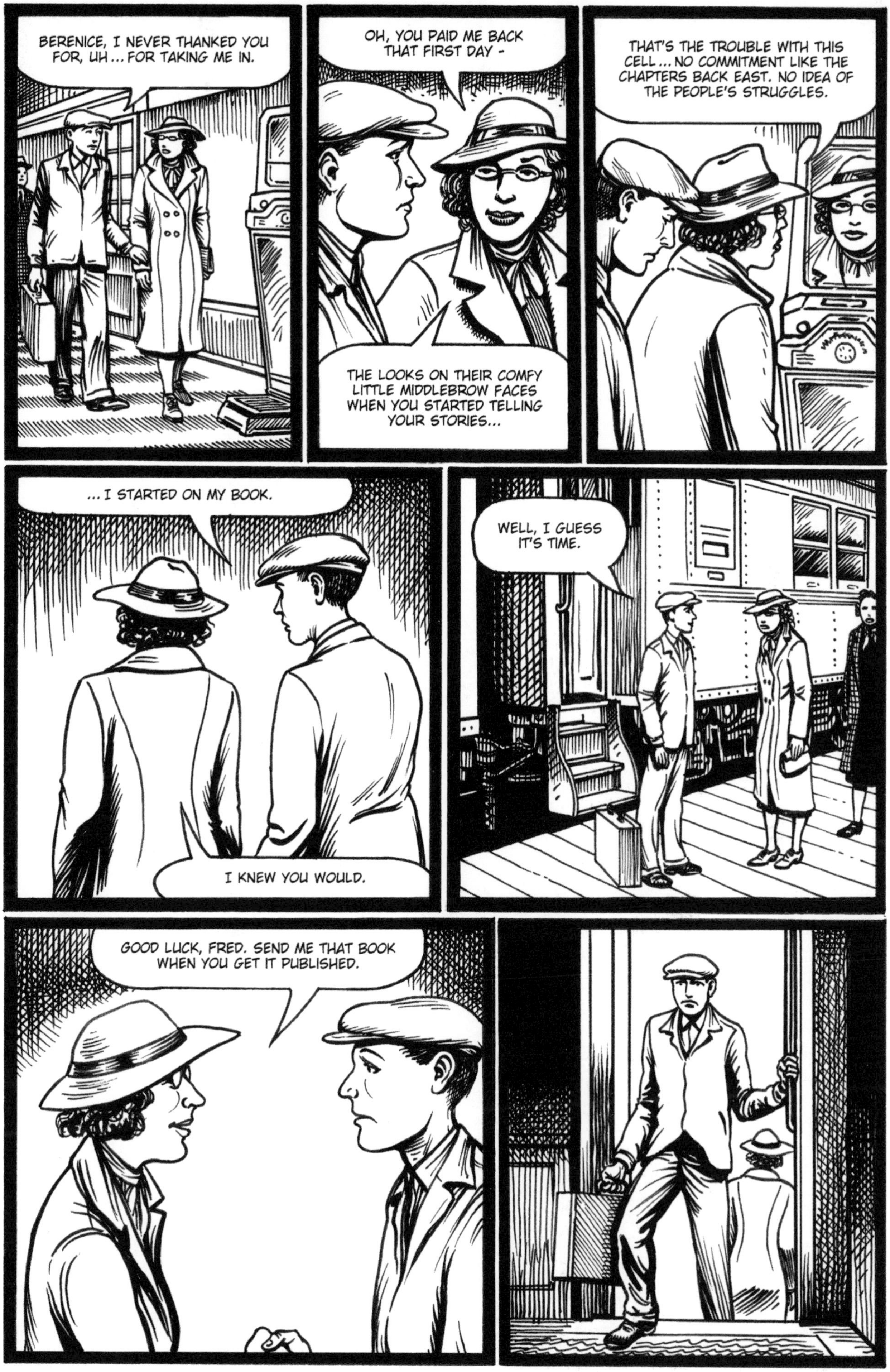
BERENICE, I NEVER THANKED YOU FOR, UH ... FOR TAKING ME IN.
OH, YOU PAID ME BACK THAT FIRST DAY -
THE LOOKS ON THEIR COMFY LITTLE MIDDLEBROW FACES WHEN YOU STARTED TELLING YOUR STORIES...
THAT'S THE TROUBLE WITH THIS CELL ... NO COMMITMENT LIKE THE CHAPTERS BACK EAST. NO IDEA OF THE PEOPLE'S STRUGGLES.
... I STARTED ON MY BOOK.
I KNEW YOU WOULD.
WELL, I GUESS IT'S TIME.
GOOD LUCK, FRED. SEND ME THAT BOOK WHEN YOU GET IT PUBLISHED.

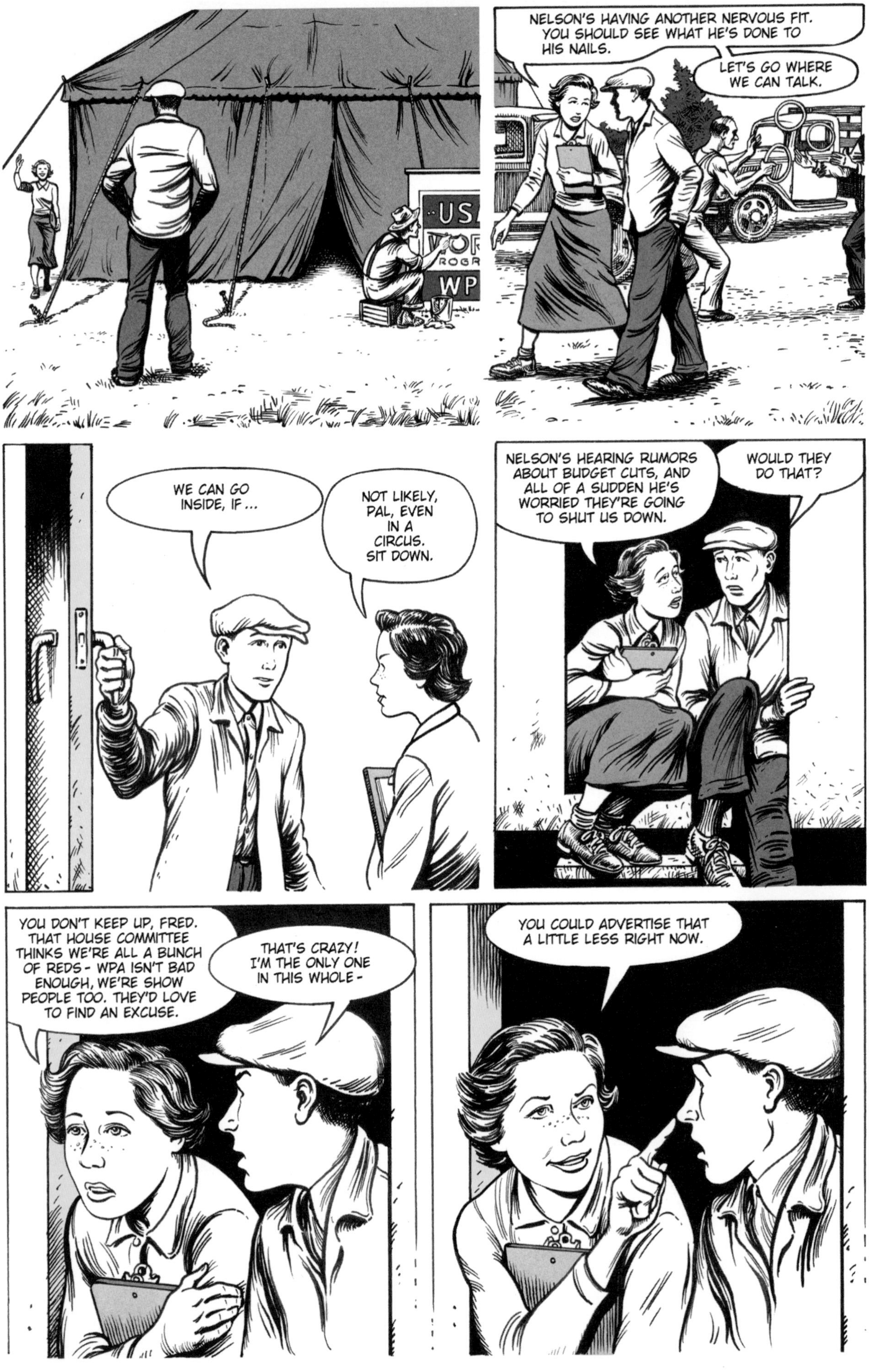
NELSON'S HAVING ANOTHER NERVOUS FIT. YOU SHOULD SEE WHAT HE'S DONE TO HIS NAILS.
LET'S GO WHERE WE CAN TALK.
WE CAN GO INSIDE, IF ...
NOT LIKELY, PAL, EVEN IN A CIRCUS. SIT DOWN.
NELSON'S HEARING RUMORS ABOUT BUDGET CUTS, AND ALL OF A SUDDEN HE'S WORRIED THEY'RE GOING TO SHUT US DOWN.
WOULD THEY DO THAT?
YOU DON'T KEEP UP, FRED. THAT HOUSE COMMITTEE THINKS WE'RE ALL A BUNCH OF REDS - WPA ISN'T BAD ENOUGH, WE'RE SHOW PEOPLE TOO. THEY'D LOVE TO FIND AN EXCUSE.
THAT'S CRAZY! I'M THE ONLY ONE IN THIS WHOLE -
YOU COULD ADVERTISE THAT A LITTLE LESS RIGHT NOW.

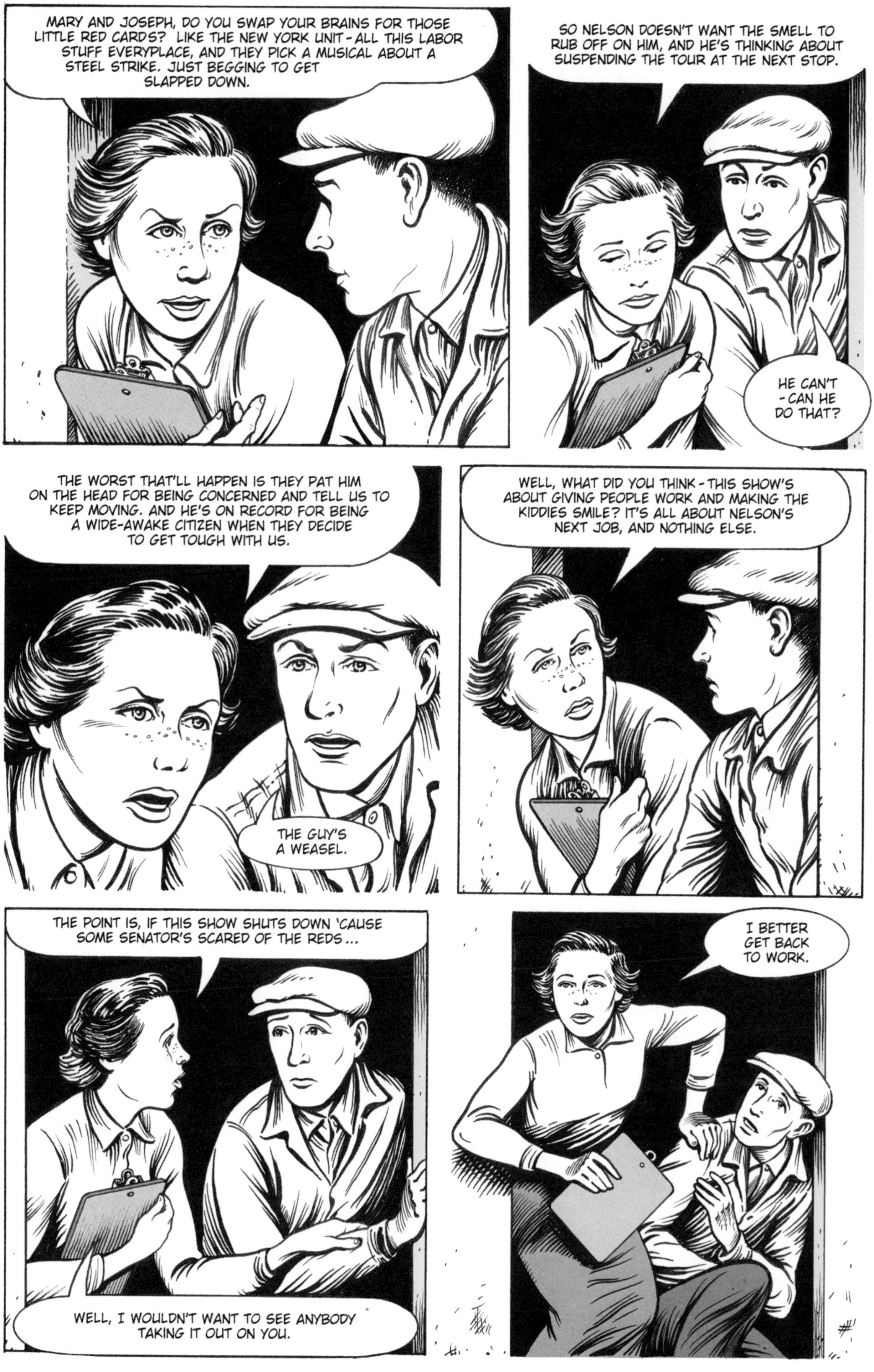
MARY AND JOSEPH, DO YOU SWAP YOUR BRAINS FOR THOSE LITTLE RED CARDS? LIKE THE NEW YORK UNIT - ALL THIS LABOR STUFF EVERYPLACE, AND THEY PICK A MUSICAL ABOUT A STEEL STRIKE. JUST BEGGING TO GET SLAPPED DOWN.
SO NELSON DOESN'T WANT THE SMELL TO RUB OFF ON HIM, AND HE'S THINKING ABOUT SUSPENDING THE TOUR AT THE NEXT STOP.
HE CAN'T - CAN HE DO THAT?
THE WORST THAT'LL HAPPEN IS THEY PAT HIM ON THE HEAD FOR BEING CONCERNED AND TELL US TO KEEP MOVING. AND HE'S ON RECORD FOR BEING A WIDE-AWAKE CITIZEN WHEN THEY DECIDE TO GET TOUGH WITH US.
THE GUY'S A WEASEL.
WELL, WHAT DID YOU THINK - THIS SHOW'S ABOUT GIVING PEOPLE WORK AND MAKING THE KIDDIES SMILE? IT'S ALL ABOUT NELSON'S NEXT JOB, AND NOTHING ELSE.
THE POINT IS, IF THIS SHOW SHUTS DOWN 'CAUSE SOME SENATOR'S SCARED OF THE REDS...
WELL, I WOULDN'T WANT TO SEE ANYBODY TAKING IT OUT ON YOU.
I BETTER GET BACK TO WORK.

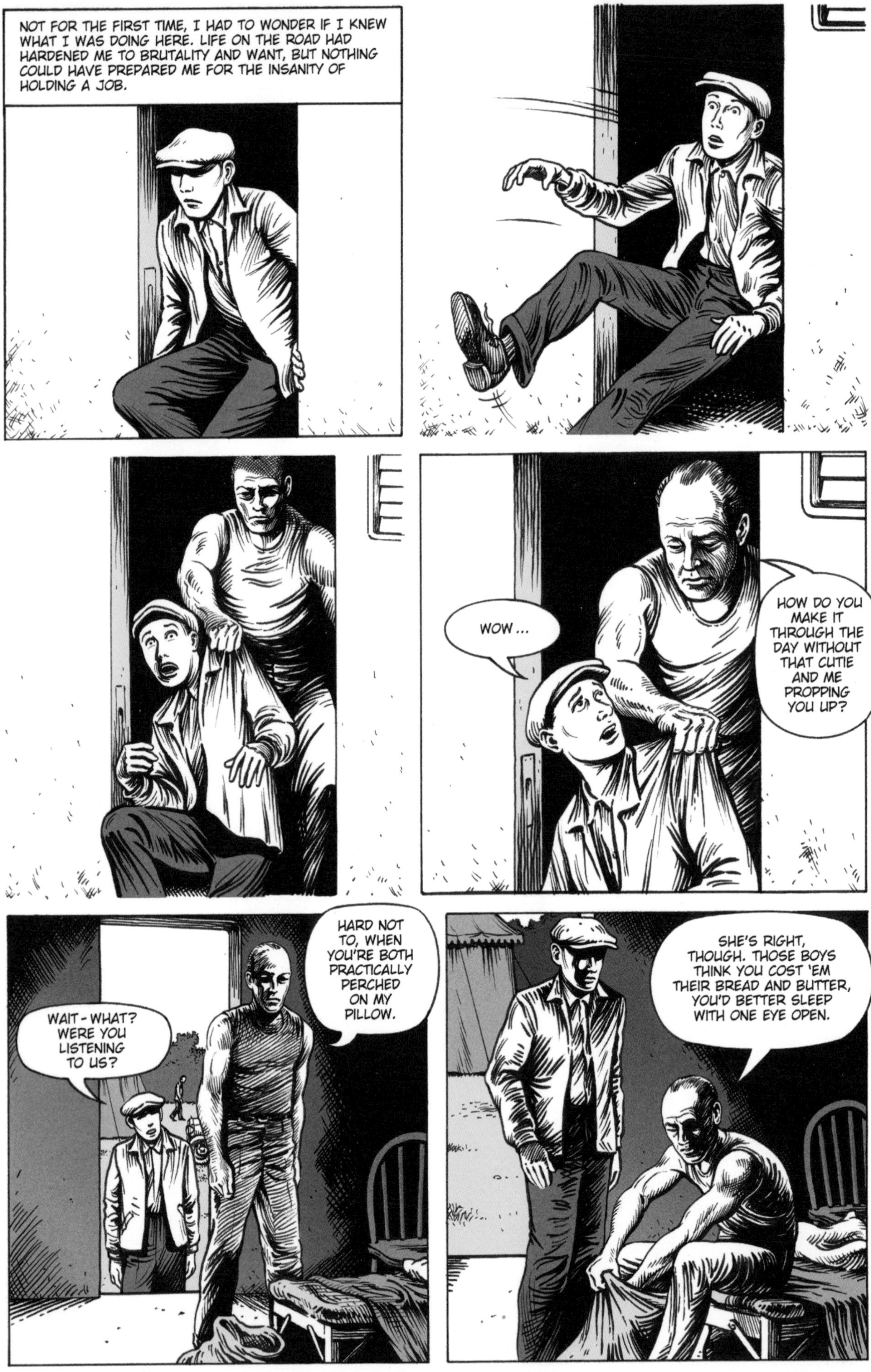
NOT FOR THE FIRST TIME, I HAD TO WONDER IF I KNEW WHAT I WAS DOING HERE. LIFE ON THE ROAD HAD HARDENED ME TO BRUTALITY AND WANT, BUT NOTHING COULD HAVE PREPARED ME FOR THE INSANITY OF HOLDING A JOB.
WOW...
HOW DO YOU MAKE IT THROUGH THE DAY WITHOUT THAT CUTIE AND ME PROPPING YOU UP?
WAIT-WHAT? WERE YOU LISTENING TO US?
HARD NOT TO, WHEN YOU'RE BOTH PRACTICALLY PERCHED ON MY PILLOW.
SHE'S RIGHT, THOUGH. THOSE BOYS THINK YOU COST 'EM THEIR BREAD AND BUTTER, YOU'D BETTER SLEEP WITH ONE EYE OPEN.

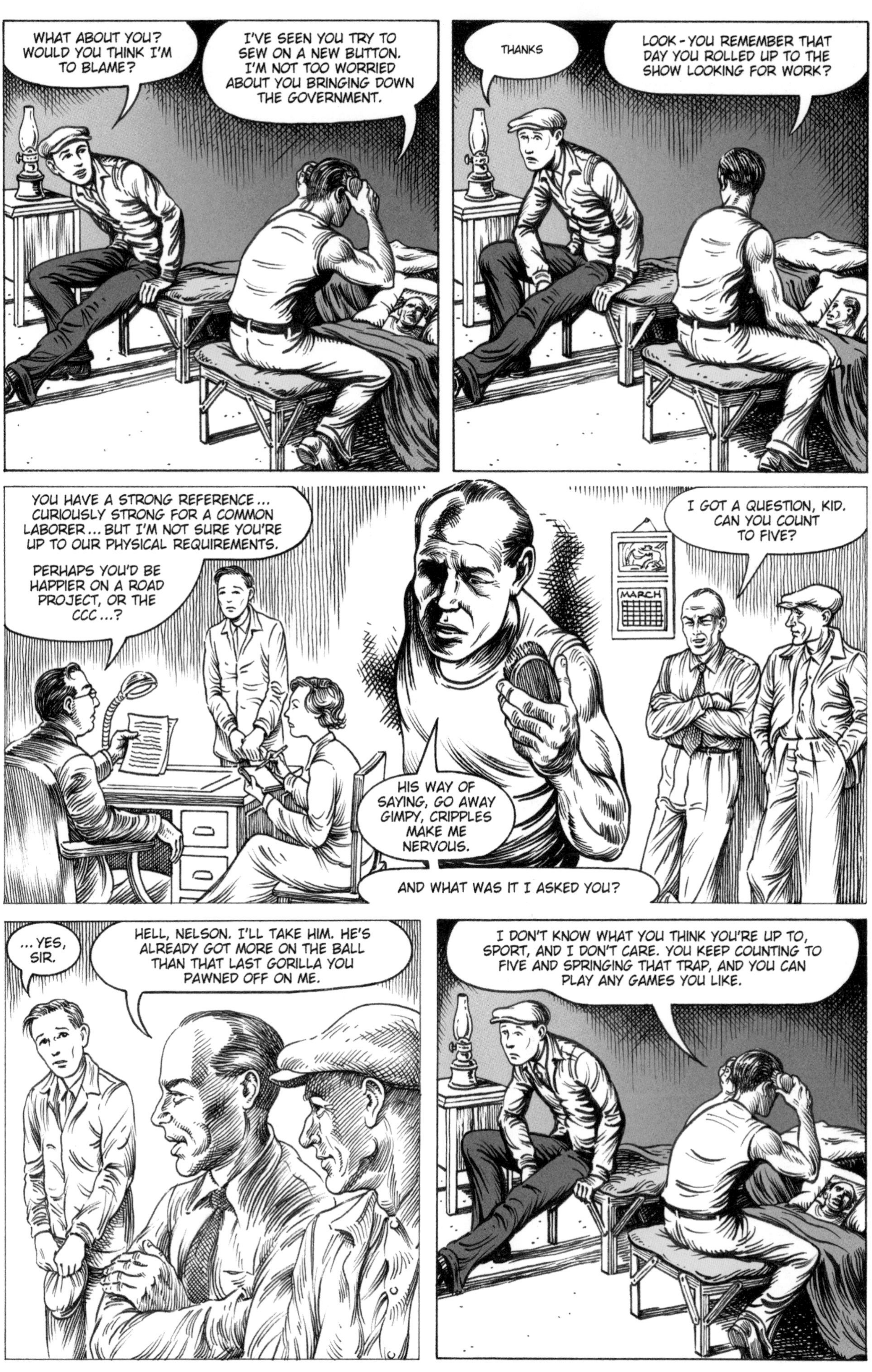
WHAT ABOUT YOU? WOULD YOU THINK I'M TO BLAME?
I'VE SEEN YOU TRY TO SEW ON A NEW BUTTON. I'M NOT TOO WORRIED ABOUT YOU BRINGING DOWN THE GOVERNMENT.
THANKS
LOOK - YOU REMEMBER THAT DAY YOU ROLLED UP TO THE SHOW LOOKING FOR WORK?
YOU HAVE A STRONG REFERENCE... CURIOUSLY STRONG FOR A COMMON LABORER... BUT I'M NOT SURE YOU'RE UP TO OUR PHYSICAL REQUIREMENTS.
PERHAPS YOU'D BE HAPPIER ON A ROAD PROJECT, OR THE CCC...?
HIS WAY OF SAYING, GO AWAY GIMPY, CRIPPLES MAKE ME NERVOUS.
MARCH
I GOT A QUESTION, KID. CAN YOU COUNT TO FIVE?
AND WHAT WAS IT I ASKED YOU?
...YES, SIR.
HELL, NELSON. I'LL TAKE HIM. HE'S ALREADY GOT MORE ON THE BALL THAN THAT LAST GORILLA YOU PAWNED OFF ON ME.
I DON'T KNOW WHAT YOU THINK YOU'RE UP TO, SPORT, AND I DON'T CARE. YOU KEEP COUNTING TO FIVE AND SPRINGING THAT TRAP, AND YOU CAN PLAY ANY GAMES YOU LIKE.

FRED, THEY JUST CALLED A CREW MEETING. BETTER HURRY.
WHAT'S UP?
I DUNNO, SOMEBODY HEARD IT WAS GONNA RAIN...
WHAT, *TONIGHT*?!

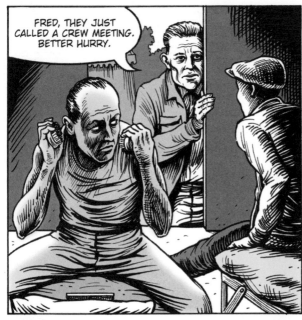

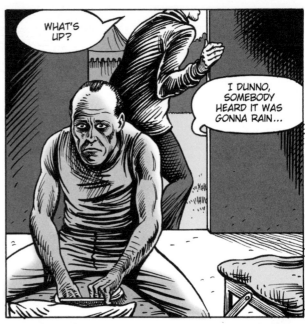

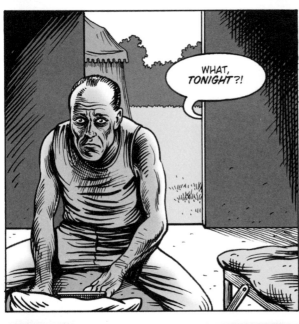

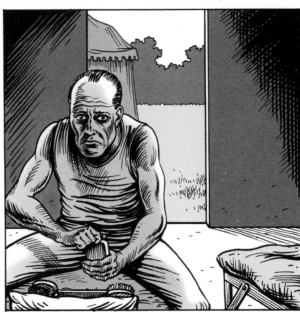

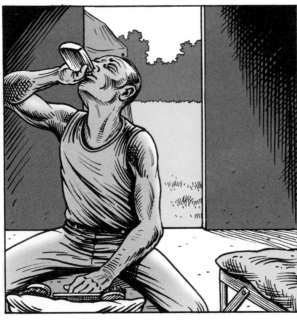

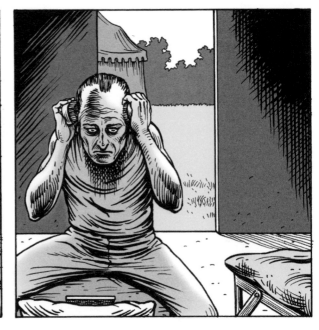

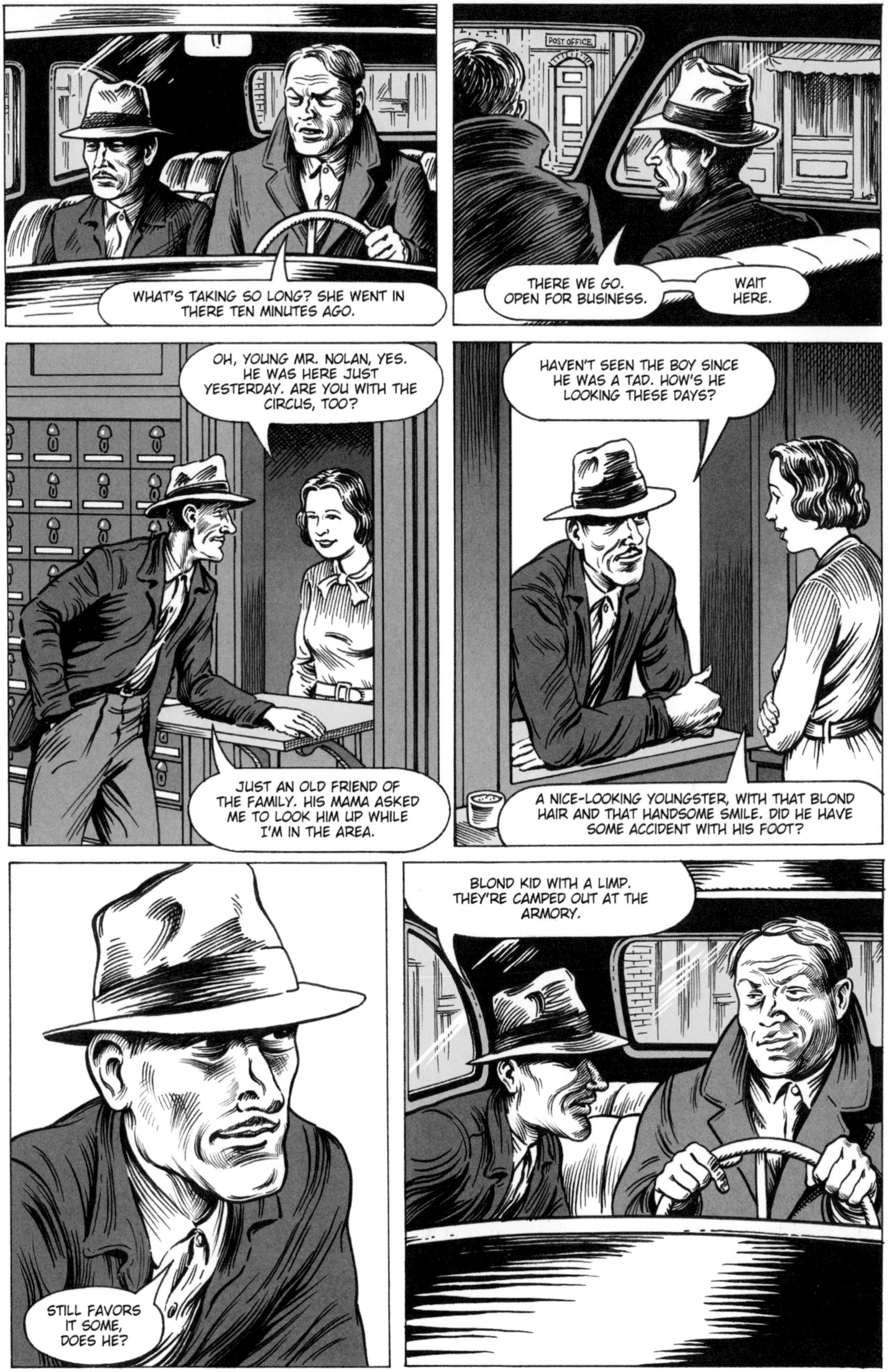

WHAT'S TAKING SO LONG? SHE WENT IN THERE TEN MINUTES AGO.
POST OFFICE
THERE WE GO. OPEN FOR BUSINESS.
WAIT HERE.
OH, YOUNG MR. NOLAN, YES. HE WAS HERE JUST YESTERDAY. ARE YOU WITH THE CIRCUS, TOO?
JUST AN OLD FRIEND OF THE FAMILY. HIS MAMA ASKED ME TO LOOK HIM UP WHILE I'M IN THE AREA.
HAVEN'T SEEN THE BOY SINCE HE WAS A TAD. HOW'S HE LOOKING THESE DAYS?
A NICE-LOOKING YOUNGSTER, WITH THAT BLOND HAIR AND THAT HANDSOME SMILE. DID HE HAVE SOME ACCIDENT WITH HIS FOOT?
STILL FAVORS IT SOME, DOES HE?
BLOND KID WITH A LIMP. THEY'RE CAMPED OUT AT THE ARMORY.

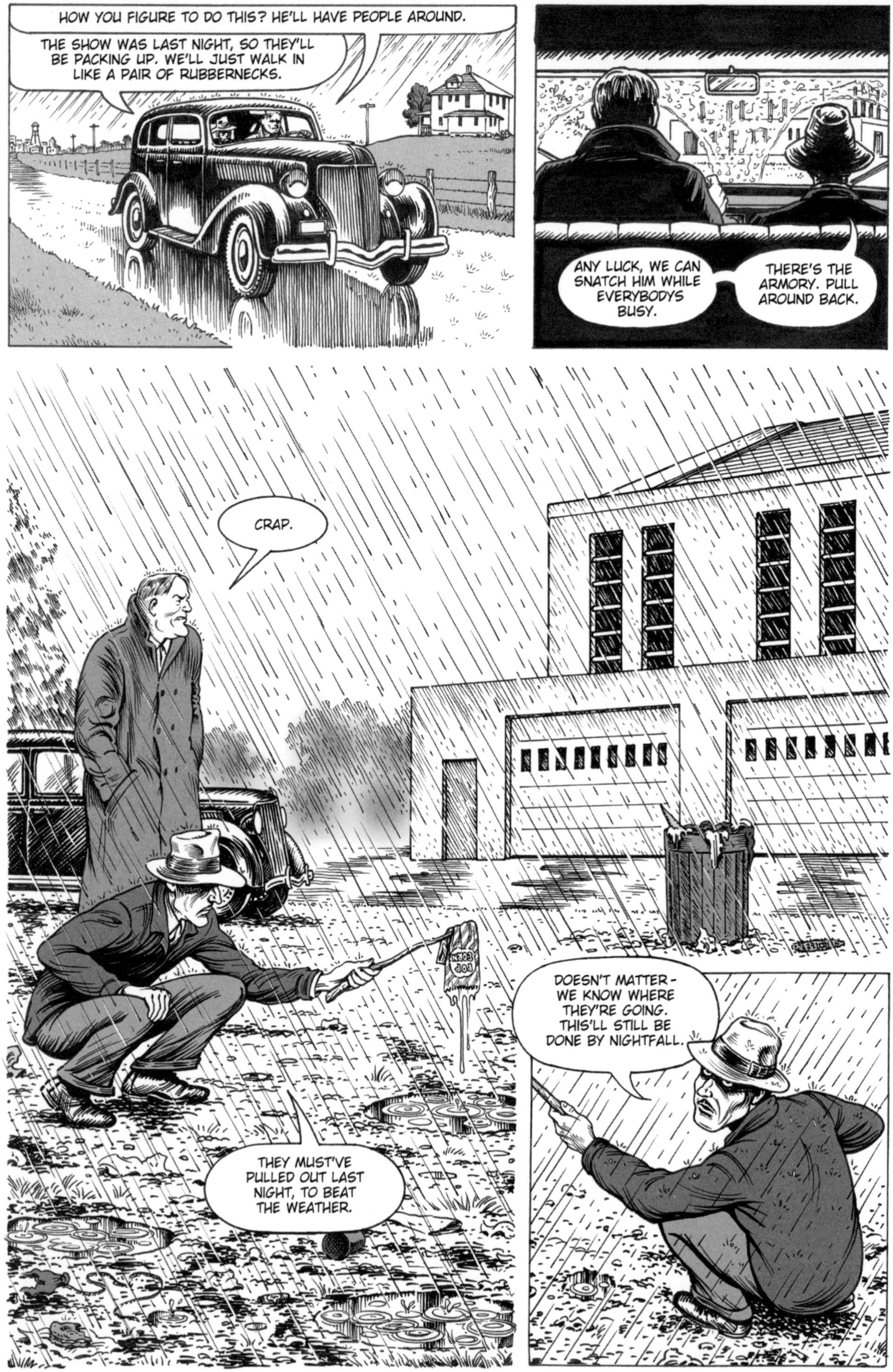
HOW YOU FIGURE TO DO THIS? HE'LL HAVE PEOPLE AROUND.
THE SHOW WAS LAST NIGHT, SO THEY'LL BE PACKING UP. WE'LL JUST WALK IN LIKE A PAIR OF RUBBERNECKS.
ANY LUCK, WE CAN SNATCH HIM WHILE EVERYBODYS BUSY.
THERE'S THE ARMORY. PULL AROUND BACK.
CRAP.
THEY MUST'VE PULLED OUT LAST NIGHT, TO BEAT THE WEATHER.
DOESN'T MATTER - WE KNOW WHERE THEY'RE GOING. THIS'LL STILL BE DONE BY NIGHTFALL.

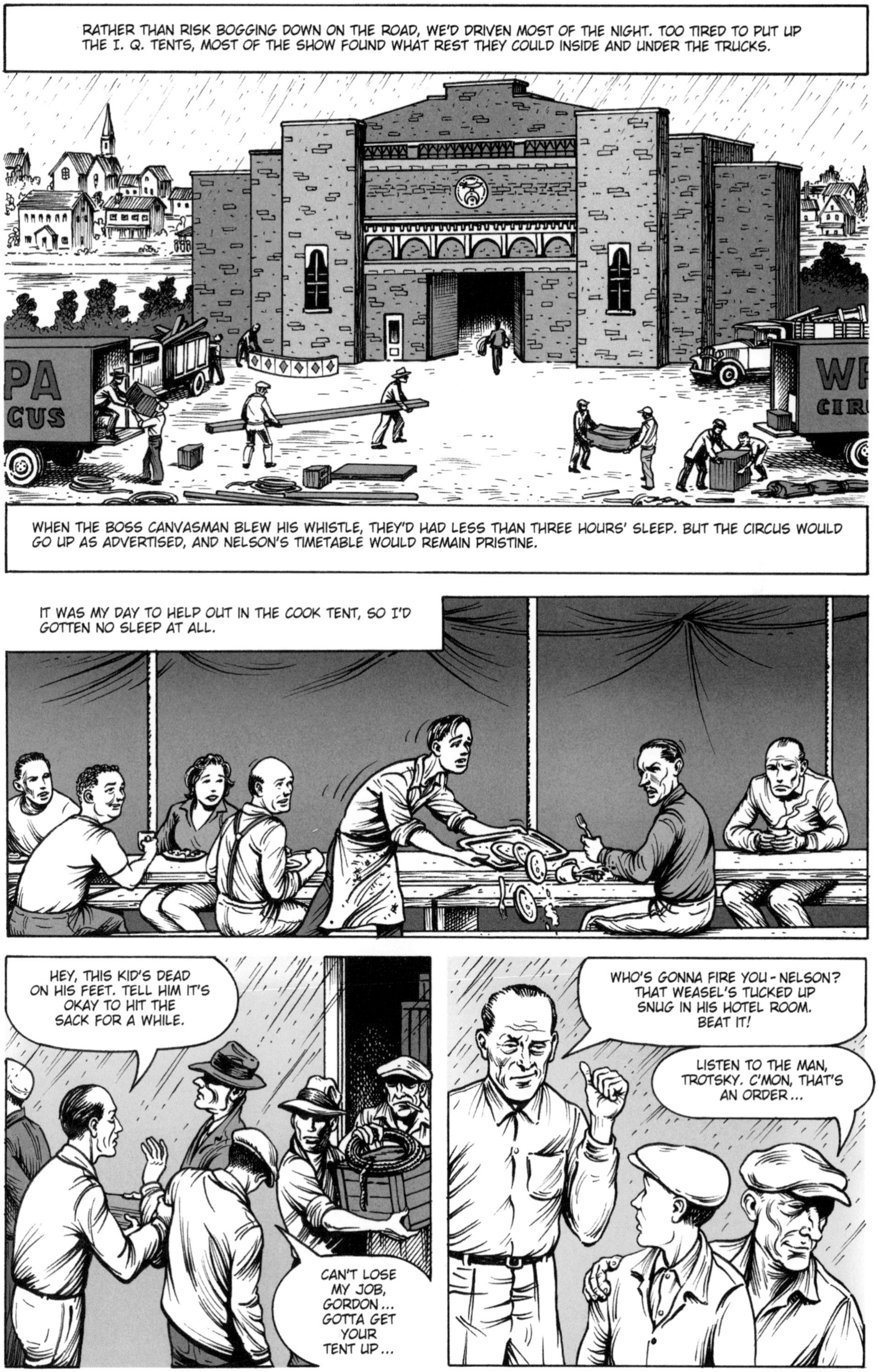
RATHER THAN RISK BOGGING DOWN ON THE ROAD, WE'D DRIVEN MOST OF THE NIGHT. TOO TIRED TO PUT UP THE I. Q. TENTS, MOST OF THE SHOW FOUND WHAT REST THEY COULD INSIDE AND UNDER THE TRUCKS.
WPA CIRCUS
WHEN THE BOSS CANVASMAN BLEW HIS WHISTLE, THEY'D HAD LESS THAN THREE HOURS' SLEEP. BUT THE CIRCUS WOULD GO UP AS ADVERTISED, AND NELSON'S TIMETABLE WOULD REMAIN PRISTINE.
IT WAS MY DAY TO HELP OUT IN THE COOK TENT, SO I'D GOTTEN NO SLEEP AT ALL.
HEY, THIS KID'S DEAD ON HIS FEET. TELL HIM IT'S OKAY TO HIT THE SACK FOR A WHILE.
CAN'T LOSE MY JOB, GORDON... GOTTA GET YOUR TENT UP...
WHO'S GONNA FIRE YOU - NELSON? THAT WEASEL'S TUCKED UP SNUG IN HIS HOTEL ROOM. BEAT IT!
LISTEN TO THE MAN, TROTSKY. C'MON, THAT'S AN ORDER...

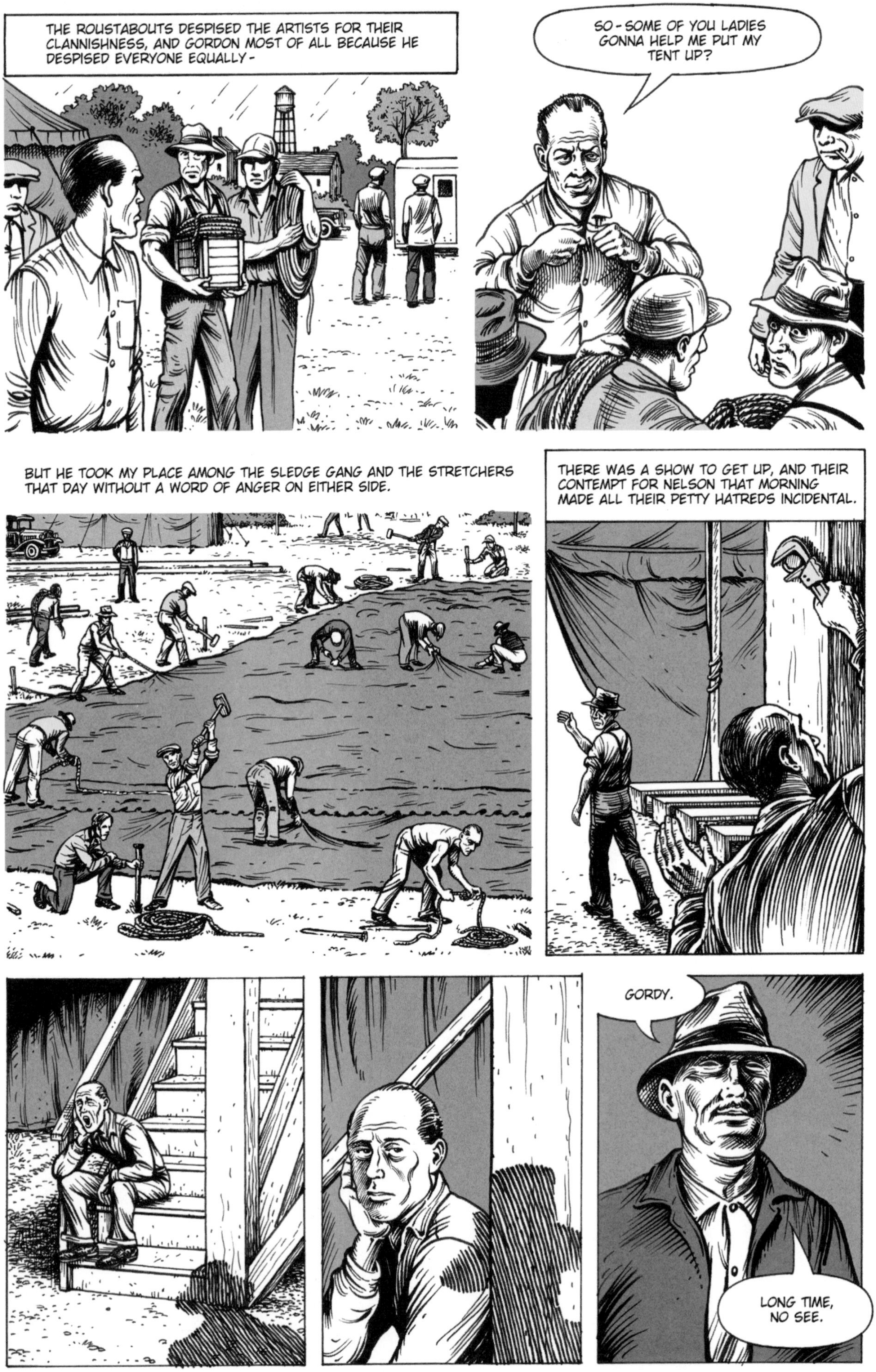
THE ROUSTABOUTS DESPISED THE ARTISTS FOR THEIR CLANNISHNESS, AND GORDON MOST OF ALL BECAUSE HE DESPISED EVERYONE EQUALLY-
SO - SOME OF YOU LADIES GONNA HELP ME PUT MY TENT UP?
BUT HE TOOK MY PLACE AMONG THE SLEDGE GANG AND THE STRETCHERS THAT DAY WITHOUT A WORD OF ANGER ON EITHER SIDE.
THERE WAS A SHOW TO GET UP, AND THEIR CONTEMPT FOR NELSON THAT MORNING MADE ALL THEIR PETTY HATREDS INCIDENTAL.
GORDY.
LONG TIME, NO SEE.

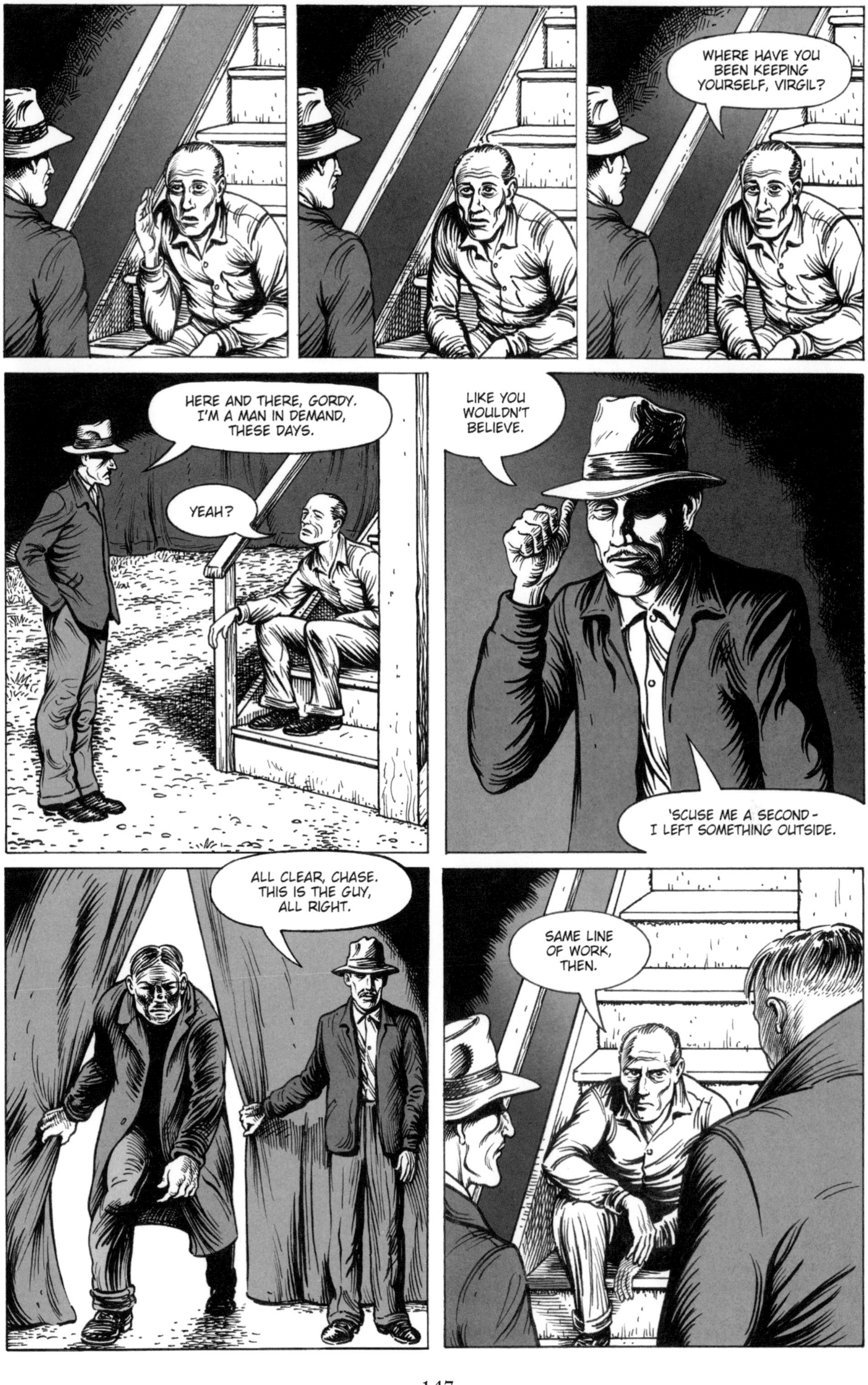
WHERE HAVE YOU BEEN KEEPING YOURSELF, VIRGIL?
HERE AND THERE, GORDY. I'M A MAN IN DEMAND, THESE DAYS.
YEAH?
LIKE YOU WOULDN'T BELIEVE.
'SCUSE ME A SECOND - I LEFT SOMETHING OUTSIDE.
ALL CLEAR, CHASE. THIS IS THE GUY, ALL RIGHT.
SAME LINE OF WORK, THEN.

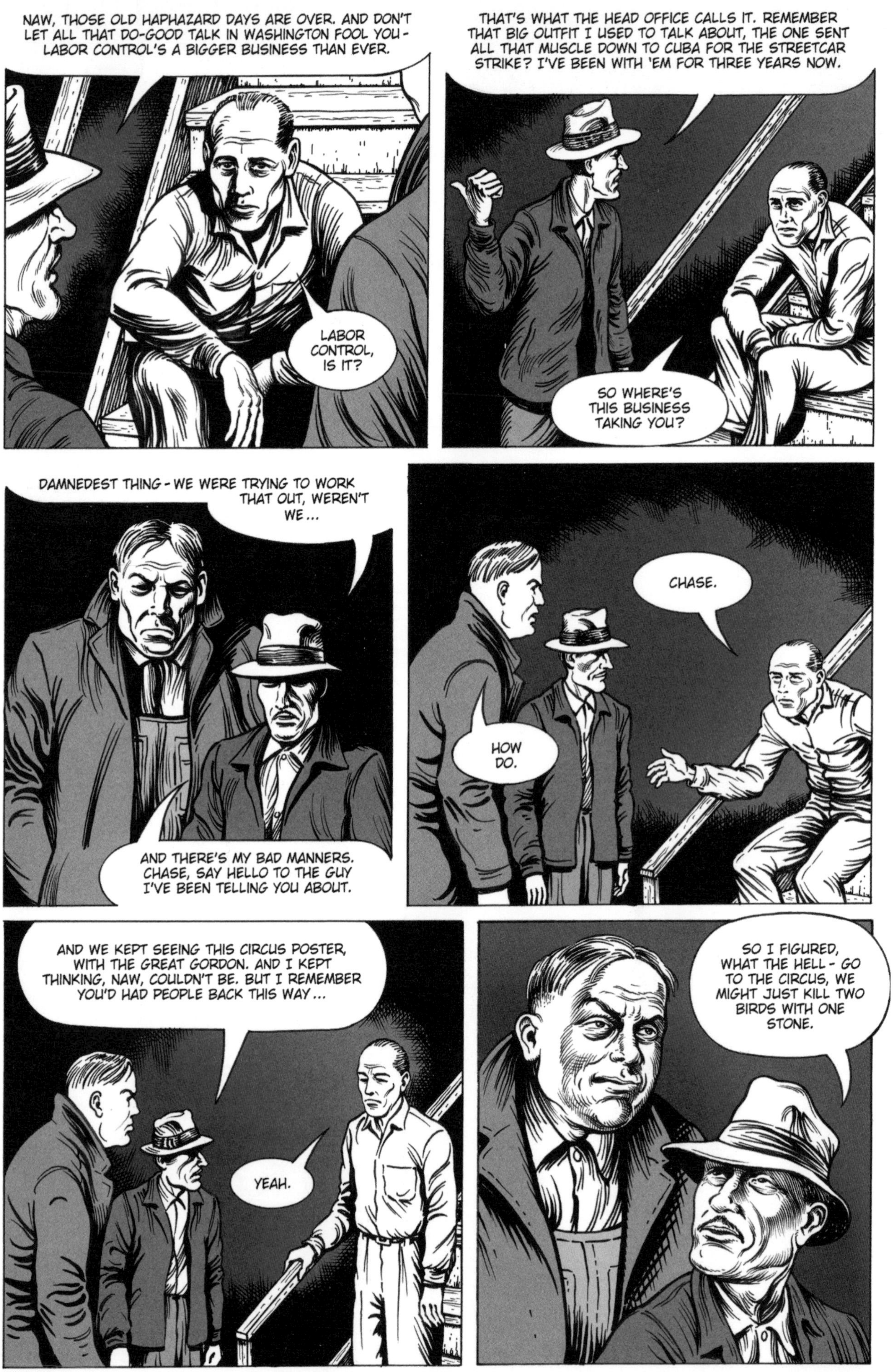
NAW, THOSE OLD HAPHAZARD DAYS ARE OVER. AND DON'T LET ALL THAT DO-GOOD TALK IN WASHINGTON FOOL YOU - LABOR CONTROL'S A BIGGER BUSINESS THAN EVER.
LABOR CONTROL, IS IT?
THAT'S WHAT THE HEAD OFFICE CALLS IT. REMEMBER THAT BIG OUTFIT I USED TO TALK ABOUT, THE ONE SENT ALL THAT MUSCLE DOWN TO CUBA FOR THE STREETCAR STRIKE? I'VE BEEN WITH 'EM FOR THREE YEARS NOW.
SO WHERE'S THIS BUSINESS TAKING YOU?
DAMNEDEST THING - WE WERE TRYING TO WORK THAT OUT, WEREN'T WE...
AND THERE'S MY BAD MANNERS. CHASE, SAY HELLO TO THE GUY I'VE BEEN TELLING YOU ABOUT.
CHASE.
HOW DO.
AND WE KEPT SEEING THIS CIRCUS POSTER, WITH THE GREAT GORDON. AND I KEPT THINKING, NAW, COULDN'T BE. BUT I REMEMBER YOU'D HAD PEOPLE BACK THIS WAY...
YEAH.
SO I FIGURED, WHAT THE HELL - GO TO THE CIRCUS, WE MIGHT JUST KILL TWO BIRDS WITH ONE STONE.

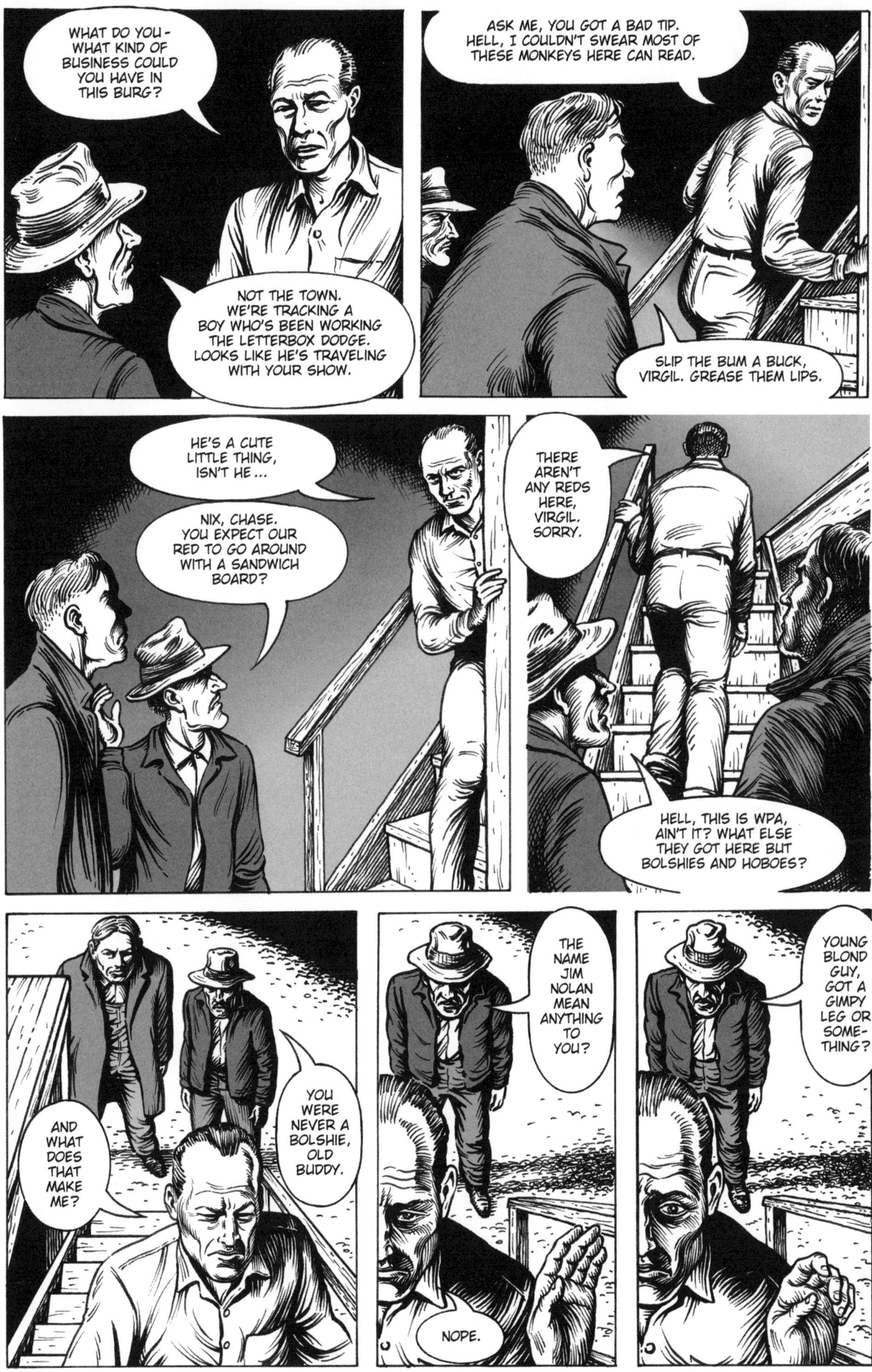
WHAT DO YOU - WHAT KIND OF BUSINESS COULD YOU HAVE IN THIS BURG?
NOT THE TOWN. WE'RE TRACKING A BOY WHO'S BEEN WORKING THE LETTERBOX DODGE. LOOKS LIKE HE'S TRAVELING WITH YOUR SHOW.
ASK ME, YOU GOT A BAD TIP. HELL, I COULDN'T SWEAR MOST OF THESE MONKEYS HERE CAN READ.
SLIP THE BUM A BUCK, VIRGIL. GREASE THEM LIPS.
HE'S A CUTE LITTLE THING, ISN'T HE...
NIX, CHASE. YOU EXPECT OUR RED TO GO AROUND WITH A SANDWICH BOARD?
THERE AREN'T ANY REDS HERE, VIRGIL. SORRY.
HELL, THIS IS WPA, AIN'T IT? WHAT ELSE THEY GOT HERE BUT BOLSHIES AND HOBOES?
YOU WERE NEVER A BOLSHIE, OLD BUDDY.
AND WHAT DOES THAT MAKE ME?
THE NAME JIM NOLAN MEAN ANYTHING TO YOU?
NOPE.
YOUNG BLOND GUY, GOT A GIMPY LEG OR SOME-THING?

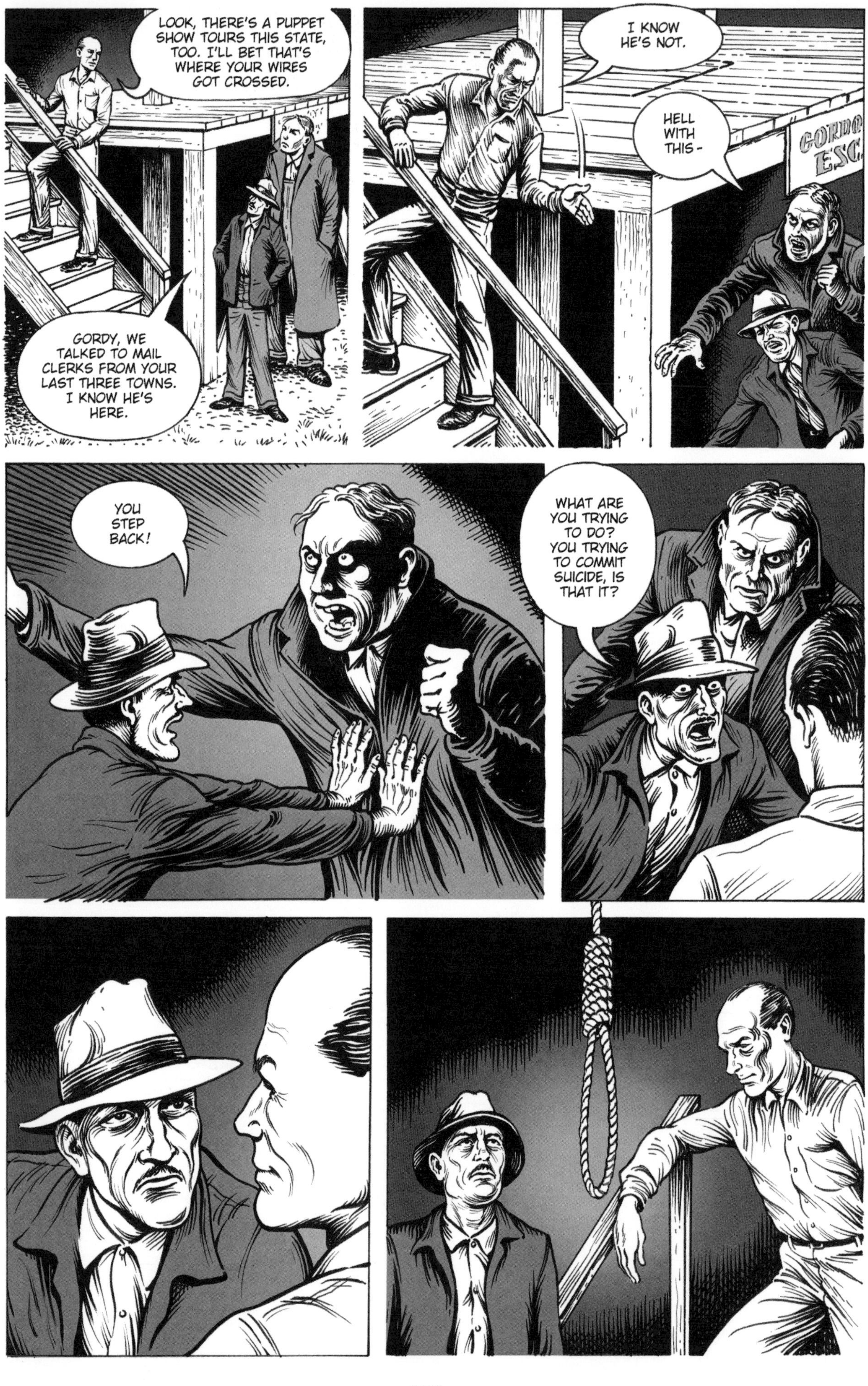
LOOK, THERE'S A PUPPET SHOW TOURS THIS STATE, TOO. I'LL BET THAT'S WHERE YOUR WIRES GOT CROSSED.
GORDY, WE TALKED TO MAIL CLERKS FROM YOUR LAST THREE TOWNS. I KNOW HE'S HERE.
I KNOW HE'S NOT.
HELL WITH THIS -
GORDO
ESC.
YOU STEP BACK!
WHAT ARE YOU TRYING TO DO? YOU TRYING TO COMMIT SUICIDE, IS THAT IT?

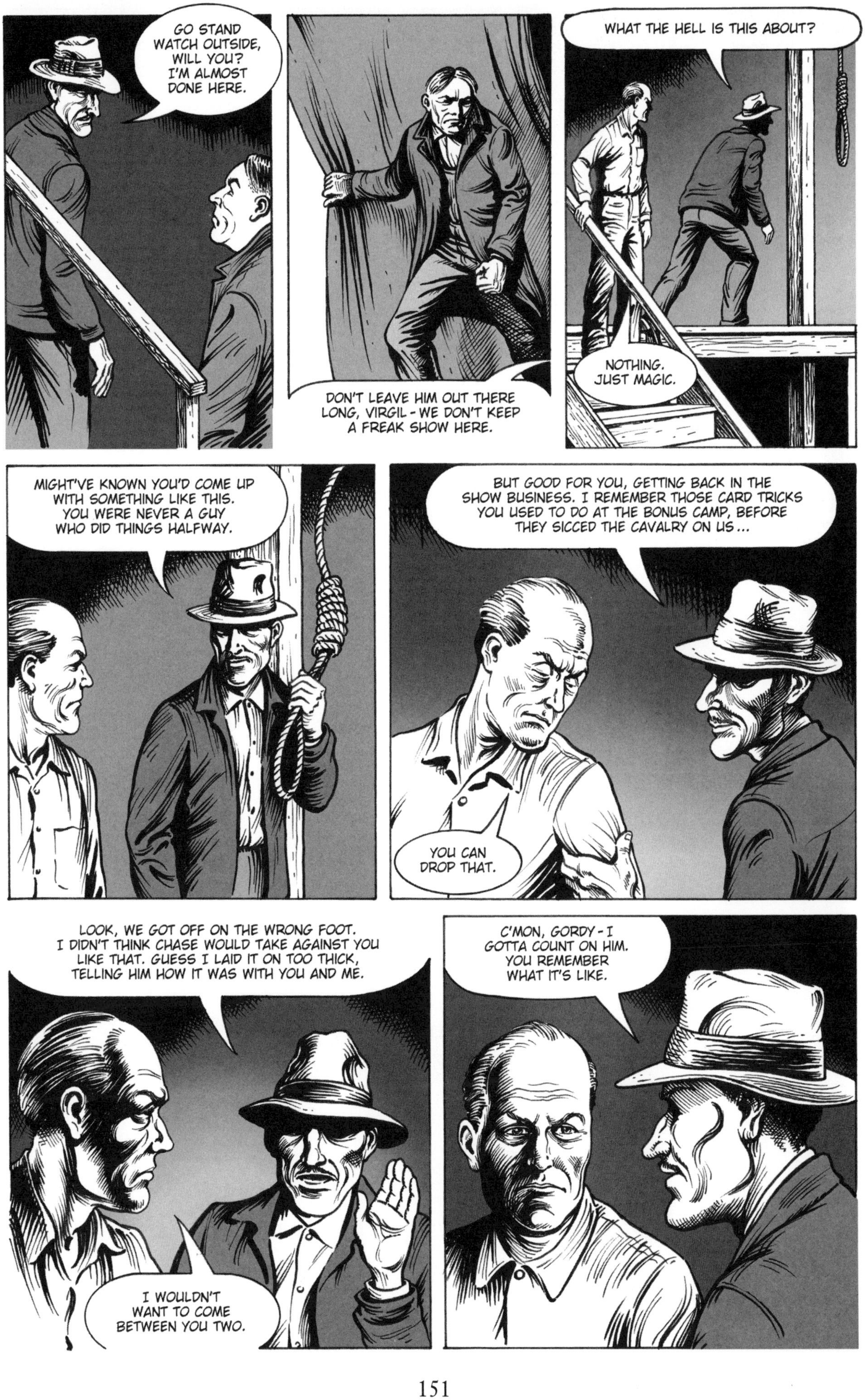
GO STAND WATCH OUTSIDE, WILL YOU? I'M ALMOST DONE HERE.
DON'T LEAVE HIM OUT THERE LONG, VIRGIL - WE DON'T KEEP A FREAK SHOW HERE.
WHAT THE HELL IS THIS ABOUT?
NOTHING. JUST MAGIC.
MIGHT'VE KNOWN YOU'D COME UP WITH SOMETHING LIKE THIS. YOU WERE NEVER A GUY WHO DID THINGS HALFWAY.
BUT GOOD FOR YOU, GETTING BACK IN THE SHOW BUSINESS. I REMEMBER THOSE CARD TRICKS YOU USED TO DO AT THE BONUS CAMP, BEFORE THEY SICCED THE CAVALRY ON US ...
YOU CAN DROP THAT.
LOOK, WE GOT OFF ON THE WRONG FOOT. I DIDN'T THINK CHASE WOULD TAKE AGAINST YOU LIKE THAT. GUESS I LAID IT ON TOO THICK, TELLING HIM HOW IT WAS WITH YOU AND ME.
I WOULDN'T WANT TO COME BETWEEN YOU TWO.
C'MON, GORDY - I GOTTA COUNT ON HIM. YOU REMEMBER WHAT IT'S LIKE.

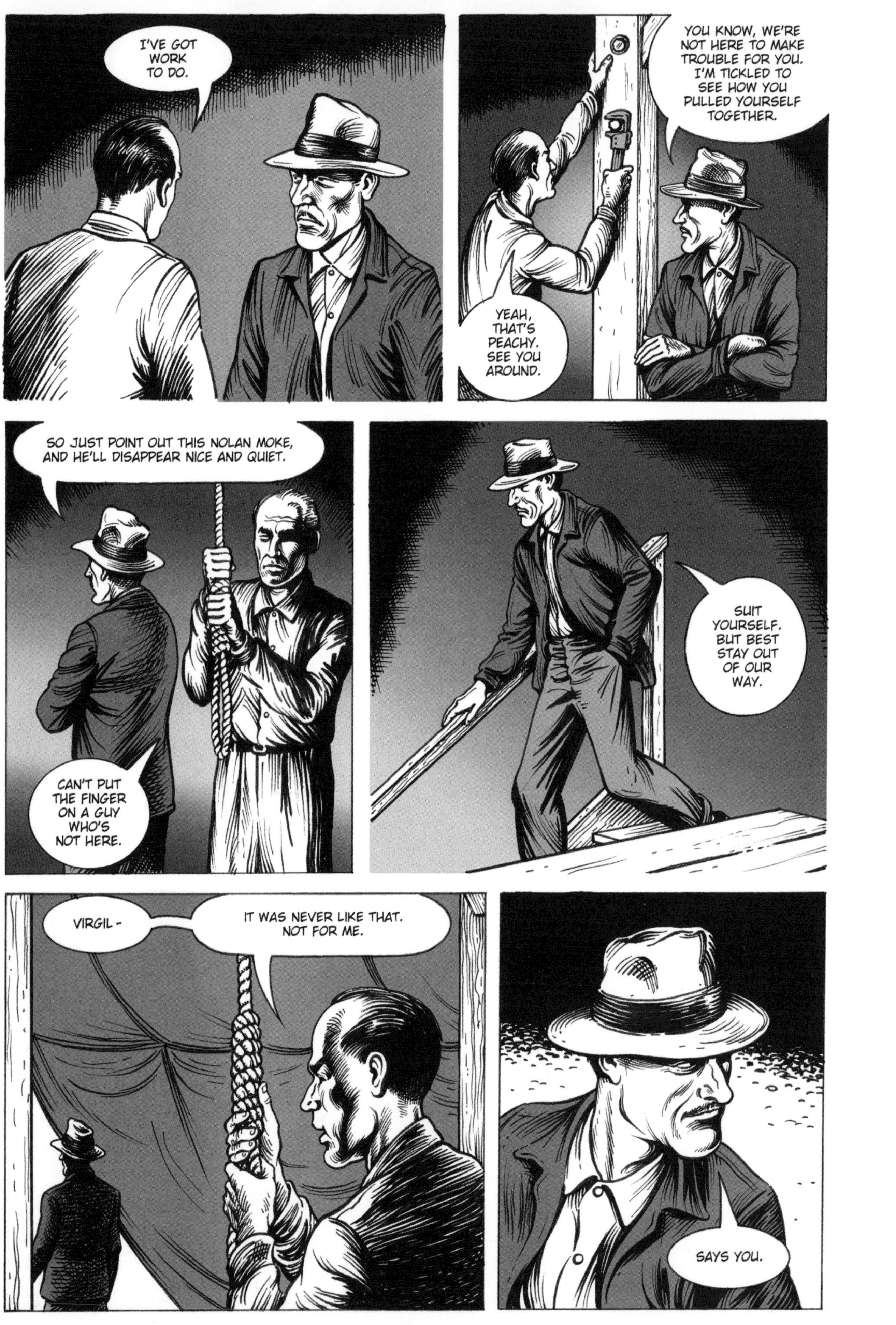
I'VE GOT WORK TO DO.
YOU KNOW, WE'RE NOT HERE TO MAKE TROUBLE FOR YOU. I'M TICKLED TO SEE HOW YOU PULLED YOURSELF TOGETHER.
YEAH, THAT'S PEACHY. SEE YOU AROUND.
SO JUST POINT OUT THIS NOLAN MOKE, AND HE'LL DISAPPEAR NICE AND QUIET.
CAN'T PUT THE FINGER ON A GUY WHO'S NOT HERE.
SUIT YOURSELF. BUT BEST STAY OUT OF OUR WAY.
VIRGIL -
IT WAS NEVER LIKE THAT. NOT FOR ME.
SAYS YOU.

LET'S GO. C'MON, WE'RE PACKING YOU OUT OF HERE.
DID WE DO THE SHOW ...?
YOU'RE GOING TO SEE THAT WOMAN, THAT GUIDEBOOK WRITER, LIKE YOU WANTED.
TAKE THIS THING, WILL YOU?
BUT...NO...HOW CAN I...
YOU REMEMBER WHAT EILEEN WAS SAYING ABOUT NELSON CALLING A LAYOVER HERE? YOU GET STUCK IN THIS RUBE STAND, YOU'LL MISS YOUR BIG MEETING.
WAIT-NELSON GAVE THIS THE OKAY?
NELSON WON'T KNOW THE DIFFERENCE. I'LL GET SOMEBODY TO COVER FOR YOU, AND LAUGH UP MY SLEEVE THE WHOLE TIME YOU'RE GONE.
HAVE YOU BEEN, YOU KNOW-
I'M COLD SOBER. AND WE GOTTA DO THIS NOW, WHILE EVERYBODY'S STILL BUSY OUT ON THE LOT.
WHY, GORDON? YOU DIDN'T WANT ME TO GO.
'CAUSE THAT PRISSY LITTLE GINK STEPPED ON MY TOES ONE TIME TOO MANY TODAY. EITHER YOU HELP ME PULL THIS GAG OFF, OR I'LL JUST GO STOMP HIS SPECS AND SET FIRE TO THAT DESK OF HIS.

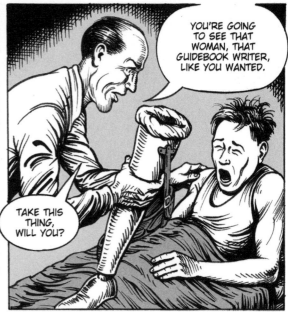

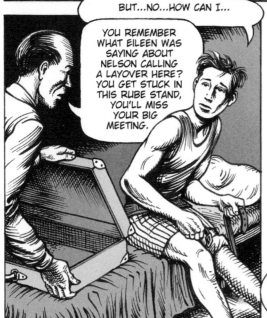

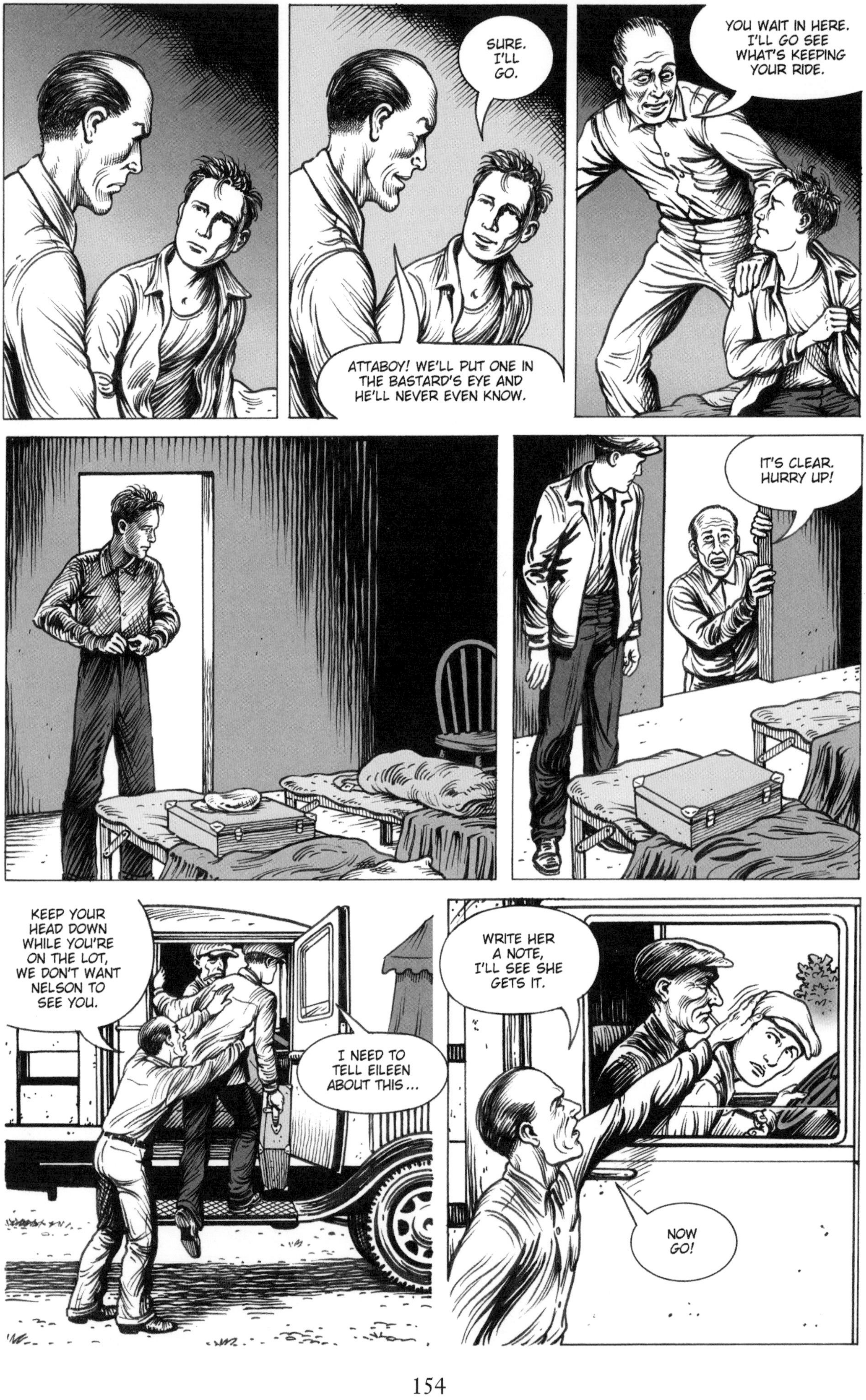
SURE. I'LL GO.
ATTABOY! WE'LL PUT ONE IN THE BASTARD'S EYE AND HE'LL NEVER EVEN KNOW.
YOU WAIT IN HERE. I'LL GO SEE WHAT'S KEEPING YOUR RIDE.
IT'S CLEAR. HURRY UP!
KEEP YOUR HEAD DOWN WHILE YOU'RE ON THE LOT, WE DON'T WANT NELSON TO SEE YOU.
I NEED TO TELL EILEEN ABOUT THIS...
WRITE HER A NOTE, I'LL SEE SHE GETS IT.
NOW GO!

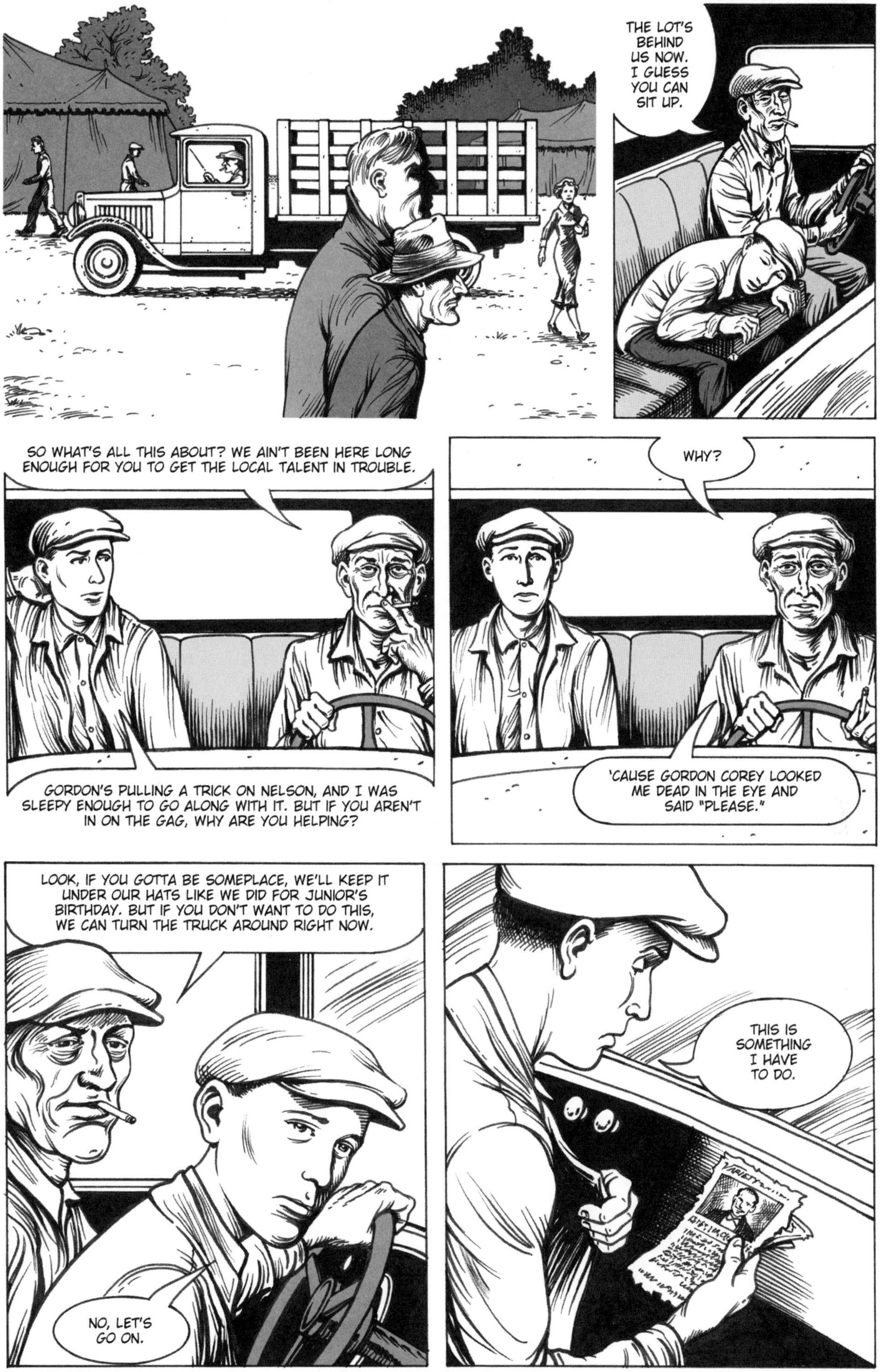
THE LOT'S BEHIND US NOW. I GUESS YOU CAN SIT UP.
SO WHAT'S ALL THIS ABOUT? WE AIN'T BEEN HERE LONG ENOUGH FOR YOU TO GET THE LOCAL TALENT IN TROUBLE.
GORDON'S PULLING A TRICK ON NELSON, AND I WAS SLEEPY ENOUGH TO GO ALONG WITH IT. BUT IF YOU AREN'T IN ON THE GAG, WHY ARE YOU HELPING?
WHY?
'CAUSE GORDON COREY LOOKED ME DEAD IN THE EYE AND SAID "PLEASE."
LOOK, IF YOU GOTTA BE SOMEPLACE, WE'LL KEEP IT UNDER OUR HATS LIKE WE DID FOR JUNIOR'S BIRTHDAY. BUT IF YOU DON'T WANT TO DO THIS, WE CAN TURN THE TRUCK AROUND RIGHT NOW.
NO, LET'S GO ON.
THIS IS SOMETHING I HAVE TO DO.

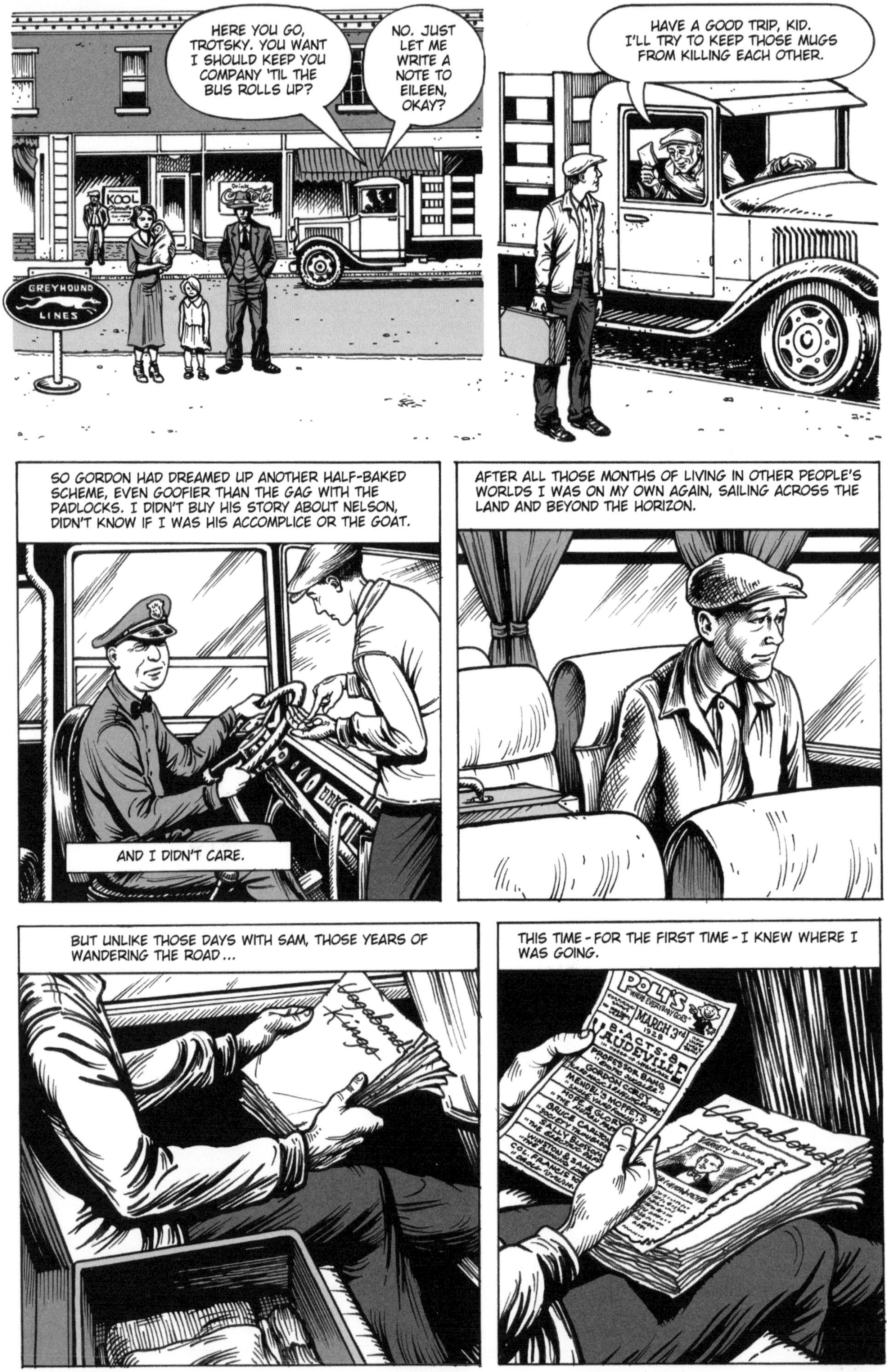

HERE YOU GO, TROTSKY. YOU WANT I SHOULD KEEP YOU COMPANY 'TIL THE BUS ROLLS UP?
NO. JUST LET ME WRITE A NOTE TO EILEEN, OKAY?
GREYHOUND LINES
KOOL
HAVE A GOOD TRIP, KID. I'LL TRY TO KEEP THOSE MUGS FROM KILLING EACH OTHER.
SO GORDON HAD DREAMED UP ANOTHER HALF-BAKED SCHEME, EVEN GOOFIER THAN THE GAG WITH THE PADLOCKS. I DIDN'T BUY HIS STORY ABOUT NELSON, DIDN'T KNOW IF I WAS HIS ACCOMPLICE OR THE GOAT.
AND I DIDN'T CARE.
AFTER ALL THOSE MONTHS OF LIVING IN OTHER PEOPLE'S WORLDS I WAS ON MY OWN AGAIN, SAILING ACROSS THE LAND AND BEYOND THE HORIZON.
BUT UNLIKE THOSE DAYS WITH SAM, THOSE YEARS OF WANDERING THE ROAD...
Vagabond Kings
THIS TIME - FOR THE FIRST TIME - I KNEW WHERE I WAS GOING.
POLI'S
MARCH 3rd 1928
8 ACTS 8 VAUDEVILLE

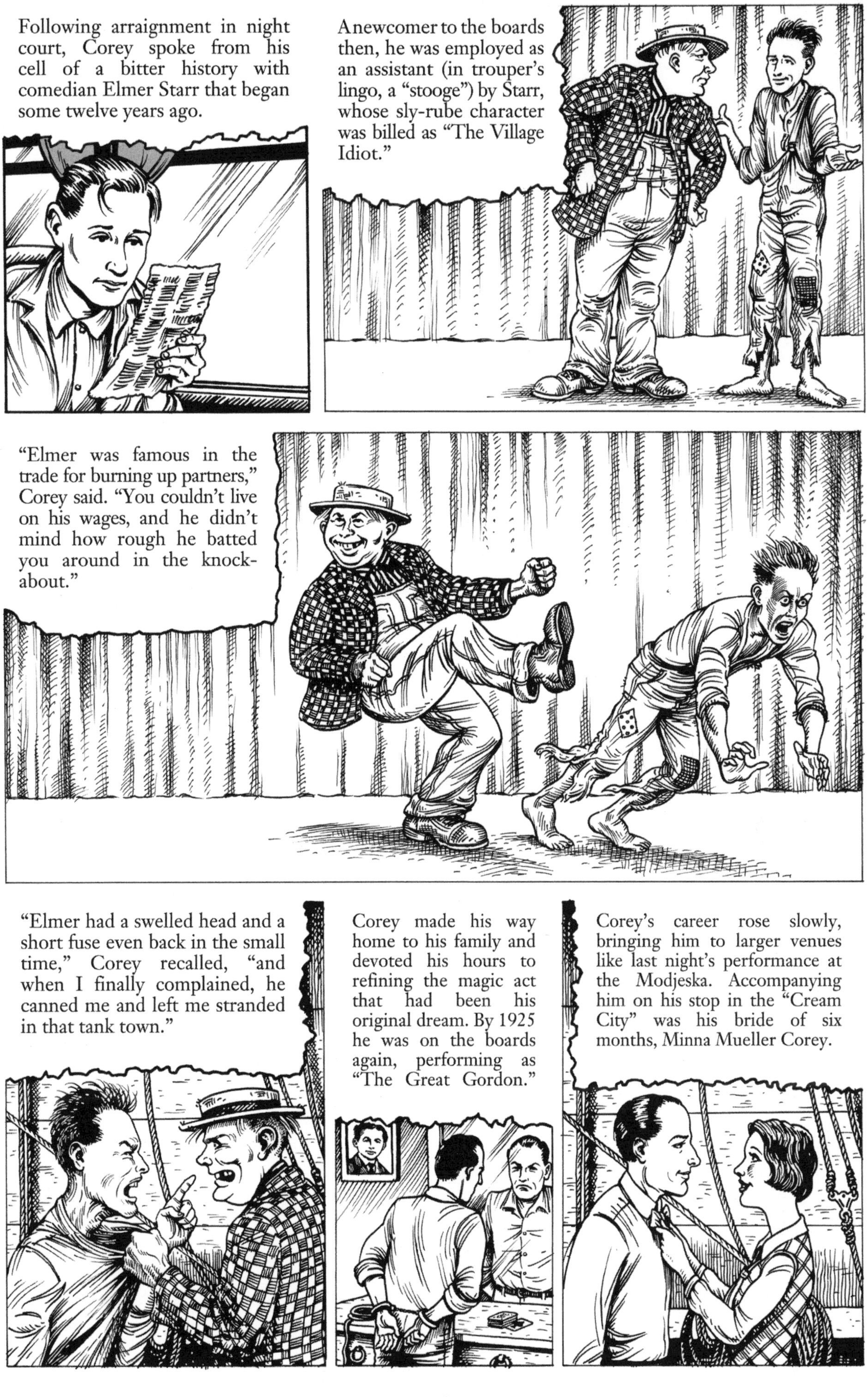
Following arraignment in night court, Corey spoke from his cell of a bitter history with comedian Elmer Starr that began some twelve years ago.
A newcomer to the boards then, he was employed as an assistant (in trouper's lingo, a "stooge") by Starr, whose sly-rube character was billed as "The Village Idiot."
"Elmer was famous in the trade for burning up partners," Corey said. "You couldn't live on his wages, and he didn't mind how rough he batted you around in the knock-about."
"Elmer had a swelled head and a short fuse even back in the small time," Corey recalled, "and when I finally complained, he canned me and left me stranded in that tank town."
Corey made his way home to his family and devoted his hours to refining the magic act that had been his original dream. By 1925 he was on the boards again, performing as "The Great Gordon."
Corey's career rose slowly, bringing him to larger venues like last night's performance at the Modjeska. Accompanying him on his stop in the "Cream City" was his bride of six months, Minna Mueller Corey.

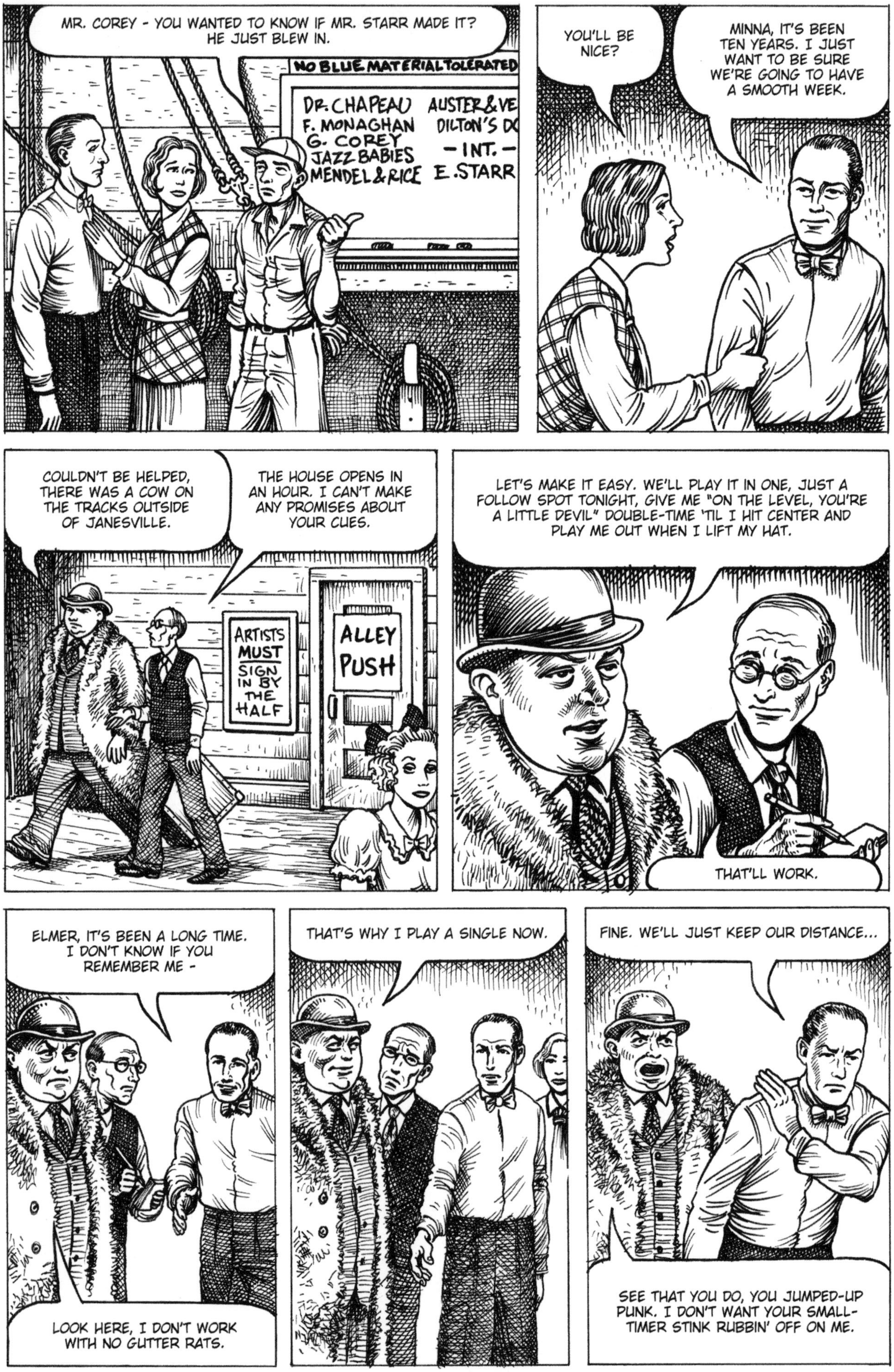
MR. COREY - YOU WANTED TO KNOW IF MR. STARR MADE IT? HE JUST BLEW IN.
NO BLUE MATERIAL TOLERATED
DR. CHAPEAU
F. MONAGHAN
G. COREY
JAZZ BABIES
MENDEL & RICE
AUSTER & VE
DILTON'S DO
- INT. -
E. STARR
YOU'LL BE NICE?
MINNA, IT'S BEEN TEN YEARS. I JUST WANT TO BE SURE WE'RE GOING TO HAVE A SMOOTH WEEK.
COULDN'T BE HELPED, THERE WAS A COW ON THE TRACKS OUTSIDE OF JANESVILLE.
THE HOUSE OPENS IN AN HOUR. I CAN'T MAKE ANY PROMISES ABOUT YOUR CUES.
ARTISTS MUST SIGN IN BY THE HALF
ALLEY PUSH
LET'S MAKE IT EASY. WE'LL PLAY IT IN ONE, JUST A FOLLOW SPOT TONIGHT, GIVE ME "ON THE LEVEL, YOU'RE A LITTLE DEVIL" DOUBLE-TIME 'TIL I HIT CENTER AND PLAY ME OUT WHEN I LIFT MY HAT.
THAT'LL WORK.
ELMER, IT'S BEEN A LONG TIME. I DON'T KNOW IF YOU REMEMBER ME -
LOOK HERE, I DON'T WORK WITH NO GUTTER RATS.
THAT'S WHY I PLAY A SINGLE NOW.
FINE. WE'LL JUST KEEP OUR DISTANCE...
SEE THAT YOU DO, YOU JUMPED-UP PUNK. I DON'T WANT YOUR SMALL-TIMER STINK RUBBIN' OFF ON ME.

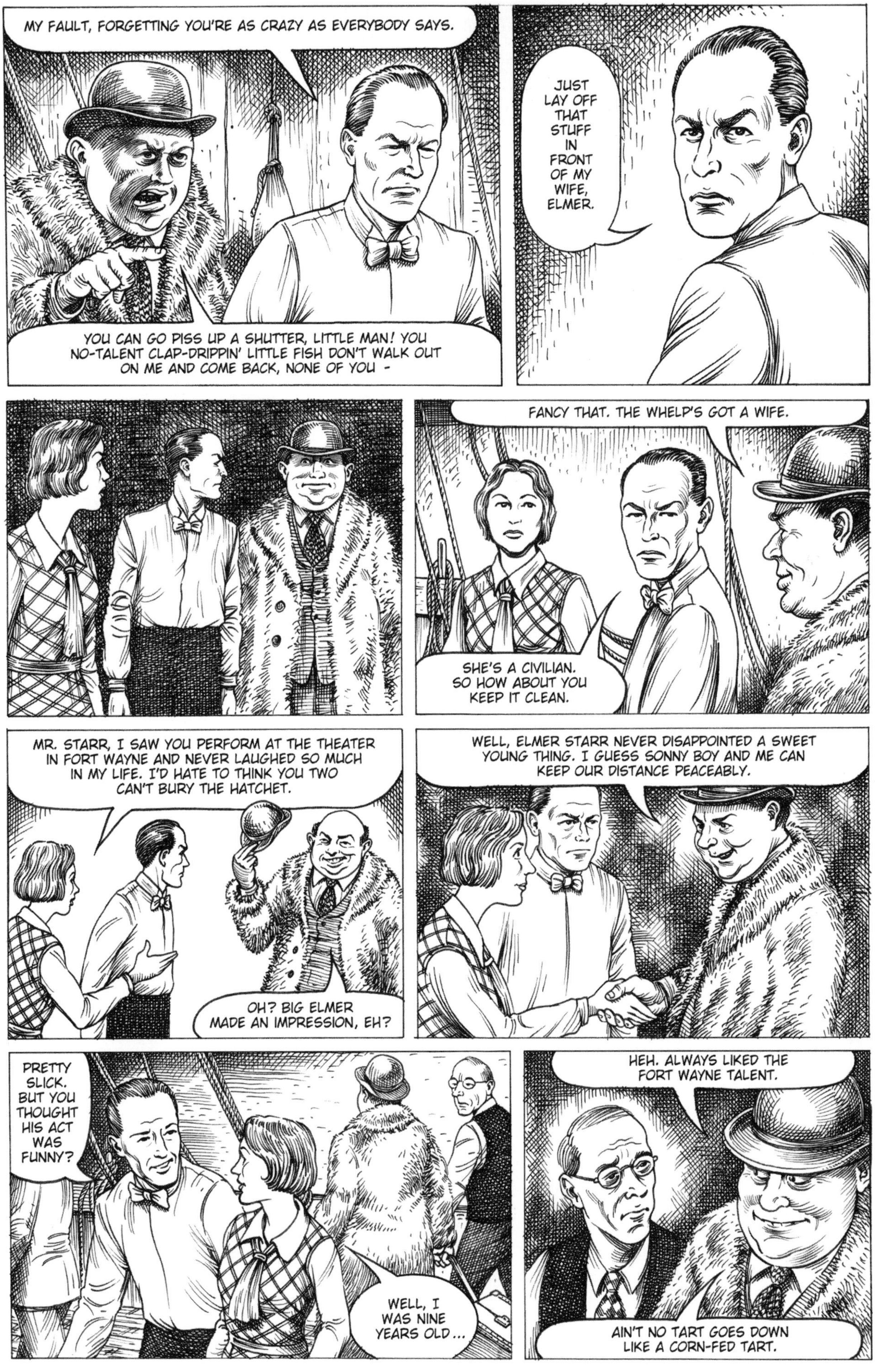
MY FAULT, FORGETTING YOU'RE AS CRAZY AS EVERYBODY SAYS.
YOU CAN GO PISS UP A SHUTTER, LITTLE MAN! YOU NO-TALENT CLAP-DRIPPIN' LITTLE FISH DON'T WALK OUT ON ME AND COME BACK, NONE OF YOU -
JUST LAY OFF THAT STUFF IN FRONT OF MY WIFE, ELMER.
FANCY THAT. THE WHELP'S GOT A WIFE.
SHE'S A CIVILIAN. SO HOW ABOUT YOU KEEP IT CLEAN.
MR. STARR, I SAW YOU PERFORM AT THE THEATER IN FORT WAYNE AND NEVER LAUGHED SO MUCH IN MY LIFE. I'D HATE TO THINK YOU TWO CAN'T BURY THE HATCHET.
OH? BIG ELMER MADE AN IMPRESSION, EH?
WELL, ELMER STARR NEVER DISAPPOINTED A SWEET YOUNG THING. I GUESS SONNY BOY AND ME CAN KEEP OUR DISTANCE PEACEABLY.
PRETTY SLICK. BUT YOU THOUGHT HIS ACT WAS FUNNY?
WELL, I WAS NINE YEARS OLD...
HEH. ALWAYS LIKED THE FORT WAYNE TALENT.
AIN'T NO TART GOES DOWN LIKE A CORN-FED TART.

"The week started out fine," Corey continued. "I even wowed them at the matinees. Management was happy, the customers were clapping…

"and I had my doll in the wings."

"The few times I saw Elmer backstage, we cut each other dead. That was the first time I'd ever known him to keep his word, so it was okay by me."

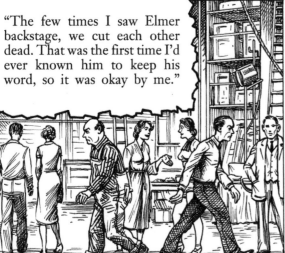

In his cell, Corey fell silent. After a moment's reflection, he continued more somberly:

"Minna got quieter and quieter after the first couple of days, but I wasn't paying attention. I was too d—d full of myself."

"In the three months we'd been married, she'd hardly ever missed a show. Near the end of the week she started staying in the dressing room."

"Tonight my swelled head got the better of me. After I'd finished my turn, I got tough and made her tell me what was eating her."

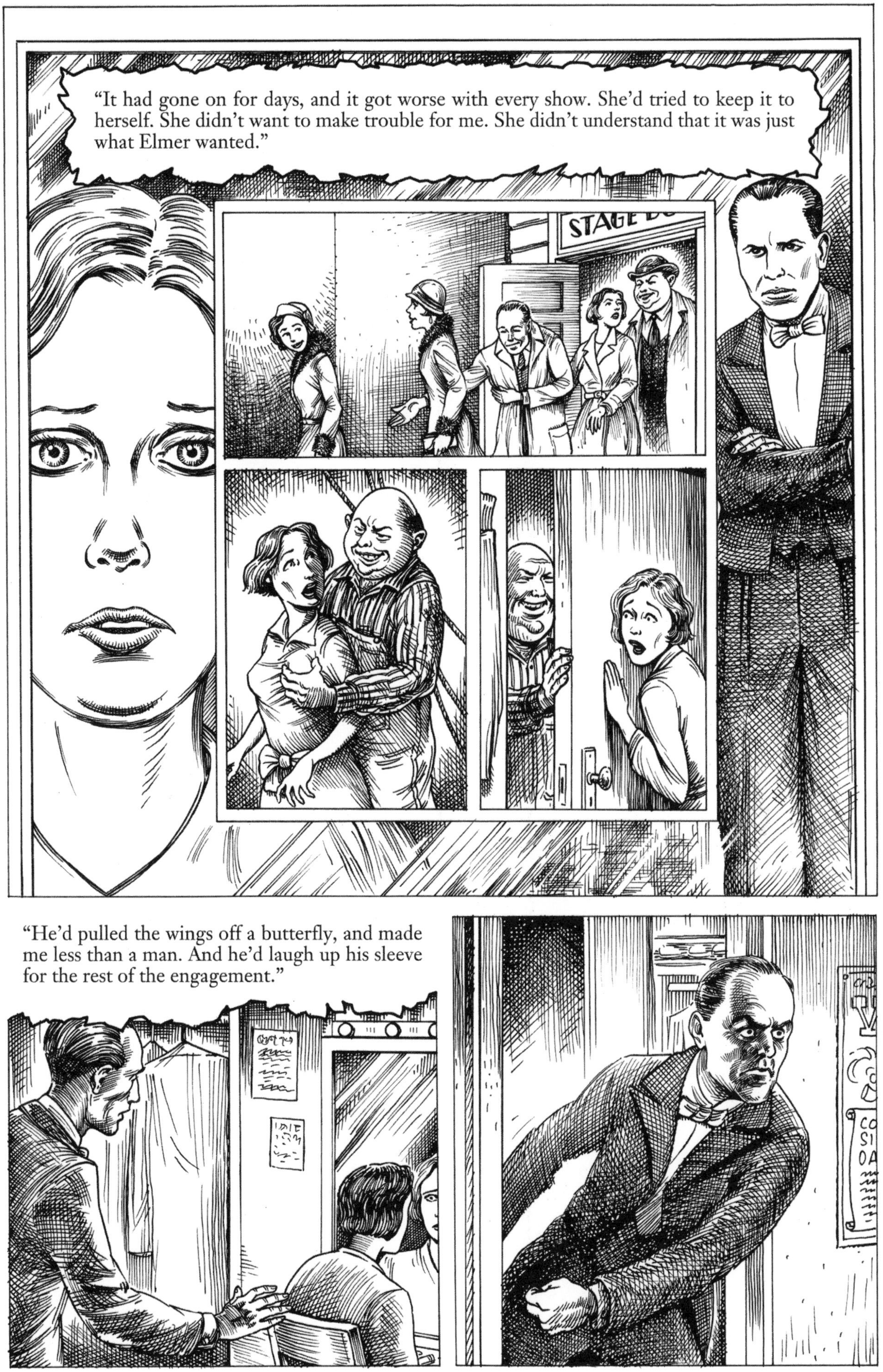
"It had gone on for days, and it got worse with every show. She'd tried to keep it to herself. She didn't want to make trouble for me. She didn't understand that it was just what Elmer wanted."
STAGE
"He'd pulled the wings off a butterfly, and made me less than a man. And he'd laugh up his sleeve for the rest of the engagement."

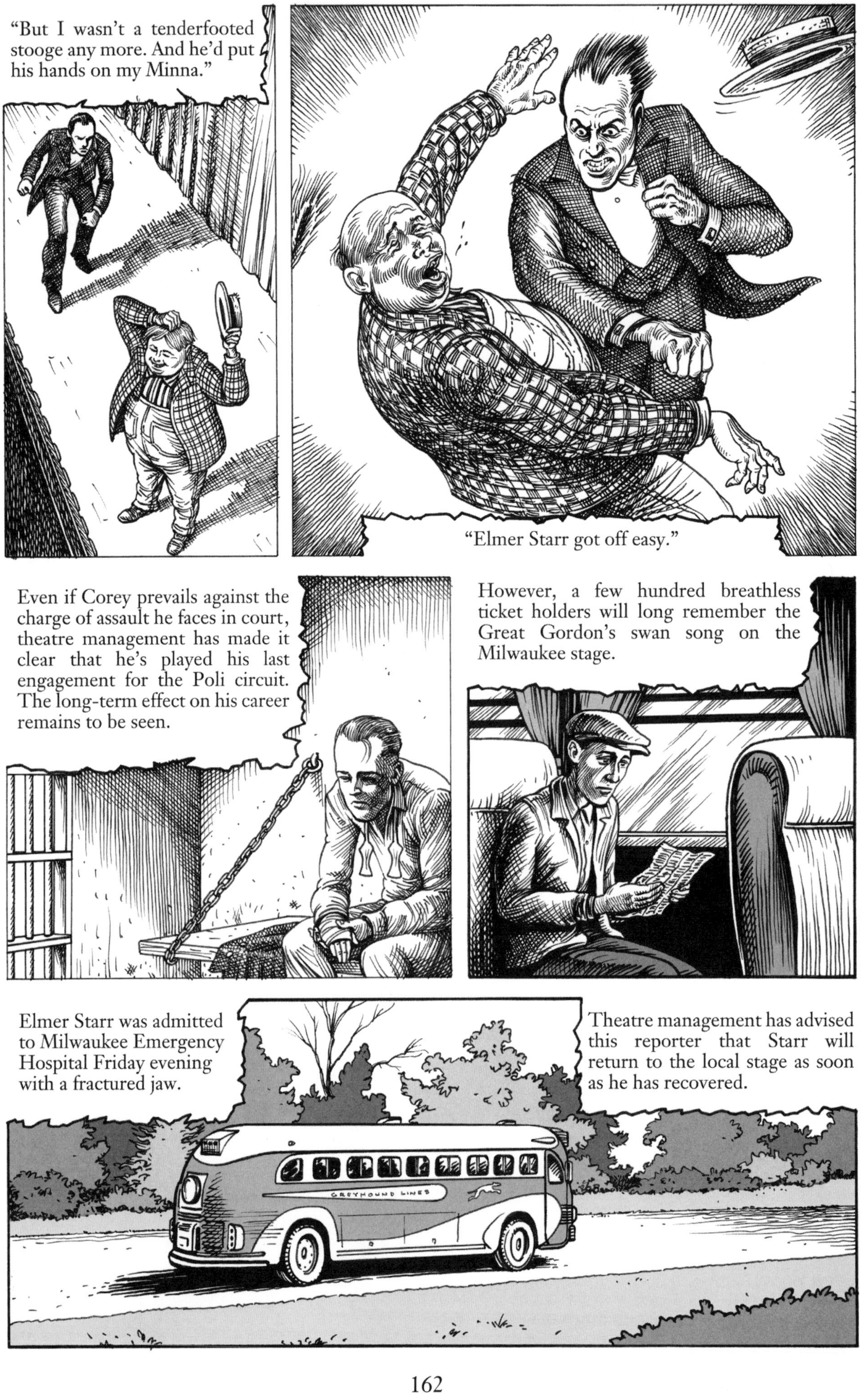
"But I wasn't a tenderfooted stooge any more. And he'd put his hands on my Minna."
"Elmer Starr got off easy."
Even if Corey prevails against the charge of assault he faces in court, theatre management has made it clear that he's played his last engagement for the Poli circuit. The long-term effect on his career remains to be seen.
However, a few hundred breathless ticket holders will long remember the Great Gordon's swan song on the Milwaukee stage.
Elmer Starr was admitted to Milwaukee Emergency Hospital Friday evening with a fractured jaw.
Theatre management has advised this reporter that Starr will return to the local stage as soon as he has recovered.
GREYHOUND LINES

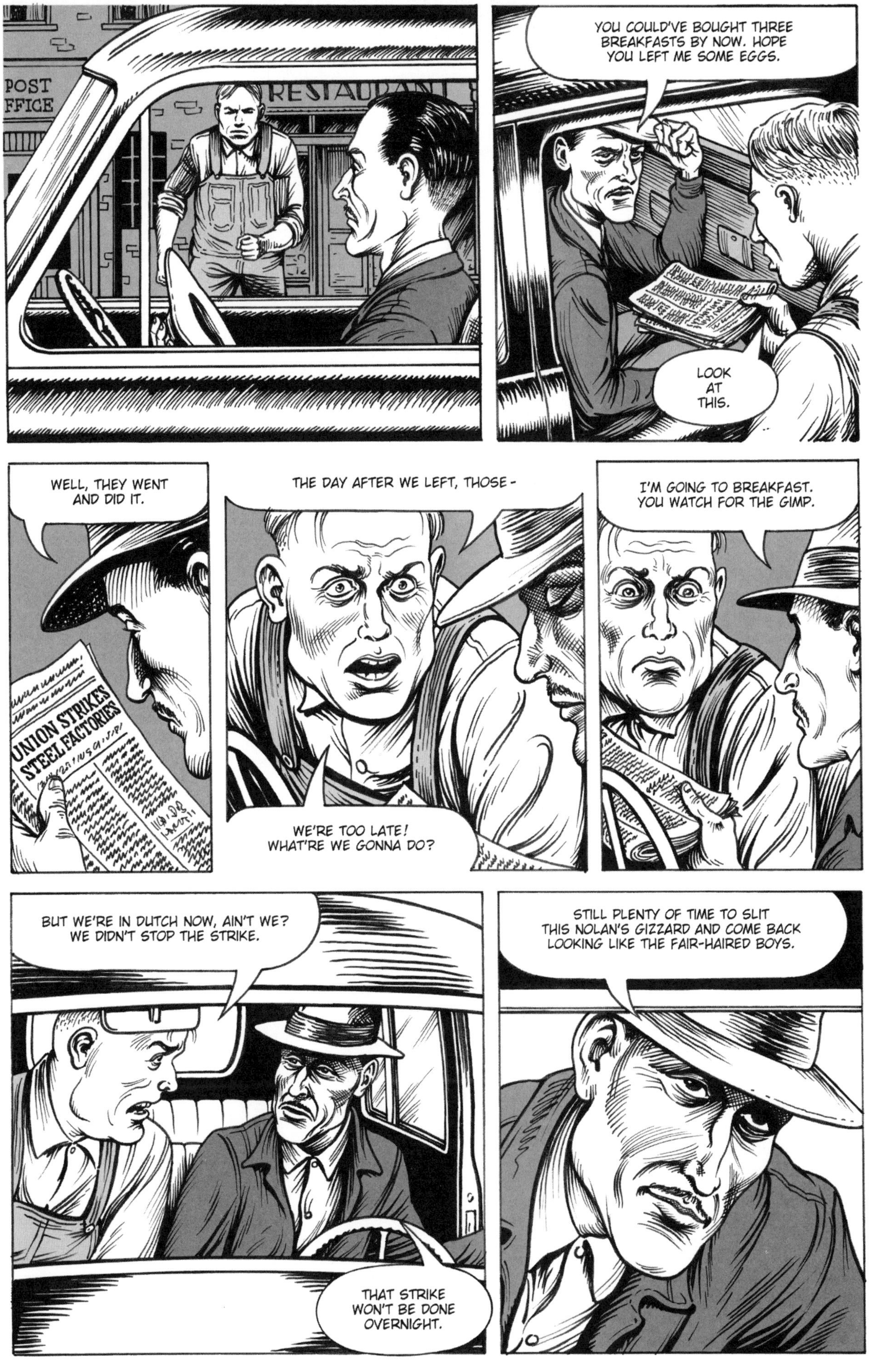
YOU COULD'VE BOUGHT THREE BREAKFASTS BY NOW. HOPE YOU LEFT ME SOME EGGS.
LOOK AT THIS.
WELL, THEY WENT AND DID IT.
UNION STRIKES STEEL FACTORIES
THE DAY AFTER WE LEFT, THOSE -
WE'RE TOO LATE! WHAT'RE WE GONNA DO?
I'M GOING TO BREAKFAST. YOU WATCH FOR THE GIMP.
BUT WE'RE IN DUTCH NOW, AIN'T WE? WE DIDN'T STOP THE STRIKE.
THAT STRIKE WON'T BE DONE OVERNIGHT.
STILL PLENTY OF TIME TO SLIT THIS NOLAN'S GIZZARD AND COME BACK LOOKING LIKE THE FAIR-HAIRED BOYS.

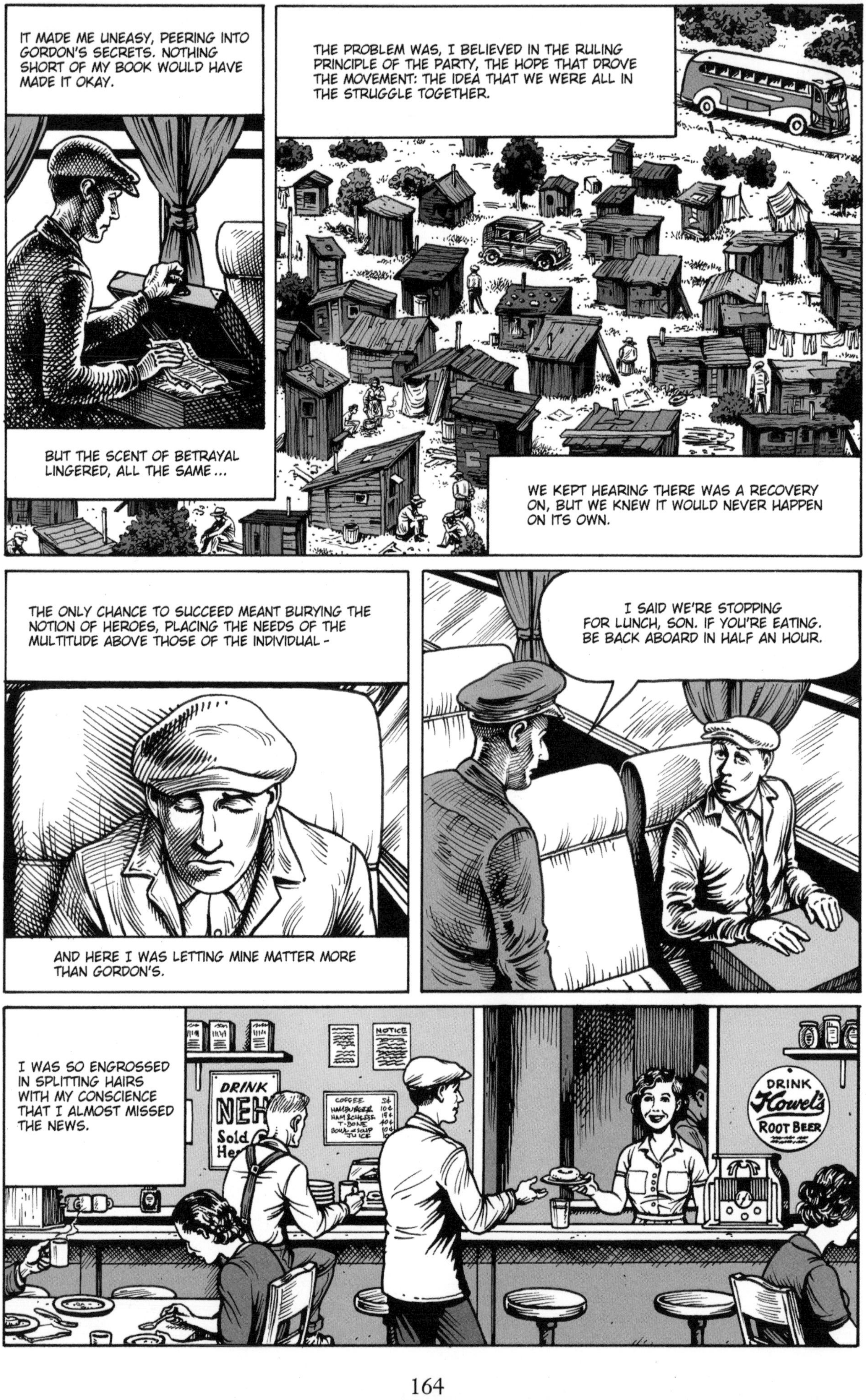
IT MADE ME UNEASY, PEERING INTO GORDON'S SECRETS. NOTHING SHORT OF MY BOOK WOULD HAVE MADE IT OKAY.
BUT THE SCENT OF BETRAYAL LINGERED, ALL THE SAME...
THE PROBLEM WAS, I BELIEVED IN THE RULING PRINCIPLE OF THE PARTY, THE HOPE THAT DROVE THE MOVEMENT: THE IDEA THAT WE WERE ALL IN THE STRUGGLE TOGETHER.
WE KEPT HEARING THERE WAS A RECOVERY ON, BUT WE KNEW IT WOULD NEVER HAPPEN ON ITS OWN.
THE ONLY CHANCE TO SUCCEED MEANT BURYING THE NOTION OF HEROES, PLACING THE NEEDS OF THE MULTITUDE ABOVE THOSE OF THE INDIVIDUAL -
AND HERE I WAS LETTING MINE MATTER MORE THAN GORDON'S.
I SAID WE'RE STOPPING FOR LUNCH, SON. IF YOU'RE EATING. BE BACK ABOARD IN HALF AN HOUR.
I WAS SO ENGROSSED IN SPLITTING HAIRS WITH MY CONSCIENCE THAT I ALMOST MISSED THE NEWS.
NOTICE
DRINK
NEH
Sold
DRINK Howel's ROOT BEER

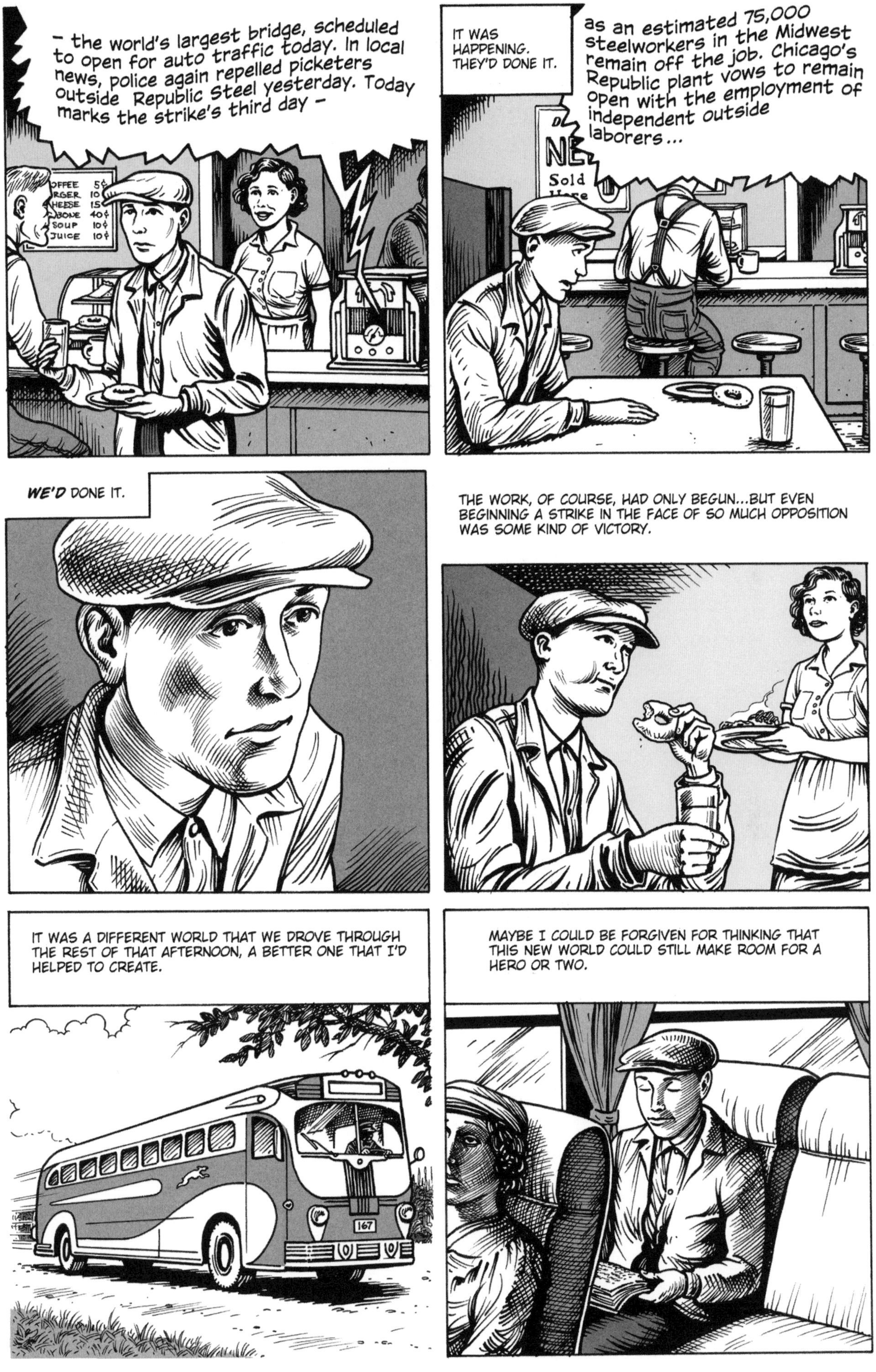
– the world's largest bridge, scheduled to open for auto traffic today. In local news, police again repelled picketers outside Republic Steel yesterday. Today marks the strike's third day –
OFFEE 5¢
RGER 10
HEESE 15
BONE 40¢
SOUP 10¢
JUICE 10¢
IT WAS HAPPENING. THEY'D DONE IT.
as an estimated 75,000 steelworkers in the Midwest remain off the job. Chicago's Republic plant vows to remain open with the employment of independent outside laborers...
Sold
WE'D DONE IT.
THE WORK, OF COURSE, HAD ONLY BEGUN...BUT EVEN BEGINNING A STRIKE IN THE FACE OF SO MUCH OPPOSITION WAS SOME KIND OF VICTORY.
IT WAS A DIFFERENT WORLD THAT WE DROVE THROUGH THE REST OF THAT AFTERNOON, A BETTER ONE THAT I'D HELPED TO CREATE.
167
MAYBE I COULD BE FORGIVEN FOR THINKING THAT THIS NEW WORLD COULD STILL MAKE ROOM FOR A HERO OR TWO.

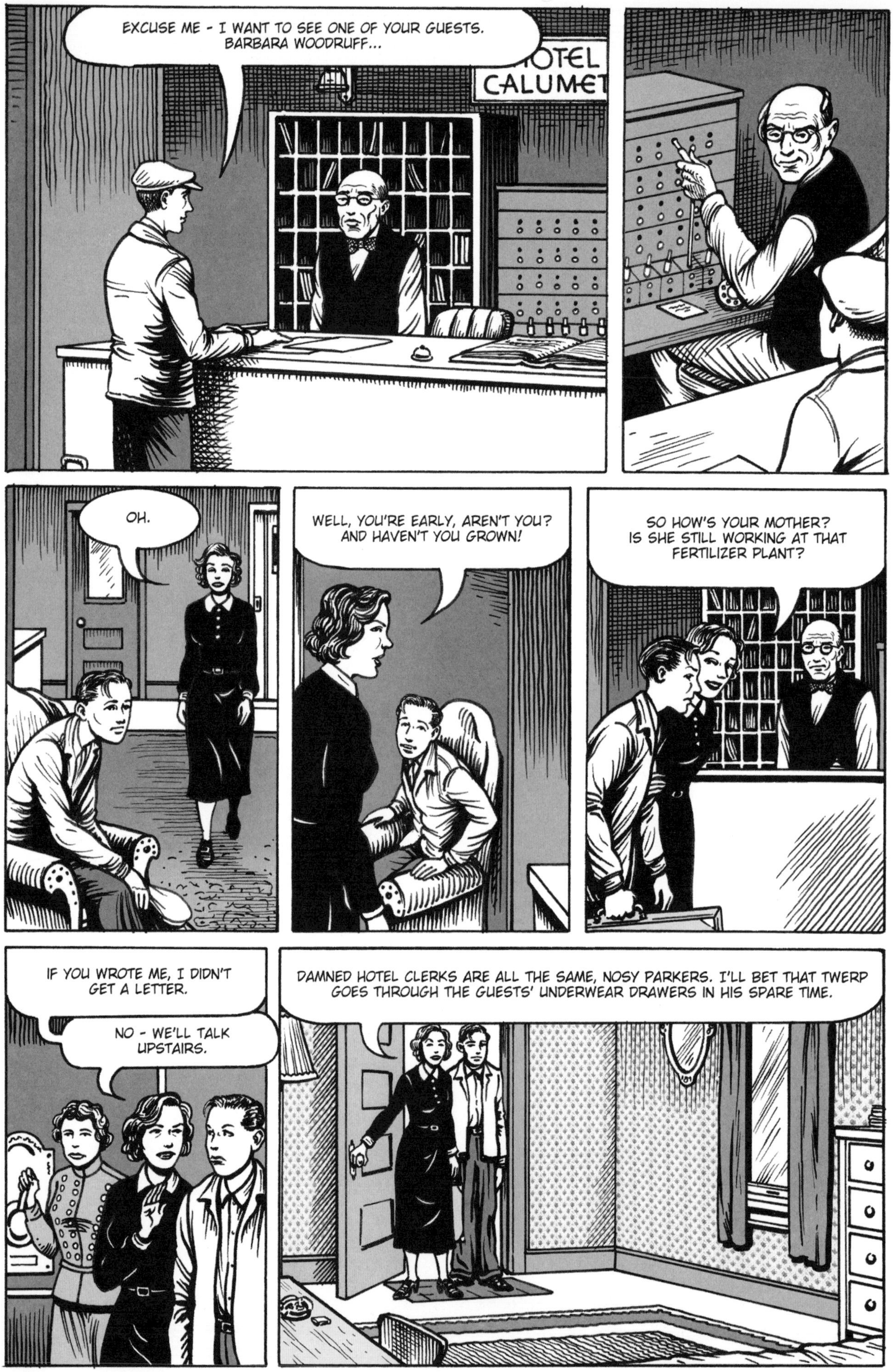
EXCUSE ME - I WANT TO SEE ONE OF YOUR GUESTS. BARBARA WOODRUFF...
HOTEL CALUMET
OH.
WELL, YOU'RE EARLY, AREN'T YOU? AND HAVEN'T YOU GROWN!
SO HOW'S YOUR MOTHER? IS SHE STILL WORKING AT THAT FERTILIZER PLANT?
IF YOU WROTE ME, I DIDN'T GET A LETTER.
NO - WE'LL TALK UPSTAIRS.
DAMNED HOTEL CLERKS ARE ALL THE SAME, NOSY PARKERS. I'LL BET THAT TWERP GOES THROUGH THE GUESTS' UNDERWEAR DRAWERS IN HIS SPARE TIME.

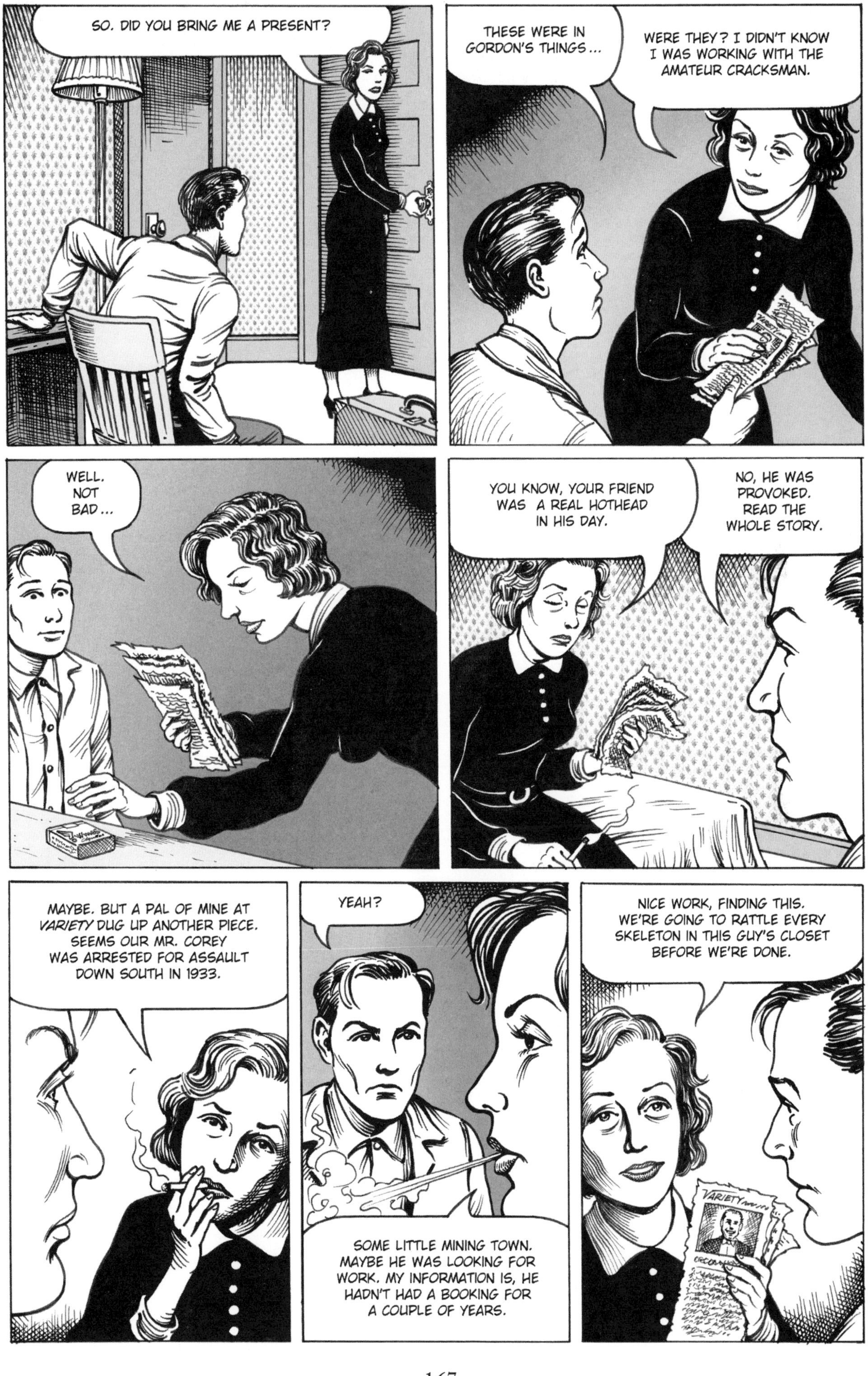
SO. DID YOU BRING ME A PRESENT?
THESE WERE IN GORDON'S THINGS...
WERE THEY? I DIDN'T KNOW I WAS WORKING WITH THE AMATEUR CRACKSMAN.
WELL. NOT BAD...
YOU KNOW, YOUR FRIEND WAS A REAL HOTHEAD IN HIS DAY.
NO, HE WAS PROVOKED. READ THE WHOLE STORY.
MAYBE. BUT A PAL OF MINE AT *VARIETY* DUG UP ANOTHER PIECE. SEEMS OUR MR. COREY WAS ARRESTED FOR ASSAULT DOWN SOUTH IN 1933.
YEAH?
SOME LITTLE MINING TOWN. MAYBE HE WAS LOOKING FOR WORK. MY INFORMATION IS, HE HADN'T HAD A BOOKING FOR A COUPLE OF YEARS.
NICE WORK, FINDING THIS. WE'RE GOING TO RATTLE EVERY SKELETON IN THIS GUY'S CLOSET BEFORE WE'RE DONE.

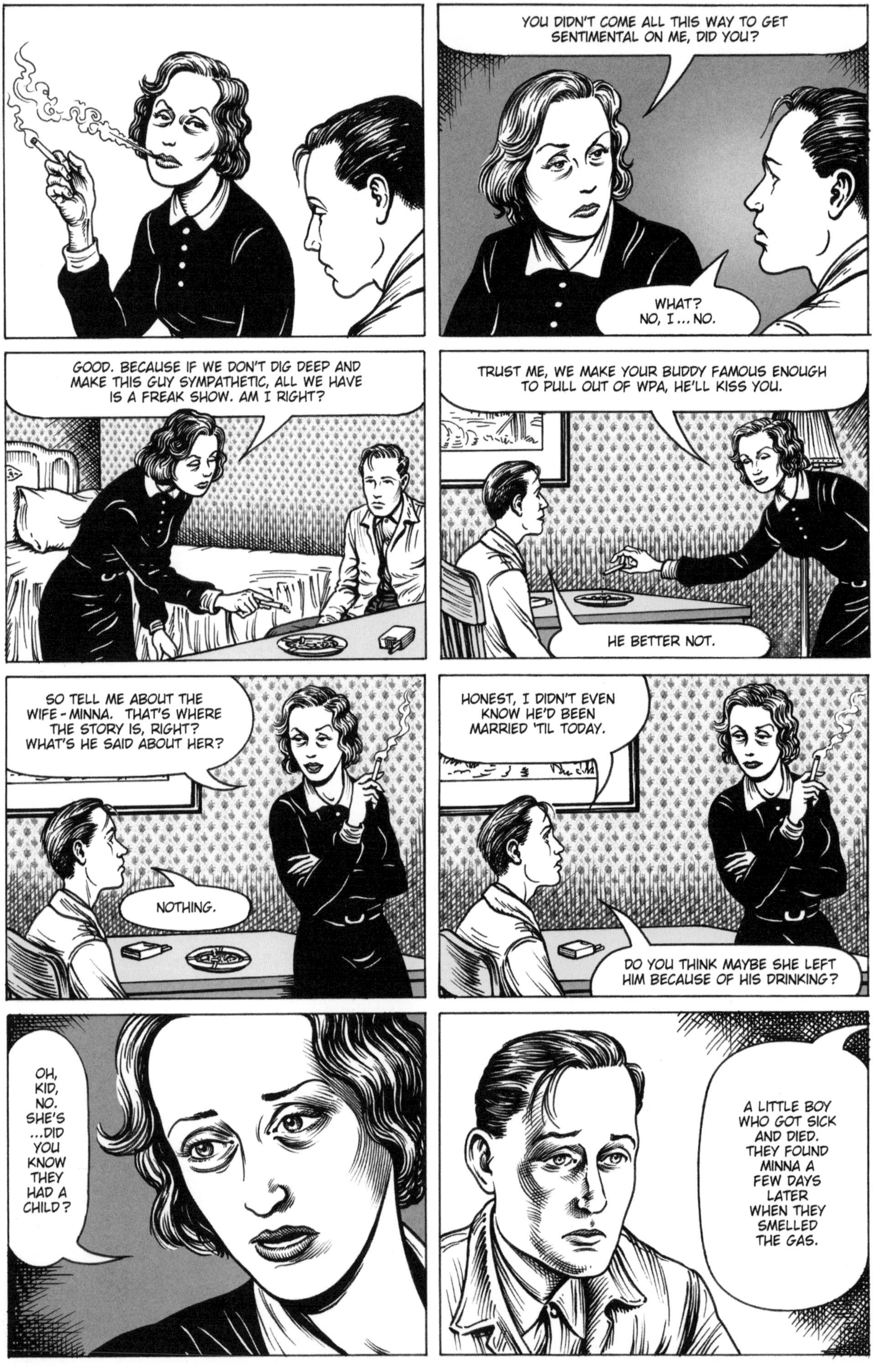
YOU DIDN'T COME ALL THIS WAY TO GET SENTIMENTAL ON ME, DID YOU?
WHAT? NO, I... NO.
GOOD. BECAUSE IF WE DON'T DIG DEEP AND MAKE THIS GUY SYMPATHETIC, ALL WE HAVE IS A FREAK SHOW. AM I RIGHT?
TRUST ME, WE MAKE YOUR BUDDY FAMOUS ENOUGH TO PULL OUT OF WPA, HE'LL KISS YOU.
HE BETTER NOT.
SO TELL ME ABOUT THE WIFE - MINNA. THAT'S WHERE THE STORY IS, RIGHT? WHAT'S HE SAID ABOUT HER?
NOTHING.
HONEST, I DIDN'T EVEN KNOW HE'D BEEN MARRIED 'TIL TODAY.
DO YOU THINK MAYBE SHE LEFT HIM BECAUSE OF HIS DRINKING?
OH, KID, NO. SHE'S ...DID YOU KNOW THEY HAD A CHILD?
A LITTLE BOY WHO GOT SICK AND DIED. THEY FOUND MINNA A FEW DAYS LATER WHEN THEY SMELLED THE GAS.

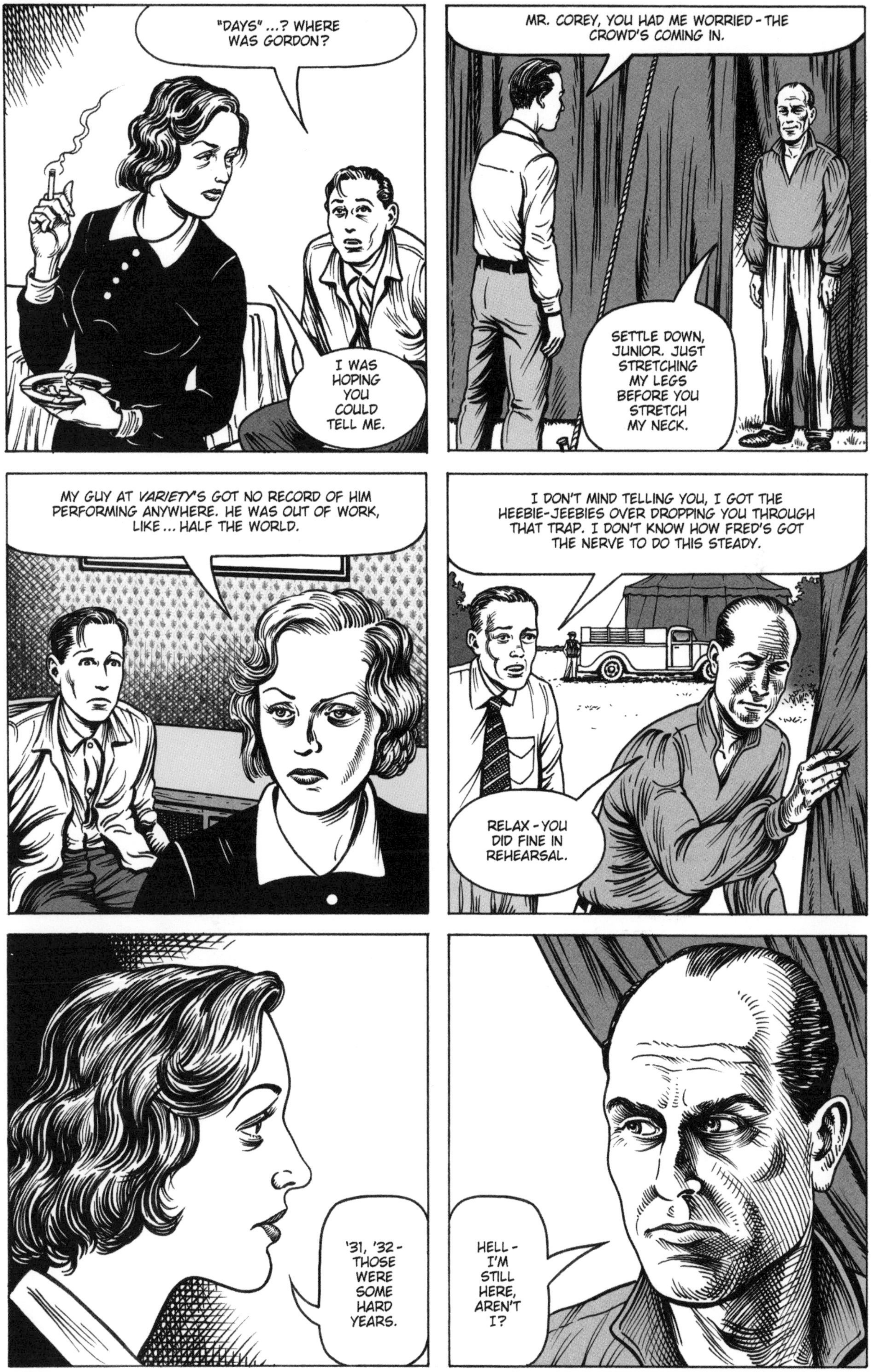
"DAYS" ...? WHERE WAS GORDON?
I WAS HOPING YOU COULD TELL ME.
MR. COREY, YOU HAD ME WORRIED - THE CROWD'S COMING IN.
SETTLE DOWN, JUNIOR. JUST STRETCHING MY LEGS BEFORE YOU STRETCH MY NECK.
MY GUY AT *VARIETY*'S GOT NO RECORD OF HIM PERFORMING ANYWHERE. HE WAS OUT OF WORK, LIKE ... HALF THE WORLD.
I DON'T MIND TELLING YOU, I GOT THE HEEBIE-JEEBIES OVER DROPPING YOU THROUGH THAT TRAP. I DON'T KNOW HOW FRED'S GOT THE NERVE TO DO THIS STEADY.
RELAX - YOU DID FINE IN REHEARSAL.
'31, '32 - THOSE WERE SOME HARD YEARS.
HELL - I'M STILL HERE, AREN'T I?

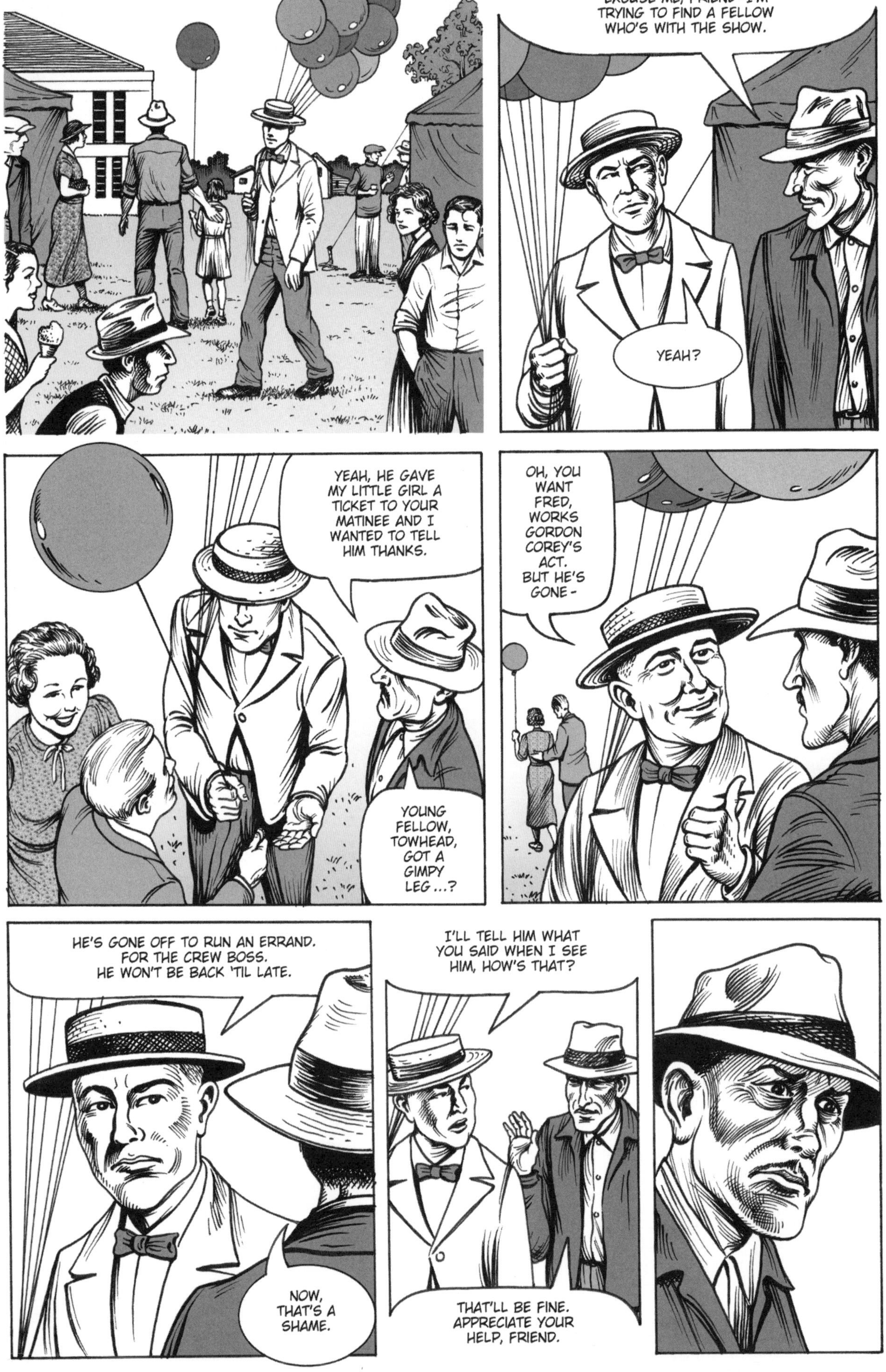
EXCUSE ME, FRIEND-I'M TRYING TO FIND A FELLOW WHO'S WITH THE SHOW.
YEAH?
YEAH, HE GAVE MY LITTLE GIRL A TICKET TO YOUR MATINEE AND I WANTED TO TELL HIM THANKS.
YOUNG FELLOW, TOWHEAD, GOT A GIMPY LEG ...?
OH, YOU WANT FRED, WORKS GORDON COREY'S ACT. BUT HE'S GONE-
HE'S GONE OFF TO RUN AN ERRAND. FOR THE CREW BOSS. HE WON'T BE BACK 'TIL LATE.
NOW, THAT'S A SHAME.
I'LL TELL HIM WHAT YOU SAID WHEN I SEE HIM, HOW'S THAT?
THAT'LL BE FINE. APPRECIATE YOUR HELP, FRIEND.

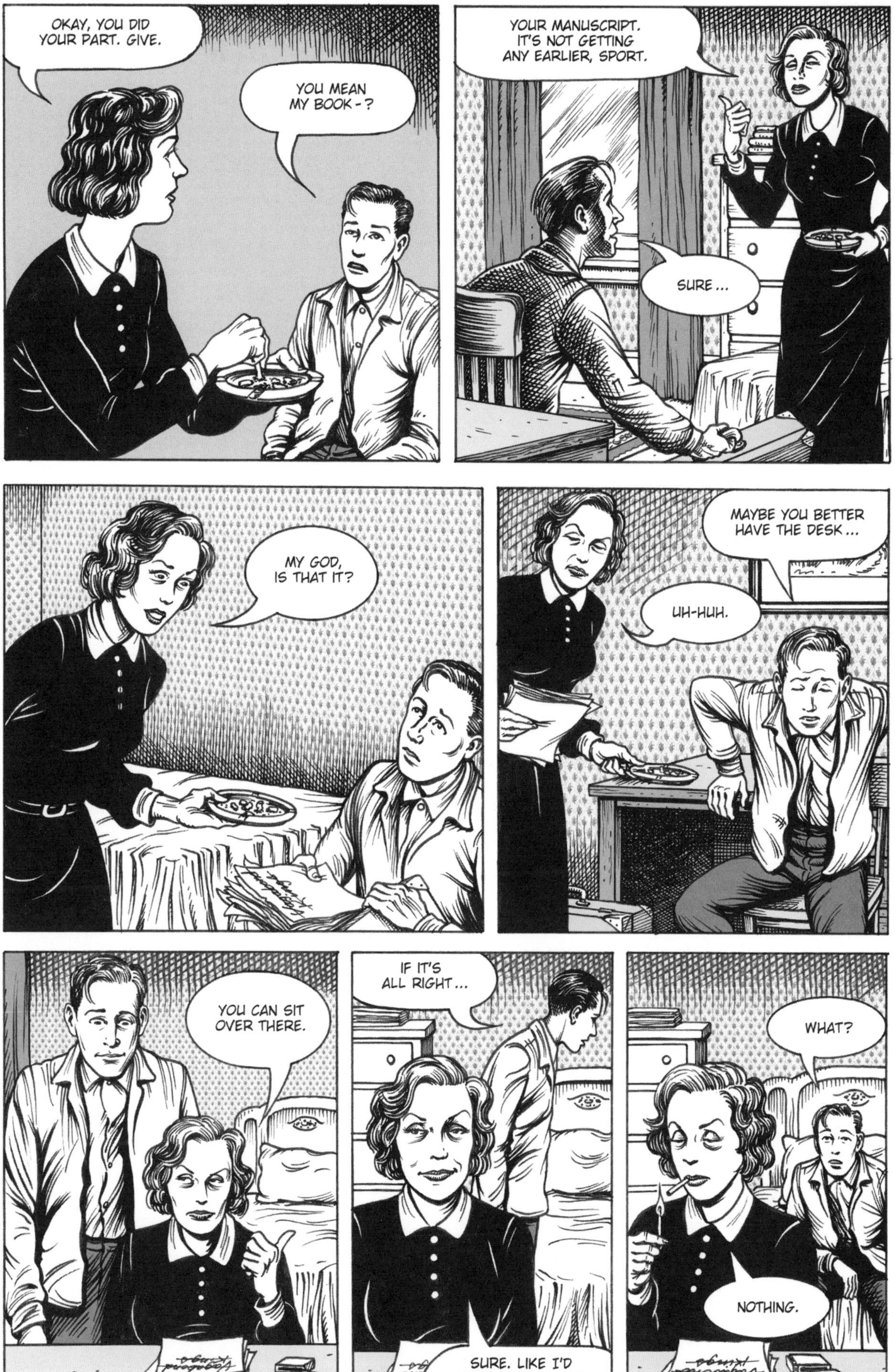
OKAY, YOU DID YOUR PART. GIVE.
YOU MEAN MY BOOK - ?
YOUR MANUSCRIPT. IT'S NOT GETTING ANY EARLIER, SPORT.
SURE ...
MY GOD, IS THAT IT?
MAYBE YOU BETTER HAVE THE DESK ...
UH-HUH.
YOU CAN SIT OVER THERE.
IF IT'S ALL RIGHT ...
SURE. LIKE I'D REMEMBER WHAT TO DO WITH A -
WHAT?
NOTHING.

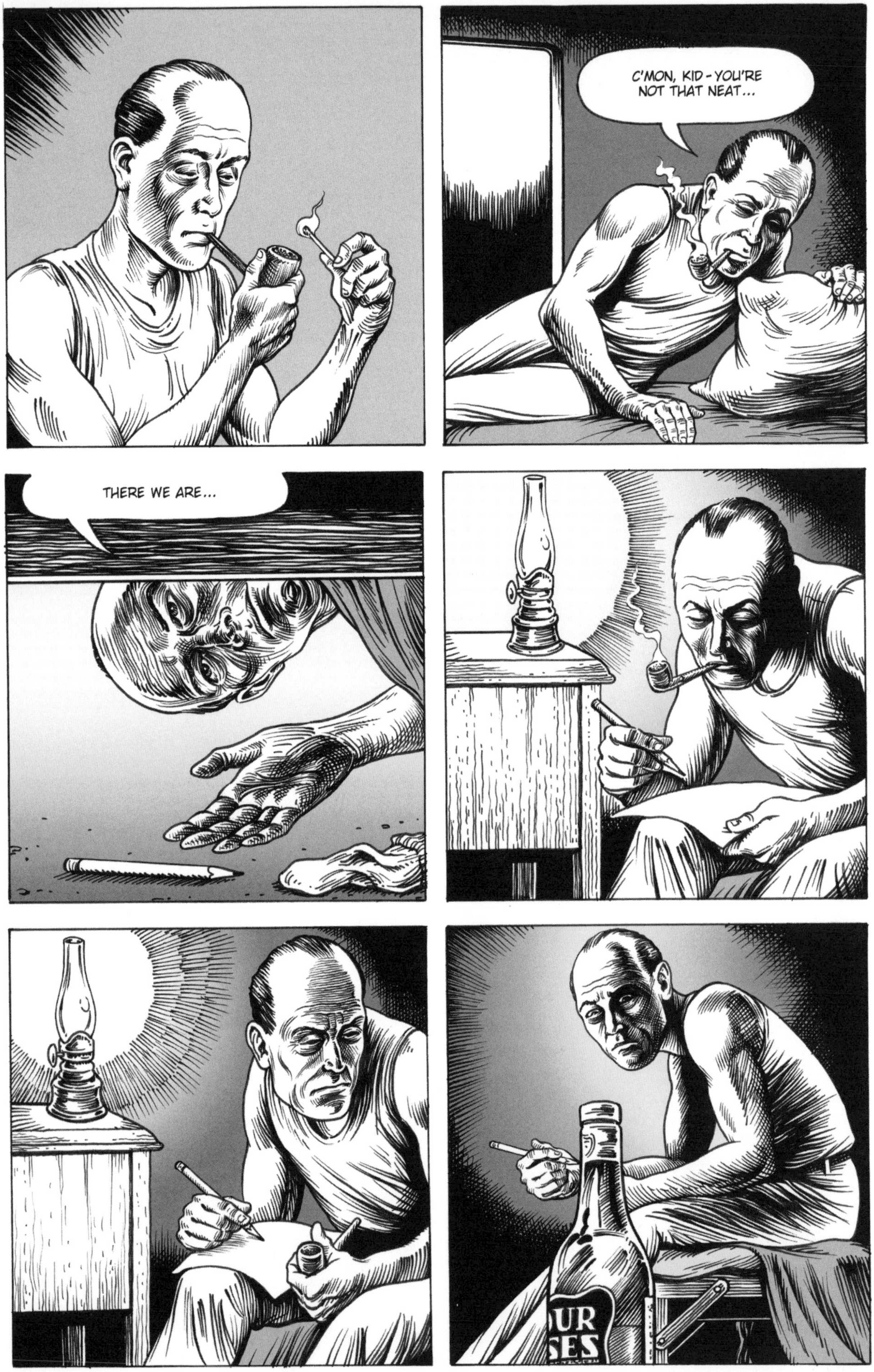
C'MON, KID - YOU'RE NOT THAT NEAT...
THERE WE ARE...

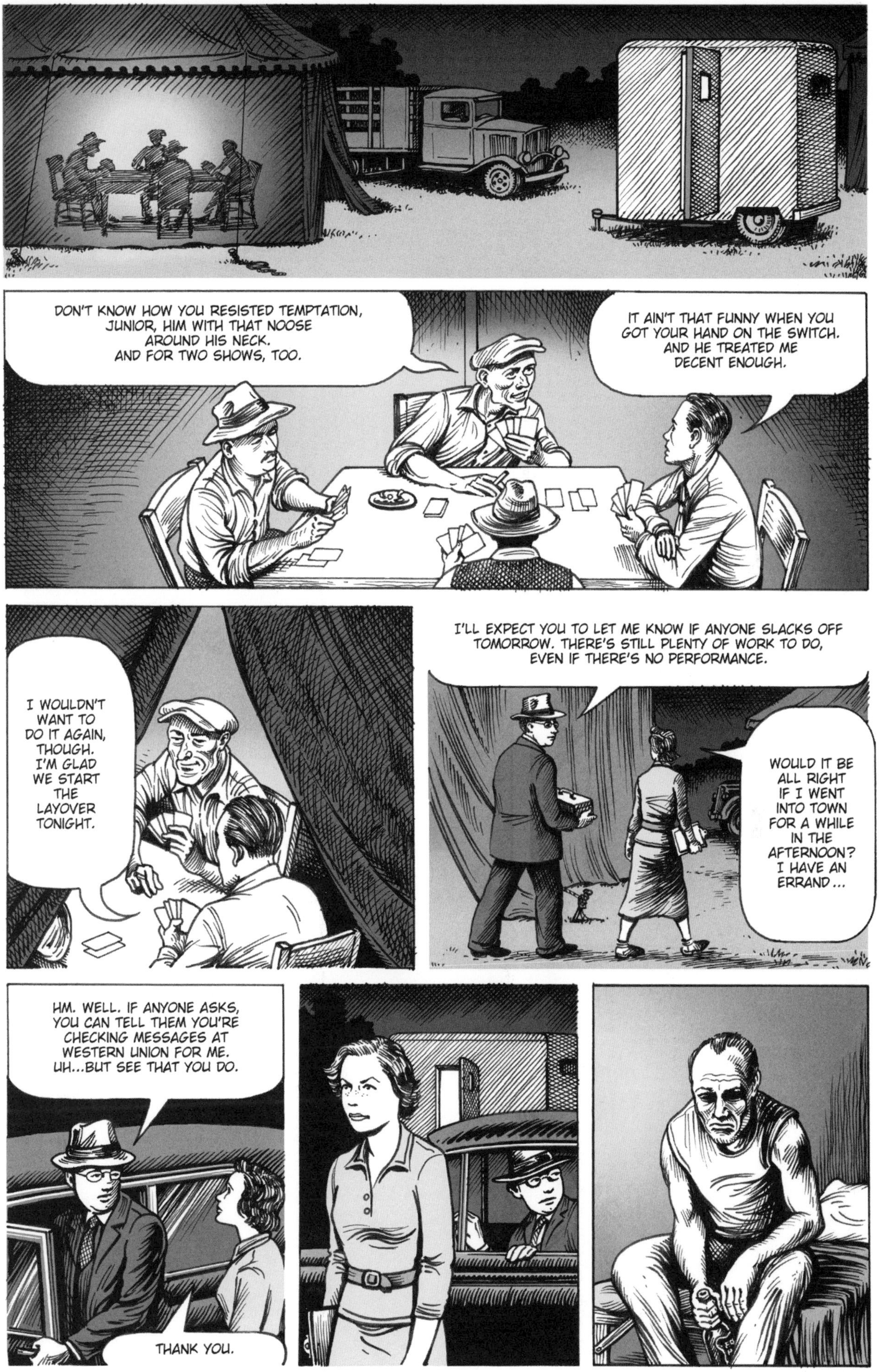

DON'T KNOW HOW YOU RESISTED TEMPTATION, JUNIOR, HIM WITH THAT NOOSE AROUND HIS NECK. AND FOR TWO SHOWS, TOO.
IT AIN'T THAT FUNNY WHEN YOU GOT YOUR HAND ON THE SWITCH. AND HE TREATED ME DECENT ENOUGH.
I WOULDN'T WANT TO DO IT AGAIN, THOUGH. I'M GLAD WE START THE LAYOVER TONIGHT.
I'LL EXPECT YOU TO LET ME KNOW IF ANYONE SLACKS OFF TOMORROW. THERE'S STILL PLENTY OF WORK TO DO, EVEN IF THERE'S NO PERFORMANCE.
WOULD IT BE ALL RIGHT IF I WENT INTO TOWN FOR A WHILE IN THE AFTERNOON? I HAVE AN ERRAND...
HM. WELL. IF ANYONE ASKS, YOU CAN TELL THEM YOU'RE CHECKING MESSAGES AT WESTERN UNION FOR ME. UH...BUT SEE THAT YOU DO.
THANK YOU.

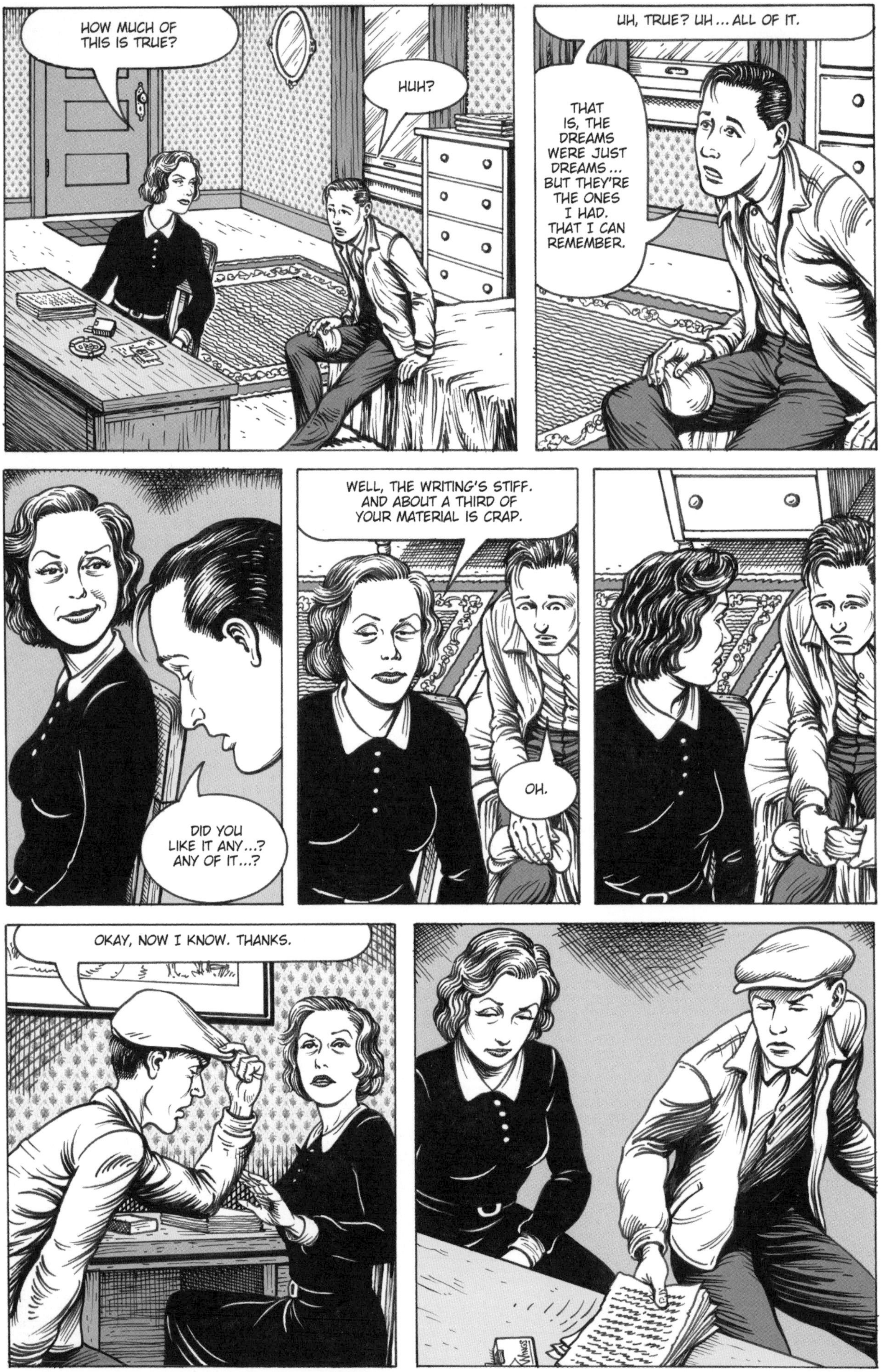
HOW MUCH OF THIS IS TRUE?
HUH?
UH, TRUE? UH ... ALL OF IT.
THAT IS, THE DREAMS WERE JUST DREAMS ... BUT THEY'RE THE ONES I HAD. THAT I CAN REMEMBER.
DID YOU LIKE IT ANY...? ANY OF IT...?
WELL, THE WRITING'S STIFF. AND ABOUT A THIRD OF YOUR MATERIAL IS CRAP.
OH.
OKAY, NOW I KNOW. THANKS.

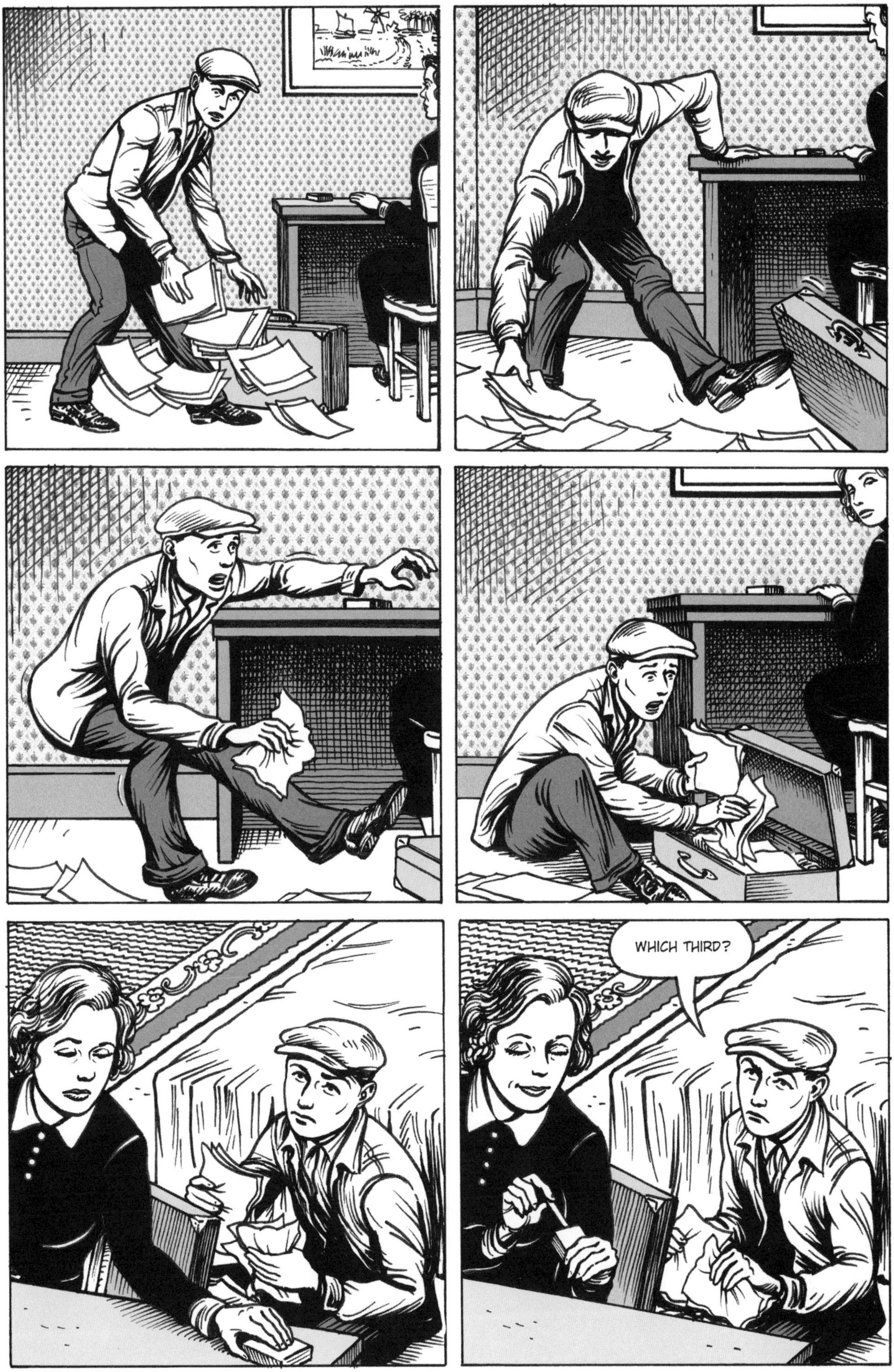
WHICH THIRD?

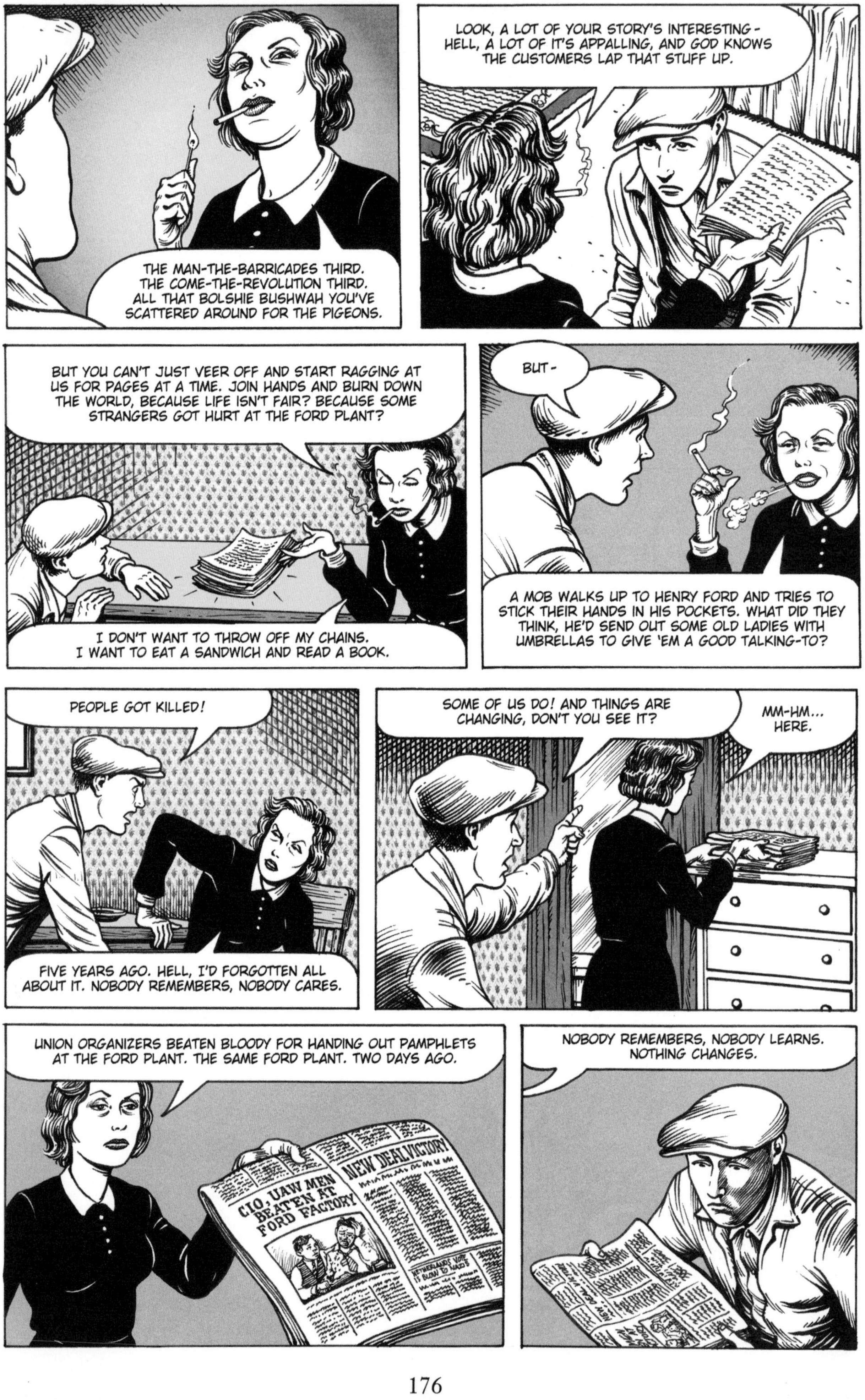
THE MAN-THE-BARRICADES THIRD. THE COME-THE-REVOLUTION THIRD. ALL THAT BOLSHIE BUSHWAH YOU'VE SCATTERED AROUND FOR THE PIGEONS.
LOOK, A LOT OF YOUR STORY'S INTERESTING - HELL, A LOT OF IT'S APPALLING, AND GOD KNOWS THE CUSTOMERS LAP THAT STUFF UP.
BUT YOU CAN'T JUST VEER OFF AND START RAGGING AT US FOR PAGES AT A TIME. JOIN HANDS AND BURN DOWN THE WORLD, BECAUSE LIFE ISN'T FAIR? BECAUSE SOME STRANGERS GOT HURT AT THE FORD PLANT?
I DON'T WANT TO THROW OFF MY CHAINS. I WANT TO EAT A SANDWICH AND READ A BOOK.
BUT -
A MOB WALKS UP TO HENRY FORD AND TRIES TO STICK THEIR HANDS IN HIS POCKETS. WHAT DID THEY THINK, HE'D SEND OUT SOME OLD LADIES WITH UMBRELLAS TO GIVE 'EM A GOOD TALKING-TO?
PEOPLE GOT KILLED!
FIVE YEARS AGO. HELL, I'D FORGOTTEN ALL ABOUT IT. NOBODY REMEMBERS, NOBODY CARES.
SOME OF US DO! AND THINGS ARE CHANGING, DON'T YOU SEE IT?
MM-HM... HERE.
UNION ORGANIZERS BEATEN BLOODY FOR HANDING OUT PAMPHLETS AT THE FORD PLANT. THE SAME FORD PLANT. TWO DAYS AGO.
NEW DEAL VICTORY
CIO, UAW MEN BEATEN AT FORD FACTORY
NOBODY REMEMBERS, NOBODY LEARNS. NOTHING CHANGES.

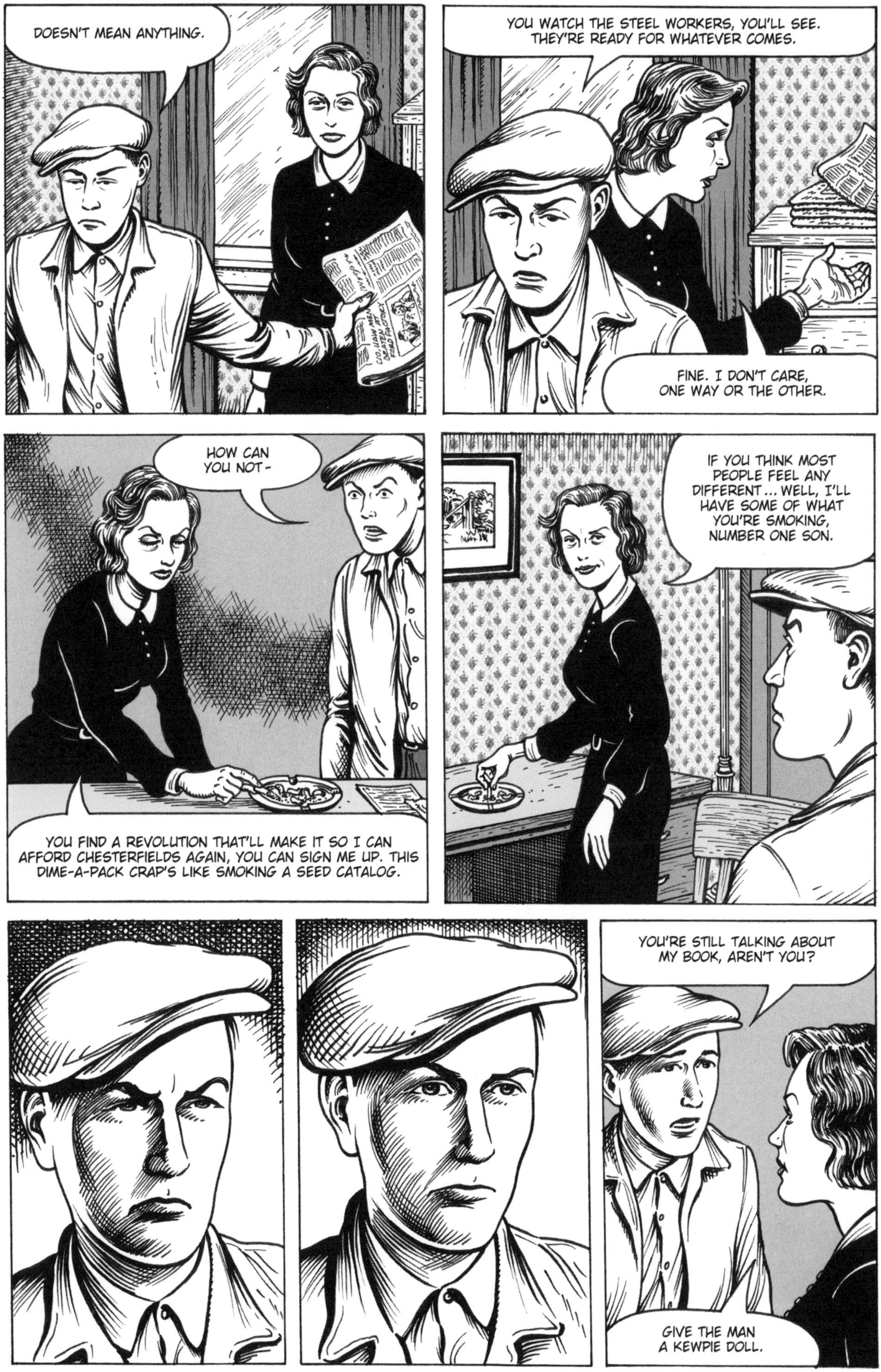
DOESN'T MEAN ANYTHING.
YOU WATCH THE STEEL WORKERS, YOU'LL SEE. THEY'RE READY FOR WHATEVER COMES.
FINE. I DON'T CARE, ONE WAY OR THE OTHER.
HOW CAN YOU NOT-
YOU FIND A REVOLUTION THAT'LL MAKE IT SO I CAN AFFORD CHESTERFIELDS AGAIN, YOU CAN SIGN ME UP. THIS DIME-A-PACK CRAP'S LIKE SMOKING A SEED CATALOG.
IF YOU THINK MOST PEOPLE FEEL ANY DIFFERENT... WELL, I'LL HAVE SOME OF WHAT YOU'RE SMOKING, NUMBER ONE SON.
YOU'RE STILL TALKING ABOUT MY BOOK, AREN'T YOU?
GIVE THE MAN A KEWPIE DOLL.

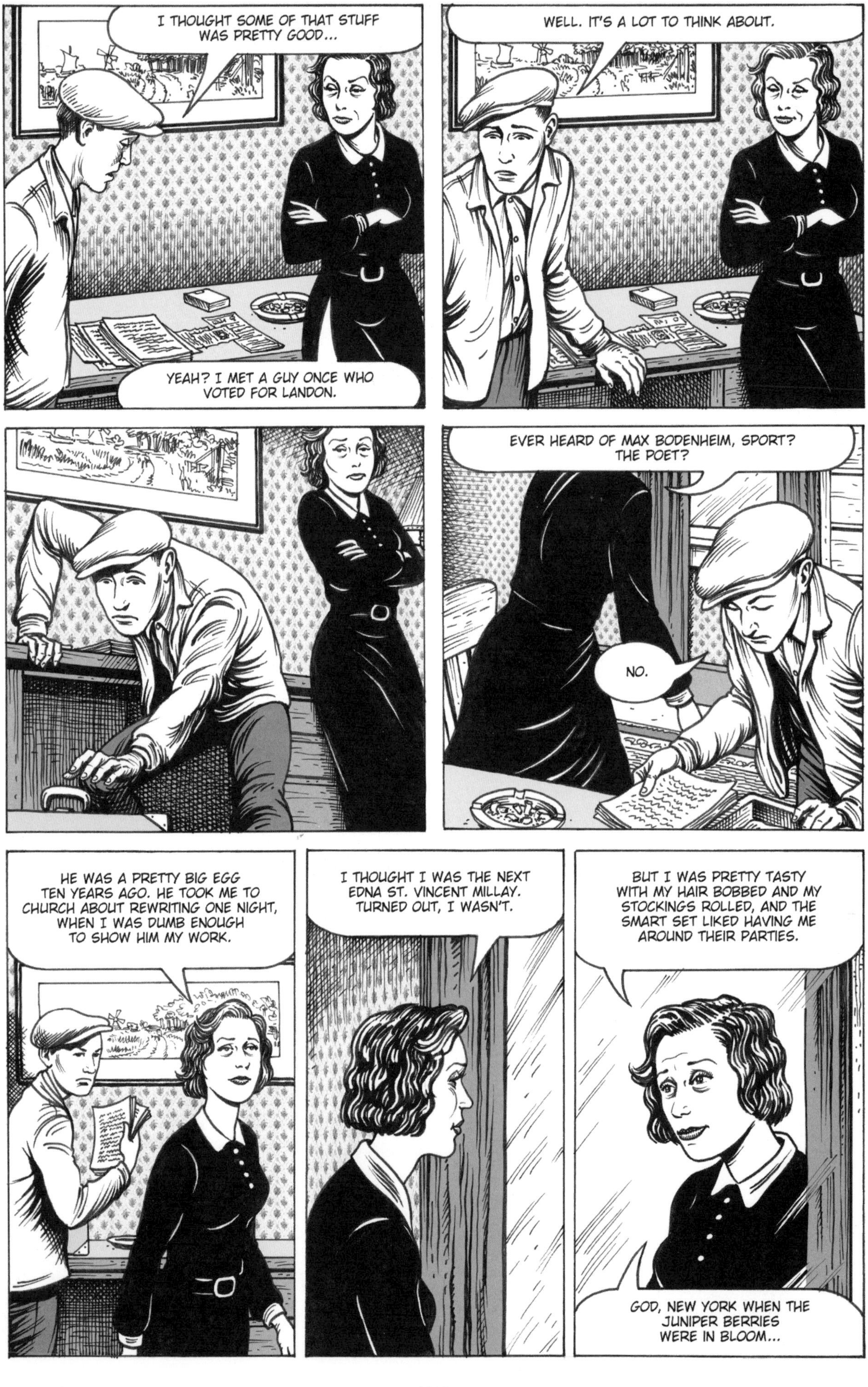
I THOUGHT SOME OF THAT STUFF WAS PRETTY GOOD...
YEAH? I MET A GUY ONCE WHO VOTED FOR LANDON.
WELL. IT'S A LOT TO THINK ABOUT.
EVER HEARD OF MAX BODENHEIM, SPORT? THE POET?
NO.
HE WAS A PRETTY BIG EGG TEN YEARS AGO. HE TOOK ME TO CHURCH ABOUT REWRITING ONE NIGHT, WHEN I WAS DUMB ENOUGH TO SHOW HIM MY WORK.
I THOUGHT I WAS THE NEXT EDNA ST. VINCENT MILLAY. TURNED OUT, I WASN'T.
BUT I WAS PRETTY TASTY WITH MY HAIR BOBBED AND MY STOCKINGS ROLLED, AND THE SMART SET LIKED HAVING ME AROUND THEIR PARTIES.
GOD, NEW YORK WHEN THE JUNIPER BERRIES WERE IN BLOOM...

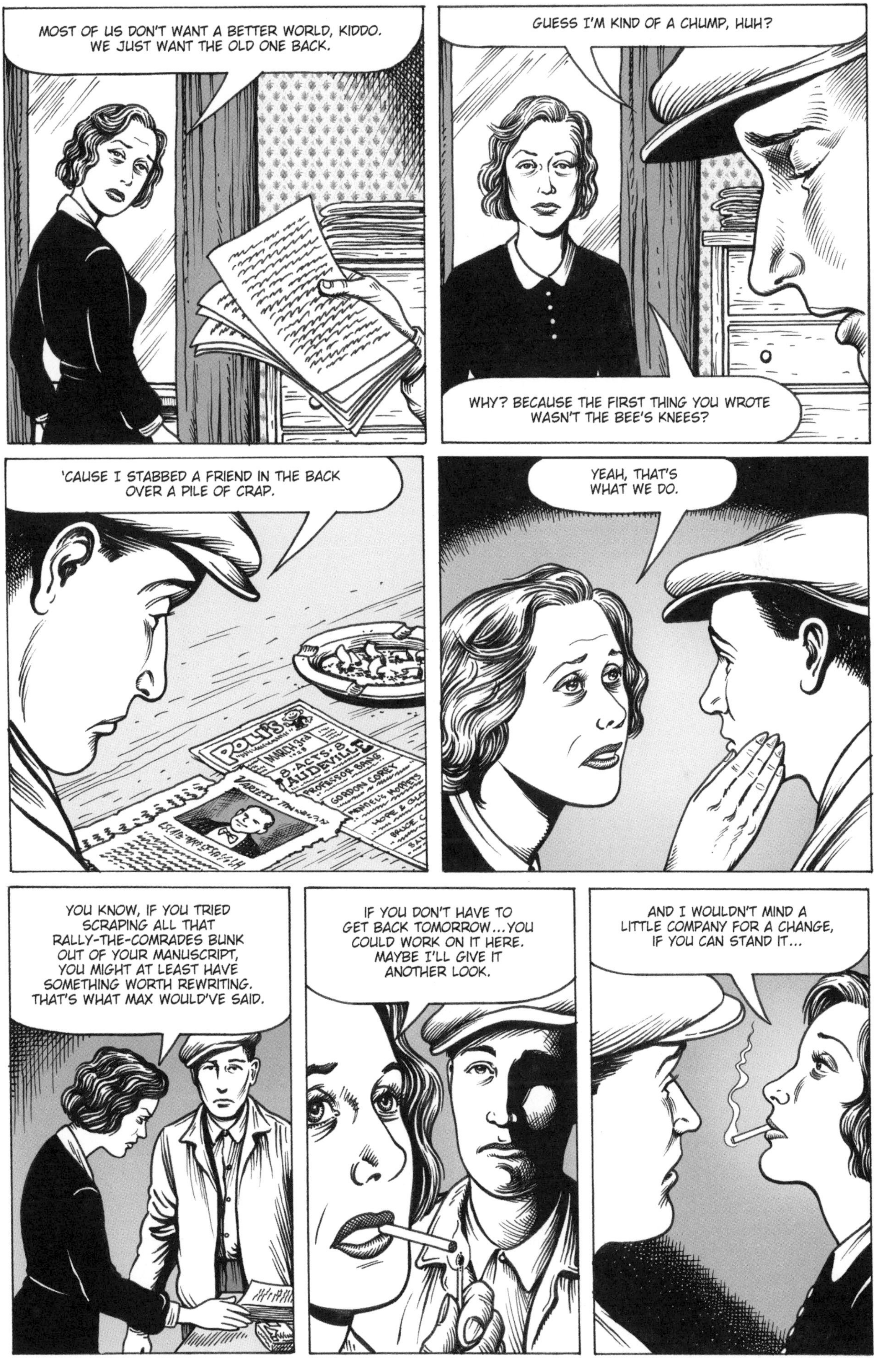
MOST OF US DON'T WANT A BETTER WORLD, KIDDO. WE JUST WANT THE OLD ONE BACK.
GUESS I'M KIND OF A CHUMP, HUH?
WHY? BECAUSE THE FIRST THING YOU WROTE WASN'T THE BEE'S KNEES?
'CAUSE I STABBED A FRIEND IN THE BACK OVER A PILE OF CRAP.
YEAH, THAT'S WHAT WE DO.
YOU KNOW, IF YOU TRIED SCRAPING ALL THAT RALLY-THE-COMRADES BUNK OUT OF YOUR MANUSCRIPT, YOU MIGHT AT LEAST HAVE SOMETHING WORTH REWRITING. THAT'S WHAT MAX WOULD'VE SAID.
IF YOU DON'T HAVE TO GET BACK TOMORROW... YOU COULD WORK ON IT HERE. MAYBE I'LL GIVE IT ANOTHER LOOK.
AND I WOULDN'T MIND A LITTLE COMPANY FOR A CHANGE, IF YOU CAN STAND IT...

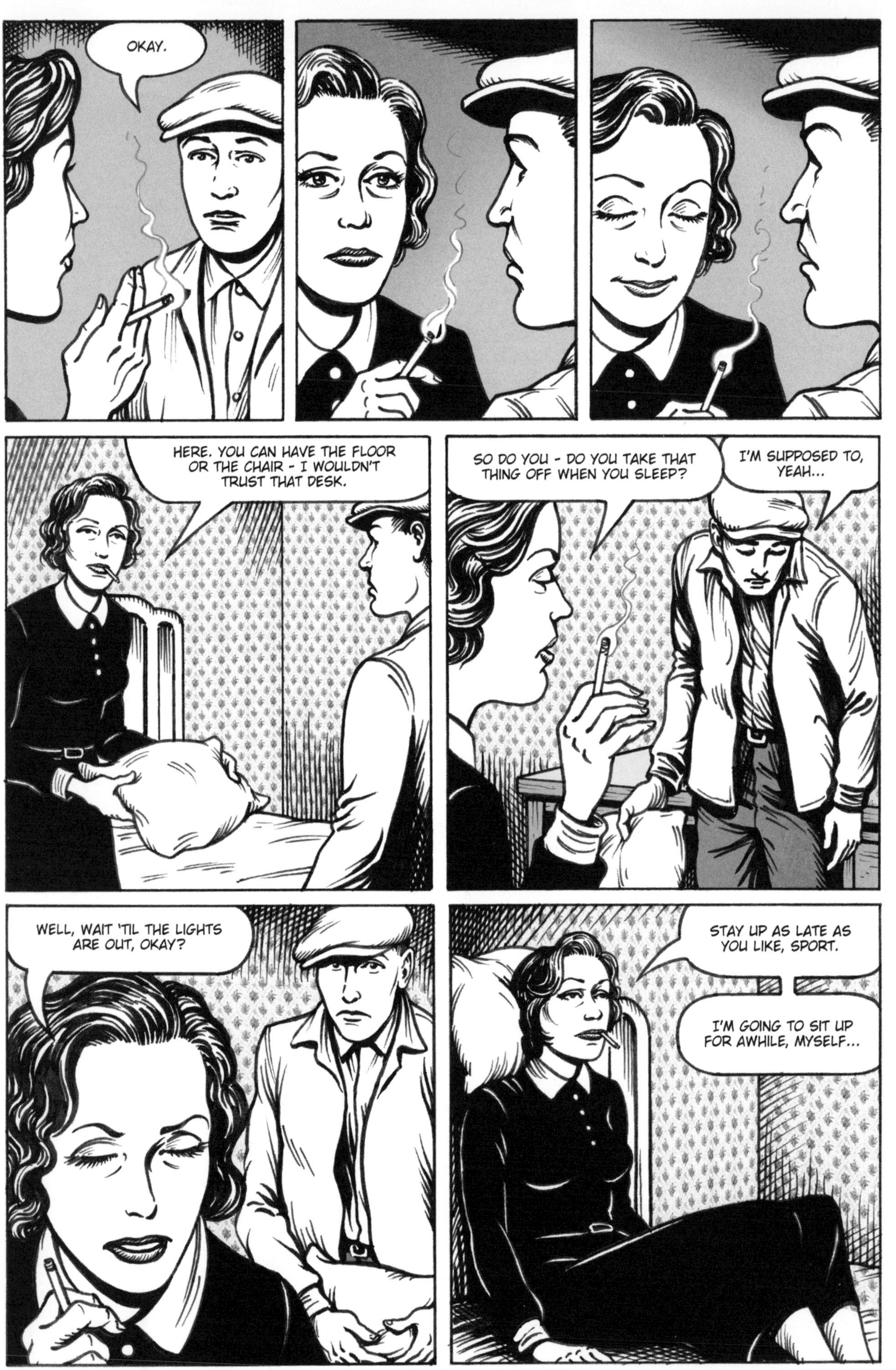
OKAY.
HERE. YOU CAN HAVE THE FLOOR OR THE CHAIR - I WOULDN'T TRUST THAT DESK.
SO DO YOU - DO YOU TAKE THAT THING OFF WHEN YOU SLEEP?
I'M SUPPOSED TO, YEAH...
WELL, WAIT 'TIL THE LIGHTS ARE OUT, OKAY?
STAY UP AS LATE AS YOU LIKE, SPORT.
I'M GOING TO SIT UP FOR AWHILE, MYSELF...

WHAT...
DAMN-!
BE A HELL OF A NOTE...
Fred
Sorry I send you packing but now you know it was for the best. If I was you I'd keep my head down for a while and maybe hide out someplace

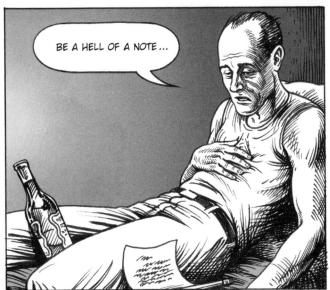

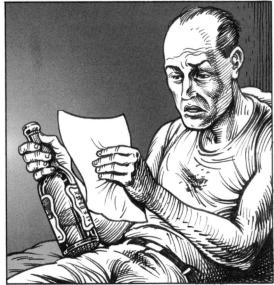

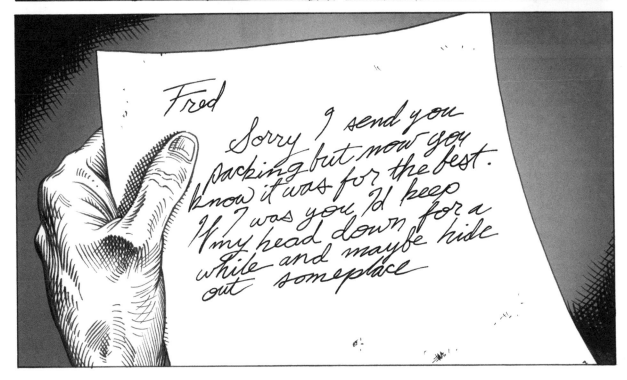

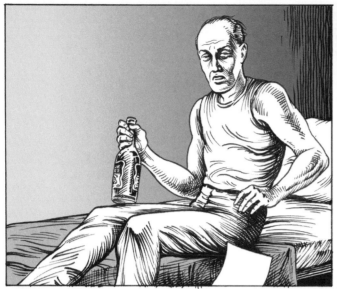

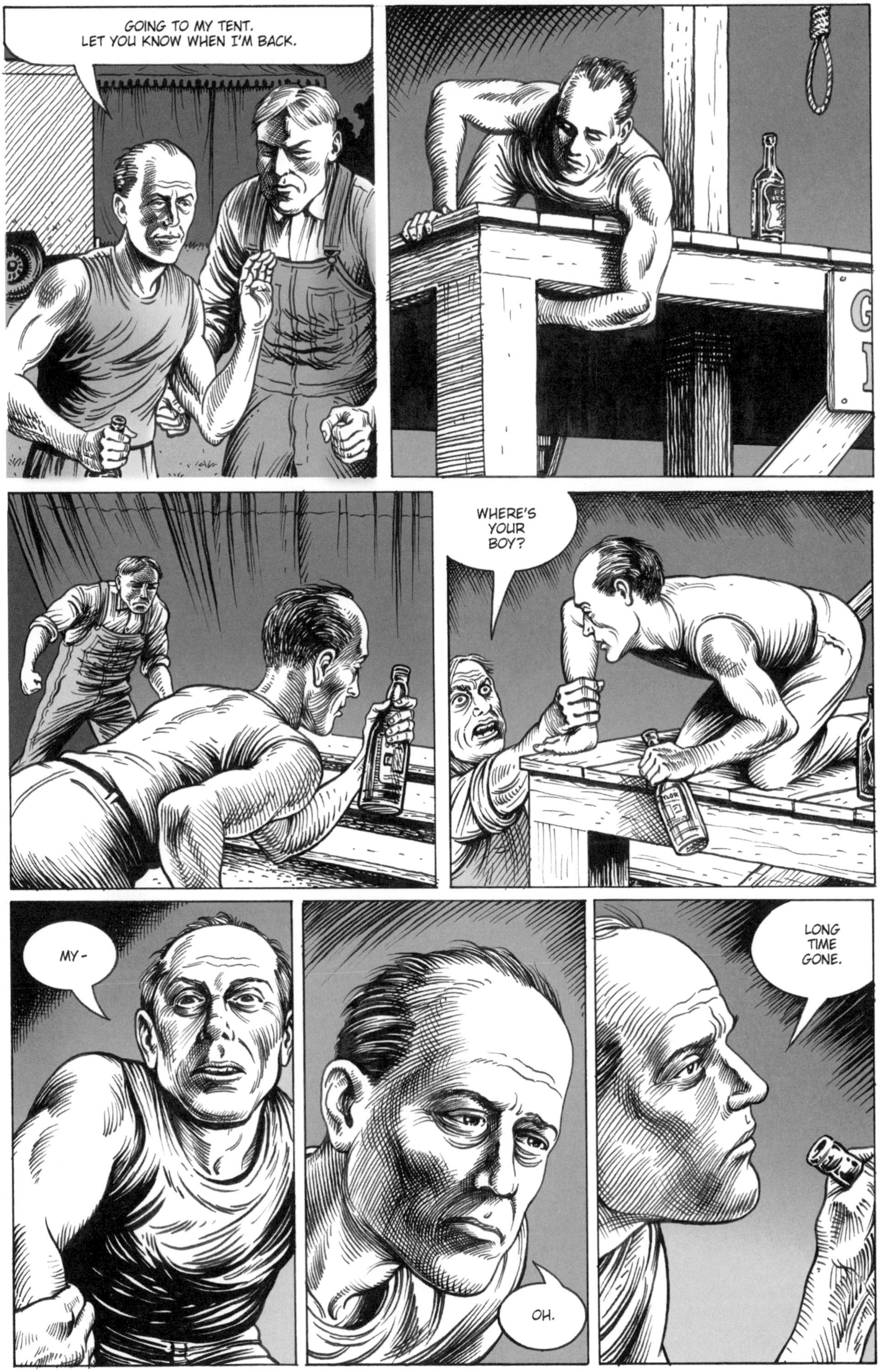
GOING TO MY TENT.
LET YOU KNOW WHEN I'M BACK.
WHERE'S YOUR BOY?
MY -
OH.
LONG TIME GONE.

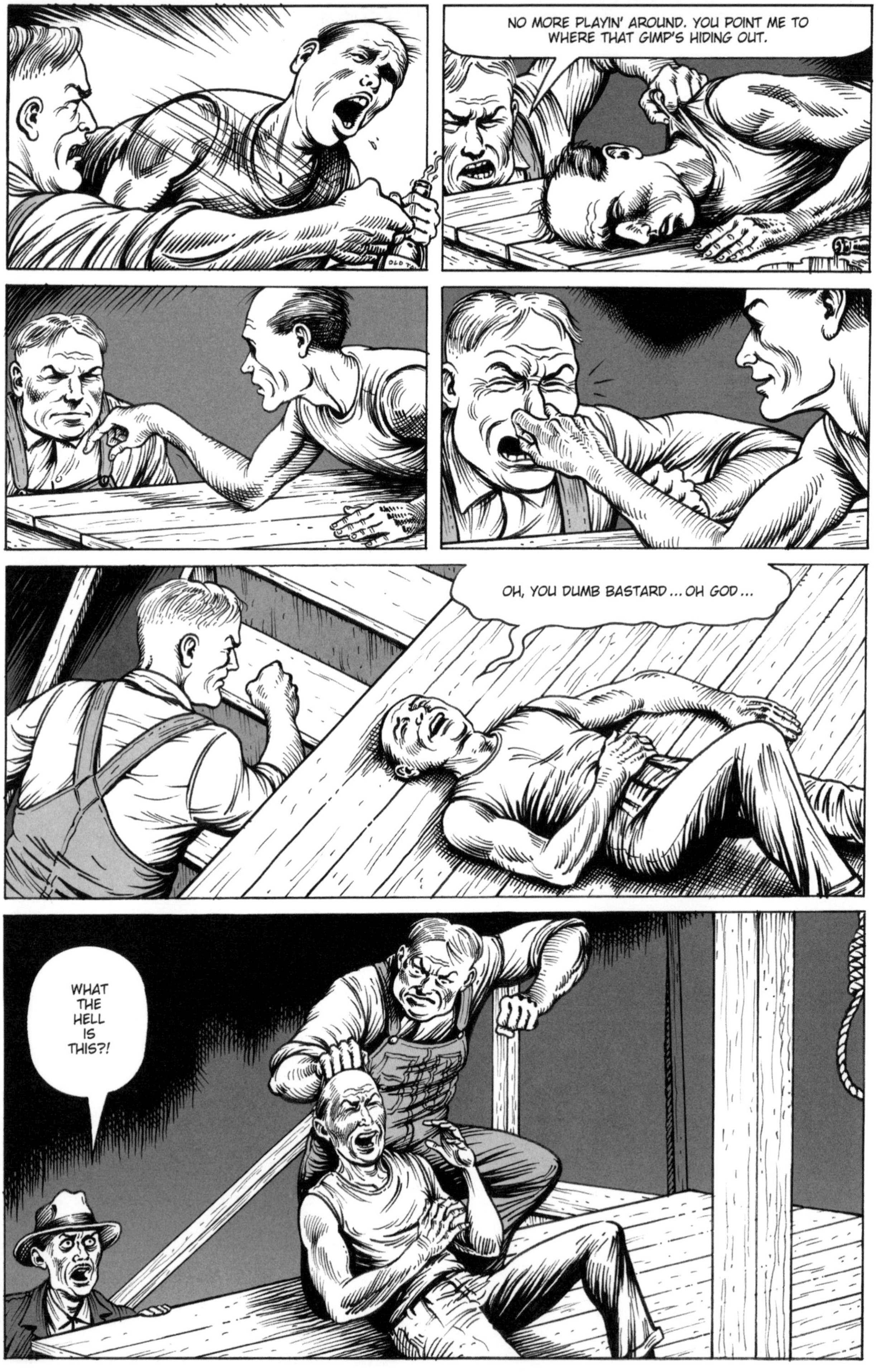
NO MORE PLAYIN' AROUND. YOU POINT ME TO WHERE THAT GIMP'S HIDING OUT.
OH, YOU DUMB BASTARD ... OH GOD ...
WHAT THE HELL IS THIS?!

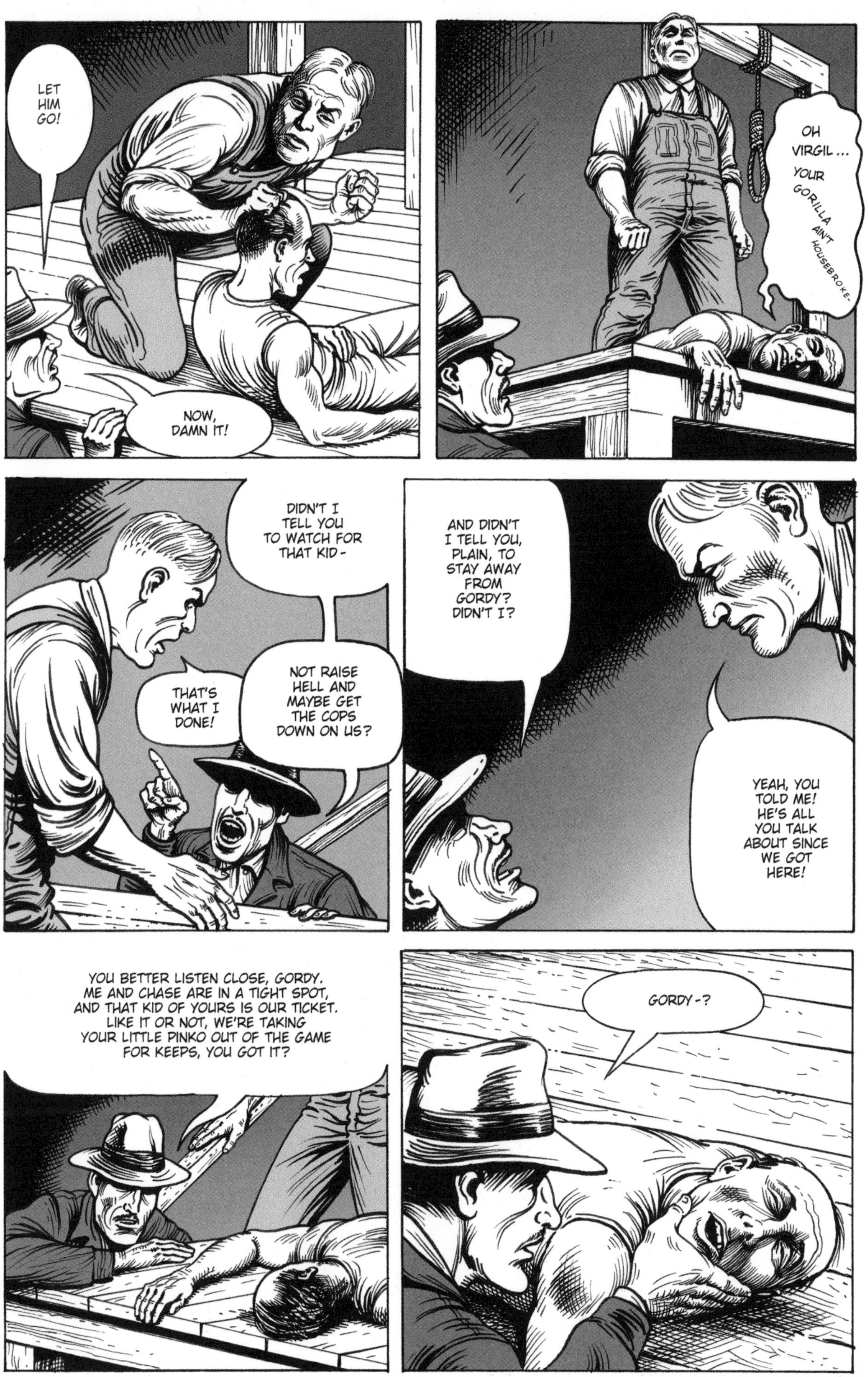
LET HIM GO!
NOW, DAMN IT!
OH VIRGIL...
YOUR GORILLA AIN'T HOUSEBROKE.
DIDN'T I TELL YOU TO WATCH FOR THAT KID-
NOT RAISE HELL AND MAYBE GET THE COPS DOWN ON US?
THAT'S WHAT I DONE!
AND DIDN'T I TELL YOU, PLAIN, TO STAY AWAY FROM GORDY? DIDN'T I?
YEAH, YOU TOLD ME! HE'S ALL YOU TALK ABOUT SINCE WE GOT HERE!
YOU BETTER LISTEN CLOSE, GORDY. ME AND CHASE ARE IN A TIGHT SPOT, AND THAT KID OF YOURS IS OUR TICKET. LIKE IT OR NOT, WE'RE TAKING YOUR LITTLE PINKO OUT OF THE GAME FOR KEEPS, YOU GOT IT?
GORDY-?

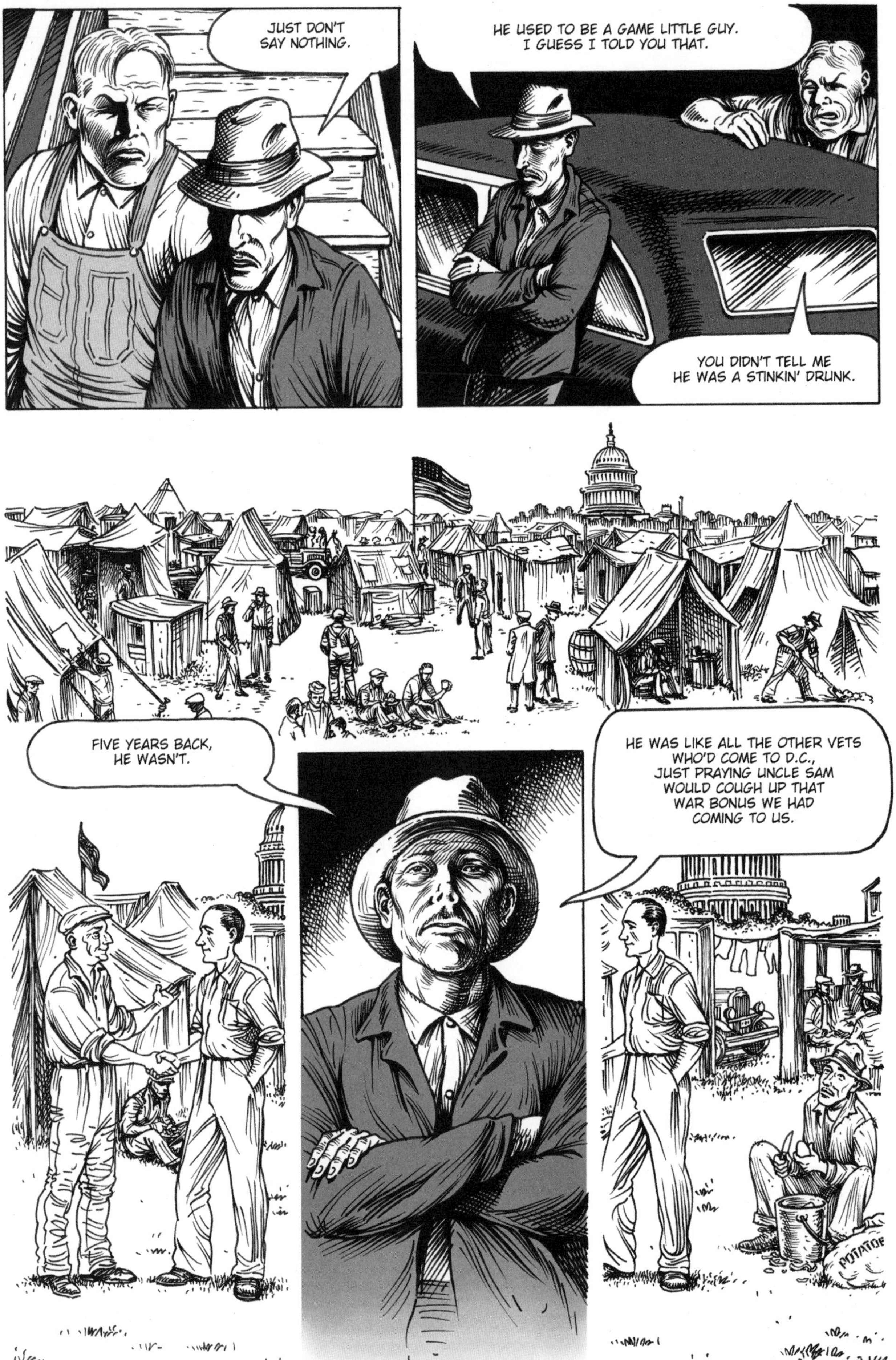
JUST DON'T SAY NOTHING.
HE USED TO BE A GAME LITTLE GUY. I GUESS I TOLD YOU THAT.
YOU DIDN'T TELL ME HE WAS A STINKIN' DRUNK.
FIVE YEARS BACK, HE WASN'T.
HE WAS LIKE ALL THE OTHER VETS WHO'D COME TO D.C., JUST PRAYING UNCLE SAM WOULD COUGH UP THAT WAR BONUS WE HAD COMING TO US.

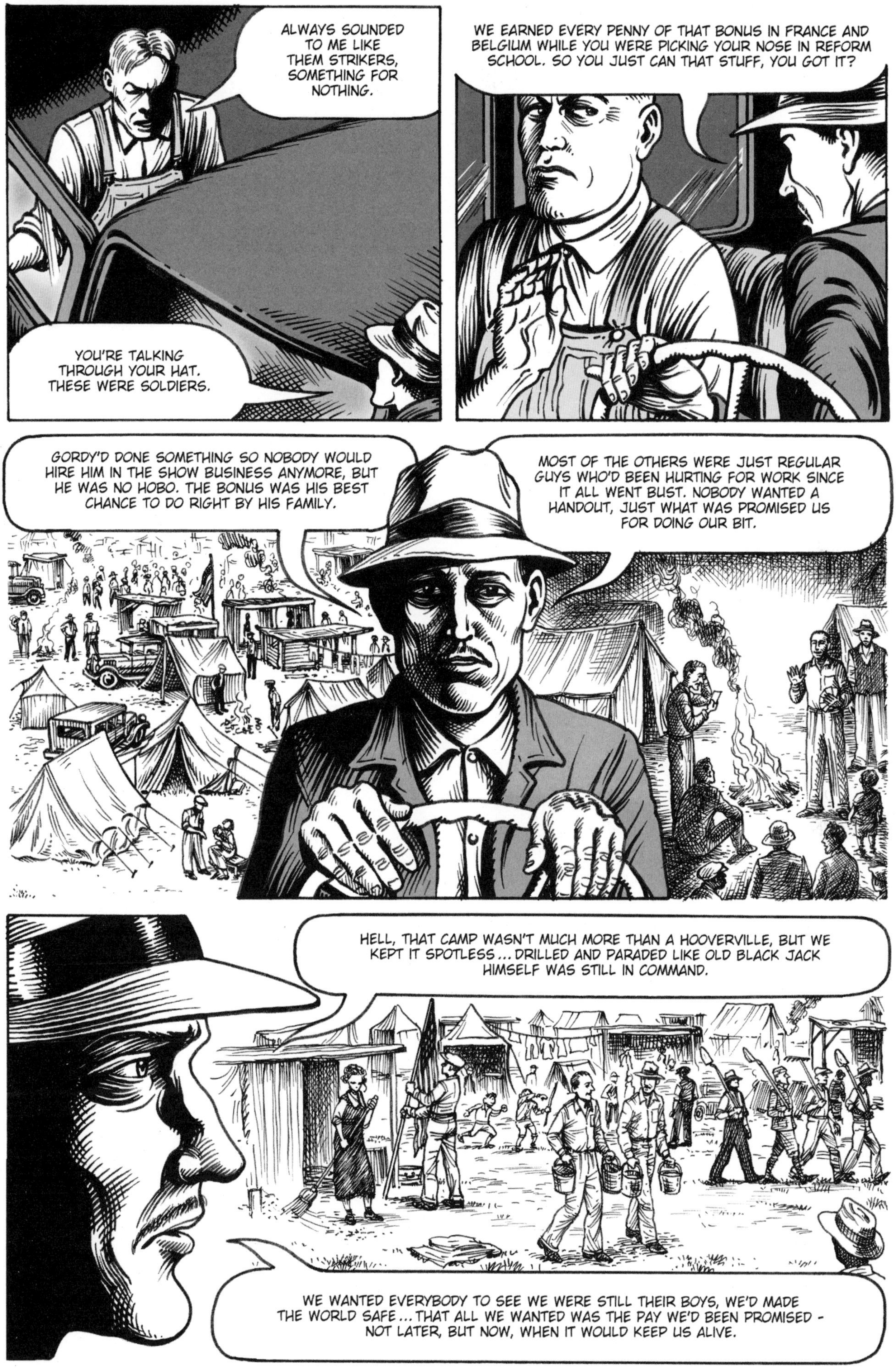
ALWAYS SOUNDED TO ME LIKE THEM STRIKERS, SOMETHING FOR NOTHING.
YOU'RE TALKING THROUGH YOUR HAT. THESE WERE SOLDIERS.
WE EARNED EVERY PENNY OF THAT BONUS IN FRANCE AND BELGIUM WHILE YOU WERE PICKING YOUR NOSE IN REFORM SCHOOL. SO YOU JUST CAN THAT STUFF, YOU GOT IT?
GORDY'D DONE SOMETHING SO NOBODY WOULD HIRE HIM IN THE SHOW BUSINESS ANYMORE, BUT HE WAS NO HOBO. THE BONUS WAS HIS BEST CHANCE TO DO RIGHT BY HIS FAMILY.
MOST OF THE OTHERS WERE JUST REGULAR GUYS WHO'D BEEN HURTING FOR WORK SINCE IT ALL WENT BUST. NOBODY WANTED A HANDOUT, JUST WHAT WAS PROMISED US FOR DOING OUR BIT.
HELL, THAT CAMP WASN'T MUCH MORE THAN A HOOVERVILLE, BUT WE KEPT IT SPOTLESS ... DRILLED AND PARADED LIKE OLD BLACK JACK HIMSELF WAS STILL IN COMMAND.
WE WANTED EVERYBODY TO SEE WE WERE STILL THEIR BOYS, WE'D MADE THE WORLD SAFE ... THAT ALL WE WANTED WAS THE PAY WE'D BEEN PROMISED - NOT LATER, BUT NOW, WHEN IT WOULD KEEP US ALIVE.

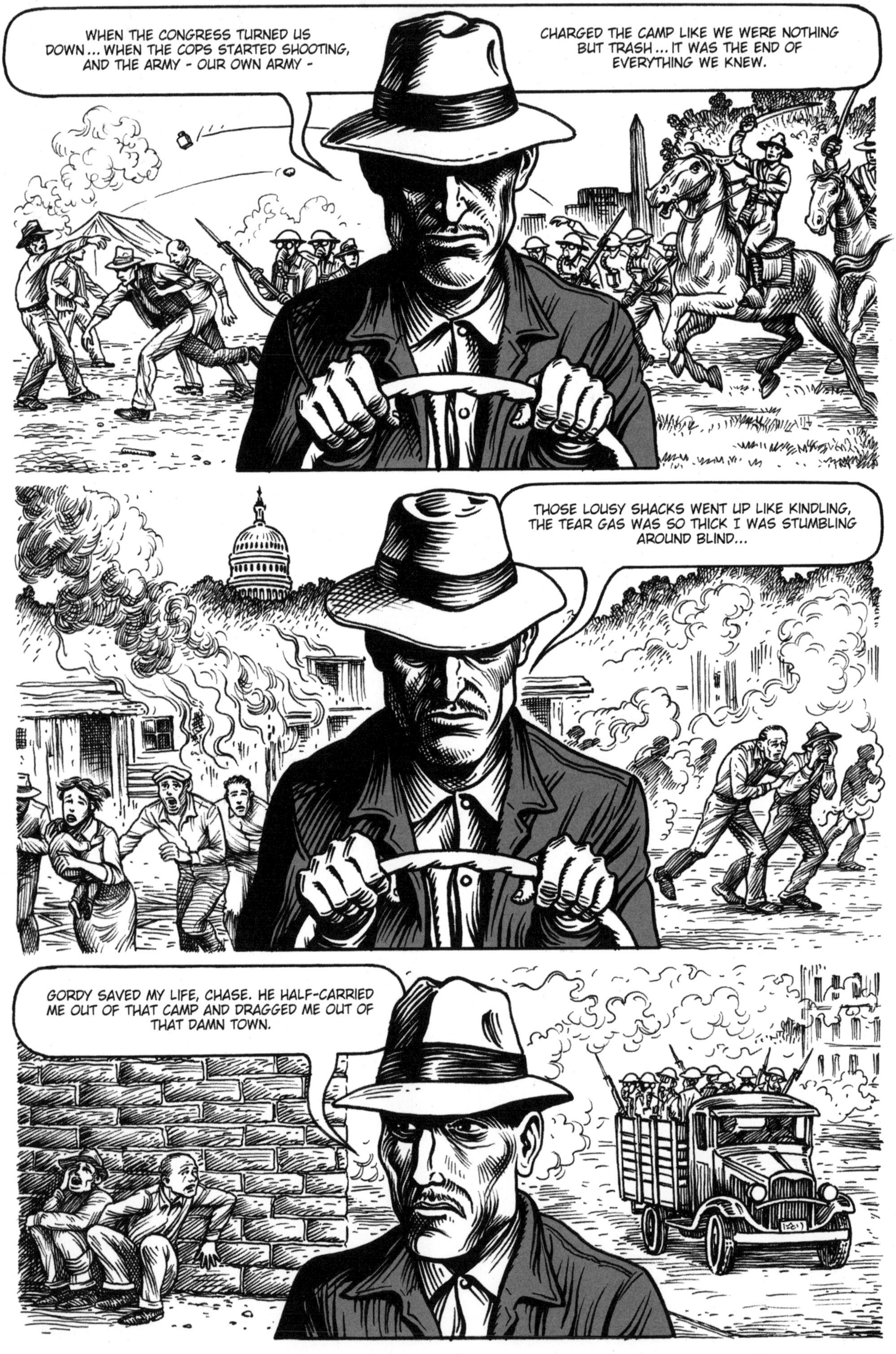
WHEN THE CONGRESS TURNED US DOWN... WHEN THE COPS STARTED SHOOTING, AND THE ARMY - OUR OWN ARMY -
CHARGED THE CAMP LIKE WE WERE NOTHING BUT TRASH... IT WAS THE END OF EVERYTHING WE KNEW.
THOSE LOUSY SHACKS WENT UP LIKE KINDLING, THE TEAR GAS WAS SO THICK I WAS STUMBLING AROUND BLIND...
GORDY SAVED MY LIFE, CHASE. HE HALF-CARRIED ME OUT OF THAT CAMP AND DRAGGED ME OUT OF THAT DAMN TOWN.

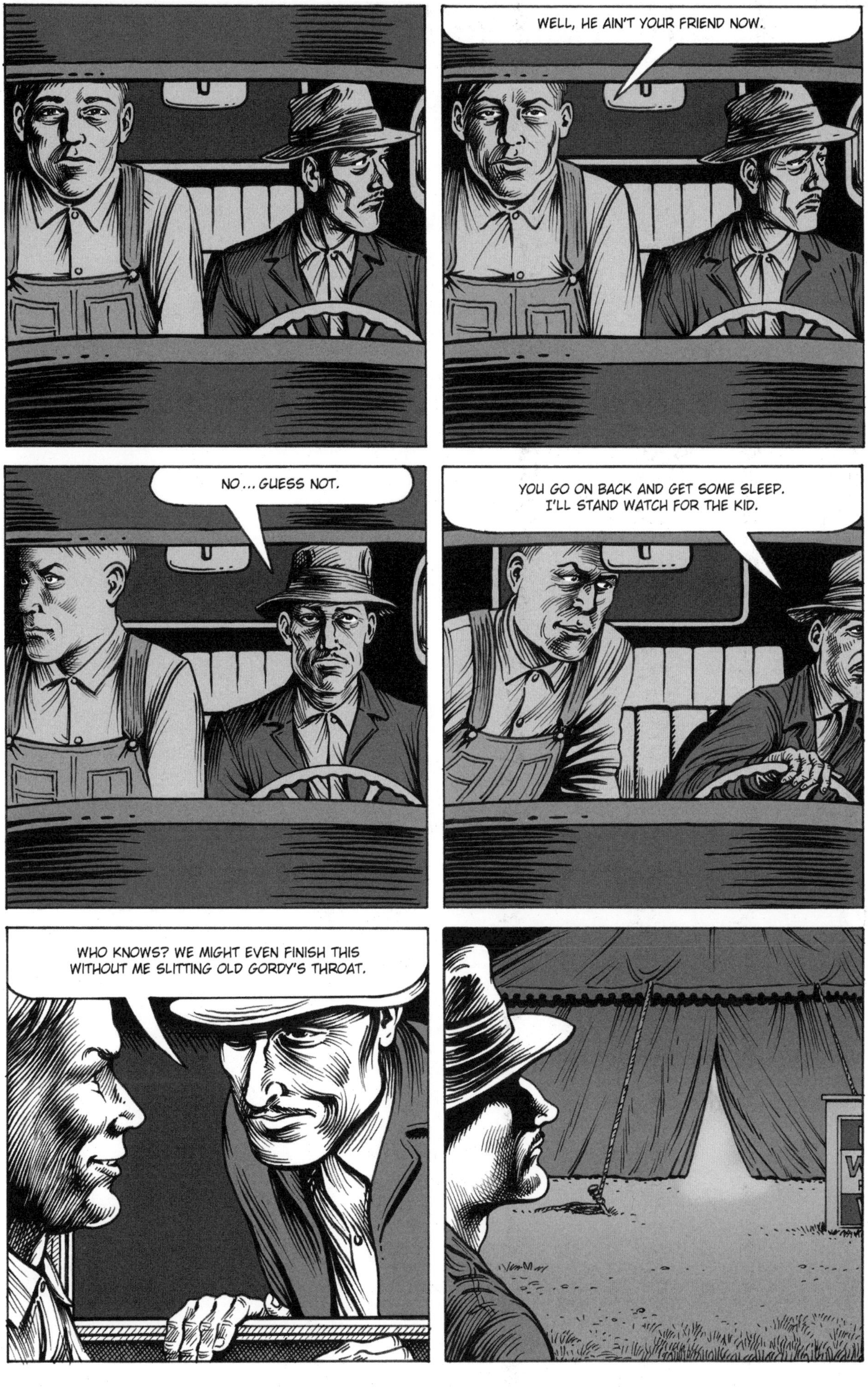
WELL, HE AIN'T YOUR FRIEND NOW.
NO... GUESS NOT.
YOU GO ON BACK AND GET SOME SLEEP. I'LL STAND WATCH FOR THE KID.
WHO KNOWS? WE MIGHT EVEN FINISH THIS WITHOUT ME SLITTING OLD GORDY'S THROAT.

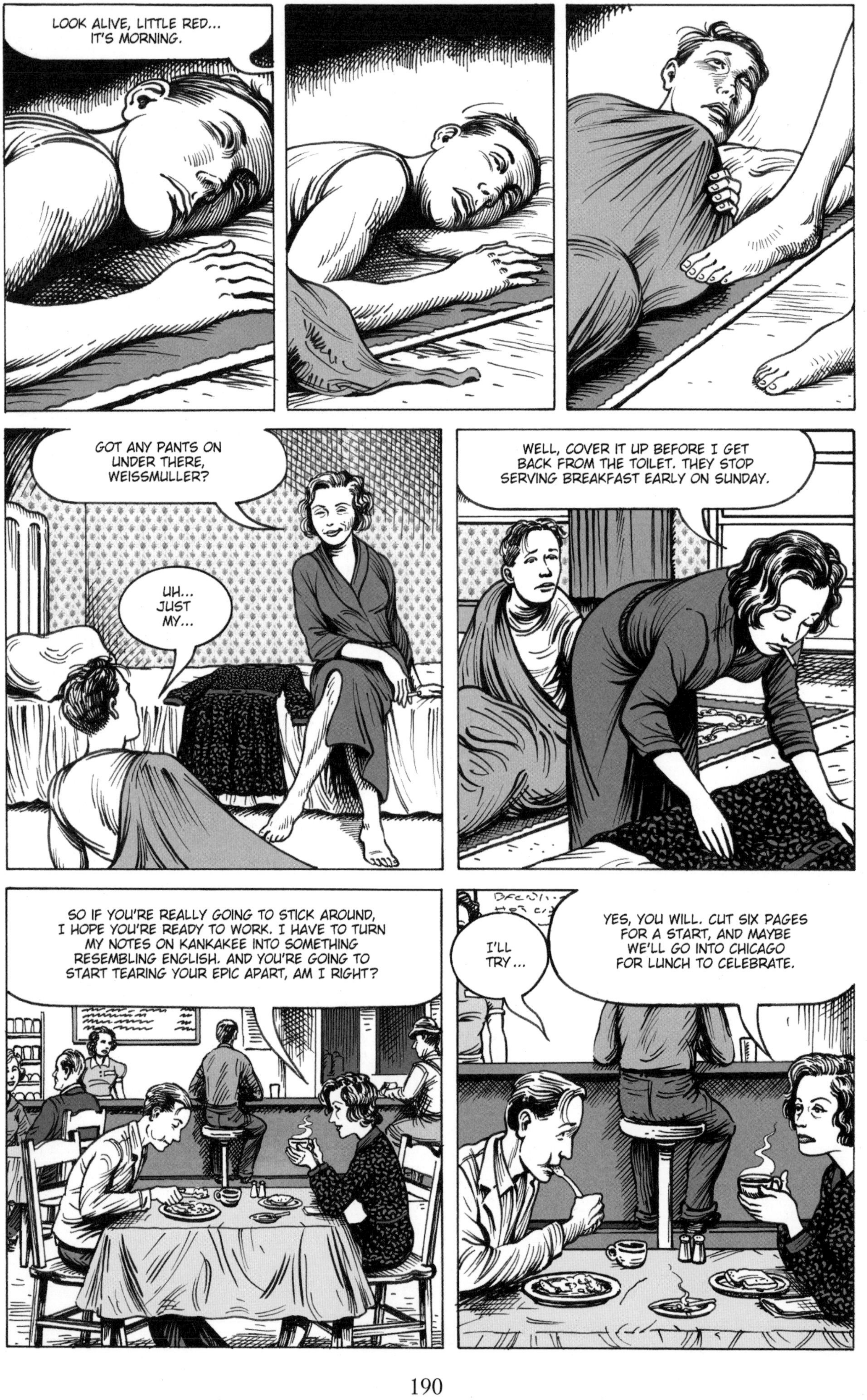
LOOK ALIVE, LITTLE RED... IT'S MORNING.
GOT ANY PANTS ON UNDER THERE, WEISSMULLER?
UH... JUST MY...
WELL, COVER IT UP BEFORE I GET BACK FROM THE TOILET. THEY STOP SERVING BREAKFAST EARLY ON SUNDAY.
SO IF YOU'RE REALLY GOING TO STICK AROUND, I HOPE YOU'RE READY TO WORK. I HAVE TO TURN MY NOTES ON KANKAKEE INTO SOMETHING RESEMBLING ENGLISH. AND YOU'RE GOING TO START TEARING YOUR EPIC APART, AM I RIGHT?
I'LL TRY...
YES, YOU WILL. CUT SIX PAGES FOR A START, AND MAYBE WE'LL GO INTO CHICAGO FOR LUNCH TO CELEBRATE.

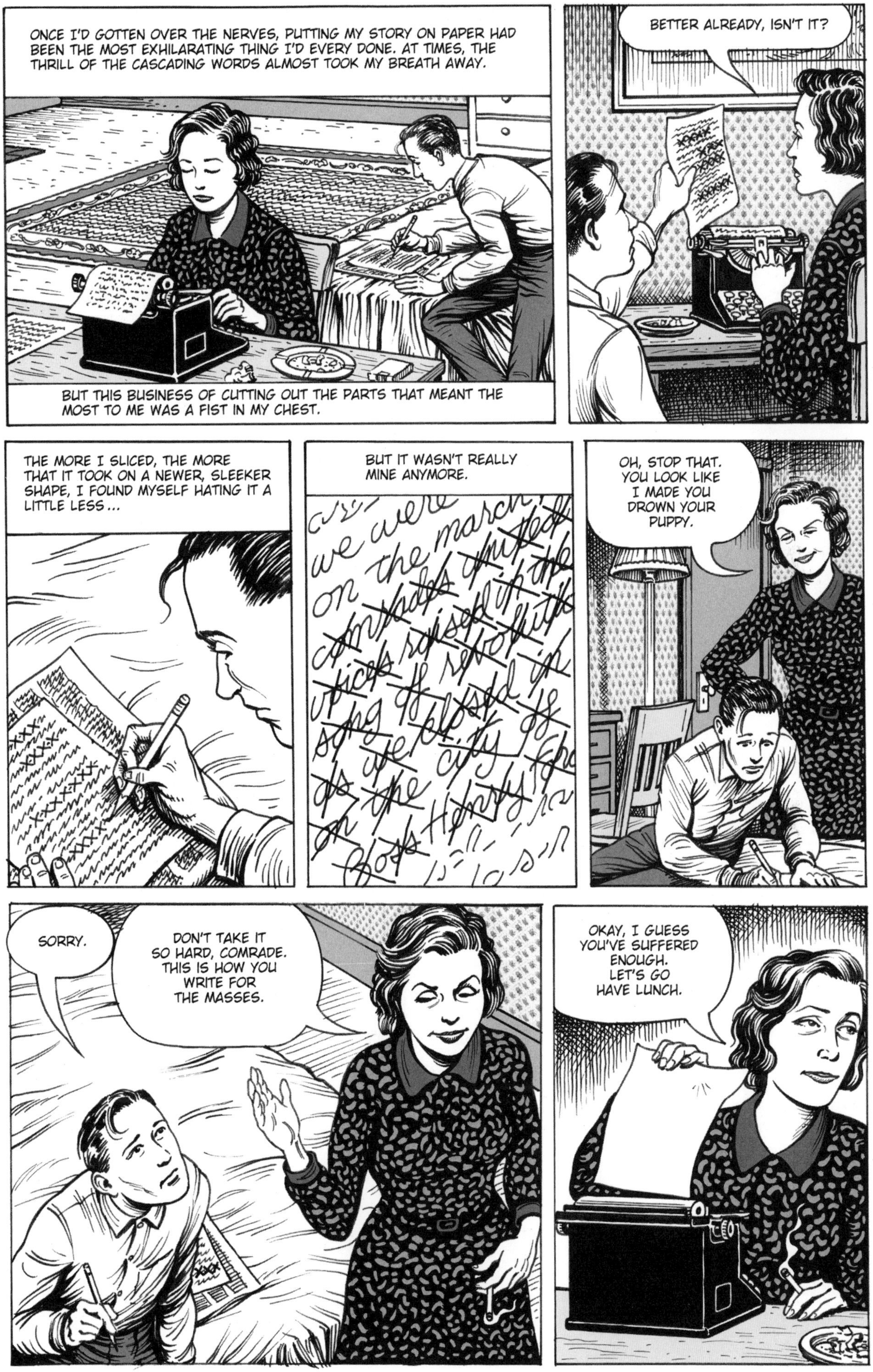
ONCE I'D GOTTEN OVER THE NERVES, PUTTING MY STORY ON PAPER HAD BEEN THE MOST EXHILARATING THING I'D EVERY DONE. AT TIMES, THE THRILL OF THE CASCADING WORDS ALMOST TOOK MY BREATH AWAY.
BUT THIS BUSINESS OF CUTTING OUT THE PARTS THAT MEANT THE MOST TO ME WAS A FIST IN MY CHEST.
BETTER ALREADY, ISN'T IT?
THE MORE I SLICED, THE MORE THAT IT TOOK ON A NEWER, SLEEKER SHAPE, I FOUND MYSELF HATING IT A LITTLE LESS...
BUT IT WASN'T REALLY MINE ANYMORE.
we were
on the march
the city
OH, STOP THAT. YOU LOOK LIKE I MADE YOU DROWN YOUR PUPPY.
SORRY.
DON'T TAKE IT SO HARD, COMRADE. THIS IS HOW YOU WRITE FOR THE MASSES.
OKAY, I GUESS YOU'VE SUFFERED ENOUGH. LET'S GO HAVE LUNCH.

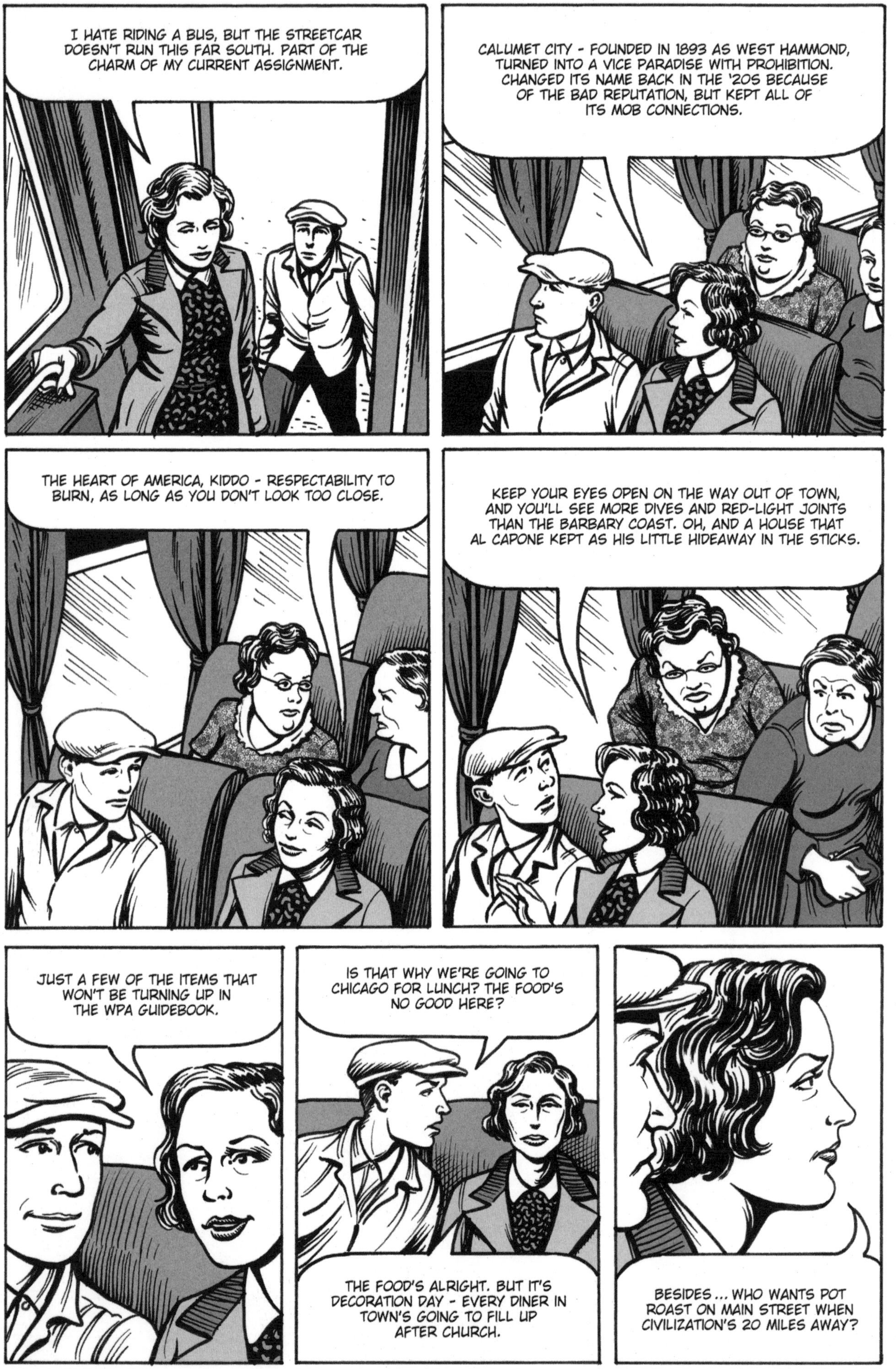
I HATE RIDING A BUS, BUT THE STREETCAR DOESN'T RUN THIS FAR SOUTH. PART OF THE CHARM OF MY CURRENT ASSIGNMENT.
CALUMET CITY - FOUNDED IN 1893 AS WEST HAMMOND, TURNED INTO A VICE PARADISE WITH PROHIBITION. CHANGED ITS NAME BACK IN THE '20S BECAUSE OF THE BAD REPUTATION, BUT KEPT ALL OF ITS MOB CONNECTIONS.
THE HEART OF AMERICA, KIDDO - RESPECTABILITY TO BURN, AS LONG AS YOU DON'T LOOK TOO CLOSE.
KEEP YOUR EYES OPEN ON THE WAY OUT OF TOWN, AND YOU'LL SEE MORE DIVES AND RED-LIGHT JOINTS THAN THE BARBARY COAST. OH, AND A HOUSE THAT AL CAPONE KEPT AS HIS LITTLE HIDEAWAY IN THE STICKS.
JUST A FEW OF THE ITEMS THAT WON'T BE TURNING UP IN THE WPA GUIDEBOOK.
IS THAT WHY WE'RE GOING TO CHICAGO FOR LUNCH? THE FOOD'S NO GOOD HERE?
THE FOOD'S ALRIGHT. BUT IT'S DECORATION DAY - EVERY DINER IN TOWN'S GOING TO FILL UP AFTER CHURCH.
BESIDES ... WHO WANTS POT ROAST ON MAIN STREET WHEN CIVILIZATION'S 20 MILES AWAY?

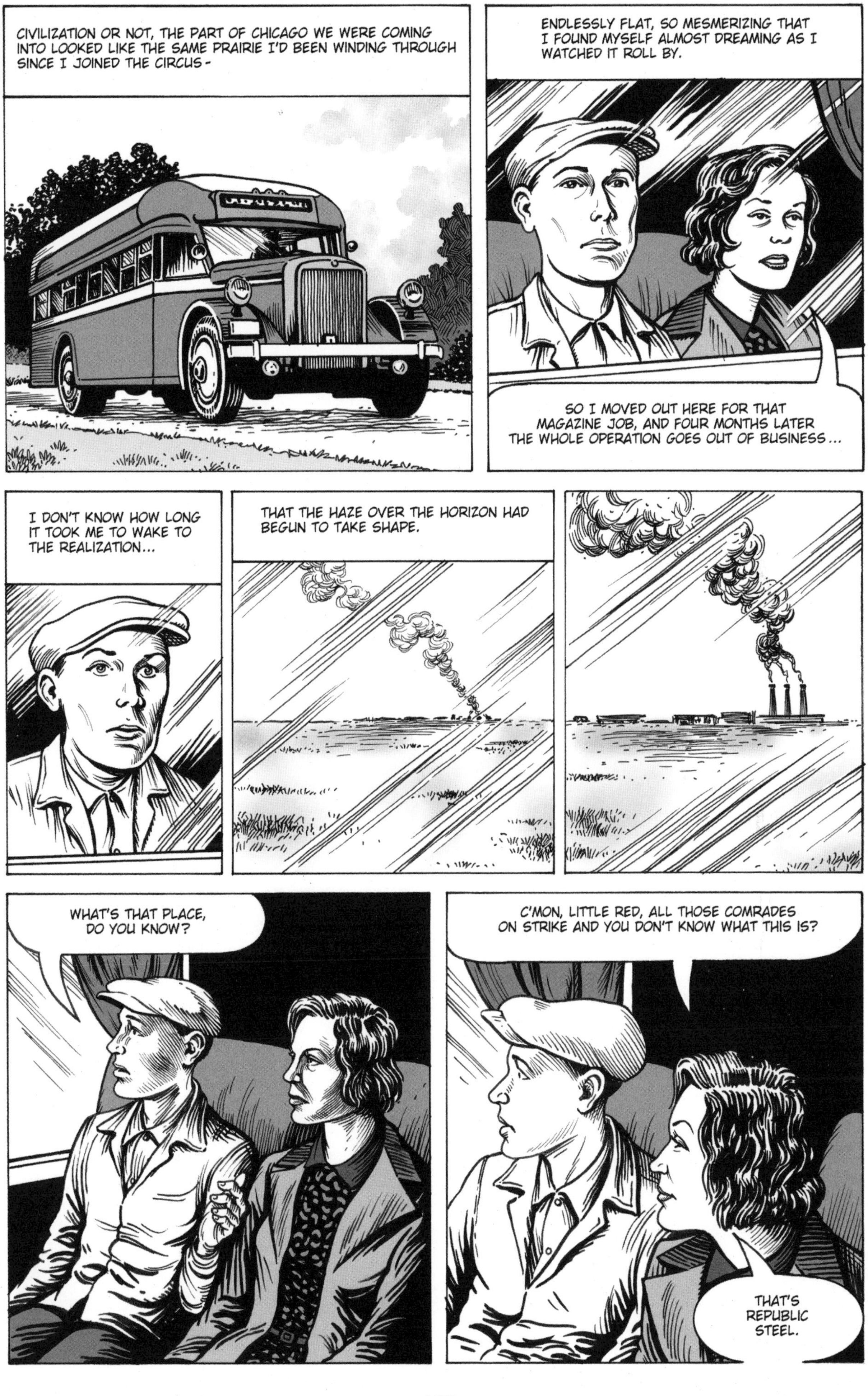
CIVILIZATION OR NOT, THE PART OF CHICAGO WE WERE COMING INTO LOOKED LIKE THE SAME PRAIRIE I'D BEEN WINDING THROUGH SINCE I JOINED THE CIRCUS -
ENDLESSLY FLAT, SO MESMERIZING THAT I FOUND MYSELF ALMOST DREAMING AS I WATCHED IT ROLL BY.
SO I MOVED OUT HERE FOR THAT MAGAZINE JOB, AND FOUR MONTHS LATER THE WHOLE OPERATION GOES OUT OF BUSINESS...
I DON'T KNOW HOW LONG IT TOOK ME TO WAKE TO THE REALIZATION...
THAT THE HAZE OVER THE HORIZON HAD BEGUN TO TAKE SHAPE.
WHAT'S THAT PLACE, DO YOU KNOW?
C'MON, LITTLE RED, ALL THOSE COMRADES ON STRIKE AND YOU DON'T KNOW WHAT THIS IS?
THAT'S REPUBLIC STEEL.

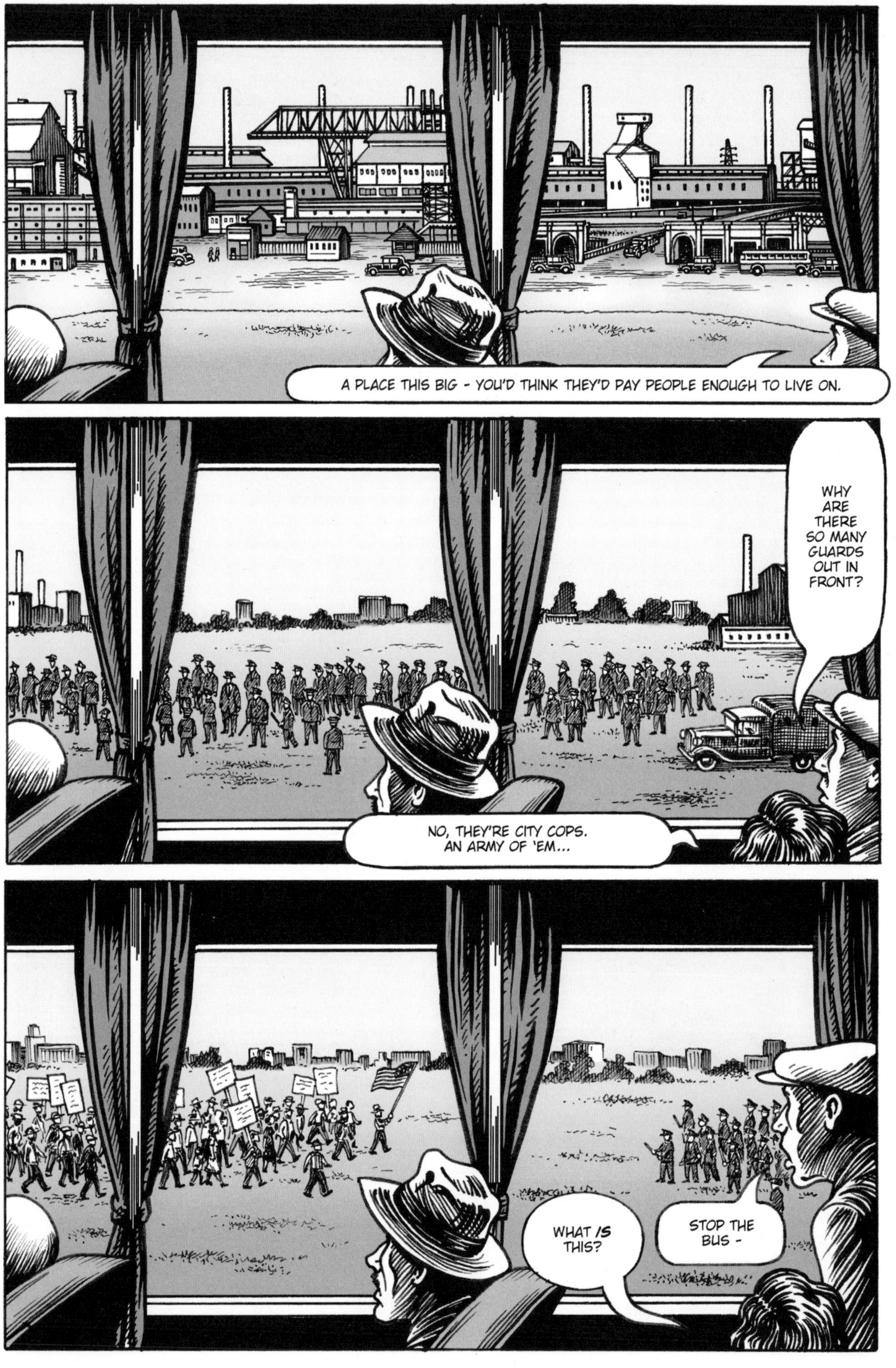
A PLACE THIS BIG - YOU'D THINK THEY'D PAY PEOPLE ENOUGH TO LIVE ON.
WHY ARE THERE SO MANY GUARDS OUT IN FRONT?
NO, THEY'RE CITY COPS. AN ARMY OF 'EM...
WHAT IS THIS?
STOP THE BUS -

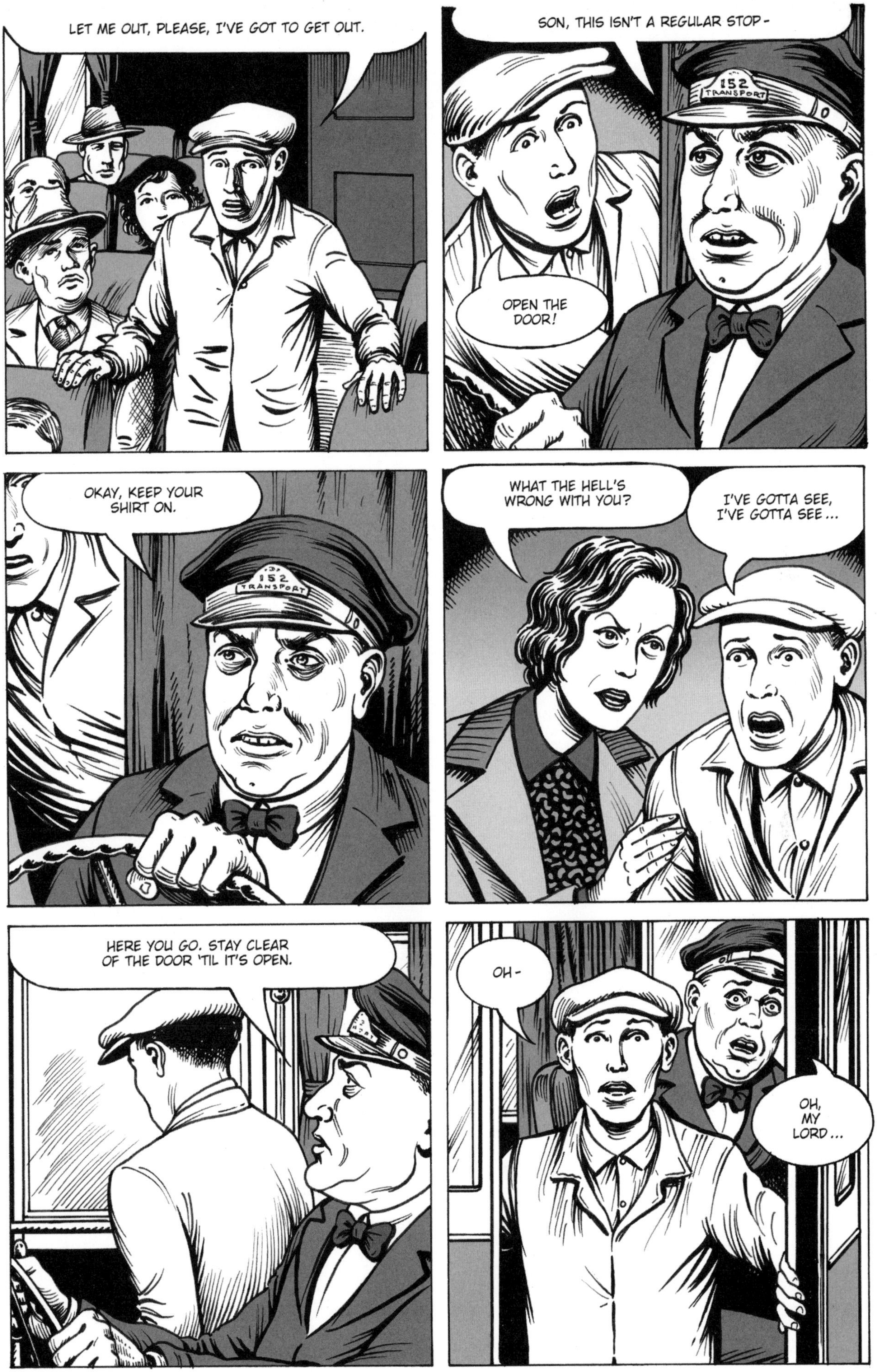
LET ME OUT, PLEASE, I'VE GOT TO GET OUT.
SON, THIS ISN'T A REGULAR STOP-
OPEN THE DOOR!
152 TRANSPORT
OKAY, KEEP YOUR SHIRT ON.
152 TRANSPORT
WHAT THE HELL'S WRONG WITH YOU?
I'VE GOTTA SEE, I'VE GOTTA SEE...
HERE YOU GO. STAY CLEAR OF THE DOOR 'TIL IT'S OPEN.
OH-
OH, MY LORD...

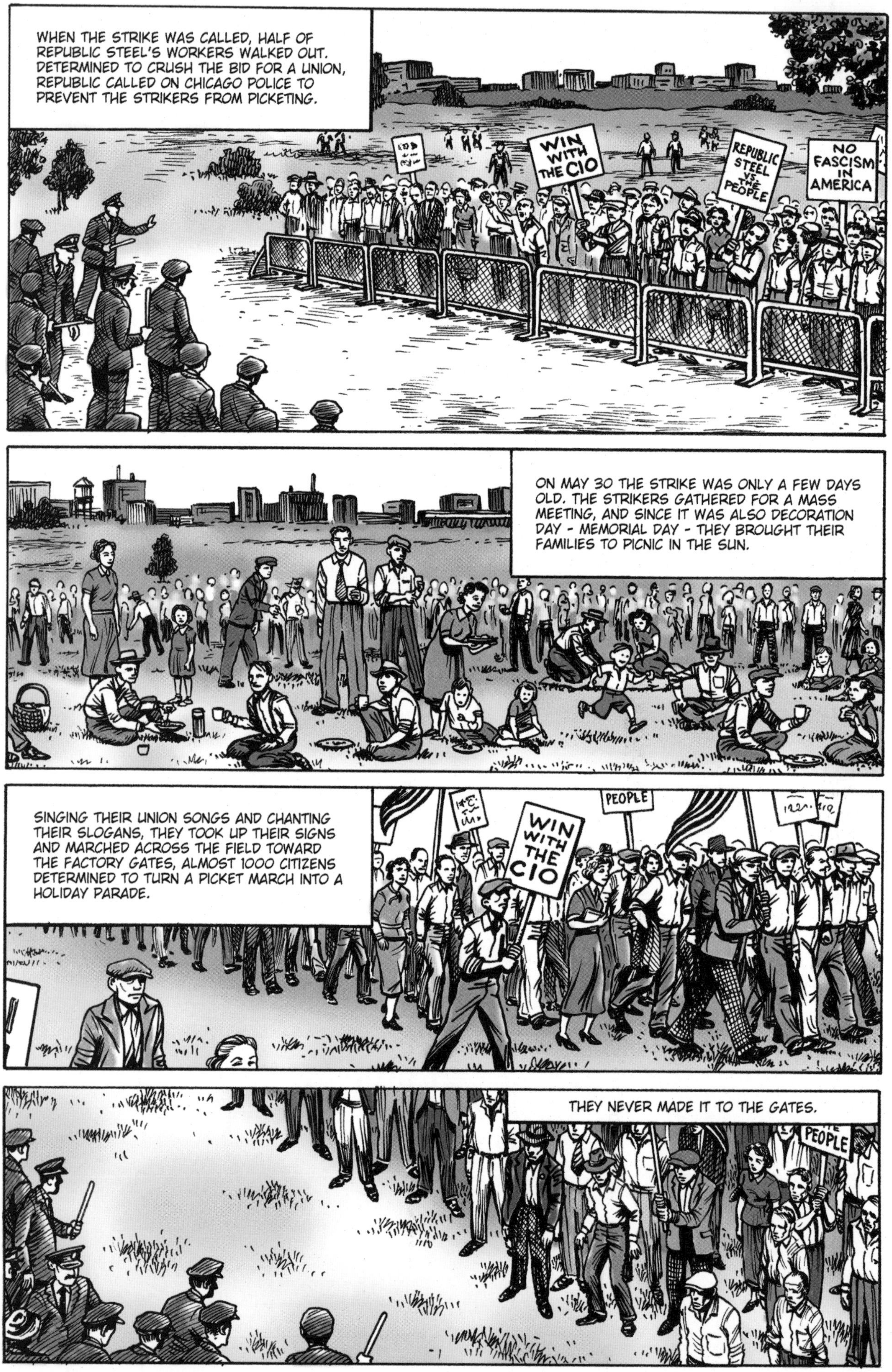
WHEN THE STRIKE WAS CALLED, HALF OF REPUBLIC STEEL'S WORKERS WALKED OUT. DETERMINED TO CRUSH THE BID FOR A UNION, REPUBLIC CALLED ON CHICAGO POLICE TO PREVENT THE STRIKERS FROM PICKETING.
WIN WITH THE CIO
REPUBLIC STEEL VS. THE PEOPLE
NO FASCISM IN AMERICA
ON MAY 30 THE STRIKE WAS ONLY A FEW DAYS OLD. THE STRIKERS GATHERED FOR A MASS MEETING, AND SINCE IT WAS ALSO DECORATION DAY - MEMORIAL DAY - THEY BROUGHT THEIR FAMILIES TO PICNIC IN THE SUN.
SINGING THEIR UNION SONGS AND CHANTING THEIR SLOGANS, THEY TOOK UP THEIR SIGNS AND MARCHED ACROSS THE FIELD TOWARD THE FACTORY GATES, ALMOST 1000 CITIZENS DETERMINED TO TURN A PICKET MARCH INTO A HOLIDAY PARADE.
PEOPLE
WIN WITH THE CIO
THEY NEVER MADE IT TO THE GATES.
PEOPLE

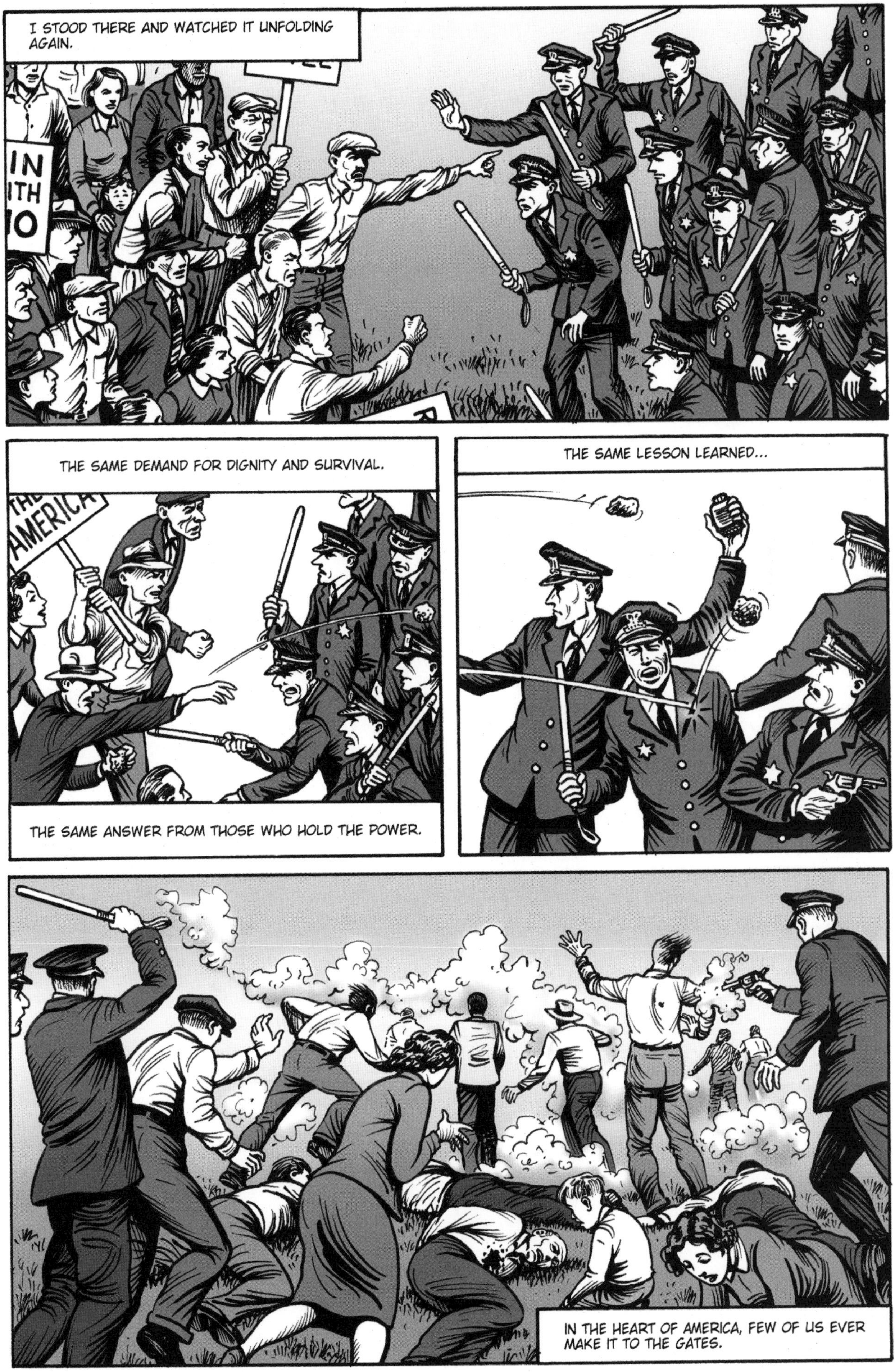
I STOOD THERE AND WATCHED IT UNFOLDING AGAIN.
IN
ITH
O
THE SAME DEMAND FOR DIGNITY AND SURVIVAL.
AMERICA
THE SAME ANSWER FROM THOSE WHO HOLD THE POWER.
THE SAME LESSON LEARNED...
IN THE HEART OF AMERICA, FEW OF US EVER MAKE IT TO THE GATES.

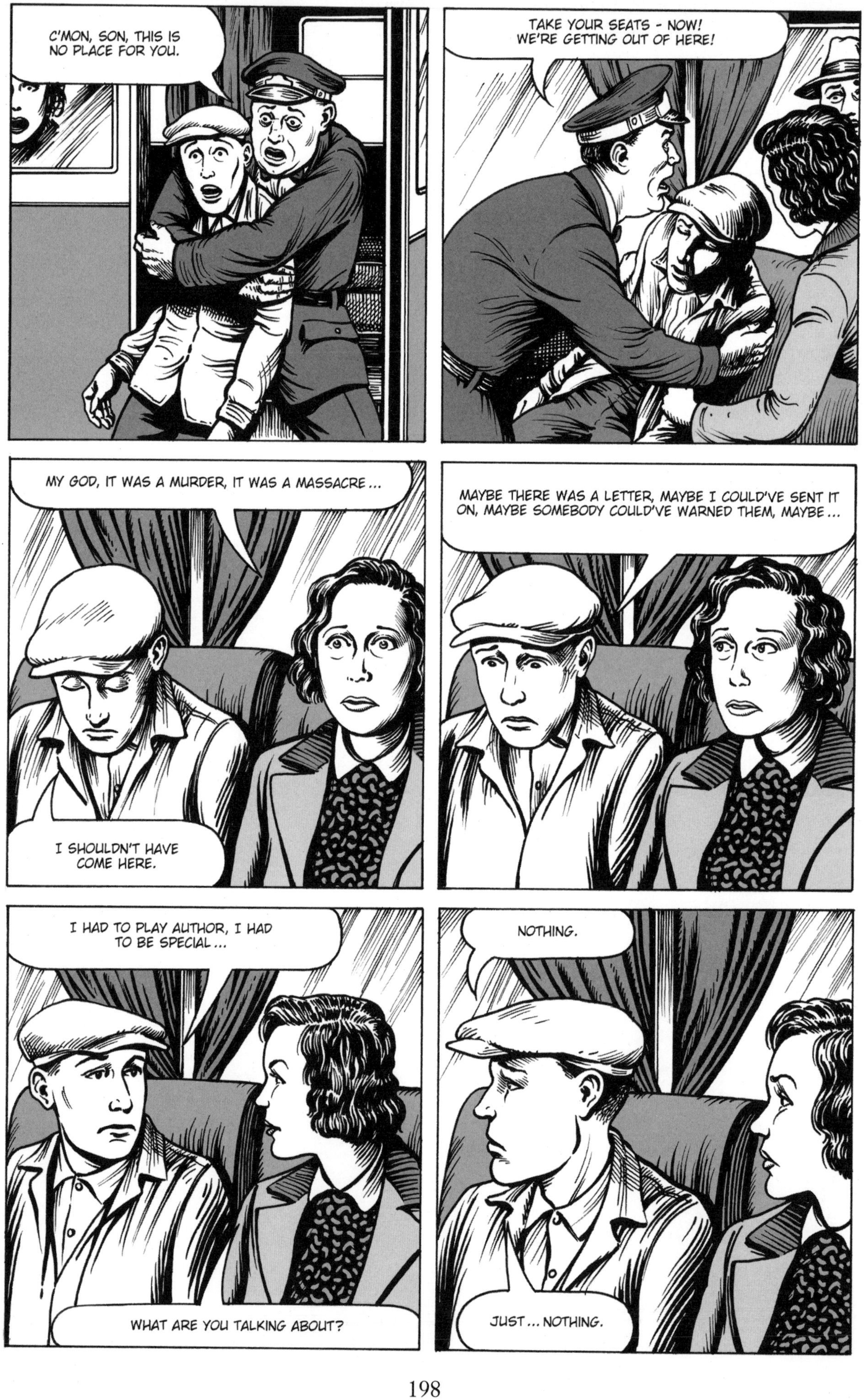
C'MON, SON, THIS IS NO PLACE FOR YOU.
TAKE YOUR SEATS - NOW! WE'RE GETTING OUT OF HERE!
MY GOD, IT WAS A MURDER, IT WAS A MASSACRE...
I SHOULDN'T HAVE COME HERE.
MAYBE THERE WAS A LETTER, MAYBE I COULD'VE SENT IT ON, MAYBE SOMEBODY COULD'VE WARNED THEM, MAYBE...
I HAD TO PLAY AUTHOR, I HAD TO BE SPECIAL...
WHAT ARE YOU TALKING ABOUT?
NOTHING.
JUST... NOTHING.

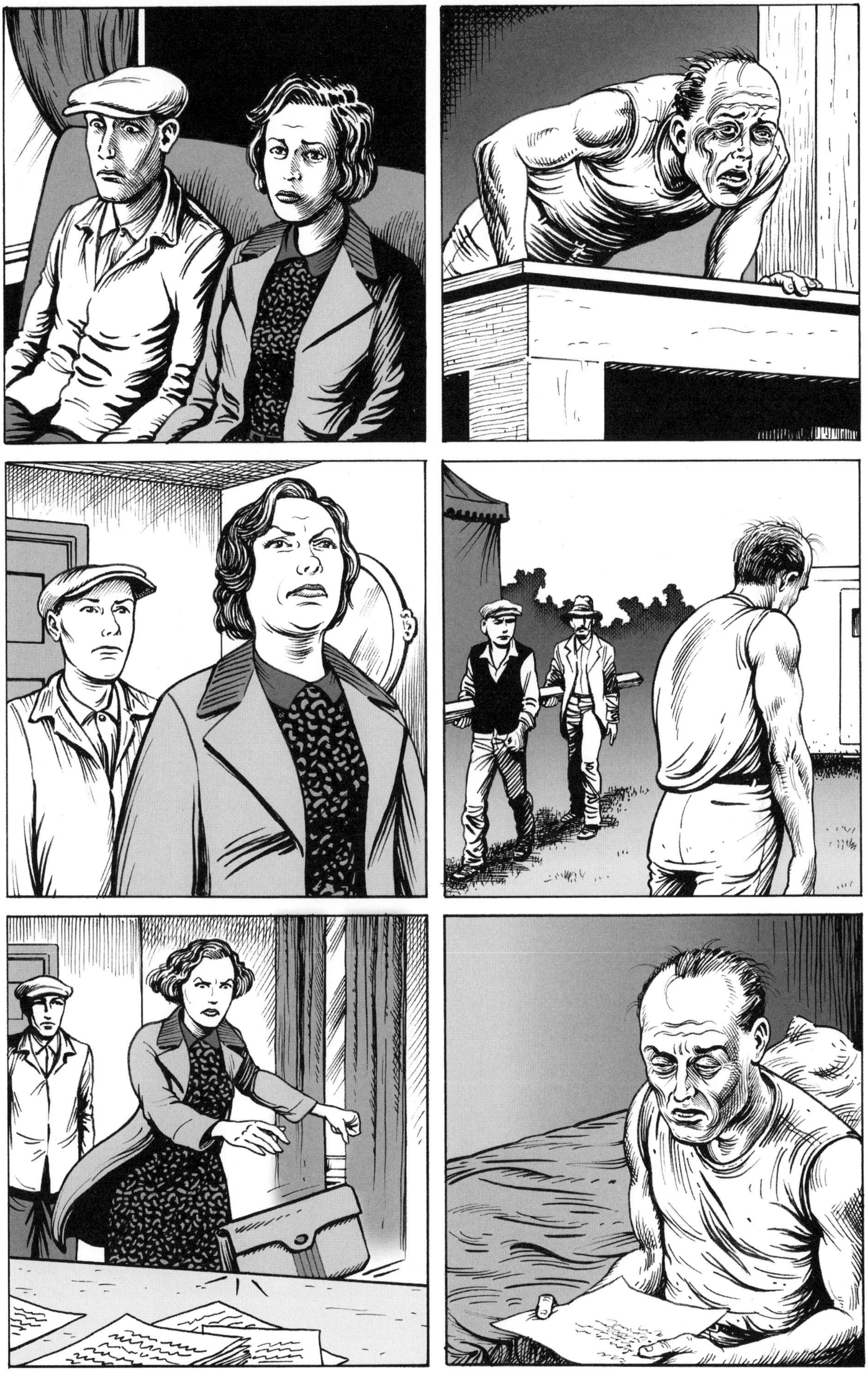

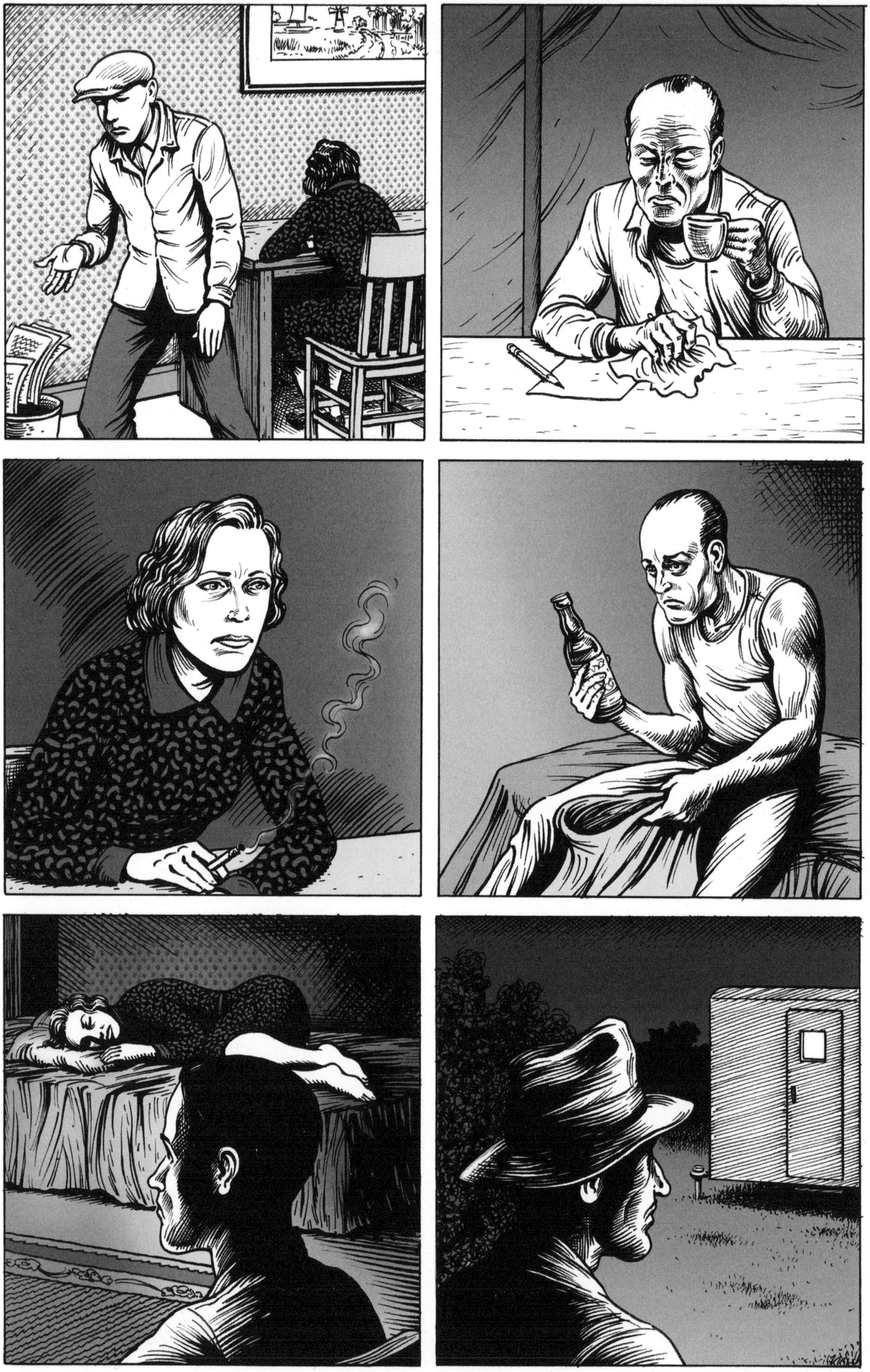

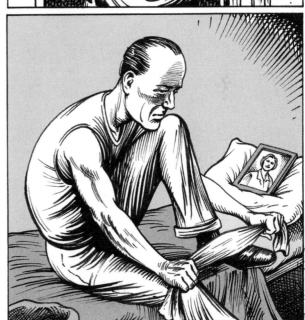
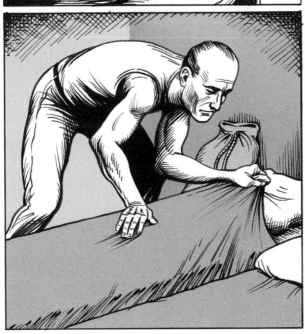

201

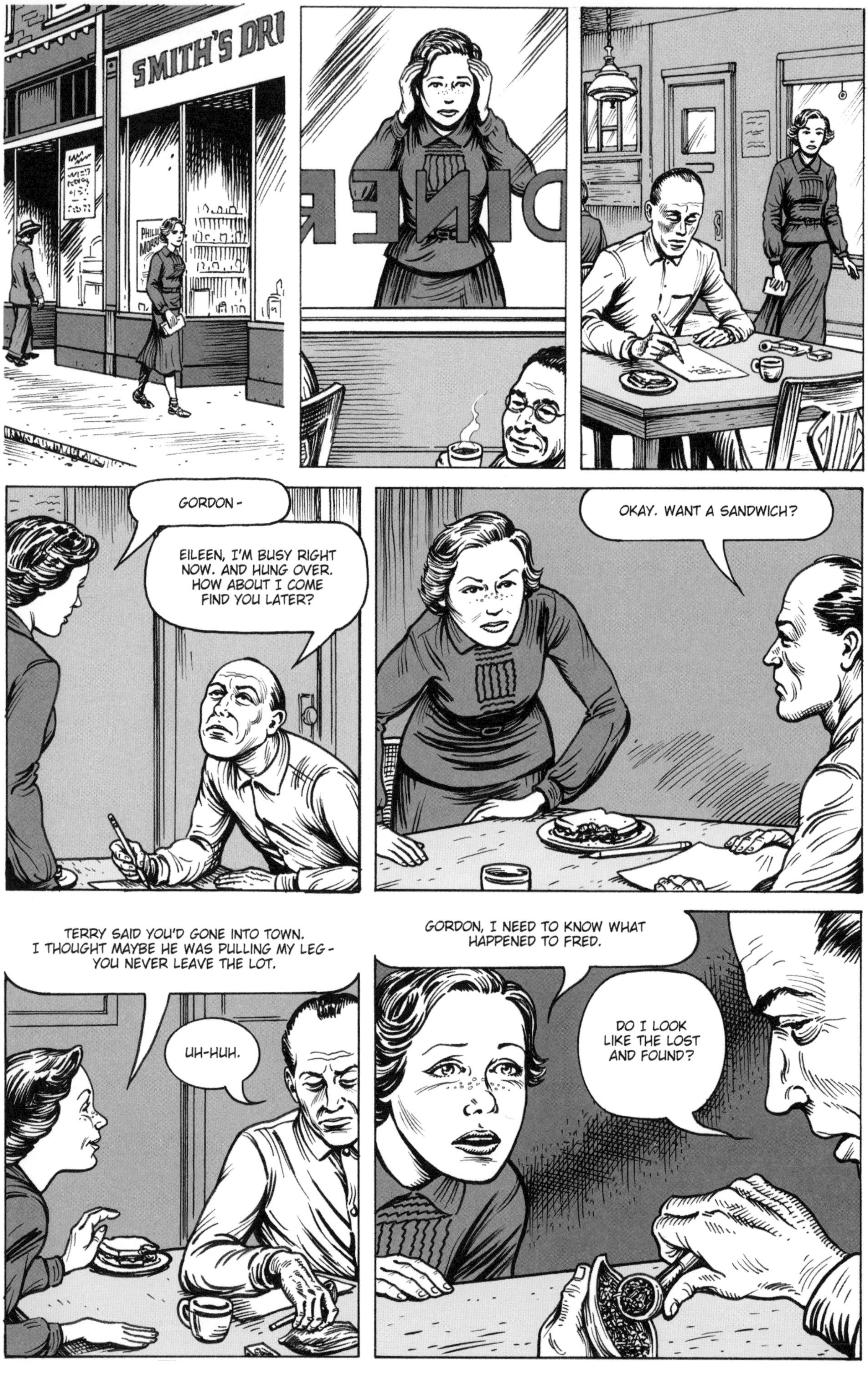
SMITH'S DRI
DINER
GORDON -
EILEEN, I'M BUSY RIGHT NOW. AND HUNG OVER. HOW ABOUT I COME FIND YOU LATER?
OKAY. WANT A SANDWICH?
TERRY SAID YOU'D GONE INTO TOWN. I THOUGHT MAYBE HE WAS PULLING MY LEG - YOU NEVER LEAVE THE LOT.
UH-HUH.
GORDON, I NEED TO KNOW WHAT HAPPENED TO FRED.
DO I LOOK LIKE THE LOST AND FOUND?

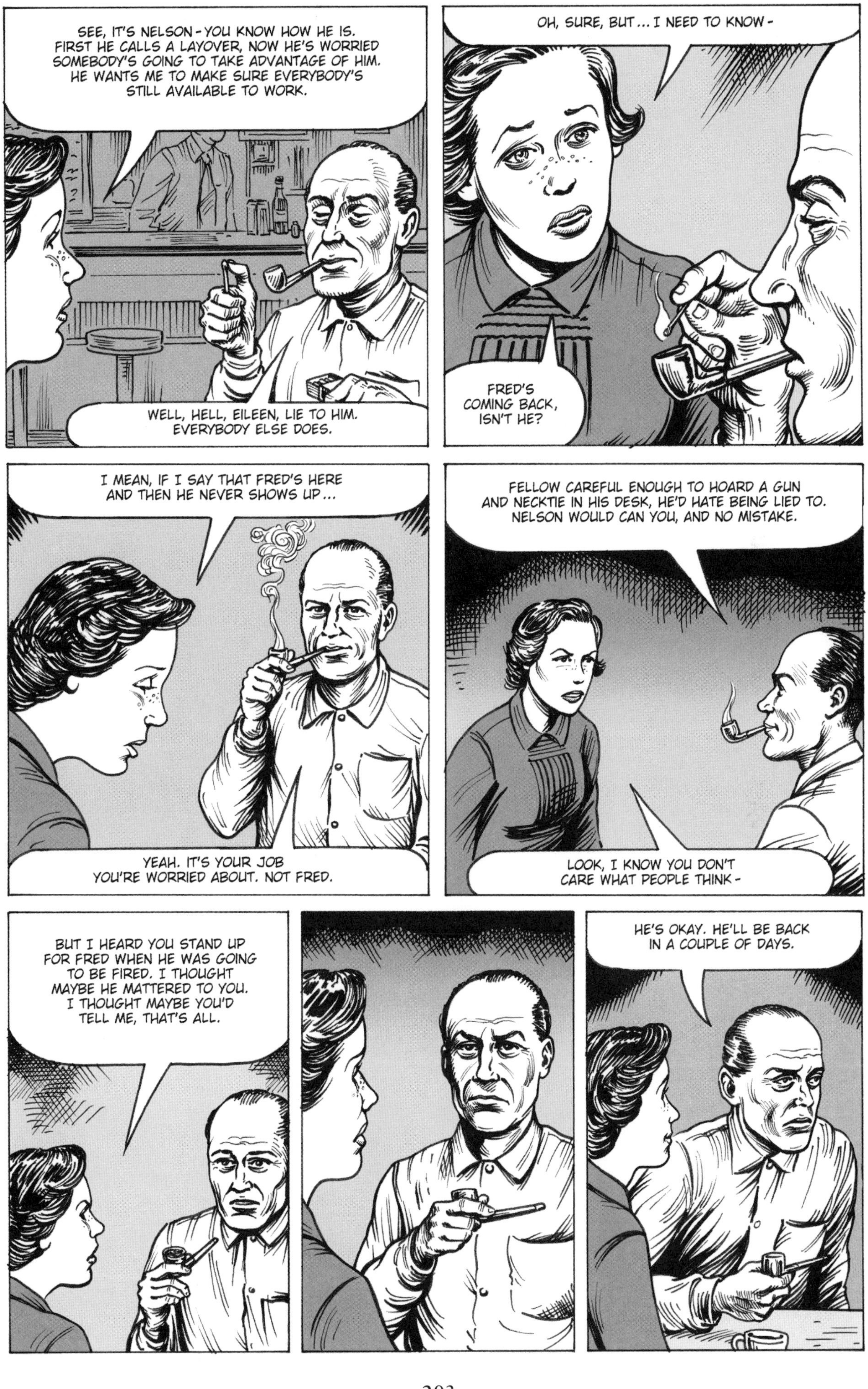
SEE, IT'S NELSON - YOU KNOW HOW HE IS. FIRST HE CALLS A LAYOVER, NOW HE'S WORRIED SOMEBODY'S GOING TO TAKE ADVANTAGE OF HIM. HE WANTS ME TO MAKE SURE EVERYBODY'S STILL AVAILABLE TO WORK.
WELL, HELL, EILEEN, LIE TO HIM. EVERYBODY ELSE DOES.
OH, SURE, BUT... I NEED TO KNOW -
FRED'S COMING BACK, ISN'T HE?
I MEAN, IF I SAY THAT FRED'S HERE AND THEN HE NEVER SHOWS UP...
YEAH. IT'S YOUR JOB YOU'RE WORRIED ABOUT. NOT FRED.
FELLOW CAREFUL ENOUGH TO HOARD A GUN AND NECKTIE IN HIS DESK, HE'D HATE BEING LIED TO. NELSON WOULD CAN YOU, AND NO MISTAKE.
LOOK, I KNOW YOU DON'T CARE WHAT PEOPLE THINK -
BUT I HEARD YOU STAND UP FOR FRED WHEN HE WAS GOING TO BE FIRED. I THOUGHT MAYBE HE MATTERED TO YOU. I THOUGHT MAYBE YOU'D TELL ME, THAT'S ALL.
HE'S OKAY. HE'LL BE BACK IN A COUPLE OF DAYS.

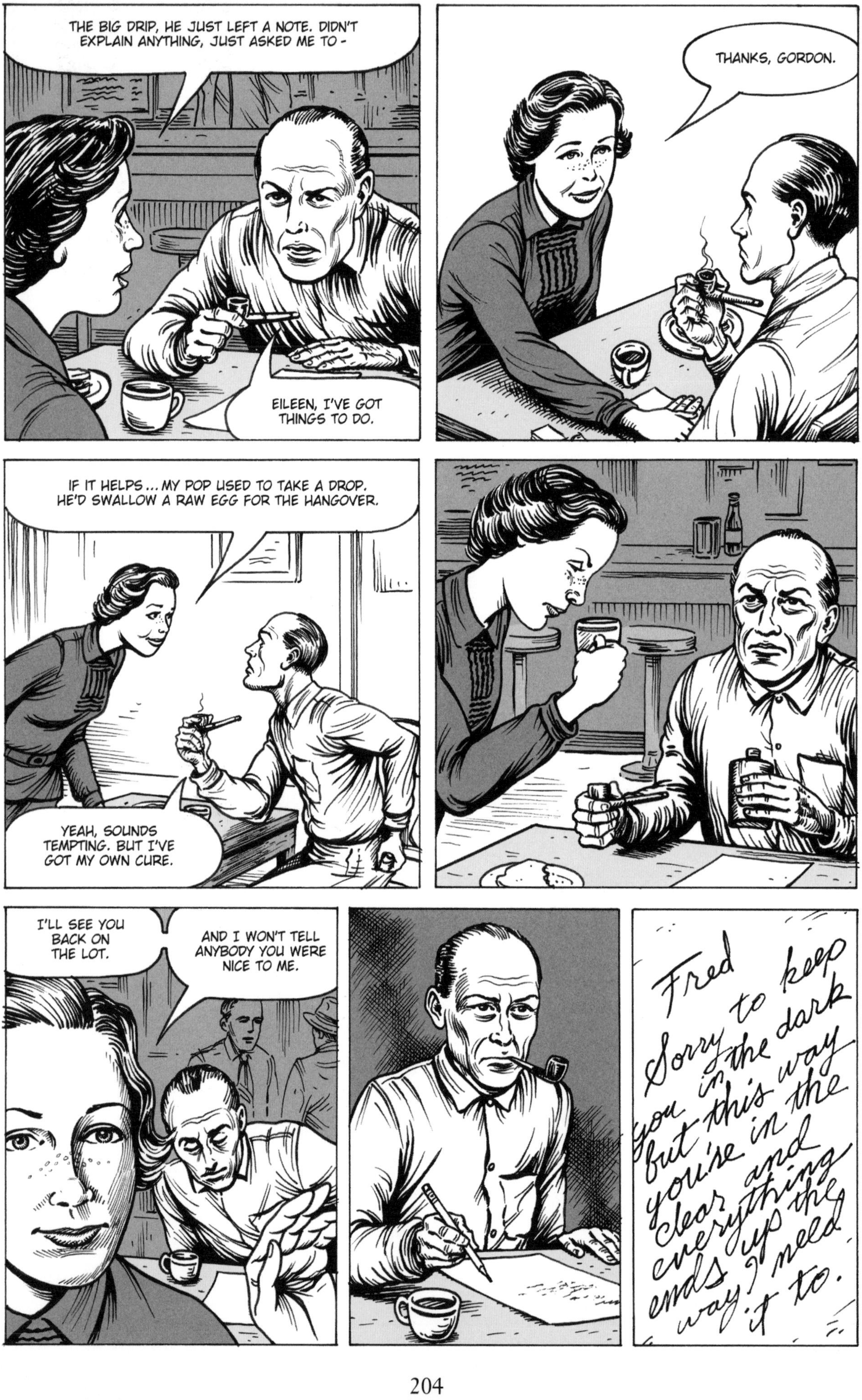
THE BIG DRIP, HE JUST LEFT A NOTE. DIDN'T EXPLAIN ANYTHING, JUST ASKED ME TO -
EILEEN, I'VE GOT THINGS TO DO.
THANKS, GORDON.
IF IT HELPS ... MY POP USED TO TAKE A DROP. HE'D SWALLOW A RAW EGG FOR THE HANGOVER.
YEAH, SOUNDS TEMPTING. BUT I'VE GOT MY OWN CURE.
I'LL SEE YOU BACK ON THE LOT.
AND I WON'T TELL ANYBODY YOU WERE NICE TO ME.
Fred
Sorry to keep you in the dark but this way you're in the clear and everything ends up the way I need it to.

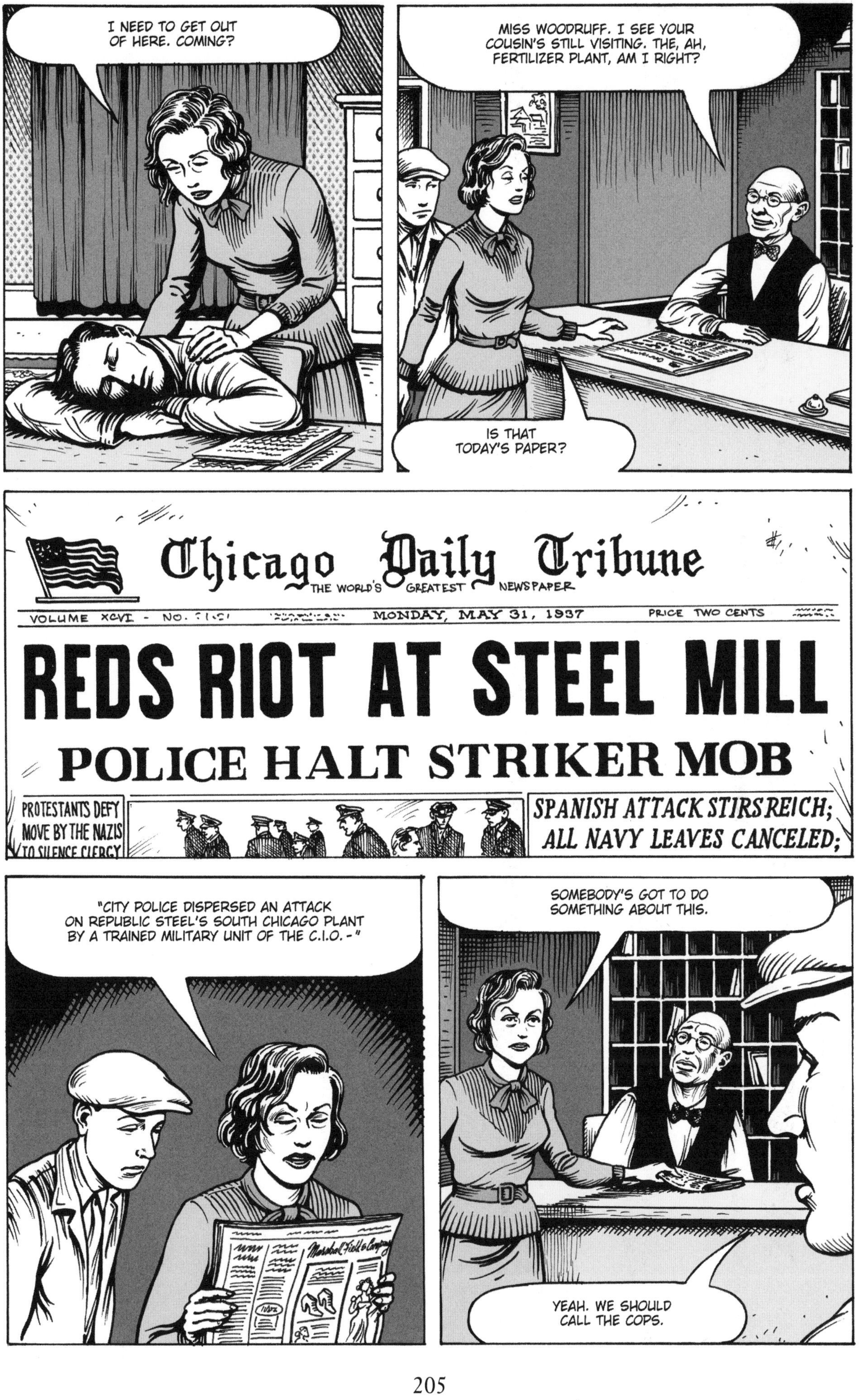
I NEED TO GET OUT OF HERE. COMING?
MISS WOODRUFF. I SEE YOUR COUSIN'S STILL VISITING. THE, AH, FERTILIZER PLANT, AM I RIGHT?
IS THAT TODAY'S PAPER?
Chicago Daily Tribune
THE WORLD'S GREATEST NEWSPAPER
VOLUME XCVI - NO.
MONDAY, MAY 31, 1937
PRICE TWO CENTS
REDS RIOT AT STEEL MILL
POLICE HALT STRIKER MOB
PROTESTANTS DEFY MOVE BY THE NAZIS TO SILENCE CLERGY
SPANISH ATTACK STIRS REICH; ALL NAVY LEAVES CANCELED;
"CITY POLICE DISPERSED AN ATTACK ON REPUBLIC STEEL'S SOUTH CHICAGO PLANT BY A TRAINED MILITARY UNIT OF THE C.I.O. -"
SOMEBODY'S GOT TO DO SOMETHING ABOUT THIS.
YEAH. WE SHOULD CALL THE COPS.

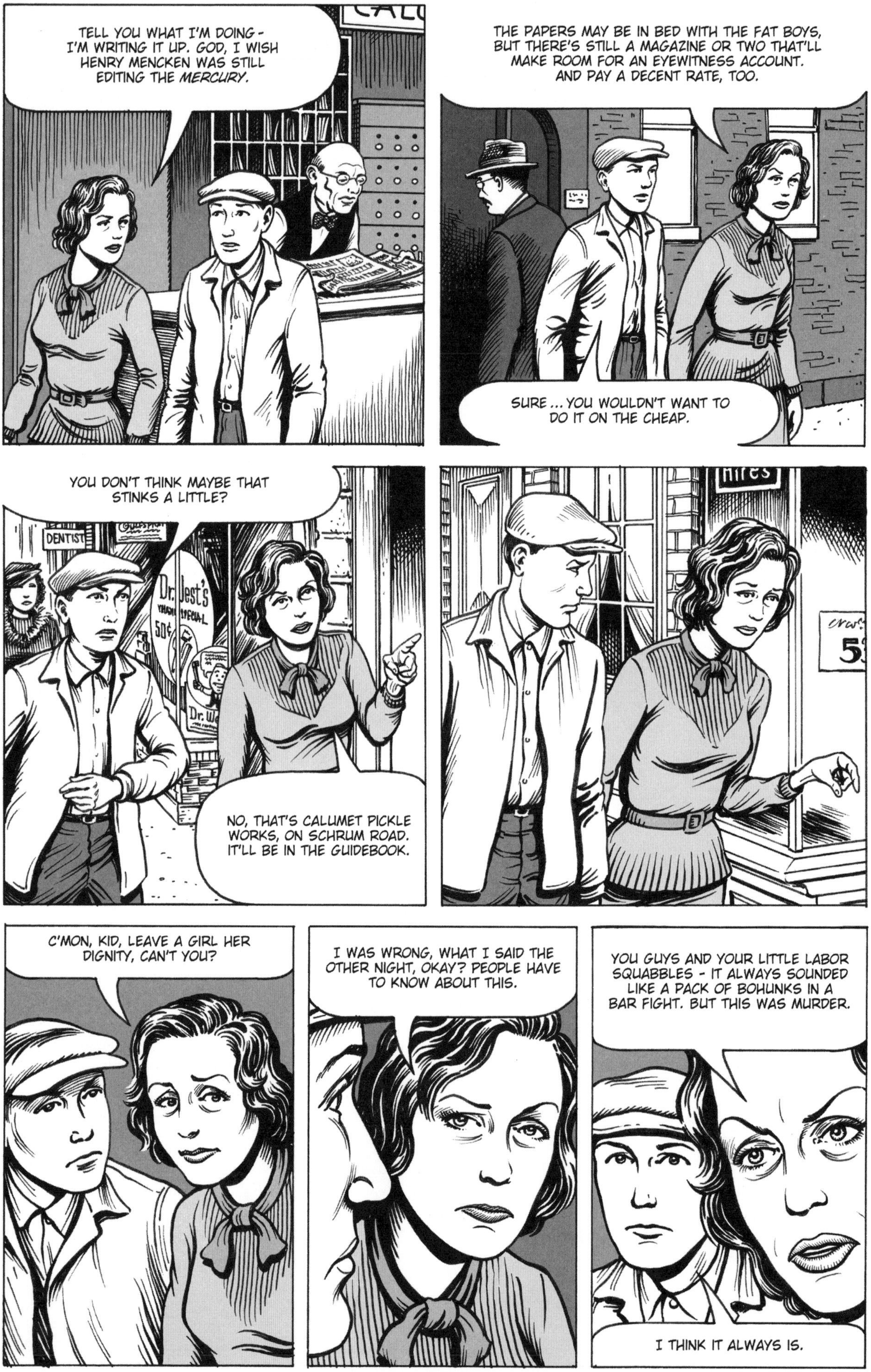
TELL YOU WHAT I'M DOING - I'M WRITING IT UP. GOD, I WISH HENRY MENCKEN WAS STILL EDITING THE *MERCURY.*
THE PAPERS MAY BE IN BED WITH THE FAT BOYS, BUT THERE'S STILL A MAGAZINE OR TWO THAT'LL MAKE ROOM FOR AN EYEWITNESS ACCOUNT. AND PAY A DECENT RATE, TOO.
SURE ... YOU WOULDN'T WANT TO DO IT ON THE CHEAP.
YOU DON'T THINK MAYBE THAT STINKS A LITTLE?
DENTIST
NO, THAT'S CALUMET PICKLE WORKS, ON SCHRUM ROAD. IT'LL BE IN THE GUIDEBOOK.
C'MON, KID, LEAVE A GIRL HER DIGNITY, CAN'T YOU?
I WAS WRONG, WHAT I SAID THE OTHER NIGHT, OKAY? PEOPLE HAVE TO KNOW ABOUT THIS.
YOU GUYS AND YOUR LITTLE LABOR SQUABBLES - IT ALWAYS SOUNDED LIKE A PACK OF BOHUNKS IN A BAR FIGHT. BUT THIS WAS MURDER.
I THINK IT ALWAYS IS.

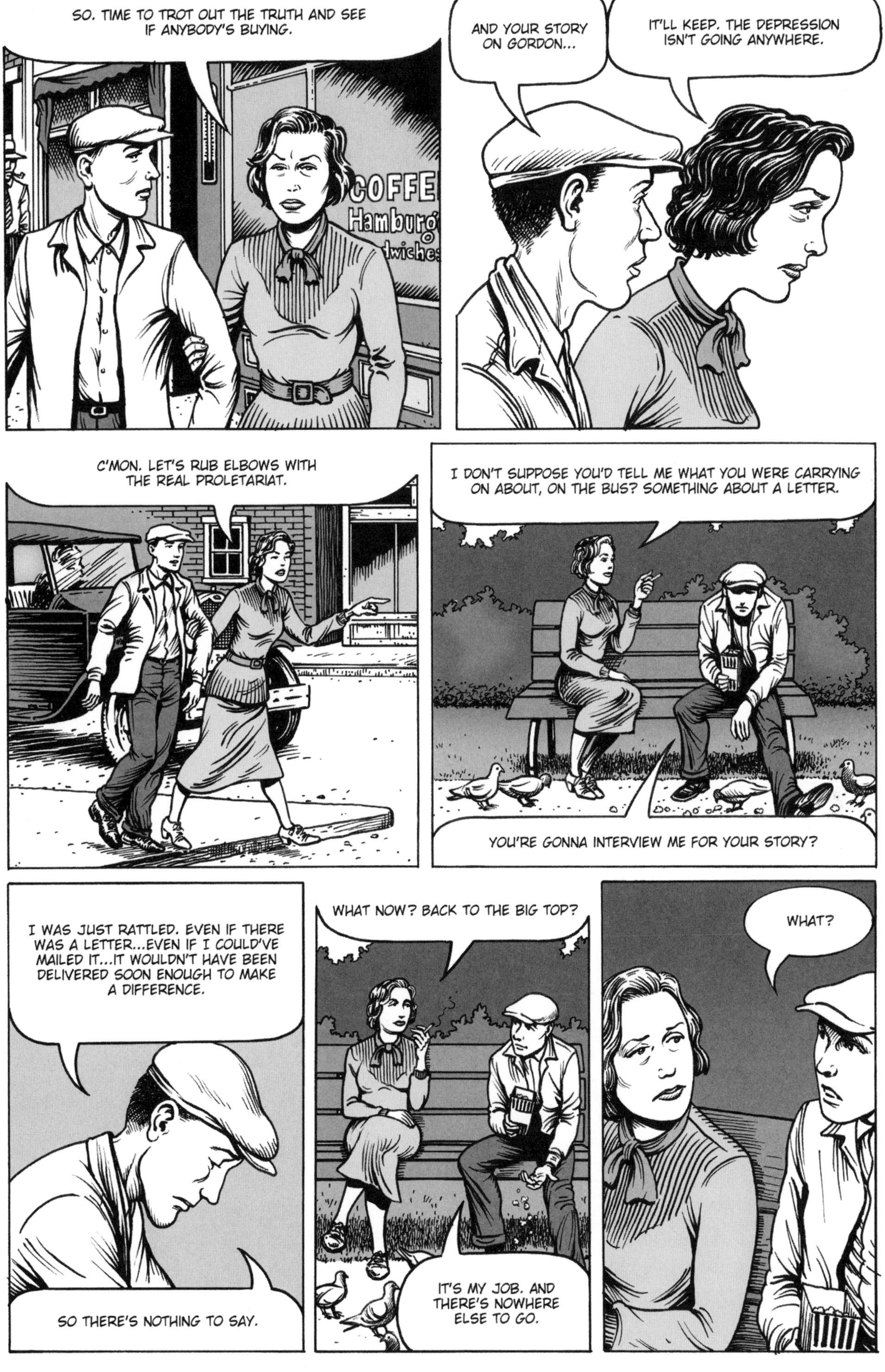
SO. TIME TO TROT OUT THE TRUTH AND SEE IF ANYBODY'S BUYING.
COFFEE
Hamburg
dwiches
AND YOUR STORY ON GORDON...
IT'LL KEEP. THE DEPRESSION ISN'T GOING ANYWHERE.
C'MON. LET'S RUB ELBOWS WITH THE REAL PROLETARIAT.
I DON'T SUPPOSE YOU'D TELL ME WHAT YOU WERE CARRYING ON ABOUT, ON THE BUS? SOMETHING ABOUT A LETTER.
YOU'RE GONNA INTERVIEW ME FOR YOUR STORY?
I WAS JUST RATTLED. EVEN IF THERE WAS A LETTER...EVEN IF I COULD'VE MAILED IT...IT WOULDN'T HAVE BEEN DELIVERED SOON ENOUGH TO MAKE A DIFFERENCE.
SO THERE'S NOTHING TO SAY.
WHAT NOW? BACK TO THE BIG TOP?
IT'S MY JOB. AND THERE'S NOWHERE ELSE TO GO.
WHAT?

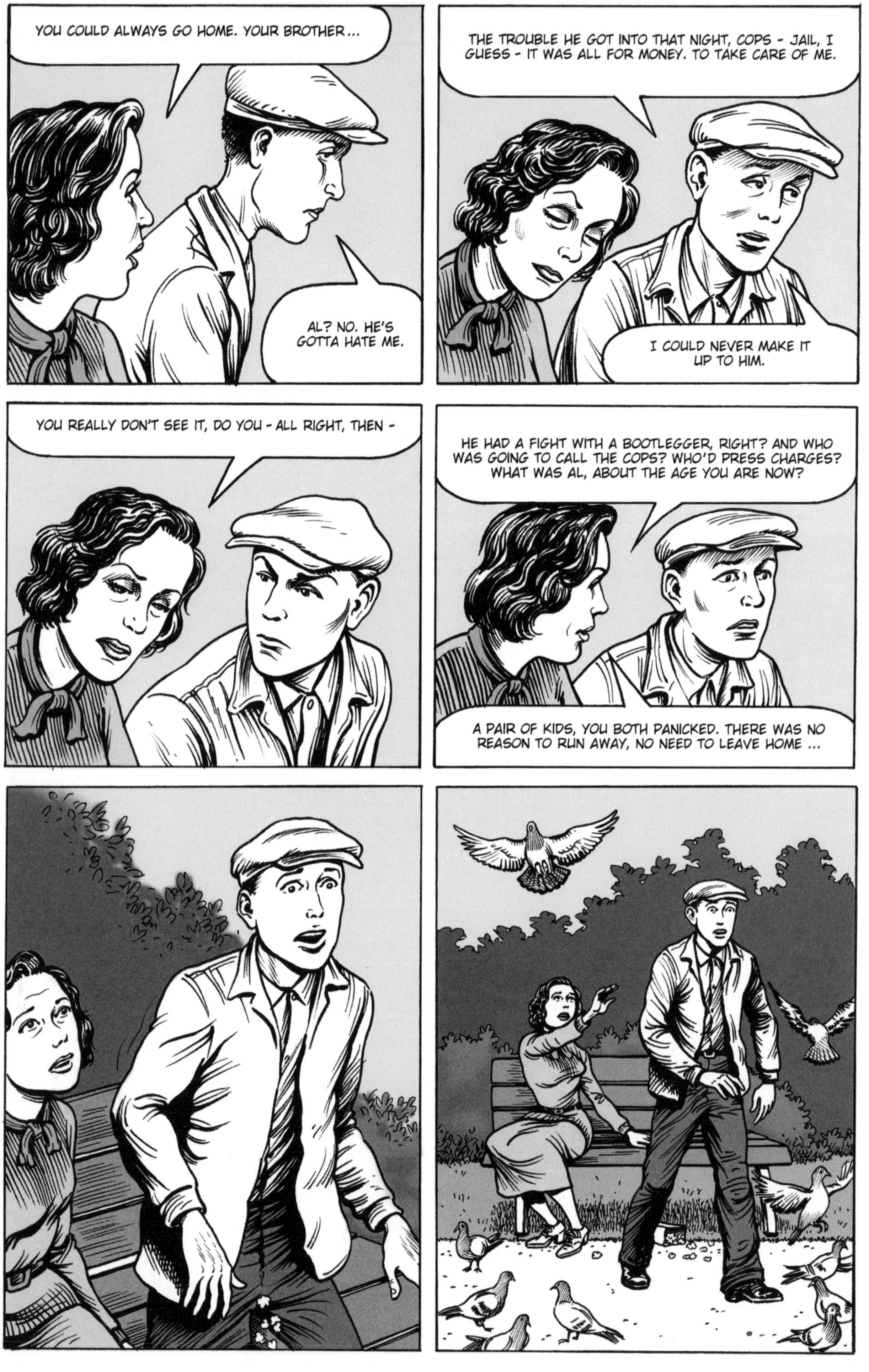
YOU COULD ALWAYS GO HOME. YOUR BROTHER...
AL? NO. HE'S GOTTA HATE ME.
THE TROUBLE HE GOT INTO THAT NIGHT, COPS - JAIL, I GUESS - IT WAS ALL FOR MONEY. TO TAKE CARE OF ME.
I COULD NEVER MAKE IT UP TO HIM.
YOU REALLY DON'T SEE IT, DO YOU - ALL RIGHT, THEN -
HE HAD A FIGHT WITH A BOOTLEGGER, RIGHT? AND WHO WAS GOING TO CALL THE COPS? WHO'D PRESS CHARGES? WHAT WAS AL, ABOUT THE AGE YOU ARE NOW?
A PAIR OF KIDS, YOU BOTH PANICKED. THERE WAS NO REASON TO RUN AWAY, NO NEED TO LEAVE HOME ...

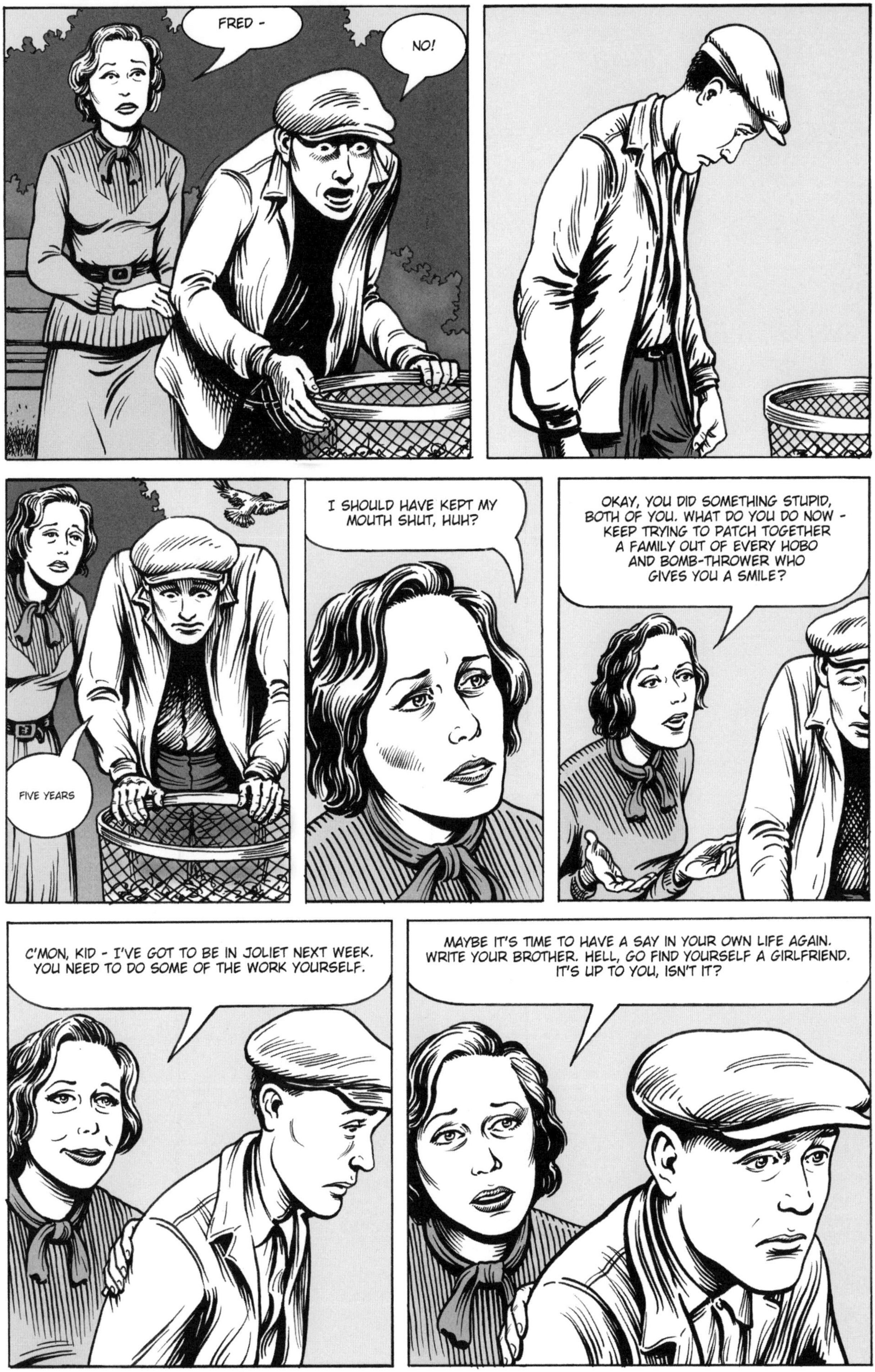
FRED -
NO!
FIVE YEARS
I SHOULD HAVE KEPT MY MOUTH SHUT, HUH?
OKAY, YOU DID SOMETHING STUPID, BOTH OF YOU. WHAT DO YOU DO NOW - KEEP TRYING TO PATCH TOGETHER A FAMILY OUT OF EVERY HOBO AND BOMB-THROWER WHO GIVES YOU A SMILE?
C'MON, KID - I'VE GOT TO BE IN JOLIET NEXT WEEK. YOU NEED TO DO SOME OF THE WORK YOURSELF.
MAYBE IT'S TIME TO HAVE A SAY IN YOUR OWN LIFE AGAIN. WRITE YOUR BROTHER. HELL, GO FIND YOURSELF A GIRLFRIEND. IT'S UP TO YOU, ISN'T IT?

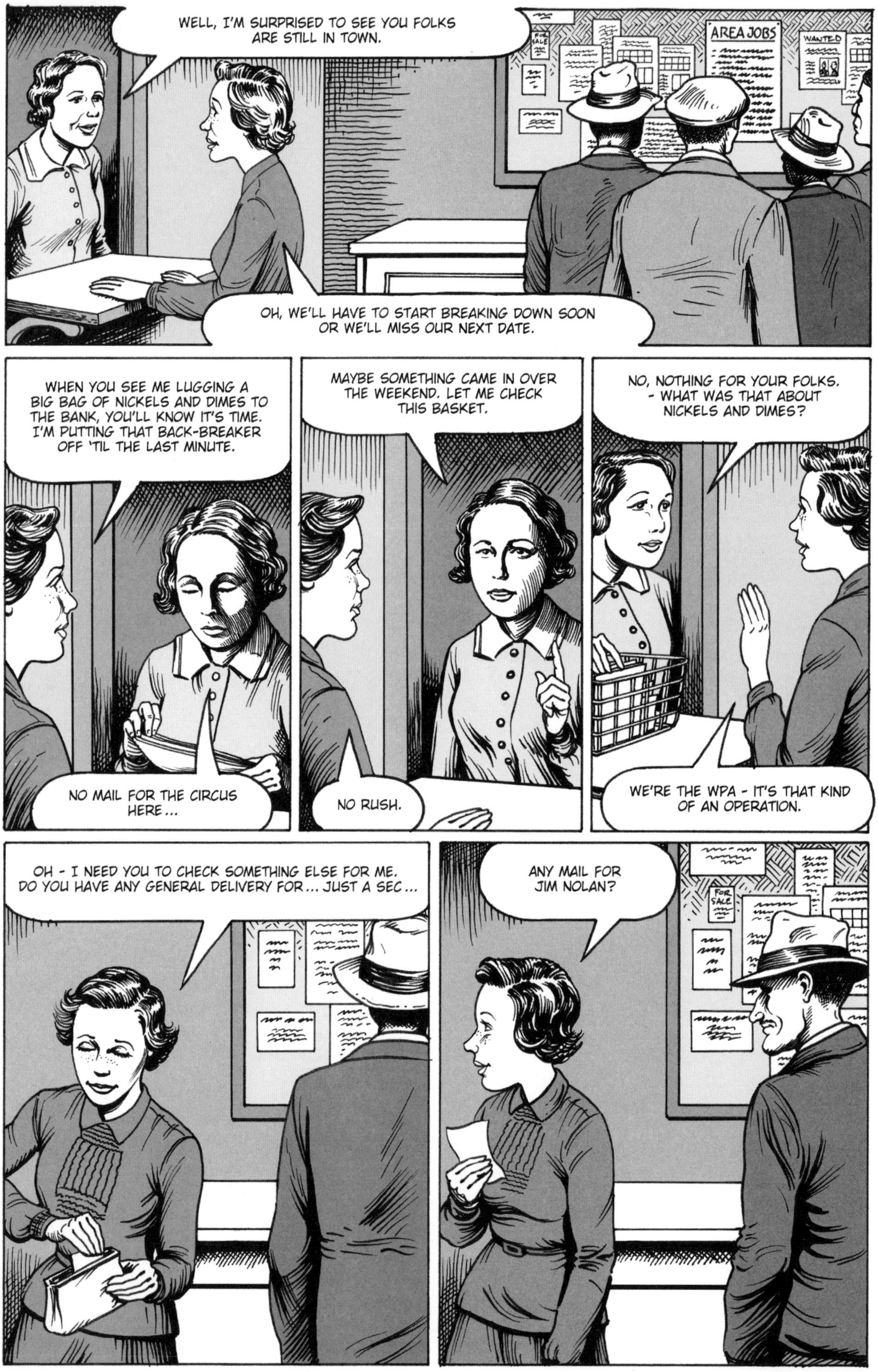
WELL, I'M SURPRISED TO SEE YOU FOLKS ARE STILL IN TOWN.
AREA JOBS
WANTED
FOR SALE
OH, WE'LL HAVE TO START BREAKING DOWN SOON OR WE'LL MISS OUR NEXT DATE.
WHEN YOU SEE ME LUGGING A BIG BAG OF NICKELS AND DIMES TO THE BANK, YOU'LL KNOW IT'S TIME. I'M PUTTING THAT BACK-BREAKER OFF 'TIL THE LAST MINUTE.
NO MAIL FOR THE CIRCUS HERE...
MAYBE SOMETHING CAME IN OVER THE WEEKEND. LET ME CHECK THIS BASKET.
NO RUSH.
NO, NOTHING FOR YOUR FOLKS. - WHAT WAS THAT ABOUT NICKELS AND DIMES?
WE'RE THE WPA - IT'S THAT KIND OF AN OPERATION.
OH - I NEED YOU TO CHECK SOMETHING ELSE FOR ME. DO YOU HAVE ANY GENERAL DELIVERY FOR... JUST A SEC...
ANY MAIL FOR JIM NOLAN?
FOR SALE

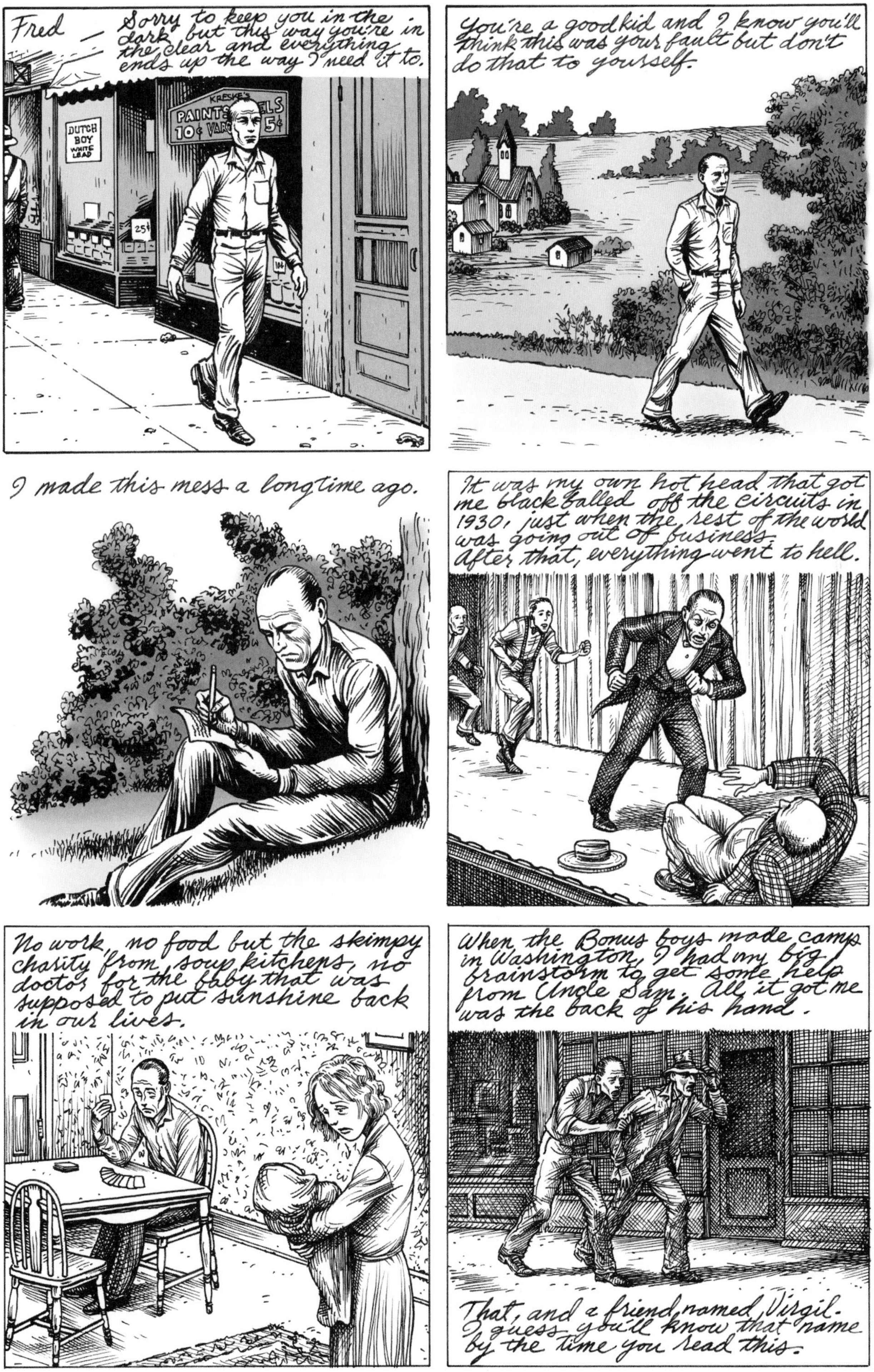
Fred — Sorry to keep you in the dark but this way you're in the clear and everything ends up the way I need it to.
KRESKE'S
DUTCH BOY WHITE LEAD
25¢
You're a good kid and I know you'll think this was your fault but don't do that to yourself.
I made this mess a longtime ago.
It was my own hot head that got me blackballed off the circuits in 1930, just when the rest of the world was going out of business. After that, everything went to hell.
No work, no food but the skimpy charity from soup kitchens, no doctor for the baby that was supposed to put sunshine back in our lives.
When the Bonus boys made camp in Washington, I had my big brainstorm to get some help from Uncle Sam. All it got me was the back of his hand.
That, and a friend named Virgil. I guess you'll know that name by the time you read this.

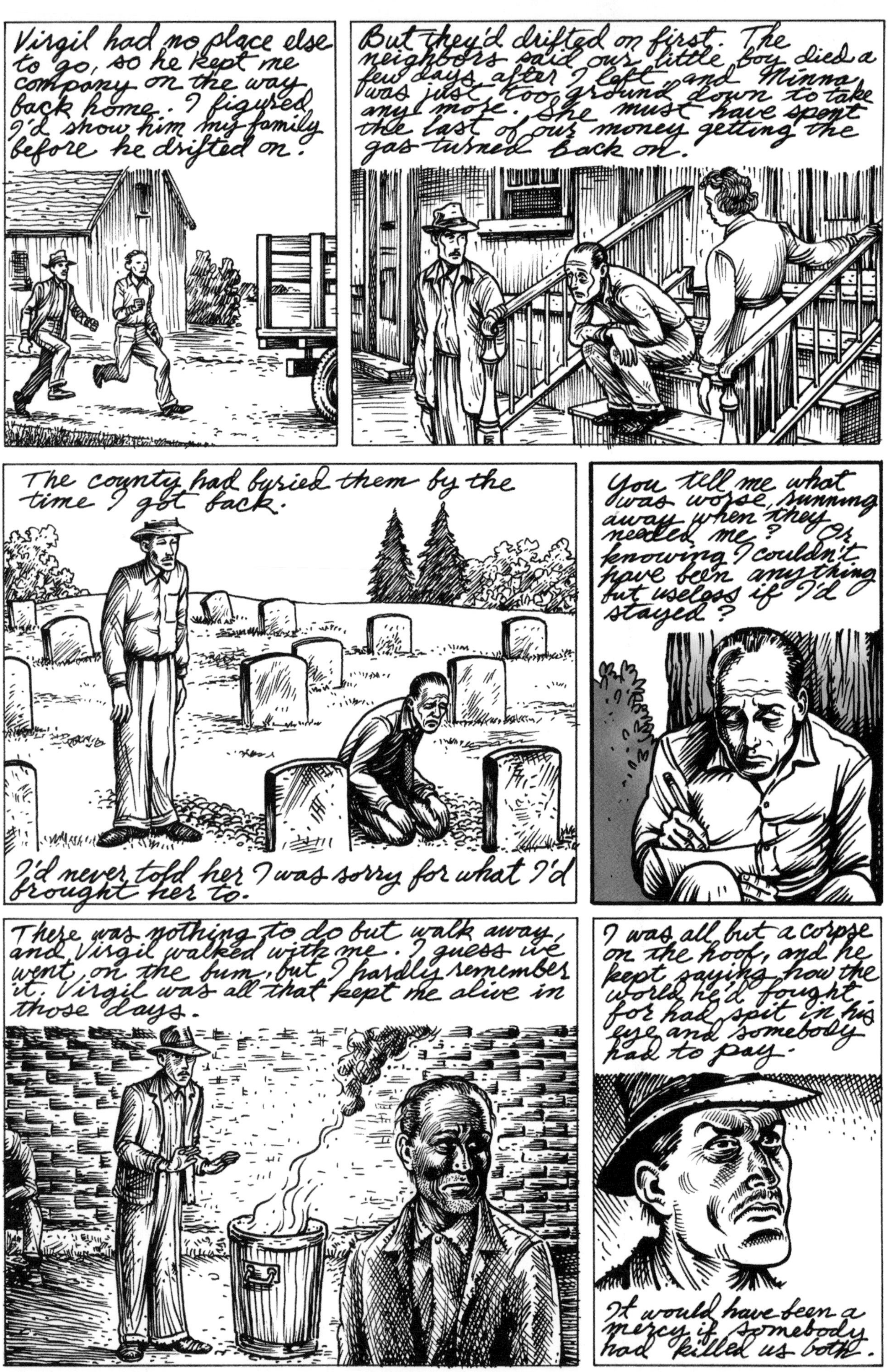
Virgil had no place else to go, so he kept me company on the way back home. I figured I'd show him my family before he drifted on.
But they'd drifted on first. The neighbors said our little boy died a few days after I left and Minna was just too ground down to take any more. She must have spent the last of our money getting the gas turned back on.
The county had buried them by the time I got back.
I'd never told her I was sorry for what I'd brought her to.
You tell me what was worse, running away when they needed me? Or knowing I couldn't have been anything but useless if I'd stayed?
There was nothing to do but walk away, and Virgil walked with me. I guess we went on the bum, but I hardly remember it. Virgil was all that kept me alive in those days.
I was all but a corpse on the hoof, and he kept saying how the world he'd fought for had spit in his eye and somebody had to pay.
It would have been a mercy if somebody had killed us both.

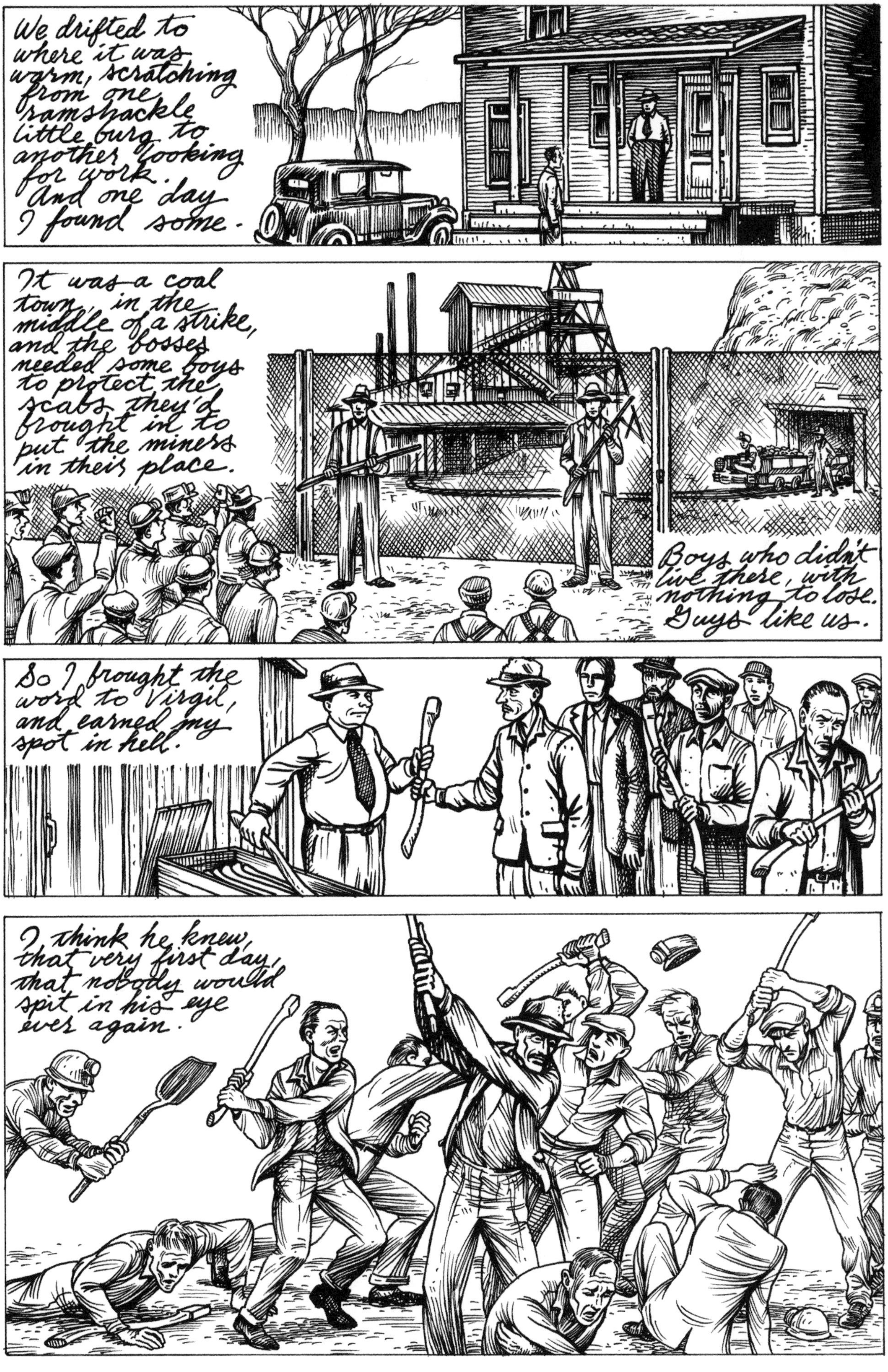
We drifted to where it was warm, scratching from one ramshackle little burg to another looking for work. And one day I found some.
It was a coal town, in the middle of a strike, and the bosses needed some boys to protect the scabs they'd brought in to put the miners in their place.
Boys who didn't live there, with nothing to lose. Guys like us.
So I brought the word to Virgil, and earned my spot in hell.
I think he knew, that very first day, that nobody would spit in his eye ever again.

We did two nights in the local can, just till the mine boss could slip us out of town. He liked our work, and said he knew a guy who could do us some good.

We got passed along to an outfit that called itself a detective agency, but that was the bunk. It's real game was hiring out muscle to put down strikers all over the country.

I'd never heard of such a thing. But it was a big operation and getting bigger, and we were just the kind of thugs they needed.

I won't lie to you, kid. For a year or so I was mixed up in things you'd be crazy not to hate me for.

Hell, I was crazy, and there were days I hated me worse than anybody.

Virgil, though, was a man on the rise. And since he had it in his head that he owed me something, he carried me along from one godawful job to the next.

But even a worthless scum can get his fill of wading through blood and brains and busted bones. After a while, I just couldn't take any more.

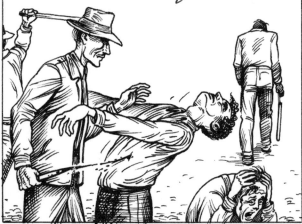

So I went on the fade for a good long while, and tried to burn the slaughterhouse out of my dreams.

214

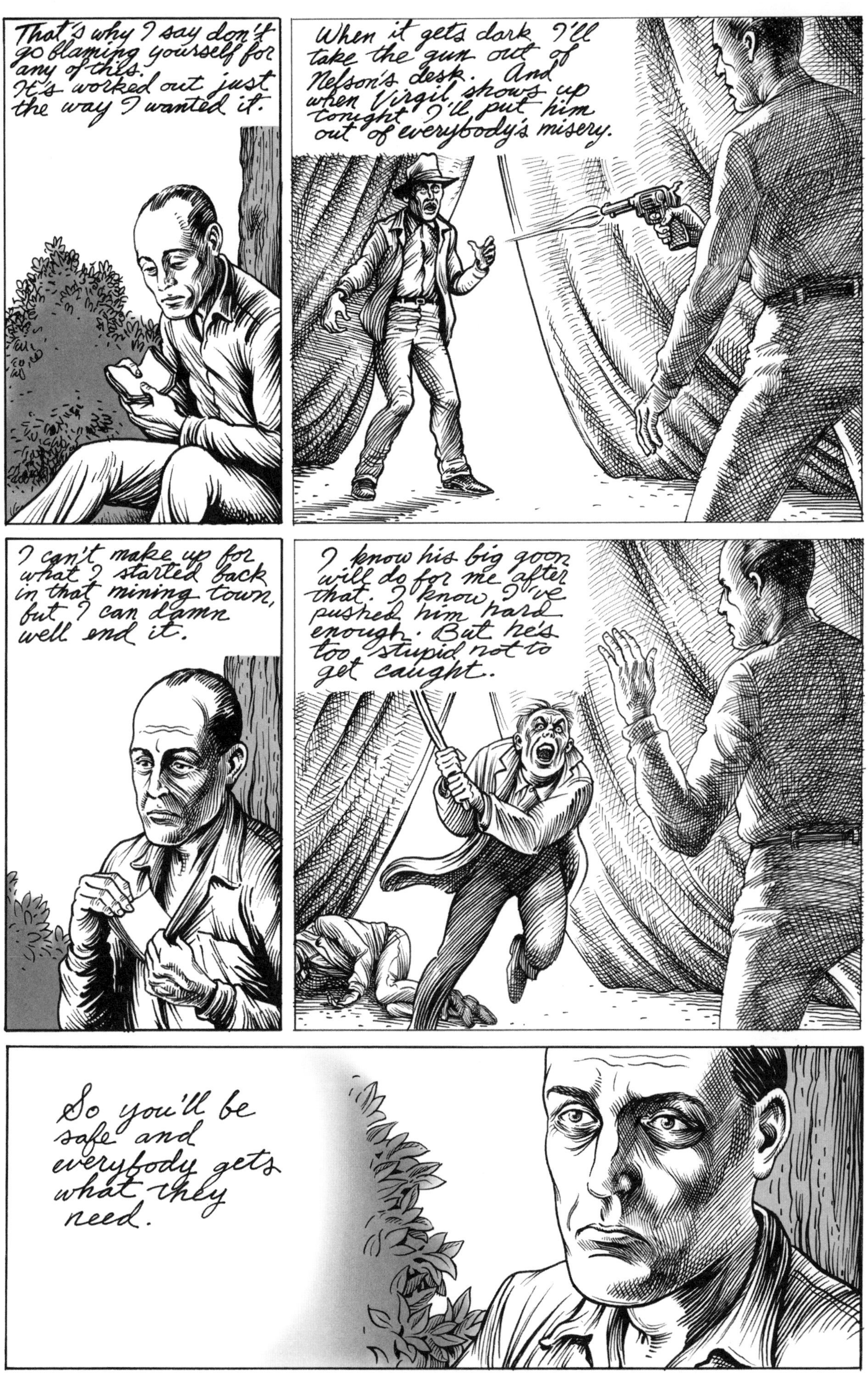
That's why I say don't go blaming yourself for any of this. It's worked out just the way I wanted it.
When it gets dark I'll take the gun out of Nelson's desk. And when Virgil shows up tonight I'll put him out of everybody's misery.
I can't make up for what I started back in that mining town, but I can damn well end it.
I know his big goon will do for me after that. I know I've pushed him hard enough. But he's too stupid not to get caught.
So you'll be safe and everybody gets what they need.

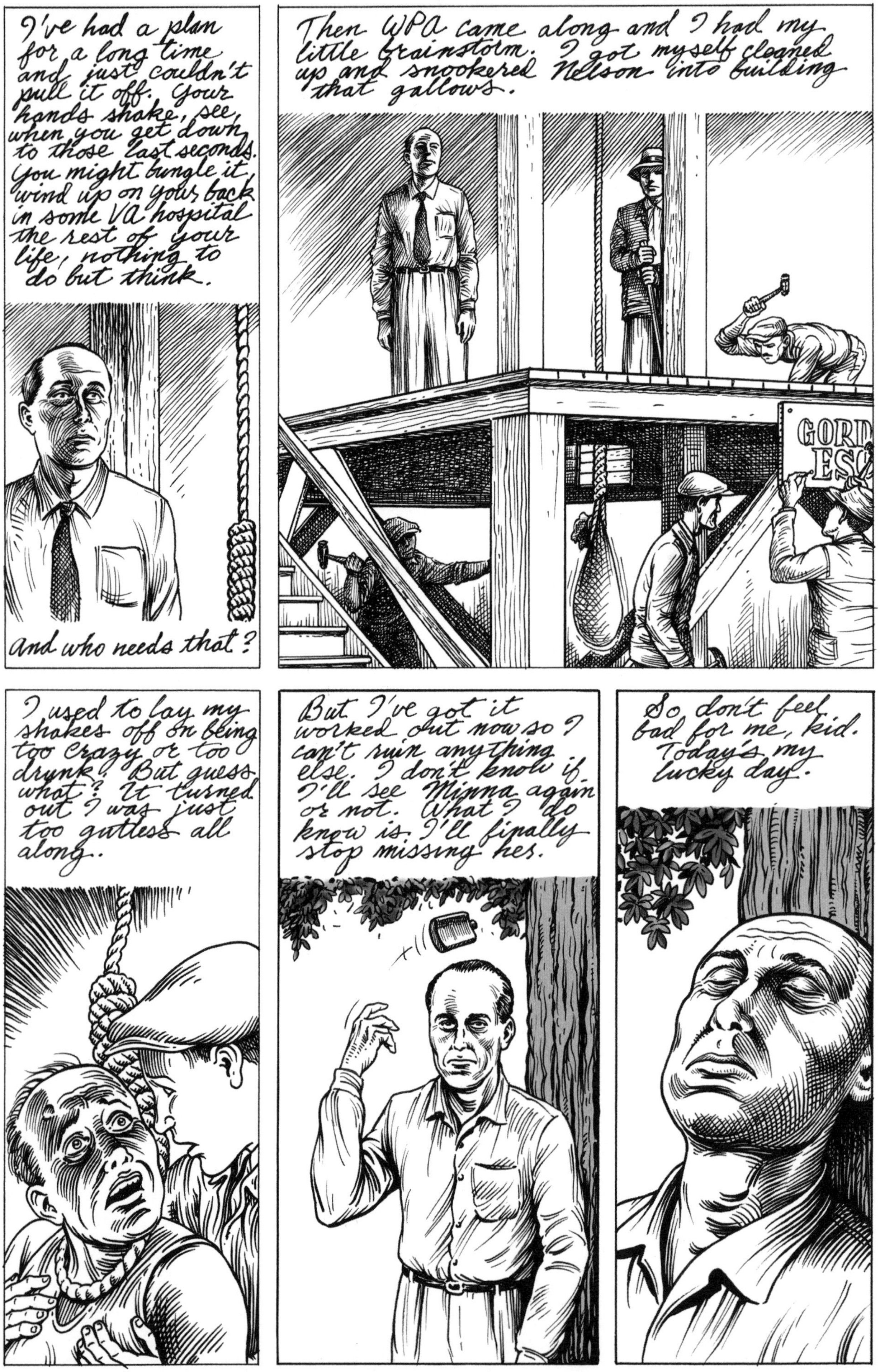

I've had a plan for a long time and just couldn't pull it off. Your hands shake, see, when you get down to those last seconds. You might bungle it wind up on your back in some VA hospital the rest of your life, nothing to do but think.
And who needs that?
Then WPA came along and I had my little brainstorm. I got myself cleaned up and snookered Nelson into building that gallows.
GORD
ESC
I used to lay my shakes off on being too crazy or too drunk. But guess what? It turned out I was just too gutless all along.
But I've got it worked out now so I can't ruin anything else. I don't know if I'll see Minna again or not. What I do know is, I'll finally stop missing her.
So don't feel bad for me, kid. Today's my lucky day.

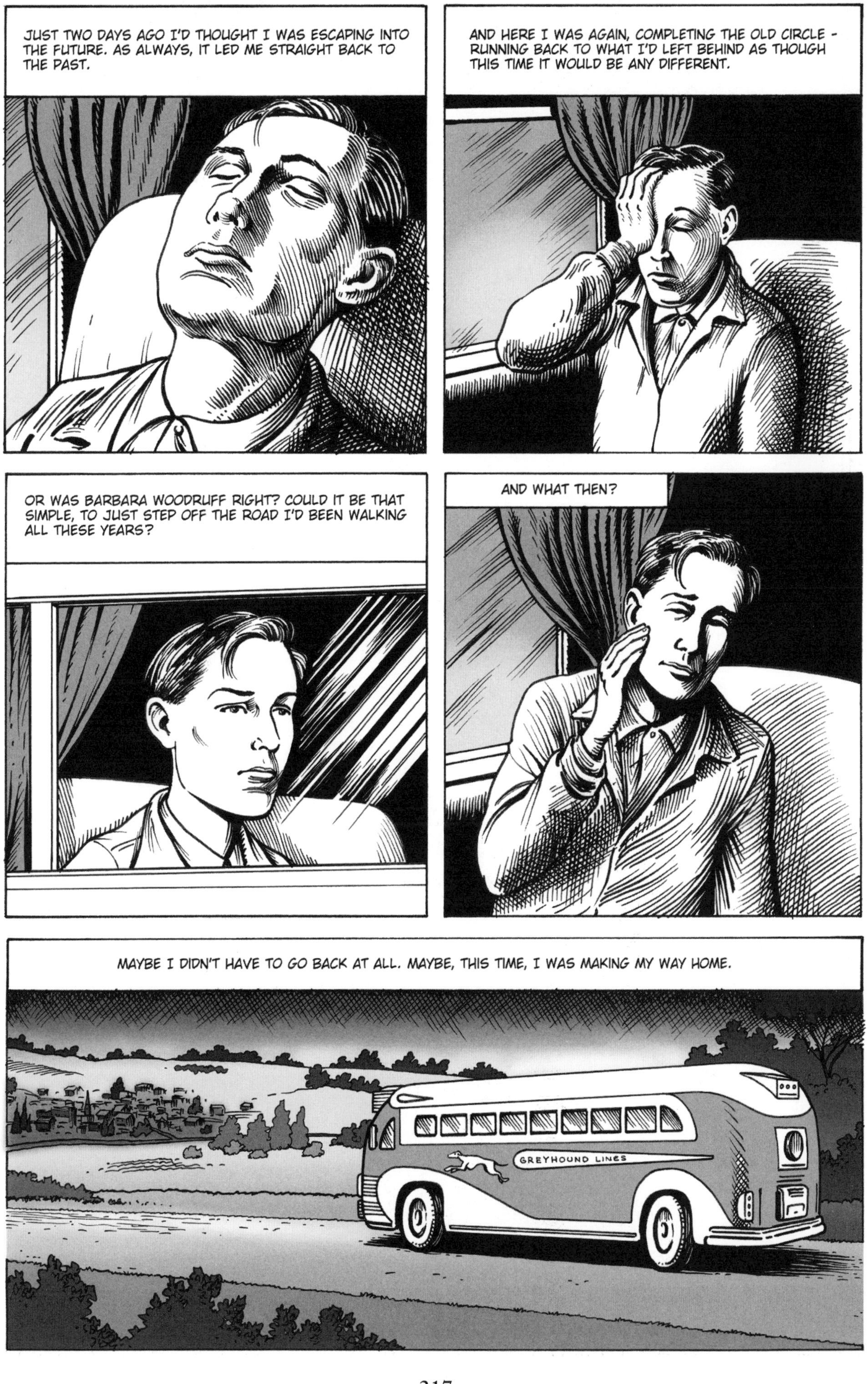
JUST TWO DAYS AGO I'D THOUGHT I WAS ESCAPING INTO THE FUTURE. AS ALWAYS, IT LED ME STRAIGHT BACK TO THE PAST.
AND HERE I WAS AGAIN, COMPLETING THE OLD CIRCLE - RUNNING BACK TO WHAT I'D LEFT BEHIND AS THOUGH THIS TIME IT WOULD BE ANY DIFFERENT.
OR WAS BARBARA WOODRUFF RIGHT? COULD IT BE THAT SIMPLE, TO JUST STEP OFF THE ROAD I'D BEEN WALKING ALL THESE YEARS?
AND WHAT THEN?
MAYBE I DIDN'T HAVE TO GO BACK AT ALL. MAYBE, THIS TIME, I WAS MAKING MY WAY HOME.
GREYHOUND LINES

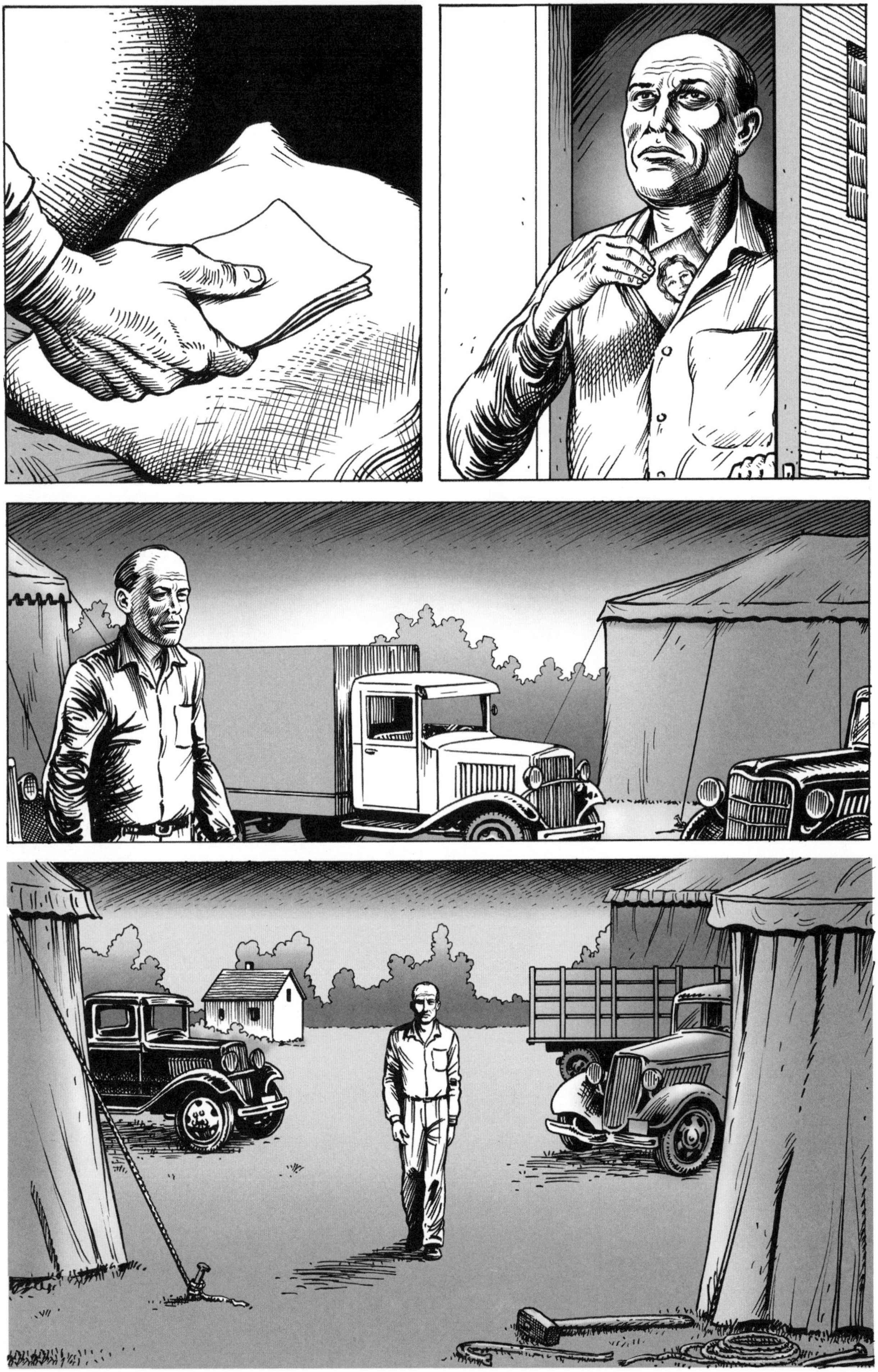

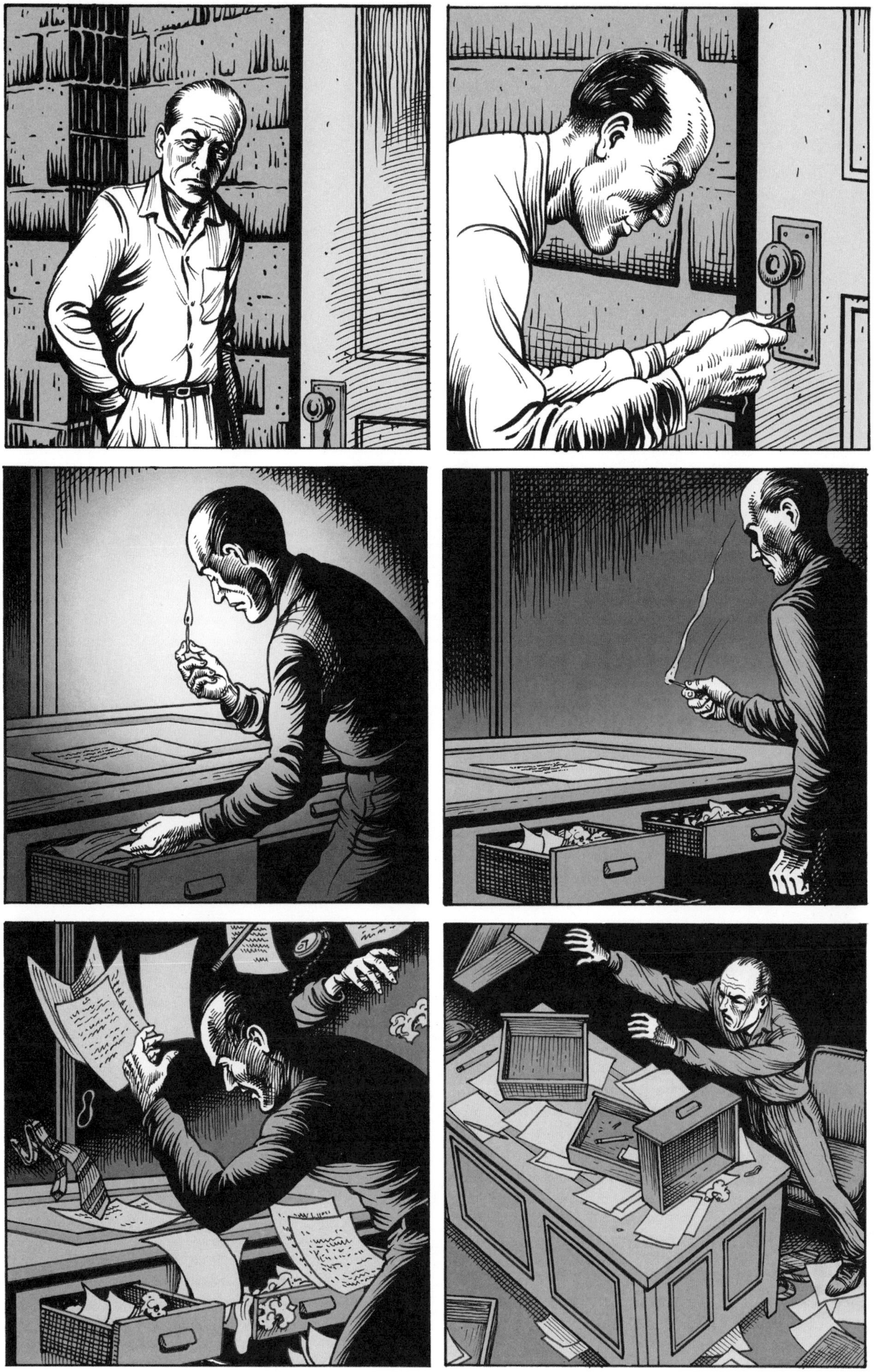

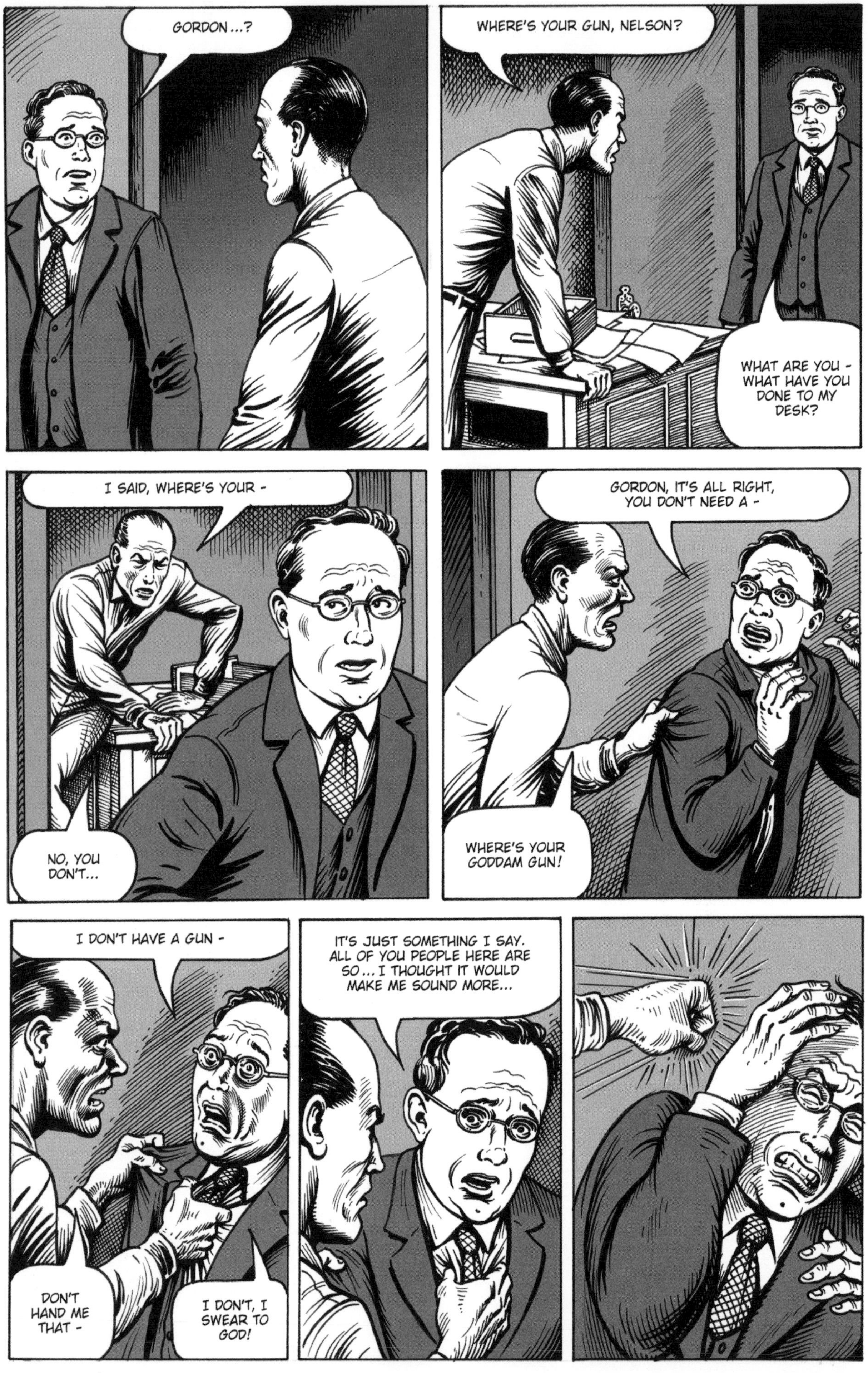

GORDON...?
WHERE'S YOUR GUN, NELSON?
WHAT ARE YOU - WHAT HAVE YOU DONE TO MY DESK?
I SAID, WHERE'S YOUR -
NO, YOU DON'T...
GORDON, IT'S ALL RIGHT, YOU DON'T NEED A -
WHERE'S YOUR GODDAM GUN!
I DON'T HAVE A GUN -
DON'T HAND ME THAT -
I DON'T, I SWEAR TO GOD!
IT'S JUST SOMETHING I SAY. ALL OF YOU PEOPLE HERE ARE SO... I THOUGHT IT WOULD MAKE ME SOUND MORE...

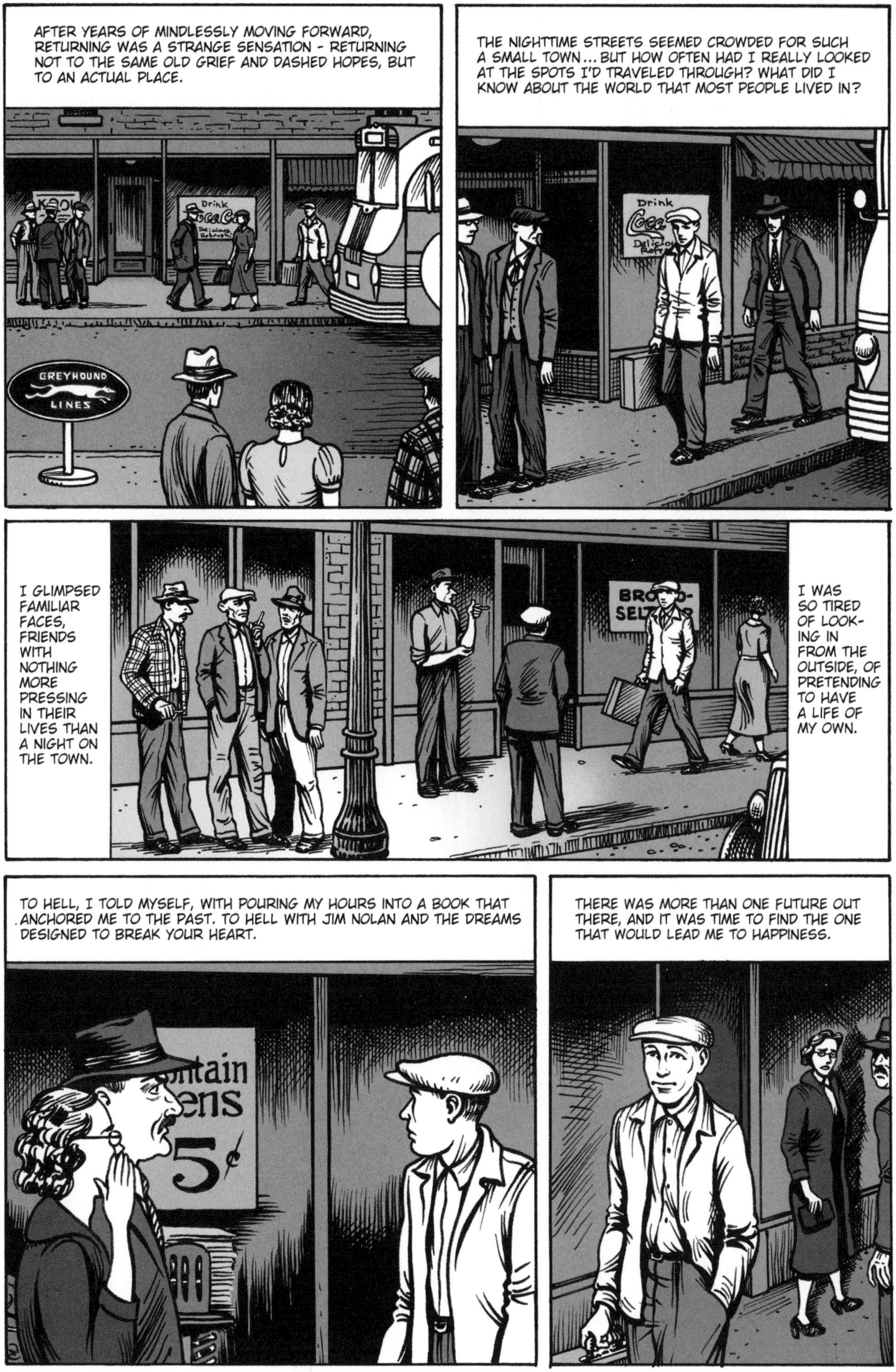
AFTER YEARS OF MINDLESSLY MOVING FORWARD, RETURNING WAS A STRANGE SENSATION - RETURNING NOT TO THE SAME OLD GRIEF AND DASHED HOPES, BUT TO AN ACTUAL PLACE.
Drink
GREYHOUND
LINES
THE NIGHTTIME STREETS SEEMED CROWDED FOR SUCH A SMALL TOWN... BUT HOW OFTEN HAD I REALLY LOOKED AT THE SPOTS I'D TRAVELED THROUGH? WHAT DID I KNOW ABOUT THE WORLD THAT MOST PEOPLE LIVED IN?
Drink
Coca
I GLIMPSED FAMILIAR FACES, FRIENDS WITH NOTHING MORE PRESSING IN THEIR LIVES THAN A NIGHT ON THE TOWN.
I WAS SO TIRED OF LOOKING IN FROM THE OUTSIDE, OF PRETENDING TO HAVE A LIFE OF MY OWN.
TO HELL, I TOLD MYSELF, WITH POURING MY HOURS INTO A BOOK THAT ANCHORED ME TO THE PAST. TO HELL WITH JIM NOLAN AND THE DREAMS DESIGNED TO BREAK YOUR HEART.
5¢
THERE WAS MORE THAN ONE FUTURE OUT THERE, AND IT WAS TIME TO FIND THE ONE THAT WOULD LEAD ME TO HAPPINESS.

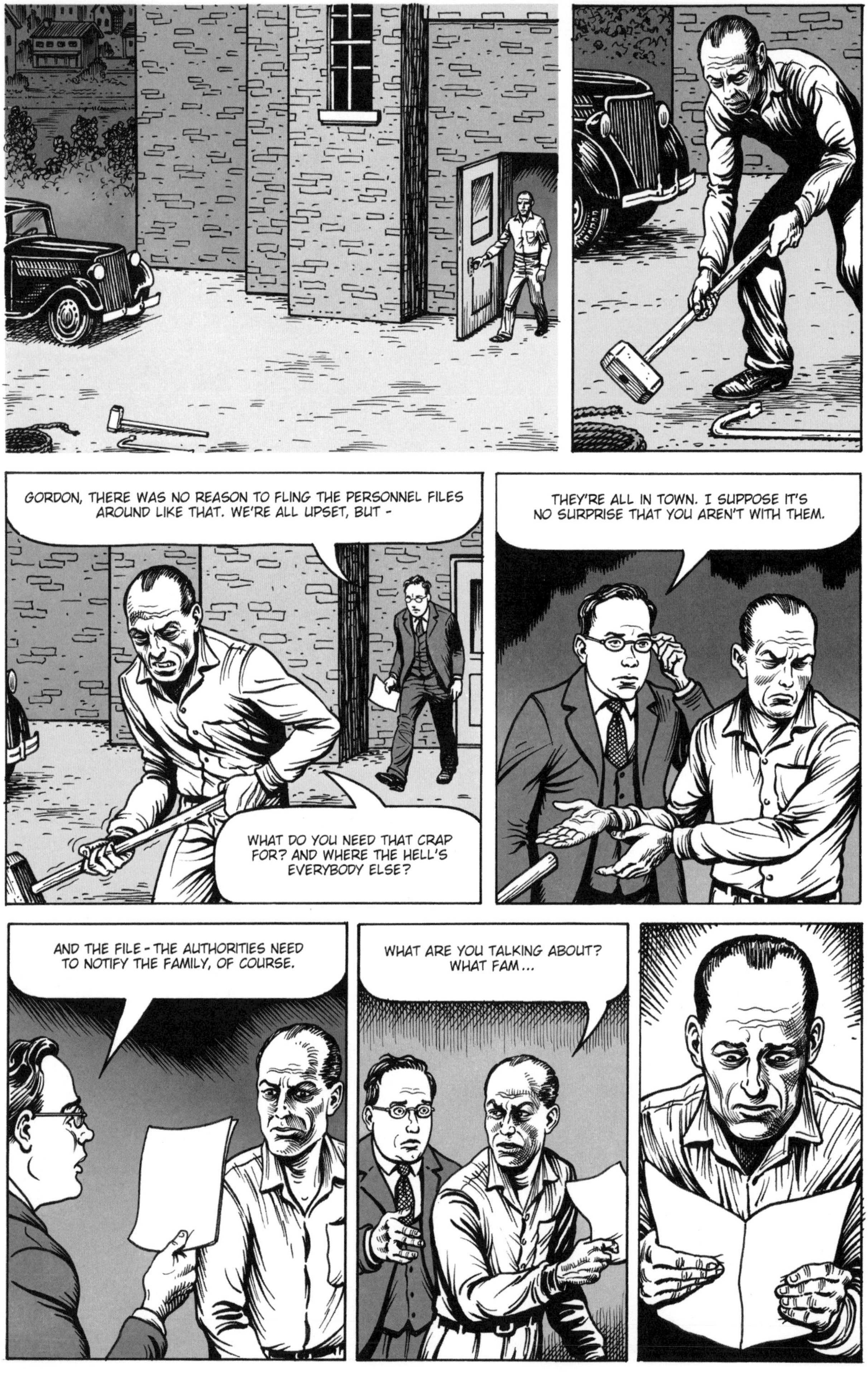
GORDON, THERE WAS NO REASON TO FLING THE PERSONNEL FILES AROUND LIKE THAT. WE'RE ALL UPSET, BUT -
WHAT DO YOU NEED THAT CRAP FOR? AND WHERE THE HELL'S EVERYBODY ELSE?
THEY'RE ALL IN TOWN. I SUPPOSE IT'S NO SURPRISE THAT YOU AREN'T WITH THEM.
AND THE FILE - THE AUTHORITIES NEED TO NOTIFY THE FAMILY, OF COURSE.
WHAT ARE YOU TALKING ABOUT? WHAT FAM ...

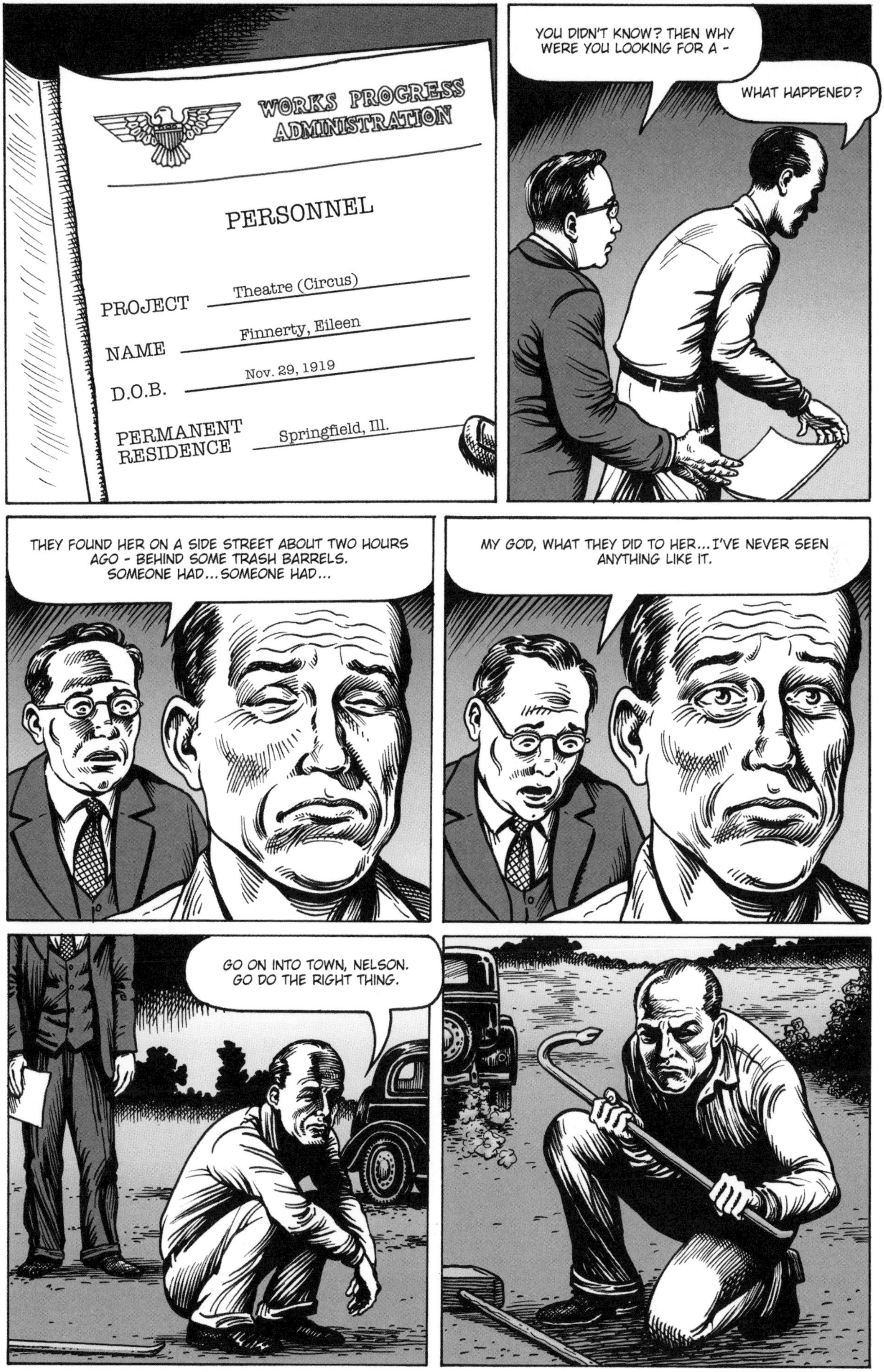
WORKS PROGRESS ADMINISTRATION
PERSONNEL
PROJECT Theatre (Circus)
NAME Finnerty, Eileen
D.O.B. Nov. 29, 1919
PERMANENT RESIDENCE Springfield, Ill.
YOU DIDN'T KNOW? THEN WHY WERE YOU LOOKING FOR A -
WHAT HAPPENED?
THEY FOUND HER ON A SIDE STREET ABOUT TWO HOURS AGO - BEHIND SOME TRASH BARRELS. SOMEONE HAD... SOMEONE HAD...
MY GOD, WHAT THEY DID TO HER... I'VE NEVER SEEN ANYTHING LIKE IT.
GO ON INTO TOWN, NELSON. GO DO THE RIGHT THING.

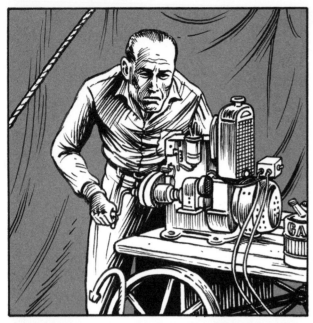

ONE
FOR
THE
ROAD.

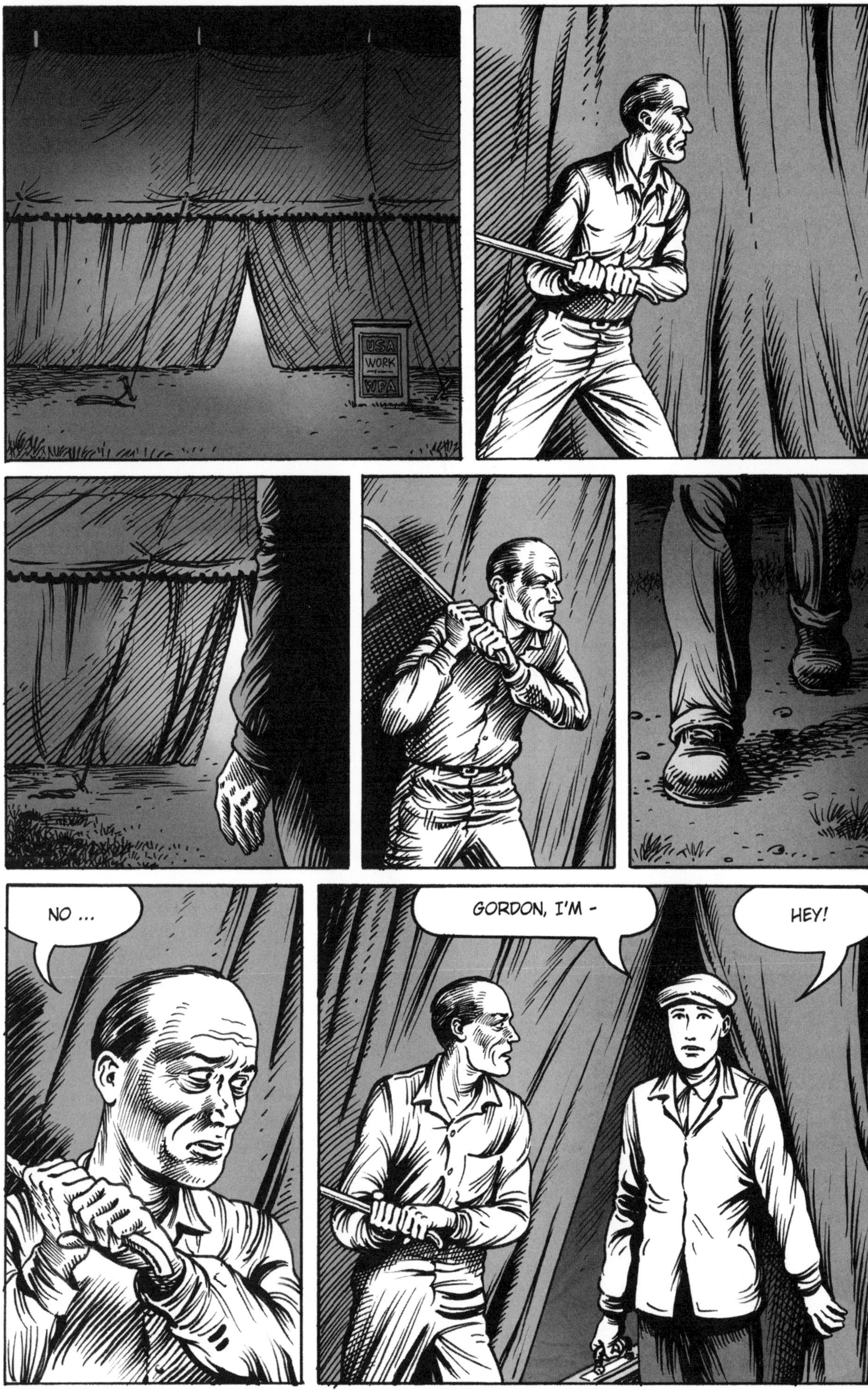
USA
WORK
WPA
NO ...
GORDON, I'M -
HEY!

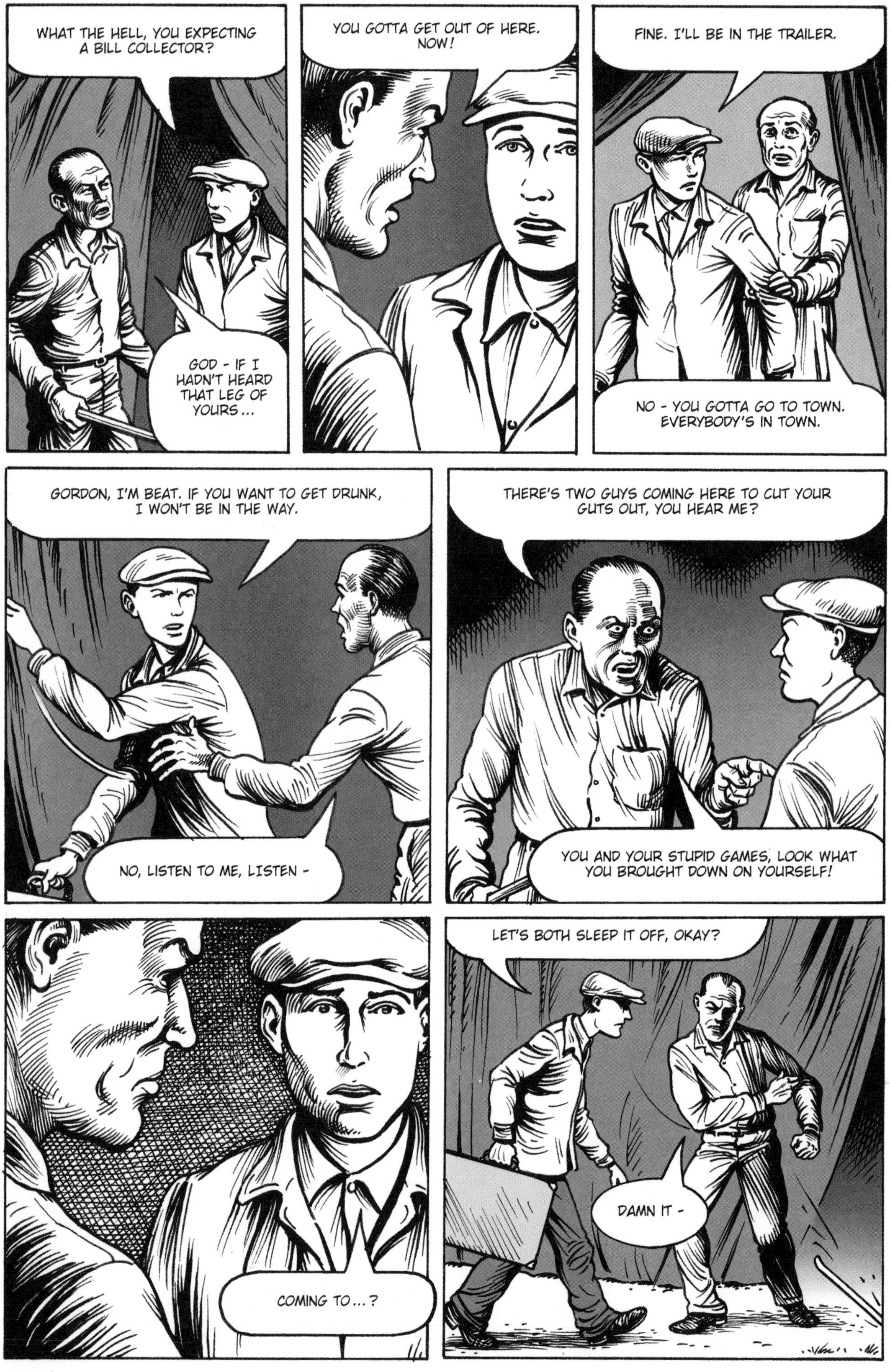
WHAT THE HELL, YOU EXPECTING A BILL COLLECTOR?
GOD - IF I HADN'T HEARD THAT LEG OF YOURS...
YOU GOTTA GET OUT OF HERE. NOW!
FINE. I'LL BE IN THE TRAILER.
NO - YOU GOTTA GO TO TOWN. EVERYBODY'S IN TOWN.
GORDON, I'M BEAT. IF YOU WANT TO GET DRUNK, I WON'T BE IN THE WAY.
NO, LISTEN TO ME, LISTEN -
THERE'S TWO GUYS COMING HERE TO CUT YOUR GUTS OUT, YOU HEAR ME?
YOU AND YOUR STUPID GAMES, LOOK WHAT YOU BROUGHT DOWN ON YOURSELF!
COMING TO...?
LET'S BOTH SLEEP IT OFF, OKAY?
DAMN IT -

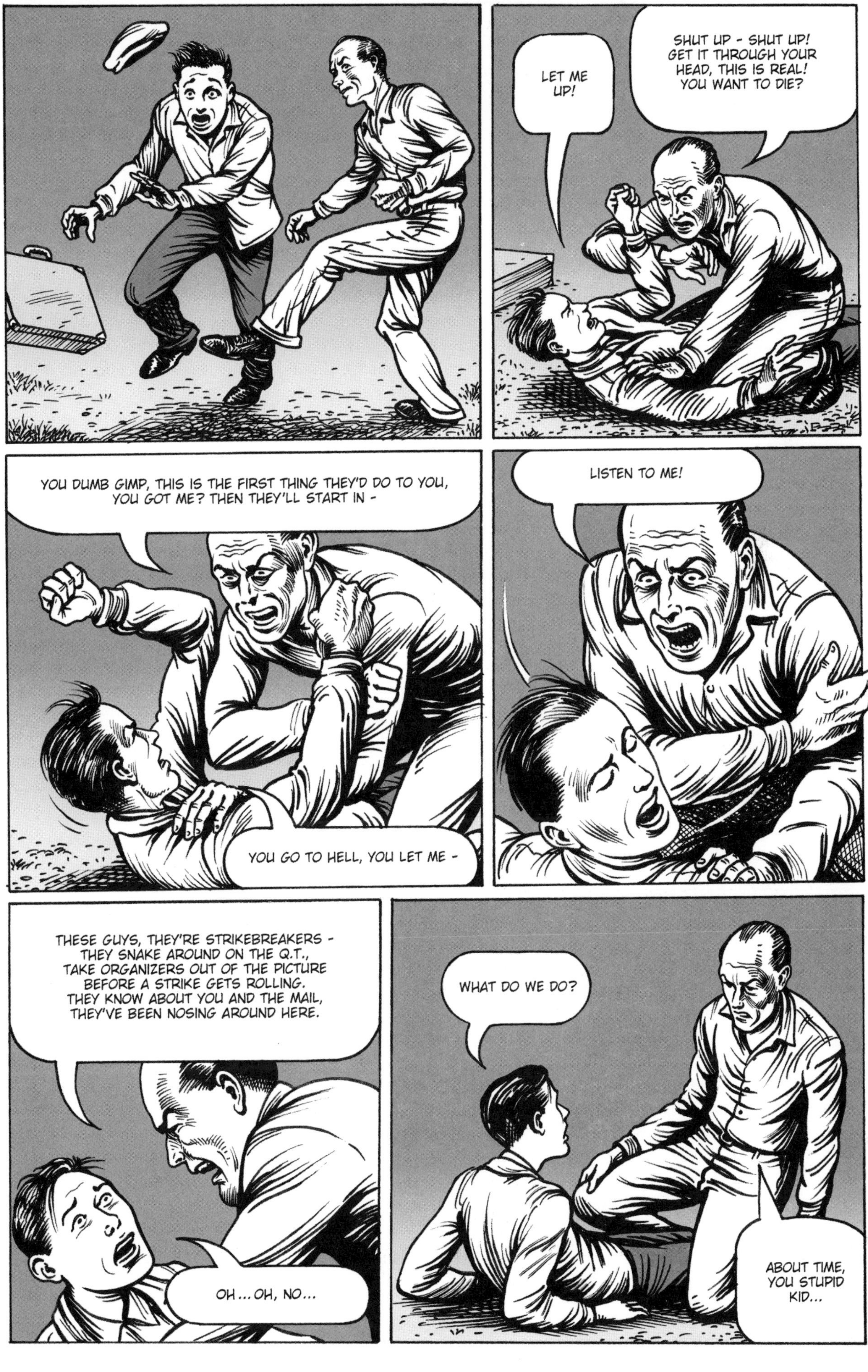
LET ME UP!
SHUT UP - SHUT UP! GET IT THROUGH YOUR HEAD, THIS IS REAL! YOU WANT TO DIE?
YOU DUMB GIMP, THIS IS THE FIRST THING THEY'D DO TO YOU, YOU GOT ME? THEN THEY'LL START IN -
YOU GO TO HELL, YOU LET ME -
LISTEN TO ME!
THESE GUYS, THEY'RE STRIKEBREAKERS - THEY SNAKE AROUND ON THE Q.T., TAKE ORGANIZERS OUT OF THE PICTURE BEFORE A STRIKE GETS ROLLING. THEY KNOW ABOUT YOU AND THE MAIL, THEY'VE BEEN NOSING AROUND HERE.
OH ... OH, NO ...
WHAT DO WE DO?
ABOUT TIME, YOU STUPID KID ...

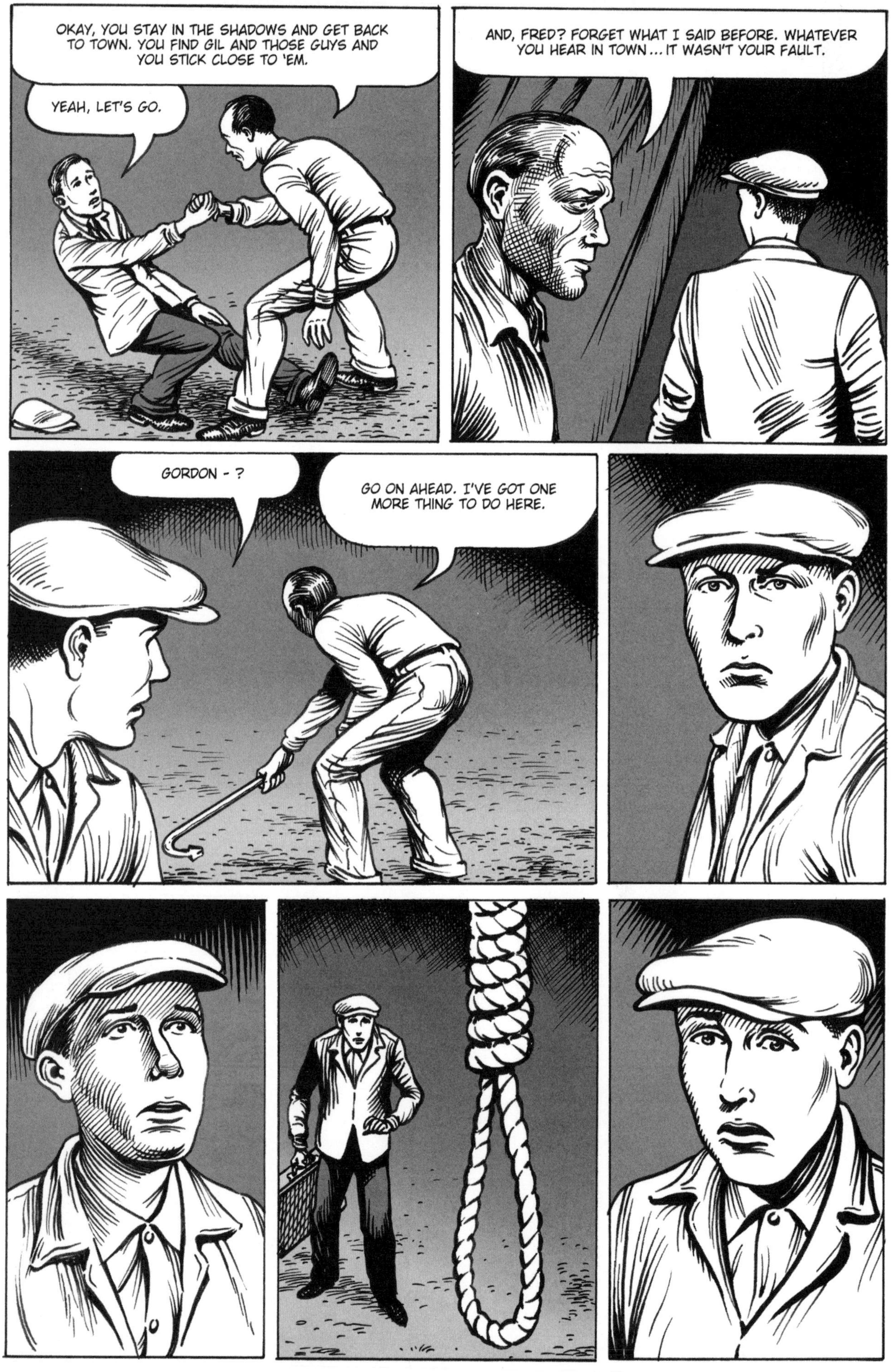
OKAY, YOU STAY IN THE SHADOWS AND GET BACK TO TOWN. YOU FIND GIL AND THOSE GUYS AND YOU STICK CLOSE TO 'EM.
YEAH, LET'S GO.
AND, FRED? FORGET WHAT I SAID BEFORE. WHATEVER YOU HEAR IN TOWN... IT WASN'T YOUR FAULT.
GORDON - ?
GO ON AHEAD. I'VE GOT ONE MORE THING TO DO HERE.

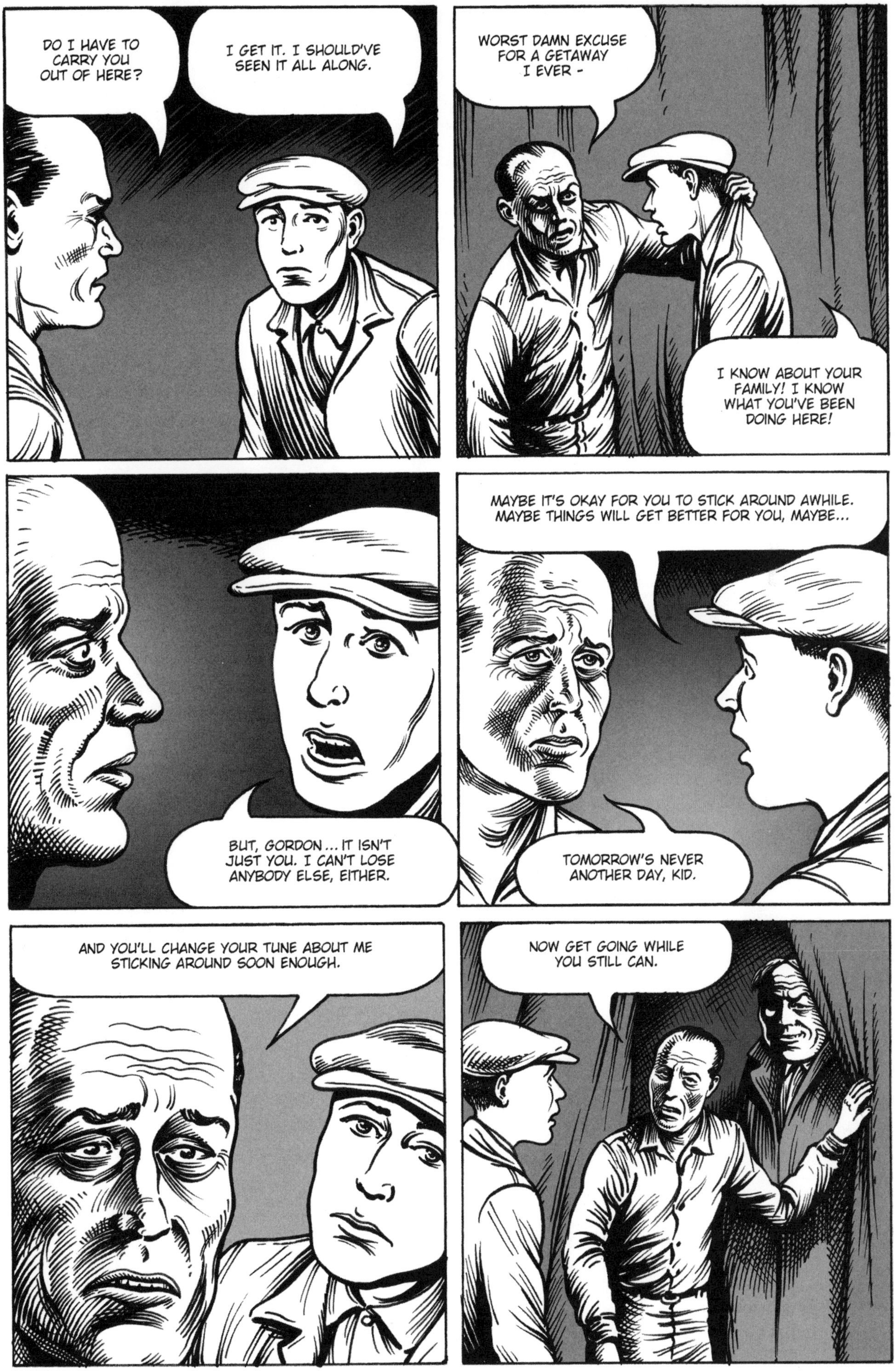
DO I HAVE TO CARRY YOU OUT OF HERE?
I GET IT. I SHOULD'VE SEEN IT ALL ALONG.
WORST DAMN EXCUSE FOR A GETAWAY I EVER -
I KNOW ABOUT YOUR FAMILY! I KNOW WHAT YOU'VE BEEN DOING HERE!
BUT, GORDON ... IT ISN'T JUST YOU. I CAN'T LOSE ANYBODY ELSE, EITHER.
MAYBE IT'S OKAY FOR YOU TO STICK AROUND AWHILE. MAYBE THINGS WILL GET BETTER FOR YOU, MAYBE...
TOMORROW'S NEVER ANOTHER DAY, KID.
AND YOU'LL CHANGE YOUR TUNE ABOUT ME STICKING AROUND SOON ENOUGH.
NOW GET GOING WHILE YOU STILL CAN.

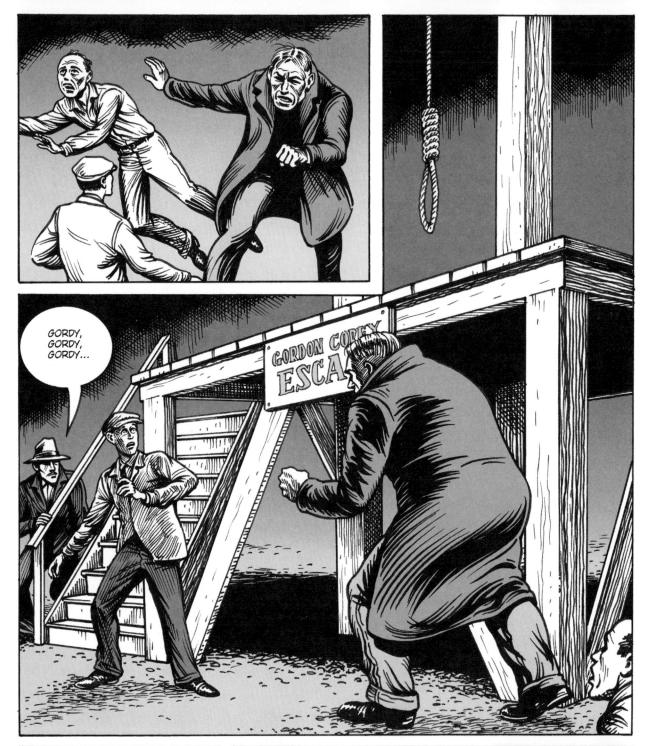

GORDY, GORDY, GORDY...

GORDON COREY ESCA...

AND MR. NOLAN. THE MAN THAT'S GONNA SAVE OUR BACON.

HOLD HIM, CHASE.

THIS WON'T TAKE LONG.

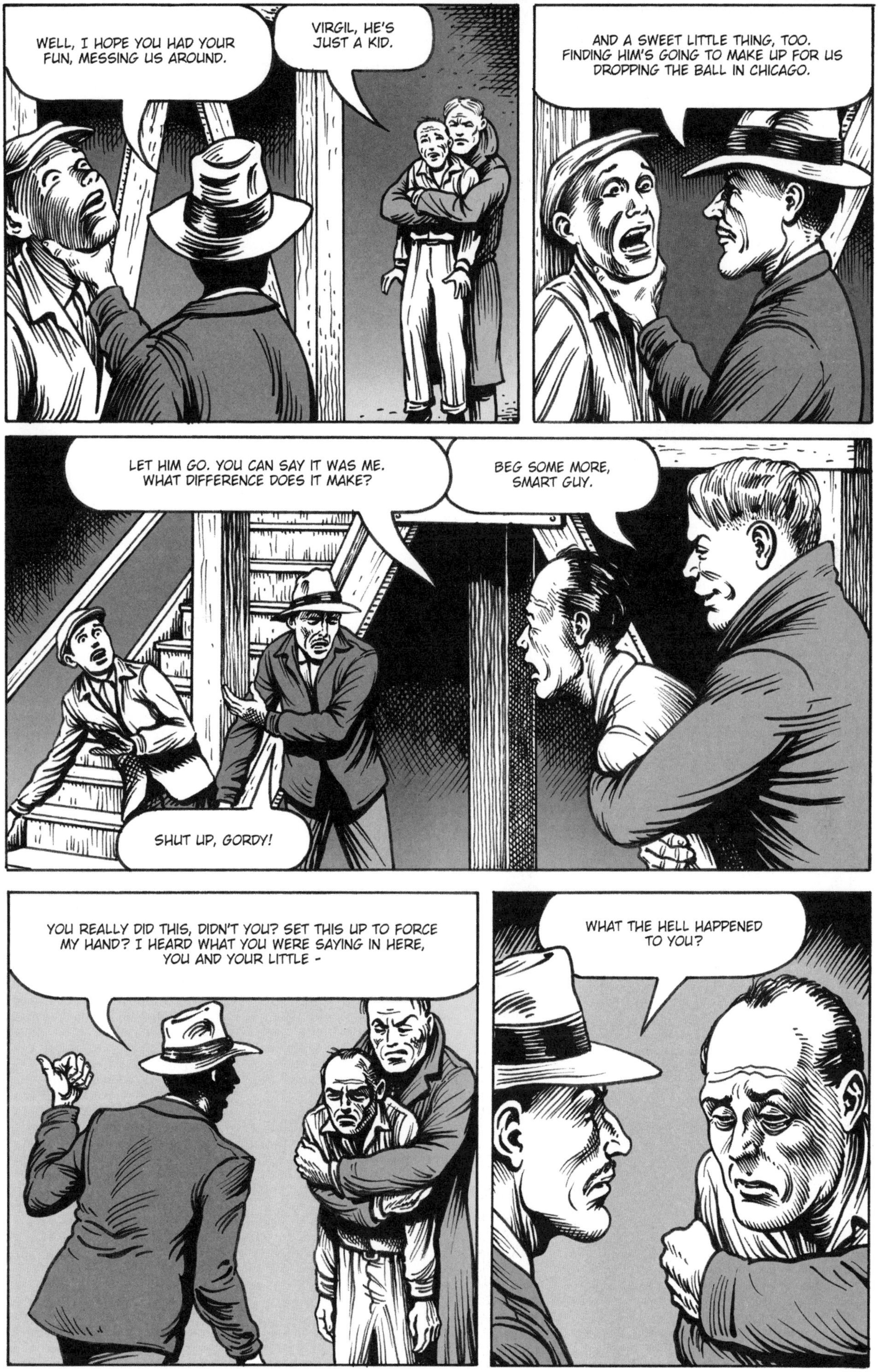
WELL, I HOPE YOU HAD YOUR FUN, MESSING US AROUND.
VIRGIL, HE'S JUST A KID.
AND A SWEET LITTLE THING, TOO. FINDING HIM'S GOING TO MAKE UP FOR US DROPPING THE BALL IN CHICAGO.
LET HIM GO. YOU CAN SAY IT WAS ME. WHAT DIFFERENCE DOES IT MAKE?
BEG SOME MORE, SMART GUY.
SHUT UP, GORDY!
YOU REALLY DID THIS, DIDN'T YOU? SET THIS UP TO FORCE MY HAND? I HEARD WHAT YOU WERE SAYING IN HERE, YOU AND YOUR LITTLE -
WHAT THE HELL HAPPENED TO YOU?

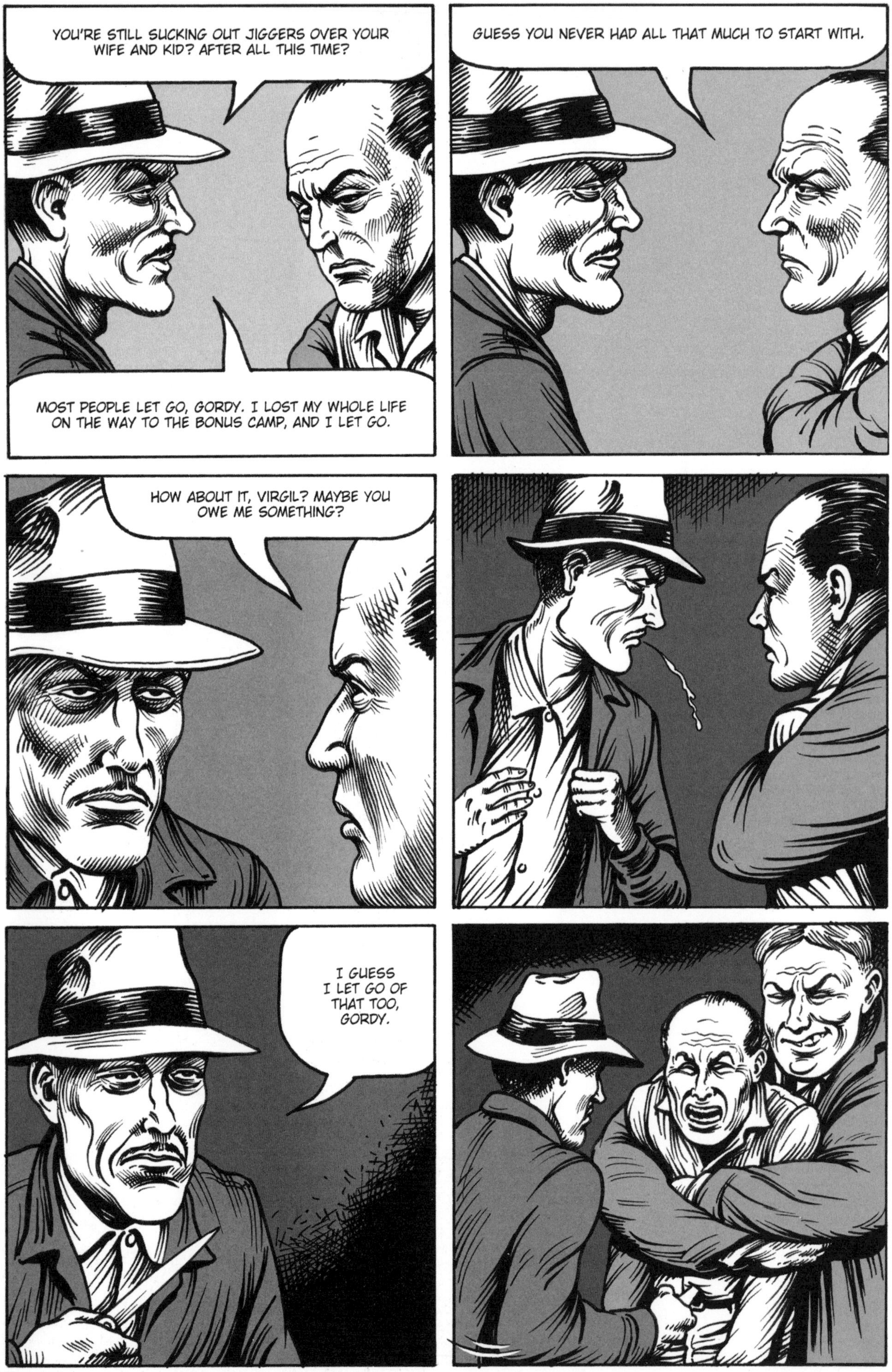
YOU'RE STILL SUCKING OUT JIGGERS OVER YOUR WIFE AND KID? AFTER ALL THIS TIME?
MOST PEOPLE LET GO, GORDY. I LOST MY WHOLE LIFE ON THE WAY TO THE BONUS CAMP, AND I LET GO.
GUESS YOU NEVER HAD ALL THAT MUCH TO START WITH.
HOW ABOUT IT, VIRGIL? MAYBE YOU OWE ME SOMETHING?
I GUESS I LET GO OF THAT TOO, GORDY.

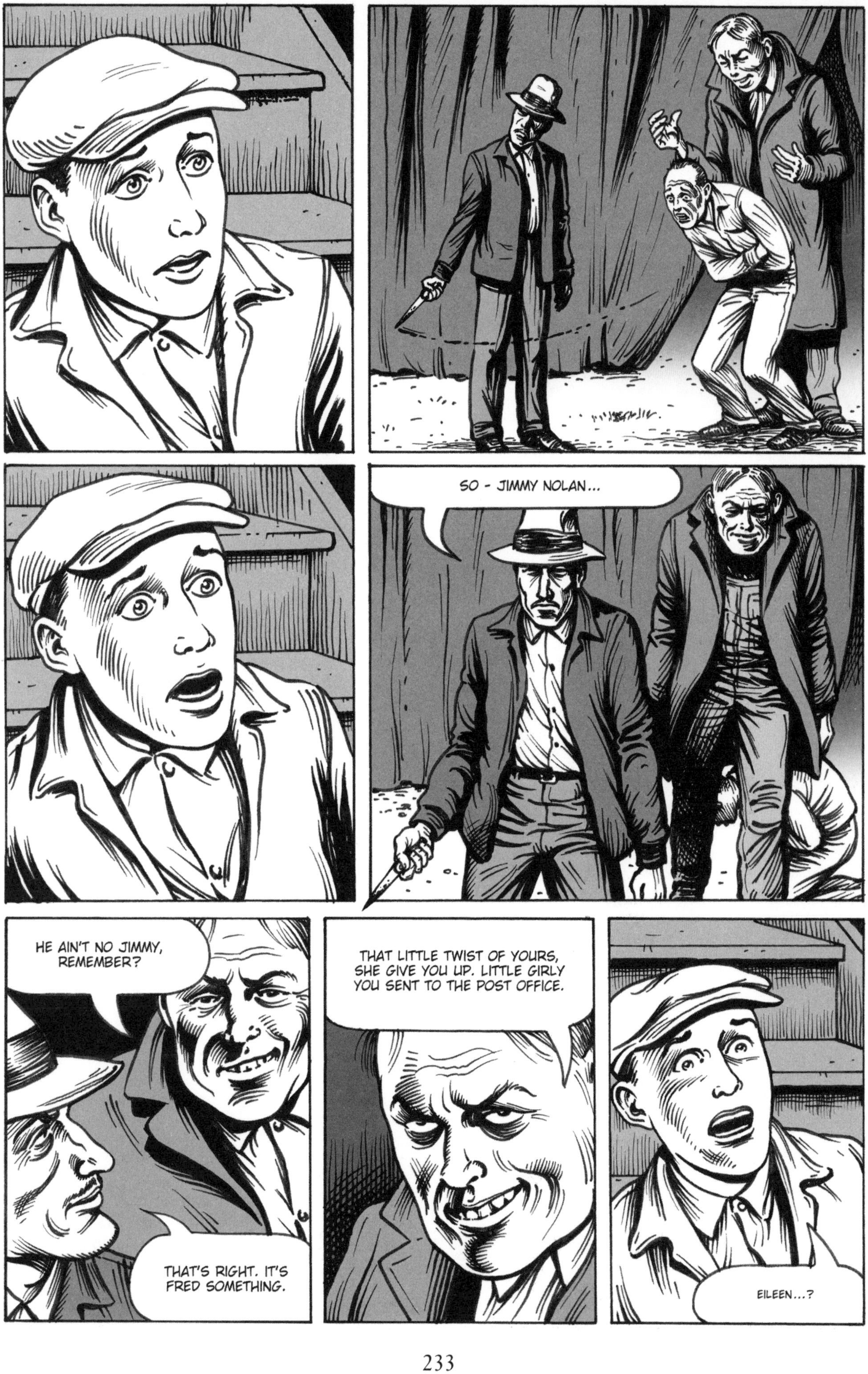
SO - JIMMY NOLAN...
HE AIN'T NO JIMMY, REMEMBER?
THAT'S RIGHT. IT'S FRED SOMETHING.
THAT LITTLE TWIST OF YOURS, SHE GIVE YOU UP. LITTLE GIRLY YOU SENT TO THE POST OFFICE.
EILEEN...?

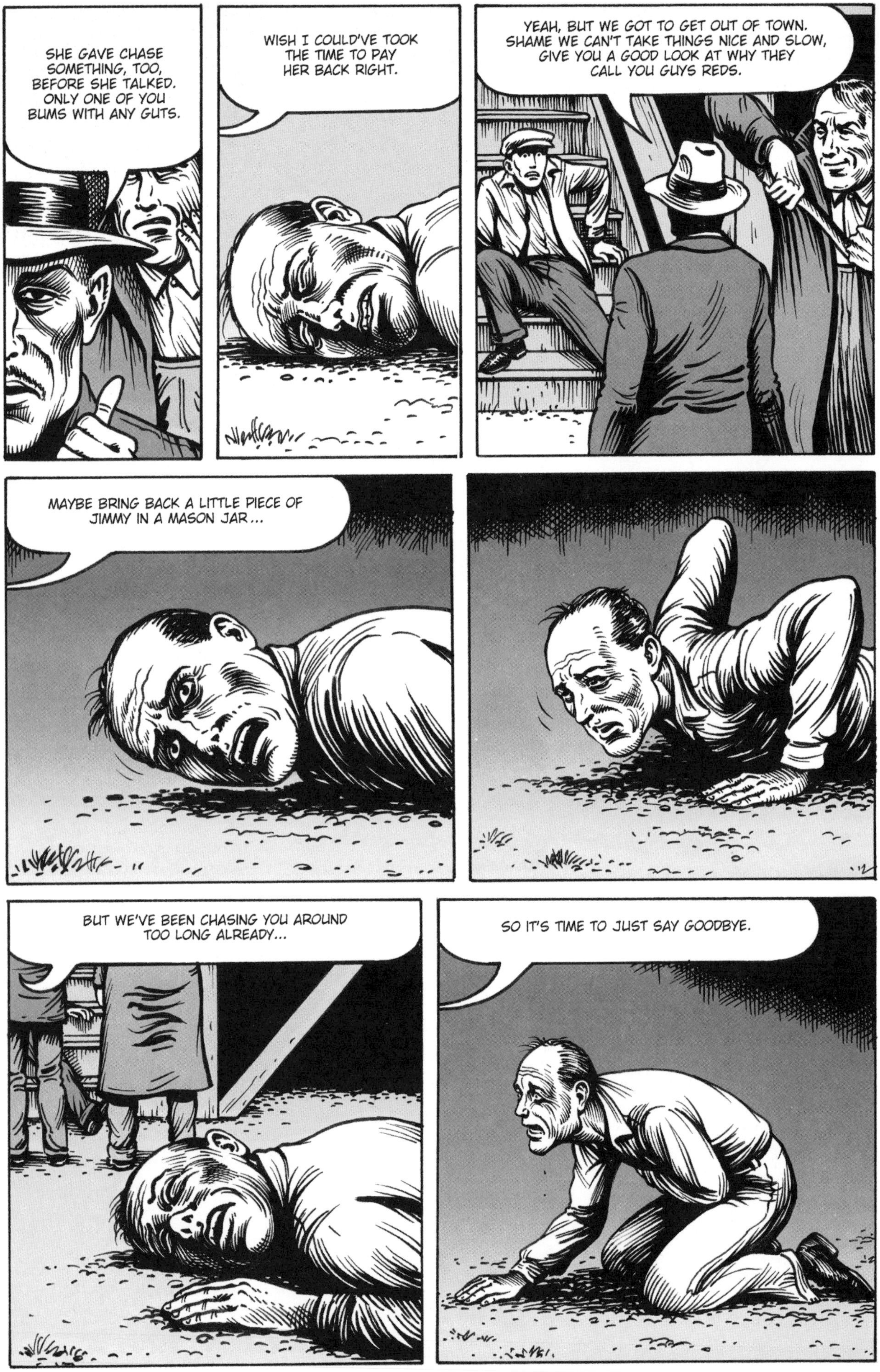
SHE GAVE CHASE SOMETHING, TOO, BEFORE SHE TALKED. ONLY ONE OF YOU BUMS WITH ANY GUTS.
WISH I COULD'VE TOOK THE TIME TO PAY HER BACK RIGHT.
YEAH, BUT WE GOT TO GET OUT OF TOWN. SHAME WE CAN'T TAKE THINGS NICE AND SLOW, GIVE YOU A GOOD LOOK AT WHY THEY CALL YOU GUYS REDS.
MAYBE BRING BACK A LITTLE PIECE OF JIMMY IN A MASON JAR...
BUT WE'VE BEEN CHASING YOU AROUND TOO LONG ALREADY...
SO IT'S TIME TO JUST SAY GOODBYE.

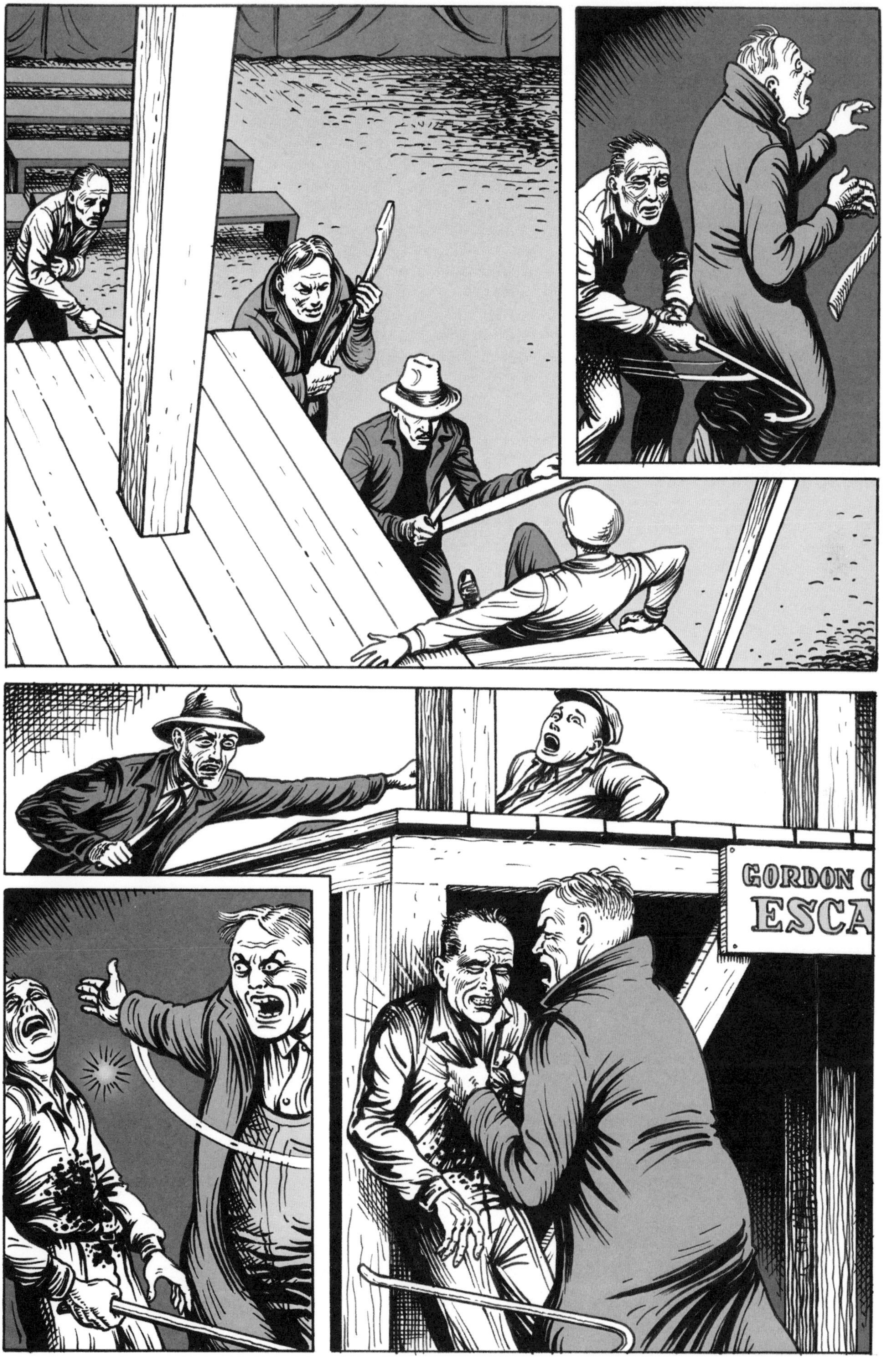
GORDON C
ESCA

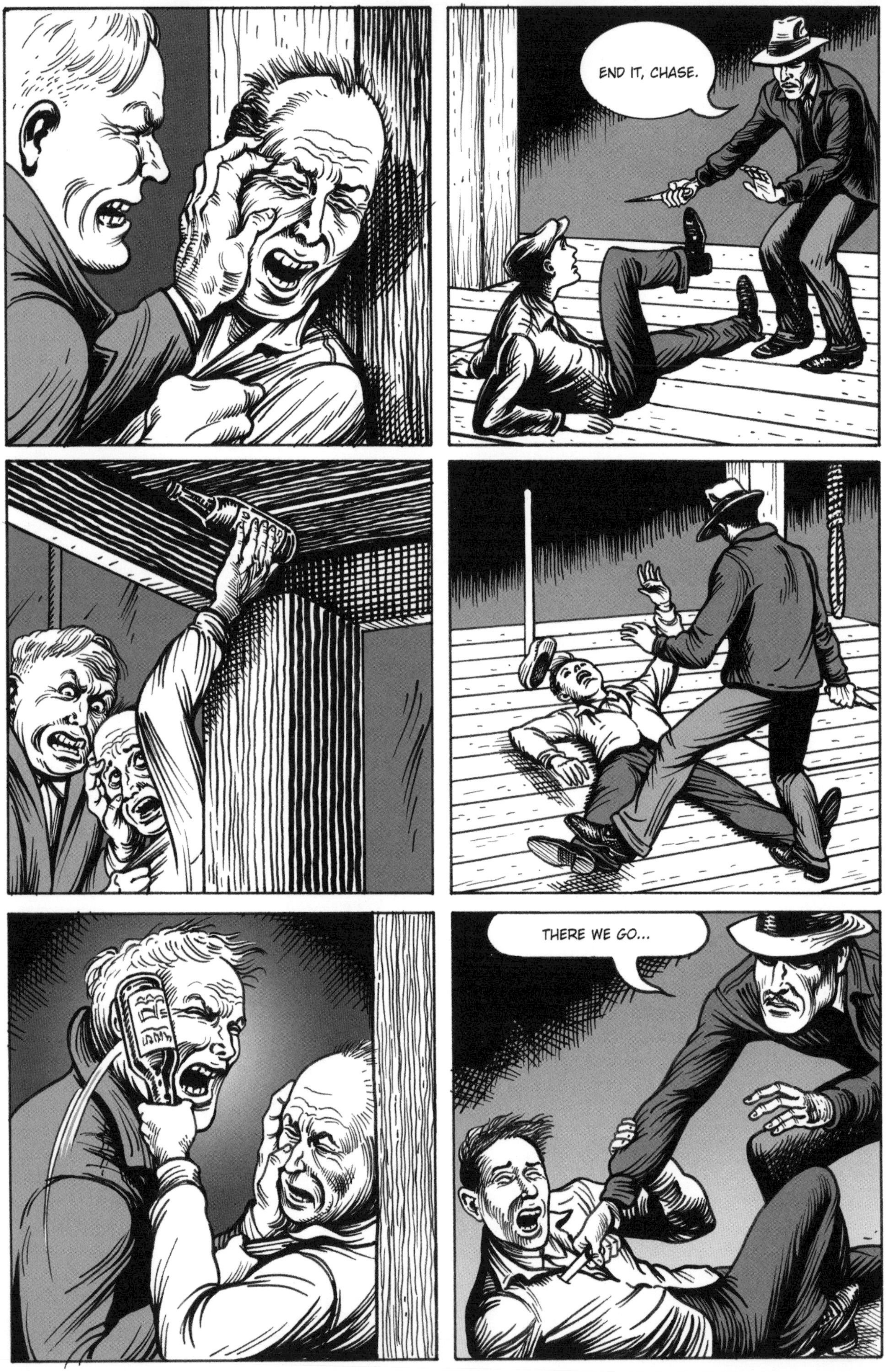
END IT, CHASE.
THERE WE GO...

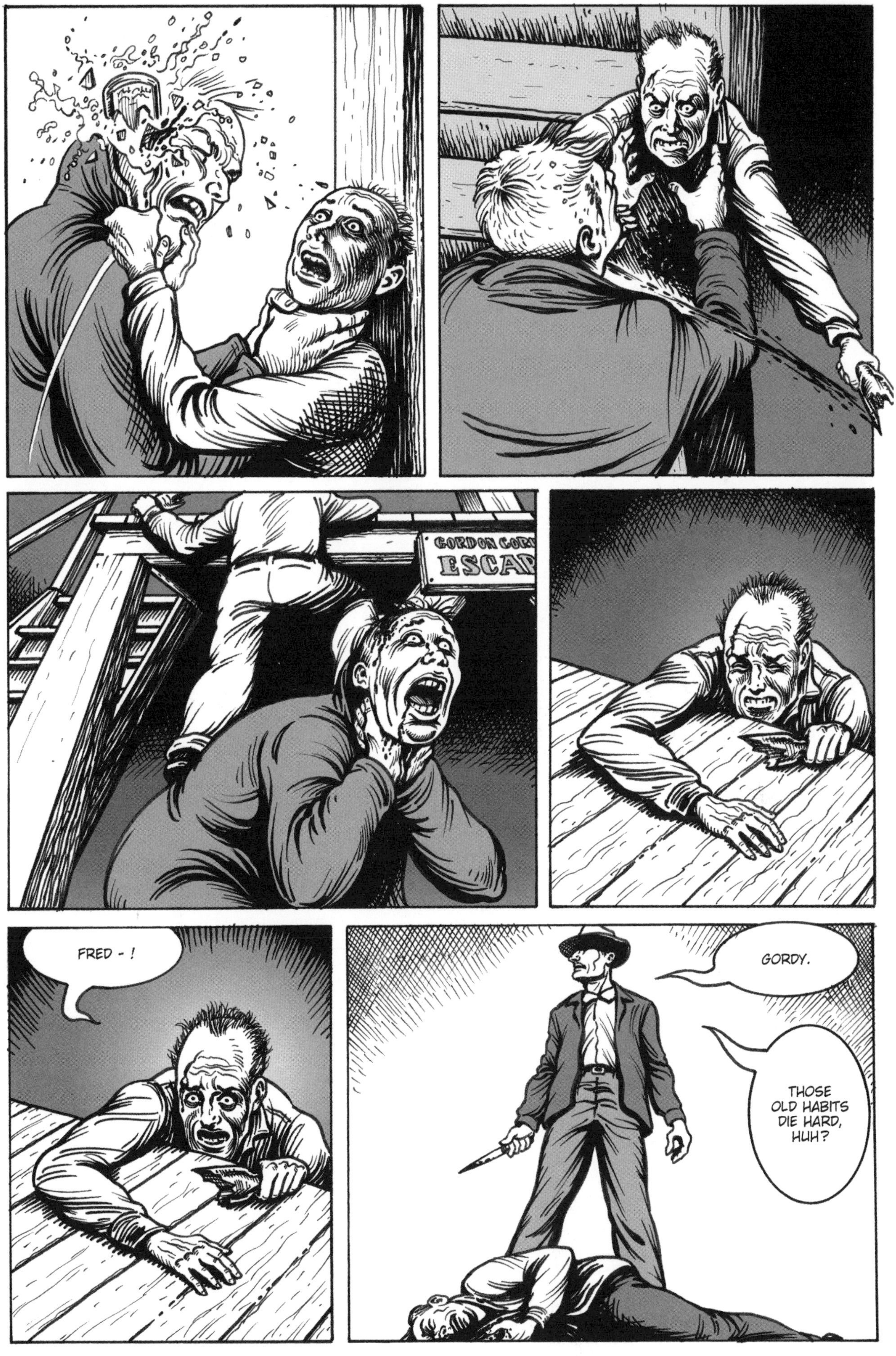
GORDON CORY
ESCAP
FRED - !
GORDY.
THOSE OLD HABITS DIE HARD, HUH?

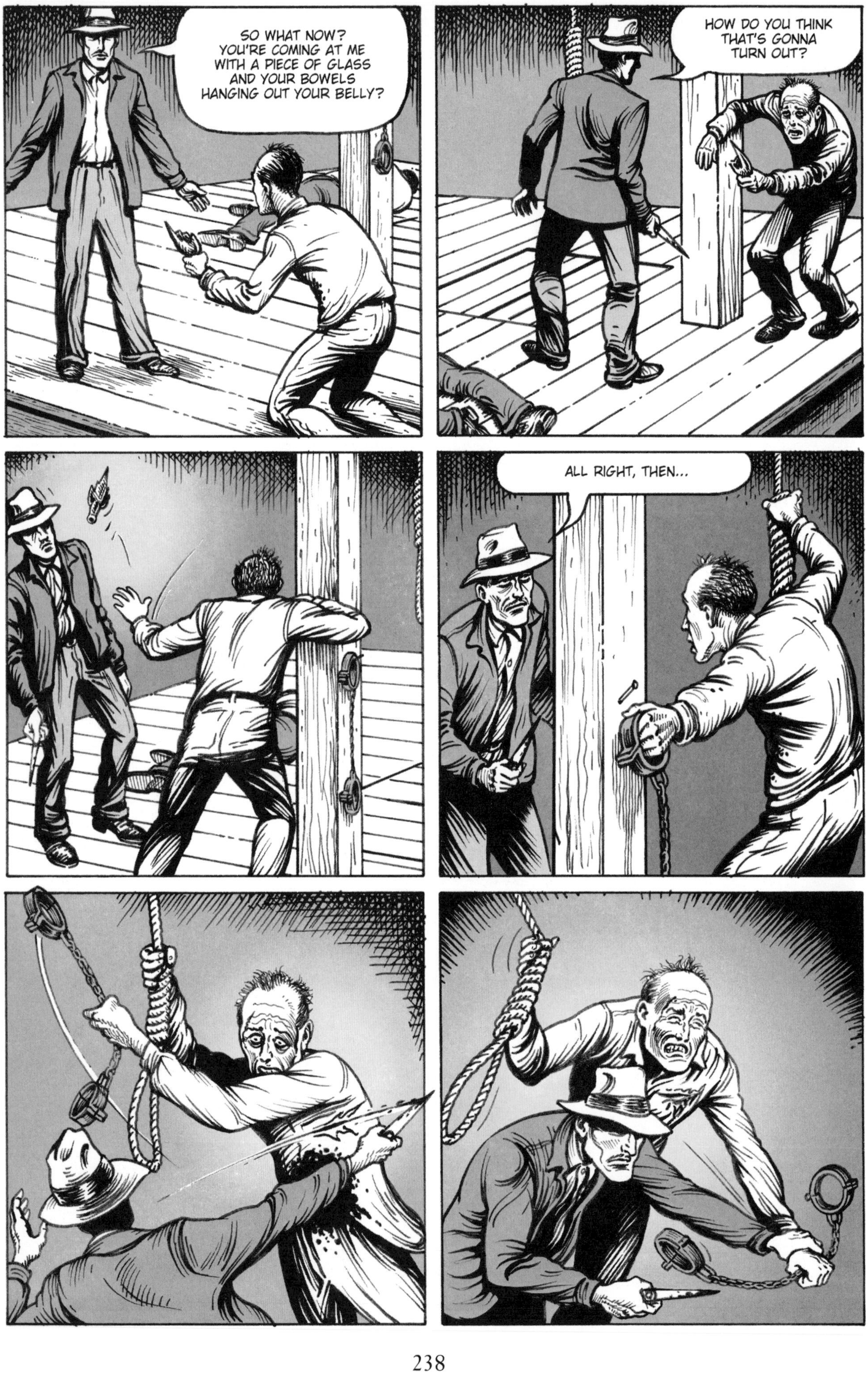
SO WHAT NOW? YOU'RE COMING AT ME WITH A PIECE OF GLASS AND YOUR BOWELS HANGING OUT YOUR BELLY?
HOW DO YOU THINK THAT'S GONNA TURN OUT?
ALL RIGHT, THEN...

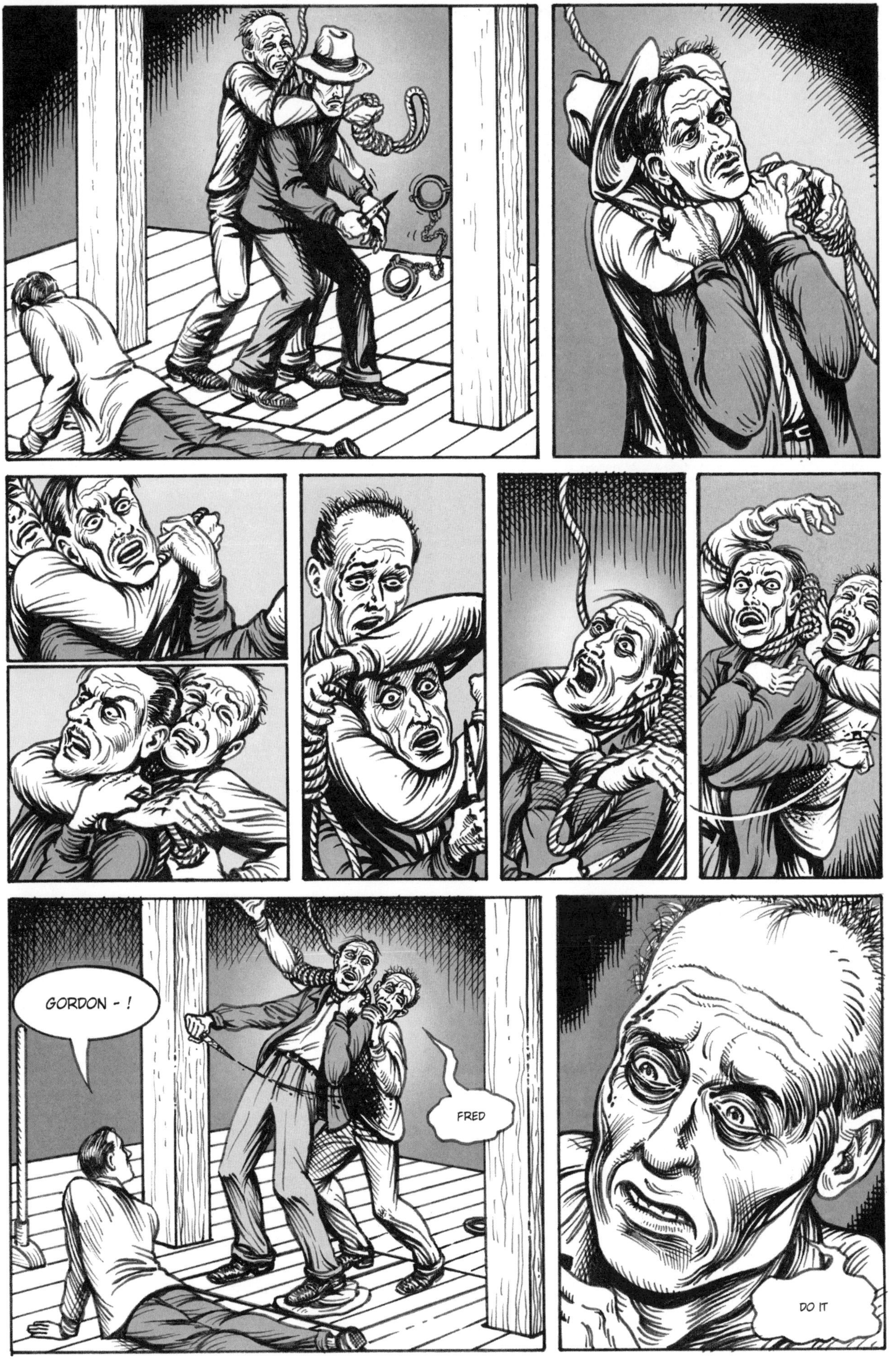
GORDON - !
FRED
DO IT

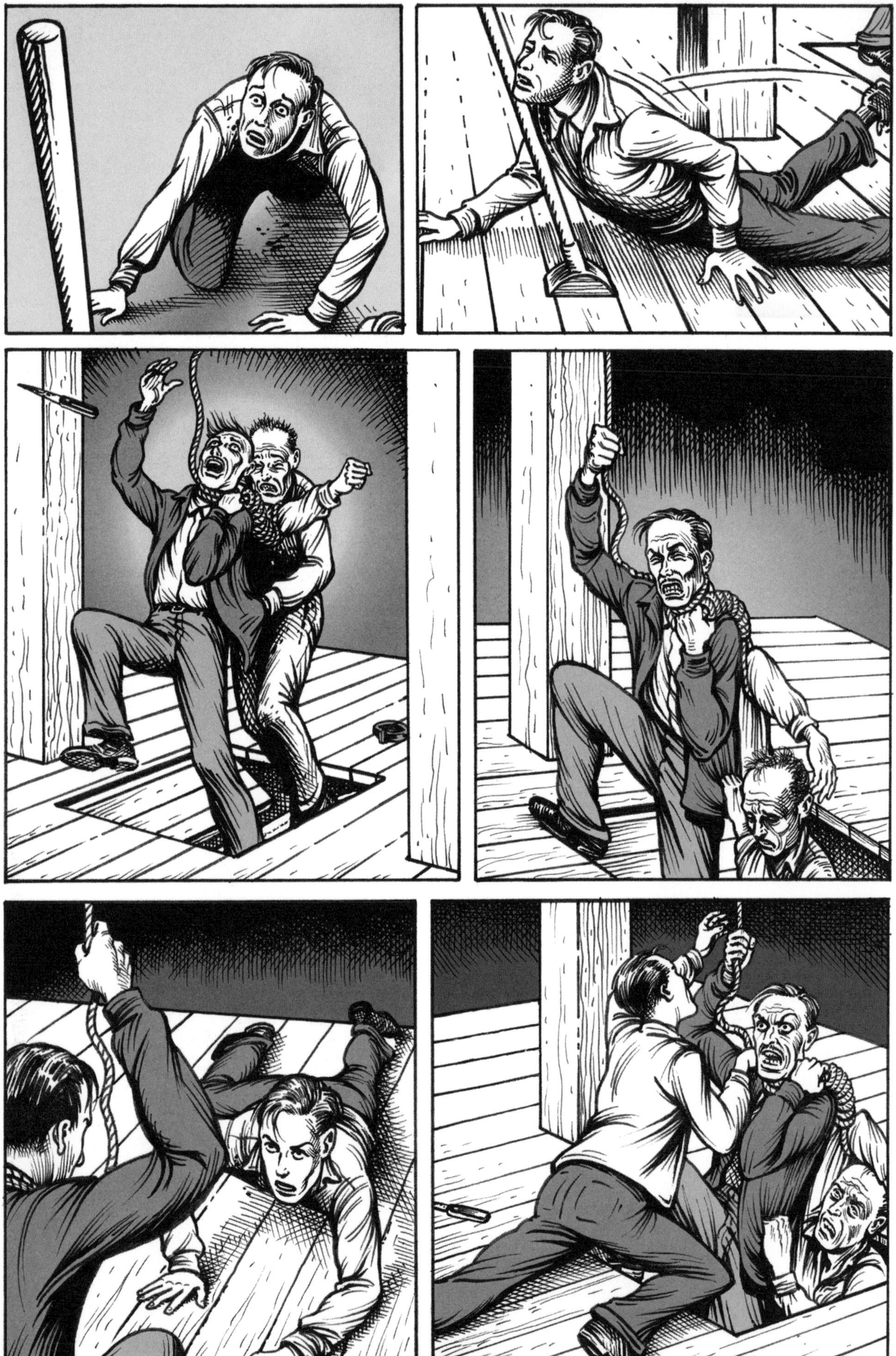

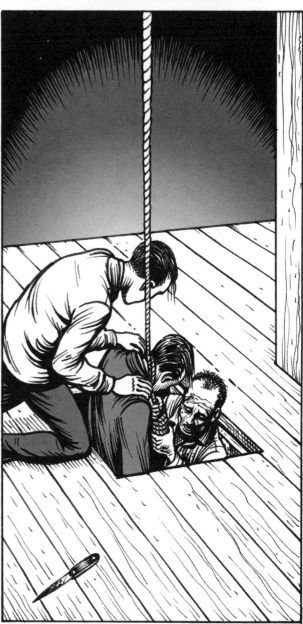

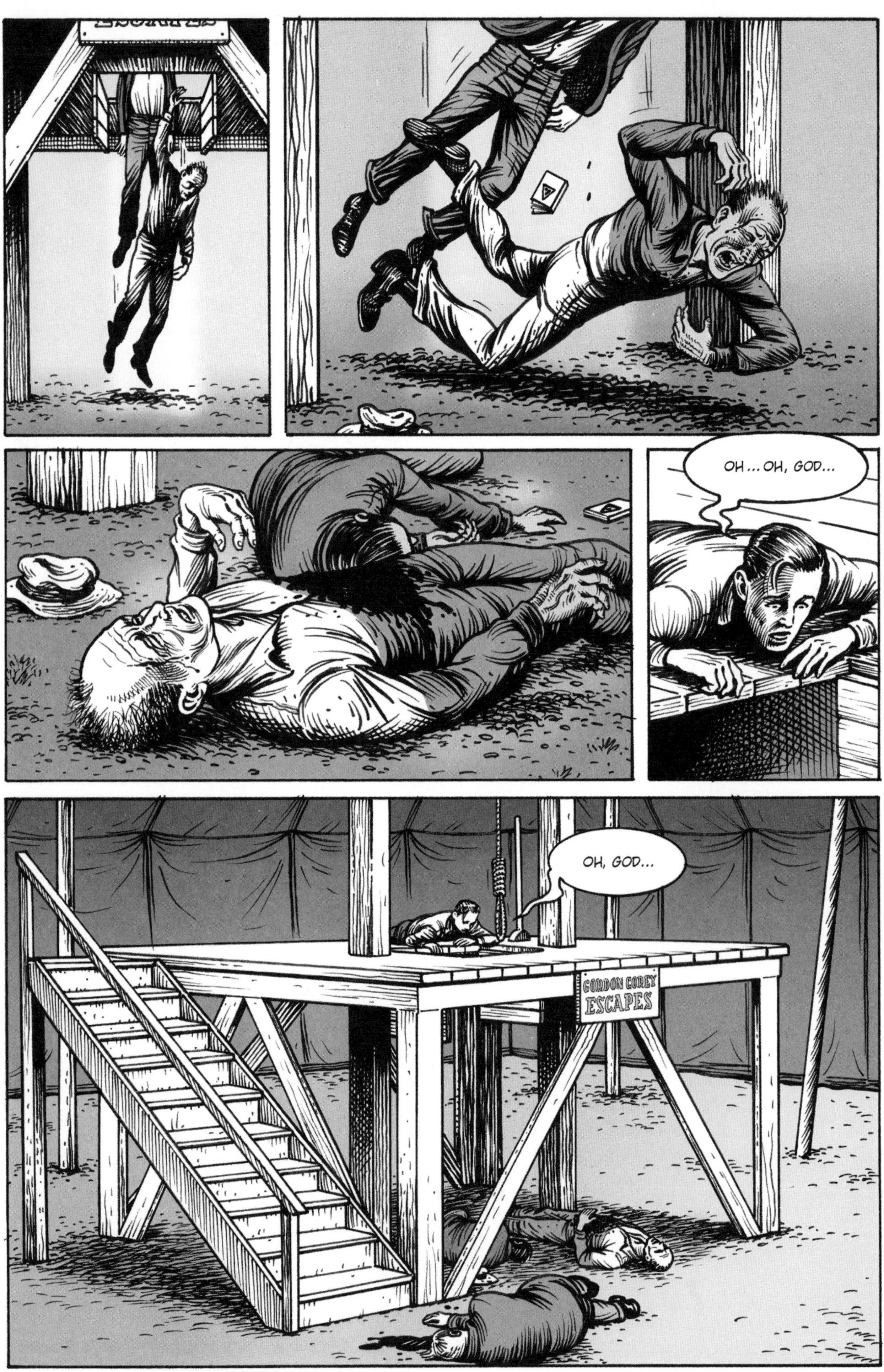
OH... OH, GOD...
OH, GOD...
GORDON COREY
ESCAPES

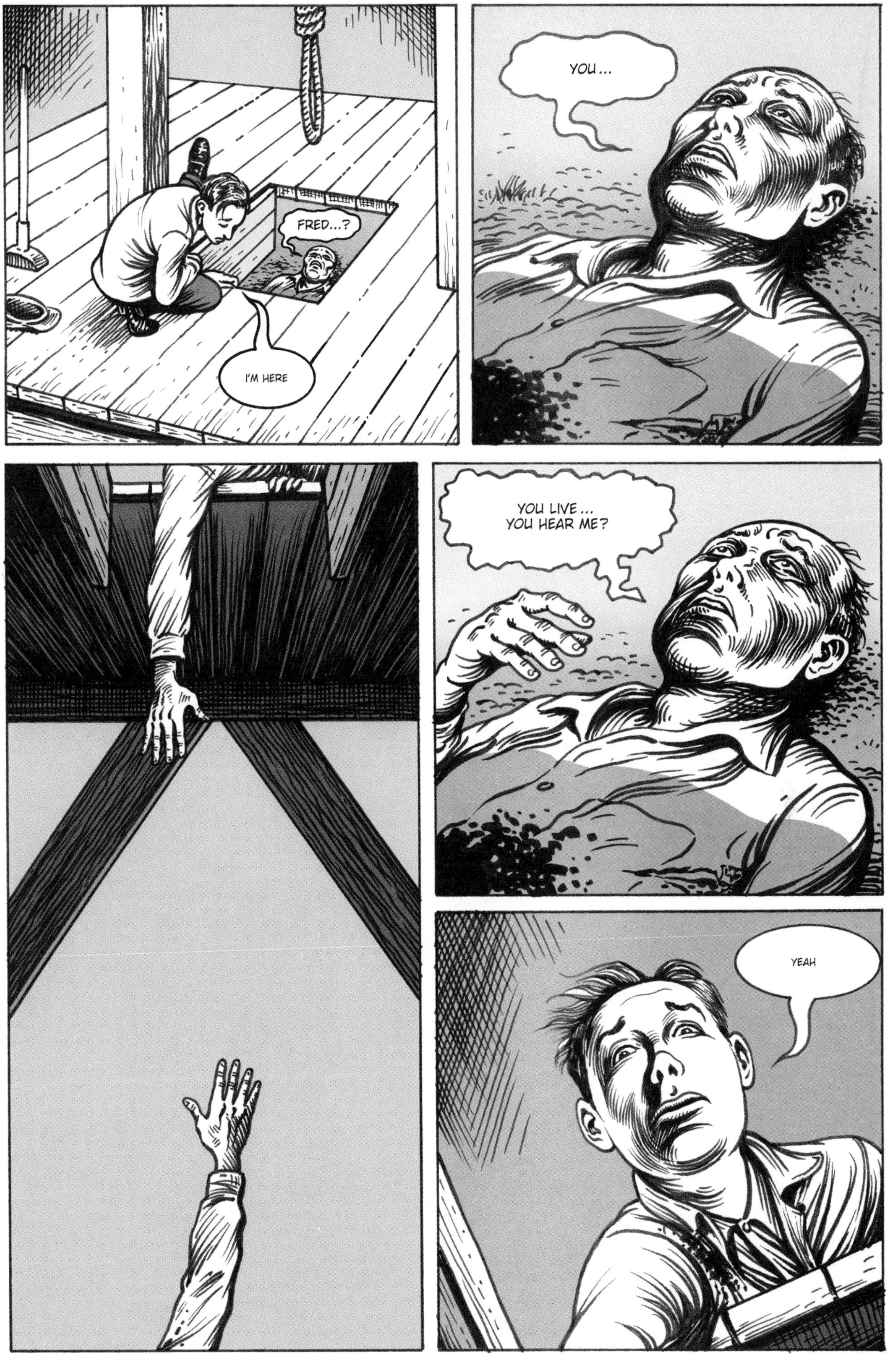
FRED...?
I'M HERE
YOU...
YOU LIVE...
YOU HEAR ME?
YEAH

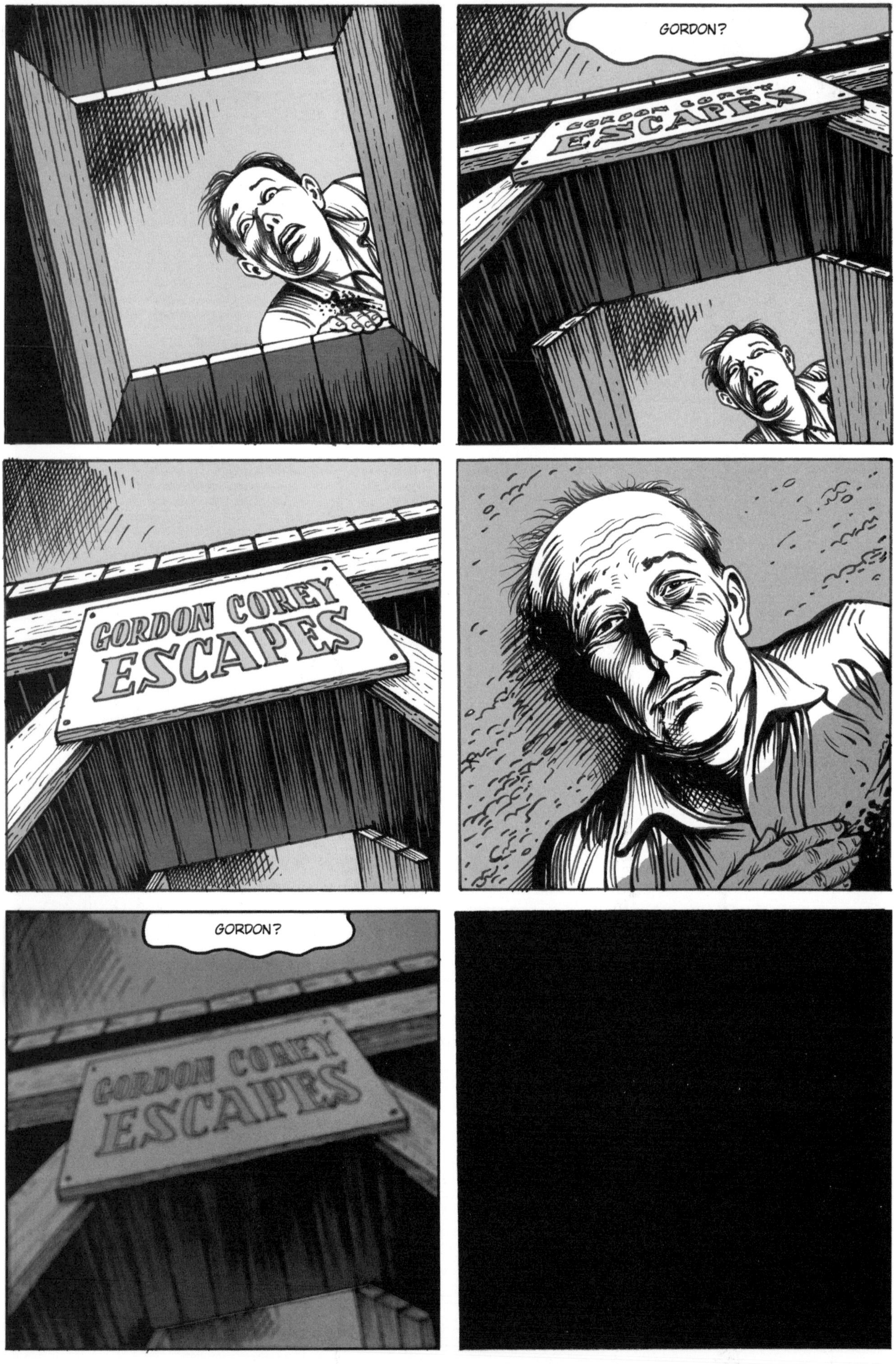
GORDON?
GORDON COREY ESCAPES
GORDON COREY ESCAPES
GORDON?
GORDON COREY ESCAPES

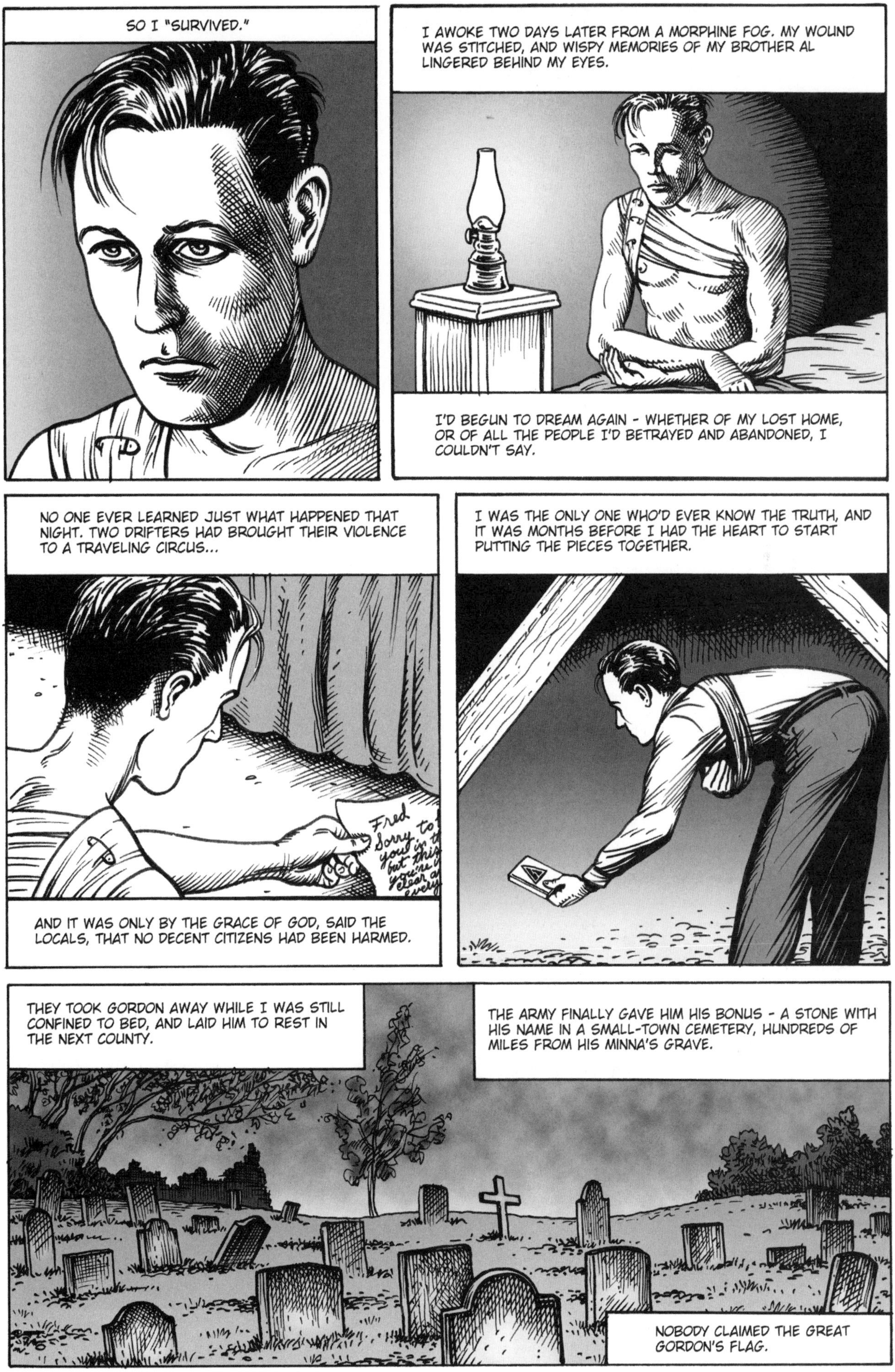
SO I "SURVIVED."
I AWOKE TWO DAYS LATER FROM A MORPHINE FOG. MY WOUND WAS STITCHED, AND WISPY MEMORIES OF MY BROTHER AL LINGERED BEHIND MY EYES.
I'D BEGUN TO DREAM AGAIN - WHETHER OF MY LOST HOME, OR OF ALL THE PEOPLE I'D BETRAYED AND ABANDONED, I COULDN'T SAY.
NO ONE EVER LEARNED JUST WHAT HAPPENED THAT NIGHT. TWO DRIFTERS HAD BROUGHT THEIR VIOLENCE TO A TRAVELING CIRCUS...
AND IT WAS ONLY BY THE GRACE OF GOD, SAID THE LOCALS, THAT NO DECENT CITIZENS HAD BEEN HARMED.
I WAS THE ONLY ONE WHO'D EVER KNOW THE TRUTH, AND IT WAS MONTHS BEFORE I HAD THE HEART TO START PUTTING THE PIECES TOGETHER.
THEY TOOK GORDON AWAY WHILE I WAS STILL CONFINED TO BED, AND LAID HIM TO REST IN THE NEXT COUNTY.
THE ARMY FINALLY GAVE HIM HIS BONUS - A STONE WITH HIS NAME IN A SMALL-TOWN CEMETERY, HUNDREDS OF MILES FROM HIS MINNA'S GRAVE.
NOBODY CLAIMED THE GREAT GORDON'S FLAG.

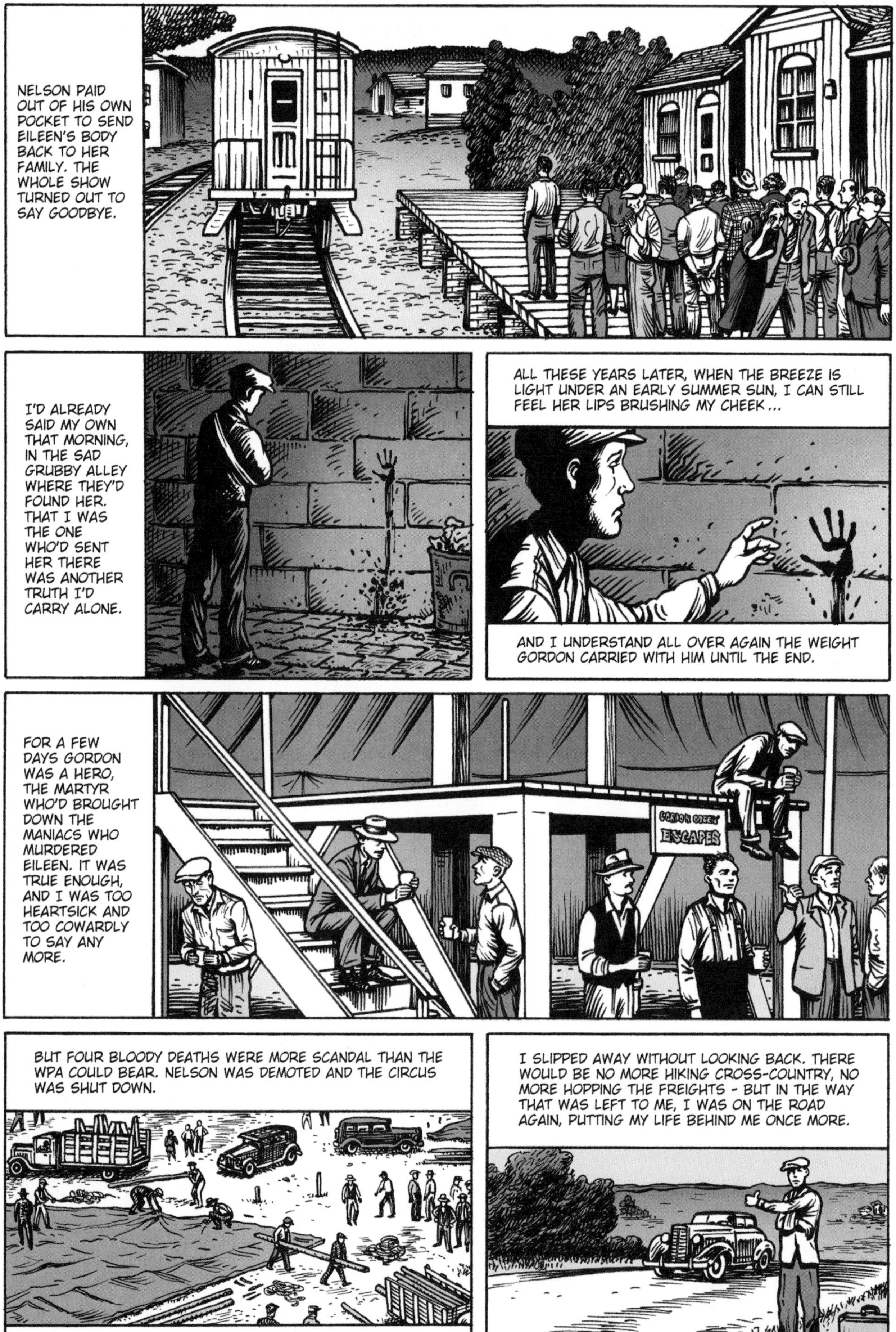
NELSON PAID OUT OF HIS OWN POCKET TO SEND EILEEN'S BODY BACK TO HER FAMILY. THE WHOLE SHOW TURNED OUT TO SAY GOODBYE.
I'D ALREADY SAID MY OWN THAT MORNING, IN THE SAD GRUBBY ALLEY WHERE THEY'D FOUND HER. THAT I WAS THE ONE WHO'D SENT HER THERE WAS ANOTHER TRUTH I'D CARRY ALONE.
ALL THESE YEARS LATER, WHEN THE BREEZE IS LIGHT UNDER AN EARLY SUMMER SUN, I CAN STILL FEEL HER LIPS BRUSHING MY CHEEK...
AND I UNDERSTAND ALL OVER AGAIN THE WEIGHT GORDON CARRIED WITH HIM UNTIL THE END.
FOR A FEW DAYS GORDON WAS A HERO, THE MARTYR WHO'D BROUGHT DOWN THE MANIACS WHO MURDERED EILEEN. IT WAS TRUE ENOUGH, AND I WAS TOO HEARTSICK AND TOO COWARDLY TO SAY ANY MORE.
ESCAPES
BUT FOUR BLOODY DEATHS WERE MORE SCANDAL THAN THE WPA COULD BEAR. NELSON WAS DEMOTED AND THE CIRCUS WAS SHUT DOWN.
THEY DIDN'T TOAST GORDON'S MEMORY MUCH AFTER THAT.
I SLIPPED AWAY WITHOUT LOOKING BACK. THERE WOULD BE NO MORE HIKING CROSS-COUNTRY, NO MORE HOPPING THE FREIGHTS - BUT IN THE WAY THAT WAS LEFT TO ME, I WAS ON THE ROAD AGAIN, PUTTING MY LIFE BEHIND ME ONCE MORE.

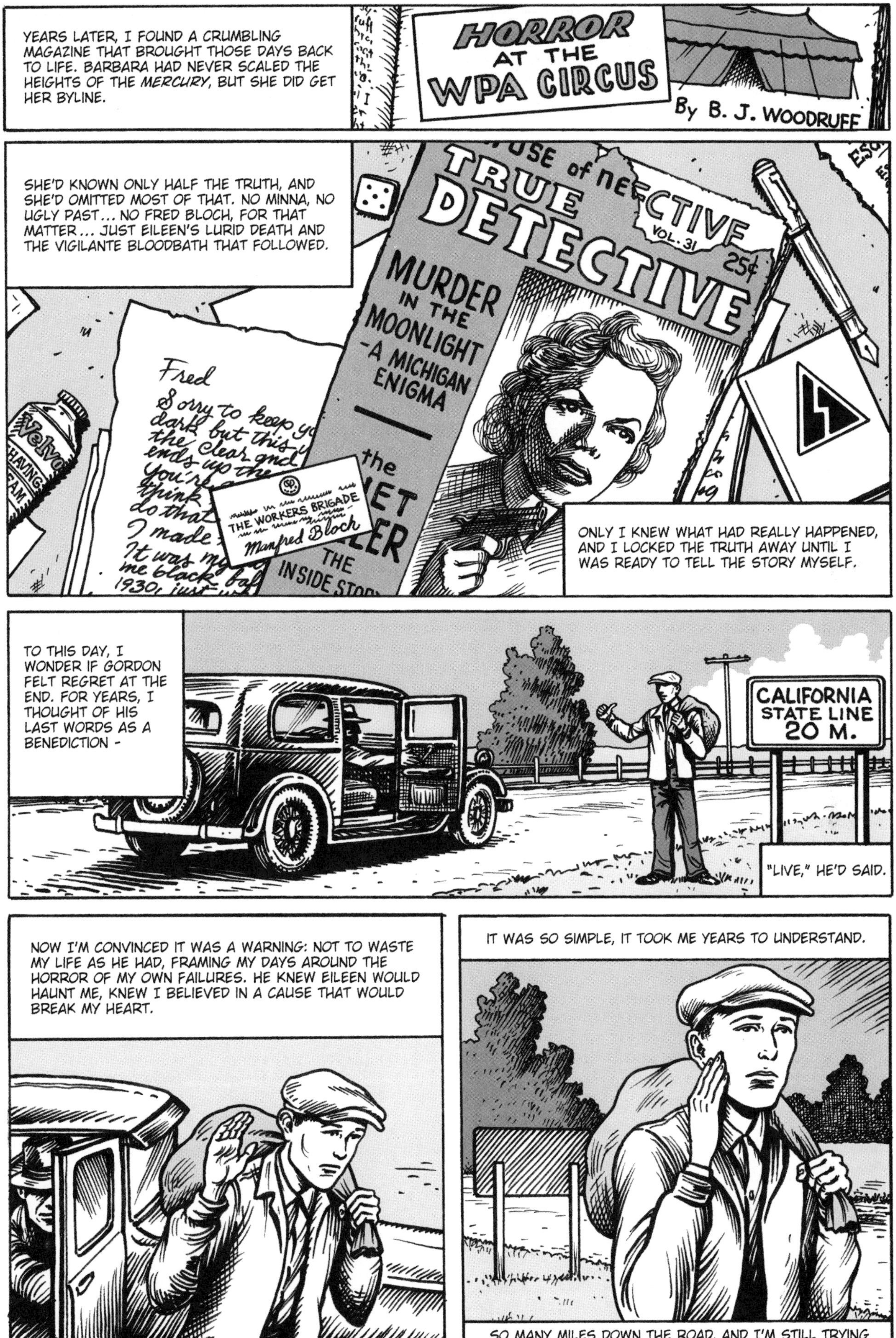
YEARS LATER, I FOUND A CRUMBLING MAGAZINE THAT BROUGHT THOSE DAYS BACK TO LIFE. BARBARA HAD NEVER SCALED THE HEIGHTS OF THE *MERCURY*, BUT SHE DID GET HER BYLINE.
HORROR AT THE WPA CIRCUS
By B. J. WOODRUFF
SHE'D KNOWN ONLY HALF THE TRUTH, AND SHE'D OMITTED MOST OF THAT. NO MINNA, NO UGLY PAST... NO FRED BLOCH, FOR THAT MATTER... JUST EILEEN'S LURID DEATH AND THE VIGILANTE BLOODBATH THAT FOLLOWED.
TRUE DETECTIVE
VOL. 31
25¢
MURDER IN THE MOONLIGHT -A MICHIGAN ENIGMA
THE INSIDE STORY
Fred
THE WORKERS BRIGADE
Manfred Bloch
ONLY I KNEW WHAT HAD REALLY HAPPENED, AND I LOCKED THE TRUTH AWAY UNTIL I WAS READY TO TELL THE STORY MYSELF.
TO THIS DAY, I WONDER IF GORDON FELT REGRET AT THE END. FOR YEARS, I THOUGHT OF HIS LAST WORDS AS A BENEDICTION -
CALIFORNIA STATE LINE 20 M.
"LIVE," HE'D SAID.
NOW I'M CONVINCED IT WAS A WARNING: NOT TO WASTE MY LIFE AS HE HAD, FRAMING MY DAYS AROUND THE HORROR OF MY OWN FAILURES. HE KNEW EILEEN WOULD HAUNT ME, KNEW I BELIEVED IN A CAUSE THAT WOULD BREAK MY HEART.
IT WAS SO SIMPLE, IT TOOK ME YEARS TO UNDERSTAND.
SO MANY MILES DOWN THE ROAD, AND I'M STILL TRYING TO TAKE THAT STEP.

JAMES VANCE and **DAN E. BURR** are pioneers of the literary graphic novel. Their previous work, *Kings in Disguise*, swept the Eisner and Harvey Awards and has been hailed as one of the best graphic novels of all time by *Time* and the *Guardian*. Vance has written scripts for *The Crow*, *The Spirit*, and other popular comics. He lives in Tulsa, Oklahoma. Burr has been an illustrator for DC Comics's *Big Book Series*. He lives in Milwaukee, Wisconsin.

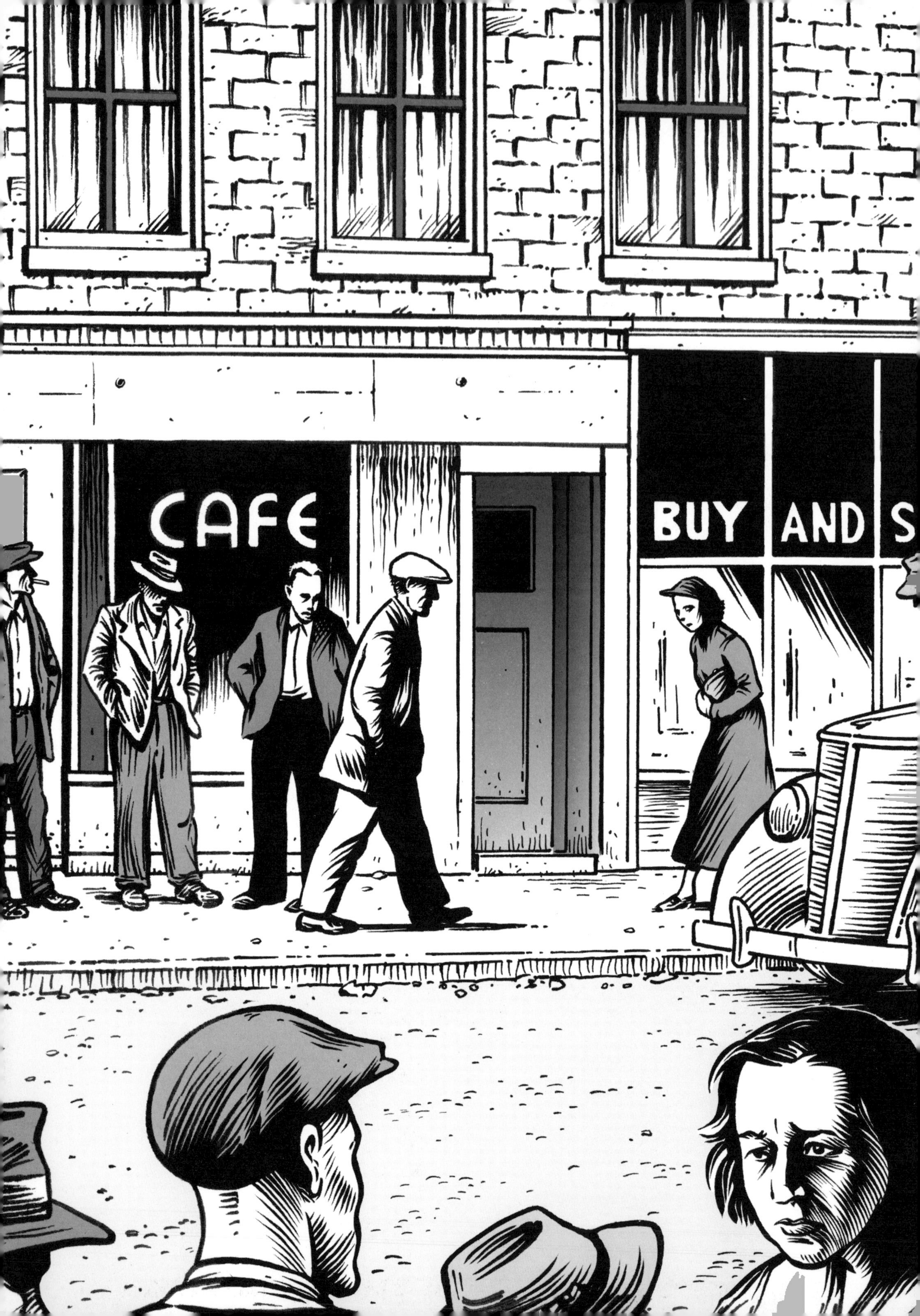
CAFE
BUY AND S